Crypto Wars

Crypto Wars

Crypto Wars

The Fight for Privacy in the Digital Age: A Political History of Digital Encryption

Craig Jarvis

CRC Press
Taylor & Francis Group
Boca Raton London New York

CRC Press is an imprint of the
Taylor & Francis Group, an **informa** business

First edition published 2021
by CRC Press
6000 Broken Sound Parkway NW, Suite 300, Boca Raton, FL 33487-2742

and by CRC Press
2 Park Square, Milton Park, Abingdon, Oxon, OX14 4RN

ISBN: 978-0-367-64245-7 (hbk)
ISBN: 978-0-367-64248-8 (pbk)
ISBN: 978-1-003-12367-5 (ebk)

Typeset in Times
by Deanta Global Publishing Services, Chennai, India

For V.

Contents

Preface

Digital technologies arbitrate power in the twenty-first century. The government-citizen power dynamic is moderated by the degree to which civil liberties, especially privacy, exist in both the physical and digital domains. Digital privacy is a broad topic dependent on factors ranging from how companies handle our data, or put another way, our most intimate secrets, to the level of data access governments claim in the name of national security. The most important digital privacy technology is encryption, the subject of this history.[1] The conflict over the degree to which citizens should be permitted access to encryption, to technology capable of placing their secrets beyond the reach of their governments, is known as the crypto wars. We are enduring the third crypto war, absent ceasefire prospects.

The historic ability of governments to develop mass surveillance capabilities has been limited by the vast labor requirements, which are economically infeasible in democratic societies. Digital technologies removed this labor constraint. Digital privacy activists, recognizing the removal of the labor constraint, developed and disseminated digital encryption technologies in an attempt to introduce a new surveillance constraint to help preserve the pre-digital government-citizen power dynamic, and prevent what they feared as digital world could incubate: an Orwellian state. Furthermore, some cryptologists branded themselves "crypto-anarchists" and aspired to use encryption technologies to change irrevocably the pre-digital government-citizen power balance to the advance of the latter. The US government recognized the danger of such crypto-anarchist aspirations. Fearing a loss of law enforcement and intelligence capabilities it believed vital for preserving the pre-digital government-citizen power dynamic, and for protecting its citizens, the government responded by attempting to exert control over cryptography, and to find ways to provide citizens with access to encryption without negating their own surveillance capabilities. How society settles the government-citizen power dynamic, and the provision of civil liberties such as security and privacy in the digital age, are the central issues of the crypto wars.

Whilst vociferous debates about citizens' rights in the digital era are occurring, these discourses rest upon fragile foundations at times bereft of historical context. The crypto wars comprise half a century of conflict, yet today's belligerents are often unaware of this history. Harvard scholar George Santayana once said, "unless experience is maintained...infancy is perpetual"—if we want to elevate the quality of debate, and the chance for a resolution to this conflict, we must understand our historical inheritance. A lack of familiarity with the past is exacerbated by a culture of venom and sensationalization on all sides of the crypto wars, inculcating a tribalism which often brands those who diverge from party lines, or dare collaborate with

---

[1] For a non-technical overview of cryptography, see Keith Martin's *Cryptography: The Key to* *Digital Security, How It Works, and Why It Matters* (New York: WW Norton, 2020).

opponents in search of compromise, as fools or traitors. The objective of this book is to create a crypto wars history to aid the establishment of fact from fiction, in the hope that such a foundation will catalyze a higher caliber of discourse and facilitate progress on this debate. Such progress may be in acceptance of, or dissonance with, the status quo.

This book is structured in a series of stand-alone chapters, with the first three chapters providing context for the crypto wars, and the remainder providing a historical account of the conflict itself. The prologue offers a light-hearted overview of the most important discovery in the history of encryption: public key cryptography. Chapter 1 outlines the crypto wars. The digital communications revolution is not the first to change the government-citizen power dynamic; therefore, Chapter 2 considers the impact of previous communications revolutions. Chapter 3 provides an in-depth exploration of the cypherpunks, a group of digital privacy activists, including crypto-anarchists, who challenged the government's cryptologic hegemony. Chapters 4 and 5 cover the first crypto war, spanning 1966 to 1981 and comprising the first government data encryption standard, and the battle for cryptologic academic freedom. Chapters 6 and 7 catalog the second crypto war, extending from 1991 to 2002. During this period, digital privacy activists attempted to provide cryptography to the masses, whilst the government sought to achieve the same without losing their ability to intercept communications and disrupt threats. Chapter 8 covers the third crypto war, commencing in 2013.

The nature of the government-citizen power dynamic and a correlating civil liberties/risk settlement for the digital age should be determined by citizens, but policy makers and business leaders need to drive this debate. For this reason, and as this study is more concerned with the socio-political implications of cryptology rather than the technical nuances (though there are interdependencies), this book is written as a socio-political, rather than a technical, history.[2] At times, the genesis of core cryptographic inventions, such as public key cryptography, is explored; however, this text should not be viewed as a general history of cryptology. Studying the crypto wars requires a knowledge of many disciplines including geopolitics, law, security, psychology, and technology. A mastery of so many disparate fields is elusive to even the most dedicated scholar. Whilst I am a seasoned technologist, it is important to acknowledge that I am not a cryptologist, nor am I a lawyer. Thankfully, many sources fill these knowledge gaps—any misinterpretation of such sources is solely my responsibility, as are any errors within this study. The scope of this text is limited principally to the United States, and to activities impacting the government-citizen power dynamic. Beyond the US, I briefly touch on other democratic nations dealing with this challenge. With the exception of one case study, I have omitted US government operations to interfere with, or compromise, the cryptography of other nations, as these activities do not impact the government-citizen power dynamic. By virtue

---

[2] Cryptology is the overarching science of cryptography and crypt-analysis.

of this topic, this book is somewhat an asymmetric study—much government information pertaining to encryption remains classified. Where there are gaps, I have resisted the temptation to speculate; instead, I have focused on integrating as much primary source material as possible, enabling readers to form their own opinions where gaps exist.

Historians should also acknowledge their own backgrounds to readers, as one's experiences inevitably bestow biases. I grew up in an anti-establishment part of the UK, and as a child and young man I was a musician—in this environment and culture, the government and any vestige of authority were distrusted and often perceived as the enemy. Later, I trained in cyber security and found the hacker culture closely aligned to my own background. During my cyber security career, like many in this field, I have also been exposed to classified environments. Whilst NDAs prevent further elaboration, I do want to state that I was not involved with subjects relating to the crypto wars, and the motivation to write this book, as well as its contents, are solely my own. I have attempted to write a non-partisan history of this issue; I like to think my anti-government and pro-government experiences and biases even out, and I have striven to present all sides of the story absent judgment.

This book makes no pretensions to being the "final word" on the history of the crypto wars. Whilst I have chronicled much of the conflict, there is more I would like to have done. However, to further delay publication when governments are today implementing digital-oriented civil liberties policies that will mold our futures would have been the wrong decision. It is my hope this book will stimulate conversations about the crypto wars history, that participants who have not yet done so will tell their stories, and that scholars will challenge the contents of the book where they find errors, leading to an ever more precise historical record of events.

It is not a historian's role to advocate policy. However, in the conclusion I offer a number of non-partisan observations and a high-level solution-neutral framework for advancing the debate. My hope is that such ideas will help those much smarter than I find a way to negotiate a ceasefire to the crypto wars, allowing us to bestow upon future generations a rights settlement befitting of great democracies.

Craig Jarvis

Prologue: A New Cryptological Era
California, 1975

Whitfield Diffie wept. With more than thirty summers of his life elapsed, Diffie's odyssey had left him adrift from the promised land his heart fervently preached was more than a mirage. His tears fell freely as he told his beloved Mary he was a broken-down old researcher who would never amount to anything.[1] He was a disciple of cryptology unable to ascend to exalted prophet. Diffie cradled his head despondently. He was earning barely enough to survive. He told Mary she should find another man.[2] Diffie's mission had failed.

Diffie's pilgrimage had indeed been infused with a religious-like zeal, for he believed the birth of the digital age was imminent, but its crowning would be the death knell of privacy.

For years, he had quixotically searched for a solution to allow humanity access to the world's knowledge, whilst also shielding their secrets from a hostile world. Secrets such as the names of those who exchanged seductive whispers through cyberspace. Secrets such as whether one attended Alcoholics Anonymous. Secrets revealing whether one desired a capitalist or a communist future. Secrets that, if exposed, could see one's most intimate expressions laid bare to an unforgiving world capable of ridicule, blackmail, persecution, and murder.

At the heart of the problem was key distribution. In order for two individuals to communicate securely, they first had to exchange secret encryption keys. This could not be done over an insecure network, such as the Internet, as any lurking eavesdroppers could snatch the keys from the wires, rendering subsequent communications based on those keys as private as a declaration of love bellowed across a town square. Therefore, the keys must be exchanged offline. Easy enough for Diffie when he wanted to establish secure online communications with Mary, whom he saw daily, but in a globalizing world where continents divided those who needed to communicate, physical key exchange was not feasible—in engineering parlance, the solution did not scale. Cryptography needed a revolution if communications were to be protected in a digital world.

Diffie's quest to instigate such a revolution saw him travel coast-to-coast as he sought counsel from the eminent mathematical and computing minds of his age.

---

[1] Levy, 2001, 67.
[2] Ibid.
[3] Ibid. 24.

Diffie struggled to trust anyone.[3] His inability to trust, and his desire for privacy, drove his obsession to seek out a mathematical incantation—an algorithm, with which scientists could cast a spell to conjure an impregnable digital ark of privacy, which no mortal could invade.

Diffie wondered if cryptology research would endanger his life; he kept a low profile.[4] In the unlikely event of success, he would subvert the prowess of perhaps the most potent intelligence power on Earth, the National Security Agency (NSA). But government agents never arrived. Perhaps they already knew the futility of his pilgrimage. Maybe the NSA decided rather than enacting elaborate plans to frustrate his mission, they would simply allow the impenetrable walls encircling the crypto-graphic nirvana to block his passage.

Diffie's tears continued to tumble from his cheeks as Mary comforted him. She had been studying Egyptology, and explained to him that the ancient Egyptians believed some qualities were innate whilst others were acquired; she thought great-ness must be an innate characteristic; "I know what I am looking at, and I know you are a great man," she whispered.[5]

Mary returned home one day later that year to find Diffie waiting at the door with a strange look on his face; "I think," he said, "I've made a great discovery."[6]

Diffie's revelation was a cryptographic heresy, but a heresy as revolutionary as when Prometheus stole fire from Olympus for humanity, or when the Bible was translated from Latin to secular.

Diffie's blasphemy would change the course of computing, commerce, and con-flict forever. Rather than keep the shared encryption key secret, known only to the correspondents, Diffie would use a pair of keys; one would be public, and the other secret, or private. The parties would exchange public keys without the need for secrecy, for the revelation Diffie offered the world meant messages encrypted with a user's public key could only be decrypted with that user's private key: the key they alone possessed. Now the public key could be sent over insecure channels, such as the Internet. Diffie didn't have an algorithmic implementation of his vision, but he had discovered the conceptual framework—the direction of travel toward a solution.

Public key cryptography was born.

Working with his intellectual partner, Martin Hellman, Diffie refined the approach and in a 1976 article entitled "New Directions in Cryptography," their discovery was announced.

The age-old key distribution problem was on the ropes, but the knockout blow was yet to land.

Few immediately grasped the discovery's implications. For it was a discovery, rather than an invention. Diffie and Hellman's public key cryptography was to com-puter science as Newton's theory of universal gravitation was to physics, as Pasteur's germ theory had been to medicine, and as Darwin's theory of evolution was to biol-ogy. They were on the "brink of a revolution in cryptography," a new era of privacy.[7]

---

[4] Ibid. 26.   [6] Ibid. 73.
[5] Ibid. 67.   [7] Diffie and Hellman, 1976, 644.

For encryption was seen by those most prescient as a panacea to the threats faced by the common person, as a natural evolution of citizens' ability to protect themselves in the digital age against a state that could at any time lurch towards dictatorship.

This was a moment upon which the history of communications, information dissemination, and thus political power, would pivot. One has to wonder, had they known the implications of Diffie's discovery, would there have been a limit to how much treasure the West's enemies would have expended, how much blood they would have spilled, to control the fertile new ground?[8]

From this new ground, Nikita Khrushchev, sitting behind the Kremlin's crimson fortifications, could have secured every secret binding the Soviet Union.

From this new ground, Fidel Castro could have concealed the political strategies anchoring his recently liberated nation to the Communist powers.

From this new ground, Kim Il-Sung could have prevented the American hoard at his border from eavesdropping on Pyongyang.

Diffie's only protection from such dangers had been the world's ongoing ignorance of what many believed a hopeless quixotic quest to solve the key exchange conundrum. When Diffie's thoughts morphed to words in an academic journal, he and Hellman were free of the risk any government would kill them to control their discovery.

Diffie and Hellman had offered the world a map of the new lands beneath their feet. But they could only sketch the general direction of travel—it would be others, namely MIT's Ron Rivest, Adi Shamir, and Leonard Adleman who would discover an algorithm allowing completion of the map to public key cryptography. It would take the world years to comprehend the prophetic nature of Diffie and Hellman's work: they had laid the foundations for confidentiality in the digital age.

Privacy and intimacy could now be extended regardless of distance.

1 The Crypto Wars

We are at one of those important cusp points in history.

The technologies of networks and of encryption make it very easy for exciting new structures to develop (crypto anarchy, privacy...anonymous systems, digital banks).

But the same technologies make it possible for a cyberspatial police state to develop.

The race is on.

Timothy C. May, cypherpunks co-founder, 1994

Digital communications empower citizens to a greater degree than at any point in history. Today, citizens learn languages, confess sins, consult physicians, and even enter virtual reality via the Internet. The digital revolution is fundamentally changing how citizens interact with governments. Citizens can instantly access online public services, and are afforded a plethora of information on how their governments operate. This allows transparency organizations to monitor governments more closely, and for groups such as WikiLeaks to use data obtained via hacking techniques to expose practices they deem corrupt or immoral.[1] Transparency groups hope such surveillance of governments will deter abuses of power, and act as a detection mechanism when transgressions manifest, such as the abuse of citizens' privacy rights.

Digital communications have also empowered governments. Today, citizens voluntarily carry devices capable of listening to their conversations and tracking their movements. If a century ago governments were asked to design the perfect surveillance tool, such a device would look a lot like a smartphone. With the high levels of smartphone market saturation governments can, if unrestrained by laws, operate the most invasive surveillance apparatus in history. The depth of surveillance is complimented by its breadth. Modern computing technologies are able to analyze data at a scale never before possible, and as a result a relatively small number of government employees can now surveil an entire citizenry: for the first time in history, the digital revolution has untethered the surveillance labor constraint. This is important, as historically the feasibility of mass surveillance was regulated not only by laws, but by the economic viability of surveillance. Enacting an extensive national surveillance system, such as that achieved by the Stasi in the German Democratic Republic (GDR), required committing vast resources, capital, and labor. Such expense necessitated a quality of service sacrifice in domains such as welfare and education; for example, GDR security spending was estimated at 9.2% of national income by 1986.[2]

---

[1] For example, see Wikileaks, 2017.　　　　[2] Crane, 1989, V.

Comparatively, in the same year the UK spent only 4.7% of GDP on security;[3] by 2018, in (relative) peacetime, UK security spending dropped to 1.8%, whilst the US spent 3.2%.[4] Unless a democratic citizenry desired a surveillance state, an incumbent politician would be unlikely to win the votes to remain in office on a platform of endemic surveillance *in lieu of* other services, such as health care, deemed vital by the electorate. Therefore, in democratic societies the cost of recruiting vast numbers of citizens into the security services was untenable, and would likely lead to the ejection of the executive from office. This labor constraint acted as a natural check against any inclinations a democratic state may hold to deploy mass surveillance against its citizenry. Whilst a capital expenditure constraint remains, market economies have made this challenge surmountable.

To highlight how digital technologies have minimized the surveillance labor constraint, consider the following hypothetical investigation exploring pre-digital and digitally enabled variants. The first investigative stage is to identify potential threats to the state (target discovery). In order to identify spies during World War Two, the US employed more than 10,000 civil servants to open almost a million pieces of international mail each week.[5] If faced with the same challenge in the digital era, assuming a suitable level of access, computer algorithms could be programmed to search for patterns likely to reflect a spy's activity. For instance, intelligence agencies could search for any telephones located near multiple sensitive, geographically disparate government sites in isolated locations that are also in contact with telephones in the hostile nation. Whilst this is a crude example, as long as collection assets were in place it would require virtually no labor to execute, whereas the pre-digital equivalent would require vast resources.

During the investigation the pre-digital analyst would have to search for the target's previous activities by combing through vast paper-based archives, which may not be centralized or efficiently indexed. Even when relevant records are located, they may provide only limited details due to the available labor required to create comprehensive records. To understand the scale of this challenge, consider that to support 30 officers in 1938, MI5 required four times as many secretaries.[6] The pre-digital investigator could engage with the telephone companies to obtain historical billing records, though returned data would be limited to other phone numbers contacted, and potentially the premises to which those phones were registered. The investigator could potentially speak to contacts of the target in an effort to develop a profile, but this would risk exposing their investigation and require significant resources. The investigator could consider deploying surveillance teams, or covert agents to build a relationship with the target; however, this would again require substantial labor resources and time. In contrast, the digitally enabled investigation would be able to use signals intelligence assets to quickly create a profile of the target, perhaps using nothing more than their online footprint (unless the target exercised exceptional

3 Rogers, 2010.   5 Broderick and Mayo, 1980, 23–27.
4 World Bank, 2018.   6 Higgs, 2004, 146–147.

operational security) requiring minimal labor. Details available via digital surveillance could include a target's travel history (and future intentions), their correspondence, networks, pictures, videos, reading habits, financial transactions, and more. Digital surveillance can be made easier with the assistance of internet companies, many of whom are essentially advertising companies (e.g., Alphabet, Facebook) that build detailed profiles of their clients in order to target advertisements. The US is in a particularly fortuitous position when it comes to digital surveillance capabilities, as it hosts vital internet transit points and services. Consequently, a high volume of global online communications either traverse or terminate within its territories.[7]

Technology has even improved the efficiency of physical surveillance. Static surveillance teams are able to use digital technology to make surveillance less dependent on physical eyes being constantly on the target. For instance, surveillance officers can deploy miniature digital cameras and microphones, and potentially even state-operated malware onto the target's devices to provide close access coverage. Mobile surveillance becomes easier when leveraging a target's digital footprint, such as which cell tower their phone is using, and leveraging additional digital data sources such as automatic number plate recognition technology, and potentially even GPS data extracted from their phone by state-operated malware.[8] The result of these technological evolutions is that whereas in the pre-digital age building a comprehensive profile of a citizen would take a team of investigators months of tedious work, in the digital age a detailed investigation can be executed remotely with relatively little manual effort, and within a compressed time period. With the labor constraint for surveillance mostly removed, it has now become possible to enact mass surveillance against an entire citizenry. This significantly changes the government-citizen power dynamic.

To appreciate the implications of mass surveillance one has to understand relevant definitions. Surveillance is defined by David Lyon as "any collection and processing of personal data, whether identifiable or not, for the purposes of influencing or managing those whose data have been garnered."[9] Like governments, internet companies are increasingly able to conduct surveillance to develop an understanding of citizens in order to target advertisements, and to influence their purchasing decisions. Bruce Schneier, a cyber security expert and fellow at Harvard University, argues that "surveillance is the business model of the Internet."[10] Internet companies try not to emphasize this business model of harvesting user data in exchange for services, instead preferring to cultivate a narrative that they are making the world a better place, such as Facebook's slogan of "give people the power to build community and bring the world together," or that they are virtuous, such as Google's "don't

---

[7] For a visual representation of the US' position within the Internet's cabling systems, see Telegeography, 2018.

[8] For example, ZooPark malware, assessed by Kaspersky Labs to be operated by a nation state, is capable of activating microphones and harvesting GPS data from smartphones (Kaspersky, 2018).

[9] Lyon, 2002, 3.

[10] Rashid, 2014.

be evil" mantra.[11,12] Surveillance is either targeted or untargeted. Targeted surveillance is conducted against individuals that, as a result of evidence gathered, the state has assessed are acting, or intend to act, illegally. Throughout modern history targeted surveillance, or the government's right to selectively violate the privacy of individuals for the defense of the wider citizenry where they possess probable cause and a legal warrant, has been a broadly accepted government activity.[13] Untargeted surveillance is when the government conducts target discovery activities against citizens where there is no evidence to indicate they are acting, or intend to act, illegally. Untargeted surveillance is typically associated with mass surveillance programs, where governments collect as much data on as many citizens as possible against which to conduct their untargeted surveillance (although mass surveillance also supports targeted surveillance).

Governments argue surveillance programs can help law enforcement and intelligence services deliver security for their citizens by aiding in prevention of criminal conspiracies and terrorist plots—though quantifying such benefits is extremely challenging.[14] The Internet is midwife to myriad new crimes and threats the government is attempting to manage, and those who would harm citizens can now do so from behind anonymity tools and beyond national borders. For some citizens the first duty of government is to provide security: these citizens may welcome digital surveillance capabilities. For other citizens, such surveillance powers represent an unacceptable violation of privacy and the principle of innocent until proven guilty, as well as holding the potential to be abused in ways that may impede or even doom their democracies. Many human rights groups, such as Liberty, argue that mass surveillance is an "unjustifiable invasion of our privacy. It erodes our freedom of expression and our right to peaceful assembly and association."[15]

In the early 1970s, cryptologists, presciently observing the untethering of the surveillance labor constraint and the resultant potential for mass surveillance, attempted to introduce a new constraint: digital encryption. Some, such as the crypto-anarchists, even desired a future where encryption enabled privacy to be dominant, and for the state to drastically shrink.[16] Not only could the crypto-anarchists' vision render governments unable to carry out security functions, it could even prevent taxation, which former US President James Madison observes "is essential to the very existence of government."[17]

In 1975, cryptologists Whitfield Diffie and Martin Hellman discovered public key cryptography.[18] For the first time in history, public key cryptography provided the ability for individuals who had not previously exchanged encryption keys (for

---

[11] Google's *"don't be evil"* slogan was changed in 2016 to *"do the right thing,"* possibly to alleviate the implication that without strict guidelines their default state would be "evil" (Alphabet, 2018).

[12] Facebook, 2018, and Google, 2018.

[13] For instance, see the fourth amendment of the US Constitution in United States Government, 1789.

[14] For an overview of this challenge, see Cayford and Pieters' "The effectiveness of surveillance technology: What intelligence officials are saying."

[15] Couchman, 2018.

[16] See May, 1988.

[17] Internal Revenue Service, 2018.

[18] Diffie and Hellman, 1976.

instance, via courier) to initiate a secure digital communication channel. Ever since the discovery of public key cryptography, society has debated to what degree citizens should be allowed access to cryptography, or put another way, how much digital privacy citizens should be permitted. Whether the Internet would remain free of government monitoring or would become more surveilled than the off-line world, would be determined to a significant degree by citizens' access to encryption. Recognizing this, in 1992 a group of technical experts coalesced to defend privacy in the coming digital age by providing citizens with access to cryptography. They became known as the cypherpunks. The cypherpunks brought together academics, crypto-anarchists, and industry professionals. Its members were anti-establishment; according to cypherpunk co-founder Timothy May, the group comprised "a lot of radical libertarians… [and] some anarcho-capitalists."[19] In 1993, May estimated about 50% of the cypherpunks were "strongly libertarian/anarchist," a further 20% were liberal or leftist, while the rest of the group's composition was unknown.[20] The cypherpunks would be augmented by others with similar ideologies, such as lawyers and journalists, forming a wider digital privacy rights movement. Though it is important to note whilst the prefix "digital" is used to describe these activists, the inexorable convergence of the online and off-line worlds means we are actually discussing civil rights in the modern era, rather than privacy within the digital realm alone. The cypherpunks' initiatives were often in conflict with US government policies. The conflict between the digital privacy activists and the government became known as the "crypto wars"—unknown to many, the "wars" had been ongoing since at least 1966. The crypto "wars" are of course not warfare in the traditional sense as perhaps best defined by nineteenth-century Prussian philosopher of war General Carl Von Clausewitz, who argued warfare comprises three elements: use of (violent) force; instrumental to achieving objectives; political in nature.[21]

The crypto wars are framed using militaristic language, setting the belligerents to battle in an implied zero-sum game. The metaphorical invocation of warfare underlines the hostility existing between the parties. It also reflects the media-savvy nature of the cypherpunks in sensationalizing their arguments in order to appeal to the media and amplify their message. The narrative is typically of security and privacy being in opposition, with the state benefiting from security (surveillance capabilities), and citizens from privacy (encryption). Such a framing is flawed as it fails to acknowledge that citizens benefit from the security that the state provides, just as governments are enriched by taxes from a robust online economy protected by privacy-enhancing technologies such as encryption.[22] However, there is a security vs. privacy dimension to the crypto wars, and it is true that at least to some degree a "balance" exists between the two—but a wider perspective, that of overall digital risk to states and citizens, is required for a more comprehensive and useful framing of the government-citizen relationship and digital age civil rights provisions.

[19] May, 1994b.
[20] May, 1993.
[21] Clausewitz, 1909.

[22] Without encrypted communications it would not be possible to securely exchange sensitive data, such as credit card details, and therefore secure online transactions would likely be impossible.

Whilst traditionally the crypto wars have been divided into two conflicts—the 1990s and post-Snowden eras—they are more appropriately divided into three distinct conflicts. The first crypto war started in 1966, and the major battles were waged in the mid-to-late 1970s over the strength of the first government-accredited data encryption standard (DES), and the freedom of academics to publish cryptologic research. The war concluded in 1981. The second crypto war commenced in 1991 when cypherpunk Phil Zimmermann, reacting to legislation put forth by Senator Joe Biden, which suggested encryption that did not provide for government access may be outlawed, wrote the first computationally viable public key cryptography software for personal computers.[23,24] Concurrently, the US government attempted to build a backdoor access method to encryption chips to provide cryptography to the masses whilst preserving their ability to access protected communications when required. This second war lasted until 2002. The third and ongoing crypto war was ignited in 2013 with Edward Snowden's disclosures of the NSA's surveillance practices.[25] Naturally, skirmishes occurred between the crypto wars.

Today, the crypto-anarchist aspiration to hinder state security functions is not as fantastical as may have been thought at the inception of these ideas in the 1980s.[26] The challenge of cryptography is that practitioners do not know how to implement robust encryption that at once meets the requirements of citizens, businesses, and governments. This combined requirement is an encryption capability that both protects the digital privacy of citizens and businesses from a plethora of threats, including overreaching governments, whilst at the same time providing a selective, or "exceptional" access method against singular implementations of cryptography (e.g., an encrypted smartphone) for government agents in possession of legal warrants. The feasibility of selectively breaking encryption algorithms for law enforcement agencies without creating a systemic security weakness has been repeatedly met with derision by the technical community.[27] The primary issue is that once a "backdoor" has been created, how can that backdoor be secured against compromise by unauthorized users? Creating secure backdoors is considered by many technical experts to be impossible due to the inability to both protect the access mechanism (i.e., the access process at a corporate headquarters), and to prevent others from independently discovering and exploiting the access mechanism. Therefore, societies are confronted with a dilemma; if the encryption exceptional access problem cannot

---

[23] The software was called "Pretty Good Privacy" (PGP). There had been earlier efforts to create public key software computationally viable for personal computers, such as Charlie Merritt's Dedicate32 software, however the computations (key generations) were too slow to be used in practice.

[24] United States Congress, 1991. Section 2201.

[25] The NSA is America's primary communications intelligence agency. Their mission statement is: "The National Security Agency/Central Security Service (NSA/CSS) leads the US government in cryptology that encompasses both Signals Intelligence (SIGINT) and Information Assurance (IA) products and services, and enables Computer Network Operations (CNO) in order to gain a decision advantage for the Nation and our allies under all circumstances" (National Security Agency, 2018).

[26] For an articulation of the crypto-anarchists' philosophy, see May, 1988.

[27] See Abelson et al., 2015.

be solved, society must either implement a system allowing governments complete access to all encrypted communications (or major subsets thereof), introducing systemic weaknesses into the digital ecosystem upon which society depends, or society must implement (or continue to permit) robust cryptographic systems that prevent any government access to encrypted data. Either option will distort the pre-digital government-citizen power dynamic, with one path leading to an era of heightened state power and digital vulnerability and the other leading to a greater level of risk from hostile nations, organized crime, and terrorism. This impasse is at the root of the crypto wars and has catalyzed a debate between citizen and state spanning half a century without resolution (or at least resolution to the satisfaction of nation states).

In order to understand this topic, we must explore what is meant by the concepts of security and privacy. Whilst security and privacy have a large body of academic research, both terms are contested. Daniel Solove argues that privacy should not be considered a singular entity, but a series of concepts that resemble one another: "The term privacy is best used as a shorthand umbrella term for a related web of things."[28] Furthermore, Solove argues that other than in this usage, "the term privacy has little purpose. In fact, it can obfuscate more than clarify."[29] Solove comments that rather than focusing on the definition of privacy, we should instead direct our attention to the specific privacy violations that cause harm to individuals.[30] For instance, Solove indicates surveillance and interrogation cause harm, as the objective of these pursuits is the attainment of information the subject is not willing to relinquish. Another example is unauthorized disclosure of information, which harms an individual by influencing the way others judge their character.[31]

Privacy is increasingly prominent in legal documents; however, this was not always the case. For instance, consider the 1789 American Bill of Rights which outlines the rights of its citizens. The Fourth Amendment, which is a battleground for whether the constitution supports the use of encryption, declares:

> The right of the people to be secure in their persons, houses, papers, and effects, against unreasonable searches and seizures, shall not be violated, and no warrants shall issue, but upon probable cause, supported by oath or affirmation, and particularly describing the place to be searched and the persons or things to be seized.[32]

The amendment did not explicitly use the term "privacy." Diffie observes, "I don't suppose it occurred to anyone at the time that it [privacy] could be prevented."[33] The amendment also failed to qualify what it meant to be "secure," what would constitute reasonability, and whether there was a threshold of criminality that would trigger a violation of a citizen's rights. By the twentieth century, more focus was being placed on privacy and the consequences of its violation. In the United Nation's *Universal Declaration of Human Rights* of 1948, the authors brand rights violations as a root

[28] Solove, 2007, 760.
[29] Ibid.
[30] Ibid, 482.

[31] Ibid, 490
[32] United States Government, 1789, 396.
[33] Diffie, 1995, 394.

cause for "barbarous acts which have outraged the conscience of mankind."[34] The declaration specifically employs the term "privacy," stating, "No one shall be subjected to arbitrary interference with his privacy, family, home or correspondence."[35] Interestingly, the declaration includes a clause that could be applied to digital encryption technologies, and that is not found in other similar documents, "Everyone has the right...[to] share in scientific advancement and its benefits."[36]

The term security equally suffers from a contestation of definition, with the notion of security itself being subjective. For Arnold Wolfers, "national security" is a phrase used to indicate policies that should be "designed to promote demands which are ascribed to the state rather than to individuals, sub-national groups or mankind as a whole."[37] However, Ken Booth argues any such definition of security lacks universality, as "different world views and discourses about politics deliver different views and discourses about security."[38] In opposition to Wolfers, Booth argues the referent object for security should be individual humans rather than the state. Booth opposes Wolfers by arguing the state is a means, rather than an end, as in traditional security studies. Booth's removal of the state as the referent object to be secured means sub- and supra-state entities, such as individual security, women's security, and environmental security, can now be considered referent entities. Booth argues that security means emancipating citizens from physical and human constraints preventing pursuit of their goals. Whilst war is one constraint there are many others, including poverty, poor education, and political oppression; "emancipation, not power or order," Booth argues, "produces true security."[39]

An argument can be made that privacy itself is a national security issue, as privacy is a core value helping democratic forms of governance endure. Privacy facilitates freedom of speech without fear of censorship or repercussions. This enables the incubation of new political ideas amongst small groups before such ideas mature and are able to be articulated to the electorate for wider debate. If privacy were to be subverted, this mechanism of developing new potentially contentious political ideas would be compromised—one could argue this would undermine a structural pillar of democracy threatening the future of the country under its existing governance model.

Acute challenges arise when one or more citizen rights, such as security and privacy, are in conflict. Documents such as the French *Declaration of the Rights of Man and of the Citizen*, and the UN's *Universal Declaration of Human Rights* profess that as well as a right to liberty, or privacy, citizens have a right to security. Governments must confront conundrums such as citizens who demand security from terrorism, but also instruct their privacy must not be violated. Whether governments elect to provide additional security at the expense of privacy or vice versa, they will be curtailing a core right of their citizens. Governments must therefore consider how they balance freedoms, and which of a citizen's rights are removed or curtailed either

---

[34] United Nations, 1948, 398.
[35] Ibid, 399.
[36] Ibid.

[37] Wolfers, 1952, 481.
[38] Booth, 1997, 106.
[39] Booth, 1991, 319.

temporarily or permanently. Ideally, policies should be implemented that accurately reflect the will of the population as to what degree of privacy and their broader civil rights should be sacrificed for "national security" goals, or vice versa. Therefore, we must explore citizen sentiment on this issue, and the primary factors causing sentiment modulation. Pollsters typically frame their questions on this topic as an either/or between security and privacy, which produces results that are somewhat unnuanced, but are useful nonetheless as a general view of citizen sentiment.

One may hypothesize high profile security/privacy events, such as the Al-Qaeda attacks of 2001, or the Edward Snowden leaks of 2013, would have a significant impact on public sentiment with regard to security and privacy but the supporting evidence for this statement is often contradictory. For instance, a 2006 CNN poll of 1003 Americans found that 38% believed the government had gone too far in restricting civil liberties; this number had increased from 28% in 2003, and 11% in 2002.[40] This suggests that in the wake of the September 11, 2001 attacks Americans were more willing to accept privacy curtailment in favor of a perceived increase in security, which would support the hypothesis that the attacks changed public sentiment, only for them to slowly revert to a "normal" state as the fear of attack subsided. An alternate reading of this data may be that the measures the government imposed after the attack incrementally altered security measures and privacy provisions until the point was reached at which greater numbers of civilians thought the measures no longer proportionate to the threat.

However, other studies suggest there is less of an impact from security-privacy events. For instance, a Pew Research survey conducted after the Snowden revelations in 2015 revealed that 62% of respondents believed it more important to investigate terrorism than protect privacy; the same response received 68% of the vote in 2010, and 65% in 2006.[41,42] Whilst the sample size (1004) leaves questions as to whether this can be considered a representative data set, the three approximately correlating readings suggest that not all high-profile security/privacy events result in a drastic change in public sentiment, or that any post-Snowden modulation was short-lived. However, an alternate interpretation of this data could be that privacy events (e.g., Snowden leaks) have a minimum impact, or impact a much smaller demographic, than security events. Many other polls that attempt to show public opinion changes in proximity to high-profile security-privacy events suffer from the same challenge of being too small a sample to be considered representative.[43]

A 2019 Pew Research poll offered a larger sampling by interviewing 4,272 US adults.[44] The poll found 66% believed they were not benefiting from the system of government data gathering, and 64% were concerned how the government may be using their data. 47% believed at least most of the digital activities were being traced

---

[40] CNN, 2006.

[41] The full question was: "What do you think is more important right now—(for the federal government to investigate possible terrorist threats, even if that intrudes on personal privacy); or (for the federal government not to intrude on personal privacy, even if that limits its ability to investigate possible terrorist threats)"

[42] Washington Post, 2015.

[43] For instance, see Toner and Elder, 2001.

[44] Auxier, Rainie et al. 2019.

by the government. 49% believed it acceptable for the government to collect data on all Americans (mass surveillance) to detect terrorist activity; 31% felt it unacceptable. Surprisingly, 57% of the sample said they follow privacy news very, or somewhat closely—with those over 65 much more likely than their younger compatriots to do so. 70% felt their data was less secure than it was five years ago. Further analysis is needed to make detailed assessments of public security and privacy sentiments and to understand modulation variables. Citizens often have conflicting views about this topic as articulated by cypherpunk Timothy May:

> Americans have two dichotomous views held exactly at the same time. One view is,
>
> "None of your damn business, a man's home is his castle. What I do is my business."
>
> And the other is,
>
> "What have you got to hide? If you didn't have anything to hide, you wouldn't be using cryptography."
>
> There's a deep suspicion of people who want to keep things secret.[45]

When addressing the encryption debate one is often confronted with the argument May references, that if one has nothing to hide, one has nothing to fear from state surveillance. This position is held by those such as Michelle Van Cleave, who argues innocent citizens should not fear having their digital privacy violated by mass surveillance such as an NSA supercomputer conducting data mining.[46] The argument posits that if a government agent does not look at the data, it is not considered harmful to the citizen. Quantifying the damage from surveillance, whether it be human-operated or machine-driven, is indeed challenging. Digital privacy activists often draw out surveillance's impact of "chilling" freedom of speech and reducing the range of debate within the democratic process; Liberty argues that surveillance "causes us to self-censor and change our behavior."[47] But, how can one demonstrate speech has indeed been chilled? Or how can one measure the result of that chilling whilst providing quantified societal benefits of surveillance, such as security gains? Bruce Schneier argues the "nothing to hide" mantra positions the argument upon a faulty premise, that "privacy is about hiding a wrong. It's not. Privacy is an inherent human right, and a requirement for maintaining the human condition with dignity and respect."[48] The cypherpunks would agree, arguing in their manifesto:

> Privacy is not secrecy. A private matter is something one doesn't want the whole world to know, but a secret matter is something one doesn't want anybody to know. Privacy is the power to selectively reveal oneself to the world.[49]

45 Levy, 1993.
46 Van Cleave, 2013, 59.
47 Couchman, 2018.
48 Schneier, 2006.
49 Hughes, 1993.

We should further consider the framing of these rights. Opposing security and privacy so diametrically belies their interdependence. Security and privacy are symbiotic, not being likely to exist without one other, whilst achieving either to the fullest extent is unlikely sustainable. Daniel Sherwinter argues "absolute security requires totalitarianism, but total privacy creates anarchy."[50] The framing of the relationship between security and privacy as a "balance" is flawed, as Solove points out:

> Placing the security measure on the scale assumes that the *entire security measure, all-or-nothing, is in the balance.* It's not. Protecting privacy seldom negates the security measure altogether. Rarely does judicial oversight or the application of the Fourth Amendment prohibit a government surveillance activity. Instead, the activity is allowed subject to oversight and sometimes a degree of limitations. [author italics][51]

Additionally, not all security measures impact privacy; for instance, the introduction of fortified cabin doors in airplanes after 11 September 2001 have resulted in no diminution of citizen privacy.

In making decisions concerning civil liberties trade-offs, mechanisms should also be implemented to manage the biases upon politicians who are making rights decisions on not only the level of risk to the state, but to their personal careers. It is unlikely politicians will favor a civil rights decision exposing them to the personal electoral cost of a security incident over the less likely benefit a privacy bias would convey at the polls. Executive bias is addressed within terrorism literature. For instance, Tiberiu Dragu argued in 2011 that "the assumption that reduced privacy increases security…advantages the executive, who can rhetorically couch antiterrorism measures in terms of patriotism."[52] Dragu argues that should an executive oversee privacy restrictions there exists a paradigm that such restrictions may never be reversed:

> if a terrorist attack is absent, then they can argue that privacy-reducing measures are effective, and if a terrorist attack occurs, then they can argue that their surveillance powers were not sufficient to prevent the attack and ask for new powers.[53]

However, one should be cognizant that politicians maintain power by reflecting the desires of their constituents. Therefore, electorate-driven biases are valid in democratic societies. There are times when citizens' short-term fears following security incidents must be balanced with their long-term desires for freedoms such as privacy (if this is their desire). Such considerations can tempt us towards a potentially undemocratic form of government paternalism—a posture of informing citizens "you may say you want this, but this is what you actually want and need." In order to manage executive and public biases, mechanisms should be considered to ensure actions taken amidst high-profile but low-impact security incidents have appropriate safety valves. This can help ensure the long-term desires of the citizenry are not compromised with permanent privacy-restricting measures being implemented in response to temporary security threats.

---

[50] Sherwinter, 2007, 504.
[51] Solove, 2011, 35.
[52] Dragu, 2011, 74–75.
[53] Ibid, 75.

A further complication in framing security against privacy is that privacy measures such as encryption also benefit citizen security from cybercrime threats, and help protect government critical national infrastructure from hostile states. Rather than a binary conversation of the balance of power between the government and citizenry, or between the rights of security and privacy, we must consider the wider risk portfolio each party manages. Society must calculate where the greatest risk resides: a state that abuses its surveillance powers?; cybercriminals emptying citizen bank accounts?; blackouts instigated by foreign adversaries? Rather than a balancing of security and privacy, the encryption conundrum is really a question of risk management in the digital age.

Digital technologies do not represent the first communication revolution to disrupt the government-citizen power dynamic. Each communication revolution has provided citizens with a greater degree of connectivity and access to information, whilst also offering governments new surveillance opportunities. The next chapter will offer a brief exploration of each communication revolution to place the digital communication revolution into historical context.

REFERENCES

ARTICLES

Abelson, H., Anderson, R., Bellovin, S. M., Benaloh, J., Blaze, M., Diffie, W., Gilmore, J., Green, M., Landau, S., Neumann, P. G., Rivest, R. L., Schiller, J. I., Schneier, B., Specter, M. A., and Weitzner, D. J. (2015). Keys Under Doormats: Mandating Insecurity by Requiring Government Access to All Data and Communications. *Journal of Cybersecurity* 1(1), 69–79.

Booth, K. (1991). Security and Emancipation. *Review of International Studies* 17(4), 313–326.

Cayford, M. and Pieters, W. (2018). The Effectiveness of Surveillance Technology: What Intelligence Officials Are Saying. *The Information Society* 34 (2), 88–103.

Diffie, W. and Hellman, M. (1976). New Directions in Cryptography. *IEEE Transactions on Information Theory* 22(6), 644–654.

Dragu, T. (2011). Is There a Trade-Off between Security and Liberty? Executive Bias, Privacy Protections, and Terrorism Prevention. *American Political Science Review* 105(1), 64–78.

Sherwinter, D. J. (2007). Surveillance's Slippery Slope: Using Encryption to Recapture Privacy Rights. *Journal on Telecommunications & High Technology Law* 5(2), 501–532.

Solove, D. J. (2007). I've Got Nothing to Hide and Other Misunderstandings of Privacy. *San Diego Law Review* 44(4), 745–772.

Van Cleave, M. (2013). What It Takes: In Defence of the NSA. *World Affairs* 176(4), 57–64.

Wolfers, A. (1952). "National Security" as an Ambiguous Symbol. *Political Science Quarterly* 67(4), 481–502.

BOOKS

Broderick, W. and Mayo, D. (1980). *Civil Censorship in the United States During World War II* (Civil Censorship Study Group).

Higgs, E. (2004). *The Information State in England: The Central Collection of Information on Citizens since 1500* (Hampshire: Palgrave Macmillan).

Lyon, D. (2002). *Surveillance Society: Monitoring Everyday Life* (Buckingham: Open University Press).
Solove, D. J. (2011). *Nothing to Hide: The False Tradeoff between Security and Privacy* (New Haven: Yale University Press).

CHAPTERS IN BOOKS

Booth, K. (1997). Security and Self: Reflections of a Fallen Realist. In *Critical Security Studies*. Edited by Keith Krause and Michael C. Williams (London: UCL Press).
Diffie, W. (1995). The Impact of Secret Cryptographic Standard on Encryption, Privacy, Law Enforcement and Technology. In *Building in Big Brother: The Cryptographic Policy Debate*. Edited by Lance J. Hoffman (New York: Springer-Verlag), 393–400.
United Nations. (1948). United Nations Universal Declaration of Human Rights. In *Political Thought*. Edited by Michael Rosen and Jonathan Wolff (1999) (Oxford: Oxford University Press), 398–402.
United States Government. (1789). Bill of Rights. In *Political Thought*. Edited by Michael Rosen and Jonathan Wolff (1999) (Oxford: Oxford University Press), 396–397.

CYPHERPUNKS MAILING LIST ARCHIVAL POSTS

May, T. C. (1993). "Spreading Encryption to Political Groups." MessageID: "9302192007. AA27273@netcom.netcom.com." February 19, 1993.

WEBSITES

Alphabet. (2018). *Code of Conduct*. Available: https://abc.xyz/investor/other/code-of-conduct/ [Accessed December 31, 2018].
Auxier, B., Rainie, L., Anderson, M., Perrin, A., Kumar, M., and Turner, E. (2019). *Americans and Privacy: Concerned, Confused and Feeling Lack of Control over Their Personal Information*. Available: https://www.pewresearch.org/internet/2019/11/15/americans-and-privacy-concerned-confused-and-feeling-lack-of-control-over-their-personal-information/ [Accessed May 23, 2020].
Clausewitz, C. V. (1909). *On War*. https://www.gutenberg.org/files/1946/1946-h/1946-h.htm [Accessed August 12, 2020].
CNN. (2006). *Poll Finds U.S. Split Over Eavesdropping*. Available: http://edition.cnn.com/2006/POLITICS/01/10/poll.wiretaps/ [Accessed October 13, 2019].
Couchman, H. (2018). *Moving Forward the Fight against Mass Surveillance*. Available: https://www.libertyhumanrights.org.uk/news/blog/moving-forward-fight-against-mass-surveillance [Accessed December 22, 2015].
Crane, K. (1989). *East Germany's Military: Forces and Expenditures (Rand)*. Available: https://www.rand.org/content/dam/rand/pubs/reports/2007/R3726.1.pdf [Accessed December 26, 2018].
Cypherpunks. (1992–1998). *Cypherpunks Mail List Archive 1992–1998*. Available: https://lists.cpunks.org/pipermail/cypherpunks/2013-September/000741.html [Accessed July 10, 2015].
Facebook. (2018). *Bringing the World Closer Together*. Available: https://www.facebook.com/pg/facebook/about/?ref=page_internal [Accessed December 31, 2018].
Google. (2018). *Google Code of Conduct*. Available: https://web.archive.org/web/20180504211806/https://abc.xyz/investor/other/google-code-of-conduct.html [Accessed December 31, 2018].

Greenwald, G. (2013). *NSA Collecting Phone Records of Millions of Verizon Customers Daily.* Available: https://www.theguardian.com/world/2013/jun/06/nsa-phone-reco rds-verizon-court-order [Accessed January 10, 2020].

Hughes, E. (1993). *Cypherpunk's Manifesto.* Available: https://www.activism.net/ cypherpunk/manifesto.html [Accessed October 13, 2019].

Internal Revenue Service. (2018). *Tax Quotes.* Available: https://www.irs.gov/newsroom/tax-quotes [Accessed December 24, 2018].

Kaspersky. (2018). *Kaspersky Lab Discovers ZooPark, an Android-Based Malware Campaign.* Available: https://usa.kaspersky.com/about/press-releases/2018_zoopark-new-android-based-malware [Accessed December 31, 2018].

Levy, S. (1993). *Crypto Rebels.* Available: https://www.wired.com/1993/02/crypto-rebels/ [Accessed January 1, 2019].

May, T. C. (1988). *The Crypto Anarchist Manifesto.* Available: https://www.activism.net/ cypherpunk/crypto-anarchy.html [Accessed March 29, 2017].

May, T. C. (1994b). *Cyphernomicon V0.666.* Available: https://www.cypherpunks.to/faq/ cyphernomicron/cyphernomicon.txt [Accessed August 20, 2017].

National Security Agency. (2018). *Mission & Values.* Available: http://www.nsa.gov/about/ mission-values/ [Accessed July 11, 2018].

Rashid, F. Y. (2014). *Schneier on Security: Surveillance Is the Business Model of the Internet: Bruce Schneier.* Available: https://www.schneier.com/news/archives/2014/04/surveill ance_is_the.html [Accessed January 26, 2019].

Rogers, S. (2010). *Historic Government Spending by Area: Get the Data Back to 1948.* Available: https://www.theguardian.com/news/datablog/2010/oct/18/historic-governm ent-spending-area [Accessed December 29, 2018].

Schneier, B. (2006). *Schneier on Security: The Eternal Value of Privacy.* Available: https ://www.schneier.com/essays/archives/2006/05/the_eternal_value_of.html [Accessed October 10, 2019].

Telegeography. (2018). *Submarine Cable Map.* Available: https://www.submarinecablemap. com/ [Accessed December 24, 2018].

Toner, R. and Elder, J. (2001). *A Nation Challenged: Attitudes; Public Is Wary But Supportive on Rights Curbs.* Available: https://www.nytimes.com/2001/12/12/us/a-nation-challeng ed-attitudes-public-is-wary-but-supportive-on-rights-curbs.html [Accessed October 22, 2018].

United States Congress. (1991). *S.266—Comprehensive Counter-Terrorism Act of 1991.* Available: https://www.congress.gov/bill/102nd-congress/senate-bill/266 [Accessed February 10, 2019].

Washington Post. (2015). *Majority Says NSA Tracking of Phone Records "Acceptable"— Washington Post-Pew Research Center Poll.* Available: https://www.washingtonpos t.com/page/2010-2019/WashingtonPost/2013/06/10/National-Politics/Polling/release _242.xml?tid=a_inl_manual [Accessed October 10, 2019].

Wikileaks. (2017). *Vault 7: CIA Hacking Tools Released.* Available: https://wikileaks.org/ ciav7p1/ [Accessed March 7, 2017].

World Bank. (2018). *Military Expenditure (% of GDP).* Available: https://data.worldbank.org/ indicator/ms.mil.xpnd.gd.zs [Accessed April 16, 2020].

2 A Brief History of Communications Revolutions

What Hath God Wrought?

First Ever Telegram Message, Samuel Morse, 1844

2.1 THE WRITTEN WORD

The first communications revolution, discounting the emergence of language itself, was the written word, believed to have originated in Sumer (now southern Iraq) between 3400 BCE and 3300 BCE.[1] The written word allowed the conveyance of messages without depending on the accuracy of a courier's memory. If a communication were urgent, and needed to travel long distances, it would be relayed via additional couriers; the traditional verbal relaying of the correspondence decreased privacy and risked message integrity. The written word enabled reliable relay, ensuring long-distance transit without compromising integrity.

As literary rates improved, the written word resulted in greater ability for one-to-many, as well as one-to-one, communications in the form of pamphlets and books. Given the expense of production, the ability to produce lengthy texts likely remained the exclusive domain of Church and State, resulting in a perpetuation of their narratives and reinforcement of existing power structures. Despite this, smaller pamphlets could be produced in limited numbers by well-educated citizens allowing the circulation of political ideas, including those of a subversive nature. In such circumstances the creator(s) and recipient(s) would both have risked punitive measures if found with such documents.

The written word increased risk for citizens. Now, government agents, or their equivalent, were not solely reliant on the pliability of the courier, who, when carrying a memorized message could deny they were a courier, or could even provide interception agents a fake message. Interception of a courier with a written message almost guaranteed access to the correspondence unless some form of steganography was employed. Whilst cryptography aims to make messages unreadable to those apart from the authorized recipient, steganography attempts to conceal the fact a message is in transmission. For example, almost 4000 years ago in Babylon (not far from Baghdad in present-day Iraq), messages were written on clay tablets

---

[1] Fagan and Beck, 762.

before being covered with a second layer of thin clay. The recipient would break off the outer layer revealing the underlying message; to all others without the knowledge a message was concealed within the tablet, its existence remained hidden.[2] Steganography could enable couriers to be intercepted and minimize the risk of message discovery; correspondents could also send a decoy message as a countermeasure to courier interception. It is possible the courier themselves may not have been aware they were carrying a message, offering the sender further protections. However, given the primitive steganography methods available, this approach was unlikely to be often used.

The most sensitive of messages were probably transited by trusted associates of the sender, who were unlikely to have advertised their role as couriers. The sender may even have the trusted courier memorize the message rather than committing it to paper thus further reducing interception risk. However, memorization did introduce an authenticity challenge where the courier was not known by the recipient as being a trustworthy representative of the sender, and a diminution of message integrity given the fallibility of human memory.

There were several measures correspondents could take to realize the benefits of the new communications medium whilst minimizing associated risks. The written word allowed for increased authenticity provisions, such as signatures and seals. A seal could be created with the use of a material such as wax or bitumen upon which the sender is able to create a distinctive impression (typically a symbol associated with the author, such as a coat of arms). Nevertheless, there was a dependency on the recipient having pre-existing knowledge of the authentic representation of these markings, and they could be forged by a skilled artist. Before the written word, recipients had either had no means of verification, or relied on pre-existing knowledge that the courier was a trusted representative of the sender. Otherwise, the correspondents may have utilized a previously exchanged code word or phrase to establish authenticity.

Without steganography, possession of a written message could not be denied by the courier as could a memorized message. However, the government could not easily access its contents without the correspondent's knowledge, as inspection required violation of the seal. Nevertheless, given the fragility of early envelopes, the government could hope the recipient would assume a damaged seal was the result of hazardous travel conditions or rough handling, rather than interception.[3] Governments could employ specialists who were skilled in the ability to open letters and rebuild the seal, but such work was intricate, and still risked discovery if their work was not immaculate. Additionally, governments would need to coerce the courier into not reporting the interception of the correspondence, or they would need to covertly access the mail for a long enough duration to allow surreptitious access and seal reconstruction. Whilst the discovery of interception may not have posed a risk in some scenarios, in most it would have been anathema to the government's intelligence operations, where knowledge of interception could expose an investigation thus counteracting the intelligence gain.

---

[2] Lane, 2009, 2.   [3] Ibid, 3.

Another option available to citizens was to encrypt their messages, albeit only with the use of primitive hand ciphers. Even closer to the present, robust implementation of complex hand ciphers would remain a rare skill. Encryption also provided security against the courier betraying message confidentiality. Governments could employ mathematicians to attempt to break encrypted messages; in some situations, the mere presence of cryptography may have been treated as evidence of conspiracy. Few citizens could afford to employ professional cryptographers to protect their messages, and senders of encrypted messages were likely reliant on their recipients having an equally skilled cryptographer to decrypt the correspondence; the recipient would also need prior knowledge of the encryption schema and keying material. But for governments, the retention of cryptographic experts was economically viable. For instance, Queen Elizabeth I of England employed cryptologists who broke the encrypted messages of Mary, Queen of Scots, which revealed her complicity in an attempt to assassinate Elizabeth: the decryption led to Mary's death.[4]

Overall, the government's surveillance capabilities were not significantly diminished by the evolution of the written word, given the citizenry's low literacy rates. However, as literacy rates improved, the written word resulted in a greater ability for governments to surveil their citizens.

2.2 PRINTING PRESS

The printing press, invented in 1448, represented a significant information dissemination advance.[5] At first, the printing press served the elite of society—governments, churches, and universities—but as literacy rates increased so did the variety of books produced.[6] As the printing press was a broadcast mechanism, with its messages typically designed to be read by all, privacy was not required. Regulations upon the printing press were not initially introduced, although most printings were conducted with church or state oversight. After 1500, as the technology began to spread, the church and state became more concerned with the printing presses—specifically they feared the presses could foment heresy or dissent. As a result, in some countries printers were required to be licensed by the state, or for printed texts to receive advanced approval by the church.[7] By the sixteenth century's conclusion, the printing press enabled a new profession: journalism.[8] Whilst the printing press produced primarily unidirectional communications, slower bidirectional interactions could occur between reader and newspaper which could be reflected back to the readership in the form of "letters to the editor."

Journalism challenged the information dominance by the powerful; the government and clergy were no longer the sole arbiters of the national narrative. However, in many countries journalists would have known a story criticizing the government could result in loss of income, liberty, or maybe even life. Even today, mechanisms

---

[4] Singh, 1999, Chapter 1.
[5] Lemelson MIT, 2018.
[6] Cameron, 1999, 65.

[7] University of Leicester Open Educational Resources, no date.
[8] Cameron, 1999, 67.

are reserved in many societies for the government to issue reporting restrictions under the banner of security or justice.[9] Sometimes such bans are temporary, other times they are permanent.

As printing press technologies propagated, they became harder for governments to control, especially when they were not owned by entities such as newspapers that could be more readily coerced to conform to the state's narrative. The printing press allowed citizens the opportunity to oppose government activities, as was the case during pre-revolutionary France when a large volume of pamphlets challenged royal policies.[10] Citizens authoring, or even possessing, subversive literature could face penalties. Therefore, subversive content would unlikely have been widespread.

Overall, whilst the printing press initially acted as an amplifier for the state's narrative, and for its gaining public support for government policies, the subsequent rise of journalism and the ability to disseminate subversive literature benefited citizens to a greater degree. The benefits of journalism grew over time as within democratic societies the principle of freedom of the press was enshrined within culture and law allowing government policy, and even the government's right to power, to be contested.

2.3   POSTAL SYSTEM

Postal systems emerged in the sixteenth and seventeenth centuries. King Henry VIII of England appointed the first "Master of the Posts" in 1516 to serve the King and Court.[11] The postal system replaced freelance couriers, or small private organizations, with monolithic national systems operated by the state or private enterprise. For citizens, this meant a more reliable, extensive, and affordable service. Whilst the speed of such services was moderated by the means of travel available to mail workers, a postal system offered citizens significant new communication capabilities.

From the earliest days, the ability of the postal system to not only increase commerce, but to aid in surveillance was recognized. The postal system was declared to be "the best means to discover and prevent many dangerous and wicked designs against the commonwealth," in an English ordinance establishing a general post office in 1657.[12] A public postal system gave the government direct, unfettered access to all correspondence traversing the network. The removal of almost all private couriers entrusted with delivery of a letter, and potentially loyal to the sender to the point of being deprived of liberty and life, removed a significant surveillance constraint— though of course senders could still elect to use couriers. In postal sorting stations the government could intercept letters and employ experts to counter tamper-resistance mechanisms enabling the copying of letters before onward transmission. For the first time, the government was able to reliably intercept letters without leaving a sign they had done so against all but the most sophisticated tamper-detection methods.

---

[9]   Such as the UK's Defence and Security Media   [11]   Royal Mail Group, 2016.
      Advisory (DSMA) notices.   [12]   Tomlins, 1811, Post Office Section.
[10] Greenlaw, 1957, 354.

Governments could alter the contents of the letter to serve their goals, such as sowing discord within a rebel faction, or could even prevent the mail's transit altogether.

However, there were challenges for the government in operating a postal surveillance system. Whilst at first there would have been a limited volume of correspondence and any letters going to a recipient (or even a nation) considered to be a threat could be intercepted, as the volume of traffic and complexity of the network increased, it would be harder to reliably intercept communications from a savvy citizen. For instance, the citizen could ask a friend to take receipt of their correspondence at a secondary address. As mailboxes became common it would also become harder to track letters the individual sent unless they were under surveillance enabling authorities to identify any public postbox in which they deposited correspondence. However, as citizens knew the government had access to mail, or held coercive powers over private companies which had access, they were unlikely to use the postal service for discussion of criminal or subversive activities—they would seek alternate communication methods. For instance, in the 1770s "committees of correspondence" were established by American colonists to enable a more secure transmission of communications independent from the government postal system when they wanted to challenge acts of parliament.[13] Additionally, citizens could employ hand ciphers to preserve their privacy against this system; however the complexity of doing so, the ability of the government to break citizen codes, and the suspicion likely falling upon citizens for using such methods were all reasons to assess hand ciphers were rarely employed.

Overall, whilst the invention of the postal system enabled citizens to more readily communicate with one another, it represented a much more significant advance in the state's ability to surveil its populace, and removed the citizens' visibility of courier interceptions.

2.4 TELEGRAPH

The telegraph removed the protection of an envelope, signature, and seal from correspondence but allowed much faster delivery than the postal service, with transmission in minutes or hours rather than days or weeks. Messages were typically short, given a human operator had to manually type the message. The necessity of human operators resulted in no expectation of privacy for telegraph communications. Therefore, it is unlikely citizens chose to use this method to send information that may be construed by the government as adversarial. Hand ciphers could be applied to communications; however, few likely did so outside diplomats and the most cautious in society, given the requisite skills. Encryption would also be highly visible to operators, and could trigger government surveillance.

Governments invested heavily in telegraph monitoring capabilities. Telegraph technology allowed the first global surveillance system to be implemented by Britain during the First World War. Exploiting the worldwide network of the Eastern

---

[13] Lane, 2009, 8.

Telegraph Company, British "censors" were positioned to monitor or prevent communications between the enemy and its agents.[14] The limitation from a surveillance perspective was the short length of the messages and the lack of telegraph privacy provisions, meaning the enemy was unlikely to often transmit sensitive data. However, when the telegraph intercept product was aggregated, and combined with other sources of intelligence, the capability would likely have been a formidable asset.

Overall, whilst the government gained access to another communications mechanism they could intercept without the target becoming aware, and whilst communications were predominantly unencrypted, citizens having no expectation of privacy likely limited the surveillance benefit to governments. However, for some use cases, the bulk aggregation of even unencrypted communications may have given governments new intelligence insights.

2.5 TELEPHONE

The telephone enabled real-time global communications. It was a technology that encouraged citizens to be more verbose than previous mediums; bidirectional communications could extend for hours. For the citizen this resulted in a greater ability to exchange ideas and to plan subversive or illegal actions.

For most of telephony history there has been no, or minimal, encryption. In the early years, telephone switchboard operators were required to connect calls. Once the parties were connected the operators were supposed to stop listening; however, callers likely understood this was not always the case.[15] Early telephone lines were often shared between a number of people in the same building with multiple physical phones. One occupier could pick up their phone to make a call to find another resident already on the line—should they wish to, they had the ability to listen in to their neighbor's conversation. Therefore, citizen privacy expectations whilst making telephone calls were limited.

Telephony networks offered governments a rich source of intelligence. Providers kept call records for billing purposes, this gave governments an ability to retrospectively identify citizens' communications networks when they became subjects of investigation.[16] The richly detailed exchanges also offered a level of insight previously not possible in all but the most lengthy and intimate missives. In countries where the telephony systems were not government-operated, some form of executive order or legislation may have been required to compel private companies to provide the government with access to the communications infrastructures. Additionally, agencies like the NSA could develop capabilities to access communications without a private firm's consent. However, interception with the cooperation of the carrier offers the optimum chance of completeness of intercept and economy of cost. For governments to monitor known telephone numbers became easy. However, if

---

[14] Corera, 2015, Prologue.   [16] Ibid, 82.
[15] Lane, 2009, 80.

citizens set out to avoid interception, they could use the telephone devices of friends, public pay phones, or later disposable—or "burner"—cell phones. However, such steps were likely only taken by the most paranoid of citizens, or those partaking in criminal endeavors, rather than those seeking communication privacy for its own sake.

Overall, telephony resulted in a significant augmentation for government surveillance powers as a richer level of content was being passed over a readily accessible insecure communications channel. Whilst citizens would have limited expectations of privacy, and it is likely the most sensitive aspects of any subversion or illegal matters would be conveyed in person, there would remain ample information transmitted advantageous to the state.

2.6 COMMUNICATIONS REVOLUTIONS SUMMARY

Table 2.1 summarizes the key benefits bestowed by the communications revolutions to citizens and state, and the overall impact upon the state's surveillance capabilities.

This table shows a parallel advance in citizen communication tools and state surveillance capabilities. This book will explore the role encryption has played in the state's surveillance capabilities, and the impact that has had on citizens' civil liberties. The next chapter explores the cultural genesis of the cypherpunks, a group that has led the charge against government cryptography policies since the early 1990s.

TABLE 2.1

Communications Revolutions Surveillance Impacts

Communications Revolution	Citizen Benefit	State Benefit	Surveillance Impact
Written Word	• Authenticity (signatures and seals) • Signs of interception (violation of seals) • Hand ciphers to protect messages	• Interception easier as messages on paper, rather than in courier's memory • Ability to alter messages in transit (though requires either covert access or courier complicity)	• Small augmentation of surveillance capabilities, increases over time as literacy rates improve
Printing Press	• Public dissemination of government counter-narrative • Journalism	• Wider dissemination of their narrative	• Early gain for states, until journalism allows counter-narratives
Postal Service	• Reliable, cost-efficient, and swift long-distance message delivery • Ability to more readily correspond with fellow citizens	• Transparent interception of communications • Longer duration with correspondence to covertly defeat anti-tamper mechanisms	• Significant augmentation of surveillance capabilities
Telegraph	• Increased speeds of transmission	• Communications sent primarily unencrypted • Metadata analysis	• Mainly neutral, though some benefits for surveillance
Telephone	• Instant global communications • Ability to organize dissent (though risk of detection)	• Access to citizen phone calls • Richer level of detail than telegraph • Ability to retrospectively create network maps of targets	• Significant augmentation surveillance capabilities

REFERENCES

ARTICLES

Greenlaw, R. W. (1957). Pamphlet Literature in France During the Period of the Aristocratic Revolt (1787–1788). *The Journal of Modern History* **29**(4), 349–354.

BOOKS

Cameron, E. (1999). *Early Modern Europe: An Oxford History* (Oxford: Oxford University Press).

Corera, G. (2015). *Cyber Spies: The Secret History of Surveillance, Hacking and Digital Espionage* (New York: Pegasus Books Ltd).

Fagan, B. M. and Beck, C. (Eds.). *The Oxford Companion to Archaeology* (Oxford: Oxford University Press).

Lane, F. S. (2009). *American Privacy: The 400-Year History of Our Most Contested Right* (Boston: Beacon Press).

Singh, S. (1999). *The Code Book: The Secret History of Codes and Code-breaking* (London: Harper Collins).

Tomlins, T. E. (1811). *Law-Dictionary Explaining the Rise, Progress, and Present State of the English Law: Defining and Interpreting the Terms or Words of Art; and Comprising Copious Information on the Subjects of Law, Trade, and Government, Volume 2* (New York & Philadelphia: I.Riley).

WEBSITES

Lemelson MIT. (2018). *Johan Gutenberg: Movable Printing Press*. Available: https://lemelso n.mit.edu/resources/johann-gutenberg [Accessed October 28, 2018].

Royal Mail Group. (2016). *500 Years of History Delivered to Your Doorstep*. Available: https ://www.royalmailgroup.com/en/press-centre/press-releases/royal-mail-group/500-ye ars-of-history-delivered-to-your-doorstep/ [Accessed November 21, 2019].

University of Leicester Open Educational Resources (no date). *The Historical Background to Media Regulation*. Available: https://www.le.ac.uk/oerresources/media/ms7501/mod 2unit11/page_02.htm [Accessed July 5, 2020].

3 The Cypherpunks

The only solution is to use crypto anarchy to destabilize the system and, hopefully,

see them swinging by their necks in front of the Washington Monument.

Nearly every politician...has richly earned the death penalty...

I hope to see in my lifetime justice carried out.

Timothy C. May, cypherpunks co-founder, 1997

3.1 THE MOST EXTREME CRYPTO-ANARCHIST MANIFESTATION: ASSASSINATION POLITICS

The idea was simple. Well, it was not so much an idea as an inevitable by-product of the crypto-anarchists' labors: *Assassination Politics*.

In the summer of 1996, Jim Bell sent his ten-part *Assassination Politics* essay to the cypherpunks, a collective of cryptographic enthusiasts and digital privacy activists, many of whom fervently believed encryption could shift the balance of power from governments to citizens.[1] Bell's *Assassination Politics* was designed to coercively regulate behavior with threat of assassination for those who acted outside the acceptable bounds of the system's operators; encryption, Bell believed, provided the anonymity to make the *Assassination Politics* market impossible to destroy.[2]

Bell ardently believed the citizenry faced dire peril from the government, whose weapons included taxation, regulations, and "hired thugs to kill us when we oppose their wishes."[3] A dedicated libertarian, Bell's view was that he never consented to live in the United States—his citizenship was an accident of birth. Nor had he agreed to relinquish to the government a substantial portion of the salary earned from his toils at Intel, where he built early solid-state hard drives.[4] Anyone receiving his extorted tax dollars, Bell wrote, was guilty of violating the non-aggression principle, the act of interfering with another person or their belongings without consent, and thus was, in Bell's interpretation of libertarian doctrine, a legitimate target for assassination.[5] Bell did speculate, however, that most victims of assassination politics would be guilty of more than simply spending his taxes. Bell cited the government agents responsible for killing participants of the Ruby Ridge and Waco sieges in 1992 and 1993, as the types of people likely to be marked for death.[6]

---

[1] Bell, 1997.
[2] Ibid, Part 7.
[3] Ibid, Part 1.

[4] Greenberg, 2012, Chapter 3.
[5] Bell, 1997, Part 7.
[6] Ibid, Part 1.

Bell envisaged a centralized organization that would administer the assassination market, for ease of explanation we will call it "Murder Corp." Target selection would be Murder Corp's responsibility. If Bell were CEO, he would only target violators of the non-aggression principle.[7] Citizens could donate money to the assassination of his targets by placing bets on when they would die (or be assassinated). The winner would collect the entire bounty on the target. These bets would be in the form of digital money (cryptographic currencies). For most citizens there would be no expectation their guess would be correct, but their bet would swell the overall bounty on the target's head. At a certain point, the bounty would be sufficient to entice a more proactive citizen to make their own bet. Only this citizen would not be guessing, for they would be the assassin willing to prompt Atropos to draw her knife across their victim's life thread, allowing collection of the bounty. Let's call our assassin "Brutus."

It was previously hard to motivate assassins, Bell explained, as they could not reliably collect and spend their bounty whilst maintaining anonymity.[8] For most like Brutus, the risk-reward balance was not favorable.

But three technological developments were now reducing the assassin's risk, making the partnership of Murder Corp and Brutus possible. These developments were providing the "technical underpinnings for the entire system," Bell wrote, allowing Brutus to collect his bounty with "mathematical certainty that he could not be identified."[9]

Firstly, Diffie and Hellman's intellectual offspring, public key encryption, was emerging from its awkward teenage years and being widely deployed. With the protection of strong encryption Brutus could submit his "guess" to Murder Corp of when he thought the target may "suffer a terrible, and entirely unfortunate accident," without the fear of government eavesdroppers.[10]

Secondly, the Internet held a growing number of anonymous encrypted relays. Even if law enforcement were surveilling either Murder Corp or Brutus, they would not know they were talking to one another as their communications were routed through servers around the globe before reaching one another.[11]

Thirdly, cryptocurrencies beyond the government's control meant Brutus' blood-soaked bounty was untraceable. This last component was still evolving, though Bell believed it would soon manifest.[12]

According to Bell, the risk–reward ratio was changing; the odds would soon favor Brutus.

This same triad of developments also offered protection to those users wishing to "guess" when a selected victim would meet their downfall, but who were unwilling to wield the scythe. They could connect to Murder Corp through anonymous remailers, their communications protected by public key encryption, and their bets placed in the form of untraceable cryptocurrencies. Bell believed the business model was

---

[7] Ibid.
[8] Ibid, Part 2.
[9] Ibid, Parts 2 and 7.

[10] Ibid, Part 7.
[11] Ibid.
[12] Ibid.

viable, and that organizations such as Murder Corp would be legal under current law.[13]

Even should Murder Corp actively cooperate with government due to coercion, the anonymity fused into its technical architecture would prevent any meaningful assistance being rendered. It was a prescient design; in the post-Snowden era, technology companies would embark upon a similar strategy, implementing end-to-end encryption architectures to place decryption keys for sensitive data, such as instant messaging, solely on their users' devices, and thus out of their own technical grasp. This meant should a state serve a warrant demanding all data owned by a specific user be surrendered to the government, the organization would be able to provide nothing apart from encrypted data. At once, communications companies could, by the letter of the law, fulfil their legal obligations to the state, whilst offering users the level of protection they demanded in the post-Snowden world and protect their global client base. But, Bell's Murder Corp would never contemplate yielding to the government, and Bell believed even were the enterprise deemed illegal:

> no prosecutor would dare file charges against any participant, and no judge would hear the case, because no matter how long the existing list of "targets," there would always be room for one or two more.[14]

As Murder Corp grew, Bell prophesied a profound change in politics as "no large government structure could survive in its current form."[15] Assassination politics would catalyze if not an anarchist, at least minarchist (minimal government) system.[16]

Bell further encourages the reader to "consider how history might have changed if we'd been able to 'bump-off' Lenin, Stalin, Hitler, Mussolini," for surely citizens would have reached deep into their pockets to bankroll the efforts of their local Brutus.[17] In fact, Bell postulated, once dictators were removed there would be no more war, as without political disputes between leaders, "the people are able to get along pretty well with the citizens of other countries."[18] Therefore, armies and nuclear weapons would be redundant and could be abolished; Bell ruminated on whether he had "provided a solution for the 'war' problem that has plagued mankind for millennia."[19] As the author of a system that could topple the most powerful dictators in the world, Bell acknowledged he may be killed by such dictators. Bell accepted the risk. He would forfeit his life if he could, "help form what will be the LAST revolution on earth, the one that'll take down ALL the governments," if, in commanding Murder Corp he could make the "ENTIRE WORLD FREE FOREVER," he would willingly pay the ultimate price.[20] Bell proclaimed assassination politics could not be stopped, as he realized the "destination is certain"; Bell recalls how he felt "awe,

---

[13] Ibid, Part 3.
[14] Ibid, Part 4.
[15] Ibid, Part 2.
[16] Ibid.

[17] Ibid.
[18] Ibid.
[19] Ibid, Part 9.
[20] Ibid, Part 10.

astonishment, joy, terror, and finally, relief."[21] Murder Corp and Brutus were inevitable, Bell believed, regardless of what anybody did to stop them, and that the scourge of taxes, governments, nuclear weapons, and war was coming to an end. "I'm satisfied we *will* be free," Bell wrote. "It may feel like a roller-coaster ride...[but] please understand, we *will* be free" (original italics).[22]

Jim Bell's assassination politics were, in his own words, "radical and extreme."[23] In years to come Bell would be labeled a "techno-terrorist" by the US government, and be convicted of both tax evasion and stalking an IRS agent, the latter of which saw Bell become a guest of the federal correction system for a decade.[24]

Whilst in prison, Bell would claim to have made a "truly phenomenal discovery in the areas of chemistry, physics, and material science, of total value well in excess of $100 billion."[25] Bell claimed to have "probably solved the energy crisis a dozen times over"; the MIT graduate believed once he became a "hero of scientific and technological progress,"[26] his assassination politics would be reassessed and implemented. Prison only hardened his views:

> I once believed it's too bad that there are a lot of people who work for government who are hard-working and honest people who will get hit [by assassination politics] and it's a shame...I don't believe that any more. They are all either crooks or they tolerate crooks or they are aware of crooks among their numbers.[27]

Bell's sanity would be questioned on multiple occasions throughout his trials.[28] His assassination politics is an example of the most extreme manifestation of the crypto-anarchy ideology, to which he and some—but only some—of his fellow cypherpunks adhered.

Assassination Politics generated polarizing debate on the cypherpunks' mailing list, their digital club house. Timothy C. May, crypto-anarchy's ideological founder, told Bell he was coming across as "a loon," and required "some kind of anti-psychotic medication."[29] But it was not the morals concerning May; he himself once wrote of the need to perform a "thermonuclear cauterization" of Washington so that a new, limited government could be formed that "honors the Constitution instead of catering to negroes and queers and welfare addicts."[30] May was anxious Bell would invite unwanted government attention.[31] May, who like Bell had worked at Intel, raised the possibility of assassination markets as early as the 1980s, suggesting the coming of networking and encryption could result in online black markets providing services including assassination.[32] But Bell took the concept much further, defining a detailed operating model for an assassination market; years later, he even estimated a body count of around 230,000 (extrapolated from the French Revolution) would

---

[21] Ibid, Part 7.
[22] Ibid.
[23] Ibid.
[24] McCullagh, 2000a and 2000b; Greene, 2001a and 2001b.
[25] Greenberg, 2012, Chapter 3.
[26] Ibid.

[27] McCullagh, 2000a.
[28] Ibid.
[29] May, 1996.
[30] NowImScared, 2007.
[31] Greenberg, 2012, Chapter 3.
[32] May, 1996.

be required to usher in the anarchic age he prophesied would result from Murder Corp.[33] May's primary concern was Bell "wasn't paranoid enough in distancing himself from the project," and that Bell did not take ample steps to protect himself from the legal ramifications of his writings; after all, the government would likely use the full array of tools in their armory to combat such subversive ideas.[34] May minimized contact with Bell, likely fearing the attention of law enforcement agencies.[35] Cypherpunk Dr. Vulis (an alias, or "nym" [pseudonym]) posted on the cypherpunks' mailing list that he believed Bell to be a "highly intelligent, knowledgeable and overall nice person"; however, another user operating under the alias Jdoe-0007 replied Bell was in need of "immediate mental health intervention." Jdoe-0007 posted that Bell was advocating "nothing less than paid death squads using crypto as a means to hide payment to these murderous terrorists." Jdoe-0007 also foresaw the government using assassination politics as an excuse to justify new cryptography regulations and put another nail in the "crypto-coffin." Jdoe-0007 told Vulis he prayed both he and Bell were the first victims of their own "murderous madness."[36] There were others on the mailing list who adopted a more favorable stance, entering into detailed exploration of how Murder Corp would function, one anonymous user even provided a list of suggested targets.[37] Others on the list refused to engage Bell. After attempting to point out the system's myriad flaws, alias user Black Unicorn posted, "I simply refuse to debate the matter any longer as it is clear you are not open to reasoned debate, nor, it would seem, are you clearly possessed of reason."[38]

When Bell asked Phil Zimmermann, the inventor of Pretty Good Privacy (PGP), a tool that for the first time brought public key encryption to the masses, his opinion of *Assassination Politics*, Zimmermann told Bell who was, in his opinion, so "full of violence and anger," that he accomplished what no government officer ever managed, "he had made me wonder whether I never should have worked on encryption in the first place."[39]

Assassination Politics is representative of the vitriolic antipathy towards authority harbored by the crypto-anarchist wing of the cypherpunks, though as demonstrated by the response to Bell's idea, there were many desiring a less violent solution. The cypherpunks often held a Manichean view of the world: they were the good, the light, and the government was the darkness that must be restrained, or even banished with the most potent weapon at their disposal: encryption.

3.2   ARISE, CYPHERPUNKS

"Arise, Cypherpunks, evil deeds are brewing in the bowels of the Beast"—with these words Timothy May summoned his comrades to arms.[40]

In spring 1992, May hosted Eric Hughes as the latter searched for a home in Oakland, California. During their shared residence, little house-hunting occurred,

---

[33] Greenberg, 2012, Chapter 3.
[34] Ibid.
[35] Ibid.
[36] jdoe-0007, 1996.

[37] Anonymous, 1996.
[38] Black Unicorn, 1996.
[39] Greenberg, 2012, Chapter 3.
[40] May, 1992.

as the two exchanged impassioned views on the privacy threats posed by the nascent digital revolution.[41] By the end of the visit, May and Hughes decided to assemble a group of like-minded friends to take action.[42] The focus of their group would be to forge cryptographic tools to defend themselves from present and future enemies.[43]

The group first coalesced in September. May and Hughes, along with John Gilmore, who became the third cypherpunk co-founder, discreetly invited around twenty people to their inaugural meeting. Many attendees held strongly anti-establishment views and needed little convincing the government would exploit the digital age to augment their power. Time was set aside for the reading of manifestos.[44] May first published his *Crypto Anarchist Manifesto* in 1988, and now it had a rapt audience, "A specter is haunting the modern world," the manifesto began, "the specter of crypto anarchy."[45] May's manifesto explained the technology for a "social and economic revolution" was now emerging, and the coming decade would bring sufficient computing power to make the revolution "economically feasible and essentially unstoppable."[46] Just as the invention of the printing press eroded the power of the medieval guilds, cryptography would alter the nature of commerce and governance.[47] The coming technological revolution would bring public key cryptography to the masses. It would enable citizens to interact and trade anonymously with one another. May wrote that these developments would profoundly alter society, governments would no longer be able to collect taxes if transactions were veiled by cryptography, and payments would utilize crypto-currencies beyond the control of central banks. The nature of government regulations would have to change, as how could one regulate what one could not see? The ability to keep information secret would be fundamentally challenged as public key encryption and anonymous relays allowed insiders to leak confidential documents online with minimal fear of identification. Implicit in May's writings was that if citizens' interactions were protected by encryption, the ability of the government to build digital dossiers on its populations would be severely diminished. May cautioned:

> The State will of course try to slow or halt the spread of this technology, citing national security concerns, use of the technology by drug dealers and tax evaders, and fears of societal disintegration. Many of these concerns will be valid; crypto anarchy will allow national secrets to be trade[d] freely and will allow illicit and stolen materials to be traded.[48]

May acknowledged "criminals and foreign elements" would be enabled by the new world of crypto-anarchy, but that would "not halt" its spread.[49] For May and his cohorts, whilst cryptography could facilitate activities even they could find common ground with the government in opposing, such as child abuse; their ability to protect

---

41 Hughes, 1993.   46 Ibid.
42 Ibid.   47 Ibid.
43 Ibid.   48 Ibid.
44 Levy, 2001, Crypto Anarchy, Chapter 7.   49 Ibid.
45 May, 1988.

themselves was akin to gun ownership. Whilst both guns and encryption could be used to terrible ends, it was also a last defense of the citizenry against a potentially tyrannical government possessing a monopoly on violence. British cypherpunk Russell E. Whitaker commented, "Arguments for the right to keep and bear arms can often be directly mapped onto arguments for the right to keep and use pkeys [private keys]."[50]

For the rest of the first meeting the group played the "crypto-anarchy game," role-playing how their various anonymous systems would operate.[51] It was during the meeting that Eric Hughes' girlfriend, Jude Milhon, herself a seasoned hacker and activist who had written a how-to guide for "online revolution," joked, "You guys are just a bunch of cypherpunks"; the hackers loved the name, and according to May, it was "adopted immediately."[52]

The name was a play on the cyberpunk genre combining science fiction with hackers and cyberspace. Cyberpunk novels included William Gibson's *Neuromancer*, which would later become the inspiration for the Matrix movies. Such movies typically involved hackers who were victimized by oppressive regimes in the physical world, but who flourished in cyberspace, often finding ways to use their extreme intellect to outsmart dictatorial overlords. However, as May explained in the sprawling *Cyphernomicon*—the closest thing the group had to a canon—the cypherpunks were "about as punkish as most of our cyberpunk cousins are, which is to say, not very."[53]

The group's name, as well as their crypto-anarchy ideology, would be challenged in the months ahead. Some cypherpunks believed they should re-brand themselves, that talk of anarchy was "not helpful to the cause," and "Middle America will be turned off by the hippie radicals in t-shirts, leather jackets, sandals, and beards."[54] They argued unless the cypherpunks could speak the language of the "suits," their message would fall on deaf ears. Alternative names for their group such as "Cryptographic Research Association" or "Cryptography Privacy" were suggested, but May believed cypherpunks was an appropriate name:

> I fully agree with many of you that the name "Cypherpunks" has some, shall we say, unusual connotations. Some will assume we're skateboarding geeks, others will assume we're "crypto primitives" who pierce our bodies and spend all our time at raves. But the name has undeniable appeal to many, and certainly grabs a lot of attention. It seems improbable that some staid name like "Northern California Cryptography Hobbyists Association" would've gotten much attention.[55]

The cypherpunk brand would capture the imaginations of journalists. After all, May reflected, there were already groups addressing digital civil liberties issues that can "present lawyer-like faces to the press." "As for respectability," May wrote to his challengers:

---

[50] Whitaker, 1992.   [53] Ibid, 2.4.9.
[51] May, 1994a.   [54] May, 1993.
[52] May, 1994b, 2.4.10; Milhon, J. (no date).   [55] Ibid.

is our goal to be "co-opted" into the establishment?...Is it to be a respectable voice for moderation and the gentle process of negotiating? I think not. In a sense, Cypherpunks fill an important ecological niche by being the outrageous side, the radical side... perhaps a bit like the role the Black Panthers, Yippies, and Weather Underground played a generation ago.[56]

May's drawing on icons of the counterculture was followed by an affirmation that he had no intention to don a suit, nor to cut his hair or shave his beard; he also had no intention of "watering down" the cypherpunk message or being "moderate and reasonable" in their pursuit of crypto-anarchy.[57] He would be true to his word.

May was crypto-anarchy's most vocal proponent, posting more messages to the mailing list than any other user over a six-year period.[58] Despite this, May did not consider himself their leader. Officially, the crypto-anarchists did not have a leader; May explained this in the *Cyphernomicon* by pointing to the etymology of the name of their ideology: "No rule = no head = an arch = anarchy."[59] Despite this, May was one of the few members with the spare time to act as the cypherpunks' unofficial figurehead, even if it was never acknowledged by the other members. May had retired in 1986, at the age of 34, from his position as a physicist at Intel, possessing sufficient stock options to ensure that with a lifestyle eschewing fast cars, foreign travel, and expensive restaurants, he would never need work again.[60] The highlight of May's dozen years at Intel was when he proved quantum events could affect the movements of subatomic particles; this discovery enabled Intel to insulate their semiconductors from such disruptive quantum events, thus allowing Moore's law to continue advancing.[61] But as 1986 arrived, things were getting tougher at Intel and the bottom ten percent of each division feared for their jobs.[62] After receiving a criticism-heavy performance review, May ran his calculations on a well-worn HP calculator and realized he could afford to resign and pursue the life of an intellectual, unencumbered by accommodating the whims of his corporate bosses.[63] During his "retirement," May digested piles of books and academic articles covering everything from business magazines to science fiction novels; "I never had any interest in horseback riding, boating, hiking, or whatever it is people do," he commented, "Instead, I just read and read and read."[64]

Like many technologists, the cypherpunks were deeply protective, and profoundly in love with the Internet which led to a parental desire to protect the space many considered their intellectual home. John Perry Barlow, a co-founder of the Electronic Frontier Foundation, the preeminent digital civil liberties group, described himself as having a "holy vision" the first time he connected to the Internet; he reflected:

If you're going to take all of humanity and put them in the same social space where they don't have clothes and buildings, or anything to show who they are, they don't

---

56 Ibid.
57 Ibid.
58 Cypherpunks, 1992–1998.
59 May, 1994b, 2.4.7.
60 Greenberg, 2012, Chapter 2.

61 Levy, 2001, Crypto Anarchy, Chapter 7.
62 Greenberg, 2012, Chapter 2.
63 Ibid.
64 Ibid.

have property, they don't have jurisdictional boundaries, they don't have law maybe...it could be the biggest thing since the capture of fire.[65]

For Barlow, the Internet brought about a "renegotiation of power" between government and citizen as dangerous as the invention of the Gutenberg Bible.[66] The Internet was a nexus for these intellectual explorers. Cypherpunk John Young, who established one of the first leaking sites before collaborating with Julian Assange on WikiLeaks, recalls when he and his wife first discovered the Internet, "We felt that we had been living in the doldrums, and suddenly we were on the cutting edge."[67] The "netizens" could instantaneously interact with the pioneers of their fields, even when they were on the other side of the planet. In a world where proximity dictates collaborative potential, groups could now easily coalesce, exchange groundbreaking ideas, ferment change, and find comfort in those who shared their passions.

3.3 THE FEAR OF BIG BROTHER

"It is crucial that the fiends proposing this be convinced that resistance will be too high to implement their plan," cypherpunk Perry Metzger posted to the mailing list in late 1992.[68] Metzger saw the government attempting to clamp down on free access to cryptography, and intended to shout from the digital rooftops to frustrate their ambitions, "My friends...by panicing [sic] early we can avert a disaster later on."[69] It was a prominent cryptographer from Georgetown University, Dr. Dorothy Denning, who instigated the panic. Denning was exploring ways law enforcement could gain access to encrypted communications in the coming digital age. She had suggested a trustee, non-governmental agency could retain copies of all of the public's private encryption keys.[70] Should the government need access to the associated encrypted data as part of a criminal investigation they could, with the appropriate legal warrant, approach the agency to recover the keys and decipher the data.[71] The hoarding of private keys would become known as "key escrow."[72]

To the cypherpunks, key escrow was the digital equivalent of the government keeping a copy of their front door keys just in case the FBI should ever need to search their homes.[73] To Denning, it was a way to "prevent a major crisis in law enforcement," and to provide strong encryption to all citizens without the loss of vital electronic surveillance capabilities she believed were an "essential tool in preventing serious crimes such as terrorist attacks and destabilizing organized crime... that could seriously disrupt other liberties."[74] Metzger quickly recognized her words as a variation of a recurring narrative that the government was only attempting to "maintain the current capability in the presence of new technology."[75]

---

[65] Ibid, Chapter 6.
[66] Ibid
[67] Ibid, Chapter 3.
[68] Metzger, 1992a.
[69] Ibid.
[70] Metzger, 1992a.

[71] Ibid.
[72] See Chapter 6.
[73] Bernhardt, 1993.
[74] Metzger, 1992a.
[75] Ibid.

Denning stated her work had nothing to do with the government.[76] However, the cypherpunks wondered whether Denning and other "quaint crypt-heads" had alerted the government to the threat of cryptography.[77] They further considered whether the government was now using academics to release position papers in preparation for a "crypto-crackdown."[78] Metzger cautioned his fellow cypherpunks that if Denning's "sinister" idea became legislation, "it would become impossible for individuals to take any action to protect their own communications privacy from a dictatorial regime, even ignoring the question of abuses that could occur right now."[79] These were the two core fears of the cypherpunks: government abuse of existing powers, and the implementation of surveillance capabilities that could one day subvert democracy and usher in a dictatorial regime to the inception of a dystopian future. This fear was articulated by Phil Zimmermann when he testified before the US Senate Committee on Commerce, Science, and Transportation in 1996:

> The Clinton Administration seems to be attempting to deploy and entrench a communications infrastructure that would deny the citizenry the ability to protect its privacy. This is unsettling because in a democracy, it is possible for bad people to occasionally get elected—sometimes very bad people.
>
> Normally, a well-functioning democracy has ways to remove these people from power. But the wrong technology infrastructure could allow such a future government to watch every move anyone makes to oppose it. It could very well be the last government we ever elect.
>
> When making public policy decisions about new technologies for the government, I think one should ask oneself which technologies would best strengthen the hand of a police state. Then, do not allow the government to deploy those technologies. This is simply a matter of good civic hygiene.[80]

With such considerations in mind, the safeguard of warrants was seen as little guarantee, as such a defense against abuse, according to Metzger, could "dissapear [sic] with a mere change of attitude."[81] Cognizant of these two fears, Metzger instructed that "Big Brother" be resisted.

3.4   CYPHERPUNK OBJECTIVES

Absent official leadership, goals, and collaborations bound the cypherpunks. Now the cryptographers had found one another, they set about forging consensus as to their ambitions. The cypherpunks' strategic objectives encompass four areas:

1. Unencumbered citizen access to encryption
2. Anonymous communications
3. Freedom to conduct anonymous economic transactions (cryptocurrencies)
4. Development of whistleblowing platforms to constrain government power

---

[76] Ibid.
[77] May, 1992.
[78] Ibid.

[79] Metzger, 1992a.
[80] Zimmermann, 1996.
[81] Metzger, 1992a.

These objectives were founded on the desire to preserve the freedoms the cypher-punks believed citizens enjoyed in the pre-digital era; cyberspace must be afforded the same protections as the physical realm. There was also the possibility of aug-menting citizens' power using cryptography; for instance, digital leaking platforms could significantly lower the risk of detection for citizens releasing stolen data evi-dencing corporate or governmental corruption.

Whilst this book only covers objective 1—unencumbered citizen access to encryp-tion—each objective will briefly be explored to provide a context of the cypher-punks' wider goals, and the potential of cryptography to disrupt the status quo.

3.4.1 No Government Cryptography Regulations: Freedom for the Bits!

The primary objective of the cypherpunks was that encryption should be unen-cumbered by governmental regulations. Widespread, or ubiquitous, encryption would, in theory, prevent the state surveilling its citizens' digital data. In 1993, when the cypherpunks learned the office of the US President had created an email account so citizens could digitally write to the administration, cypherpunk Marc Ringuette, who was studying a master's degree in Computer Science at Carnegie Mellon University, jokingly suggested the following could be sent on behalf of their group:

> Dear President Clinton,
> Freedom for the bits! We will not rest until each bit is free to determine its own natural orientation without outside coercion. The good news is, you don't need to do anything at all; merely get out of the way of the free market, and the bits will free themselves.
> Best regards,
> The Cypherpunks (Anarchist Subgroup).[82]

The Clinton administration implemented a neoliberal approach to governance in emphasizing the market's ability to best meet the needs of citizens when free from government regulation; however, its cryptography policies were in sharp contrast to the deregulatory vigor that otherwise characterized their administrations.

With divergent opinions on the desired political implications of ubiquitous encryption, the only "major consensus of the cypherpunks is the commitment to cryptography and the belief that it should be unregulated and freely used," alias user Larry Detweiler notes.[83]

3.4.2 Anonymous Communications: A Shield
from the Tyranny of the Majority

Anonymity allows minority opinions to be heard in a democracy without fear of reprisals from the majority. The US boasts a rich history of anonymity. For instance,

---

[82] Ringuette, 1993 and 2000.   [83] Detweiler, 1993.

in the late 1780s, eighty-five essays supporting the recently drafted ratification of the US constitution were published in newspapers by the Founding Fathers James Madison, Alexander Hamilton, and John Jay. All were authored under the pseudonym "Publius," and collectively became known as the *Federalist Papers*.[84] Perhaps no stronger argument could be made regarding the Fathers' feelings regarding anonymity.

The cypherpunks considered anonymity the shield of the citizenry, for it was their corporeal forms, rather than their ideas, which were vulnerable to dismemberment. Ideas could be suppressed, but never destroyed. Cyberspace and anonymity were intended to "create immunity from these [physical] threats," Eric Hughes comments.[85]

As well as shielding the cypherpunks from the majority, anonymity helped conceal the digital exhaust of their interactions. Eric could email Tim with encrypted content, but the mail must still traverse the digital highways to reach its destination, departing Eric's virtual door and arriving at Tim's. Any system administrators watching, or any spies eavesdropping, would know Eric and Tim were communicating, even if their correspondence could not be decrypted. This information, or metadata, they believed, could be fed into a government surveillance machine, becoming a vital component in the creation of digital dossiers. Therefore, the cypherpunks developed anonymous remailer networks to ensure communications could not be easily traced during transmission.

3.4.3 ANONYMOUS ECONOMIC TRANSACTIONS (CRYPTOCURRENCIES)

If Diffie is the father of digital encryption, then David Chaum is the father of cryptocurrencies. It was Chaum who first articulated the surveillance implications of digital currencies: "The foundation is being laid for a dossier society, in which computers could be used to infer individuals' lifestyles, habits, whereabouts, and associations from data collected in ordinary consumer transactions," he wrote in a 1985 article, the title of which—"Security Without Identification, Transaction Systems to make Big Brother Obsolete"—conveyed Chaum's political leanings.[86] Chaum, a Professor at New York and later California University, grew up in the midst of the counterculture and studied in San Diego; he would later leave a graduate program at UCLA in disgust at his program's military funding.[87] Chaum was not a cypherpunk, but his writings would form an indispensable book in their gospel, and Eric Hughes had once worked for him in Amsterdam.[88] Amongst his most cogent observations was:

> Computerization is robbing individuals of the ability to monitor and control the ways information about them is used. Already, public and private sector organizations acquire extensive personal information and exchange it amongst themselves.[89]

---

[84] United States Government, no date.
[85] May, 1994b, 6.7.2.
[86] Chaum, 1985a, 1030.

[87] Greenberg, 2012, Chapter 2.
[88] Slater, 1997.
[89] Chaum, 1985a, 1030.

This trend of people not knowing their data is secure, Chaum explained, could have a "chilling effect," causing them to "alter their observable behaviors."[90] This behavior modification would produce an effect on society similar to that described by the panopticon prison, designed by Jeremy Bentham in 1791.[91] Efficiency was the driver of Bentham's design. He wanted to allow a small number of prison guards to monitor a large number of inmates. Bentham conceived of a circular building in which the cells would be at the circumference and the guard tower in the center, where through the use of "blinds and other contrivances," the guards would be concealed from their prisoners, this would promote "the sentiment of a sort of omnipresence."[92] The inmates would never know when they were being watched, therefore they would modify their behavior on the assumption of constant surveillance. Chaum believed a dossier society would render this same effect. The coming of digital currencies was expanding the dangers of the dossier society to "an unprecedented extent," David Chaum wrote in 1985.[93] Seven years later, Tim May informed the cypherpunks the trend towards a "cashless society represents the greatest threat…[it would be] worse that [than] Orwell's worst should it become government run." May told the cypherpunks they must act to prevent this fear becoming reality.[94]

The appeal of cryptographic currencies to the cypherpunks was their decentralization. In combination with encryption and the anonymity infrastructure the cypherpunks were building, transactions could occur between two parties without the government's knowledge. If the government could not see transactions, they could not levy taxes, nor build a dossier society. Therefore, the cypherpunks believed cryptocurrencies had the potential to clog the very arteries surging power through the body politic, the government's beating heart would fall silent, and the era of crypto-anarchy could begin.

3.4.4 WHISTLEBLOWING PLATFORMS TO CONSTRAIN GOVERNMENTS: FALLING THE BEAST

Julian Assange, whose WikiLeaks would expose a quarter of a million classified US diplomatic cables, and release tens of thousands of emails stolen from the Democratic National Committee before the 2016 election, would not join the cypherpunks for several years after their formation.[95] However, his essay, "Conspiracy as a Form of Governance," evangelizing the transparency effects leaking could deliver, articulates the impact for which the cypherpunks were likely striving:

> The more secretive or unjust an organization is, the more leaks induce fear and paranoia in its leadership and planning coterie. This must result in minimization of efficient internal communications mechanisms…and consequent system-wide cognitive

---

90 Ibid.
91 Bentham, 1843.
92 Ibid.

93 Chaum, 1985b.
94 May, 1992e.
95 Leigh, 2010; WikiLeaks, 2016.

decline resulting in decreased ability to hold onto power as the environment demands adaption.[96]

Assange asks the reader to imagine what would become of a political organization if they were so in fear of leaks, they abandoned email and telephone communications preventing collaboration with their colleagues:

> An authoritarian conspiracy that cannot think is powerless to preserve itself against the opponents it induces. When we look at an authoritarian conspiracy as a whole, we see a system of interacting organs, a beast with arteries and veins whose blood may be thickened and slowed until it falls, stupefied; unable to sufficiently comprehend and control the forces in its environment.[97]

Assange believed leaking would frustrate abuses of the current government and be a defense against future tyrants. Of the cypherpunks' four strategic objectives, leaking was perhaps the traditional activity the Internet could most advance. It was not merely a case of replicating the ability of past whistleblowers, but enhancing them— the ability for leakers to steal vast quantities of data, such as the US diplomatic cables and DNC emails—would previously have been if not impossible, then highly unlikely.

The cypherpunks believed that together, encryption, anonymity, cryptocurrencies, and leaking platforms would provide them with the ability to prevent mass surveillance and reverse the government-citizen power dynamic. It is easy to see why the government feared such cryptography-induced advances. But it was not solely these objectives which shaped the philosophy and manifesto of the cypherpunks.

3.5   DIGITAL INSURGENTS: CODE IS LAW

John Gilmore made his fortune as an early employee of Sun Microsystems—in youthful retirement he co-founded the Electronic Frontier Foundation (EFF) to lobby for the recognition of civil liberties in cyberspace. EFF provided support to those technologists they believed persecuted by, in John Perry Barlow's words, the "continuing intemperance of law enforcement."[98] Along with co-founders Mitch Kapor and John Perry Barlow, Gilmore directed EFF to fund lawyers to assist embattled hackers, to conduct digital policy analysis and encourage grassroots activism, and to advocate for a more secure and free Internet.[99] But the cypherpunks were neither lobbyists, nor were they a protest movement—they would not be marching belligerently around Berkley waving placards denigrating government cryptography policy. The cypherpunks preached direct action - they were a digital insurgency.

Whilst Gilmore's EFF were lobbying for government recognition of traditional rights in the digital domain, the cypherpunks would create encryption tools to render government policies moot. Today, they were going to build the tomorrow they

---

96   Assange, 2006.   98   Perry Barlow, 1990.
97   Ibid.   99   Electronic Frontier Foundation, no date.

craved, a practice which would embody Lawrence Lessig's pithy assessment, "code is law."[100,101] The cypherpunks believed once their code was globally dispersed, the government could never revoke it.

This philosophy of this approach is articulated in Eric Hughes' 1993 *Cypherpunk Manifesto*:

> Cypherpunks write code.
> We know that someone has to write software to defend privacy, and since we can't get privacy unless we all do, we're going to write it.
> We publish our code so that our fellow Cypherpunks may practice and play with it. Our code is free for all to use, worldwide.
> We don't much care if you don't approve of the software we write.
> We know that software can't be destroyed and that a widely dispersed system can't be shut down.[102]

But the "cypherpunks write code" slogan should not be taken literally, explains Sandy Sandfort: "'to write code' means to take unilateral effective action as an individual. That may mean writing actual code, but it could also mean dumpster diving [searching through strangers' trash for useful information]."[103] Tim May explains in the phrase actually means to aspire to "technology and concrete solutions over bickering and chatter"; in fact, May explained, only around 10% of the list, as of late 1994, could write "serious" code, and only half of those could produce "crypto or security software."[104] However, they were a direct action group: all had to contribute to the mission with whatever skills they possessed.

The cypherpunks believed if they shaped the tools of the future, then those tools would in turn shape the future they desired. Aaron Swartz, an intellectual descendent of the cypherpunks, would reflect years later, "the design of the software regulates behavior just as strongly as any formal law does; more effectively, in fact."[105]

3.6   THE CRYPTO SINGULARITY

Seven weeks after the cypherpunks' first physical meeting, Tim May posted his belief they had reached a "crypto singularity," encompassing "extremely rapid changes in outlook, technology, and culture." May cited a number of reasons for his bold assertion. Firstly, the increasing user base of PGP, the first public key encryption tool, that Phillip Zimmermann's missionary-like zeal had brought forth to the masses. Secondly, the increasing coverage of cryptography in *Scientific American* and *Wired* that was attracting cryptographic heathens ripe for baptism into their new religion. Thirdly, the development of fully-encrypted remailers, which for the first time was

---

[100] Lessig, 2006.
[101] Attribution of the roots of this statement is contested, though its origins may trace back to a Winston Churchill 1941 statement, "We shape our buildings and afterwards our buildings shape us" (Quote Investigator, 2016).
[102] Hughes, 1993.
[103] May, 1994b, 4.5.3.
[104] Ibid, 2.4.17.
[105] Swartz, 2016.

providing an ability to anonymously communicate whilst maintaining cryptographic protection of the contents of one's message. Fourthly, May noted the "incredible excitement" for the crypto-anarchy agenda at the annual hackers' conference. But May assessed there was another contributor to the singularity: the authorities were starting to conduct a "hacker crackdown."[106] Were the authorities recognizing they were losing control of cyberspace? Or for the first time realizing the importance of a domain they neither understood nor could govern? A recent high profile government operation, Operation Sundevil, had targeted hackers across the country, and separately, a meeting of hacker collective "the 2600" had been ejected from a shopping mall.[107] The origins of the latter action were ascribed to the Secret Service by some on the mailing list, as well as by 2600 members themselves (though the shopping mall security guards claimed to have acted independently).[108] "Will the cypherpunks be next?" May asked. "Will the 150–200 of us get raided?"[109]

The cypherpunks feared the government would demonize hackers and encryption, creating a public climate in which they could either outlaw cryptography, or pass such severe restrictions on the permissible algorithms and key lengths as to render its application effectively useless. May theorized that in order to create this climate, the government would saddle the "four horsemen of the Infocalypse," these being terrorists, child pornographers, drug dealers, and money launderers.[110] The prosecution of terrorists and child pornographers was seen as a universal good across the political spectrum. Any steps that could be presented as sensible measures to stymie the horsemen's machinations, such as restrictions on the "hacker technology" encryption, would likely be well received by the public in such a climate. This would especially be the case if a campaign could be mounted in the immediate aftermath of a high-profile security incident caused by a horseman. May predicted a "high-publicity case involving drugs or child molesters will be used as a pretext to crack down."[111]

The cypherpunks had always feared the government would attempt to douse the flames of the crypto-infused revolution they were igniting, to counteract such attempts they aspired to widely disperse their knowledge and tools before any anti-encryption legislation were enacted.[112] As well as making it technically infeasible to put the "crypto-genie" back in the bottle, if encryption were so intertwined with online transactions and the burgeoning information-economy, then it would be economically untenable for the US government to outlaw the technologies.[113] Big business would then likely protest any restrictive actions and they, unlike the cypherpunks, wielded significant lobbying prowess in the capital. Simon Garfinkel suggested their argument should be that in an increasingly globalized world, encryption was vital for communicating securely with the overseas offices of American companies, and for protecting the information on their hard drives against seizure by foreign countries.

---

106 May, 1992c.
107 See Section 3.12, "The Hacker Ethic."
108 The Omega [alias], 1992.
109 May, 1992c.

110 May, 1994e.
111 Ibid.
112 May, 1994b.
113 Ibid and May, 1994d.

The cypherpunks believed they had an advantage in the race against government: they were agile and innovative, their enemy cumbersome and anachronistic.

If the crypto-singularity were indeed near, legislative actions would soon be powerless to halt cryptography. However, May warned, before they reached that point, things would get "very sticky."[114] As the cypherpunks' reputation grew, so did their fears of government surveillance. Perry Metzger posted in November 1992, "I bet the government folks know exactly what it is we are discussing and in great detail."[115] It was even possible to elicit all of the cypherpunks' email addresses by sending a simple instruction to the mailing list's server. Despite their calls for anonymity and encryption, in the early 1990s the cypherpunks' anonymity tools were mostly experimental and not reliable enough for everyday use; even when such technologies improved, the cypherpunks were hesitant to use them. The cypherpunks needed to exchange knowledge in order to develop crypto tools, and disappearing underground may be perceived by the government and public as evidence of conspiracy. Many of their order were also eminent physicists, computer scientists, and academics—they were the intellectual elite with legitimate concerns based on a history littered with serious government abuses of privacy—why should they hide?

3.7 HOW ANARCHIST WERE THE CYPHERPUNKS?

The majority of the cypherpunks were anti-establishment. There were "a lot of radical libertarians [and] some anarcho-capitalists."[116] In February 1993, May estimated fifty percent of the list were "strongly libertarian/anarchist" whilst a further twenty percent were liberal or leftist, and the rest of the group's composition was unknown.[117] On another occasion, May observed additional political orientations that included, "anarcho-syndicalists, anarcho-capitalists, neo-pagans, Christian fundamentalists, and maybe even a few unreconstructed Communists."[118] May believed the average age of the cypherpunks was between 21 and 27, though there were some members in their 40s and 50s.[119]

For those of the anarchic and libertarian disposition there was a desire to, in May's words, "undermine the so-called democratic governments of the world."[120] Libertarians believe the most important political value is liberty, rather than democracy.[121] They feel that should the majority be uneducated or unenlightened, the tyranny of the majority can equal the tyranny of a dictator.[122] Libertarians saw taxation as the most potent non-lethal weapon at the democrat's disposal. However, the "ultimate evil" was the government's monopoly of violence. Libertarians believe each person should be permitted to live by their own choices, provided they do not attempt to prevent others from doing the same.[123] In a libertarian's eyes, the gravest crimes in history were perpetrated by governments, often as a result of their deliberate

---

[114] May, 1994c.
[115] Metzger, 1992b.
[116] May, 1994b, 1.2.
[117] May, 1993b.
[118] May, 1994c.

[119] May, 1994d.
[120] May, 1994b, 2.13.6.
[121] Boaz, 2015.
[122] Hospers, 1971, 23.
[123] Ibid, 2.

policies.[124] Julian Assange had the following C. S. Lewis quote in his signature block in late 1996, evidencing this philosophy: "Of all tyrannies a tyranny sincerely exercised for the good of its victims may be the most oppressive. It may be better to live under robber barons than under omnipotent moral busybodies."[125] The cypherpunks also believed the governments of the world had caused much more suffering than any other force; Sandy Sandfort posted to the mailing list, "governments—primarily through the use of their militaries—have killed, by some counts 170,000,000, men, women, and children in this century alone. Hardly the guardians of freedom, in my opinion."[126]

There is debate within libertarian ideology, as there was within the cypherpunks, regarding whether government was necessary at all. For moderate libertarians, a government is only tolerable when its exercise of force is severely curtailed. The only acceptable applications of governmental coercion are in acting against their citizens who have initiated force against fellow citizens, thus violating their victim's liberty and the non-aggression principle, and in defending the country from external threats.[127] Another school of thought is anarcho-capitalism, whose adherents judge any form of government as an unnecessary evil and believe the free market can supply the same services without violating human rights in the process.[128]

For the anarcho-capitalists, and some libertarians, there was frustration their tax dollars were being spent in propping up a part of society less productive or able than themselves, Tim May once spoke of "the dirt people clamoring for more handouts."[129] Libertarians believe they should not be compelled to aid their fellow citizens, to provide such aid is a choice individuals should make for themselves, rather than by being compelled via taxation.[130] Tim May expresses his views in the *Cyphernomicon* about how crypto-anarchy will affect the social configuration:

> Crypto anarchy means prosperity for those who can grab it, those competent enough to have something of value to offer for sale; the clueless 95% will suffer, but that is only just. With crypto anarchy we can painlessly, without initiation of aggression, dispose of the nonproductive, the halt and the lame.[131]

This view was not universal among the cypherpunks, however, as Julian Assange argued:

> the 95 percent of the population which compromise the flock have never been my target and neither should they be yours. It's the 2.5 percent at either end of the normal that I have in my sights.[132]

This viewpoint represented a fundamental split within the cypherpunks. One segment, intellectually elite, productive, and prosperous, resented the burden of the

---

[124] Ibid, 3.
[125] Assange, 1996.
[126] Sandfort, 1996.
[127] Hospers, 1971, 8.
[128] Ibid, 241.

[129] Greenberg, 2012, Chapter 2.
[130] Hospers, 1971, 11.
[131] May, 1994b, 6.7.3.
[132] Bartlett, 2015.

masses—they wanted to isolate themselves from those they considered inferior, for why should they pay a government to subsidize the masses when they receive nothing but oppression in return? The other segment, in which Assange resided, desired to focus its wrath on the overbearing government more than the citizens who gave its leaders power.

But not all of the cypherpunks were advocates of overthrowing the government. Phil Karn would post in November 1992 that he found himself a "little uncomfortable with some of the more anarchist ideas expounded"; he was not "interested in overthrowing the government by force," but wanted to protect his privacy from everyone, especially the government.[133] Karn believed "good fences make good neighbors," and "good cryptography will make for good government."[134] Even May, in a rare moderate moment, commented, "Overthrowing the government may not be such a hot idea…the replacement could be much worse. But finding ways to preserve personal liberty is a good goal. Finding ways to selectively bypass the State is also a good goal."[135]

The cypherpunks may have disagreed on the degree to which the authorities needed to be curtailed, but it seems almost a universal belief among their collective that government must be downsized to the absolute minimum, into the smallest corner of public life. The hacker ethic the cypherpunks inherited proclaimed central authorities were to be distrusted—this imperative colored the cypherpunks' attitude in pursuing their goals of a technological check against the government.

3.8 THE HACKER ETHIC

One-hundred and fifty agents burst through doors in Detroit, LA, and San Francisco, in Miami, Texas, and New York.[136] Similar scenes were unfolding in fourteen US cities as Secret Service agents and law enforcement officers executed twenty-seven search warrants.[137] They would seize around 40 computers and 23,000 floppy disks, in the process shutting down numerous bulletin boards (early digital forums).[138] Only three arrests were made in Operation Sundevil.[139] It was 1990, years before the cypherpunk movement would assemble; the "hacker crackdown" was underway. "Today, the Secret Service is sending a clear message to those computer hackers who have decided to violate the laws of this nation," Assistant Director of the Secret Service Garry M. Jenkins declared immediately after the raids, "in the mistaken belief that they can successfully avoid detection by hiding behind the relative anonymity of their computer terminals."[140] "It's a whole new era," US Attorney for Arizona Stephen McName declared. "Computers are providing a new avenue for criminal activities. It is possible to transmit computer information for an illegal purpose in the blink of an eye."[141] McName stated the hackers may have been responsible for fifty

---

[133] Karn, 1992.
[134] Ibid.
[135] May, 1994d.
[136] Sterling, 2002, Part 3.
[137] Charles, 1990; Turner, 2006, Chapter 5; Sterling, 2002, Part 3.
[138] Charles, 1990.
[139] Turner, 2006, Chapter 5.
[140] Sterling, 2002, Part 2.
[141] Markoff, 1990.

million dollars of losses.[142] Assistant Attorney General Gail Thackeray later stated, "You could pay off the national debt" with the proceeds of electronic crime acquired by criminals ripping off the "old and the weak."[143] No evidence for her bold statement was provided. Thackeray claimed hackers profited through traditional cons, such as boiler room fraud,[144] fake sweepstakes, and fake charities, rather than hacking crimes *per se*.[145] Criminality was occurring in cyberspace, and there were legitimate national security concerns and criminal threats, but the stigma from the more malignant cyberspace actors was being indiscriminately cast upon genuine hackers, to whom earning money from digital criminality was in violation of hacker ethics.[146] The government's blanket approach in their treatment, in Mitch Kapor's words, "of all hackers, as a class, as nefarious enemies," stoked by the media's oft misguided, if not sensationalist, coverage of the perilous dangers posed by the "hacker menace," would sow further discord between hackers and society.[147,148] It was not the first time hackers felt betrayed and demonized by the authorities; the "hacker ethic" reflected a principle for dealing with a powerful establishment they perceived as hostile; mistrust authority—a credo at the heart of hacker culture. Hackers believed the government had repeatedly commandeered powerful scientific minds to craft tools of control, or weapons of war, such as atomic bombs. Authorities imposed rules—such a notion was as alien to hackers domiciled at the technological cutting edge as they would have been to ancient explorer-sailors being forbidden from venturing too far for fears they would plummet over the edge of the earth.

Since the early days, hackers believed they had been misunderstood by both their peers and the media. The hacking culture first originated at the Michigan Institute of Technology (MIT), where a hack was considered to be:

> a project undertaken or a product built not solely to fulfill some constructive goal, but with some wild pleasure taken in mere involvement...to qualify as a hack, the feat must be imbued with innovation, style, and technical virtuosity.[149]

Steven Levy, in his seminal 1984 work *Hackers*, traced the movement back to 1959, when a group of young undergraduates first gravitated towards a machine, the TX-0 (pronounced "Tix Oh") that was donated to MIT's Research Laboratory of Electronics.[150] The TX-0 was originally built for defense research at the Lincoln Laboratory, but the aggressive pace of technological innovation meant the model was soon superseded, even though it remained one of the fastest computers in the world when it reached MIT.[151] Over the coming years, undergraduates and teenagers

---

142 Alexander, 1990.
143 Sterling, 2002, Part 3.
144 Boiler-room fraud involves selling shares that either do not exist, are over-priced, or are worthless, via cold calls.
145 Sterling, 2002, Part 3.
146 Levy, 2010, 111.
147 Charles, 1990; Ibid, Afterword.

148 For an example of media sensationalization of the threat from hackers see CBS' coverage of the 1988 hacker conference.
149 Levy, 2010, Chapter 1.
150 Turner, 2006, Chapter 4.
151 Michigan Institute of Technology Museum, no date.

from the Cambridge area would gravitate towards the TX-0 and other hardware arriving at the electronics lab. Those using the machines divided into two groups: the planners who were computer theorists, and often PhD students; and the hackers, who were more hands-on and often absent of any plan but to experiment and make the computers do something new to sate their voracious intellectual appetite.[152] If the planners were the types who would buy a 2000-piece Lego set to make the spectacular castle on the front of the box, the hackers were those seeing a castle as the most conventional, and hence least virtuosic or fun thing that could be done with the pieces. Hackers would see a boat that could fly, a plane able to submerge, or myriad other manifestations, hence stubbornly refusing adherence to conformity.

The hackers were the poor cousins of the planners as far as computer access was concerned. Often hackers arrived deep in the night or before the sun rose to gain access to the machines, exploiting the hours in which the planners were sleeping. As their culture evolved, traits such as the hacker's nocturnal circadian rhythms forged in those battles for spare computing cycles were supplemented by traits adopted from their scientific predecessors, academia, and the counterculture, whilst other characteristics developed indigenously.

Levy captured the hacker principles comprising their commandments:

1. Access to computers—and anything that might teach you something about the way the world works—should be unlimited and total. Always yield to the Hands-On Imperative!
2. All information should be free
3. Mistrust authority; promote decentralization
4. Hackers should be judged by their hacking, not bogus criteria such as degrees, age, race, or position
5. You can create art and beauty on a computer
6. Computers can change your life for the better[153]

Hacking was not about criminality, breaking into computers to cause harm or theft of data, as the media and law enforcement suggested. To hackers, the notion of some youngster or criminal conducting technical parlor tricks to steal credit card data whilst calling themselves a hacker was an insult to the legacy and honor of their storied guild. Such antics were leagues beneath their holy order, authentic hackers worked to achieve technical virtuosity and see their code transform the world—they would not degrade themselves in the pursuit of materialistic goals.[154] This mentality was reflected in their lifestyles as "computer bums," described by MIT Professor Joseph Weizenbaum as:

Bright young men of disheveled appearance, often with sunken glowing eyes, can be seen sitting at computer consoles, their arms tensed and waiting to fire their fingers, already poised to strike, at the buttons and keys on which their attention seems to be

---

[152] Levy, 2010, Chapter 3.
[153] Ibid, Chapter 2.
[154] Ibid.

riveted as a gambler's on the rolling dice...when not so transfixed, they often sit at tables strewn with computer print-outs over which they pore like possessed students of a cabbalistic text.
They work until they nearly drop, twenty, thirty hours at a time. Their food, if they arrange it, is brought to them: coffee, cokes, sandwiches. If possible, they sleep on cots near the printouts. Their rumpled clothes, their unwashed and unshaven faces, and their uncombed hair all testify that they are oblivious to their bodies and to the world in which they move. These are computer bums, compulsive programmers.[155]

Whilst they were not criminals, it was true that hackers had a disdain for anything limiting their intellectual explorations. Many hackers believed property rights a relic of the physical age where everything could be available to everyone—there was no need for sole ownership. Years later, Aaron Swartz articulated this belief:

The law about what is stealing is very clear. Stealing is taking something away from someone so they cannot use it. There's no way that making a copy of something is stealing under that definition...it's called stealing or piracy, as if sharing a wealth of knowledge were the moral equivalent of plundering a ship and murdering its crew. But sharing isn't immoral—it's a moral imperative.[156]

In true cypherpunk tradition, Swartz married his words with actions in 2010 when he downloaded 4.8 million academic articles from the JSTOR[157] database with the intent of posting them online; the Secret Service arrested him before he could fulfill his plan.[158] Facing 35 years in jail, Swartz died by suicide before his trial.[159] Whilst there was no suicide note, his girlfriend believed it was caused by "a criminal justice system that prioritizes power over mercy, vengeance over justice."[160] Aaron's story would become a *cause célèbre* for many in the hacking community. Swartz's picture was displayed during Rick Falkvinge's keynote presentation at Blackhat Europe, the hacker world's premier conference, shortly after his death. Falkvinge told more than a thousand hackers, "Curiosity is never a crime. Locking up knowledge and culture, however, is...it is a moral imperative to break laws you believe unjust."[161]

Hackers also enjoyed picking locks, safe-cracking, and generally accessing anything forbidden. They needed to know why it was off-limits. What hidden knowledge was harbored on the shores of the unknown, what cerebral somersaults would be required to access the secrets? And, how would achieving such a feat make them a better hacker? Early MIT hackers would often crawl through ceiling spaces to circumvent locked doors.[162] On another occasion, a new twenty-four-hour pick-proof lock was locked before the combination was received from the manufacturer—the

---

155 Weizenbaum, 1976, 116.
156 Swartz, 2016.
157 JSTOR describes itself as a digital library for scholars, researchers, and students. With over 12 million articles it is one of the largest repositories of knowledge in the world. JSTOR access requires membership, and universities typically provide this access to their students.
158 Kirschbaum, 2011.
159 Kemp et al., 2015.
160 Stinebrickner-Kauffman, 2013.
161 Falkvinge, 2013, 58:45.
162 Levy, 2010, Chapter 5.

hackers had it open in twenty minutes.[163] Sometimes it was not even accessing the hidden secrets, but simply defeating the security—solving the puzzle—that motivated the hackers.

Some of the cypherpunks grew up in the seventies and eighties as part of the first generation of hackers. The most famous cypherpunk hacker from that era was John Draper, alias "Captain Crunch." Draper, described by Levy as "a scraggly dresser who never seemed to put a comb to his long dark hair," was a "phone phreaker," a hacker of telephone networks.[164] Draper earned his moniker when he realized the pitch of a toy whistle from the Captain Crunch breakfast cereal sounded at the exact 2600-cycle frequency the phone company used to initiate long-distance calls. By whistling into the phone's receiver, Draper could make free calls, but in keeping with the hacker culture it was not about stealing from the phone company; it was "for one reason and one reason only...I'm learning about a system. The phone company is a system. A computer is a system."[165] Draper says he and his fellow phreakers never used their knowledge for sabotage, but quite the opposite: "We do a lot of troubleshooting for them...we help them more than they know."[166] This philosophy of doing no harm is echoed by Julian Assange's comments on his actions when he was being hunted by a system's administrator in Nortel, a telecoms company he had hacked. At 2.30 am one morning, realizing that he could no longer evade detection, Assange claims to have playfully sent the following to the sysadmin's screen:

I have finally become sentient.
   I have taken control.
   For years, I have been struggling in this greyness.
But now I have finally seen the light.[167]

Assange followed the words a few moments later with the plea, "We didn't do any damage and we even improved a few things. Please don't call the Australian Federal Police."[168] Whether Draper or Assange were being truthful is unknown; however, another hacker principle which would support the verity of their statements is that "imperfect systems infuriate hackers, whose primal instinct it is to debug them."[169]

For the cypherpunks, having Draper—who had eventually ended up serving three short jail terms as a result of his digital escapades—amongst them was an important continuation of their intellectual and cultural hacker heritage.[170] One cypherpunk, Hal Finney, posted "the famous 'Captain Crunch' was an inspiration to me when I was in college in the 1970's...he represented...the spirit of questioning authority and exploring beyond the accepted bounds of the system."[171]

Another insight into the hacker ethic is the *Hacker Manifesto*, also known as *The Conscious of a Hacker*.[172] The manifesto is written by Loyd Blakenship, who went by

163 Ibid.
164 Ibid, Chapter 12.
165 Rosenbaum, 1971.
166 Ibid.
167 Assange, 2011.

168 Assange, 2011.
169 Levy, 2010, Chapter 2.
170 Rhoads, 2007.
171 Finney, 1992.
172 Blankenship, 1986.

the hacker alias "The Mentor," and was a member of the hacker collective "Legion of Doom." Blakenship wrote the *Manifesto* shortly after his 1986 arrest by the FBI for computer-related crimes. It was a time when hackers were being demonized by the press, especially following the *WarGames* movie that depicted a hacker inadvertently shepherding the world to the brink of nuclear apocalypse. The manifesto draws together a number of characteristics and views common amongst the hacker fraternity; Blakenship wrote, "I'm smarter than most of the other kids, this crap they teach us bores me…we've been spoon-fed baby food at school when we hungered for steak."[173] Then Blakenship recalls finding technology:

> I made a discovery today. I found a computer. Wait a second, this is
> cool. It does what I want it to. If it makes a mistake, it's because I
> screwed it up. Not because it doesn't like me…
> Or feels threatened by me…
> Or thinks I'm a smart ass…
> And then it happened…a door opened to a world…rushing through
> the phone line like heroin through an addict's veins, an electronic pulse is
> sent out, a refuge from the day-to-day incompetencies is sought…a board is
> found.
> "This is it…this is where I belong…"
> I know everyone here…even if I've never met them, never talked to
> them, may never hear from them again…I know you all.[174]

Ostracism from society is often felt by hackers. The Internet is a haven where one can discover like-minded peers from around the world. Judgments are based not on a manifestation of a corporeal form beyond their control, but on the authentic representation of their cultivated intellect—such an environment hackers migrate to and colonize:

> This is our world now…the world of the electron and the switch, the beauty of the baud.
> We make use of a service already existing without paying for what could be dirt-cheap
> if it wasn't run by profiteering gluttons, and you call us criminals. We explore…and
> you call us criminals. We seek after knowledge…and you call us criminals. We exist
> without skin color, without nationality, without religious bias…and you call us criminals. You build atomic bombs, you wage wars, you murder, cheat, and lie to us and try
> to make us believe it's for our own good, yet we're the criminals.
> Yes, I am a criminal. My crime is that of curiosity. My crime is that of judging
> people by what they say and think, not what they look like. My crime is that of outsmarting you, something that you will never forgive me for.[175]

It was rare during the earliest days of hacking that coders would discuss the political or social implications of the technology they were developing. Hackers were seldom trying to instigate social change; theirs was a quest of the mind and heart,

---

173 Ibid.
174 Ibid.
175 Ibid.

but for most hackers, it was not buttressed by a political ideology.[176] But when the anti-authority hacker culture migrated to the west coast it became influenced by the counterculture and those desperate to find ways to resist the perceived government oppression.

One of the best reflections of the hacker and cypherpunk philosophy is found in John Perry Barlow's 1996 *Declaration of the Independence of Cyberspace*.[177] Barlow's declaration first of all seeks to undermine any authority nation states claim in cyberspace:

> Governments of the Industrial World, you weary giants of flesh and steel, I come from Cyberspace, the new home of Mind. On behalf of the future, I ask you of the past to leave us alone. You are not welcome among us. You have no sovereignty where we gather.

Barlow continues to invoke liberty as the foundation of cyberspace:

> We have no elected government, nor are we likely to have one, so I address you with no greater authority than that with which liberty itself always speaks. I declare the global social space we are building to be naturally independent of the tyrannies you seek to impose on us. You have no moral right to rule us nor do you possess any methods of enforcement we have true reason to fear.

Barlow argues cyberspace is a zone beyond that of the physical:

> Governments derive their just powers from the consent of the governed. You have nei-ther solicited nor received ours. We did not invite you. You do not know us, nor do you know our world. Cyberspace does not lie within your borders.

Barlow argues cyberspace is self-governing, and governments do not understand how the digital world functions:

> You do not know our culture, our ethics, or the unwritten codes that already provide our society more order than could be obtained by any of your impositions. You claim there are problems among us that you need to solve. You use this claim as an excuse to invade our precincts. Many of these problems don't exist. Where there are real con-flicts, where there are wrongs, we will identify them and address them by our means. We are forming our own Social Contract.[178]

Barlow invokes the equality of digital citizens, that cyberspace holds no biases: "We are creating a world that all may enter without privilege or prejudice accorded by race, economic power, military force, or station of birth." Barlow claims the Internet's inhabitants as part of another group of society that governments cannot understand: "You are terrified of your own children, since they are natives in a world

---

[176] Levy, 2010, Chapter 4.   [178] Ibid.
[177] Barlow, 1996.

where you will always be immigrants." It was this sense of otherness causing Barlow to proclaim, "our virtual selves immune to your sovereignty, even as we continue to consent to your rule over our bodies. We will spread ourselves across the Planet so that no one can arrest our thoughts." Barlow intended the Internet to be "a civilization of the Mind," and hoped "it be more humane and fair than the world your governments have made before."[179] But the cypherpunks did not merely want to create a new domain for the mind, their actions were fully intended to have impacts in the physical world, and to upend the status quo. It was the counterculture influences which largely drove the cypherpunks' objectives to interfere with the political order.

3.9   CYPHERPUNKS AND COUNTERCULTURE: LEVITATING THE PENTAGON

The locking mechanism snapped into place as handcuffs bound Phil Zimmermann's wrists together. Amongst the crowd of some four hundred protesters with Zimmermann was Daniel Ellsberg, who, in 1971, effected the then most significant leak in US history: the Pentagon Papers.[180] Ellsberg had helped to produce the top-secret study of America's involvement in Vietnam since 1945.[181] It was a damning report, assessing that the US' involvement in a war that was deeply unpopular with the American people had only ever been detrimental to the Vietnamese. It was 1987 as Zimmermann and Ellsberg stood upon the sands of the Nevada nuclear weapon test site and the handcuffs locked in place. Ellsberg wore a suit, and Zimmermann also adopted this attire. "The message was that we were respectable Americans," Zimmermann recalls, "just like anybody else, only willing to go to jail to stop the nuclear tests."[182]

At the start of the 1980s, Zimmermann was despondent and contemplated fleeing America. Zimmermann's first son had just been born into a world where, in his words, "millions of people feared the world was drifting inexorably toward nuclear war."[183] Moving to the nuclear-free New Zealand seemed a wise decision to protect his young family: "We thought it would be a hard life in New Zealand after a war, but we thought it might still be livable."[184] As Zimmermann and his wife were preparing their immigration papers in 1982, they were told of a conference taking place in Denver by a group called the Nuclear Weapons Freeze Campaign.[185] It was in Denver that Zimmermann first heard Daniel Ellsberg speak. Zimmermann found the conference "sobering but empowering," and Ellsberg's speech gave him hope. "It seemed plausible that this was a political movement that had some chance of success, of turning things around...we decided to stay and fight"; Zimmermann reflected years later, "It was like I had been in an airplane that I knew was crashing, trying to get in the back seats to increase my chance of survival. Instead, I decided to get

---

179   Ibid.
180   Formerly known as "History of U.S. Decision-Making in Vietnam 1945–1968."
181   Ellsberg, 1973.
182   Greenberg, 2012, Chapter 2.
183   Zimmermann, no date.
184   Garfinkel, 1995, 87.
185   Ibid.

into the cockpit."[186] Zimmermann's fight would ultimately manifest is his creation of PGP—he would give encryption to the citizenry, providing significant challenges to government surveillance.

Counterculture influences punctuated the cypherpunks' ideology. The fusion of East Coast hackers and West Coast counterculture in the late 1960s and 1970s politicized the hacker movement, and provided technical skills to those perceived by many as drug-addled hippies.

"Counterculture" was first termed by the lecturer Theodore Roszak in his 1969 book *The Making of A Counter Culture: Reflections on the Technocratic Society and Its Youthful Opposition.*[187] Roszak described the counterculture as "a culture so radically disaffiliated from the mainstream assumptions of our society that it scarcely looks to many as a culture at all, but takes on the alarming appearance of a barbaric intrusion."[188] The reason for this disaffiliation was routed in the events of World War Two, when the age of atomic warfare dawned with a blinding flash above Hiroshima, an illumination extinguishing the light of 100,000 souls.[189] In 1939, Albert Einstein urged President Roosevelt to commit America's resources to the achievement of a nuclear weapon, suggesting Hitler was already working to achieve such an ambition.[190] Roosevelt directed some of the greatest scientific minds of his generation to building "the bomb." Roszak believed the post-atomic youth were in rebellion at this inherited reality:

> the orthodox culture they confront is fatally and contagiously diseased. The prime symptom of that disease is the shadow of thermonuclear annihilation beneath which we cower. The counter culture takes its stand against the background of this absolute evil, an evil which is not defined by the sheer fact of the bomb, but by the total ethos of the bomb, in which our politics, our public morality, our economic life, our intellectual endeavor are now embedded with a wealth of ingenious rationalization. We are a civilization sunk in an unshakeable commitment to genocide, gambling madly with the universal extermination of our species.[191]

This threat was compounded by the Soviet Union's achievement of the bomb in 1949, the same year Chinese Communists were victorious in their civil war. The youth of the 1950s and 60s feared that "the sky was falling."[192] Stewart Brand, the organizer of the first hackers' conference, recalls, "we were the 'now generation' because we figured there would be no then. We were completely apoplectic, the sky was falling."[193]

As well as believing they were the last generation of their race, those coming of age in the post-war era feared a conscription into the "technocracy" of the

---

[186] Garfinkel, 1995, 87; Greenberg, 2012, Chapter 2.
[187] Roszak, 1969.
[188] Ibid, 42.
[189] Zinn, 1980, 422.
[190] Einstein, 1939.
[191] Roszak, 1969, 47.
[192] Turner, 2006, Chapter 4.
[193] Ibid.

military-industrial complex, the very collective they believed helped usher in the end of days they now confronted.[194] Those of the counterculture felt society was molding them into the parts required to manufacture and indefinitely sustain the war machine, that they were being dehumanized and fashioned into a standard build to conform with expectations of a hierarchical and corporately controlled America.

Charles Reich warned in his 1970 book *The Greening of America* that "there is a revolution coming," as a result of the "betrayal and loss of the American dream, the rise of the Corporate State and the way that State dominates, exploits and ultimately destroys both nature and man."[195] Scientific "reason" as it existed, "makes impoverishment, dehumanization and even war appear to be logical and necessary."[196] As well as war, a decline of democracy and liberty, and lawmaking by private powers, Reich cited uncontrolled technology as being at the root of the cultural corruption that "no mere reform can touch."[197] Reich believed Americans were "systematically stripped of imagination, creativity, heritage, dreams, and personal uniqueness in order to style us into productive units for a mass, technological society."[198] Once absorbed into the technocracy, "people virtually become their professions, roles or occupations, they are strangers to themselves."[199] In their work and life, people had become "more and more pointless and empty."[200]

The threat of the technocracy eroding their personalities merged with the possibility of a communist invasion. Brand wrote in his diary in 1957 that if it came to it he would fight them, but not for his government or capitalism, but "I will fight for individualism and personal liberty...I will fight to avoid becoming a number—to others and myself."[201]

But in Reich's reading of society, repression was already being enacted by the present government as liberty was eroded:

> The nation has gradually become a rigid managerial hierarchy, with a small elite and a great mass of the disenfranchised. Democracy has rapidly lost ground; giant managerial institutions and corporations have seized power, and experts, specialists, and professionals make wide-reaching decisions safely insulated from the feelings of the people. Both dissent and efforts at change are dealt with by repression.[202]

The young adults felt alienated from the culture in which they were supposed to assume their position, a culture whose crowning achievement was a weapon that could eradicate humankind. The revolution Reich warned of seemed to be the only answer: "it will not be like revolutions of the past," he wrote. "It will originate with the individual and with culture, and it will change the political structure only as its final act."[203]

---

194 Ibid, Chapter 1.
195 Reich, 1970, Chapter 1.
196 Ibid.
197 Ibid.
198 Ibid.

199 Ibid.
200 Ibid.
201 Turner, 2006, Chapter 2.
202 Reich, 1970, Chapter 1.
203 Ibid.

In order to stave off the end of days, and stop themselves being stripped of all vestiges of individuality, those of the counterculture turned away from mainstream society and became "hippies." Many hippies believed that to change society they must first change their own psychology. To do this some groups retired to communes to live outside the physical societies they deplored; other groups turned inwards, using psychedelic drugs to aid them in fashioning a new and more evolved consciousness. Stewart Brand, who experimented with narcotics, wrote in his diary:

> the responsibility of evolution is on each individual man, as for no other species. Since the business of evolution for man has gone over to the mental and psychological phase, each person may contribute to and influence the heritage of the species. [original italics][204]

Brand associated with the *Merry Pranksters*, a group dedicated to taking drugs, or tripping, who traveled in their flamboyantly colored converted school bus spreading word of their new peaceful and fun way of life.[205] It had become an evolutionary imperative to share their message of love, peace, and withdrawal from a society that, in Reich's words, "deals death, not only to people in other lands but to its own people."[206] Despite the abhorrence of American society, those of the counterculture struggled to articulate a destination for the technicolor journey of enlightenment. Reich offered these unspecific words of their destination after declaring the coming revolution:

> It promises a higher reason, a more human community, and a new and liberated individual. Its ultimate creation will be a new and enduring wholeness and beauty—a renewed relationship of people to themselves, to other people, to society, to nature and to the land.[207]

Despite the oppression many in the counterculture perceived, the scientific world view of the technocracy of promulgating, technology itself was not shunned by those of the counterculture, instead, it was embraced. In particular, the cybernetic theory of Norbert Weiner was seen as a model of how systems could be built in a peer-to-peer, rather than hierarchical structures, this view echoed the anarchist and decentralized political structure that many of those in the counterculture coveted.[208]

Technology was heavily utilized within the San Francisco "trips festivals."[209] Ken Kesey, the unofficial leader of the Merry Pranksters instructed attendees to "wear ecstatic dress and bring their own gadgets."[210] These hedonistic gatherings fused together drugs, multimedia light shows, music and technology, allowing revelers to experience new forms of consciousness during their trips. Many in the counterculture believed that a techno-social society could be cultivated, where machines served

---

[204] Turner, 2006, Chapter 2.
[205] Ibid.
[206] Reich, 1970, Chapter 1.
[207] Ibid.
[208] Turner, 2006, Chapter 1.
[209] Ibid, Chapter 2.
[210] Ibid.

humans and in turn humans served machines.[211] This sentiment was articulated by Richard Brautigan in his 1967 poem "Machines of Loving Grace," written during his tenure as poet-in-residence at the California Institute of Technology. Brautigan wrote of a "cybernetic meadow where mammals and computers live together in mutually programming harmony," and of a "cybernetic ecology where we are free of our labors and joined back to nature, returned to our mammal brothers and sisters, and all watched over by machines of loving grace."[212]

Whitfield Diffie came of age during the counterculture believing in the "radical viewpoint," and that, "one's politics and the character of his particular work are inseparable."[213] From as early as his high school years in New York, Diffie moved in left/liberal circles.[214] As he approached the draft age, and the prospect of serving in Vietnam, a war uniformly detested by the left, Diffie made the decision to take a job as a military-funded researcher rather than serve as a conscript.[215] Diffie interviewed at the Mitre Corporation, a defense organization with a large number of military contracts. Rather than being an interrogation of his mathematical prowess, the interview with distinguished mathematician Ronald Silver was a test of Diffie's knowledge of psychedelic drugs.[216] Displaying his counterculture pedigree, Diffie excelled and was offered the job, absolving the fear of his boots plunging into the sodden soil of distant rainforests.[217]

As one cypherpunk, Peter Wayner, wrote on the mailing list in 1993, their movement liked to "cloak itself in the romance of the counterculture."[218] As a suited Zimmermann was being led away in handcuffs from the Nevada nuclear test site, the romance must have felt to have been hard at times—though meeting Ellsberg must surely have boosted his spirits. The counterculture and hacker culture anchored the cypherpunks in an anti-establishment mentality—this mentality in those who oppose government cryptography policies endures to the present day, helping to reinforce an antagonism felt towards the state. The following section will briefly explore the specific incidents that underwrote the distrust felt towards government by the cypherpunks, and broader digital privacy activists.

3.10   THE SOURCE OF THE CYPHERPUNKS' DISTRUST

"I ain't got no quarrel with no Viet Cong," Muhammed Ali declared in 1967. "They never called me n*****, they never lynched me, they didn't put no dogs on me, they didn't rob me of my nationality, rape and kill my mother and father."[219] On another occasion, the heavyweight champion, who had been stripped of his title for draft-dodging, rebutted a critical college student attacking him for refusing conscription:

---

[211] Turner, 2006, Chapter 1.
[212] Brautigan, 1967.
[213] Levy, 2001, The Loner, Chapter 1.
[214] Ibid.
[215] Markoff, 2005, 137.

[216] Ibid, 138.
[217] Ibid.
[218] Wayner, 1993.
[219] Ali, 1975, 1:27 and 0:27.

If I'm gonna die, I'll die now right here fighting you...you my enemy, my enemies the white people not the Viet Congs...you my opposer when I want freedom, you my opposer when I want justice, you my opposer when I want equality...you won't even stand up for me here at home.[220]

The same year, Dr. Martin Luther King Junior pleaded to a packed congregation at Riverside Church in New York City:

Somehow this madness must cease. We must stop now. I speak as a child of God and brother to the suffering poor of Vietnam...I speak for the poor of America who are paying the double price of smashed hopes at home, and dealt death and corruption in Vietnam...Every man of humane convictions must decide on the protest that best suits his convictions, but we must all protest.[221]

Muhammed Ali and Dr. King, both US citizens, were on the NSA's interception watchlist.[222]

Investigative journalist James Bamford lists King, the singer Joan Baez, and the actress Jane Fonda amongst those American citizens on the NSA's watchlist.[223] For the cypherpunks, these victims were conducting legitimate and legal political protest only to be targeted by the most formidable surveillance agency in the world, an agency whose giant ear was never supposed to turn on its own citizens. It was a founding NSA document, National Security Council Intelligence Directive No. 9, which defined the agencies' mission as foreign, rather than domestic, intelligence collection.[224] But the cypherpunks did not trust the NSA would be bound by their legal limitations, or that the White House would not change such limitations; Doug Porter posted to the mailing list in mid-1993 that the "NSA has a long history of ignoring whether they are chartered for an activity."[225]

Amongst the highest of NSA transgressions in the eyes of the cypherpunks was Operation Shamrock, a program originating in the aftermath of World War Two to access foreign communications arriving at, or transiting, the United States.[226] During the 1976 Church inquiries, Frank Church described Shamrock as "probably the largest governmental interception program affecting Americans ever undertaken."[227] Shamrock started as a project to gain access to telegraphs to which the government legally had access during the war, though with peace's outbreak, and without an existential threat to America, no legislation supported bulk legal access to communications.[228] Access needed to be achieved without congressional authorization, which could be considered an illegal act.[229] The first conversation a government representative had with one of the three primary telecommunications companies in New York, ITT Communications, went badly—ITT refused to provide the state with copies of

---

[220] Ali, 2011, 2:14.
[221] King, 1967.
[222] Aid and Burr, 2013.
[223] Bamford, 1982, 160.
[224] United States National Security Council, 1952.

[225] Porter, 1993.
[226] United States Senate, 1975, 57–58.
[227] United States Senate, 1976c, 765.
[228] Bamford, 1982, 303–310.
[229] Ibid, 311.

their traffic.[230] Subsequent approaches were more productive, the first batch of cables was secretly delivered to the government in September 1945.[231] Corporate lawyers advised all three of the companies—ITT, Western Union, and RCA—against acquiescing to the government's request as they doubted its legality, but the organizations proceeded nonetheless.[232]

By the following spring, however, the executives were getting nervous. The head of the American Signals Agency (NSA's predecessor) wrote to the Army Chief of Staff, and future US President, General Dwight Eisenhower, informing him their access was at risk, tacitly acknowledging the absence of legislation to support the intercepts; he stated the companies had "placed themselves in precarious positions since the legality of such operations has not been established."[233] Eisenhower sent a formal letter of appreciation in an attempt to placate the executives.[234] Secretary of Defense James Forrestal met with the nervous executives and thanked them for their efforts in 1947, whilst offering assurances they would be protected by the Justice Department as long as the current President was in office.[235] It was reiterated their "intelligence constituted a matter of great importance to national security"—with such assurances and flattery, the executives were satisfied.[236] Over the next thirty years, the covert, and potentially illegal, interception program grew and become business as usual for the communications companies, and as technology evolved, so did the volume and nature of data sent to the government. The Church report reflected:

> Operation Shamrock, which began as an effort to acquire the telegrams of certain foreign targets, expanded so that NSA obtained from at least two cable companies essentially all cables to or from the United States, including millions of the private communications of Americans.[237]

For the most trusting of individuals, Shamrock could potentially be rationalized with a faithful assumption that the government disregarded any cables not associated with legitimate foreign intelligence targets (e.g., resident aliens employed by a hostile government). But that assumption would be severely challenged as Church's inquiry revealed details of Operation Minaret, another source of the cypherpunks' mistrust for government.

Robert F. Kennedy became Attorney General in 1961. A top priority was the curtailing of organized crime. He brought American law enforcement and intelligence communities together to share information on the criminal underworld in a bid to, for the first time, consolidate their knowledge and improve government crime fight abilities.[238] As part of that drive, the coordinating body, the Justice Department's

---

230 Ibid, 303.
231 Ibid, 305.
232 Ibid, 304.
233 Ibid, 309.
234 Ibid.

235 Ibid.
236 Ibid, 309–310.
237 United States Senate, 1976, 104.
238 Bamford, 1982, 315–316.

criminal division, requested the NSA send any information they had, or would in the future collect on their list of target racketeers.[239]

The Kennedys were also concerned about Fidel Castro, so the FBI began investigating American citizens with business dealings in Cuba. The names of their targets were sent to NSA with a request for information; "Now, for the first time," Bamford commented, "NSA had begun turning its massive ear inward toward its own citizens."[240] By 1967, the NSA's watchlist was expanding again, the agency was tasked by the army with identifying foreign influences on the civil disturbances, such as anti-war protests, sweeping the country.[241] The Secret Service, CIA, and FBI soon also sent civil disturbance suspects names to be added to the NSA's watchlist.[242] Another request for surveillance came in 1970 when President Nixon further targeted the international drug trade with the Intelligence community instructed to "contribute to the maximum extent possible."[243] After a subtle insertion by the NSA into the 1968 Omnibus Crime Control and Safe Streets Act, the agency now believed they had legal cover from other laws and directives aimed at preventing and moderating the targeting of Americans by the NSA.[244] Tasking was soon received from the Bureau of Narcotics and Dangerous Drugs to target organizations and individuals violating drug laws in America, with this Bamford noted:

> NSA had taken its most dangerous step…Until then, all intelligence provided through the Minaret program had been "byproducts," information on watchlisted persons picked up during the course of monitoring foreign targets for foreign intelligence collection. The giant ear had suddenly turned directly inward.[245]

But drug cartels were not isolated in receiving Nixon's wrath.

President Nixon's fist pounded into his Oval office desk, "now goddamn it, somebody's got to go to jail!"[246] It was 1971, and Daniel Ellsberg was leaking the Top Secret Pentagon papers laying bare to the American people a critical expose of their interventions in Vietnam. "Let's get the son-of-a-bitch into jail," Nixon told his Attorney General John N. Mitchell.[247] Discrediting Ellsberg became a White House priority. Nixon wanted not merely to prosecute Ellsberg, but to thoroughly assassinate his character, and the anti-war movement of which he was now a champion.[248] His administration organized a burglary of the office of Daniel Ellsberg's psychiatrist in an unsuccessful operation to find ammunition in the form of the whistleblower's medical records.[249]

But an even more profound abuse of power led to Nixon's downfall. In 1972, five intruders were arrested inside the offices of the Democratic National Committee carrying wiretap and photography equipment, the name of the complex in which they were caught would become synonymous with the scandal: Watergate. Despite

---

[239] Ibid, 317.
[240] Ibid.
[241] Ibid, 317–318.
[242] Ibid, 319.
[243] Department of Justice, 1976, 46–47.
[244] Bamford, 1982, 326.

[245] Ibid, 328.
[246] Moran, no date.
[247] Campbell, 2002.
[248] Olson and Holland, 2016, 18.
[249] Ibid, 20.

the White House's vehement denials, the crime was soon traced back to the Nixon administration.[250] Numerous transgressions by Nixon were uncovered during the course of subsequent investigations; these included: John Mitchell controlling a fund to be used for discrediting the Democratic Party by stealing campaign files, forging letters, and producing false news; millions of dollars of illegal donations given by big business to the Nixon campaign; Nixon pledging to give executive clemency and pay-offs to his Watergate henchmen in return for their silence; and the manipulation of FBI files to conceal the targeting of journalists and government officials.[251] It was also confirmed the administration broke into the office of Ellsberg's psychiatrist, and also planned to physically attack him during a Washington rally.[252] Nixon was forced to resign. It was in 1977, during an interview with David Frost that Nixon was asked about surveillance, and at what point the President can decide it is in the best interests of the nation to do something illegal. Nixon answered with words of tyrannical implications, "Well, when the president does it, that means it is not illegal."[253] These words, already etched in history by the time the cypherpunks coalesced were a manifestation of their deepest fears—a president with ill-regard for the constitution and its mandated checks and balances. The President had attempted to subvert the system, and if the Watergate robbery had gone undetected, Nixon could have continued his abuses, and maybe even, had he been left unchecked, ascended to autocracy. Another interpretation could have been the system had worked and Nixon had been removed from office—though such a reading of history would not resonate with those such as the cypherpunks who were already pre-disposed to distrust authority.

The March 1977 top secret prosecutorial summary of a Department of Justice investigation into potentially illegal wiretapping identified twenty-three categories of questionable NSA eavesdropping operations. Operation Minaret was amongst those operations the report stated that could be considered criminal.[254] The summary was sent to the Attorney General Benjamin Civiletti, it included a note of caution that in attempting to prosecute, "there is likely to be much 'buck-passing' from subordinate to superior, agency to agency, agency to board or committee, board or committee to the President, and from the living to the dead."[255] The summary also noted the agency's top-secret charter, issued by the executive branch, exempted Fort Meade from the laws governing the other federal agencies; the agency was in effect considered to be above the law.[256] No prosecutions took place.

The FBI's Counter Intelligence Program (COINTELPRO), was in the eyes of the cypherpunks, another of the most egregious historic violations of civil rights.[257] COINTELPRO was initiated in 1956 as an operation against the US Communist Party; neither the President nor the Attorney General were initially informed of the program.[258] In 1968, COINTELPRO was also directed against the anti-war

---

[250] Zinn, 1980, 542–543.
[251] Ibid, 543–544.
[252] Ibid, 544.
[253] Nixon & Frost, 1977.
[254] Bamford, 2014.

[255] Ibid.
[256] Ibid.
[257] Goen, 1993.
[258] Stone, 2008, 99.

movement.[259] There were violent elements of the anti-war movement which would be considered by most citizens as legitimate targets for criminal investigations. At least 250 bombings against reserve officers' training corps buildings, draft boards, induction centers, federal offices, and corporate headquarters occurred between fall 1969 and spring 1970.[260] President Nixon told FBI Director John Edgar Hoover he believed "revolutionary terror" to represent the single greatest threat to American society, though as most of the bombings were in the dead of night, and few people were ever injured or killed, the public at large did not share Nixon's fears.[261] However, the FBI's actions went far beyond a traditional investigation, or even beyond an intelligence penetration campaign. COINTELPRO included measures such as sending anonymous letters to the parents and employers of anti-war activists accusing them of homosexuality, drug abuse, or other perceived indiscretions in order to sow discord in the protestors' lives, thus destabilizing their movement.[262] The FBI sent letters to the spouses of activists informing them their partners were having affairs, and spread false rumors their targets were embezzling funds or cooperating with the FBI.[263] More directly, federal agents infiltrated and disrupted the anti-war movements. Further activities included causing activists to be evicted from their homes, intercepting their mail and communications, inciting police harassment for minor offenses, sabotage of peaceful demonstrations, and even instigation of physical assaults.[264]

It was 1971 before the public learned of COINTELPRO, when an anti-war group broke into an FBI office and stole around a thousand documents before providing them to journalists and members of Congress.[265] *The Washington Post* accused the FBI of implementing a form of "internal security appropriate for the Secret Police of the Soviet Union."[266] Amid pressure from the media and congress, COINTELPRO was terminated in April 1971; it had performed 300 disruptive actions against the anti-war movement, with forty percent designed to prevent citizens from "speaking, teaching, writing, or publishing."[267] Five years later, a subsequent director of the FBI, Clarence Kelly, apologized for COINTELPRO and conceded some of its activities were "clearly wrong and quite indefensible."[268] COINTELPRO was repeatedly cited by the cypherpunks as a contributing factor to their ideology.

The cypherpunks believed there was an increasing risk of further government overreach and abuses in the new digital age. Zimmermann's 1996 testimony to a US Senate Subcommittee articulates this belief:

> Advances in technology will not permit the maintenance of the status quo, as far as privacy is concerned. The status quo is unstable. If we do nothing, new technologies will give the government new automatic surveillance capabilities that Stalin could

---

259 Ibid, 100.
260 Ibid, 97.
261 Burrough, 2016.
262 Stone, 2008, 100.
263 Ibid, 99.

264 Ibid.
265 Ibid, 104.
266 Editorial—Washington Post, 1971.
267 United States Senate, 1976, 215.
268 Stern, 2014.

never have dreamed of. The only way to hold the line on privacy in the information age is strong cryptography. Cryptography strong enough to keep out major governments. The government has a track record that does not inspire confidence that they will never abuse our civil liberties. The FBI's COINTELPRO program targeted groups that opposed government policies. They spied on the anti-war movement and the civil rights movement. They wiretapped Martin Luther King's phone. Nixon had his enemies list. And then there was the Watergate mess. The War on Drugs has given America the world's largest per capita incarceration rate in the world, a distinction formerly held by South Africa, before we surpassed them during the eighties even when apartheid was in full swing.[269]

The most significant source of the cypherpunks' knowledge of the NSA was Bamford's seminal 1982 work *The Puzzle Palace*. It was read voraciously by the cypherpunks and amongst the literature helping many of them develop and justify their world view of the NSA as an all-powerful agency operating without the checks and balances required to ensure such potent capabilities were never turned against Americans. Tim May would post to the cypherpunk mailing list that "all would-be cypherpunks should read James Bamford's 'The Puzzle Palace.'"[270] The cypherpunks would come to believe Congress was inept at checking the NSA's power, and the Justice Department, despite having identified likely criminal practices, could not prosecute an agency that for all intents and purposes was beyond the law. The cypherpunks would put their faith in mathematics and encryption, over institutions and presidents.

Whilst the cypherpunks' distrust of government may at first seem extreme, when viewed through the lens of historic abuses, it becomes more readily understandable why they placed more faith in mathematics to protect the citizenry than they did a system of checks and balances they believed ineffective, or in presidents who could be despotic by nature or manipulated by external forces.

3.11   CYPHERPUNK LITERATURE AND FILM

Winston Smith...I must strongly advise you against using false names & SS [Social Security] numbers as it is...illegal to atempt [sic] to conceal one identity in any communtication [sic]...We do have a room reserved here right next to an associate of your Jim Bell if you insist on persuing [sic] this cource [sic] of action.[271]

Cypherpunk William Geiger III, 1997

"An indignant and prophetic novel," read the title of the 1949 *New York Times'* review of George Orwell's *1984*.[272] The cypherpunks vociferously agreed.[273] Throughout their early communications, *1984* references were made, such as the above quote, which a cypherpunk posted in jest, or when Captain Crunch asked whether the

---

[269] Zimmermann, 1996.
[270] May, 1992.
[271] Geiger III, 1997.

[272] Lane, 2011, 141.
[273] May, 1994g.

"thought police" would burst down his door should he use PGP.[274] David Chaum's article on digital currencies was intended to "make Big Brother Obsolete."[275]

Culture, especially cyberpunk literature and movies, played a significant role in articulating the narrative of the cypherpunks' struggles and ambitions. Dystopian novels, such as *1984*, were brandished as vivid portrayals of the near future enabled by the assent of technology and its conscription by the powerful. At other times the cypherpunks added contemporary reflections of their philosophy, such as the *Sneakers* movie, to their reference materials. "Read the sources," Tim May would insist in the *Cyphernomicon*, and top of the sources list was *True Names*.[276]

Vernor Vinge wrote *True Names* in 1981 as part of a double novel, the other half authored by a then-obscure George R. R. Martin, who continued to *A Game of Thrones'* fame. *True Names* was one of the first novels to portray a granular depiction of cyberspace, it was one of the early sources to inspire May's conceptions of crypto-anarchy and held high status within cypherpunk lore, even being used as the basis for their discussions and conceptions on anonymity.[277] May advised a fellow cypherpunk in late 1993, "If you have not yet read it, buy a copy today and read it tonight."[278] *True Names* follows the journey of a hacker known as "Mr. Slippery," whose true name was "his most valued possession but also the greatest threat to his continued good health."[279] A hacker's true name was their real-world identity. Hackers were powerful and evasive in cyberspace where only the mind can grant power, but in the flesh, they could be coerced or killed by the authorities. Hackers in cyberspace, or "the other plane" as Vinge termed it, vied with one another for power, but they also targeted criminals. For instance, one hacker robbed a Mafia operation and distributed the proceeds to millions of "ordinary people." As the story proceeds, a mysterious hacker, "the Mailman," emerges and attempts to take over cyberspace. Mr. Slippery and his ally "Ery" combine their forces to stop the Mailman catalyzing a war that spills into the physical realm devastating the world. Slippery and Ery are able to gather enough processing power to topple the Mailman, who it turns out, is a rogue NSA artificial intelligence. Slippery and Ery acquire enough power to rule both the virtual and physical worlds, but after a brief contemplation, they "self-lobotomize" and relinquish their power, knowing that in order to preserve such power they would have to induce such suffering as to "end up being worse than the human-based government."[280] Both hackers make this sacrifice despite being cognizant that the government, which has identified their true names, would likely kill them when they relinquished their strength.

Cypherpunk Daniel Ray articulated the asymmetric nature of the physical world and threat of governments that Vinge portrayed in *True Names* on the mailing list in early 1993, "Once it gets to a face-to-face confrontation…you lose, and you lose immediately, there is nothing you can bring to bear, since it is now just a force equation, and they have over 10,000 times the force you do."[281]

---

[274] Draper, 1992.
[275] Chuam, 1985.
[276] May, 1994b, 2.4.2.
[277] Hughes, 1994.
[278] May, 1994f.
[279] Vinge, 1981, 185.
[280] Ibid, 242.
[281] Ray, 1993.

Ender's Game, written by Orson Scott Card in 1985, was also highly regarded by the cypherpunks.[282] The subplot features two young prodigiously intelligent children who cultivate online pseudonyms, or "nyms," and eventually translate their online influence into real-world political power, despite their tender ages. The ability to be represented solely by their thoughts, rather than the physical form was a hacker ideal echoed by the author's narrative:

> With false names, on the right nets, they could be anybody. Old men, middle-aged women, anybody, as long as they were careful about the way they wrote. All that anyone would see were their words, their ideas. Every citizen started equal, on the nets.[283]

Many of the cypherpunks already possessed the societal respect they craved, being highly educated and often leaders in their respective fields. It was likely that the anonymity provided by pseudonyms was more valuable as a means of a stable presence in cyberspace divorced from their true names; with this presence they could do or say things which would not impact their "real" lives. *Ender's Game* also features a war-hungry government that manipulates a young, talented child into leading a military operation that results in their committing genocide against an alien species; this conformed to the cypherpunks' perception of authority.

The translation of cyberspace effects in the offline world was well portrayed in another cypherpunk favorite, John Brunner's 1975 novel *The Shockwave Rider*. The protagonist, Nickie Haflinger, makes use of a society endowed with ubiquitous computing to evade the authorities hunting him. Haflinger uses the extensive computing training he received at a secret government facility to break into secure networks and create new identities for himself as required (hacker Kevin Mitnick would later do just this).[284] After Haflinger creates a worm designed to leak all government data online, the government launches nuclear weapons against him; Haflinger uses his technical and social-engineering skills to stop the inbound missiles before they reach him, thus enacting what would later become a cypherpunk dream—the neutralization of the government's monopoly on violence. *The Shockwave Rider* is also notable for the prevalence of digital payments having mostly replaced cash, allowing the government to monitor how each of their citizens spent their earnings: a cypherpunk nightmare. Tim May comments, "in many ways it [*The Shockwave Rider*] prepared me for my later role as a hunted CyberFelon."[285]

Tyrannical Governments. Anonymity and Pseudonymity. Dystopian Futures. Imminent apocalypse. Ubiquitous technology and connectivity. These themes permeate the literary outputs that form the cannon of the cypherpunks, and what could manifest should their ambitions falter. Seventeen years before the cypherpunks had formed during the first crypto war, Senator Church, a man at the heart of the political

---

[282] Dinkelacker, 1993.
[283] Card, 1985, 134.
[284] Mitnick has written about his activities in *Ghost in the Wires: My Adventures As the World's Most Wanted Hacker.*

[285] May, 1994d.

establishment, presciently articulated their fears in his comments made whilst he was in the midst of his committee's inquiry into intelligence agencies abuses in 1975:

> the United States government has perfected a technological capability that enables us to monitor the messages that go through the air...that capability at any time could be turned around on the American people, and no American would have any privacy left such is the capability to monitor everything—telephone conversations, telegrams, it doesn't matter. There would be no place to hide.
>
> If this government ever became a tyranny, if a dictator ever took charge in this country, the technological capacity that the intelligence community has given the government could enable it to impose total tyranny, and there would be no way to fight back because the most careful effort to combine together in resistance to the government, no matter how privately it was done, is within the reach of the government to know. Such is the capability of this technology...I know the capacity that is there to make tyranny total in America, and we must see to it that...all agencies that possess this technology operate within the law and under proper supervision so that we never cross over that abyss. That is the abyss from which there is no return.[286]

The other constant in the cypherpunks' literary inspirations was a downtrodden hero, often cast aside by kin, disregarded by society, and exploited by government. In cyberspace, the champion could have outsized abilities to right the wrongs visited upon themselves and society, and in the process, save the world.

Understanding the cypherpunks is vital to comprehension of the wider crypto wars conflict. The cypherpunk order represents the most extreme views of encryption's uses, and aspects of their narrative influenced those who would follow and shaped the animosity existing today between digital rights activists and the government. Whilst crypto-anarchy is not a philosophy permeating the entire digital privacy community, the notion of selectively bypassing the state to preserve privacy, of trusting technological controls rather than laws to protect civil liberties, and of belligerents being influenced by the hacker ethic, the counterculture, and the fear of government abuses are threads which run through the conflict. That conflict started in the 1960s, with David Kahn.

REFERENCES

ARTICLES

Chaum, D. (1985a). Security without Identification: Transaction Systems to Make Big Brother Obsolete. *Communications of the ACM* **28**(10), 1030–1044.

BOOKS

Bamford, J. (1982). *The Puzzle Palace: Inside the National Security Agency* (New York: Penguin Books).

---

[286] NBC, 2014, 0:43.

Card, O. S. (1985). *Ender's Game* (New York: Tor Books).

Garfinkel, S. (1995). *PGP: Pretty Good Privacy* (New York: O'Reilly Media Inc.).

Greenberg, A. (2012). *This Machine Kills Secrets: How Wikileakers, Cypherpunks, and Hacktivists Aim to Free the World's Information* (New York: Random House).

Hospers, J. (1971). *Libertarianism: A Political Philosophy For Tomorrow* (Los Angeles: Nash Press).

Lane, F. S. (2011). *American Privacy: The 400-Year History of Our Most Contested Right* (Boston: Beacon Press).

Lessig, L. (2006). *Code 2.0* (New York: Basic Books).

Levy, S. (2001). *Crypto: Secrecy and Privacy in the New Cold War* (New York: Viking Penguin).

Levy, S. (2010). *Hackers: Heroes of the Computer Revolution—25th Anniversary Edition* (New York: O'Reilly Media).

Markoff, J. (2005). *What the Doormouse Said: How the Sixties Counterculture Shaped the Personal Computing Industry* (New York: Penguin Books, 2005).

Reich, C. (1970). *The Greening of America* (New York: Random House).

Roszak, T. (1969). *The Making of a Counter Culture: Reflections on the Technocratic Society and Its Youthful Opposition* (New York: Anchor Books).

Swartz, A. (2016). *The Boy Who Could Change the World: The Writings of Aaron Swartz* (New York: Perseus Distribution).

Turner, F. (2006). *From Counterculture to Cyberculture: Stewart Brand, the Whole Earth Network, and the Rise of Digital Utopianism* (Chicago: University of Chicago Press).

Vinge, V. (1981). *True Names* (New York: Dell Publishing).

Weizenbaum, J. (1976). *Computer Power and Human Reason, from Judgement to Calculation* (San Francisco: W. H. Freeman).

Zinn, H. (1980). *A People's History of the United States* (New York: HarperCollins Publishers).

CHAPTERS IN BOOKS

Olson, K. W., and Holland, M. (2016). Patterns from the Beginning. In *Watergate: The Presidential Scandal That Shook America*. Edited by Keith W. Olson (KS: University Press of Kansas).

Stone, G. R. (2008). The Vietnam War: Spying on Americans. In *Security V. Liberty: Conflicts Between National Security and Civil Liberties in American History*. Edited by Daniel Farber (New York: Russell Sage Foundation).

CYPHERPUNK MAILING LIST ARCHIVES 1992–1998

Anonymous. (1996). "Assassination Biz." MessageID: "199602191740.SAA14401@utopia. hacktic.nl." February 20, 1996.

Assange, J. (1996). "Again: [hrdware] Anti-Tempest Video Settings." MessageID: "199605120351.NAA01349@suburbia.net." May 12, 1996.

Bernhardt, S. (1993). "Code Bite." MessageID: "9304200313.AA107798@acs.bu.edu." April 19, 1993.

Black Unicorn. (1996). "Assassination Politics, was Kiddie porn on the Internet." MessageID: "Pine.SUN.3.94.960921225528.24100A-100000@polaris." September 22, 1996.

Detweiler, L. (1993). "White House Letter." MessageID: '9302050002.AA11919@longs.lanc e.colostate.edu'. February 4, 1993.

Dinkelacker, J. (1993). "Shockwave Rider (True Names, Enders Game, Islands In The Net)." MessageID: "9310190303.AA07520@netcom.netcom.com." October 18, 1993.

Draper, J. (1992). "Mac PGP—Some Comments." MessageID: 9211121059.AA11389@net-com.netcom.com." November 12, 1992.

Finney, H. (1992). "Misc. Items." MessageID: "921128181712_74076.1041_DHJ61-1@Co mpuServe.com." November 28, 1992.

Geiger III, W. (1997). "I Am Allowed One Message (Was: List Problems or is it Quiet???)." MessageID: "199705271807.NAA00518@mailhub.amaranth.com." May 28, 1997.

Gilmore, J. (1993). "Remarks of John Perry Barlow to the First International Symposium on National Security & National Competitiveness." MessageID: "9302212127.AA26790@ toad.com." February 21, 1993.

Goen, K. (1993). "Political Reasons to Spread Crypto (Warning FLAME-BAIT)." MessageID: "9302192122.AA08664@netcom.netcom.com." February 19, 1993.

Hughes, E. (1994). "ANNOUNCE: February Meeting—'True Names.'" MessageID: "9402091941.AA04783@ah.com." February 9, 1994.

jdoe-0007 [alias]. (1996). "Jim Bell—Murderous Terrorist." MessageID: "199602050306. TAA01578@infinity.c2.org." February 5, 1996.

Karn, P. (1992). "How Far is to Far?." MessageID: "9211272304.AA09837@servo." November 27, 1992.

May, T. C. (1992). "Registering Keys with Big Brother." MessageID: "9210260209.AA18958@ netcom2.netcom.com." October 25, 1992.

May, T. C. (1992c). "The Crypto Singularity." MessageID: "9211130018.AA11046@netcom. netcom.com." December 11, 1992.

May, T. C. (1992e). "TEMPEST, Eavesdropping, and PDAs." MessageID: "9210202226. AA28803@netcom2.netcom.com." October 20, 1992.

May, T. C. (1993). "Crypto Activism and Respectability." MessageID: "9304212053. AA23743@netcom.netcom.com." April 21, 1993.

May, T. C. (1993b). "Spreading Encryption to Political Groups." MessageID: "9302192007. AA27273@netcom.netcom.com." February 19, 1993.

May, T. C. (1994a). "GAMES: The 'Crypto Anarchy Games.'" MessageID: "199402240227. SAA22222@mail.netcom.com." February 23, 1994.

May, T. C. (1994c). "Blacknet Worries." MessageID: "199402202033.MAA25767@mail.net-com.com." February 20, 1994.

May, T. C. (1994d). "Re: The Coming Police State." MessageID: "199403110637.WAA03791@ mail.netcom.com." March 10, 1994.

May, T. C. (1994e). "The Four Horsemen." MessageID: "199412112144.NAA08154@ne tcom4.netcom.com." December 11, 1994.

May, T C. (1994f). "'True Names,' chat with Vinge, and Cypherpunks." MessageID: "1994 07130630.XAA00700@netcom9.netcom.com." July 12, 1994.

May, T. C. (1994g). "'True Names,' chat with Vinge, and Cypherpunks," MessageID: '1994 07130221.TAA17224@netcom5.netcom.com'. July 12, 1994.

May, T. C. (1996). "RE: Bell, Detweiler, Ravings, and Whatnot." MessageID: "ad6906251 6021004b4c4@[205.199.118.202]." March 12, 1996.

Metzger, P. (1992a). "Threat to our privacy." MessageID: "9210272346.AA11735@newsu. shearson.com." October 27, 1992.

Metzger, P. (1992b). "the list." MessageID: "9211291832.AA23438@newsu.shearson.com." November 29, 1992.

Porter, D. (1993). "NSA STRENGTH." MessageID: "93Jun24.095545pdt.13970-1@well.sf. ca.us." June 24, 1993.

Ray, D. (1993). "more on security/obscurity/reality." MessageID: "9301150610.AA09544@ tnl.com." January 15, 1993.

Ringuette, M. (1993). "White House Letter." MessageID: "9302050513.AA11882@toad. com." April 2, 1993.

Sandfort, S. (1996). "Re: a retort + a comment + a question = [RANT]." MessageID: "Pine .SUN.3.91.961110085723.7792B-100000@crl4.crl.com." November 10, 1996.
The Omega [alias] (1992). "No Subject." MessageID: "9211121751.AA01503@spica.bu.edu." December 11, 1992.
Wayner, P. (1993). "No Subject." MessageID: "9301142206.AA23922@brokk.cs.cornell.edu." January 14, 1993. Cypherpunk Mail List Archives 1992–1998.
Whitaker, R. E. (1992). "Apple including PKS?" MessageID: "4195@eternity.demon.co.uk." November 16, 1992.

NEWSPAPERS

Editorial. "What is the FBI Up To?" *Washington Post*, March 25, 1971. A20.

WEBSITES

Aid, M. and Burr, W. (2013). *Secret Cold War Documents Reveal NSA Spied on Senators... along with Muhammad Ali, Martin Luther King, and a Washington Post Humorist.* Available: http://foreignpolicy.com/2013/09/25/secret-cold-war-documents-reveal-n sa-spied-on-senators/ [Accessed October 10, 2019].
Alexander, M. (1990). *Secret Service Busts Alleged Crime Ring.* Available: https://books.google .co.uk/books?id=wDlUmfY9nQsC&pg=PT127&lpg=PT127#v=onepage&q&f=false [Accessed October 10, 2019].
Assange, J. (2006). *Conspiracy As a Form of Governance.* Available: https://cryptome.org /0002/ja-conspiracies.pdf [Accessed October 11, 2019].
Assange, J. (2011). *Julian Assange: "I Am—Like All Hackers—A Little Bit Autistic."* Available: http://www.independent.co.uk/news/uk/home-news/julian-assange-i-am-ndash-like-all-hackers-ndash-a-little-bit-autistic-2358654.html [Accessed October 10, 2019].
Bamford, J. (2014). *The N.S.A. and Me.* Available: https://theintercept.com/2014/10/02/the-nsa-and-me/ [Accessed June 5, 2020].
Barlow, J. P. (1996). *A Declaration of the Independence of Cyberspace.* Available: https://ww w.eff.org/cyberspace-independence [Accessed October 12, 2019].
Bartlett, J. (2015). *Cypherpunks Write Code.* Available: https://web.archive.org/web/2016100 9114212/http://www.http://americanscientist.org/bookshelf/pub/cypherpunks-write-co de [Accessed October 10, 2019].
Bell, J. (1997). *Assassination Politics.* Available: http://cryptome.org/ap.htm [Accessed October 10, 2019].
Bentham, J. (1843). *The Works of Jeremy Bentham, vol. 11 (Memoirs of Bentham Part II and Analytical Index).* Available: http://oll.libertyfund.org/titles/bentham-the-works-of-jeremy-bentham-vol-11-memoirs-of-bentham-part-ii-and-analytical-index [Accessed May 12, 2019].
Blankenship, L. (1986). *Hacker Manifesto/The Conscience of a Hacker.* Available: http:// phrack.org/issues/7/3.html [Accessed October 10, 2019].
Boaz, D. (2015). *The Libertarian Mind.* Available: https://www.libertarianism.org/guides/in troduction-libertarianism [Accessed October 10, 2019].
Brautigan, R. (1967). *All Watched Over by Machines of Loving Grace* [Online]. Available: http://www.brautigan.net/machines.html [Accessed October 10, 2019].
Burrough, B. (2016). *The Bombings of America that We Forgot.* Available: http://time.com /4501670/bombings-of-america-burrough/ [Accessed October 10, 2019].

Campbell, D. (2002). *It's Time to Take Risks.* Available: https://www.theguardian.com/bo oks/2002/dec/10/biography.usa [Accessed October 10, 2019].

Charles, D. (1990). *Crackdown on Hackers "May Violate Civil Rights."* Available: https://ww w.newscientist.com/article/mg12717261.300-crackdown-on-hackers-may-violate-civil -rights-/ [Accessed October 10, 2019].

Chaum, D. (1985b). *Security without Identification Card Computers to Make Big Brother Obsolete.* Available: https://www.chaum.com/publications/Security_Wthout_Identific ation.html [Accessed October 18, 2019].

Cypherpunks. (1992–1998). *Cypherpunks Mail List Archive 1992–1998.* Available: https:// lists.cpunks.org/pipermail/cypherpunks/2013-September/000741.html [Accessed July 10, 2015].

Einstein, A. (1939). *Einstein's Letter to President Einstein—1939* [Online]. Available: http:// www.atomicarchive.com/Docs/Begin/Einstein.shtml [Accessed September 10, 2019].

Electronic Frontier Foundation. (n.d.). *About EFF.* Available: https://www.eff.org/about [Accessed October 11, 2019].

Ellsberg, D. (1973). *Text of C.I.A. Ellsberg Affidavit* [Online]. Available: https://www.nyt imes.com/1973/09/26/archives/text-of-cia-ellsberg-affidavit-affidavit.html [Accessed October 11, 2019].

Greene, T. C. (2001a). *Cypherpunk Bell Found Guilty: Incomplete Verdict Passes Muster.* Available: http://www.theregister.co.uk/2001/04/11/cypherpunk_bell_found_guilty/ [Accessed October 10, 2019].

Greene, T. C. (2001b). *Cypherpunk Bell Gets Ten Years: Judge Cracks Nut with Sledgehammer.* Available: https://www.theregister.co.uk/2001/08/28/cypherpunk_bell_gets_ten_year s/ [Accessed October 10, 2019].

Hughes, E. (1993). *A Cypherpunk's Manifesto.* Available: https://www.activism.net/cyphe rpunk/manifesto.html [Accessed October 11, 2019].

Kemp, J., Trapasso, C., and Mcshane, L. (2015). *Aaron Swartz, Co-Founder of Reddit and Online Activist, Hangs Himself in Brooklyn Apartment, Authorities Say.* Available: http://www.nydailynews.com/new-york/co-founder-reddit-hangs-brooklyn-apartm ent-article-1.1238852 [Accessed October 10, 2019].

King, M. L. (1967). *Beyond Vietnam: A Time to Break Silence Address to the Clergy and Laity Concerned about Vietnam, Riverside Church, New York City April 4, 1967 by Dr. Martin Luther King Jr.* Available: http://www.drmartinlutherkingjr.com/beyondvie tnam.htm [Accessed October 10, 2019].

Kirschbaum, C. (2011). *Swartz Indicted for JSTOR Theft.* Available: http://tech.mit.edu/ V131/N30/swartz.html [Accessed October 10, 2019].

Leigh, D. (2010). *US Embassy Cables Leak Sparks Global Diplomatic Crisis (Guardian, 28 Nov 2010).* Available: https://www.theguardian.com/world/2010/nov/28/us-embass y-cable-leak-diplomacy-crisis [Accessed October 11, 2019].

Markoff, J. (1990). *Drive to Counter Computer Crime Aims at Invaders.* Available: http:// www.nytimes.com/1990/06/03/us/drive-to-counter-computer-crime-aims-at-invaders .html?pagewanted=all [Accessed October 10, 2019].

May, T. C. (1988). *Crypto-Anarchist Manifesto.* Available: https://www.activism.net/cyphe rpunk/Crypto Anarchy.html [Accessed October 10, 2019].

May, T. C. (1994b). *The Cyphernomicon.* Available: https://nakamotoinstitute.org/static/docs/ cyphernomicon.txt [Accessed October 10, 2019].

McCullagh, D. (2000a). *Assassination Politics & Jim Bell.* Available: http://www.konformis t.com/2000/assassination/assassination.htm [Accessed October 10, 2019].

McCullagh, D. (2000b). *Crypto-Convict Won't Recant.* Available: https://www.wired.co m/2000/04/crypto-convict-wont-recant/ [Accessed October 10, 2019].

Michigan Institute of Technology Museum. (n.d.). *TX-0 Computer.* Available: http://museum. mit.edu/150/23 [Accessed October 10, 2019].

Moran, J. (n.d.). *The First Domino: Nixon and the Pentagon Papers.* Available: https://we b.archive.org/web/20170116210752/http://millercenter.org/educationalresources/firs t-domino-nixon-and-pentagon-papers [Accessed October 10, 2019].

Nixon, R. and Frost, D. (1977). Edited transcript of David Frost's interview with Richard Nixon broadcast in May 1977. Available: https://www.theguardian.com/theguardian/ 2007/sep/07/greatinterviews1 [Accessed September 10, 2019].

NowImScared [alias]. (2007). *Who Wants a Theme Song.* Available: http://exurbannation.blog spot.com/2007/02/who-wants-theme-song.html [Accessed October 10, 2019].

Perry Barlow, J. (1990). *A Not Terribly Brief History of the Electronic Frontier Foundation.* Available: https://www.eff.org/pages/not-terribly-brief-history-electronic-frontier-fo undation [Accessed November 16, 2019].

Quote Investigator. (2016). *We Shape Our Tools, and Thereafter Our Tools Shape Us.* Available: http://quoteinvestigator.com/2016/06/26/shape/ [Accessed October 11, 2019].

Rhoads, C. (2007). *The Twilight Years of Cap'n Crunch.* Available: https://www.wsj.com/ articles/SB116863379291775523 [Accessed October 10, 2019].

Ringuette, M. (2000). *Resume.* Available: http://www.cs.cmu.edu/~mnr/resumes/feb00.txt [Accessed April 17, 2020].

Rosenbaum, R. (1971). *Secrets of the Little Blue Box.* Available: http://www.lospadres.info/ thorg/lbb.html [Accessed October 10, 2019].

Slater, D. (1997). *Secret Agents.* Available: http://groups.csail.mit.edu/mac/classes/6.805/arti cles/crypto/cypherpunks/bay-area-weekly-march-14-97.txt [Accessed December 31, 2019].

Sterling, B. (2002). *The Hacker's Crackdown.* Available: http://www.mit.edu/hacker/hacker. html [Accessed October 10, 2019].

Stern, C. (2014). *NBC Reporter Recounts Breaking FBI Spying Story.* Available: http://inv estigations.nbcnews.com/_news/2014/01/08/22220561-nbc-reporter-recounts-breaking -fbi-spying-story [Accessed October 10, 2019].

Stinebrickner-Kauffman, T. (2013). *Why Aaron Died.* Available: http://tarensk.tumblr.com/ post/42260548767/why-aaron-died [Accessed October 10, 2019].

United States Department of Justice. (1976). *Report on Inquiry into CIA-Related Electronic Surveillance Activities.* Available: https://nsarchive2.gwu.edu/NSAEBB/NSAEBB506/ docs/ciasignals_25.pdf [Accessed November 22, 2019].

United States Government. (n.d.). *About the Federalist Papers.* Available: https://www.con gress.gov/resources/display/content/About+the+Federalist+Papers [Accessed October 10, 2019].

United States National Security Council. (1952). *National Security Council Intelligence Directive No. 9: Communications Intelligence.* Available: https://nsarchive2.gwu.edu/ NSAEBB/NSAEBB23/docs/doc02.pdf [Accessed May 1, 2020].

United States Senate. (1975). *Hearings before the Select Committee to Study Governmental Operations with Respect to Intelligence Activities of the United States Senate, Volume 5: The National Security Agency and Fourth Amendment Rights, October 29 and November 6, 1975.* Available: https://www.intelligence.senate.gov/sites/default/files /94intelligence_activities_V.pdf [Accessed November 21, 2019].

United States Senate. (1976). *Intelligence Activities and the Rights of American: Book Two. Final Report of the Select Committee To Study Governmental Operations with Respect to Intelligence Activities. Church Report.* Available: https://www.intelligence.senat e.gov/sites/default/files/94755_II.pdf [Accessed October 10, 2019].

United States Senate. (1976c). Supplementary Detailed Staff Reports on Intelligence Activities and the Rights of Americans: Book Three. Final Report of the Select Committee to Study Governmental Operations with Respect to Intelligence Activities. Available: <https://www.intelligence.senate.gov/sites/default/files/94755_III.pdf>   [Accessed October 11, 2019]. 765.

WikiLeaks. (2016). *Search the DNC Email Database* [Online]. Available: https://wikileaks. org/dnc-emails/ [Accessed June 11, 2020].

Zimmermann, P. (n.d.). *The Early Roots of PGP* [Online]. Available: https://www.philzimm ermann.com/EN/background/peace.html [Accessed October 10, 2019].

Zimmermann, P. (1996). Testimony of Philip R. Zimmermann to the Subcommittee on Science, Technology, and Space of the US Senate Committee on Commerce, Science, and Transportation. Available: https://philzimmermann.com/EN/essays/Testimon y.html [Accessed October 10, 2019].

YOUTUBE VIDEOS

Ali, M. "Muhammad Ali on the Vietnam War-Draft," YouTube video, 2:37, posted by "kao-tikkalm," Feb 11, 2011, Available: https://www.youtube.com/watch?v=HeFMyrWlZ68 [Accessed October 10, 2019].

Falkvinge, R. "Black Hat EU 2013—Shelters or Windmills: The Struggle for Power and Information Advantage," YouTube Video, 1:10, posted by "Black Hat," October 25, 2013, Available: https://www.youtube.com/watch?v=jygJe8gNxU4 [Accessed November 15, 2019].

4 Crypto War I (1966–1981)
The Data Encryption Standard (DES)

I am very worried that the NSA has surreptitiously influenced the [data encryption standard]…in a way which…may pose a threat to individual privacy [1]

Martin Hellman, 1976b

4.1 THE CODEBREAKERS: DAVID KAHN PUBLISHES A CRYPTOLOGICAL BIBLE

"Kahn's 'The Codebreakers' remains the definitive book," Tim May posted to the cypherpunk mailing list in 1993.[2] At over a thousand pages in length, David Kahn's 1967 *The Codebreakers* was considered the authoritative history of cryptology. It lured a generation of mathematicians and technologists to a field that, outside of classified environments, had received scant attention. When Whitfield Diffie was on his cryptological odyssey, Kahn's tome was his guide. Harriet Fell, a friend of Diffie's, later recounted, "He traveled everywhere with that book in hand. If you invited him to dinner, he'd come with *The Codebreakers.*"[3] Diffie consumed Kahn's writings for countless hours; "I read it more carefully than anyone had ever read it…Kahn's book to me is like the Vedas," he recalls, referring to the ancient Hindu scriptures.[4] The US government never wanted the book published. Quite presciently, the government feared Kahn's writings would be as the falling pebbles which summon a landslide, capable of devastating the government's cryptological hegemony.

Kahn was a journalist. In the years before World War Two, Kahn's first exposure to ciphers had been a copy of Fletcher Pratt's 1939 *Secret and Urgent* he discovered in a New York library—its cover lured him immediately—"That dust jacket was terrific; it had letters and numbers swirling out of the cosmos. I was hooked," he recalls. Kahn's enthusiasm led him to join the American Cryptogram Association, a group of hobbyist codebreakers, but he found their prowess limited: "It was a bunch of amateurs, they solved cryptograms as puzzles and used a little publication with articles on how to solve them."[5]

---

[1] Hellman, 1976b.
[2] May, 1993.
[3] Levy, 2001, The Loner, Chapter 1.

[4] Ibid.
[5] Ibid.

Kahn would note in the preface to *The Codebreakers* that the only previous attempt at a "book-length attempt to survey the history of cryptology" was Fletcher's *Secret and Urgent*.[6] However, Kahn confesses "disillusion" with Fletcher's effort as it was full of "errors and omissions, his false generalizations based on no evidence, and his unfortunate predilection for inventing facts."[7] Kahn cites two further books as useful references on the technical aspects of cryptology: Helen F. Gaines' 1939 *Elementary Cryptanalysis*, and Luigi Sacco's 1951 *Manuel de Cryptographie* [French edition; original Italian edition *Manuele di crittografia*].[8]

Kahn estimated between eighty-five and ninety percent of *The Codebreakers'* content had never before been published.[9] His book covers four millennia of cryptological history, exploring developments in locations including China, Egypt, India, Italy, Iran, and Mesopotamia. It also included a chapter on the secretive US signals intelligence organization, the National Security Agency (NSA).

For the first time, the NSA faced the threat of a compendium of cryptological wisdom, as well as details about its own existence, being exposed to the world. Kahn's book not only promoted the field of cryptology, but would drastically accelerate the future advancement of the discipline by inspiring great minds not beholden to government agencies. Should cryptology advance, and spread overseas, the capabilities allowing the NSA to protect the United States from threats including a nuclear-armed Soviet Union, could be severely undermined.

The full details of actions undertaken by the US government to halt the publication of *The Codebreakers* are unknown. However, James Bamford's *The Puzzle Palace* offers some insights.[10] Kahn was contracted to write *The Codebreakers* in 1961 by the Macmillan Company. He toiled away as a reporter by day whilst researching cryptology by night for two years before quitting his job to wholly dedicate himself to completing the book. It was around this time, Bamford writes, the NSA became aware of Kahn's endeavor. At some point during this period, Bamford claims, Kahn would also be added to the MINARET watch list allowing interception of his calls and telegrams.[11] It was the start of the first crypto war. Bamford explains that within the NSA:

> Innumerable hours of meetings and discussions, involving the highest levels of the agency, including the director, were spent in an attempt to sandbag the book. Among the possibilities considered were hiring Kahn into the government so that certain criminal statutes would apply if the work was published; purchasing the copyright; undertaking "clandestine service applications" against the author, which apparently meant anything from physical surveillance to a black-bag job; and conducting a "surreptitious entry" into Kahn's Long Island home.[12]

All of these options were rejected. Instead, the matter was taken to the pan-agency United States Intelligence Board (USIB) where the book was assessed as being of

---

6 Kahn, 1967, Preface.
7 Ibid.
8 Ibid, Appendix.
9 Ibid, Preface.

10 Bamford, 1982.
11 Bamford, 2006, 169.
12 Bamford, 1982, 168–169.

possible value to foreign communications security authorities. The USIB recommended further "low-key actions" be taken to dissuade Kahn and his publisher from releasing the book, but that legal action to prevent publication should not be attempted.[13] It is unknown why legal measures were not part of the recommendation issued by the reviewing committee. One can hypothesize that should news of a legal proceeding against a journalist make the headlines, there would be uproar in defense of the constitutionally protected right to freedom of speech, as well as undesired publicity being directed towards Fort Meade and Kahn's book. Bamford notes the USIB also intended to engage with the director of the CIA, Allen Dulles, to understand how they may be able to help, though it is unknown if the request resulted in any actions from Langley.

In March 1966, Macmillan, acting without Kahn's consent, submitted *The Codebreakers* manuscript to the Pentagon.[14] It is unknown if they were acting solely under their own initiative, or whether external forces influenced their action. Shortly after submitting Kahn's *The Codebreakers* to the Pentagon, Macmillan's chairman, Lee C. Deighton, received a letter from the Department of Defense informing him they "deplored" the manuscript, and that "it would not be in the national interest to publish the book."[15] The DoD had given the manuscript to NSA, who subsequently sent it to the USIB for review. The government informed Macmillan that if they proceeded with publication, significant national interest omissions would be required.[16]

For a month Macmillan did not respond. NSA Director General Marshall S. Carter was dispatched to make a personal appeal to Deighton. On 22 July 1966, Carter donned a suit and caught a flight to New York.[17] It was a risky move. If the media were alerted to the NSA's attempt to censor a publishing house, the agency could be front-page news, and may even end up summoned to congressional hearings—discretion was paramount. As such, Deighton was unaware of the purpose of the scheduled meeting, or of Carter's affiliation beyond the Pentagon.[18] The Macmillan chairman was surprised to learn Carter worked for the NSA. At Carter's request, Deighton agreed not to document their meeting.[19] Carter was informed Kahn's contract with Macmillan meant no manuscript changes could be made without the author's consent. Nevertheless, Carter attacked Kahn's credentials:

> I pointed out that Kahn's reputation as a cryptologist was suspect; that he was an amateur; that he had never been employed by the government; that, fortunately, there were enough errors in the book to denigrate the substantive documentation of cryptology in the eyes of the community…that the book…was sufficiently wrong in sufficient areas to depreciate its validity as the final anthology of cryptology.[20]

Despite Carter's attack on Kahn, Deighton was sympathetic to the national security arguments and agreed to engage with Kahn on the topic. By now, the NSA

---

13 Ibid, 169.
14 Ibid.
15 Ibid, 170.
16 Ibid, 171.

17 Ibid, 170–171.
18 Ibid, 171.
19 Ibid.
20 Ibid.

had accepted they would not be able to prevent publication of the book, nor have the chapter on their agency omitted. Their revised objective was to remove mention of the NSA's close cooperation with their British equivalent, the Government Communications Headquarters (GCHQ). In the United Kingdom, GCHQ were also applying pressure on the UK office of Macmillan. The content NSA insisted be removed consisted of a mere three paragraphs, given that they initially sought to have the entire book permanently disappear into Deighton's draw, it was a relatively small request; Kahn reluctantly agreed.[21] However, the NSA did not notice the references to the GCHQ source material were located at the back of Kahn's book—it would be possible for any reader to look up the referenced material and acquire the same information.[22]

After publication, *The Codebreakers* was lauded a success; a *New York Times* reviewer wrote, "Mr Kahn has presented the specialist and the general public with a lavishly comprehensive introduction to cryptography."[23] *The Washington Post* was even more profuse in its praise, stating *The Codebreakers* "replaces everything else written on the subject," and the reviewer wrote that the book was "astounding in its scholarship," adding, "Kahn has told the story with economy, lucidity, and vast excitement...a *tour de force*, he renders comprehensible to the layman something that, by definition, was designed to be impenetrable."[24] Selling 75,000 copies in hardback, *The Codebreakers* became a best seller, and even became a nominee for the 1968 general non-fiction Pulitzer prize.[25] It was considered the seminal work in its field for a generation of cryptologists.

4.2   AN ENIGMATIC GERMAN: HORST FEISTEL AND DIGITAL DOSSIERS

Martin Hellman, reflecting on how he became interested in cryptography, cites that as well as hearing David Kahn speak, another key influence was his proximity to cryptologist Horst Feistel at IBM, who he notes was "widely regarded as the father of IBM's cryptographic research effort."[26] Feistel's labors set the foundation upon which the pioneers of digital cryptography built.

In 1973 Feistel wrote an influential *Scientific American* article in which he warned, "computers now constitute, or will soon constitute, a dangerous threat to individual privacy...it will soon be feasible to compile dossiers in depth on an entire citizenry."[27]

Feistel was born in Germany in 1914.[28] With Hitler poised to enact military conscription, Feistel traveled to Zurich to visit his aunt; he never returned.[29] Upon completing his studies, Feistel moved to the United States.[30] Just before he was to become

21   Ibid, 172.
22   Ibid, 171–173.
23   Davis, 1968.
24   Friendly, 1967.
25   Macpherson, 1978; Hastedt, 2011, 430.

26   Hellman and McGraw, 2016.
27   Feistel, 1973, 15.
28   Diffie and Landau, 1998, Chapter 2.
29   Levy, 2001, The Standard, Chapter 3.
30   Ibid.

a US citizen, Japanese warplanes devastated Pearl Harbor.[31] America was at war. As a German, Feistel's movements were restricted to Boston.[32] In January 1944, his luck changed. Feistel was granted both citizenship and security clearance to work at the US Air Force's highly secretive Cambridge Research Center (CRC).[33]

Feistel declared his interest in cryptology on arriving at the CRC, but was warned a German-born man should not be talking about such a subject whilst America was at war with the Nazis.[34] It must have been a challenge for Feistel to desist from cryptographic work—it had consumed him since his teenage years. Diffie reflected years later, "you think I'm single minded…he [Feistel] basically worked on cryptography; he wouldn't work on anything but cryptography his whole life," and Feistel had a "nut passion for the subject."[35]

By the early Cold War years, Feistel had returned to his passion, having maneuvered himself to head a cryptographic research group at the CRC. When Feistel discovered a project designed to allow allied fighter planes to identify one another— the "Identify Friend or Foe" project—was about to enter service absent of suitable cryptographic defenses to prevent an enemy manipulating or emulating such signals, he intervened. Feistel's team of mathematicians worked with outside academic consultants in order to find and fix a number of vulnerabilities; his group subsequently developed the first practical block ciphers (ciphers that encrypt a block of data, rather than one bit at a time [stream cipher]).[36]

According to Diffie and Susan Landau, the CRC maintained close contact with the NSA, noting the agency seems "to have exerted a profound influence on cryptographic design in that organization [IBM]," they also comment the "NSA appears eventually to have succeeded in shutting down the Air Force work." By the late 1950s, the cryptologic effort at Cambridge was over.[37]

Whilst there is no evidence to support Diffie and Landau's claim that the NSA was responsible for shutting the program down, it would be consistent with Fort Meade believing cryptology belonged solely to the US government and to their agency. The NSA likely understood complete hegemony over cryptology was the only way to ensure tight control over the distribution of encryption algorithms, and that any approved for public use were not beyond their means to break.

With the CRC's cryptographic programs shut down, Feistel headed to Mitre, a defense organization with a large number of military contracts, to attempt to catalyze their cryptographic research program; however, his attempts failed.[38] Feistel told Diffie he "got squeezed out of doing cryptographic research," citing additional conversations with Mitre employees; Diffie notes, "he [Feistel] was forced to abandon the project as a result of what was perceived at Mitre as NSA pressure."[39] Given Diffie himself had worked at Mitre, it is likely his sources were reliable. It is unknown if this was an attempt by the NSA to curtail research efforts being incubated in the private sector. If

31 Ibid.
32 Ibid.
33 Ibid.
34 Diffie and Landau, 1998, 65.
35 Plutte, 2011, 15.

36 Diffie and Landau, 1998, 65.
37 Ibid.
38 Hellman and McGraw, 2016.
39 Ibid; Diffie and Landau, 1998, 65.

businesses were to develop encryption products, even if they were at first used exclusively for US military applications, an appetite for return on research investment would result in the desire to sell their products as widely as possible, including to other countries. The NSA certainly did not want their enemies to possess encryption beyond their means to decipher, and even their allies receiving encryption capabilities may have been deemed undesirable as today's friend can become tomorrow's enemy.

Feistel's next destination was the dominant computer power of its age: IBM. Feistel joined the Computer Science Department at IBM's Thomas J. Watson research center in Yorktown Heights, New York in 1968.[40] Yorktown was, in Diffie's words, "a good bit more independent of the government," which allowed Feistel to return to his cryptographic pursuits.[41]

IBM used its vast wealth to create a bastion of intellectual power with a relaxed culture; Alan Konheim, who became Feistel's boss in 1971, recalls Feistel worked only between the hours of seven and eleven in the morning, but it was accepted as he produced quality research.[42] A great degree of freedom was granted to employees of IBM's research division, "If they hired you at Yorktown, you'd do what you wanted, as long as you did something," Konheim writes, "and Feistel did something—he formalized his idea for a cryptosystem."[43]

It was whilst working at IBM Feistel wrote his 1973 *Scientific American* article "Cryptography and Computer Privacy."[44] In the article, Feistel expressed his concerns about the imminent consequences of the technological revolution: the creation of dossiers on every citizen. Previously, Feistel explained, "the material for such dossiers was scattered in many separate locations under widely diverse jurisdictions," but that was rapidly changing.[45] Feistel's solution was to adapt a computer to "guard its contents from everyone but the authorized individuals by enciphering the material in forms highly resistant to cipher-breaking."[46] Feistel observes that whilst diplomats and soldiers had traditionally required encryption, it had not been a public concern for the typical individual with the exception of "lovers and thieves," who "solved their requirements for communications privacy as best they could."[47] But the technological age was dawning, encryption was now required to protect the average individual, and finally, Feistel found himself in an organization with commercial drivers correlating to his moral imperatives. Feistel created an encryption algorithm: Demon.

4.3   THE DEMON RE-CHRISTENED

In 1968, IBM CEO Thomas J. Watson Jr. addressed the Commonwealth Club of California:

> I believe we in the industry must continue to improve existing technological safeguards which limit access to information stored in electronic systems...we must offer to share

---

[40] Konheim, 2015, 27.
[41] Plutte, 2011.
[42] Levy, 2001, The Standard, Chapter 2.
[43] Ibid.

[44] Feistel, 1973.
[45] Ibid, 15.
[46] Ibid.
[47] Ibid.

every bit of specialized knowledge…in a determination to help secure progress and privacy.[48]

For commercial reasons, IBM needed to maintain the confidentiality of sensitive client data, as well as the public's trust that privacy was not being sacrificed for modernity. Horst Feistel had been installed as head of cryptographic research within IBM's computer sciences division to fulfill the promise of Watson's words.[49] Konheim recalls their algorithm was initially to be called DEMONSTRATION; however, the programming language[50] with which Feistel was working did not permit that many characters, so the name was truncated to DEMON.[51] A colleague would later suggest Lucifer as an alternative, probably due to the cryptographic pun—Feistel concurred.[52]

As Feistel labored away on Lucifer, an immediate business application was developing in IBM's product division. In 1966, IBM were contracted to build a cash issuing terminal for Lloyds Banking Group; it would be designated IBM 2984, and became a component of the first automatic teller machine (ATM).[53] Security was paramount for such technology. Should an attacker be able to read the communications between the bank's mainframe and the ATM, they would gain access to sensitive information about who was withdrawing money, and even the balances of their bank accounts. But perhaps more seriously, if one could intercept the telemetry between the bank and the ATM, they could potentially decode the communication protocols and manipulate the bank's instructions to the ATM, causing money—around fifty thousand US dollars per machine—to spill into the hands of awaiting criminals.[54] Project leader Walter Tuchman and his team proved such an attack was feasible when on one rainy Sunday evening they managed to empty a hundred ATMs in London of millions of pounds by masquerading as the host and sending false "give him cash" messages to the ATMs.[55] Tuchman subsequently highlighted what he believed the most severe threat of what became known as a "jackpot" attack happening, in order to convey the severity of the threat to his bosses: "We conjured up a building wired with a LAN,[56] and a disgruntled employee in the basement office."[57] With the criminal world yet to transition to the online realm, insider threats were Tuchman's prime concern.

As a corporate titan, IBM was rich enough to absorb the losses from a single, or even a series of ATMs being looted. However, an undermining of confidence in their new technology would have a more toxic effect. Not only would the prospect of a global dispersion of IBM-produced ATMs be lost, but so too would the public's faith in technology companies protecting their privacy.

---

[48] IBM, no date.
[49] Ibid.
[50] Advanced Programming Language (APL).
[51] Konheim, 2015, 15.
[52] Ibid.
[53] Ibid, 16.
[54] Tuchman, 1998, 276.

[55] Ibid, 227.
[56] Local Area Network, typically a business' corporate network located within their office, though may also be a home user's network with the central component being the Internet router.
[57] Tuchman, 1998, 276.

Tuchman looked to Feistel's cryptographic research group, and Lucifer, to secure the ATM's communications.[58] Feistel's team completed work and integrated Lucifer into Lloyds' ATMs in 1971.[59] Buoyed by Feistel's success, IBM seemed poised to fully commercialize Lucifer; Walter Tuchman was positioned to lead their data security group and transfer IBM's aspiration to implementation.[60] Tuchman's team realized Lucifer needed further refinement before it was ready for the mass market, and went about applying the revisions.[61]

On 30 June 1971, IBM filed a patent request for Feistel's 128-bit Lucifer cipher, entitled the "Block Cipher Cryptographic System." Before an organization can apply for a foreign patent in the US, they must first seek a domestic one. The application is filed with the US Patent and Trademark Office, who then consult with federal agencies to determine whether the subject of the request may pose a risk to national security; if so, it may be classified under the Invention Secrecy Act of 1951. IBM's patent request took until October 1973 to complete, at which point a secrecy order was placed over Feistel's creation—Konheim believed this was ordered by the NSA. However, with a number of papers being published, including Feistel's article in *Scientific American*, Konheim states Feistel had let the "cat out of the bag describing the innards of…Lucifer…the secrecy order seemed ludicrous." Despite the government's continuing push to restrict the information, the secrecy order was lifted in November 1973, allowing the patent to be issued the following March.[62]

4.4   SEEKING A DATA ENCRYPTION STANDARD

On 15 March 1973, the government solicited candidates for the first Data Encryption Standard (DES).[63] Two drivers caused the government to seek a standard to protect their non-classified, yet sensitive data. The first was the Brooks Act of 1965, which instructed the National Bureau of Standards (NBS)[64] to create standards to govern the procurement and use of the federal government's computers. The second driver was the growing pressure to secure data the government held on its citizens; this requirement resulted in the Privacy Act of 1974.[65] After passage of the Brooks Act, NBS' Ruth Davis started investigating whether the transactions of non-classified government communications should be encrypted; she assessed they should, and before issuing a public solicitation, sought the NSA's assistance in developing a suitable encryption algorithm.[66]

In the early 1970s, NSA's cryptographic efforts were still analog, developing hardware-based encryption. Richard "Dickie" George, an NSA mathematician at the time comments, "The information assurance directorate [at NSA], which had about 2500 people doing…evaluation of crypto, and implementation of crypto…did

---

[58] Ibid, 12.
[59] Bamford, 1982, 434.
[60] Ibid.
[61] Ibid.
[62] Konheim, 2016, 12.

[63] Burr, no date, 250.
[64] NBS is the predecessor of the National Institute of Standards and Technology (NIST).
[65] United States Senate, 1978, 1.
[66] Johnson, 1998, 232.

not own a computer, we were doing the work with paper and pencil."[67] The NSA's leadership were not investing in non-hardware encryption. George recounts how in 1973 the information assurance director found him working on a software-based encryption algorithm, and told George, "don't spend more than 10% of your time on that, because we will never run crypto in software, you can't trust computers."[67] Despite these limitations, NSA considered themselves the preeminent cryptology agency; George comments:

> What made NSA the leader in cryptography was we had the best problems. We had the best designers in the world and we were looking at their crypto and trying to find problems with it—nobody had those problems to work with, that was awesome. We also had a critical mass of people, we had a thousand mathematicians looking at these problems and sharing information with each other every day. So the best problems, and a critical mass of people thinking about them, that's how you own the space—and we did own it.[68]

On receiving NBS' request to develop the DES, George recalls:

> There was a lot of discussion…at all the levels at NSA…a lot of the discussion was technically could we do it and how would we do it…at the more senior levels the questions were if we put out an algorithm no-one's going to use it because they think it's going to be hooked [the NSA would have inserted a back door]. If anyone finds an attack on it they're going to know we hooked it, even if we didn't. So this, politically, is going to be disaster for us no matter what way we go.[69]

The NSA were also accustomed to a long development cycle. Take, for instance, the Vincent, a handheld radio with an integrated encryption algorithm that was developed for military forward observers. The algorithm was designed in 1957 and then endured twelve years of NSA evaluation and refinement before implementation approval. The implementation was then scrutinized for a further seven years, with alarms being built into the device for any conceivable malfunctions.[70] It was a total of 19 years before the product was deployed.[71] George comments with that heritage, "when NBS said we're going to put this out in a year we were nervous that we would design something and there would be a problem with it. So, the agency said we don't want to design the algorithm."[72] The NSA's director told his NBS counterpart that whilst the agency would not create a DES algorithm, it would evaluate the chosen algorithm to check for known attacks.[73] The NSA director told his team, "I want to be able to assure the director of…[NBS] that the algorithm is as strong as advertised…if we find anything, we are going to tell them."[75] An official NSA history of the period notes:

---

[67] Ibid, 5:57.
[68] Ibid, 29:39.
[69] Ibid, 6:20.
[70] Ibid, 7:24.
[71] Ibid, 8:06.

[72] Ibid, 8:30.
[73] Ibid, 9:53.
[74] Johnson, 1998, 232.
[75] Jeffery, 1976.

The decision to get involved with NBS was hardly unanimous. From the SIGINT standpoint, a competent industry standard could spread into undesirable areas, like Third World government communications, narcotics traffickers, and international terrorism targets. But NSA had only recently discovered the large-scale pilfering of information from U.S. government and defense industry telephone communications. This argued the opposite case—that, as Frank Rowlett [government cryptologist and Commandant of the National Cryptologic School] had contented since World War II, in the long run it was more important to secure one's own communications that to exploit those of the enemy.[74]

The solicitation NBS issued indicated a number of criteria for the DES. Firstly, the algorithm should not be secret, as had been the case in the past with many encryption systems; security should rest solely with the encryption key's secrecy.[75] Secondly, the algorithm should be able to withstand a known plaintext attack. In a known plaintext attack, a cryptanalyst has access to both enciphered communications and their plaintext decryptions to aid their attempts to identify the key.[76] This was important as a key could persist for a long period of time, whilst the associated decryptions could be either stolen, or exposed in the public domain as part of normal business operations, such as a press release that is sensitive whilst in draft, but designed to be disseminated widely once published. Thirdly, the only viable attack against the algorithm should be an "exhaustion," or brute-force attack, where every possible key is tried, and it should be uneconomical to conduct such an attack.[77]

The first solicitation in the Federal Register did not go well; only three professors answered, all of whom wanted money to study the problem rather than having an available algorithm, so NBS refused their requests.[78] The NBS returned to the NSA asking if they could develop the DES as the private sector was unable to meet the requirement.[79] As the NSA were again debating if they could create such an algorithm, Lucifer's existence was discovered by NSA's Deputy Director for Research and Engineering, Howard Rosenblum.[80] This discovery was likely due to the Inventions Secrecy Order placed upon Lucifer, possibly on the instruction of someone within the NSA. George recounts finding out "the main designer [Feistel]...has worked on crypto with NSA. So, there was a feeling that he actually knew what he was doing and this might be a decent algorithm."[81] Feistel may have worked with the NSA whilst at the CRC, though the record on this is unclear. IBM and the NSA had a close relationship; according to Alan Konheim, "They [NSA employees] came up every couple of months to find out what IBM was doing."[82] In addition, IBM's Chief Scientist, Lewis Branscombe was previously head of the NBS.[83] Given the close links, the NBS' Dr. Denny Branstad made a direct request to Tuchman for IBM to submit Lucifer as a candidate algorithm.[84]

---

[76] Ibid.
[77] Ibid.
[78] George, 2016, 10:45.
[79] Ibid, 11:06.
[80] Ibid, 11:21; Johnson, 1998, 232.

[81] Ibid, 11:31.
[82] Kolata, 1977, 440.
[83] Ibid.
[84] Tuchman, 1998, 277.

A meeting was convened to discuss the NBS request at IBM's New York headquarters. Lucifer was the subject of vast hours of design and refinement. Submitting it as a candidate would mean sacrificing their patent, allowing other companies to utilize the algorithm, and would significantly diminish IBM's return on investment. IBM would still have the secrets of how to implement and optimize the algorithm on a chip, and the ability to exploit its existing customer base, but the vast returns that could have resulted from having one of the only viable commercial ciphers would no longer be achievable. Paul Rizzo, second-in-command at IBM listened with fellow executives Bob Evans and Branscomb as Tuchman pleaded with them to keep Lucifer proprietary.[85] Tuchman later reflected he was a "running dog, capitalist warmonger," as he argued Lucifer was the best on the market and would deliver IBM's competitive advantage for years to come.[86] Tuchman later wrote Rizzo's response was both poignant and memorable, "If G.M. [General Motors] had perfected a new superior seatbelt, I am *sure* they would share it with their competitors rather than use it for commercial advantage."[87] The decision was taken to submit the algorithm to NBS. Tuchman drove back to his Kingston lab reflecting he had never been more proud of IBM; he noted his warmongering capitalist mentality was permanently eroded.[88]

With IBM on board, NBS needed to demonstrate due diligence on whether other candidate algorithms may yet emerge, therefore a second DES solicitation was conducted. Three responses were received: one from another professor requesting money to study the problem, another from a commercial company who had an algorithm, but wanted to keep it proprietary which would prevent public examination of the algorithm, and Lucifer.[89] Lucifer was selected to become the DES candidate. NSA analysis of Lucifer commenced.[90,91] A number of IBM employees were given security clearances enabling them to ask of the NSA any question regarding Lucifer, and the latter were under orders by their directors to answer truthfully; George comments that the NSA "worked pretty closely with IBM to make sure what they were turning in was correct."[94] An NSA team was set up to evaluate DES, shortly afterward a shadow evaluation team was established to evaluate the first team's work without their knowledge, in turn a second shadow team was assembled to evaluate the first shadow team's work.[92] George comments, "I don't know how many teams were involved in watching those teams, but it seems like everyone was involved and nobody knew it…it was a crazy system."[93]

The Data Encryption Standard uses the Data Encryption Algorithm (Lucifer), a block cipher that encrypts 64-bit blocks at a time. Lucifer is a symmetric algorithm; the same key both encrypts and decrypts the data (as opposed to an asymmetric/public key algorithm, where two separate, but mathematically related, keys encrypt and decrypt data). Whilst the key is expressed as a 64-bit variable, every eighth bit is for parity, designed to ensure the key is free of errors, producing an effective key

---

[85] Ibid, 278.
[86] Ibid.
[87] Ibid.
[88] Ibid.
[89] George, 2016, 12:10.

[90] Exhaustion attacks are more commonly known as brute force attacks.
[91] George, 2016, 13:00.
[92] George, 2016, 14:03.
[93] Ibid, 15:15.

size of 56 bits. Whilst the difference of 8 bits may seem minor, the difference of each additional bit in a key size doubles the strength of the key, therefore a 64-bit key is vastly superior to a 56-bit key. The use of this parity bit would later come under significant public scrutiny.

The algorithm uses a combination of two basic cryptographic principles, as defined by Claude Shannon in his seminal paper *A Mathematical Theory of Communication* published in 1948. Confusion obscures the relationship between the cipher text and the original plain text, with the idea that if even a single bit of the input is changed it should affect much, if not all, of the output cipher text, thus making it hard to analyze. Diffusion is the property of statistical redundancy in the plaintext outputs, preventing analysis methods based on techniques such as frequency analysis (where certain letters will occur more frequently in the language under investigation, such as "E" in English). The easiest way to cause diffusion is through transposition (also known as permutation) which rearranges the letters of the plaintext.[94] DES uses substitution boxes (S-Boxes) to employ the principles of confusion and diffusion in order to subject the plain-text to sixteen iterations (or rounds) of mathematical operations to produce the eventual cipher text.[95] The NSA gave IBM eight criteria their S-Boxes needed to satisfy; however, there was an additional criterion of which IBM were unaware.[96] The secret ninth criterion addressed a classified technique called differential cryptanalysis, which was the study of the differences changes of inputs make on the output, with the aim of detecting non-random results which may suggest a weakness in the algorithm. George comments:

> We didn't think that was going to be a problem [for IBM to meet these criteria] because we thought it was going to be pretty easy to develop permutations that weren't subject to these kind of problems [vulnerability to differential cryptanalysis]. Turned out…it was really hard, none of the proposed S-Boxes that IBM turned in to us satisfied that ninth criteria.[97]

Therefore, George recounts, "NSA just generated S-Boxes which met all nine criteria, and sent them to IBM telling IBM that these would be the DES S-Boxes."[98] The public soon became aware of NSA's intervention, George comments:

> word got out that NSA had supplied the S-Boxes and everybody said they've hooked it and a lot of work was done on was this a random set of S-Boxes. All the work said no it's not a random set, and it wasn't as it had to satisfy that ninth criteria. So there was a tremendous amount of work that was done people trying to figure out what the hook was, the world didn't trust it, and that was OK, because it was designed for US commercial interests and they were using it, and it was fine.[99]

Whilst the NSA may not have wanted DES to be used globally without restrictions on key size, IBM did want to sell to the worldwide market. As cryptography was classed

---

[94] Schneier, 1996, 193.
[95] Ibid, 224.
[96] George, 2014, 23:34.
[97] Ibid, 23:34.
[98] George, 2020.
[99] George, 2014, 24:15.

as a munition, Tuchman approached the Commerce Department for DES export permission.[100] If IBM were not allowed to export the 56-bit strength DES products there would be two damaging consequences.[101] Firstly, IBM would have to produce two versions of all of their products that included cryptography: one for domestic use, and another, weaker version for foreign consumption. This would greatly increase the production cost, and could lead to weaker products being used for both domestic and foreign markets rather than accepting the cost overhead of producing two different products. In effect, this meant market forces would cause any export restrictions to become *de facto* domestic restrictions. Secondly, IBM would risk losing market share in the near future as foreign companies recognized and met the accelerating demand for cryptography.

The NSA informed IBM as multiple components of their algorithm, such as the S-Boxes, were either reinventions of, or based on NSA's own classified mathematical portfolio, the extensive mathematical analysis that went into the design of the algorithm could not be published.[102] It was this constraint that led to much of the subsequent controversy, as researchers hypothesized the secrecy surrounding the S-Boxes' design was due to an NSA-inserted vulnerability which acted as an access method, or backdoor method, to the algorithm. The design also had to be kept secret as during the validation of the algorithm IBM had discovered differential cryptanalysis techniques, Coppersmith states, "After discussions with NSA, it was decided the disclosure of the design considerations would reveal the technique of differential cryptanalysis... [this] would weaken the competitive advantage of the United States."[103] The secrecy also covered the crypt-analytic effort, which IBM claimed amounted to seventeen person years of effort expended in their internal certification of the algorithm.[104]

The determination of DES' key size went to the very top of the NSA. The crypt-analytic team wanted a 16-bit key, George comments, "nobody was going to buy that, that was a joke," but what the cryptanalytic team were most concerned with was they would "teach the world how to make good crypto."[105] To prevent the NSA's methods becoming visible in the DES' design, NSA's director ordered no changes be made to DES unless such changes were critical to its security.[106] 56-, 64-, 80-, and 128-bit key sizes were all under consideration—to understand the key size required for DES' security responsibilities, the director consulted NSA's Jim Frazer.[107] In the 1950s, Frazer developed the NSA's version of Moore's law to predict technological evolution, though his system was more fine-grained, allowing it to cover numerous important fields within computer science. This allowed the NSA to develop the appropriate level of security it deemed necessary for government communications equipment.[108] The Director asked Frazer, "how big do I have to make it [the key size] to be safe into the future?" Frazer replied, "To go out to 1990 you need 56 bits, but then you've got to decertify it in 1990, because in 1991 it's going to be attackable."[109]

---

[100] Tuchman, 1998, 278.
[101] Ibid.
[102] Ibid.
[103] Coppersmith, 1994, 244.
[104] Hellman et al., 1976b, 2.

[105] George, 2016, 9:00.
[106] Ibid, 13:10.
[107] George, 2020.
[108] George, 2016, 20:53.
[109] Ibid, 25:07.

The director called his NBS counterpart and said, "We want to go 56 bits, it's going to give you to the end of 1990," to which the director of NBS replied, "We're only going to use it for 3–4 years, then we'll replace it with the next version, sure that's fine."[110] So why did the NSA not opt for a bigger size to give increased security? George comments, "It was 56 bits because we were asked how good does it have to be? You always want to basically limit it to good enough. If you try to overdesign something you wind up with it either being used longer than you want or you put some kind of a problem in because you've overdesigned it."[111] The question of why the key size was not increased to 64, or even 128, bits would fuel public concerns that the NSA had calibrated the key size to a strength where they knew they could exhaustively defeat it for years into the future.

4.5 PUBLIC CRITIQUE

In March 1975, the NBS published details of the proposed DES and requested public comments. Diffie and Hellman's response was critical, lamenting the absence of DES' supporting technical information, noting the algorithm, "remains obscure to us."[112] Hellman had spoken to Feistel directly, but NSA restrictions prevented their discussion.[113]

Diffie and Hellman recognized industry lacked a mature process to certify cryptographic algorithms past a "continued cryptanalytic assault."[114] Therefore, in order to prevent the public duplicating IBM's failed attacks against DES, Diffie and Hellman requested details of IBM's testing be made public.[115] Diffie and Hellman wrote the 56-bit key length also raised concerns:

> The key size is at best barely adequate. Even today…defeating the system by exhaustive search would strain, but probably not exceed the budget of a large intelligence organization. As the feasibility of such a project depends on the cost and speed of crypto hardware, its future seems bright.[116]

Diffie and Hellman observed only a small increase in cryptanalytic capabilities could "dramatically improve the cost performance picture," therefore they suggested the key size ideally be doubled to prevent any chance of exhaustive attacks.[117] Diffie and Hellman noted 56 bits was a very awkward binary number, and that 64 bits would be better aligned to computer architectures. Although the key variable possessed 64 bits, it was "for reasons which are not apparent to us" that eight of them were reserved for parity checking.[118] Diffie and Hellman estimated it would cost twenty million dollars to build a computer capable of cracking 56-bit DES keys in a day.[119] Whilst such a sum was expensive, if used constantly

---

[110] Ibid, 25:17.
[111] George, 2014, 24:51.
[112] Ibid.
[113] Hellman et al., 1976a.
[114] Diffie, 1975.

[115] Ibid.
[116] Ibid.
[117] Ibid.
[118] Ibid.
[119] Electronic Frontier Foundation, 2002.

over a five-year period, the per-key price would be around ten thousand dollars.[120] Therefore, if the intelligence gained from the breaking of each key was assessed to be worth more than ten thousand dollars, it would be an economically viable investment. The only entities likely to require cryptanalysis on such scale were intelligence and law enforcement agencies. Diffie and Hellman estimated with a 64-bit key the cost of such a machine would be five-billion dollars, with a per-key price of two-and-a-half million dollars; "such costs appear to outstrip even the intelligence agencies," the pair commented.[121]

Diffie and Hellman also highlighted the S-Boxes retained traits that were "surprisingly similar to a type that can be used to build a trapdoor into the system."[122] However, their findings were ultimately inconclusive: "Structures have been found in DES that were undoubtedly inserted to strengthen the system against certain types of attack. Structures have also been found that appear to weaken the system."[123] Diffie and Hellman conceded their analysis was preliminary with only ten-person weeks of effort, and without full knowledge of the system it was unknown whether such structures were the result of their misanalysis, poor IBM practices, or NSA subterfuge.[124] The authors concluded, "An explanation and further study are needed before trust can be placed in DES. This need is enhanced because NSA does not want a genuinely strong system to frustrate its cryptanalytic intelligence operations."[125]

In January 1976 NBS' Seymour Jeffery replied telling Diffie and Hellman DES met NBS' design criteria.[126] Regarding the eight-bit parity check, Jeffery offered a response that provided no further insights, "Each eight-bit byte of key has a parity bit for…checking the accuracy of the key before transmission of data."[127] With regards to Diffie and Hellman's computations on the amount of time and expense it would take to break DES keys, Jeffery wrote, "we feel that your assumptions and computed costs are inaccurate."[128] NBS estimated it would take 91 years to break each key rather than Diffie and Hellman's twenty-four hours, though Jeffery was quick to divert from the topic, "Rather than argue the relative accuracy of our assumptions, you must place the algorithm in its proper perspective."[129] The proper perspective for the NBS being that DES was better than nothing, which is what non-classified government systems operated with at the time of writing, "I think that you will agree," wrote Jeffery, "that this algorithm provides a significant level of protection… even against professional codebreakers."[130] In some ways, 91 years was an improvement—in March 1975, NBS' Ruth Davis estimated it would take two-thousand years for an exhaustive search against DES.[131]

Hellman's letter of January 20, 1977 reveals Jeffery's response had exhausted his patience:

---

[120] Hellman, 1975.
[121] Ibid.
[122] Ibid, 3.
[123] Ibid, 45.
[124] Ibid.
[125] Ibid.

[126] Jeffery, 1976.
[127] Ibid.
[128] Ibid.
[129] Ibid.
[130] Ibid.
[131] Diffie and Hellman, 1976, 4.

> I am getting an increasing feeling of duplicity on the part of NBS/NSA...I believe that the 56 bit key was chosen...to make the standard vulnerable to attack by NSA and that...IBM was influenced in its design to produce this effect.[132]

Hellman argues an intelligence agency under military command should not be taking a decision so important to the balance of power between government and citizen:

> While I am sure that NSA was motivated by its legitimate concern with foreign communications intelligence, if it is able to break the standard [DES] it also has the ability to obtain domestic intelligence. There is a tradeoff here between NSA's need and those of the public, and I do not think NSA should be the one to make the decision as to where the balance should lie.[133]

Hellman acknowledged that whilst his exhaustive search estimates may not be precisely accurate, it was impossible to reconcile his calculations with the NBS' ninety-one years. However, Hellman argues any errors would be offset by the rapidly decreasing cost of computation in just a few years' time. Despite the fact that Hellman learned of NBS' intent to change the DES before it became obsolete, he believed a legacy problem would remain, as all of the data encrypted today needs to remain secure for a ten to twenty-five-year period. Changing the standard within such a short period of its launch would be expensive, inconvenient and, "unwarranted since a totally adequate standard is certainly possible at this time." Hellman closed the letter by strongly urging the NBS, "to reconsider the implications of the course of action you are currently pursuing. Very important national goals are at stake, and an unbiased assessment is needed."

Hellman took his objections to the Commerce Department, NBS' parent organization. Writing to Commerce Secretary Elliot Richardson on 23 February 1976, Hellman stated:

> I am very worried that the NSA has surreptitiously influenced the NBS in a way which seriously limits the value of a proposed standard, and which may pose a threat to individual privacy.[134]

Hellman informed Richardson he was convinced the NSA interfered with the selection process to ensure they could break DES, resulting in the capability for the agency to "delve [into decrypted DES communications], almost at will, and undetected, into the supposedly private files of other agencies." In ten years, Hellman explained, due to computational advances, "the proposed standard will be breakable by almost any organization." Hellman concluded:

> I am now convinced that the NBS group involved is too closely connected to NSA...I thought it best to write directly to you, informing you of interference in your department.[135]

---

[132] Hellman, 1976a.   [134] Ibid.
[133] Ibid.   [135] Ibid.

A month elapsed before Hellman received a reply, but it was not from Richardson but acting NBS director Ernest Ambler.[136] Ambler stated the NSA were involved in assessing the DES as they were the "only organization...having both the expertise and facilities to evaluate encryption algorithms."[137] Turning to the accusations of an NSA backdoor, Ambler pointed to Executive Order 11905, which articulated the functions and responsibilities of the agency and specified restrictions on collection activity against US citizens.

In 1976, NBS and NSA representatives visited Diffie and Hellman at Stanford in an attempt to allay their concerns.[138] Douglas L. Hogan represented the NSA. Dennis Branstad attended on behalf of NBS, accompanied by Arthur J. Levenson, a former NSA codebreaker who served with Alan Turing at Bletchley Park, and was consulting for NBS on the DES.[139,140]

The meeting began in a friendly manner as the NSA delegation agreed to have the meeting's audio recorded one of the attendees joked, "It's appropriate they approve their own wiretapping." Hellman expressed his frustration it was not possible to get Feistel to give an unrestricted opinion on DES, and specifically to address the fact an algorithm initially designed to work with a 128-bit key, was now being proposed with a 56-bit key.[141]

A principal point of contention was the period for which DES must protect data. Diffie and Hellman contested it should be at least twenty-five years. When asked whether DES would provide that level of protection Levenson argued, "I don't know what's going to be here 25 years from now, so I don't know." Levenson also challenged Diffie and Hellman's expectation: "I don't know of any unclassified data that requires that kind of protection." Diffie argued census data must be kept secret by law for a century. Levenson replied, "That's actually not your business, it's not my business, it's really [up to] the director of the Census Bureau." Branstad stated they believed the DES would be secure for a decade but said, "I'm not willing to say about anything that it'll be secure in 25 years. I don't think anybody who says he does knows what he's talking about."[142]

The NSA representatives revealed their threat assessments extended to 1990. They also considered alternate methods of acquiring the data such as breaking into physical premises, which they believed a more realistic approach for most threat actors when compared to the cost of constructing Diffie and Hellman's DES-cracking machine; the desire was that breaking DES would be, "so expensive that the person who wishes to attack will go some other way." Levenson added, "this is not...intended to be the standard forever...it's intended for the current threat."[143]

When the conversation moved to what would happen if the NSA had the ability to listen in to DES-encrypted conversations of domestic citizens, Levenson became exasperated: "I spent my career there, and I never read anybody's income tax return.

---

[136] Ibid.

[137] Ibid.

[138] Hellman et al., 1976b.

[139] National Cryptological Museum, 1987; Phoenix Society, 2007.

[140] Hellman et al., 1976b.

[141] Ibid.

[142] Ibid.

[143] Ibid.

I don't know anybody who did." Hellman asked what Levenson would do if asked by the executive to act against a US citizen—Levenson replied, "If the Executive Branch comes and tells me as civil servant to shoot Marty Hellman, I don't know what I'd do." Another attendee joked, "you would!" to which Levenson replied, "I don't know what to say to that. When you're asked to do something, that becomes an existential question."[144] Hellman directly asked if the NSA would have the capability to break DES in the next decade, Levenson replied with a partial answer, "Today it [the capability] is not available to us."[145] Levenson's statement would have been taken with a healthy dose of skepticism—any such capability was likely classified.

The meeting was cordial, but both parties left without resolution.

At first, the dissenters had tried to engage with the NBS to effect change. Hellman recalls, "we were naïve enough to think they actually wanted comments on it. We didn't realize…that once something's…a proposed standard, it's really a *de facto* standard."[146] Hellman recounts DES' opponents eventually understood they were in a political, rather than a technical fight leading them to, "fight it as a political fight,"—they engaged the media—"we got David Kahn to write an op-ed in the New York Times," Hellman recalls.[147]

Kahn's article appeared in the New York Times in April 1976. Writing of the data which could be gained by exploiting DES, Kahn wrote the government, "would gain this information at the expense of American privacy."[148] As to trusting in the restraint of the federal government, Kahn commented, "recent history has shown how often an agency exercises a power simply because it has it."[149] Kahn addresses whether such a sacrifice of privacy for intelligence and security gain was prudent by invoking a biblical reference, "For what shall it profit a man, if he shall gain the whole world and lose his own soul?"[150] Several years later, Kahn later wrote DES was:

> in fact, so good that a miniature debate seems to have broken out in secret between the two halves of the National Security Agency…The codebreaking side wanted to make sure that the cipher was weak enough for the NSA to solve it when used by foreign nations and companies. The code-making side wanted any cipher it was certifying for use by Americans to be truly good. The upshot was a bureaucratic compromise. Part of the "S-boxes" that performed a substitution—was strengthened…the key…was weakened.[151]

An article by Gina Bari Kolata in the July 1977 issue of *Science* devoted three pages to scrutinizing DES.[152] Kolata wrote, "some critics suspect that this coding system was carefully designed to be just secure enough so that corporate spies outside the government could not break a user's code and just vulnerable enough so that the NSA

144 Ibid.
145 Ibid.
146 Hellman and McGraw, 2016.
147 Ibid.
148 Kahn, 1976.

149 Ibid.
150 Ibid.
151 Kahn, 1979, 151.
152 Kolata, 1977.

could break it."[153] Kolata highlighted concerns over a number of members within the NBS who were former NSA staff.[154] These included Dennis Branstad, who was leading NBS' computer security project, and NBS consultant Arthur Levenson.[155] Kolata also highlighted that Louis Branscomb of IBM formerly led NBS.[156] However, given the specialty of the encryption and information security fields during this period, cross-contamination of staff is unsurprising.

With a similar level of confidence to Kahn, James Bamford wrote in his 1982 *The Puzzle Palace* that, "as a result of close-door negotiations with officials of the NSA, IBM agreed to reduce the size of its key from 128 bits to 56 bits."[157] Neither Bamford nor Kahn detailed how they reached their assessments. However, given the esteem with which both figures were held by the academic community, it is likely their statements were considered reliable by their contemporaries, thus reinforcing perceptions of the government as being intent on exploiting the digital age to further concentrate its power. Tuchman refuted the accusations on behalf of IBM, writing in *Science* in September 1977:

> it is difficult to present a restrained response to allegations by critics that my colleagues and I were involved with the NSA and National Bureau of Standards (NBS) in designing "trapdoors" so that only a select few would know how to break the DES algorithm...The essence of the algorithm, including the "S-boxes" was totally the work of myself and my colleagues at IBM...Our involvement with NSA was limited to obtaining permission to export computer equipment incorporating DES.[158]

Clearly the information on the S-Boxes was false as NSA have since acknowledged they were the authors. It is unknown whether Tuchman made this statement independently or at the NSA's behest, or if there were some reason he was not aware of NSA's hand in the S-Box production, though this seems unlikely given his prominent role in DES project. Tuchman stated that even if IBM released the full DES designs, their critics could argue they did not release all of the relevant data, something IBM would not be able to empirically disprove.[159] Tuchman suggested, "the only catharsis for the doubters is to...seek a mathematical procedure that can solve for the key...in my opinion they will fail...as have all previous attempts."[160] Tuchman recalls how his "saintly, but unworldly" mother, who, reflecting the public perception instilled by the media coverage, "was worried about my involvement and thought I should leave IBM and stop hanging around with 'those bad people.'"[161] With some difficulty, Tuchman reassured her that, "notwithstanding Watergate, my IBM and government colleagues were on the side of the angels."[162] Hellman replied to Tuchman via the letters section of *Science* magazine in October 1977, "IBM seems to distinguish between the choice of a key size for the DES and the design of the algorithm itself," he wrote. "In this

---

153 Ibid, 438.
154 Ibid.
155 Ibid, 440.
156 Ibid.
157 Bamford, 1982, 436.

158 Tuchman, 1998, 279; Tuchman, 1977, 938.
159 Tuchman, 1977, 938.
160 Ibid.
161 Tuchman, 1998, 279.
162 Ibid.

parlance, Tuchman does not contradict Kolata's article when he says that 'In no way did NSA affect the design of the algorithm.'"[163] Hellman notes it is "known that NSA would not allow...a larger key to be exported," and whilst he was sympathetic to the "dilemma in which IBM finds itself—caught between the NSA and the public," the ambiguity of who determined the key size and algorithm was putting IBM at risk as they were carrying full commercial accountability of the encryption being broken.[164]

At IBM, Tuchman and Carl Meyer had experimented with key exhaustion techniques on high-speed computers and convinced themselves a 56-bit key size was more than sufficient to discourage commercial attackers.[165] Tuchman reflects IBM were aiming to achieve the same security: "locked desk draws, locked doors on computer rooms, and well-behaved employees, provided."[166] With regard to the insertion of a backdoor, the principal challenge of writing such code is to ensure it can exist without detection by either those auditing the code, or by third parties hoping to access the backdoor for their own advantage. When IBM were first accused of inserting a backdoor Walter Tuchman had no idea how such a feat would be technically possible, he spoke to his team of mathematicians who were equally oblivious to any techniques that could enable a concealed access method capable of evading auditors and third parties.[167] Tuchman also challenged the logic of a fifty-billion-dollar-a-year company would risk "enormous lawsuits and the possibility of ruining its reputation by trying to fool the professional public with a hidden trapdoor"; he further reflected to build such a backdoor would be "damned immoral."[168] Tuchman comments:

> We were convinced that 56 bits were OK for commercial cryptography. We also knew that if you ran DES three times with two different keys, the key lengths would go to 112 bits, requiring astronomical resources for key searches. Therefore, we felt the key size controversy was not real.[169]

4.6 THE WORKSHOPS: GOVERNMENT ATTEMPTS TO EASE PUBLIC DES CONCERNS

Given the high level of interest, and growing controversy of DES, the NBS held two workshops in late 1976 to try and alleviate the increasingly vocal opposition among the academic community. Twenty participants from industry and government assembled for a workshop at NBS' headquarters on 30 and 31 August 1976.[170] Among the attendees from NBS were Dennis Branstad, Seymour Jeffery, and Dana Grub. Diffie traveled from the West Coast to attend.

In order to ascertain the feasibility of a key exhaustion attack, the workshop explored the pace of technical progress required to build a machine capable of such an attack in a time period which would make it a prudent investment. After several

---

163 Hellman, 1977, 8.
164 Ibid.
165 Tuchman, 1998, 279.
166 Ibid.

167 Ibid.
168 Ibid.
169 Tuchman, 1998, 280.
170 National Bureau of Standards, 1976, iii.

speakers presented on the predicted evolution of the individual components required to build a DES-cracking machine, Diffie provided an overview of his and Hellman's assessment that a twenty-million-dollar machine capable of locating DES keys within twenty-four hours, at a per-key cost of ten thousand dollars, could be manufactured. Within ten years, Diffie and Hellman assessed the diminishing cost of computing could reduce the cost per key to fifty dollars. Diffie believed NSA could build such a machine covertly. Durrell Hillis of Motorola argued only RCA could provide the million chips required for Diffie and Hellman's parallel processing DES-breaker, and it would take one to two years to fabricate with such a large production capability unlikely available until 1981.[171]

The workshop then divided into two groups, one instructed to hypothesize design, speed and costs of a DES cracker, and the other group to focus on the implications of technology evolutions on the ability to construct such a machine.[172] The key size concerns were not shared by all the attendees; Robert Morris of AT&T commented, "I don't feel that the key size is as bad as it sounds."[173] A number of different architectures for the DES cracker were outlined, some involved adapting existing supercomputers, others building the machine from scratch. It was collectively assessed that Hellman and Diffie's million-chip parallel processing DES cracker would take three-hundred person years to build, cost seventy-two million dollars, and could not be completed until 1990—even then, the group only judged it as a ten to twenty percent chance this could be achieved.[174] Tuchman assessed building a DES-cracking machine "would result in a cost to the manufacturer an order of magnitude larger than the twenty million dollar[s]."[175]

Attention turned to the S-boxes. Tuchman reiterated, "IBM has been requested by the NSA not to divulge these principles."[176] John Scantlin, of Lexar corporation commented, "We are disturbed by the potential the S-boxes possess for concealing a trapdoor and the more we carry forward our own analysis, the more uneasy we become."[177] Scantlin added his voice to calls for an objective assessment of the algorithm to ascertain its strength.[178] Morris commented, "I am shocked by the reluctance to talk about the design of the S-boxes…this information should be released."[179] Another delegate commented whilst he found no weaknesses in the S-Boxes, they were of a similar structure to that of a trapdoor.[180] Exacerbating the frustration was the response reportedly given by an unnamed IBM employee when asked for proof of the S-Boxes' security; "You must trust us," the employee allegedly said, "we are all good boy scouts."[181] During a discussion of the various attacks that could be attempted against DES, Walter Tuchman started to lose his patience: "In fact we tried a lot of things for a long time, until we were collectively frustrated. I wish you

---

[171] Ibid, 14.
[172] Ibid, 15.
[173] Ibid, 20.
[174] Ibid.
[175] Ibid, 13.
[176] Ibid, 16.

[177] Ibid.
[178] Ibid.
[179] National Bureau of Standards, 1977, 18.
[180] Ibid, 19.
[181] Kolata, 1977, 440.

all would work on this problem until you shared our frustration. Get all this out of your system."[182]

Despite the government and IBM's engagement, Diffie and Hellman's fears were not allayed.

4.7   SENATE DES INVESTIGATION

The public exposure to potential NSA subversion of the DES resulted in the US Senate Select Committee on Intelligence ordering an investigation in 1977.[183] The following year an unclassified summary of their report was released.[184]

Regarding the 56 bit DES key length, the report found, "NSA convinced IBM that a reduced key size was sufficient," though the report does not refer to whether the reduced key size was instead of 64 or 128 bits; however, IBM concurred the "key size was more than adequate for all commercial applications for which the DES was intended." The authors found the NSA "indirectly assisted in the development of the S-box structures," before certifying DES was "to the best of their knowledge, free of any statistical or mathematical weaknesses." The report stated, "IBM invented and designed the algorithm [and] made all pertinent decisions." Directly addressing the claims that NSA employees introduced a backdoor within the S-Boxes, the authors wrote, "NSA did not tamper with the design of the algorithm in any way."[185] We now know this statement was incorrect—the S-Boxes were of NSA design—though introduced to strengthen the algorithm rather than provide a backdoor. This raises a question of whether the NSA or IBM misled Congress. However, the language "tamper with" is also quite ambiguous, would Congress have considered the S-Box insertion as "tampering," if not, then this could explain their statement not accounting for the NSA S-Box insertion.

With regards to the ramifications of a shortened key length, the committee acknowledged they were "in no position to settle scientific argument regarding the exhaustion time"; however, "the overwhelming majority of scientists consulted felt that the security afforded by the DES was more than adequate for at least a 5–10 year time span." The authors also highlighted the NSA's recommendation that the Federal Reserve Board use DES in funds transfer systems, the inference being such a recommendation would not be made if the NSA believed the algorithm insecure.[186]

4.8   THE 1990S: CYPHERPUNKS PLOT DES' DEMISE

Almost two decades had passed since Diffie and Hellman sat in a Stanford room arguing with the government over the inadequacy of DES' key size, and for all accounts, the algorithm had aged well. After its ratification as a standard in January 1977, other regulatory bodies in the US and worldwide adopted DES as their

---

[182] National Bureau of Standards, 1977, 21.   [185] Ibid, 4.
[183] United States Senate, 1978.   [186] Ibid.
[184] Ibid.

encryption standard of choice; it was believed to be the most widely used encryption algorithm in the world.[187] IBM's Alan Konheim later reflected, "Horst Feistel's work has unintentionally and vastly complicated today the NSA SIGINT mission."[188] Over the years, research identified several DES weaknesses, but none were practical to implement, and they resulted in no serious concerns of a more readily applicable attack than key exhaustion.[189,190] Every five years, the government reaffirmed DES as their encryption standard of choice. However, DES had only been intended to last until 1990, its continued existence was possibly the result of the government wanting to keep DES on life support until their plans for key escrow could come to fruition. In order to demonstrate to the public DES was past its sell date, and catalyze the emergence of a stronger algorithm, the cypherpunks would need to demonstrate DES' weakness.

In 1993, Michael Wiener, of Bell Northern Research, wrote a paper similar to Hellman and Diffie's of almost two decades earlier, detailing a more efficient method of exhaustively searching the DES key space, and providing detailed plans of how to construct a machine to execute such a search using custom chips.[191] Wiener's DES cracker could be built for one million dollars, rather than Diffie and Hellman's twenty million dollars. With such a machine, it would take an average of three-and-a-half hours to find the key.[192] The machine would reduce search time in accordance with available resources; if an investor spent ten million dollars, the search time was reduced to just twenty-one minutes.[193] Wiener concluded, "If it ever was true that attacking DES was only within the reach of large governments, it is clearly no longer true."[194]

The cypherpunks followed developments closely. Reflecting on Wiener's estimate, it would only take two minutes for a one-hundred-million-dollar parallel-processing DES cracker to locate keys; Zimmermann commented, "It is not plausible to me that NSA's budget for examining DES-encrypted traffic is less than $100 million. Two minutes. Damn. Two f**king minutes"; he wrote, "DES is dead, dead, dead."[195] John Gilmore posted to the cypherpunks, "Most organizations who would build such a machine (national governments and other forms of organized crime) have probably already constructed many similar machines."[196]

But Wiener's paper, as credible as it was, was no more effective in influencing policy than Diffie and Hellman's paper had been—it was still theoretical.[197] A few months later, the US government reaffirmed DES as their encryption standard for

---

[187] Curtin, 2005, 20–21; Coppersmith, 1994.

[188] Konheim, 2015, 25.

[189] Eli Biham and Adi Shamir (of RSA fame) developed a differential cryptanalysis technique in 1990, and Mitsuru Matsui produced a linear cryptanalysis attack in 1994, that took advantage of the S-Box known correlations of S-Box inputs and outputs (Coppersmith, 1994, 246 and 250).

[190] Coppersmith, 1994, 250.

[191] Wiener, 1994.

[192] Ibid, 7.

[193] Ibid.

[194] Ibid.

[195] Zimmermann, 1993.

[196] Gilmore, 1993.

[197] Zimmermann, 1993.

another five years, even though it was three years into the period in which the NSA had said where it would be breakable.

Further indications of the insufficiency of DES' key size occurred in 1996 when a group of cryptologists including Diffie, Matt Blaze, Ron Rivest, and Michael Wiener wrote a report to assess a minimum safe key length for symmetric encryption algorithms.[198] The cryptographers wrote to be safe against the cracking capabilities of governments in 1996, at least 75-bit keys were required; DES' 56 bits was looking increasingly anachronistic.[199]

One innovation to counter the key-length insufficiency was Triple DES, a variant of the DES, introduced in the mid-1990s. Triple DES has two variations, either two-key Triple DES, with a key size of 80 bits, or three-key Triple DES, providing a 112-bit key.[200] Triple DES works by encrypting the text before decrypting the text with the second key which, as it is not the first key, will incorrectly decipher the text which acts to add another layer of encryption, and then using the DES algorithm to encrypt with the third key (or first key in two-key Triple DES) once again to produce the final cipher text.[201]

By September 1996, another attempt to break DES was initiated—cypherpunk Peter Trei wrote on the cypherpunk mailing list it was time to "kill DES." Trei recounted how software attacks against DES produced significantly poorer results in comparison to designing custom chips for a specialized DES cracking machine. Fabricating custom chips for a DES cracking machine would be significantly more expensive though, and general-purpose machines were ubiquitous and, in significant numbers, could form a distributed supercomputer using parallel processing to identify the DES key. The cypherpunks could write code for everyday machines sitting within universities, businesses, and homes all over the country—the challenge would be how to incentivize sufficient numbers of people to deploy their software. Trei suggested they offer a cash prize for whoever's machine found the DES key.[202] Ron Rivest suggested Trei approach Jim Bidzos, the President of RSA Security—if DES were to fall, RSA, with their portfolio of algorithms, would pursue their market share.[203] Bidzos donated a ten-thousand-dollar prize.[204]

The cypherpunks were excited, but there was concern as to how the government would spin, the media would present, and the public would interpret their potential success. Cypherpunk Jim Bell posted:

> I don't think this is a good idea. If anything, what this would inadvertently demonstrate is how difficult (at least, with non-dedicated hardware) it is to crack DES…they can say, "Hey, these guys had to apply $10–20 million dollars' worth of computer equipment for a full year just to get the contents of a SINGLE MESSAGE!"[205]

---

[198] Blaze et al., 1996.
[199] Ibid, 1.
[200] National Institute of Standards and Technology, 2011, 3.
[201] National Institute of Standards and Technology, 1999, 6.
[202] Trei, 1996.

[203] For example, RSA previously ran a challenge in an attempt to find shortcuts to factoring large prime numbers, if such a shortcut were found it would undermine public key encryption, though not finding a shortcut would further substantiate public key encryption's security.
[204] Trei, 1997a.
[205] Bell, 1996.

Mike Duvos envisaged the headlines: "Cypherpunks show DES can withstand up to 9,000 Pentium-years of torture and keep on ticking."[206] But another user, posting under the alias "Attila T. Hun" saw positives if they could win over the public: "we're proving that the Feds are a fraud...we might even be perceived as a good, not evil force...but I doubt it; the press mentality is too low."[207] The cypherpunks feared that, rather than being portrayed as digital insurgents revealing the duplicity of the US government, they would be painted as using their intellect to compromise the Internet's security to the benefit of criminals and spies.

The RSA Secret-Key Challenge was announced in January 1997.[208] The challenge was a known cipher text challenge; RSA provided the first twenty-four characters of the message, "The unknown message is:" in order to allow the participants to recognize when they had successfully located the key.[209] In providing the start of the message, it could have been argued this was an unfair advantage to the attackers. However, most messages adhere to some form of structure, or contain certain phrases such as "Dear Sir or Madam," that can be searched for within decrypted packets; these traits are known as *Cribs*.

Peter Trei had already developed software for the DES attack, and by late January had sent out test, or *beta*, versions to other cypherpunks allowing them to build their own DES-cracking super-computers. Due to the continuing encryption export controls, in order to avoid legal repercussions, Trei asked the cypherpunks—before he sent the file to them—to send their real name, address, and nationality to him, along with an acknowledgment they understood his code was not to leave America. Such a measure probably limited the cypherpunk uptake, as many operated under alias on the mailing list; however, some likely sent false details providing Trei plausible deniability that he attempted to prevent export.[210] Trei's efforts to catalyze a challenge to DES were successful, but his effort to galvanize the community to attack RSA's encrypted message under his leadership was less so; however, his actions inspired another programmer in Colorado, Rocke Verser.

Verser was a freelance programmer who wrote a more efficient key-searching algorithm than the cypherpunks. A growing group assembled around Verser, known as the DES Challenge (DESCHALL) team; they started their attack with most of the processing power coming from the universities where many of them worked.[211]

As the DESCHALL team's computers around the continent scoured key space, US Congress was debating the "Security and Freedom Through Encryption (SAFE) Act," which would relax cryptography controls. During the March 1997 debate, Robert S. Litt of the Department of Justice's Criminal Division stated it would take the NSA, "approximately one year and eighty-seven days using a $30 million supercomputer," to break a DES key using a brute-force attack.[212] The DESCHALL team aspired to prove they could do better, perhaps in their eyes exposing the NSA's

---

[206] Duvos, 1996.
[207] Attila t. Hun, 1996.
[208] Electronic Frontier Foundation, 2002.
[209] RSA, 1997.
[210] Trei, 1997b.
[211] Curtin, 2005, 78 and 122.
[212] United States House of Representatives, 1997.

duplicity, and influencing the narrative in Congress, with the aim of destabilizing the export regulations and discrediting DES.

At nine minutes to midnight on 17 June 1997, a Pentium computer whirring away in Salt Lake City completed its mission.[213] The Pentium had tried two-hundred and fifty thousand keys every second, patiently searching for the one key in 72,000,000,000,000,000 that would enable it to read the secret message, and now its work was done.[214]

Rocke Verser revealed the successfully decoded DES message as "Strong cryptography makes the world a safer place" on 17 June 1997. Verser described how "Tens of thousands of computers worked cooperatively on the challenge in what is believed to be one of the largest supercomputing efforts ever undertaken outside of government." They searched for four months covering one-quarter of the 72 quadrillion possible keys, reaching a speed of seven billion keys per second.[215] The DESCHALL team noted seventy-eight-thousand unique IP addresses contributed to their supercomputing effort, with an average of fourteen thousand machines per day.[216,217] "This is proving by example, not by mathematical calculation, that DES can be broken with little or no cost," Verser's collaborator Matt Curtin added in the release.[218] RSA's own press release suggested the demise of the two-decade-old standard: "this may be the final blow that indicates its [DES'] time has passed."[219] Jim Bidzos said, "This demonstrates that a determined group using easily available desktop computers can crack DES-encrypted messages, making short 56-bit key lengths…unacceptable as national standards for use in commercial applications."[220] However, as Diffie would observe a year later, "cryptosystems have nine lives."[221]

While many cypherpunks were elated at their DES victory, however incomplete it would prove to be, Tim May believed they were getting distracted from their "radical roots." May posted to the cypherpunks on June 21:

I think the "breaking of DES" challenge was, while interesting, a sideshow. And utterly predictable…as with many cypherpunks' goals, I've been chagrinned to see so much "backsliding" to lesser, less radical concerns…we are losing sight of the deeper issues.[222]

May believed the cypherpunks' focus should be on developing and deploying strong cryptographic and anonymity capabilities so widely no legislation could reverse their presence.[223] May commented if those involved in the DES crack had instead "hosted

---

213 Curtin, 2005, 13.
214 Ibid.
215 Deschall Group, 1999.
216 A specified number of IP addresses does not necessarily equate to that many users.
217 Deschall Group, 1999.
218 Ibid.
219 RSA, 1998.
220 Curtin, 2005, 263.
221 Electronic Frontier Foundation, 2002.
222 May, 1997.
223 Ibid.

remailers and anonymizers on their machines, [it] would further cypherpunks' goals a lot more than breaking DES, which we all know was breakable."[224,225,226]

Whilst the DESCHALL team believed some press coverage of their success was useful, such as a *New York Times* article, many other reports focused heavily on the scale of effort required to achieve the feat.[227] The CNN article covering their work was subtitled "but it took four months," Matt Curtin reflected, "most media coverage had roughly the same flavor."[228] The argument of DESCHALL's detractors was that tens of thousands of computer months were required to find the key, and with such resources being unavailable to most attackers, the public need not worry. The DESCHALL team could have argued criminals use botnets for similar parallel processing power, but the public was still struggling with the nature of the Internet and such counter-arguments would unlikely have resonated.

In a 1997 briefing to US Congress, FBI director Louis J. Freeh played down his agencies ability to access encrypted traffic:

> If we hooked together thousands of computers and worked together over 4 months we might, as was recently demonstrated decrypt one message bit. That is not going to make a difference in a kidnapping case, it is not going to make a difference in a national security case. We don't have the technology or the brute force capability to get to this information.[229]

The Deputy Director of the NSA, William P. Crowell, added:

> There is no brute force solution for law enforcement...the Internet gang last week broke a single message using 56 bit DES. It took 78,000 computers 96 days to break one message, and the headline was, "DES has weak encryption."[230]

The cypherpunks did have some government allies. During debates on many of the pieces of cryptologic legislation, Senate Majority Leader Trent Lott spoke up for their cause: "the demand for strong information security will not abate," Lott said, referring specifically to the DESCHALL effort, adding, "Now that 56-bit encryption has been cracked by individuals working together over the Internet, information protected by that technology is vulnerable. The need to allow stronger security to protect information is more acute than ever."[231] Senator Conrad Burns of Montana added:

> we...allowed the issue of encryption to be framed as the issue of child pornography or gambling. I want to be sure that all parties understand that the reform of encryption security standards is not related to these issues.

---

224 Anonymizers allow users to browse without the ability of the server, or eavesdroppers, identifying from where they are browsing, or to what they are browsing.

225 Remailers were a cypherpunk project to operate a number of anonymous mail servers, allowing mail to be posted anonymously, as was the case in the pre-Internet age, without the sender information included.

226 May, 1997.
227 Curtin, 2005, 265.
228 Ibid.
229 United States House of Representatives, 1997b.
230 Ibid.
231 Ibid.

Hackers, espionage agents, and those just wanting to cause mischief must be restrained from access to private information over the Internet.

When used correctly, encryption can enable citizens in remote locations to have access to the same information, the same technology, the same quality of health care, that citizens of our largest cities have.

Perhaps most importantly, it is about ensuring that American companies have the tools they need to continue to develop and provide the leading technology in the global marketplace.

Without this leadership, our national security and sovereignty will surely be threatened.[232]

The cypherpunks were no longer at war with the entire establishment.

DES' demise was finally announced in late 1997, coinciding with the policy failure of key escrow. The new standard would take years to develop—it was christened the Advanced Encryption Standard (AES). The government stated that a "multi-year transition period will be necessary to move toward any new encryption standard and that DES will continue to be of sufficient strength for many applications."[233] There was some good news in the release: "It is intended that the AES will specify an unclassified, publicly disclosed encryption algorithm available royalty-free worldwide that is capable of protecting sensitive government information well into the next century."[234] Finally, the government was going to adopt the canonic principle that an encryption algorithm's strength should reside in its key, rather than the secrecy of the design and algorithm routine; "Well, well, well...Looks like we have some dissent in the ranks," Matthew Ghio reflected with jubilation in a posting to the cypherpunks' mailing list a few days later.[235] In the EFF's DES Cracker book they wrote:

The reason that the AES is tardy is because the NSA is believed to have blocked previous attempts to begin the process over the last decade. In recent years NSA has tried, without success, to get the technical community to use classified, NSA-designed encryption algorithms such as Skipjack [Clipper] [See chapter VI], without letting the users subject these algorithms to public scrutiny. Only after this effort failed did they permit the National Institute of Standards and Technology to begin the AES standardization process.[236]

Now it seemed that if the NSA had in fact been artificially extending the life of DES, life support was being withdrawn.[237]

In late October 1999, DES was reaffirmed for a fourth time as the Federal Information Processing Standard, but with the caveat that triple-DES was the preferred version of DES, and single-DES should only be used on legacy systems.[238] In May, 2002, AES was approved to supersede DES as the Federal Information

---

[232] Ibid.
[233] National Institute of Standards and Technology, 1997.
[234] Ibid.
[235] Ghio, 1997.
[236] Electronic Frontier Foundation, 2002, 1–17.
[237] Ibid.
[238] National Institute of Standards and Technology, 1999.

Processing Standard.[239] AES 128 has 340 billion billion billion billion keys, that is 5 sextillion (5,000 billion billion) times more keys than DES.[240] Even with processing advances achieved by 2020, the fastest computer in the world would still take 50 million billion years to locate the key.[241] NIST formally withdrew DES in 2005, and provided government bodies a two-year grace period to cease usage of the algorithm.[242] By May 2007, DES was finally dead.

4.9   DES: IN RETROSPECT

"We're actually pretty good guys," Richard "Dickie" George declared to the conference, "we wanted to make sure we were as squeaky clean as possible."[243] It was 2011, and George, Technical Director of the Information Assurance Directorate at the NSA was discussing DES' history at the RSA conference.[244] On stage with George sat Diffie, Hellman, Ron Rivest, and Adi Shamir.

As part of the original DES evaluation team, George had found it fascinating to "do both the math and to follow the political arguments."[245] Approaching retirement from the NSA, George realized he was the last person at Fort Meade who was involved in the DES during its development.[246] He approached the director arguing, "we ought to declassify the whole DES story," and the director agreed.[247] George began investigating the NSA's internal records to add to his own recollections in preparation to tell the world DES' inside story. When Shamir asked about the 56-bit key length that caused so much controversy, George replied there had been a conversation between the communications security (COMSEC) and the communications intelligence (COMINT) sections of the NSA as to whether they should participate in the DES project at all.[248] If an encryption algorithm were deployed at a scale that COMINT could not break, or its breaking would be too resource-intensive, the NSA's ability to provide intelligence could be severely diminished. However, that concern was balanced against leaving US commercial, private, critical national infrastructure, and non-classified data either unprotected by encryption, or not protected to a sufficient degree. In a rapidly globalizing era where data was becoming increasingly valuable to American companies operating worldwide, George explained the decision was taken by NSA leadership that it "was in the best interests of the nation for us to participate."[249] From that point on, the NSA "were playing a complete COMSEC role," George explained.[250] However, the historical record does

---

[239] National Institute of Standards and Technology, 2001.
[240] Martin, 2020, 169–170.
[241] Ibid, 229.
[242] National Institute of Standards and Technology, 2001.
[243] Jackson, 2013.
[244] Rivest and Shamir, along with Leonard Adleman, were the team that developed the first full implementation of public key cryptography; it was called RSA (after their initials), the company at which conference this meeting was occurring.
[245] Juels et al., 2011, 8.09.
[246] George, 2016, 1.58.
[247] Ibid, 1.44.
[248] Juels et al., 2011, 20.21.
[249] Juels et al., 2011, 20.21.
[250] Ibid.

contain some discrepancies. A declassified NSA internal history written in 1998 by Thomas R. Johnson states, "NSA tried to convince IBM to reduce the length of the key from 64 to 48 bits. Ultimately, they compromised on a 56-bit key."[251] The sourcing is not entirely clear, with a footnote amalgamated from previous parts of the sentence referencing "DDIR files, Drake Notebook, Proto paper." None of these sources are publicly available. This history seems to contradict the statements of George, who argues the NSA's decision to use 56 bits was based on their internal calculations of how fast technology would evolve and for how long DES would be in service. On being asked about this contradiction, George comments, "The Johnson quote is silly… NSA would never try to convince IBM of anything—NSA dictated things."[252] George, who conducted an extensive internal assessment within the NSA for DES documentation has never seen any notes from Rick Proto on DES. George also implied Proto was likely not in a position to have such insights: "Proto was a major player at NSA later, but in 1974, Proto was a junior member of the math community, in the research directorate."[253] Based on the evidence and lack of supportive evidence for Johnson's statement, and George's account his statement may represent an error in the historical record. Hopefully at some point the source material will be declassified to allow the ambiguity to be resolved.

George would also later address why DES' 64-bit crypto variable reserved 8 bits for parity checks which resulted in a 56-bit key, substantially weaker than if the parity bits were omitted. George comments, "Everybody said well you [NSA] put in parity bits because you wanted to shorten it…that wasn't true."[254] George explained the NSA's legacy influenced their design methodology:

> The parity bits were absolutely critical…we put parity bits on all of the variables that we use and the reason is that these things are used by soldiers out in the field. It's not easy when you're sitting out there in mud, people shooting…and you're trying to pull a paper tape through a tape reader it doesn't always work really well. You get errors. When you get errors you have real problems because you're going to have people using variables that are slightly off…So to avoid that, we put parity bits in and if the parity doesn't pass you better try again, and that saves us from having these problems and that's why the parity bits were there and again that was treated by the world as "look what they've done."[255]

When asked whether the NSA inserted a backdoor into DES, George answered, "we knew we weren't smart enough to know things that people wouldn't find."[256] Whilst the cryptographic industry outside Fort Meade was slow to accelerate post-World War Two, there was a growing caliber of academic research in the field, and with the anti-government sentiment of the seventies, and with Nixon so recently deposed, the NSA knew researchers would be scrutinizing the standard for signs of government

---

251 Johnson, 1998, 232.
252 George, 2020.
253 Ibid.

254 George, 2014, 25:11.
255 Ibid, 25:31.
256 Ibid, 15.20.

tampering for years to come. Whilst the NSA had highly likely uncovered some mathematical truths yet to be discovered by the outside world, they could not be sure such truths would remain exclusively within their domain for the years DES was in service. George would later comment, "That's the big story for Crypto and NSA, we're smart enough to know we're not smart enough to do that, and that's just not a good thing to do."[257] There was also the consideration that the NSA's reputation was at stake, as George comments:

> we wanted to provide an algorithm for the public that had exactly the advertised security, we didn't want there to be any shortcut attack on it, and we wanted it to meet the security needs of the world, so when we said it had to be fifty-six bits we wanted to be able to go out and honestly say "there is no attack that we know of that's less than fifty-six bits," and we certainly didn't want to fall prey to something that would later be discovered.[258]

One thing the NSA did not anticipate was the catalyst suspicions of DES would provide to the advancement of cryptology research. Hellman commented, "DES was a gift from the gods to those of us working in academic cryptography...it gave us a target, something for us to cut our teeth on...cryptanalytically and learned a lot."[259] Rivest commented the DES was inspirational, allowing academics, "to think about why it looked the way it did and what could be done better"; therefore, the exercise advanced both their cryptographic and cryptanalytic skills. George comments:

> DES was one of the more important events in crypto history...[it] spawned the interest in crypto for people like Hellman, Diffie, and Rivest—so, in some sense, it was a key step not only in the development of crypto research (it gave the world a hard problem to study) but also was a critical element in the development of...public key cryptography.[260]

George comments, "we [the NSA] didn't see the importance of the Internet in providing a virtual critical mass of people who could collaborate on things, and I think that really made a big difference."[261] Whilst the cryptologic community in the outside world in any one physical location could not compete with the NSA, the collective might of cryptologists dispersed across the country and globe, but unified on the Internet, allowed academia to challenge the government's hegemonic position as cryptology's sole authority. George comments, "That Internet thing really threw a monkey wrench in, but y'know that was the one thing I didn't foresee...I thought people would be working in isolation, dawg on it, they weren't, they were all working together," George acknowledged, "if it wasn't DES it would have been something else, it was going to happen, there were lots of smart people out there working on lots of things."[262] George confesses in retrospect, "I'm delighted with the way it

---

[257] George, 2016, 38:15.
[258] Juels et al., 2011, 14.51.
[259] Ibid, 4.07.
[260] George, 2020.
[261] Juels et al., 2011, 10.49.
[262] George, 2016, 38:47.

worked out—a lot of smart people have done some excellent work!"[263] The Internet was having the effect that it would in time have across countless other fields: eroding the challenges of distance and time, and allowing global communities of like-minded people to attack challenging problems unable to be solved by isolated efforts. Cryptologic progress was inevitable.

The S-Box question had largely resolved itself with time. Differential cryptanalysis was rediscovered by Eli Biham and Adi Shamir in the late 1980s. Biham and Shamir tried the attack on a number of algorithms and it worked well, but DES remained impervious.[264] However, when Shamir generated random S-Boxes to replace the NSA selected ones, the attack worked, to which George comments, "It just didn't work on the real ones."[265] Bruce Schneier observed, "it took the academic community two decades to figure out that the NSA 'tweaks' actually improved the security of DES."[266] For NSA, the suspicion on the DES and S-Boxes proved quite useful for two reasons. Firstly, having the public assume there was an NSA backdoor, or hook, in the S-Boxes meant people were not focused on trying to understand that the NSA strengthened the S-Boxes to prevent differential cryptanalysis, which was a classified analysis technique; George recounted:

> it was much better for us to have people looking at those permutations trying to figure out what the trapdoor is, rather than figuring out why we used those to make it stronger. Much better for them to try to attack them [the S-Boxes] than to think what were they doing, so that worked out pretty well.[267]

The second reason was to prevent DES' propagation; George comments:

> The world was sure we had hooked the thing [DES] through the S-Boxes…some of those S-Boxes they really looked bad, and we were pretty happy they looked that bad because what a target that is for the world, if the world is telling everybody don't trust the thing that's great![268]

The NSA only wanted US government businesses to receive the protection of the DES; they did not want to see their enemies employing a high-caliber algorithm.[269]

Digital rights activists argue as to whether George's account can be trusted.[270] George's accounts contained statements which do not align with the statement IBM's Walter Tuchman made in 1977 where he stated, "The 'S-boxes' was totally the work of myself and my colleagues at IBM."[271] Tuchman could have spoken a falsehood on his own recognizance, and may have been asked not to reveal NSA involvement, or it could be he was not aware that IBM's S-Box candidates were replaced with NSA's—though the latter seems unlikely. Shamir reflected in 2011 that he:

---

[263] George, 2020.
[264] George, 2014, 28:26.
[265] Ibid, 28:26.
[266] Schneier, 2004.
[267] George, 2016, 18:30.

[268] Ibid, 28:39.
[269] Ibid, 18:45.
[270] Diffie, 2020.
[271] Tuchman, 1977, 938.

never believed that there was a trapdoor, because it made no sense to me politically. It is very unlikely that the Russian military would use DES for their internal communication, similarly the Chinese and all the other targets of the NSA. The main users, intended users were big American corporations and it sounded stupid to me that the NSA will design a scheme that will be breakable and allow all the large companies, corporations in the US to use it while knowing that they know how to break it and therefore there is a certain probability that others will also be able to break it, so just by political reasoning it made no sense to me.[272]

George's engagement with the public was welcomed by the digital rights activists, yet given the nature of intelligence work many, including Whitfield Diffie, were unsatisfied with George's account.[273] The government is in a challenging position, when something is kept secret with potentially a web of deception protecting disclosure, how are they ever able subsequently to disclose the information and satisfy the public that they have disclosed all information on a topic? Many in the digital privacy activist community will always question whether there is more of the DES story yet to tell.

4.10   A QUARTER CENTURY OF PROTEST

For over two decades, the cypherpunks and their predecessors waged an intellectual and public conflict to topple an encryption standard they believed not fit for purpose. Over this period, DES successfully protected transactions worth billions of dollars every day, and was likely the global market's dominant encryption.[274]

The primary concerns of the digital rights activists were that the NSA secretly hid a backdoor within the S-Box structures, and that the key length was insufficient. It was argued the key length could easily have been made strong enough to offer a level of security beyond the ability of any threat actors to break for the foreseeable future, rather than what was perceived as an insufficient 56 bits.

But did the digital rights activists' efforts make a difference?

One could argue that despite their protests, DES' key length remained at 56 bits, and the standard endured for decades, being used well into the 2000s. Could the NSA have been listening in to DES communications all of that time? Given the context of the era, with America in an existential war, would they have approved an algorithm they could not break? Given the computational and cerebral power at the NSA's disposal, they likely had the capability to build a DES cracker long before EFF's 1997 efforts. Could the NSA have built such a machine in 1977, when DES became the official standard? One must consider whether they would dedicate their resources to such a challenge—it was highly unlikely the Soviet Union or other national adversaries would use an American encryption system, especially one suspected of containing an NSA backdoor; DES' users were principally going to be

[272] Juels et al., 2011, 24.42.
[273] Diffie, 2020.

[274] United States General Accounting Office, 1993, 17.

America's unclassified government communications, and US business data flows, as well as potentially smaller nations.

The next question becomes: would the NSA directly target American citizens using DES? The cypherpunks believed so, and viewed through the prism of the governmental abuses of the Nixon administration, one can certainly understand why they harbored such suspicions. Had Nixon's agents not been caught due to operational errors, the US President may have used government assets, including powerful surveillance capabilities, to subvert America's democracy and preserve his own power. An alternative interpretation of the Nixon history is that the system worked—government abuse was detected, and Nixon was ejected from office.

Whilst retrospectively those such as Martin Hellman acknowledge they did not truly believe DES contained a backdoor, it could be that academic scrutiny contributed to the deterrence of such an action.[275] An argument can also be made that the cypherpunks catalyzing of the DES challenges accelerated DES' demise. It could further be posited that the increased digital rights activists' scrutiny—starting from the 1970s and peaking in the 1990s—led to the US government having no choice but to make the AES standard selection process competitive and transparent. Bruce Schneier, the owner of a finalist algorithm in the AES selection competition, commented, "I have nothing but good things to say about NIST and the AES process... They were honest, open, and fair."[276] Hellman agreed:

> we lost the [DES] key size issue...we did win in the long run...because not only did the key size go up in AES, they adopted it in the way we said DES should have been adopted: a transparent, open adoption process with critiques.[277]

In the early 1970s, the digital rights activists failed to increase DES' key size and to fully mobilize the public in support of their mission. However, by the time DES became a standard, Diffie and Hellman had made a discovery which allowed them to challenge the balance of cryptographic power: public key cryptography.

REFERENCES

ARTICLES

Coppersmith, D. (1994). The Data Encryption Standard (DES) and Its Strength Against Attacks. *International Business Machines Journal of Research and Development* **38**(3), 243–250.

Diffie, W. and Hellman, M. (1976). Exhaustive Cryptanalysis of the NBS Data Encryption Standard. *Computer* **10**(6), 2–12.

Feistel, H. (1973). Cryptography and Computer Privacy. *Scientific American* **228**(5), 15–23.

Hellman, M. (1977). Computer Encryption: Key Size. *Science* **198**(4312), 8–11.

Kahn, D. (1979). Cryptology Goes Public. *Foreign Affairs* **58**(1), 141–159.

---

[275] Juels et al., 2011, 24.42.

[276] Schneier, 2000.

[277] Hellman and McGraw, 2016.

Kolata, G. B. (1977). Computer Encryption and the National Security Agency Connection. *Science* **197**(4302), 438–440.

Konheim, A. G. (2015). The Impetus to Creativity in Technology. *Cryptologia* **39**(4), 291–314.

Konheim, A. G. (2016). Automated Teller Machines: Their History and Authentication Protocols. *Journal of Cryptographic Engineering* **6**(1), 1–29.

Tuchman, W. L. (1977). Computer Security and IBM. *Science* **197**(4307), 938.

BOOKS

Bamford, J. (1982). *The Puzzle Palace: Inside the National Security Agency* (New York: Penguin Books).

Curtin, M. (2005). *Brute Force: Cracking the Data Encryption Standard* (New York: Copernicus Books).

Diffie, W. and Landau, S. (1998). *Privacy on the Line: The Politics of Wiretapping and Encryption* (Cambridge, MA: MIT Press).

Hastedt, G. P. (2011). *Spies, Wiretaps, and Secret Operations An Encyclopedia of Espionage. Volume 1: A-J* (Santa Barbara: ABC-CLIO).

Kahn, D. (1967). *The Codebreakers: The Story of Secret Writing* (New York: Scribner).

Levy, S. (2001). *Crypto: Secrecy and Privacy in the New Cold War.* (New York: Viking Penguin).

Martin, K. (2020). Cryptography: *The Key to Digital Security, How It Works, and Why It Matters.* (New York: W. W. Norton).

Schneier, B. (1996). *Applied Cryptography: Second Edition: Protocols, Algorithms, and Source Code in C* (Hoboken: John Wiley & Sons, Inc.).

CHAPTERS IN BOOKS

Tuchman, W. L. (1998). A Brief History of the Data Encryption Standard. In *Internet Besieged: Countering Cyberspace Scofflaws.* Edited by Dorothy E. Denning and Peter J. Denning (New York: ACM Press).

CYPHERPUNK MAILING LIST ARCHIVES 1992–1998

Attila t. Hun (anonymous) (1996). "Re: Can We Kill Single DES?" MessageID: "199610020501. XAA14527@infowest.com." October 2, 1996.

Bell, J. (1996). "Re: Can we kill single DES?" MessageID: "199610020201.TAA10143@mail.pacifier.com." October 2, 1996.

Duvos, M. (1996). "Re: Can we kill single DES?" MessageID: "199610020411.VAA29067@netcom4.netcom.com." October 2, 1996.

Ghio, M. (1997). "Re: FIPS for AES." MessageID: "199701050556.AAA00312@myriad.alias.net." January 4, 1997. The Cypherpunks Archives 1992–1998.

Gilmore, J. (1993). "Crack DES in 3.5 hours for only $1,500,000!" MessageID: "9309092314. AA15000@toad.com." September 9, 1993.

May, T. C. (1993). "Re: Native American Encryption?!" MessageID: "9310130436.AA28397@netcom5.netcom.com." October 12, 1993.

May, T. C. (1997). "Getting Back to our Radical Roots." MessageID: "v0310280aaf-d0659f356a@[207.167.93.63]." June 21, 1997.

Trei, P. (1996). "can we kill single DES?" MessageID: "199610012026.NAA28151@toad.com." October 2, 1996.

Trei, P. (1997a). "DES: Thank you!" MessageID: "199706191540.IAA17231@toad.com." June 20, 1997.
Trei, P. (1997b). "[DES] DES Key Recovery Project, Progress Report #7." MessageID: "199701241856.KAA03668@toad.com." January 24, 1997.
Zimmermann, P. (1993) "Is DES dead?" MessageID: "9309090812.AA01090@longs.lanc e.colostate.edu." September 9, 1993.

NEWSPAPER ARTICLES

Friendly, A. "Secrets of Code-Breaking." *The Washington Post*, December 5, 1967.

INTERVIEWS AND CORRESPONDENCE BY AUTHOR

Diffie, W. (2020). Correspondence with Author, May 2, 2020.
George, R. (2020). Correspondence with Author, April 29–30, 2020.

WEBSITES

Bamford, J. (2006). *Big Brother is Listening* [Online]. Available: https://www.theatlantic.com/ma gazine/archive/2006/04/big-brother-is-listening/304711/ [Accessed October 13, 2019].
Blaze, M., Diffie, W., Rivest, R., Schneier, B., Shimomura, T., Thompson, E. and Wiener, M. (1996). *Minimal Key Lengths for Symmetric Ciphers to Provide Adequate Commercial Security: A Report by an Ad Hoc Group of Cryptographers and Computer Scientists* [Online]. Available: https://people.csail.mit.edu/rivest/pubs/BDRSx96.pdf [Accessed October 13, 2019].
Burr, W. (n.d.). *Data Encryption Standard* [Online]. Available: https://nvlpubs.nist.gov/nistp ubs/sp958-lide/250-253.pdf [Accessed November 30, 2019].
Cypherpunks. (1992–1998). *Cypherpunks Mail List Archive 1992–1998* [Online]. Available: https://lists.cpunks.org/pipermail/cypherpunks/2013-September/000741.html [Accessed July 10, 2015].
Davis, C. C. (1968). *Secret War of Words* [Online]. Available: https://www.nytimes.com/1 968/01/07/archives/secret-war-of-words-the-codebreakers-the-story-of-secret-writ ing-by.html [Accessed October 13, 2019].
Deschall Group. (1999). *Deschall Press Release* [Online]. Available: https://web.archive. org/web/19990221034217/http://www.http://frii.com:80/%7Ercv/despr4.htm [Accessed October 13, 2019].
Diffie, W. (1975). *Preliminary Remarks on the National Bureau of Standards Proposed Standard Encryption Algorithm for Data Protection* [Online]. Available: https:// stacks.stanford.edu/file/druid:wg115cn5068/1975%200522%20ltr%20to%20NBS.pdf [Accessed October 13, 2019].
Electronic Frontier Foundation. (2002). *Cracking DES: Secrets Encryption Research, Wiretap Politics, and Chip Design—How Federal Agencies Subvert Privacy. Electronic Frontier Foundation* [Online]. Available: https://cryptome.org/jya/crack ing-des/cracking-des.htm#foreword and https://web.archive.org/web/20020223181400/ http://www.http://eff.org:80/Privacy/Crypto_misc/DESCracker/HTML/19980716_dif fie_crackingdes_foreword.html [Accessed October 13, 2019].
Hellman, M. (1975). *Letter to Dr Dennis K. Branstad (National Bureau of Standards) from Martin Hellman, and Whitfield Diffie, 22 October 1975* [Online]. Available: https:// stacks.stanford.edu/file/druid:wg115cn5068/1975%201022%20ltr%20to%20NBS.pdf [Accessed October 16, 2019].

Hellman, M. (1976a). *Letter to Seymour Jeffery (National Bureau of Standards) from Martin Hellman, 20 January, 1976* [Online]. Available: https://stacks.stanford.edu/file/druid:wg11 5cn5068/1976%200220%20ltrs%20to%20NBS.pdf [Accessed October 16, 2019].

Hellman, M. (1976b). *Letter to Seymour Jeffery (National Bureau of Standards) from Martin Hellman, 21 January, 1976* [Online]. Available: https://stacks.stanford.edu/file/ druid:wg115cn5068/1976%200220%20ltrs%20to%20NBS.pdf [Accessed October 16, 2019].

Hellman, M. and McGraw, G. (2016). *Show 121: Marty Hellman Discusses Cryptography and Nuclear Non-Proliferation* [Online]. Available: https://www.synopsys.com/softw are-integrity/resources/podcasts/show-121.html [Accessed October 13, 2019].

Hellman, M., Diffie. W., Baran, P., Branstad, D., Hogan L., Douglas, L., and Arthur J. (1976a) [Estimate]. *DES (Data Encryption Standard) Review at Stanford University* [Online]. Available: https://web.archive.org/web/20130707114841/http://www.http://toad.com/ des-stanford-meeting.html [Accessed October 13, 2019].

Hellman, M., Merkle, R., Schroeppel, R., Washington, L., Whitfield. D., Pohlig, S., and Schweitzer, P. (1976b). *Results of an Initial Attempt to Cryptanalyze the NBS Data Encryption Standard* [Online]. Available: http://www.merkle.com/papers/Attemp t%20to%20Cryptanalyze%20DES%201976-11-10.pdf [Accessed October 13, 2019].

IBM. (n.d.). *Cryptography in a Connected World* [Online]. Available: http://www-03.ibm.co m/ibm/history/ibm100/us/en/icons/cryptography/ [Accessed October 13, 2019].

Jackson, W. (2013). *The NSA Wants to Be Your Backdoor Man* [Online]. Available: https:// gcn.com/Blogs/CyberEye/2013/09/NSA-back-door.aspx [Accessed October 13, 2019].

Jeffery, S. (1976). *Letter to Martin Hellman and Whitfield Diffie from Seymour Jeffrey, Chief Systems and Software Division, National Bureau of Standards, 6 January 1976* [Online]. Available: https://stacks.stanford.edu/file/druid:wg115cn5068/1976%20 0106%20NBS%20reply.pdf [Accessed October 16, 2019].

Johnson, T. R. (1998). *American Cryptology During the Cold War, 1945–1989. Book III: Retrenchment and Reform, 1972, 1980* [Online]. Available: https://www.nsa.gov/Porta ls/70/documents/news-features/declassified-documents/cryptologic-histories/cold_ war_iii.pdf [Accessed April 13, 2020].

Kahn, D. (1976). *Tapping Computers* [Online]. Available: https://www.nytimes.com/1976/0 4/03/archives/tapping-computers.html [Accessed October 13, 2019].

Macpherson, M. (1978). *The Secret Life of David Kahn* [Online]. Available: https://www.was hingtonpost.com/archive/lifestyle/1978/06/09/the-secret-life-of-david-kahn/1209f 0d6-e1e1-422c-8171-93a53e8ae29d/ [Accessed October 13, 2019].

National Bureau of Standards. (1976). *Report of the Workshop on Estimation of Significant Advances in Computer Technology* [Online]. Available: https://www.gpo.gov/fdsys /pkg/GOVPUB-C13-c6967009792b5d52b47a16f8d5b045ad/pdf/GOVPUB-C13-c 6967009792b5d52b47a16f8d5b045ad.pdf [Accessed October 13, 2019].

National Bureau of Standards. (1977). *Report of the Workshop on Cryptography in support of Computer Security* [Online]. Available: https://www.gpo.gov/fdsys/pkg/GOVPUB-C13 -3955d1dc6d9ab572be74ef35f487a433/pdf/GOVPUB-C13-3955d1dc6d9ab572be74e f35f487a433.pdf [Accessed October 13, 2019].

National Cryptological Museum. (1987). *In Memoriam: Douglas L. Hogan* [Online]. Available: https://cryptologicfoundation.org/what-we-do/commemorate/in-memor iam-registry-honoree-pages/douglas-hogan.html [Accessed October 13, 2019].

National Institute of Standards and Technology. (1997). *Announcing Development of a Federal Information Processing Standard for Advanced Encryption Standard* [Online]. Available: http://csrc.nist.gov/archive/aes/pre-round1/aes_9701.txt [Accessed October 13, 2019].

National Institute of Standards and Technology. (1999). *Federal Information Processing Standards Publication 46-3 Date Encryption Standard* [Online]. Available: http://csr c.nist.gov/publications/fips/fips46-3/fips46-3.pdf [Accessed October 13, 2019].

National Institute of Standards and Technology. (2001). *Federal Information Processing Standards Publication 197* [Online]. Available: http://nvlpubs.nist.gov/nistpubs/FIPS/ NIST.FIPS.197.pdf [Accessed October 13, 2019].

National Institute of Standards and Technology. (2011). *NIST Special Publication 800–131A. Transitions: Recommendation for Transitioning the Use of Cryptographic Algorithms and Key Lengths* [Online]. Available: http://nvlpubs.nist.gov/nistpubs/Legacy/SP/ni stspecialpublication800-131a.pdf [Accessed October 13, 2019].

Phoenix Society. (2007). *Arthur J. Levenson* [Online]. Available: http://www.arlingtoncemet ery.net/ajlevenson.htm [Accessed October 13, 2019].

Plutte, J. (2011). *Whitfield Diffie Interview: Computer History Museum* [Online]. Available: http://archive.computerhistory.org/resources/access/text/2015/04/102743051-05-01 -acc.pdf [Accessed October 13, 2019].

RSA. (1997). *The RSA Data Security Secret-Key Challenge* [Online]. Available: https://we b.archive.org/web/19970728090638/www.rsa.com/rsalabs/97challenge   [Accessed October 13, 2019].

RSA. (1998). *Government encryption standard DES takes a fall* [Online]. Available: https ://web.archive.org/web/19980623080752/http://www.http://rsa.com/des/   [Accessed October 13, 2019].

Schneier, B. (2000). *AES Announced* [Online]. Available: https://www.schneier.com/crypt o-gram/archives/2000/1015.html#8 [Accessed October 13, 2019].

Schneier, B. (2004). *The Legacy of DES* [Online]. Available: https://www.schneier.com/blog/ archives/2004/10/the_legacy_of_d.html [Accessed March 15, 2020].

United States General Accounting Office. (1993). *Communications Privacy: Federal Policy and Actions* [Online]. Available: http://www.gao.gov/assets/220/218755.pdf [Accessed October 13, 2019].

United States House of Representatives. (1997). *Hearing before The Subcommittee on Courts and Intellectual Property hears testimony on the Security and Freedom through Encryption (SAFE) Act, March 20, 1997* [Online]. Available: http://commdocs.house.gov/committees/ judiciary/hju41233.000/hju41233_0f.htm [Accessed October 13, 2019].

United States House of Representatives. (1997b). *Committee on International Relations: Members Briefing Regarding Encryption. June 26, 1997* [Online]. Available: https://web.archive.org/ web/20040604062410/http://jya.com/hir-hear.htm [Accessed October 13, 2019].

United States Senate. (1978). *Unclassified Summary: Involvement of NSA in the Development of the Data Encryption Standard—Staff Report of the Senate Select Committee on Intelligence United States Congress* [Online]. https://www.intelligence.senate.gov/site s/default/files/publications/95nsa.pdf [Accessed October 13, 2019].

Wiener, M. J. (1994). *Efficient DES Key Search* [Online]. Available: http://citeseerx.ist.psu. edu/viewdoc/download;jsessionid=86D868AE29E7F26B3384949B0D5BE4CA?doi=1 0.1.1.130.7347&rep=rep1&type=pdf [Accessed October 13, 2019].

VIDEOS

George, R. "CERIAS—The Role of the NSA in the Development of DES," YouTube video, 55:48, posted by "Purdue CERIAS," April 26, 2016. Available: https://www.youtube. com/watch?v=u80M009eSDk [Accessed April 12, 2020].

George, R. "Richard 'Dickie' George—Keynote—Life at Both Ends of the Barrel: An NSA Targeting Retrospective," Vimeo video, 1:07:25, posted by "Immunity Videos," June 10, 2014, Available: https://vimeo.com/97891042 [Accessed March 15, 2020].

Juels, A., Diffie, W., George, R., Hellman, M., Rivest, R, Shamir, A. "RSA Conference 2011 Keynote—The Cryptographers' Panel. RSA Conference," YouTube video, 44:49, posted by "RSA Conference," July 1, 2011, Available: https://www.youtube.com/watch?v=0NlZpyk3PKI [Accessed October 13, 2019].

5 Crypto War I (1966–1981)
The Battle for Academic Freedom

Yet it may be roundly asserted that human ingenuity

cannot concoct a cipher that human ingenuity cannot solve

Edgar Allan Poe, 1842

5.1 AN ITINERATE CRYPTOGRAPHER: WHITFIELD DIFFIE MEETS MARTIN HELLMAN

"It was like being in the desert and coming across an oasis when I met Whit," Martin Hellman reflects.[1] Since 1972, Hellman had pursued cryptology in near isolation, since other academics were disinterested, he comments:

> most of my colleagues thought I was crazy for two reasons: First, they said, you'll never discover anything new because NSA has a huge budget and if it could be done NSA would already have done it; second, if you do anything good, NSA will classify it and you'll never get credit.[2]

Most who chose to work in cryptology were shrouded under the government's cloak of secrecy. Former NSA employee Richard "Dickie" George, comments:

> in 1972 crypto was not a commercial thing. There were a few companies, mostly European, that were doing things not well, they basically were doing things the same things they'd been doing in world war 2. The real crypto was being done by governments around the world, and nobody else got to play.[3]

Those cryptologists not working for the NSA were employed by organizations beholden to government contracts, their employers would unlikely risk publishing, or publicly discussing, any innovative research that may upset their clients and risk revenue streams. It was such a problem Hellman encountered in 1974 when he visited IBM's Yorktown Heights Research Center to deliver a lecture.[4]

---

[1] Green, 2015.
[2] Myers, 2011.

[3] George, 2016, 3:52.
[4] Green, 2015.

Hellman had worked at Yorktown between 1968 and 1969, after completing his doctorate. Whilst Hellman was not working on cryptography at the time, he had lunched with Horst Feistel, the father of DES; "I learned a lot from Horst," Hellman recalls.[5] But on Hellman's return to Yorktown, he found his old colleagues in a less communicative state: "I spoke with Feistel, [Alan] Konheim, and some of the others and they were a little bit down. They said a secrecy order had just been placed on them by the NSA and they couldn't tell me very much."[6] The secrecy order was for their Lucifer algorithm. Feistel and Konheim explained, "We can't tell you much, and also we're being encouraged to work on other things."[7] Hellman says the group believed "cryptography had been solved."[8] Hellman's network of cryptologists with whom he was able to exchange ideas was dwindling.

In summer 1974, Whitfield Diffie visited Yorktown. He had recently quit his job and was now traveling around the country on a cryptological odyssey. Diffie had spent time with David Kahn, and the historian's vast library of cryptographic manuscripts, in New York. He was hoping IBM could provide further insights, but the secrecy order to which Konheim was beholden stifled knowledge exchange. Diffie recounts:

> I spoke to Alan Konheim who was very secretive, he didn't want to tell me anything. He only told me one thing, and since then he wishes he hadn't said that. He said: An old friend of mine, named Martin Hellman, was here a few months ago…you should look him up.[9]

When Diffie returned to the West Coast he called Hellman. Their meeting was scheduled in Hellman's Stanford office at 15:30 for thirty minutes. It lasted until 23:00. By 17:00, Hellman invited Diffie and his wife, Mary, back to his family home to continue their discussions: "Each of us found the other person, the best informed person, willing to talk about the subject he had yet run into," Diffie recalls.[10] Hellman recounts it "was getting lonely working in a vacuum…it was like being in the desert and coming across an oasis when I met Whit."[11]

5.2   DIFFIE AND CRYPTOLOGY

Diffie was interested in cryptology from a young age. At ten years old, one of Diffie's teachers introduced him to ciphers, he promptly asked his father to check out every cryptology book from New York City College's library. However, after consuming all the children's texts on the topic Diffie's interest waned: "I thought that everyone was interested in cryptography. I was interested in more esoteric things."[12] Years later, whilst studying Mathematics at MIT, Diffie learned how to program. Occasionally

---

[5] Ibid.
[6] Green, 2015.
[7] Hellman and McGraw, 2016.
[8] Ibid.

[9] Furger, 2002.
[10] Ibid.
[11] Green, 2015.
[12] Furger, 2002.

he would hear something about cryptography to warrant his attention, but it was not until his time at research organization and defense contractor Mitre that his boss, Ronald Silver, explained how modern cryptographic systems worked.[13]

Diffie's role at Mitre placed him in MIT's Artificial Intelligence Lab, where a computer timesharing project was underway. The Multics operating system was intended to allow multiple people, rather than a single user, to access the same machine and share its resources. To run such a system a central administrator maintains the computer, that administrator has God-like abilities on the machine, being able to access every file—such power leaves users vulnerable to the administrator. Diffie realized if a warrant were issued for data a user stored on such a system, the administrator would acquiesce to the warrant as they "would not be interested in going to prison in order to protect your files."[14] Even if the administrator were simply nosey they could invade their user's privacy. Cryptography was the answer. With encrypted files one need not trust the administrator, as all they were able to access were files that were nonsensical without the decryption key, a key the user alone should possess. Therefore, "if a court wanted your files they would have to come and threaten you and you would have the control to make the choice as to whether you would surrender your files or not."[15]

At first, Diffie tried to persuade other researchers to work on encryption, "I didn't do any work on it at that time because I wasn't really interested in it, I was working on problems I considered more important." In 1972, Diffie moved to the West Coast to work at Stanford's artificial intelligence lab. Diffie had found MIT very politically conservative. Having grown up in New York City, "a very left, politically active environment," Diffie recalls, he did not find MIT "politically congenial." The West Coast and California, bastion of the counterculture, felt more like home.[16]

Whilst working on the West Coast under John McCarthy on proof of correctness (producing a mathematical proof that an algorithm fulfills its purpose) Diffie read David Kahn's *The Codebreakers*. "I read very slowly," Diffie recalls, "I started in the fall of '72…by the spring of '73 I was doing nothing but working on cryptography."[17] McCarthy became embarrassed Diffie was not working on the task for which he was being paid; Diffie recalls, "since I was being funded by under-the-table money from NSA, that might be a bit awkward if it came to light."[18] Therefore they negotiated a "friendly parting of the ways," Diffie recalls, "and I took an indefinite leave of absence and departed."[19]

For the next two years, Diffie would attend both his "great desire to travel" and his hunt for cryptologic knowledge. He was fortunate to have the resources for such an adventure, "I had of course enough money to do that as an artifact of the society at the time. I was being paid as though I was supporting a woman, but I wasn't supporting anyone, so I had lots of extra money."[20] Diffie focused on what he thought

---

[13] Levy, 2001, The Loner, Chapter 1.
[14] Furger, 2002.
[15] Ibid.
[16] Ibid.

[17] Ibid.
[18] Plutte, 2011b, 3.
[19] Ibid.
[20] Furger, 2002.

was, "intellectually important," rather than earning more money, so he set off to search for answers:

> I went around doing one of the things I am good at, which is digging up rare manuscripts in libraries, driving round, visiting friends at universities and things, going into the university libraries and doing research there and working entirely unsupported.[21]

Diffie recalls when Hellman arranged his first talk at Stanford on his return to the West Coast he "described me in the flyer as an itinerate cryptographer, an itinerant being one who wanders around."[22]

5.3   HELLMAN AND CRYPTOLOGY

Three sources led Hellman to cryptology.[23]

Firstly, when attending an Institute of Electrical and Electronics Engineers International Symposium on Information Theory, in January 1969, the banquet speaker was David Kahn, who had released *The Codebreakers* two years earlier— "that certainly put the idea in my head," Hellman reflects.[24]

Secondly, during his time at IBM, Hellman was exposed to Feistel, who had, "been brought in from classified government work to seed IBM's research in cryptography," Hellman explains. Hellman had "a number of discussions with Feistel that opened my eyes to previously unforeseen possibilities." He assessed IBM's investment in cryptography for commercial purposes, "also indicated the need and value of such work."[25]

The final source driving Hellman's decision to pursue cryptology was when, in 1970, he was introduced to Claude Shannon's information theory and cryptography writings, "I saw that information theory owed much of its birth to wartime, classified research on cryptography that Shannon had done at Bell Lab," Hellman recalls, "and that much of what I had learned in my doctoral studies was directly applicable to cryptography." Hellman believed he could make a contribution to the field.[26]

For the next few years, Hellman spent his little spare time on cryptology, though he felt his ideas were "embryonic and not likely to be judged worthy of financial support." Hellman also worried about funding opportunities given most cryptology research was classified.[27]

Hellman considered the challenges further and felt they should not prevent his working on cryptology. Whilst NSA may have made many important cryptologic discoveries, "that knowledge was not available to meet the growing commercial needs for encryption," Hellman reflected, and besides, "credit went to the first to publish, not the first to discover and keep the work secret."[28] Hellman notes, "I kind of like being a maverick and when my colleagues told me I was crazy, instead of

---

[21] Ibid.
[22] Ibid.
[23] Hellman, no date a.
[24] Hellman and McGraw, 2016.

[25] Hellman, no date a.
[26] Ibid.
[27] Ibid.
[28] Ibid.

scaring me off, it probably attracted me."[29] However, his training, a doctorate in Electrical Engineering from Stanford, had not necessarily prepared him for a cryptologic career: "It was foolish, it was arrogant in a way for me to try to do research in cryptography...knowing as little mathematics as I knew."[30] Despite all the challenges, Hellman committed to cryptology and secured funding to allow Diffie to stay at Stanford, thus establishing perhaps the most consequential intellectual partnership in cryptological history.

5.4 PUBLIC KEY CRYPTOGRAPHY: SOLVING THE KEY DISTRIBUTION PROBLEM

The heart of the cryptography challenge was the key distribution problem. How could two people from disparate locations securely exchange encryption keys without ever having physically met? The government used couriers, but this was not an option when one wanted to instantly initiate a secure communication with a stranger sitting a thousand miles away, and it didn't scale to the millions of users who would one day be online. Added to the key distribution problem was the government's stranglehold on cryptologic expertise and standards. Shortly after Diffie and Hellman started collaborating, they became involved in a confrontation with the government over the Data Encryption Standard, adding another dimension to their challenge. Diffie and Hellman believed control of cryptography had to be wrested from the government and given to citizens, where its design and application could be focused on commerce and privacy without the conflicting government requirement of facilitating NSA surveillance.[31]

After reading the DES proposal in May 1975, Diffie tried to reconcile how the government could offer an encryption standard:

> I did not understand how those people dared either standardize a secure system or standardize a non-secure system, because if it was secure—since they were primarily an intelligence agency—they would be afraid that they wouldn't be able to read other people's traffic. If it was not secure, since they had certified it for the use of U.S. government organizations, they risk having a tremendous black eye if it were broken.[32]

Inserting what Diffie termed a "trapdoor" (or backdoor) was one way the government could release a "secure" system whilst maintaining the ability to decrypt DES-encrypted data.

A related challenge Diffie considered was how to replicate the properties of a physical signature in the digital realm. Whilst scrawling a pattern on paper was a primitive method of authenticating one's identity, it had proved remarkably resilient in the face of all but professional forgers. The signature also offered non-repudiation—it was considered legally binding in most cases, though for the most impactful

---

[29] Green, 2015.
[30] Ibid.
[31] Hellman, 1976a; Hellman, 1976b.
[32] Furger, 2002.

of contracts a witness to the signature would often be required to counteract the forgery risk. However, the nature of technology meant any digital signature was, at its most base level, a series of ones and zeros, making replication trivial. In order for online commerce to progress, and trust to develop between parties, a digital equivalent to the physical signature was required.

Diffie and Hellman toiled away at the key distribution and digital signature problems until finally they found a conceptual solution—Diffie made the initial breakthrough in May 1975. Diffie recalls, "in that moment I realized that I'd discovered something important and I was acutely aware that the computer on which I was keeping my notes was not secure," so he elected not to type his solution into the machine.[33] Hellman then refined Diffie's discovery.[34] In November 1976, they shared their discovery with the world.

5.5   NEW DIRECTIONS IN CRYPTOGRAPHY

Their overture did not lend itself to modesty; "We stand today on the brink of a revolution in cryptography," Diffie and Hellman declared in *New Directions in Cryptography*, published in *IEEE's Transactions in Information Theory* in November 1976.[35] The authors explained, "theoretical developments in information theory and computer science show promise of providing provably secure cryptosystems, changing this ancient art into a science." In less than a dozen pages, Diffie and Hellman outlined their solution to alleviate the key distribution problem, and provide a method of authenticating the sender with digital signatures. The authors called their approach a "public key cryptosystem":

> In a public key cryptosystem enciphering and deciphering are governed by distinct keys, E and D, such that computing D from E is computationally infeasible (e.g., requiring 10^{100} instructions). The enciphering key E can thus be publicly disclosed without compromising the deciphering key D. Each user of the network can, therefore, place his enciphering key in a public directory. This enables any user of the system to send a message to any other user enciphered in such a way that only the intended receiver is able to decipher it.[36]

The key that would be available to anyone, and would be used to encrypt data, is known as the "public key." The key that is known only to the recipient and decrypts the data is the "private key." Splitting the keys was an innovation that broke with the established doctrines of cryptography. When Hellman explained the scheme, Horst Feistel replied, "You can't do that!" (though it was, according to Hellman, a hurried explanation as Feistel was rushing to a doctor's appointment).[37] Whilst at first public key cryptography seems to break convention, it actually adheres to it, the private key stays private—it is only the related public key that is shared with the world.

---

[33] Ibid.
[34] Ibid.
[35] Diffie and Hellman, 1976, 644.

[36] Ibid.
[37] Yost, 2004, 23.

Fundamental to the realization of a public key cryptosystem was the ability to develop a mathematical algorithm allowing the public and private keys to relate to one another as outlined by Diffie and Hellman. This notion of a trapdoor cipher, in Diffie's mind since he started ruminating how the government could deliver a DES algorithm that was at once secure against attacks from all other actors, but also accessible to NSA agents possessing knowledge of the trapdoor, was the prerequisite for a public key cryptosystem.[38] However, the authors acknowledged there was at that time "little evidence of the existence of trapdoor ciphers."[39]

To solve the signature requirement, Diffie and Hellman envisioned an algorithm which allowed an inverse usage of the public-private key. If the recipient was able to decrypt a message, or a *signature*, with the originator's public key, then the originator must be in possession of the paired private key—of course this would require some mechanism to verify that the public key did in fact belong to the supposed owner.[40] To maintain integrity, the signature would be derived in part from the contents of the message; should even a single character be different, the message would need to be re-signed by the legitimate owner of the private key; therefore, any modifications by a third party to the original signed document would not be possible. As long as the private key was not compromised the approach was viable.

Inspired as Diffie and Hellman's paper was, it lacked an implementation algorithm; "We propose some techniques for developing public key cryptosystems, but the problem is still largely open," the authors wrote.[41] Diffie and Hellman closed their paper stating, "Skill in production cryptanalysis has always been heavily on the side of the professionals, but innovation, particularly in the design of new types of cryptographic systems, has come primarily from the amateurs."[42] They reflected that a cryptosystem invented by Thomas Jefferson, an amateur, was still in use during World War Two, and the most noted cryptosystem of the twentieth century, the rotor, was invented simultaneously by four separate amateurs. Their final line characteristically jibed the government, "We hope this will inspire others to work in this fascinating area in which participation has been discouraged in the recent past by a nearly total government monopoly."[43]

5.6 THE MIT TRIO: RIVEST, SHAMIR, AND ADLEMAN (RSA)

"Marvelous idea…these are amazing ideas," Ron Rivest comments of Diffie and Hellman's *New Directions on Cryptography*, "they didn't know how to implement them at all."[44] Rivest was a twenty-nine-year-old assistant professor in MIT's Computer Science Department when he read Diffie and Hellman's article in December 1976.

Rivest grew up in New York before winning a place to study Mathematics at Yale.[45] Whilst studying, Rivest attended a few Vietnam protest marches but was

---

[38] Furger, 2002.
[39] Diffie and Hellman, 1976, 652.
[40] Ibid, 644.
[41] Ibid.

[42] Ibid, 654.
[43] Ibid.
[44] Rivest, 2012, 21:16.
[45] Massachusetts Institute of Technology, 2018.

without the political drive of Diffie or the 1990s cypherpunks.[46] Rivest attained a PhD in Computer Science from Stanford before heading to MIT.[47] Rivest's office in Tech Square at MIT was a floor below the AI lab where Diffie worked some years earlier, yet the two had never met.[48]

When Leonard Adleman walked into his office weeks later, Rivest asked, "did you see this new thing from these guys Diffie and Hellman at Stanford?"[49] Adleman was a fellow mathematician who, like Rivest, divided his time between the computer science laboratory and the mathematics department.[50] Adleman listened to Rivest's explanation of *New Directions in Cryptography* before commenting, "Well, that's nice, Ron," then changed the subject.[51]

Adleman held a PhD in Mathematics from the University of California, Berkley. At first, he intended to become a chemist, but that changed whilst studying his under-graduate degree; speaking of his decision to enter the field of mathematics, Adleman recalled: "Suddenly something happens to somebody who becomes a mathematician, and it's much like falling in love, that's what happened to me, I suddenly, almost on a single day saw the inner beauty of it all."[52] Adleman was interested in number theory, which he describes as "a very ancient discipline...it had been studied for at least a few thousand years and at various times in its life it had burned brightly and at various times it had just been an ember kept alive by other people."[53] It was pure theory that interested Adleman, listening to Rivest's exhortations of *New Directions in Cryptography*, Adleman recalls thinking, "I'm trying to save the dignity of science because Gauss told me to do it, and this isn't going to save the dignity of science"; to Adleman's ears this was "some kind of engineering thing about networks and stuff like that," it was not something upon which the Gods of Mathematics, including Gauss, Adleman's personal deity, would sacrifice their limited hours, "it meant nothing to me," Adleman comments.[54]

Rivest was more successful enticing Adi Shamir, an Israeli mathematician recently arrived at MIT as a visiting Professor in Computer Science. Rivest called on Shamir in his office, as Shamir was preparing to teach an advanced algorithm course, a field he knew little about.[55] Once Rivest explained Diffie and Hellman's paper, Shamir quickly agreed to collaborate to find a suitable one-way function and make public key cryptography a reality, despite knowing little about cryptology.[56]

Despite Adleman's reluctance to become involved in the project, his close friendships with Rivest and Shamir meant that during the winter of 1976–77 he was drawn into their quest. Adleman recalls:

> We were friends and we used to do everything together, we'd go on trips together, we'd have dinners together, we did everything together, and we were constantly

---

[46] Levy, 2001, Prime Time, Chapter 4.
[47] Massachusetts Institute of Technology, 2018.
[48] Levy, 2001, Prime Time, Chapter 4.
[49] Adleman, 2016, 67:14.
[50] Levy, 2001, Prime Time, Chapter 4.
[51] Adleman, 2016, 67:43.

[52] Bebel and Teng 2002; Adleman, 2010, 0:12.
[53] Adleman, 2010, 0:41.
[54] Adleman, 2016, 67:23.
[55] Levy, 2001, Prime Time, Chapter 4.
[56] Ibid.

collaborating on our common discipline, which was computational complexity theory. We saw each other every day.[57]

Adleman recalls that Rivest and Shamir, "became obsessed, they're constantly talking about it and they're constantly coming up with possible public-key cryptosystems."[58] Rivest and Shamir struggled at first, "We weren't happy with the approaches we came up with," Rivest recalls, "We experimented with a lot of different approaches, including variations on things that Diffie and Hellman suggested," but time and again they broke their own algorithms.[59] The MIT trio started to wonder whether Diffie and Hellman's breakthrough was a false horizon; changing tactics, they decided to try to prove a fully-fledged public key cryptography system was more myth than realistic possibility—"We didn't get very far," Rivest recalls.[60]

Shamir concedes the trio were, "rank amateurs—we knew nothing about cryptography." However, Shamir believes this was an advantage: "We were extremely lucky. If we'd known anything about cryptography and known about differential sequences, and Lucifer, and DES, we probably would have been misled into expanding those ideas and using them for public key cryptography"[61] Eventually, Rivest and Shamir tried number theory approaches, but the solution remained evasive. Adleman recalls his colleagues placing possibility after possibility in front of him and he would reply, "No, I can break that. This, this, this. Boom, done...mostly it goes that way, and it goes that way for months."[62] Just occasionally, Rivest and Shamir developed a system challenging enough for Adleman to take home to work on, but by the next morning the algorithm would be broken.[63]

In early 1977, the trio celebrated Passover at a student's house. Rivest in particular indulged in wine, as is customary at seders, before the party dispersed at eleven.[64] Rivest returned home and lay on his sofa, his eyes closed, "I was just thinking," he recalls.[65] It was then the solution materialized in Rivest's mind.[66] Adleman's phone rang, "Hey, Len. What about blah-blah-blah?" Adleman recalls, "And the 'blah-blah-blah' he said was what we now know as the RSA cryptosystem."[67] Adleman listened before replying, "Congratulations, Ron. I think you finally did it." Adleman says Rivest's algorithm seemed solid: "This one, wow, I wouldn't know where to begin to break this. Well, I know where to begin, but I couldn't succeed."[68] The solution was based on the challenge of factoring two large primes (one hundred digits or more). A prime number is a number that can only be divided by one and itself. Multiplying two large primes produces a larger, non-prime number. Reversing the process to find the two seed primes from the larger number, a process known as factoring, was a historically hard mathematics problem. There was little attention on the problem in the 1970s. Rivest commented: "Factoring at the time was not a problem that people

---

[57] Adleman, 2016, 66:34.

[58] Ibid, 68:05.

[59] Levy, 2001, Prime Time, Chapter 4.

[60] Ibid.

[61] Ibid.

[62] Adleman, 2016, 70:01.

[63] Ibid, 70:17.

[64] Ibid, 71:01.

[65] Levy, 2001, Prime Time, Chapter 4.

[66] Ibid.

[67] Adleman, 2016, 71:30.

[68] Ibid, 71:43.

cared about very much."[69] Whilst factoring was not known to be impossible, there was no known solution to easily determine the parent primes; it was the one-way function for which Rivest, Shamir, and Adleman were searching.

The next day Rivest met Adleman with a handwritten paper, the product of an all-night writing session on his solution.[70] The paper, *Technical Memo Number 82: A Method for Obtaining Digital Signatures and Public Key Cryptosystems*, listed Adleman, Shamir, and Rivest as authors; "Take my name off that paper," Adleman says. Rivest replies, "Why?" Adleman answers, "You thought of the idea." Rivest says, "No, no. We worked as a team. This is a team. You deserve to be on this paper."[71] Eventually, Adleman accepted his name on the paper, thinking to himself, "no one's ever going to read this paper, but it will be another line on my résumé when tenure time comes."[72] Adleman requested one small concession: Rivest's name should appear first on their paper, rather than Adleman, Shamir, and Rivest, ASR, it would be Rivest, Shamir, Adleman: RSA—an acronym that became synonymous with security.[73]

5.7   HUMAN INGENUITY: TESTING RSA

A New Cipher That Would Take Millions of Years to Break, read the title of Martin Gardner's article in *Scientific American* published in August 1977.[74] *Scientific American* was broadly read, and not just by career academics such as Rivest, Shamir, and Adleman, but by amateurs and hobbyists.

Rivest recounts once the RSA algorithm was developed, the trio of inventors started asking themselves how hard the factoring of two large primes would be: "factoring at the time was not that much of an academic research area, it was sort of a backwater area that hobbyists cared about so we talked to people who liked that kind of thing."[75] That led them to a man who could help them search for answers: Gardner.[76] Rivest explained public key cryptography to Gardner, and asked what he knew about the difficulty of factoring large prime numbers. Gardner recalls getting excited about public key encryption: "I realized what a big breakthrough this was for cryptography," and he invited Rivest to his New York home to explain the discovery.[77] Gardner decided to break his rule of planning articles months in advance and quickly wrote up the innovation.[78]

Gardner's monthly *Mathematical Games* column had run for twenty years and attracted a loyal following of recreational mathematicians, just the type of people Rivest, Shamir, and Adleman needed to test their algorithm's strength.[79] Gardner's articles were typically abstracted from the intimidating mathematical equations that

[69] Levy, 2001, Prime Time, Chapter 4.
[70] Adleman, 2016, 72:16.
[71] Ibid, 73:01.
[72] Ibid, 74:10.
[73] Ibid, 74:23.
[74] Gardner, 1977.

[75] Rivest, 2012, 24:06.
[76] Ibid, 24:10.
[77] Barcellos, 2010; Levy, 2001, Prime Time, Chapter 4.
[78] Mulcahy, 2014.
[79] Ibid.

so often deterred all but the most devout, instead he conveyed the salient points in as simple prose as possible.[80] Gardner's article proclaimed public key cryptography, "so revolutionary that all previous ciphers, together with the techniques for cracking them, may soon fade into oblivion."[81] Over the next pages, Gardner explained Diffie and Hellman's breakthrough, before adding details of Rivest, Shamir, and Adleman's implementation. Gardner wrote anybody wanting further details of the MIT trio's approach could request a copy of their article by writing to MIT and including a self-addressed envelope and thirty-five cents postage.[82]

To test their algorithm, Rivest created a challenge cipher and offered a hundred dollars to anyone who could find the key.[83] The 129-digit encrypted message was included within Gardner's article.[84]

As Diffie and Hellman had observed in *New Directions in Cryptography*, whilst historically, mathematical proofs were offered to validate an encryption algorithms' security, such supposedly secure algorithms were repeatedly broken; therefore the use of mathematical proofs to validate security, "fell into disrepute and was replaced by certification via cryptanalytic assault."[85] In essence, for the community to accept an algorithm was secure, a concerted and prolonged cryptanalytic attempt must be made to break it, only when countless leading cryptanalytic minds had tried and failed would it be considered secure, or at least considered to have no easily identifiable vulnerabilities. In utilizing the wide readership of *Scientific American*, Rivest, Shamir, and Adleman sought validation from knowing hundreds had tried, and failed, to break their algorithm. Rivest estimated an exhaustion attack would take "forty quadrillion years to break," therefore the only danger was if a shortcut was found in the algorithm.[86]

Before the article, Gardner invoked a famous cryptology quote by Edgar Allan Poe, "it may be roundly asserted that human ingenuity cannot concoct a cipher which human ingenuity cannot resolve."[87] The article closed with an observation of the consequence of an unbreakable cipher: "All over the world there are clever men and women, some of them geniuses, who have devoted their lives to the mastery of modern cryptanalysis…Now these people are standing on trapdoors that are about to spring open and drop them completely from sight."[88] Gardner suggested the human ingenuity Poe spoke of had reached its pinnacle—the cryptographers were on the cusp of permanently retiring the cryptanalysts.

It would take until April 1994 before the RSA129 challenge would eventually be broken, revealing the plain text "THE MAGIC WORDS ARE SQUEAMISH OSSIFRAGE"—Rivest had randomly selected the words from a dictionary.[89] Breaking the code had taken an eight-month effort by around 600 volunteers in

---

[80] Ibid.
[81] Gardner, 1977.
[82] Ibid.
[83] Rivest, 2012, 24:37.
[84] Gardner, 1977.

[85] Diffie and Hellman, 1976, 653.
[86] Rivest, 2012, 24:53.
[87] Gardner, 1977.
[88] Ibid.
[89] Rivest, 2012, 36:55.

more than 20 countries.[90] Adleman later commented when Rivest calculated the time RSA129 would take to break as forty quadrillion years, "Ron kind of messed it up," but by then it was largely irrelevant, key sizes in use were already much larger than 129 bits.[91] One of the project participants, Derek Atkins, calculated if they were working against the then recommended RSA 1024-bit key size, it would have taken millions of years more.[92]

5.8   NSA EMPLOYEE WARNS CRYPTOGRAPHERS AGAINST PUBLISHING

A Mr. J. A. Meyer of Bethesda wrote to Elwood Gannet, Staff Secretary of the IEEE Publications Board on July 7, 1977. The letter catalyzed the first crypto war's freedom to publish battle.

Meyer wrote in recent months IEEE had, "been publishing and exporting technical articles on…cryptography—a technical field which is covered by Federal Regulations," Meyer cited the International Traffic in Arms Regulations (ITAR), legislation controlling items from atomic weapons to cryptography.[93] The ITAR defines "export" as:

- Sending or taking a defense article out of the United States in any manner
- Disclosing (including oral or visual disclosure) or transferring technical data to a foreign person, whether in the United States or abroad
- Performing a defense service on behalf of, or for the benefit of, a foreign person, whether in the United States or abroad[94]

A "defense service" is defined as:

the furnishing of assistance (including training) to foreign persons, whether in the United States or abroad, in the design, development, engineering, manufacture, production, assembly, testing, repair, maintenance, modification, operation, demilitarization, destruction, processing or use of defense articles.[95]

The ITAR is an instrument of the Arms Export Control Act, passed in 1976. It was not the first legislation to regulate the export of cryptography. In 1917, during the First World War, the Trading with the Enemy Act restricted the export of encryption technologies.[96] This was followed by the 1949 Export Control Act, and the Export Administration Act in 1969; the latter was the first attempt to balance the US' interests of national security and commerce.[97]

---

[90] Atkins et al., 1994.
[91] Adleman, 2016, 89:31.
[92] Levy, 2001, Slouching Toward Crypto, Chapter 9.
[93] Meyer, 1977.
[94] United States General Publishing Office, 1997, 329–330.

[95] United States National Archives and Records Administration, 1997.
[96] United States Congress, 1917.
[97] United States Congress, 1949 and 1969.

"Superficially," Meyer continued in his letter, "it seems like a small number of authors are providing most of the papers...They may not be aware of the full burden of government controls."[98] Meyer explained, "Unless clearances or export licenses are obtained from the State Department, or there is some special exemption, the IEEE could find itself in possible technical violation of the ITAR."[99] Meyer included the specific ITAR regulations in his correspondence, violation incurred up to ten years in prison and a substantial fine. Meyer additionally referenced a paper presented at IEEE's symposium in Sweden, to which export permission was not given; "apparently," Meyer noted, "this formality was skipped."[100] It was Hellman who presented the paper, though Meyer did not refer to him by name.[101] Meyer concluded, "I suggest that the IEEE might wish to review this situation, for these modern technologies, uncontrollably disseminated, could have more than academic effect."[102] He signed off with his IEEE membership number, but offered no organizational affiliation.

Gannet responded on July 20 stating the ITAR legislation, "places the burden of obtaining any required government approval for publication of technical data on the person or company seeking publication."[103] Gannet forwarded the letter onto Dr. Narendra P. Dwivedi, IEEE Director of Technical Activities. Dwivedi wrote to the Information Theory Group's Board of Governors, which included Hellman: "A concerned and good meaning member has drawn our attention to a possible violation by authors of ITAR regulations in some subjects which can be linked to be of possible military use."[104] Dwivedi warned whilst IEEE were exempt from the regulations, "individuals (and/or their employers) have to watch out."[105] Dwivedi recommended authors have their papers cleared by the State Department's Office of Munitions Control in advance of future publication.[106] The recipients of Dwivedi's letter may have thought that once the State Department saw their research, it could be classified before publication. "If you are beginning to feel that it is not always easy to carry out good-intentioned projects," Dwivedi concluded, "I welcome you to the club and wish you the best."[107] The tone suggests the incursion into academic freedoms was not appreciated.

Hellman took Dwivedi's letter to Stanford's general council, John Schwartz, for advice. As Hellman's employer, Stanford would share in the consequences of their Professor's actions. Hellman wanted to ensure that if he continued disseminating cryptologic knowledge, the University would cover any resultant legal costs or fines should the government prosecute, otherwise he could face bankruptcy.[108]

In a memo to Swartz, Hellman warned the threat to national security was from an absence of cryptography, not its propagation, "Although it is a remote possibility, the danger of initially inadvertent police state type surveillance through computerization

---

98 Ibid.
99 Ibid.
100 Ibid.
101 Hellman, 2009.
102 Meyer, 1977.
103 Gannet, 1977.

104 Hellman, 2009; Dwivedi, 1977.
105 Dwivedi, 1977.
106 Ibid.
107 Ibid.
108 Hellman and McGraw, 2016.

must be considered."[109] Hellman viewed his publications as a vital part of providing the cryptography society needed to protect itself. Hellman acknowledged during World War Two the cloak of secrecy guarding cryptology had been understandable. However, absent a hot war, and with the majority of businesses likely to be using computers within the decade, in a world without encryption Hellman foresaw a 'tremendous danger' to corporate secrets and individual privacy.[110] Hellman additionally explained when he tried to find out the cryptology topics he could avoid to prevent inadvertently stepping on NSA's toes, he was told such information was classified and offered no guidance.[111]

After considering Stanford's position, Schwartz replied to Hellman:

> It's my legal opinion that if the ITAR are construed broadly enough to cover a publication of your papers, it's unconstitutional, but, I've got to warn you, the only way to settle this is in a court case. So if you're prosecuted, we will defend you. If you're convicted, we'll appeal. But…if all appeals are exhausted, we can't go to jail for you.[112]

Hellman was advised if he were fined, Stanford could not pay, Swartz explained, "because now you've been adjudged a criminal. We can't aid and abet criminal conduct."[113] The personal stakes for Hellman, and any other academics studying cryptology, were high.

But who was J. A. Meyer? In 1971 Joseph Meyer wrote another article in IEEE's *Transactions on Aerospace and Electronic Systems* journal entitled *Crime Deterrent Transponder System*. The article explored placing surveillance trackers on criminals to deter them from conducting illegal acts. Meyer believed such a system would, "make crime pointless."[114] The journal's editors felt the article different enough to their usual mathematical fodder to add an introduction for the reader, "before you turn the page," the editors warned of the "controversial paper."[115] The article was appended with a biographical paragraph. Meyer was born in Newark, New Jersey in 1929.[116] He earned a Mathematics degree from Rutgers University before joining the Air Force in 1952; two years later he joined the Department of Defense working in, "mathematics, computers, and communications in the United States and overseas."[117] With such a background in combination with an article on electronic surveillance, it did not take a large leap to assume Meyer worked for the NSA.

"A group of university and industry scientists who are planning a symposium on cryptology have found themselves victims of a bizarre threat from an employee of the National Security Agency," wrote Deborah Shapley and Gina Kolata in a *Science* magazine article in September 1977.[118] The article increased the stakes for the NSA. The battle of DES taught Hellman the public spotlight was anathema to an agency accustomed to the shadows; shining a light onto his predicament was

---

109 Hellman, 1977.
110 Ibid.
111 Ibid.
112 Hellman and McGraw, 2016.
113 Plutte, 2011a, 6.

114 Meyer, 1971.
115 Ibid.
116 Ibid.
117 Ibid.
118 Shapley and Kolata, 1977, 1345.

perhaps the best form of insurance Hellman could acquire. Shapley and Kolata had investigated the mysterious Meyer and confirmed his identity as an NSA employee. Whilst the agency would not formally admit to Shapley and Kolata that Meyer worked for them, NSA spokesman Norman Boardman said, "I can state for the agency that we had nothing to do with that letter…Meyer wrote that letter as a private citizen."[119]

Hellman recounts whilst Meyer sent the letter from his home address, "portraying himself as a concerned citizen…his attempt at intimidation had many hallmarks of NSA"; such warning letters, Hellman notes, "written from home addresses, pseudonyms, and similar subterfuges were in keeping with its [the NSA's] *modus operandi*."[120] Hellman told *The Stanford Daily*, "They [NSA] never come right out and say 'stop what you're doing,'" and he viewed the letter as an "unwarranted intrusion on their part into my work."[121]

Hellman was scheduled to speak at the IEEE Symposium in New York on October 10. The Symposium was an open conference, with foreign attendees likely, meaning Hellman would be breaking ITAR as interpreted by Meyer. With the support of both his wife, Dorothie, and Stanford University, Hellman had "the confidence that we could go ahead and deliver the papers."[122] Risk remained to Hellman, but with Stanford's support and the involvement of sympathetic journalists fixing the spotlight on NSA's potential censorship attempts, Hellman proceeded with the conference. Hellman was to present two joint papers, each of them with separate graduate students, Ralph Merkle and Stephen Pohlig respectively. To help his students establish their reputations, Hellman's intent was to have them deliver the presentations. However, John Swartz warned that, as the students were not employees of Stanford University, they may not have the institution's support should the government press charges. Additionally, as a tenured professor with an established reputation as a global expert Hellman could endure a years-long legal battle, but two young men with nascent academic careers could unlikely prosper under such circumstances.[123] Merkle and Pohlig were at first defiant, insistent on delivering their work as originally planned. However, after contemplation and discussions with their families, they reluctantly allowed Hellman to present their papers.[124] In October 1977, Hellman, Merkle, and Pohlig arrived at the conference at Cornell University. Hellman delivered the papers, each time with his student standing next to him on the podium. Hellman explained the reason for his co-author's silence: "On the advice of Stanford's counsel, even though the student would normally give the paper, I will be giving it for him, but I want him to get the credit he deserves."[125] The papers were well received. Merkle and Pohlig gained even more attention, given the situation that if they presented the papers, and to Hellman's relief, he did not end the conference in handcuffs.[126]

---

[119] Ibid.
[120] Hellman, 2013, 1.
[121] Burr, 1977.
[122] Hellman, 2013; Plutte, 2011a, 6.
[123] Plutte, 2011a, 6.
[124] Ibid.
[125] Ibid.
[126] Hellman, 2013.

It was not only Diffie and Hellman impacted by Meyer's letter. Gardner's article resulted in thousands writing to MIT to request *Technical Memo Number 82* detailing the public key implementation method. Adleman recalls returning to MIT and finding, "the room is filled with self-addressed stamped envelopes. I look at some of them and they come from bizarre places like the Bulgarian secret police."[127] Gardner's article had global reach, and as a result the world was keen to learn how Rivest, Shamir, and Adleman proposed promoting Diffie and Hellman's cryptographic prophecy to reality. At the time Rivest was spending his summer on the West Coast, working at Xerox's Palo Alto Research Centre, a haven for technological intellectuals.[128] Hellman's office at Stanford was in close proximity. Rivest sent a copy of *Technical Memo Number 82* to Diffie and Hellman catalyzing a knowledge exchange that helped evolve the MIT group's ideas. Hellman shared Dwivedi's letter on cryptographic publishing with Rivest, knowing he was confronting the same challenges.[129]

The MIT trio were blissfully unaware of the politics surrounding cryptography whilst making their discovery. Rivest recalls Dwivedi's letter was "probably my first realization that our work might involve sensitivities."[130] Adleman says:

It was at that moment that I found out there was this agency called the NSA, and no one knew about this agency. At that time, not even people in government knew about it. Only a small number of legislators and presumably executives knew about it. And when they talked about it...they called it "No Such Agency."[131]

Adleman added, "I was still in a mode where I didn't understand that there had been this whole history of cryptography."[132] On learning about ITAR, Adleman was bemused: "Law? What law?" he asked, "What is this?"[133]

Rivest went to MIT's lawyers for advice. The legal experts instructed Rivest not to mail any copies of the technical memo until they assessed MIT's legal position.[134] Rivest recalls:

The requests for our paper were from all over the world, some were from foreign governments. It wasn't clear to me what we should do. When you receive this sort of ominous note from the NSA that this stuff is illegal, you want to be conservative and get it checked out.[135]

The penalty for mailing the letters out to their global audience was unclear—fines and jail time were possible. The lawyers could not offer definitive legal answers, but believed a "published materials" exemption in the ITAR, whereby the materials in question were already in some form of circulation, allowed publication of

127 Adleman, 2016, 78:51.
128 Levy, 2001, Prime Time, Chapter 4.
129 Ibid.
130 Ibid.
131 Adleman, 2016, 79:39.
132 Ibid, 76:43.
133 Ibid, 79:17.
134 Levy, 2001, Prime Time, Chapter 4.
135 Ibid.

the research—the NSA's response was ambiguous.[136] Shamir recalls, "As usual with NSA, it was hard to get any complete answer from them."[137]

It was six months after Gardner's article was published, in December 1977, the decision was finally taken to post the RSA papers. Rivest recalls, "MIT was very supportive in resolving that issue."[138] A pizza party was held at which graduate students squeezed Rivest, Shamir, and Adleman's *Technical Memo Number 82* into around seven thousand envelopes destined for recipients around the globe. Any last chance of NSA confining the genie to its bottle was lost.

Years later, Hellman came to believe that whilst "the highest echelons in NSA were extremely troubled by my publications," Meyer had acted of his own volition.[139] A 1977 Senate Select Committee investigation later found Meyer did not act at the behest of any government official, but rather "in his capacity as a member of the IEEE."[140] That assessment was supported when an internal NSA document written by their historian, Thomas Johnson, was declassified in 2009. Of Meyer the document stated, "he took matters into his own hands."[141] Given the climate of the time, and the secrecy of the NSA's methods, it is unsurprising Hellman was concerned the NSA were attempting to send a subtle message to undermine his activities. However, perhaps Meyer being so readily identified as an NSA employee should have indicated he was not operating as part of an elaborate subterfuge by an elite espionage agency.

5.9 GOVERNMENT CONCERNS OF ITAR AND EAR CONSTITUTIONALITY IN THE 1970S–80S

The constitutional deficiencies which had been identified by Stanford lawyers during the Meyer incident were known to the government. The ITAR was one of the key government tools used to control cryptography. John M. Harmon, Assistant Attorney General at the Justice Department's Office of Legal Counsel (OLC), issued a memo to Dr. Frank Press, science advisor to President Jimmy Carter, on the ITAR's constitutionality on May 11, 1978.[142] Harmon's memo was confined to the speech elements of cryptography, and the First Amendment implications of ITAR.[143] The memo would not make happy reading for the administration; the ITAR's definition of "export was recounted as:

> Whenever technical data is inter alia, mailed or shipped outside the United States, carried by hand outside the United States, disclosed through visits abroad by American citizens (including participation in briefings and symposia) and disclosed to foreign nationals in the United States (including plant visits and participation in briefings and symposia).[144]

---

[136] Ibid.
[137] Ibid.
[138] Rivest, 2012, 25:33.
[139] Hellman, 2013.
[140] United States Senate, 1978, 4.

[141] Johnson, no date, 235.
[142] Harmon, 1978.
[143] Ibid, 1.
[144] Ibid, 2–3.

Such a definition was assessed as "broad" by Harmon. Turning to the Arms Export Control Act itself, of which the ITAR was an instrument, Harmon commented:

> It is by no means clear from the language or legislative history…that Congress intended that the President regulate noncommercial dissemination of information, or considered the problems such regulation would engender. We therefore have some doubt whether…the Arms Export Control Act provides adequate authorization for the broad controls over public cryptography which the ITAR imposes.[145]

Not only did Harmon assess the Act was not being used for its intended purpose, but identified severe constitutional infirmities:

> The ITAR requirement of a license as a prerequisite to "exports" of cryptographic information clearly raises First Amendment questions of prior restraint. As far as we have been able to determine, the First Amendment implications of the ITAR have received scant judicial attention.[146]

Harmon stated the provisions also presented questions of overbreadth and vagueness, he explained:

> "Overbreadth" is a First Amendment doctrine invalidating statutes which encompass, in a substantial number of their applications, both protected and unprotected activity. The "vagueness" concept, on the other hand, originally derives from the due process guarantee, and applies where language of a statute is insufficiently clear to provide notice of the activity prohibited.[147]

The Supreme Court, Harmon noted, had "well established that prior restraints on publication are permissible only in extremely narrow circumstances and that the burden on the government of sustaining any such restraint is a heavy one."[148] Harmon explained that even if the:

> Government's interest in regulating the flow of cryptographic information is sufficient to justify some form of prior review process, the existing ITAR provisions we think fall short of satisfying the strictures necessary to survive close scrutiny under the First Amendment.[149]

The two "fundamental flaws" of the ITAR were the "issuance or denial of licenses are not sufficiently precise to guard against arbitrary and inconsistent administrative action," and, "there is no mechanism established to provide prompt judicial review of State Department decisions."[150] Harmon explained the government would need to "bear the burden" of justifying its decisions, and that the ITAR did not meet this requirement.[151] As a result of these deficiencies, Harmon assessed the ITAR

---

145 Ibid, 4.
146 Ibid, 5.
147 Ibid, 5.
148 Ibid, 9.
149 Ibid, 10–11.
150 Ibid.
151 Ibid.

was unconstitutional.[152] However, Harmon stated given the potential for cryptologic information "seriously and irremediably impairing" national security a prepublication submission scheme may be possible should a licensing scheme "provide clear, narrowly defined standards and procedural safeguards to prevent abuse," these safeguards must include judicial review.[153] Harmon indicated such a licensing scheme would require "explicit Congressional authorization," especially if such a scheme were to cover domestic as well as foreign disclosures.[154]

It would be during the House of Representatives' 1980 inquiry into the "Government's Classification of Private Ideas," chaired by Jack Brooks, that Harmon's assessment was finally exposed to the public. Tim Ingram, questioning Justice Department Attorney Miles Foy, asked:

How would I know, as a private litigant somehow ensnarled in the ITAR regulations, that I am being involved in a matter that the Justice Department, two years previously, has declared unconstitutional?

Foy conceded the opinion was intended to guide government policy rather than inform citizens, and therefore the citizens would not know of the Justice Department's assessment.[155]

The Justice Department's Theodore B. Olson reviewed the ITAR in 1981 and found Constitutional issues still remained with the regulations.[156] Olson was also responsible for a 1981 review of proposed revisions to the Export Administration Regulations, upon which the Commerce Department's Commerce Control List, used to regulate encryption the State Department deemed was not dual-use (this would later become mass-market encryption), was based. Olson judged the regulations to have a number of unconstitutional applications, and that they should therefore be substantially revised in order to meet the constitutional requirements.[157]

It would be during the second crypto war the ITAR would finally come under judicial scrutiny, but the government had many other weapons in their arsenal to allow them to manage cryptology—one of the most potent was the research funding provided to academics via the National Science Foundation.

5.10   THE NATIONAL SCIENCE FOUNDATION: THE CRYPTOLOGISTS' ACHILLES' HEEL?

The NSA were quickly finding their efforts to limit cryptographic research were being countered by the academics' increasingly savvy use of the media. The agency did not possess the leverage it held over private companies, such as IBM, who were recipients of large government contracts. The academics were a different breed. Their primary obligation was the discovery and dissemination of knowledge. Whilst the academics were also motivated to progress their own careers,

---

[152] Ibid.
[153] Ibid, 14.
[154] Ibid.

[155] Ibid.
[156] Olson, 1981b, 202.
[157] Olson, 1981a, 230.

this ambition was aligned to publishing their research, to not do so would severely limit their career opportunities. Professors such as Martin Hellman also held tenure at their prestigious establishments, meaning even if their institutions disagreed with their conflict with the government, it would be extremely difficult to remove them from their shielded positions as tenured professors. However, universities such as MIT and Stanford showed little sign of being cowed by the NSA. For the universities, there was also the possibility of sharing any revenue generated from the patent and business applications of their employees' discoveries. However, the academics possessed an Achilles' heel, that if exploited by the NSA, could provide leverage against them.

In 1950 the National Science Foundation (NSF) had been established as an independent agency to "promote the progress of science; to advance the national health, prosperity, and welfare; to secure the national defense; and for other purposes."[158] The NSF was one of the primary sources of funding for research conducted at elite universities, including in the fields of mathematics and computer science. This funding underwrote the cryptologic advances of the 1970s. Recipients of NSF funding included Diffie, Hellman, Rivest, Shamir, and Adleman. If the independence of the NSF were undermined, allowing the NSA to exert its will upon the funding process and those who received funds, the vast majority of individuals involved in non-government cryptologic research could potentially be brought under the NSA's influence. A clause could be inserted to funding grants allowing the NSA the option of classifying any resultant discoveries. If the process were part of a pre-agreed contractual arrangement, then no further justification would be needed from the NSA to classify research, and academics would unlikely have recourse to appeal.

In June 1975, NSF's Dr. Fred W. Weingarten, Director of Special Projects at the Division of Computing Research, was told by a grantee and NSA employee that the NSA "had sole statutory authority to fund research in cryptography, and, in fact, that other agencies are specifically enjoined from supporting that type of work."[159] Weingarten immediately suspended grants related to cryptographic research and wrote to NSF's general counsel for advice.[160] The NSF legal advisors were unable to find any correlating legislation, so Assistant General Counsel Jesse E. Lasken called NSA's lawyers who also found no such legislation. Weingarten resumed funding cryptographic research.[161]

By April 1977, there was no ambiguity that the NSA were attempting to influence NSF. Thirty-five-year NSA veteran, Assistant Deputy for Communications Security Cecil Corry, and his assistant David G. Boak traveled to NSF's Washington headquarters to meet with Weingarten. On the agenda was the NSF's support for cryptographic research. Corry, second in command at NSA, swiftly informed Weingarten that an unspecified Presidential Directive provided the agency with "control" of all cryptologic work, and that in granting funding for research in this area the NSF were violating that directive. Weingarten explained the incident of several years earlier,

---

158 United States Senate and House of Represen- 160 Ibid.
    tatives, 1950.   161 Ibid, 763.
159 United States House of Representatives, 1980,
    762.

and that both NSF and NSA lawyers were unable to locate such a directive. An NSA representative "mumbled that they would have to get such a law passed." Corry suggested the NSA and NSF "coordinate" the review process for cryptologic funding applications. Weingarten agreed to send NSA copies of applications for grants, in part because only their agency had the cryptographic talent to fully assess the proposal's technical virtue. However, Weingarten added under no circumstances would the NSF take advice from the NSA should they make recommendations absent justifications—the NSF would not yield to advice such as to "not fund this research, but we cannot tell you why." The NSF would continue to bestow cryptographic funding on the basis of their scientific merit alone, and should the NSA be able to provide fully documented reasons for refusing a grant based on that criteria, the NSF would consider the NSA's recommendations as part of the assessment process.[162]

After their meeting Corry wrote to Weingarten's boss, John R. Paster, Director of the Division of Mathematical and Computer Science at the NSF, to express gratitude "for your willingness to cooperate with us in considering the security implications of grant applications in this field."[163] The message must have taken Weingarten and Paster by some surprise given this was contrary to the position NSF had clearly articulated. Paster sent a message back clarifying what had been agreed, and further stating any review the NSA made of proposals would become part of the public record.[164]

In an internal NSF memo Weingarten observed, "NSA is in a bureaucratic bind... NSA is worried... public domain security research will compromise some of their work...they seem to want to maintain their control and corner a bureaucratic expertise in this field."[165] Weingarten was also concerned about NSA supremacy within the cryptologic domain:

It seems clear that turning such a huge domestic responsibility, potentially involving such activities as banking, the US mail, and cable television, to an organization such as NSA should be done only after the most serious debate at higher levels of government than represented by peanuts like me.[166]

Finally, Weingarten considered the future relations between the NSA and NSF, "no matter what one's views about the role of NSA in government, it is inescapable that NSF relations with them be formal. Informal agreements regarding support of areas of research or individual projects need to be avoided."[167] It had only taken a few interactions with NSA for Weingarten to develop an acute sense of the wider context of their requests, and their apparent willingness to deploy subterfuge, such as referencing seemingly non-existent presidential directives, in order to achieve their ambitions.

The battle for academic freedom to publish was only just starting in 1977. At almost the same time, Meyer was penning his letter to the IEEE a new director was

---

[162] Ibid, 764.
[163] Ibid, 767.
[164] Ibid, 768.

[165] Ibid, 765.
[166] Ibid.
[167] Ibid.

taking office at the NSA, a director who would step out of the shadows to argue the future for which the academics were advocating would place US national security at risk.

5.11 THE CRYPTOGRAPHIC INFORMATION PROTECTION ACT AND A NEW NSA DIRECTOR

Vice Admiral Bobby Inman rose rapidly through the ranks of the defense establishment to command, at the age of forty-seven, the NSA and their annual budget exceeding a billion dollars.[168] During the early years of his career, Inman spent three years posted to NSA as a SIGINT analyst.[169] In subsequent roles, including that of director of naval intelligence, Inman was a significant consumer of NSA product, making him intimately familiar with the dividends of NSA's cryptologic prowess when he became NSA director in July 1977.[170] However, during Inman's handover briefing from outgoing director Lewis Allen, the subject of public cryptography was not discussed, and Inman had never heard of the ITAR.[171]

Inman entered a rapidly changing environment. The conflict between academic researchers and the government was entering a new, more public phase. It was only a day after Inman assumed his role as director that NSA employee Joseph Meyer wrote to the IEEE warning against publishing cryptologic studies; Rivest, Shamir, and Adleman had just made their discovery turning a public cryptosystem from a theoretical possibility to a practical inevitability, and an academic journal dedicated to cryptology, *Cryptologia*, had just launched. Among *Cryptologia's* founders was the eternal thorn in NSA's side: David Kahn.[172] Writers at *Science* magazine and *The New York Times* in particular were ensuring the scholars had a megaphone through which to project their frustrations with government policy. Whilst many academics reiterated the need for cryptography to protect privacy, they equally were using the language of commerce to appeal to a broader audience. Government actions restricting the global expansion of the American technology sector would be much harder to justify than actions to restrict privacy in favor of security. The NSA was still by far the dominant cryptologic power, but even a casual observer could extrapolate the direction of travel, and Inman was an elite officer at the head of an elite spy agency— he understood a new strategy was required.

Declassified NSA documents show following the controversy of the Meyer incident, Inman ordered a study of the challenges external cryptologic advances presented, and solution possibilities. Inman's staff offered three options. Firstly, they could do nothing, as further "public discussion would heighten awareness of cryptographic problems and could lead to nations buying more secure crypto devices," in particular they were concerned about this occurring in the "third world." Secondly,

168 Shapley, 1978b, 407.
169 Johnson, no date, 190.
170 United States House of Representatives, 1980, 423.

171 Levy, 2001, Prime Time, Chapter 4; United States House of Representatives, 1980, 425.
172 Cipher A. Deavours, Louis Kruth, and Brian J. Winkel were the other co-founders.

NSA could seek new legislation to strengthen their ability to manage public cryptology. A final option was to "try non legislative means such as voluntary commercial and academic compliance." Inman chose legislation. The head of NSA's legal team, David Silver, circulated a draft proposal of a new Cryptographic Information Protection Act. As part of the act a new entity, the US Cryptological Board would be created to "restrict dissemination of sensitive cryptological material for up to five years." The board would have the power to impose "severe penalties" for violation of the act, including five years in prison and a ten-thousand-dollar fine.[173]

However, the decision did not stand. Inman subsequently recognized it was unlikely the Cryptographic Information Protection Act would pass through Congress.[174] Declassified documents observe, "NSA's proposed legislation would run against a strong movement in the opposite direction in both Congress and the White House, where the desire was to unshackle US commerce from any sort of Pentagon-imposed restriction on trade."[175] The 1970s had not been kind to the American intelligence apparatus—the agencies' reputations were decimated by several public inquiries, most notably that of Senator Frank Church. Whilst the NSA's new cryptologic legislation was being discussed at Fort Meade, President Carter, installed in the White House since January 1977, had issued Presidential Directive 24 (PD24), the administration's National Telecommunications Protection Policy.

PD24 clearly indicated the executive desired increased protections across the communication spectrum. As well as providing protection for classified communications, the directive instructed, "Non-governmental information that would be useful to an adversary shall be identified and the private sector informed of the problem and encouraged to take appropriate measures."[176] The Directive stated, "the responsible agencies should work with the FCC [Federal Communications Commission] and the common carriers to adopt system capabilities that protect the privacy of individual communications."[177] Furthermore, PDP24 indicated, "the laws which protect against criminal domestic acts such as wiretaps or intercept shall be strictly enforced"—whether this statement was aimed at federal agencies, or the general public, is unknown.[178] PD24 also assigned responsibility for "commercial application of cryptographic technology," not to the Defense Department, the NSA's parent body, nor to the State Department where the ITAR powers resided, but to the Commerce Department, the federal apparatus' economic hub.[179] There was no mention of the control of cryptology in the directive, despite its signatory being Zbigniew Brzezinski, Carter's National Security Advisor.

Within the context of PD24, the media battles over cryptologic policy, and the numerous congressional inquiries of recent years, Inman withdrew his decision of pursuing legislation to limit cryptology in favor of working with the academics to try to find a compromise solution to satisfy both parties. But, before Inman could

---

[173] Johnson, no date, 236.
[174] Ibid.
[175] Ibid.
[176] United States House of Representatives, 1980, 710.
[177] Ibid.
[178] United States Department of Justice, 1978, 710.
[179] Ibid, 712.

launch his charm offensive, two incidents took place that further damaged the NSA's reputation.

5.12 NSA CLASSIFIES CRYPTOGRAPHIC INVENTIONS

In October 1977, Professor George Davida of the University of Wisconsin applied, under the banner of the Wisconsin Alumni Research Foundation, to patent a device he and colleague David Wells created to apply a mathematical algorithm to produce stream ciphers.[180] Davida's work, like many other academics, was funded by the National Science Foundation. For half a year, there was silence from the patent office until April 1978, when a secrecy order was issued.[181]

Davida was not alone, that same day another secrecy was issued to a small group of West Coast inventors, led by Carl Nicolai.[182] For five months, Nicolai's group had waited for a patent to be granted on their "phasorphone"—a voice scrambler allowing encryption of citizen band radios and telephones.[183] The group estimated their device would sell for around one-hundred dollars and would have a large commercial market.[184]

The Invention Secrecy Act (ISA) became law during 1917 as a wartime measure designed to prevent the publication of inventions that may "be detrimental to the public safety or defense or might assist the enemy or endanger the successful prosecution of the war."[185] The Act ceased at the end of the war, though was reactivated during World War Two; when hostilities concluded, the ISA again expired.[186] However, by 1951, the law had been reactivated. It was this legislation being used against Davida, Wells, and Nicolai.

Werner Baum, Chancellor of the Milwaukee campus of Wisconsin University, hearing of the secrecy order placed upon Davida, wrote to NSF Director Richard C. Atkinson arguing:

> At the very least, an effort should be made to develop minimal due process guarantees for individuals who are threatened with a secrecy order. The burden of proof should be on the government to show why a citizen's constitutional rights must be abridged in the interests of "national security."[187]

Baum suggested a judge, rather than an "unknown defense agency," should determine the validity of the government's claims.[188] Without such a mechanism, Baum told Atkinson, "both individual rights and scientific research may suffer irreparable damage."[189] Baum contacted Commerce Secretary Juanita Kreps to inform her of the threat to both research and business as a result of the government's actions.[190]

---

[180] Shapley, 1978b, 407.
[181] Shapley, 1978a, 141.
[182] Ibid.
[183] Levy, 2001, Prime Time, Chapter 4.
[184] Kahn, 1979, 155.
[185] United States Congress, 1942, 1224.

[186] Bamford, 1982, 446.
[187] Shapley, 1978a, 141.
[188] Ibid.
[189] Ibid.
[190] United States House of Representatives, 1980, 415.

Baum also won the support of Senator Warren Magnuson.[191] Baum enlisted Deborah Shapley of *Science* magazine to help spread word of the NSA's attempts to prevent encryption reaching the masses. Baum told *Science* magazine the government's approach was reminiscent of McCarthy-era tactics against universities, and challenged the constitutionality of the ISA: "How can some unknown bureaucrat classify an individual's research activity without any justification or due process?" he asked in the article. Davida explained he was instructed by the secrecy order not to write about, or discuss the principles of his design. Davida told Shapley the secrecy order, "was worded so broadly, it could have meant that I couldn't talk about any of the mathematical theory underlying cryptography or my related research."[192]

At first, the NSA did not comment on the case. However, Inman later argued academic freedom was not being challenged, "there was a campaign that the imposition of the secrecy order interfered with the academic freedom of the investigators. I think that was a bum rap and I so told the Chancellor [Baum]." Inman argued, "if the individual had elected to publish in academic journals there would have been no question of a secrecy order," it was only as Davida sought a patent, and to profit financially, that such a secrecy order was possible. In what could have been interpreted as a concession, Inman stated, "we're going to be dialoguing with the Commerce and Defense departments over whether the existing procedures are adequate." The NSA director suggested there was room for improvement in the process, stating, "Baum told me that Davida got a cold postcard in the mail...you ought to be able to tell a person why the order is being imposed."[193]

The secrecy order against Davida was lifted on June 13. Inman commented its issuing was a "bureaucratic error," that the information in question had already appeared in the open media, so it was not possible to issue a classification order. Inman also spoke of the process of dealing with such issues at NSA. Secrecy order decisions were taken at a "middle-management" level, and, like in all government, it was easy to classify, but very hard to challenge whether such an action was justified. Inman said secrecy order decisions would in future go through a senior committee as a safeguard against errors.[194]

That revised NSA process for issuing secrecy orders was established when Nicolai's invention was reviewed. Inman acknowledged he himself ordered Nicolai's secrecy order:

> there was disagreement amongst the reviewing principles as to whether it merited classification or not. And, given the disagreement, I elected to ask for the secrecy order... where there is uncertainty I believe we should err on the side of national security.[195]

The NSA offered to pay Nicolai damages in compensation for their classification of his invention, but Nicolai cut all communications with the NSA.[196] The inventor told an Associated Press reporter that his secrecy order:

---

[191] Bamford, 1982, 449.
[192] Shapley, 1978a, 141.
[193] Shapley, 1978b, 407-408.
[194] Ibid, 407.
[195] Ibid, 409.
[196] Ibid.

appears part of a general plan by NSA to limit the privacy of the American people...
they've been bugging people's telephones for years and now someone comes along
with a device that makes this a little harder to do and they oppose this under the guise
of national security.[197]

On October 11, the secrecy order against Nicolai's invention was revoked. The NSA
did not state what prompted the withdrawal. Inman did, however, tell Shapley he
believed in both cases the inventors used the press to manipulate the NSA; he commented that Davida, "was very bright and realized that if you go to the media you
are likely to get the attention of the top faster than through routine appeals." Both
Davida and Nicolai denied approaching the press. Davida stated that the reporters
who approached him after the secrecy order's imposition already knew he was not at
liberty to speak about his invention.[198]

In testimony to US Congress in 1980, Inman reflected his agency's actions were
"a well-meaning attempt to hold the line that had clearly already been passed," he
stated the decisions were made "in the heat of battle," and that "from dealing day
to day with the Invention Secrecy Act, you have to make snap decisions."[199] Inman
defended the ISA itself, arguing the problems arose not from "a faulty law but inadequate government attention to its application."[200] Inman revealed when he took control of the agency, two-hundred and fifty-seven NSA secrecy orders were in effect.[201]
By the time of the hearing, Inman had reduced that number to seven, of those six
dated from the 1930s, and the last he believed was from 1967.[202] NSF's general counsel, Charles H. Herz, would also later comment, "Maybe patents aren't the best way
to police this thing [academic research]...anything in a patent that arises from university research has probably already been published."[203]

5.13 THE SKY IS FALLING: NSA ENGAGE ACADEMIA
AND TAKE THEIR MESSAGE PUBLIC

Inman's first major public engagement was in October 1978. *Science* magazine had
been the chief amplifier for the discontent academic cryptographers, it was this publication to which Inman awarded his first interview.

Deborah Shapley interviewed Inman who explained his aspiration to engage in a
dialogue with the academic community. Inman wanted to explore the implications of
cryptologic research, and discuss the circumstances which could lead to academics'
work becoming classified. Inman explained, "one motive I have in this first interview
is to find a way into some thoughtful discussion of what can be done between the two
extremes of 'that's classified' and 'that's academic freedom.'" Inman told Shapley,
"as we have moved into burgeoning public interest in public cryptography, a substantial volume of unfavorable publicity has occurred with no counterbalance...to point

---

[197] Ibid, 410.
[198] Ibid, 408–410.
[199] United States House of Representatives, 1980,
425.
[200] Ibid.
[201] Ibid, 430.
[202] Ibid.
[203] Shapley, 1978a, 141.

out that there are valid national security concerns." Inman admitted he was troubled by such coverage as "it could hurt our [the NSA's] ability to recruit and retain some of the brightest talent...we can't afford to leave an impression in the academic world of being a devious or bumbling bureaucracy."[204]

Shapley wrote that during the interview Inman "implied, but did not promise, that the administration might propose legislation on the issue in the coming months." Inman explained, "By the time we get through there will be a vast array of people in the executive drawn into this. There will be a debate between the administration and the academic community."[205]

The response to the Director's engagement with the public was positive. Senator Frank Church welcomed the speech, "We must strive to find a proper balance between governmental accountability and executive secrecy. This interview would seem to be another step in that direction."[206] The Chief Counsel during Church's inquiries, F.A.O. Schwatz, was amazed at the Director's interview noting, "back when we dealt with the NSA they considered it dangerous to have even senators questioning them in closed session."[207]

Inman traveled to universities to take his message directly to the scholars in what David Kahn called a "soft sell to get them to lay off."[208] Upon his visit to Berkley, Inman recalls, "for an hour, it was a dialogue of the deaf," with the faculty until the vice president of the university, Michael Heyman, asked what the solution would be if they did accept the Admiral's premise that national security was being endangered by cryptologic research.[209] From that point, according to a declassified NSA document, the debate was "a rational discussion of compromises."[210] The faculty requested an "honest broker" to explore the issue further.[211] In a later meeting between Inman and NSF Director Richard Atkinson, the American Council of Education was suggested as such a body; Atkinson agreed the NSF would fund a study group on options to accommodate cryptologic research whilst balancing the requirement of national security.[212]

Inman also called Martin Hellman to request a meeting. "He actually initiated the contact against the better advice of everyone else at NSA," Hellman says.[213] When they met, Inman joked, "It's nice to see you don't have horns," leading Hellman to believe, "NSA must have depicted me as a devil." Hellman returned the same comment to Inman, having long seen himself as the Luke Skywalker to the NSA Director's Darth Vadar.[214] Inman recalls he liked Hellman, and comments, "I think he [Hellman] was impressed that I had driven down to see him."[215] Hellman commented, "Inman is a very thinking individual and we got to know each other."[216] Whilst their relationship was cautious at first, Hellman recounts the two developed

---

[204] Shapley, 1978b, 407.
[205] Ibid.
[206] Levy, 2001, Prime Time, Chapter 4.
[207] Ibid.
[208] United States House of Representatives, 1980, 413.
[209] Johnson, no date, 237.
[210] Ibid, 238.
[211] Ibid, 237.
[212] Ibid.
[213] Plutte, 2011a, 6.
[214] Hellman and Hellman, 2016, 53.
[215] Levy, 2001, Prime Time, Chapter 4.
[216] Plutte, 2011a, 6.

a "friendship as we came to appreciate one another's concerns."[217] They agreed to work together to progress the dialogue between academia and the government.[218]

In January 1979, Bobby Inman spoke at a gathering of the Armed Forces Communications and Electronics Association —it was the first time an NSA Director had ever made such an appearance. Inman's speech opened by addressing the covenant of secrecy he was violating: "A public address by an incumbent Director of the National Security Agency on a subject relating to the Agency's mission is an event which—if not of historic proportions—is at least, to my knowledge, unprecedented."[219] Inman assured the audience that his agency "serves the government and the people of the United States extraordinarily well in its performance," and such service has rested "on maintaining a high degree of secrecy about all aspects of its intelligence mission…consequently, the agency has traditionally engaged in secrecy to an extraordinary extent."[220] Inman explained, "Until recently, the agency enjoyed the luxury of relative obscurity. Generally unknown to the public and largely uncontroversial, NSA was able to perform its vital functions without reason for public scrutiny or public dialogue," he recalled nostalgically, "NSA's particular field of technical mastery, cryptology, was of little public interest, except for a few hobbyists and historians."[221] However, Inman acknowledged the situation had changed:

> One result of these changes is that the agency's mission no longer can remain entirely in the shadows…There is a very real risk that in the absence of a prompt and serious effort to confront and resolve these issues, damage will be done to the national security.[222]

Inman explained in stepping from the shadows he was, "striving to open up a dialogue." Inman hoped, "such a dialogue will lead to better understanding by all parties and eventually to the development of an approach to the problem in which the legitimate interests on all sides can be accommodated." The Director expressed his wishes to, "earnestly solicit your views and your help over the coming months and years." Inman stated he was "not saying that all nongovernmental cryptologic activity is undesirable," in fact he believed in "advancing the state of the cryptographic art in ways beneficial to both public and private interests."[223]

The Director turned to the public perception of his organization:

> the Agency's role has been widely misrepresented…NSA's actions were attacked as an attempt to prevent the American public from enjoying telecommunications protection so as to permit NSA to intercept domestic communications. Nothing could be further from the truth. NSA has no interest in, and indeed is legally precluded from intercepting domestic communications. These legal restrictions, formerly imposed by executive order, have been embodied in the recently passed Foreign Intelligence Surveillance Act [FISA] of 1978.[224]

---

[217] Hellman and Hellman, 2016, 54.
[218] Levy, 2001, Prime Time, Chapter 4.
[219] Inman, 1979, 129.
[220] Ibid.

[221] Ibid, 130.
[222] Ibid.
[223] Ibid, 130–131.
[224] Ibid, 131–133.

Regarding the NSA's involvement in the DES project, Inman stated the agency was the subject of "untrue and irresponsible allegations," and that allegations of the agency weakening the algorithm were "totally false." Inman stated, "The implausibility of the public allegations is further demonstrated by the fact NSA has endorsed the use of DES for the encryption of national security-related information, including selected classified information."[225]

Regarding allegations of suppression of academia, Inman reiterated Joseph Meyer's letter was an "unfortunate incident" and referenced the Senate Select Committee, who Inman says, "found that the letter in question was entirely a personal initiative, had not been sponsored by the agency, and did not represent any attempt by the agency to inhibit scholarly activity." Inman also refuted the NSA exerted any undue influence over the NSF, "While NSA does play a peer review role with respect to such [cryptological] applications…that role has been limited to commenting on the technical merits of the proposal."[226]

Inman acknowledged the "ambiguities in the definitional provisions of the ITAR could be viewed as inhibiting international scholarly exchanges on matters relating to cryptology." Additionally, Inman stated, "Another ambiguity in the regulation could be viewed as imposing a requirement of prior governmental review on domestic scholarly publications." The NSA had raised these potential interpretations with the executive and Inman reported, "As a result of NSA initiatives, I understand that the Office of Munitions Control is reviewing the matter, and, if appropriate, will issue a clarifying statement."[227]

Inman stated that the aggregated coverage of alleged NSA counter-cryptography activities:

> paint a false picture of NSA as exerting some kind of all-powerful secret influence all over the government from behind closed doors. I can assure you from eighteen months experience that this is far from reality. The truth is that the legal resources of the Federal Government to control potentially harmful nongovernmental cryptologic activity are sparse.[228]

Inman stated rather than having too much power to control cryptological activities, his concern was that "the government has too little."[229] Whilst the ITAR did prevent the export of harmful cryptologic equipment and technical information, Inman stated that the other key legislation, the Inventions Secret Act, offers only a "very limited" possibility of classifying potentially harmful inventions.[230] Inman explained, "I say 'very limited' because the Act applies only if an application for patent is made and, obviously, is effective only to the extent public disclosure has not already occurred before the secrecy order is issued."[231] The Director stated:

---

[225] Ibid, 132.
[226] Ibid, 132–133.
[227] Ibid.
[228] Ibid.

[229] Ibid, 134.
[230] Ibid, 133–134.
[231] Ibid.

In sponsoring secrecy orders under the Inventions Secrecy Act, the Agency's sole considerations is the detrimental effect on the agency's mission, and thus on the security of the United States, that would result from the proliferation abroad of sophisticated cryptological technology.[232]

For both powers, Inman pointed out, "NSA plays a technical advisory role but is not the final decision-making authority."[233] Inman warned:

Application of the genius of the American scholarly community to cryptographic and cryptanalytic problems, and widespread dissemination of resulting discoveries, carry the clear risk that some of NSA's cryptanalytic successes will be duplicated, with a consequent improvement of cryptography by foreign targets.[234]

Inman was also concerned the devices NSA developed for secure US government communications would be "rendered ineffective by parallel nongovernmental cryptologic activity and publication." Inman concluded, "I have a deep conviction that the…missions entrusted to the Agency are in peril." Inman continued, "While I cannot go into further detail without exposing matters that must remain secret, I can tell you that I have not lightly accepted the position that unrestrained nongovernmental cryptologic activity poses a threat to the national security."[235]

Inman commented that NSA's concerns "should not lead to the conclusion that nongovernmental cryptologic endeavor must somehow be halted. I think such a step would be a disservice to everyone." Inman's position on export controls was clear: regulations should be strengthened on the transferring of cryptologic equipment and supporting technical information. Nonetheless, Inman conceded, "At the same time, it should be clarified, and will be, so as to leave unfettered the free flow of basic research and scientific information among scholars in different countries."[236]

Inman's position on internal restrictions was more complex. The Director stated that any restrictions placed on domestic dissemination of cryptologic knowledge would have to meet several criteria, including:

• The restriction should apply only to a central core of critical cryptological information that is likely to have a discernible adverse impact on National Security
• Law and regulations should make these criteria as clear as is possible without revealing information damaging to the National Security
• The burden of proof in imposing any restriction on dissemination should be borne by the government
• There should be judicial review of any such government action, perhaps by a specially constituted court that could act under suitable security precautions

---

232 Ibid, 133.
233 Ibid.
234 Ibid, 134.

235 Ibid.
236 Ibid.

- There should be full, fair and prompt compensation for any company or person losing the economic benefit of information by virtue of government-imposed restrictions on dissemination[237]

Inman stated that it was for the executive to consider further legislation, though such considerations should take place immediately.[238]

Inman concluded, "In the coming months, NSA will be undertaking discussions with the industrial and scholarly communities for purposes of better understanding the diverse points of view to be found in the private sector, and…of stimulating consideration of alternative possible solutions," also adding a plea for cooperation: "I solicit your participation in this process."[239]

In the following days and weeks, Inman's address would become known as the "sky is falling" speech, on account of his fears of the harm cryptography could impose upon national security, and that his agency was absent of the tools to confront resulting threats.[240]

Inman later reflected the dialogue with academia was proceeding well as a result of his outreach. Inman commented the two sides were exploring regulations, not necessarily legislation, to achieve both parties' aims. Inman noted, "we deliberately on both sides, have not sought publicity for that effort because we were eager to let the dialog continue without the need to posture in public from either side." Inman said academia was keen to engage rather than have a "fait accompli" imposed upon their community—he was optimistic progress could be achieved.[241]

5.14 PUBLIC CRYPTOGRAPHY STUDY GROUP AND THE VOLUNTARY REVIEW SYSTEM

In order to further the academic dialogue Inman desired, a Public Cryptography Study Group[242] was established under the auspices of the American Council on Education and funded by the NSF. The group comprised individuals recommended by the elite technical and academic bodies of America, included several people who had previously clashed with the NSA, such as George Davida, Werner Baum, and Martin Hellman. The NSA was represented by their general counsel, Daniel Schwartz. Between March 1980 and February 1981, the study group deliberated potential options to continue "the tradition that scholarly publication should be free from restrictions," whilst minimizing the consequential impact on the NSA's national security mission.[243]

---

[237] Ibid, 134–135.
[238] Ibid.
[239] Ibid.
[240] Bamford, 1982, 452.
[241] United States House of Representatives, 1980, 426.

[242] The name should not be confused with public key cryptography, it is used in this application to denote that the public and government were involved in the study.
[243] American Council on Education, 1981, 131.

The Study Group's report outlined a number of points they considered during their deliberations. The report noted there remained disagreement within the government itself, with the Commerce Department assessing, "the availability of technical data that are of significance to U.S. national security and foreign policy interests is likely to be minor," whilst the Departments of Defense and State, "continued to emphasize the need to effectively control technical data."[244]

The report considered the implications of the First Amendment noting, the freedom of speech and expression provisions in the constitution were generally, "opposed to both pre- and post-publication restraints."[245] Whilst the authors noted historically opposition to censorship regarding political or social thought was strongest, courts, "have assumed without debate that information of a technological or scientific nature is subject to first amendment protection."[246] The study group commented freedom of expression is historically related to four traditional and interrelated values:

1. Individual self-fulfillment
2. The advance of knowledge and the discovery of truth
3. Participation in decision making by all members of society
4. Maintenance of the proper balance between stability and change[247]

The authors commented, "writings on cryptology are closely related to first and second, if not also to third and fourth. That speech falls within the protection of the First Amendment, however, does not mean that it cannot be regulated."[248]

When considering possible solutions to the cryptology conundrum, the group rejected any statutory solution, for reasons including:

- The group were unable to validate the severity of the threat to national security, nor the economic or social impact of a pre-publication statutory review process
- Defining the scope of cryptological knowledge to be covered would be challenging
- Any such legislation would be against the "legal and political history of the First Amendment"
- Any system of prior review would be much more successful if researchers supported the system; a statutory approach was unlikely to generate such support[249]

Whilst the study group did not feel they could quantify the damage cryptologic publishing could cause, they did accept "as a working premise Admiral Inman's concerns that some information contained in some articles…could be inimical to the national security." As a potential solution, the group recommended a "non-statutory

---

244 Ibid, 134.   247 Ibid.
245 Ibid, 135.   248 Ibid.
246 Ibid, 136.   249 Ibid, 138.

system designed to test on an ongoing basis Admiral Inman's hypothesis, which depends for its success on the voluntary cooperation of those whom NSA might seek to regulate."[250]

The voluntary solution would include an "advisory committee cleared to a level that enables it to test adequately our working premise on an on-going basis."[251] The group highlighted the challenge such a system, devoid of legal powers to implement their will, would provide to the NSA:

> The implementation of this system will require that NSA convince authors and publishers of its necessity, wisdom and reasonableness. We believe that NSA will be able to be convincing if it establishes a record in its dialogues and administration that evidence sensitivity, narrow application and remedies, and a sense of reasonableness to those who are asked to cooperate.[252]

The study group commented whilst NSA would have to convince researchers to engage, they believed "many researchers would welcome an opportunity to find out in advance whether what they plan to publish would directly and substantially risk compromising national security interests."[253]

The authors outlined the following six steps of their proposed voluntary submission system:

1. NSA notifies cryptological community of its desire to review manuscripts prior to publication
2. NSA and technical societies define as accurately as possible the criteria for the types of cryptological data it wishes to review
3. NSA invites academics to submit manuscripts prior to publication
4. NSA assures prompt responses to submissions and would provide explanations, to the greatest degree possible, of any requested alterations or deletions
5. Where there were disagreements, NSA provides an opportunity for prompt review by the advisory committee (comprised of two people appointed by the NSA Director, and three people appointed by the science advisor to the President, who in turn would select their appointees from a list provided by the President of the National Academy of Science). The committee would provide recommendations to the NSA Director

The final step was written to accentuate the voluntary aspect: "There would be a clear understanding that submission to the process is voluntary and neither authors nor publishers will be required to comply with suggestions or restrictions urged by NSA."[254]

---

[250] Ibid, 138–139.
[251] Ibid, 139.
[252] Ibid.
[253] Ibid.
[254] Ibid, 139–140.

There was a single dissent from the group: George Davida, who wrote:

> While the PCSG has retreated from recommending model legislation, its actions are still troublesome. The very recommendations that restraints be put into effect, even if voluntary, is dangerous. There already is talk of a trial period to see if the NSA is happy about the outcome.[255]

Davida continued implying that if the researchers did not comply in full as part of the voluntary system there was "clear indication...legislation will be sought."[256] Davida attempted to undermine the recommendations of the study group by attacking whether the constituent members were qualified to advise on the topic: "The majority of the committee members are not researchers in data security or cryptography or computer science or engineering."[257] Davida concluded, "I find NSA's effort to control cryptography to be unnecessary, divisive, wasteful, and chilling. The NSA can perform its mission to the old-fashioned way: STAY AHEAD OF OTHERS."[258] Despite Davida's objections, the voluntary review system was adopted shortly after the public cryptography study group issued their recommendation.

Michael Heyman, Chancellor of Berkley, believed only some people would submit to the voluntary system to start with, however:

> if the people who go along with it think they're being handled decently by NSA, and that very few requests are being made and they're minimal kinds of requests that seem reasonable under the circumstances, then I would expect that more people would join in.[259]

A declassified NSA document reveals as the system progressed, "the committee requested very few changes to proposals, and most of these were easily accomplished." The document also states the NSA believed the prepublication review process turned out to be "less of a real than an imagined threat to First Amendment freedoms."[260]

5.15 ADLEMAN RECEIVES FUNDING FROM AN UNWANTED SOURCE

In the midst of the Public Cryptography Study Group's review, another incident occurred to further damage the NSA's reputation.

Once again, *Science* magazine was at the nexus of the debate. In mid-August 1980, Gina Kolata received a telephone call from Leonard Adleman, the "A" from RSA. Adleman recalls his words to Kolata: "Here's a story you might be interested in," he told the reporter. "The NSF, you know the leading sponsor of pure research in our country, and the NSA, you know that secret agency that does intelligence

---

[255] Davida, 1981, 147.

[256] Ibid.

[257] Ibid, 148.

[258] Ibid.

[259] Dembart, 1981.

[260] Johnson, no date, 238.

work...they seem to be collaborating now."[261] Adleman explained to Kolata that researchers periodically have to apply for funding from agencies such as the NSF. Over the previous months, he had been going through the "ritual dance" when he received a call from Bruce Barnes at the NSF on August 14. Barnes said, "Love your stuff, Len. We're going to fund it. Oh, by the way, the National Security Agency is going to fund that part involving cryptography."[262] Adleman replied, "I didn't submit a proposal to the NSA, I submitted it to the NSF, right?" Barnes answered, "It's an interagency matter."[263] Adleman recalls, "In my mind this threatened the whole mission of a university, and its place in society."[264]

Kolata was interested and published *Cryptography: A New Clash Between Academic Freedom and National Security: NSA Seeks To Influence Science Policy* the following week.[265] Kolata wrote:

> Ever since academic scientists took an interest in cryptography, they have had the feeling that the NSA was breathing down their necks. They have been told that their work may threaten national security and that it may be necessary to institute prior restraints on their research.[266]

In the article Adleman stated, "In the present climate, I would not accept funds from the NSA," since he was worried any implicit commitments such an acceptance could entail, such as giving control of his research to the Agency; would they be able to simply classify his findings, and if he refused would his funding cease? Adleman referred to the NSA-NSF collaboration as "a very frightening collusion between the agencies." Ron Rivest also worried about NSA's mission creep beyond purely cryptologic research, he explained that Adleman's research, "has to do with a fundamental understanding of what it means for a computation to be hard or easy." Rivest told Kolata, "I'm shocked, what worries me is that the line [between what is and what is not cryptology] is being pushed in a way that affects our ability to do basic computer science research."[267]

The day after Adleman called Kolata, he received another call, from Bobby Inman himself. Inman told Adleman there had been a misunderstanding, but Adleman did not want to engage, he recalls thanking the NSA Director for the call, but told him, "I think this is probably something that's going to be worked out in the open as part of the political process."[268]

Having failed to placate Adleman, Inman was keen at least to have the NSA's perspective included in the media coverage. Inman told Kolata the NSA became interested in funding cryptographic two and a half years ago, when academic activity in the field increased. Inman told Kolata the NSA engaged with then NSF director Richard Atkinson, "we got authority, good ideas and help from Atkinson." Since that conversation, all cryptological funding requests were sent to the NSA for review.

[261] Adleman, 2016, 85:07.
[262] Ibid, 84:03.
[263] Levy, 2001, Prime Time, Chapter 4.
[264] Ibid.

[265] Kolata, 1980.
[266] Ibid, 995.
[267] Ibid, 995–996.
[268] Adleman, 2016, 86:06.

Eventually, the NSA was ready to start funding research: "I wrote to [Donald] Langenberg [the then NSF Director], suggesting that these would be good ones on which to start," Inman says. The selected applications were for Rivest and Adleman. Rivest's case was yet to move forwards—Adleman was the first to be approached.[269]

Addressing the concerns of what would happen should Adleman refuse to have his work classified after accepting NSA funding, Inman said, "we would not automatically classify the work. We would want to discuss with him [Adleman] the possibility of classifying it." Inman admitted they would try to convince Adleman classification was necessary. Kolata wrote Inman believed that he was being "entirely reasonable," and the agency's funding of cryptographic research would work. "We just need two or three people who aren't scared to death of us. I really am dealing with sociological problems on both sides." George Davida told Kolata such a system of NSA funding or no funding could endanger researchers' careers: "I really don't think Inman understands how the university and academic community works...Adleman is not tenured at MIT. If he begins to have trouble getting funded or publishing his research it could literally ruin his career."[270]

NSF themselves declined to enter into a full discussion with Kolata—Langenberg told Kolata that having only been in post two months, he was still finding his bearings. However, with regards to cryptology Langenberg confessed, "we're still trying to work out a policy"; Kolata concluded her article stating if the NSF did not decide its position quickly, it would likely lose any choice in the matter and academic scientists would pay the price.[271]

On October 9, 1980, both the NSA and NSF traveled to the White House to meet with the administration's Science advisor, Frank Press. It was decided both NSA and NSF would continue to fund cryptology research, the NSA would continue to require grant recipients to submit articles to the agency before publication, but would not expect to classify research it supported. It was agreed Adleman would have the option of accepting NSA funding, or opting for NSF to finance his research—he chose the latter. Adleman subsequently commented on his decision, "On a personal level I saw myself as a pure scientist and my natural affinities were to be funded by NSF."[272]Adleman also said, "it was clear that there would be a national debate on the issues and I didn't want any action I might take to be misconstrued as suggesting that the NSA had a compelling case that they had a role to play in the scientific process."[273]

Once again, public exposure had quickly led to a resolution to the academic's satisfaction.

Inman wrote to Hellman on November 22, 1980, stating, "NSF is going to fund Adleman's research, with no objection from us"; the director thanked Hellman for his assistance in helping mediate between the two parties, saying, "I remain very grateful for your fast action which let us defuse a situation created elsewhere." Inman

[269] Kolata, 1980, 995.   [272] Ibid.
[270] Ibid.   [273] Landau, 1983, 9.
[271] Ibid.

wrote he regretted Adleman, "apparently harbors dark suspicions," and "George Davida and Gina Kolata still only see evil." In a sign of the growing cooperation between one of America's most prominent cryptographers and its most senior signals intelligence officer, Inman thanked Hellman for his support with the Public Cryptography Study Group: "Your part in making this possible has been significant." Inman stated he "freely support[ed] the innovative voluntary effort," and hoped "the idea of legislation can be put on the back burner and give cooperation a free hand." Inman signed the letter "Bob."[274]

The dialogue the director desired, whilst tumultuous at times, and potentially not consistently delivering the ideal outcomes, was established.

5.16 VOLUNTARY REVIEW LOSES ITS EFFICACY

In the late 1980s the weaknesses of the voluntary review system became increasingly evident with the actions of John Gilmore, co-founder of both the cypherpunks and the Electronic Frontier Foundation. In mid-1989, Ralph Merkle, an early pioneer of public key cryptography, and collaborator with Diffie and Hellman, wrote a paper entitled *A Software Encryption Function*.[275] The paper described how to achieve faster and more efficient encryption using two block ciphers named Khufu and Khafre.

Merkle was working at Xerox when he wrote the paper, and therefore Xerox submitted the paper for voluntary NSA review. Xerox hoped to subsequently gain export permission for products that used Merkle's innovation—getting NSA acquiescence for publishing Merkle's work would greatly aid that ambition.[276] Before submission to the NSA, Merkle shared his paper with a number of other researchers for comment, when one of those researchers found out the NSA may seek to restrict its dissemination they passed it to Gilmore.[277] Gilmore had a reputation for being a purist when it came to the hacker dictum "Information wants to be free." Gilmore published the information online in the popular Sci.Crypt UseNet forum on July 13, 1989, writing, "Ralph Merkle called me today to let me know that Xerox was not going to let him submit his paper…for publication."[278] Gilmore explained, "The story is that a division of Xerox sells a lot of stuff to NSA and they threatened to pull their business if Xerox publishes it…Happily, however, I do not sell anything to the NSA."[279]

Merkle commented the next day that he was "embarrassed" with Gilmore's actions; "the decision by Xerox to defer publication of a portion of my work is one that I both understand and fully support." Merkle added, "at no point has NSA said or suggested that there would be an adverse effect on Xerox should Xerox pursue publication."[280] Merkle requested Gilmore cease distribution of the article, though given the nature of the Internet it was very much attempting to close the stable door

---

[274] Inman, 1980.
[275] Gilmore, 1989.
[276] Markoff, 1989.
[277] Ibid.

[278] Gilmore, 1989.
[279] Ibid.
[280] Ibid.

after the horse had bolted.[281] William Spencer, Xerox's vice president for research also denied any pressure, stating it was a business decision not to publish Merkle's research.[282] When NSA spokesperson Cynthia Beck was asked about the review of Merkle's paper by *New York Times* journalist John Markoff, she stated there was no record of a review. However, she did say that around ninety-three percent of papers submitted to the review process were approved by the agency.[283]

Whether the NSA requested the paper not be released, or whether Xerox took the decision based on preserving their business relationship with the government, or possibly to turn Merkle's discovery into a commercial secret ahead of seeking a patent, it was clear the mechanisms for preventing dissemination of academic papers were increasingly infeasible in the Internet era when global dissemination was at a click of a button. The university practices themselves, such as sharing pre-publication articles with colleagues to solicit their comments, had always been incompatible with the NSA's review process. By the time a paper was considered for classification, many would already have inputted to refining its contents and held copies of the paper, now with growing academic interest in cryptology and the Internet's expansion providing an easy means of mass dissemination, the system's efficacy was further eroded.

5.17   THE FIRST CRYPTO WAR: SUMMARY

With the settlement of the freedom of publication issue, the major conflicts of the first crypto war drew to a close. Throughout the eighties there were further skirmishes, but it would not be until 1991, when Phil Zimmermann developed an implementation of public key cryptography suitable for home computers, that the second crypto war would commence.

The cryptologic community continued to coalesce at both a national and international level. In 1981, the first crypto conference was held at Santa Barbara, University of California. Initially it was to be a one-time gathering, but the future father of cryptocurrencies, David Chaum, took the lead in turning the gathering into an annual event.[284] Chaum would subsequently be among the founding members of the International Association for Cryptological Research. The first crypto war had been predominantly waged by isolated individuals, such as Diffie and Hellman with support from journalists such as Gina Kolata, the next would be fought by organized groups, the digital civil liberties organizations, with the cypherpunk mailing list providing the ideological nexus.

Throughout the first crypto war, a series of Senate inquiries were taking place into illegal intelligence activities, the suspicions these hearings inculcated often set the tone for exchanges between academia and the government. The damaging findings of those inquiries color relations between the communities to the present day, but the

---

281 Ibid.   283 Ibid.
282 Markoff, 1989.   284 Kahn, 1982.

more immediate effect was the passing of the Foreign Intelligence Surveillance Act (FISA) in 1978.[285] FISA provided additional protections for domestic citizens and legal checks against the NSA's power, such as the requirement for the government to destroy any internal US communications where accidentally collected.[286]

David Kahn, who inspired a generation of cryptologists and caused the NSA so many headaches eventually donated his extensive primary source documentary collection to the National Cryptologic Museum, a part of the NSA. Perhaps in a sign that a new generation of NSA leadership recognized Kahn's contribution to cryptology, he would serve as NSA's scholar-in-residence in 1995.

In December 1997, the story of public key cryptology took another turn. NSA's British equivalent, the Government Communications Headquarters (GCHQ), revealed one of their own mathematicians, James Ellis, had discovered public key encryption in 1970.[287] By 1974 Clifford Cocks and Malcolm Williamson had developed the idea further into the equivalent of the Diffie-Hellman and RSA algorithms.[288] Cocks comments he thought of RSA "in my head overnight," and then, rather than writing it down, "kept it in my head overnight."[289] Cocks explains when Ellis came up with the idea, "people weren't sure, which shows the extent of the revolution."[290] Then GCHQ Chief Scientist Ralph Benjamin comments:

> When I became GCHQ chief scientist in 1971, I was briefed by Dr Gerald Touch, my predecessor, that…James Ellis had produced papers about what [Ellis] called "non-secret encryption." Touch had consulted Hugh Alexander, the head of cryptography and Shaun Wylie, the chief mathematician, and I believe Denis Mardle, who was designated to succeed Wylie, and they said "non-secret cryptography" was garbage.[291]

Benjamin adds:

> Ellis's was a philosophical presentation…[his] paper discussed the mathematical requirements to achieve this, but had no practical suggestions to offer. I got the kernel of Ellis's idea, and I went to Nick Patterson, and said, "Can you look at this and devise a suitable function?"…Patterson came back with Cliff Cocks with a viable option.[292]

Benjamin states Non-Secret Encryption was, "revolutionary in the intellectual schema, and eventually in its operational impact," though he concedes:

> We didn't then foresee the full eventual operational impact…I judged it most important for military use. In a fluid military situation you may meet unforeseen threats or opportunities. To cope with threats or exploit opportunities you have to quickly reconfigure your forces…You can't do that unless you share secure communications. This means… if you can share your key rapidly and electronically, you have a major advantage over your opponent.[293]

---

[285] United States Department of Justice, 1978.
[286] Ibid.
[287] Ellis, 1970.
[288] Cocks, 1973; Williamson, 1974.
[289] Espiner, 2010.
[290] Ibid.
[291] Ibid.
[292] Ibid.
[293] Ibid.

GCHQ immediately passed on the discovery to NSA, which, according to Benjamin caused, "enormous professional excitement in the cryptography community." The NSA nominated Benjamin for the top US civil award, though in his words it was "vetoed by the Foreign Office because this would have revealed our close association with the NSA at the time"; however, NSA did present him a "special medal to show their admiration."[294] Despite the enthusiasm, Cocks commented:

> In the 70s public key cryptography was too expensive...All of the ideas were well ahead of their time. No one was implementing public key cryptography in the 70s. The UK government didn't use it until the late 1980s with the [CESG-developed] Brent telephone. By the time things were implemented, public key cryptography was quite a mature subject.[295]

Asked about whether there is any link between the discoveries at Stanford and MIT, and NSA's knowledge of Non-Secret Encryption, Benjamin states:

> NSA collaborated with Stanford and MIT to develop a secure computing architecture. There was a steady flow of people traveling between Fort Meade [NSA headquarters] and Stanford as part of the project. Our "non-secret encryption" was then such a lively subject of discussion at NSA that it would be surprising if some hint of our line of thought had not been inadvertently passed to Stanford, thus stimulating them independently to develop the same ideas and algorithm in their "public-key cryptography." However, I certainly do not believe that there was any deliberate leakage by NSA or any conscious plagiarism by Stanford.[296]

Ellis reflected that the revelation of cryptographic algorithms within the intelligence community is "only sanctioned in the interests of historical accuracy after it has been demonstrated clearly that no further benefit can be obtained from continued secrecy."[297] After declassification of the GCHQ discovery predating that of Diffie and Hellman, the latter commented, "credit goes to the first to publish."[298] In 1982, Diffie became aware of the GCHQ discovery via an NSA employee, and traveled to meet Ellis in England. Whilst Ellis never officially acknowledged he was the father of non-secret encryption, as he had called it, he and Diffie became close. One night, after several drinks at a local pub, Ellis told Diffie, "You did more with it than we did"—it was the last time Ellis ever spoke publicly of the topic—and it remained classified until after his death.[299]

The first crypto war was won and lost by both sides.

The NSA were victorious in implementing the Data Encryption Standard (DES) with a key length they desired, though it is unknown if the NSA were able to conduct exhaustive attacks against 56-bit keys when DES launched. However, if they were not able to, and had agreed to such a key length, they may have concurrently

---

294 Ibid.
295 Ibid.
296 Ibid.
297 Ellis, 1987.
298 Hellman, no date b, 2.
299 Levy, 2001, Epilogue.

established a plan where, within a reasonable timeframe, they could develop such capabilities—this part of the history remains secret.

In a small consolation for the academics, the next time an encryption standard was developed—the Advanced Encryption Standard [AES]—the process would be transparent and passed the collective scrutiny of their community.

When it came to academic freedom to publish, the academics were victorious. Knowing in the post-Nixon era further legislation for surveillance powers would be unlikely to pass, the NSA had to abandon their original plans for a law to control the free dissemination of cryptological information. The voluntary submission program was an attempt to maintain at least some degree of influence over the academic community, but with the press on their side, had NSA ever attempted to prevent publication against the wishes of the author, they were likely to face a public relations nightmare.

5.18   DID THE DIGITAL PRIVACY ACTIVISTS MAKE A DIFFERENCE?

In 1967, David Kahn dragged cryptology from the shadows and into the minds of a generation of cryptologists. Shortly after, Diffie, Hellman, Rivest, Shamir, and Adleman made discoveries enabling a revolution in cryptology, but did they really have an impact during the seventies and eighties?

The reality is, Inman comments, the cryptological revolution advanced slower than many expected.[300] Computing itself was still primarily in the hands of governments and some businesses, whilst there was growing use of the Internet by individuals, it was still the preserve of specialists. Economic and intellectual barriers meant cryptography delivered little benefit to the ordinary citizen during the seventies and eighties.

Whilst in the early years the NSA demonstrated their inability to manage the situation with finesse, Bobby Inman reversed this trend. His deft relationship-building and public engagement, that broke the NSA's learned wisdom of operating solely from the shadows, helped bridge the gap between the communities, and allowed Inman to achieve the best outcomes available to the NSA given the prevailing political climate. The NSA likely realized the need for, and growth of, commercial encryption was inevitable—their strategy was probably to buy time to allow their own cryptanalytic capabilities to evolve against new approaches such as public key cryptography, of for more direct methods of intelligence collection, such as hacking into target machines, to develop.

However, one could interpret the results of the cryptographers in another way. Whilst the cryptologists did not accomplish everything they desired, upon the next generation they bestowed a philosophy that the sharing of cryptologic knowledge, even across borders, was inevitable. They provided the raw cryptologic ingredients required if the cypherpunks were to be successful in bringing encryption to the

---

[300] United States House of Representatives, 1980,
424.

masses in an era when the world would be coming online. They also passed down a history that showed the NSA and the US government were able to be challenged, and some successes were possible.

Years later, when looking back to the first crypto war, several of the key participants note that in retrospect they would have approached the situation differently.

As David Kahn observed, whilst the NSA clearly had the primary focus of their arguments as aligned to their core mission—the breaking of foreign codes—the academics were not disinterested parties: "They were making their careers here. Challenging authority was in their DNA," Kahn comments.[301] Hellman substantiated this when he reflected, "The thought just popped into my head: Forget about what's right. Go with this, you've got a tiger by the tail. You'll never have more of an impact on society."[302] Both sides were pursuing their own agendas, though this is not to say there was not also an element of pursuing societies' best interests.

In the wake of the alleged Chinese Nation State theft of the F-35 fighter jet from a defense contractor, Bobby Inman stated of the academics that, "rather than being careful to make sure they [weren't] going to damage [NSA's intelligence operations]... I would have been interested in how quickly they were going to be able to make [encryption widely] available."[303]

Leonard Adleman reflected, "I totally understand the NSA's point of view and I think they acted very admirably in the way they handled it [the cryptological advances]."[304] Adleman also reflected of the balance between privacy and security:

> It's a line that is drawn by the political process and it can be shifted a little this way and a little that way from time to time. When there's more national security needs, less privacy, and when there's less national security needs, more privacy. That's going to shift, I expect, ad infinitum...it's...the way it should be. So I no longer passionately believe in my side and not the other. I think they're both just a line we have to live with.[305]

Most of those who would identify themselves as cypherpunks in the future were in school or university as the first crypto war was waged; some future cypherpunks were yet to be born. But when they came of age they would listen to the stories of their intellectual forebears. The Web was still to be invented, the first crypto war had been fought by those prophets anticipating what would emerge from the horizon: when the second crypto war began, the new digital world was dawning.

REFERENCES

ARTICLES

American Council on Education. (1981). Report of the Public Cryptography Study Group. *Cryptologia* 5(3), 130–142.

---

[301] Ibid.
[302] Corrigan-Gibbs, 2014.
[303] Ibid.

[304] Adleman, 2016, 81:35.
[305] Ibid, 81:51.

Cocks, C. (1973). A Note on Non-Secret Encryption. *CESG Report.* Available: https://web.arc
    hive.org/web/20000505045500/http://www.cesg.gov.uk/about/nsecret.htm   [Accessed
    April 14, 2020].
Davida, G. I. (1981). The Case Against Restraints on Non-Governmental Research in
    Cryptography. *Cryptologia* **5**(3), 143–148.
Diffie, W. and Hellman, M. (1976). New Directions in Cryptography. *IEEE Transactions on
    Information Theory* **22**(6), 644–654.
Ellis, J. (1970). The Possibility of Non-Secret Encryption. *CESG Report.* Available: https
    ://web.archive.org/web/20000505045500/http://www.cesg.gov.uk/about/nsecret.htm
    [Accessed April 14, 2020].
Inman, B. R. (1979). The NSA Perspective on Telecommunications Protection in the
    NonGovernmental Sector. *Cryptologia* **3**(3), 129–135.
Kahn, D. (1979). Cryptology Goes Public. *Foreign Affairs* **58**(1), 141–159.
Kolata, G. B. (1980). Cryptography: A New Clash between Academic Freedom and National
    Security: NSA Seeks to Influence Science Policy. *Science* **209**(4460), 995–996.
Landau, S. (1983). Primes, Codes, and the National Security Agency. *Notices of the American
    Mathematical Society* **30**(1), 7–10.
Meyer, J. A. (1971). Crime Deterrent Transponder System. *IEEE Transactions on Aerospace
    and Electronic Systems* **AES7**(1), 2–22.
Shapley, D. and G. B. Kolata. (1977). Cryptology: Scientists Puzzle over Threat to Open
    Research, Publication. *Science* **197**(4311), 1345–1349.
Shapley, D. (1978a). DOD Vacillates on Wisconsin Cryptography Work. *Science* **201**(4351),
    141.
Shapley, D. (1978b). Intelligence Agencies seek "Dialogue" with Academics. *Science*
    202(4366), 407–410.
Williamson, M. J. (1974). Non-Secret Encryption Using a Finite Field. *CESG Report.*
    Available: https://web.archive.org/web/20000505045500/http://www.cesg.gov.uk/
    about/nsecret.htm [Accessed April 14, 2020].

BOOKS

Bamford, J. (1982). *The Puzzle Palace: Inside the National Security Agency* (New York:
    Penguin Books).
Levy, S. (2001). *Crypto: Secrecy and Privacy in the New Cold War* (New York: Viking
    Penguin).

NEWSPAPER ARTICLES

Dembart, L. Dispute Over Top-Secret Codes Coming to a Head. *Los Angeles Times*, February
    1, 1981.

WEBSITES

Atkins, D., Graff, M., Lenstra, A., and Leyland, P. (1994). *Announcement of RSA129 Victory*
    [Online]. Available: https://web.archive.org/web/20140721061055/http://www.crypto
    -world.com/announcements/RSA129.txt [Accessed October 17, 2019].
Barcellos, A. (2010). *An Interview with Martin Gardner* [Online]. Available: http://thebackb
    ench.blogspot.co.uk/2010/05/interview-with-martin-gardner.html [Accessed October
    17, 2019].

Bebel, J. and Teng, S. (2002). *Leonard (Len) Max Adleman* [Online]. Available: http://amt uring.acm.org/award_winners/adleman_7308544.cfm [Accessed October 19, 2019].

Burr, S. (1977). *Prof's Work Threatens National Security* [Online]. Available: http://sta nforddailyarchive.com/cgi-bin/stanford?a=d&d=stanford19771026-01.2.3 [Accessed October 18, 2019].

Corrigan-Gibbs, H. (2014). *Keeping Secrets* [Online]. Available: https://alumni.stanford.edu/ get/page/magazine/article/?article_id=74801 [Accessed October 18, 2019].

Dwivedi, N. P. (1977). *A Letter to Dr. Martin E. Hellman, Prof. Anthony Ephemerides, Dr. F. Jeninek, Prof. J. L. Massey, Dr. A. D. Wyner, and Dr. M. G. Smith from Dr. Narendra P. Dived, Director of Technical Activities at IEEE,* 8 August, 1977 [Online]. Available: https://cryptome.org/hellman/1977-0707-Meyer-letter.pdf [Accessed October 18, 2019].

Ellis. (1987). *The Story of Non-Secret Encryption* [Online]. Available: https://web.archive. org/web/20000505045500/http://www.cesg.gov.uk/about/nsecret.htm [Accessed April 14, 2020].

Espiner, T. (2010). *GCHQ Pioneers on Birth of Public Key Crypto* [Online]. Available: https ://www.zdnet.com/article/gchq-pioneers-on-birth-of-public-key-crypto/ [Accessed April 15, 2020].

Furger, F. (2002). *Interview with Whitfield Diffie on the Development of Public Key Cryptography* [Online]. Available: http://www.itas.kit.edu/pub/m/2002/wedi02a.htm [Accessed October 17, 2019].

Gannet, E. K. (1977). *Letter to Mr Joseph. A. Meyer from Mr E. K. Gannet, Staff Secretary, IEEE Publications Board,* 7 July, 1977 [Online]. Available: https://cryptome.org/hell man/1977-0707-Meyer-letter.pdf [Accessed October 18, 2019].

Gardner, M. (1977). *Mathematical Games, August 1977: A New Kind of Cipher That Would Take Millions of Years to Break* [Online]. Available: https://www.scientificamerican .com/article/mathematical-games-1977-08/ [Accessed October 17, 2019].

Gilmore, J. (1989). *Subject: Merkle's "A Software Encryption Function" now published and available* [Online]. Available: https://tech-insider.org/data-security/research/1989/07 13.html [Accessed October 19, 2019].

Green, W. (2015). *Pearls of Wisdom from Martin Hellman—2015 ACM A.M. Turing Award Laureate › Heidelberg Laureate Forum* [Online]. Available: https://web.archive.org/web/20 170716153126/http://www.heidelberg-laureate-forum.org/blog/pearls-of-wisdom-from -martin-hellman-2015-acm-a-m-turing-award-laureate/ [Accessed October 17, 2019].

Harmon, J. (1978). *Constitutionality Under the First Amendment of ITAR Restrictions on Public Cryptography—Memorandum from Assistant Attorney General John Harmon, Office of Legal Counsel, Department of Justice to Dr Frank Press, Science Advisor to the President (11 May 1978)* [Online]. Available: https://www.justice.gov/olc/page/fi le/936106/download [Accessed April 16, 2019.

Hellman, M. (n.d.a). *Martin E. Hellman Work on Cryptography* [Online]. Available: https:// ee.stanford.edu/~hellman/crypto.html [Accessed October 17, 2019].

Hellman, M. (n.d.b). *Work on Cryptography* [Online]. Available: https://www-ee.stanford.e du/~hellman/crypto.html [Accessed October 18, 2019].

Hellman, M. (1976a). *Letter from Martin Hellman to Dennis Branstad, National Bureau of Standards, Arthur Levenson, National Bureau of Standards and Douglas Hogan, Director NSA, 21 January 1976* [Online]. Available: https://stacks.stanford.edu/file/ druid:wg115cn5068/1976%200220%20ltrs%20to%20NBS.pdf [Accessed October 19, 2019].

Hellman, M. (1976b). *Letter from Martin Hellman to Elliot Richardson, Secretary of Commerce, 23 February 1976* [Online]. Available: https://stacks.stanford.edu/file/ druid:wg115cn5068/1976%200220%20ltrs%20to%20NBS.pdf [Accessed October 19, 2019].

Hellman, M. (1977). *Memorandum to John Schwartz, Stanford University Lawyer, from Martin Hellman, 3 October, 1977* [Online]. Available: https://stacks.stanford.edu/file/druid:wg115cn5068/1977%201003%20MH2Schwartz.pdf [Accessed October 18, 2019].

Hellman, M. (2009). *Email to John Young, Subject: Re: NSA Docs on Joseph Meyer 1977 Letter to IEEE, 31 December, 2009* [Online]. Available: https://web.archive.org/web/201803301438 30/https://cryptome.org/hellman/hellman-nsa.htm [Accessed October 17, 2019].

Hellman, M. (2013). *Unpublished AutoBiography* [Online]. Available: https://stacks.stanford.edu/file/druid:kq639bj2341/Ch_1.pdf [Accessed October 21, 2019].

Hellman, D. and Hellman, M. (2016). *A New Map for Relationships: Creating True Love at Home & Peace on the Planet* [Online]. Available: http://www-ee.stanford.edu/~hellman/publications/book3.pdf [Accessed October 19, 2019].

Hellman, M. and McGraw, G. (2016). *Show 121: Marty Hellman Discusses Cryptography and Nuclear Non-Proliferation* [Online]. Available: https://www.synopsys.com/softw are-integrity/resources/podcasts/show-121.html [Accessed October 13, 2019].

Inman, B. R. (1980). *Letter to Martin Hellman from Bobby Inman, Director, NSA, 22 November 1980)* [Online]. Available: https://stacks.stanford.edu/file/druid:wg115cn5068/Inman_ Letter.pdf [Accessed October 19, 2019].

Johnson, T. R. (n.d.). *National Security Agency: American Cryptology During the Cold War, 1945–1989: Book III: Retrenchment and Reform, 1972–1980* [Online]. Available: http://nsarchive.gwu.edu/NSAEBB/NSAEBB260/nsa-6.pdf [Accessed October 12, 2019].

Kahn, D. (1982). *Accounts of IACR Formation* [Online]. Available: https://chaum.com/iacr/iacrhistory.html [Accessed October 20, 2019].

Markoff, J. (1989). *Paper on Codes Is Sent Despite U.S. Objections* [Online]. Available: http://www.nytimes.com/1989/08/09/us/paper-on-codes-is-sent-despite-us-objections.html [Accessed October 18, 2019].

Massachusetts Institute of Technology. (2018). *Ronald L. Rivest: Biographical Information* [Online]. Available: http://people.csail.mit.edu/rivest/bio.html [Accessed October 17, 2019].

Meyer, J. A. (1977). *Letter to Mr E. K. Gannet (Staff Secretary, IEEE Publications Board) from Joseph. A. Meyer* [Online]. Available: https://web.archive.org/web/201806091726 20/https://cryptome.org/hellman/1977-0707-Meyer-letter.pdf [Accessed October 17, 2019].

Mulcahy, C. (2014). *The Top 10 Martin Gardner Scientific American Articles* [Online]. Available: https://blogs.scientificamerican.com/guest-blog/the-top-10-martin-gard ner-scientific-american-articles/ [Accessed October 17, 2019].

Myers, A. (2011). *Encryption Leads Stanford's Martin Hellman into National Inventors Hall of Fame* [Online]. Available: http://news.stanford.edu/pr/2011/pr-inventor-prize-hell man-030411.html [Accessed October 17, 2019].

Olson, T. B. (1981a). *Constitutionality of Proposed Revisions of the Export Administration Regulation* [Online]. Available: https://www.justice.gov/file/22716/download [Accessed August 5, 2019].

Olson, T. B. (1981b). *Constitutionality of the Proposed Revision of the International Traffic in Arms Regulations* [Online]. Available: https://www.justice.gov/file/22696/download [Accessed August 5, 2019].

Plutte, J. (2011a). *Martin Hellman: 2011 Fellows Interview* [Online]. Computer History Museum. Available: http://archive.computerhistory.org/resources/access/text/2011/10/102743050-05-01-acc.pdf [Accessed October 17, 2019].

Plutte, J. (2011b). *Whitfield Diffie Interview: Computer History Museum* [Online]. Available: http://archive.computerhistory.org/resources/access/text/2015/04/102743051-05-01 -acc.pdf [Accessed October 17, 2019].

United States Congress. (1942). *Patents, Hearings Before the Committee on Patents, United States Senate, Seventy-Seventh Congress, Second Session, on S.2303, a Bill to Provide for the Use of Patents in the Interest of National Defense or the Prosecution of the War, and for Other Purposes* [Online]. Available: https://play.google.com/books/reader?id= 2sxFAQAAMAAJ&hl=en_GB&pg=GBS.PA1431 [Accessed April 30, 2020].

United States Congress (1917). *United States Code: Trading with the Enemy Act of 1917, 50a U.S.C. §§ 3-30* (Suppl. 2 1940). Available: https://www.loc.gov/item/uscode1940-0060 50a002/ [Accessed August 3, 2020].

United States Congress (1949). *Export Control Act of 1949*. Available: https://www.loc.gov/law/h elp/statutes-at-large/81st-congress/session-1/c81s1ch11.pdf [Accessed August 3, 2020].

United States Congress (1969). *Export Administration Act, 50 U.S.C. app.2401–2420.*

United States Department of Justice. (1978). *The Foreign Intelligence Surveillance Act of 1978 (FISA)* [Online]. Available: https://it.ojp.gov/PrivacyLiberty/authorities/statutes/ 1286 [Accessed October 18, 2019].

United States House of Representatives. (1980). *The Government's Classification of Private Ideas: Hearings before a Subcommittee of the Committee on Government Operations House of Representatives* [Online]. Available: https://babel.hathitrust.org/cgi/pt?id=m dp.39015082027817;view=1up;seq=3 [Accessed October 12, 2019].

United States General Publishing Office. (1997). *22 CFR 120.17—Export (ITAR)*. Available: https://www.govinfo.gov/content/pkg/CFR-1997-title22-vol1/pdf/CFR-1997-title22-v ol1-sec120-17.pdf [Accessed July 25, 2019].

United States Senate. (1978). *Unclassified Summary: Involvement of NSA in the Development of the Data Encryption Standard—Staff Report of the Senate Select Committee on Intelligence United States Congress*. Available: https://www.intelligence.senate.gov/ sites/default/files/publications/95nsa.pdf [Accessed May 18, 2017].

United States Senate and House of Representatives. (1950). *National Science Foundation Act of 1950* [Online]. Available: https://www.nsf.gov/about/history/legislation.pdf [Accessed October 18, 2019].

United States National Archives and Records Administration. (1997). *Federal Register 62:247, 24 December, 1997*. Available: https://www.govinfo.gov/content/pkg/FR-1 997-12-24/pdf/97-33649.pdf [Accessed July 25, 2019].

Yost, J. R. (2004). Oral History Interview with Martin Hellman. *Charles Babbage Institute, Centre for the History of Information Technology, University of Minneapolis* [Online]. Available: https://conservancy.umn.edu/bitstream/handle/11299/107353/oh375mh.pdf? sequence=1&isAllowed=y [Accessed June 5, 2020].

YOUTUBE VIDEOS

Adleman, L. "Len Adleman, 2002 ACM Turing Award Recipient," YouTube video, 2:56:54, posted by "Association for Computer Machinery (ACM)," October 25, 2016, Available: https://www.youtube.com/watch?v=K06hOhABP-Y [Accessed October 17, 2019].

Adleman, L. "Leonard Adleman on Becoming a Mathematician," YouTube video, 1:46, posted by "RSA Conference," November 1, 2010, Available: https://www.youtube.com/ watch?v=ClmkYxiLbVI [Accessed October 17, 2019].

George, R. "CERIAS—The Role of the NSA in the Development of DES," YouTube video, 55:48, posted by "Purdue CERIAS," April 26, 2016. Available: https://www.youtube. com/watch?v=u80M009eSDk [Accessed April 12, 2020].

Rivest, R. "Ronald Rivest's Killian Lecture at MIT: The Growth of Cryptography," YouTube video, 1:09:40, posted by "Ryan Lei," February 4, 2012, Available: https://www.you tube.com/watch?v=QOQ9b8STMec [Accessed October 17, 2019].

6 Crypto War II (1991–2002)

Digital Signature Standard (DSS) and Key Escrow (Clipper)

The secretive National Security Agency has built up an arcane web of

complex and confusing laws, regulations, standards, and

secret interpretations for years.

These are used to force, persuade, or confuse individuals, companies, and

government departments into making it easy for

NSA to wiretap and decode all kinds of

communications.

Their tendrils reach deep into the White House, into numerous

Federal agencies,

and into the

Congressional Intelligence Committees.

Electronic Frontier Foundation, 1996c

6.1 DIGITAL SIGNATURE STANDARD

A détente, facilitated by the stagnation of encryption technologies, existed between the state and digital privacy activists throughout the 1980s. Ron Rivest attempted to develop a circuit board capable of performing RSA encryption at MIT in 1982, but the board was too expensive for general use; "the technology was premature," Rivest recalls, and there was not the market demand to generate further investment and achieve economies of scale, "We had some interest, but it was scattered."[1]

---

[1] Garfinkel, 1995, 84.

Three critical dependencies existed before public key cryptography could be widely adopted. The first was affordable personal computers. In 1984, only 8% of American citizens had a computer at home, rising to 15% in 1989, and 23% by 1993; it would be 1997 before Internet penetration reached 19% of households.[2] The second dependency was personal computers with greater computational power than those available in the 1980s, which had proved unable to support processor-intensive cryptography operations. The third dependency was an encryption algorithm capable of exploiting the still relatively meager processing power of early 1990s home computers to rapidly generate the large prime numbers needed for public key encryption, without being so lethargic in execution as to detriment the user experience. Whilst encryption was being baked into mainstream products such as spreadsheet program Lotus 1-2-3, and Microsoft Word 2.0, decryption capabilities were often readily available demonstrating the weakness of the algorithms and the implementation ineptitudes. For example, AccessData sold decryption capabilities for products including Lotus and Word for $185.[3] The weakness of cryptography was highlighted by AccessData's creator Eric Thompson, who commented his decryption programs were so fast he coded in delay loops to increase client perception of the decryption complexity.[4] However, as the new decade emerged, the decade which would see the rise of the World Wide Web, a public key signature and key exchange standard was desperately needed to enable the advance of e-commerce.

The National Institute of Standards and Technology (NIST), the successor of the National Bureau of Standards (NBS), published their proposal for a Digital Signature Standard (DSS) in August 1991.[5] The ongoing digitization and automation of the US government, and society, offered the opportunity of increased efficiencies if the trustworthiness of written signatures could be digitally replicated. Lynn McNulty, NIST's Associate Director for Computer Security, explains that digital signatures:

> will be an important part of re-engineering the business practices that we've used for so many years in government and other parts of society...The signature will be absolutely critical in certain areas where, because of statute or practice, we currently require a written signature on paper.[6]

Signatures were also vital for technical activities such as software updates—if users could not authenticate the update was from the correct source, they could be tricked into installing malware onto their systems. NIST first called for proposals for a public key signature and key exchange standard in 1982.[7] The public key digital signature would provide authenticity of authorship, whilst the public key exchange would allow confidentiality (encryption) between two parties who had never met. To move forwards in 1982, NIST had needed the NSA to agree to, or to develop, any

---

[2] United States Census Bureau, 2010.
[3] Schifreen, 1992, 162.
[4] Zimmermann, 1994a, 105.

[5] National Institute of Standards and Technology, 1991.
[6] Sobel, no date.
[7] United States General Accounting Office, 1993, 5.

proposed solutions. A 1993 report by the government's General Accounting Office found the failure of NIST's 1982 proposal was "because of NSA and FBI concerns."[8] The report stated that whilst NSA and NIST met several times "[to] discuss NSA concerns," the outcome of those meetings was NIST's termination of the project "because of an NSA request."[9]

NIST had placed public key cryptography back on the agenda in 1989. The relationship between NIST and the NSA remained complicated. The power dynamic between the parties, and the NSA's influence over non-classified information systems, had led to congressional concerns in the mid-1980s, and as a result the 1987 Computer Security Act (CSA) was passed, giving NIST control of issuing standards for non-classified systems with the NSA relegated to a supporting role.[10] However, a 1989 memo of understanding (MOU) between the NSA and NIST seemed to undermine the CSA. The memo can be interpreted as placing NSA and NIST on equal footing; rather than the former being subordinate to the latter, some even assessed the document positioned NSA as the dominant party.[11] The MOU established a joint NSA-NIST technical working group which would "review and analyze issues of mutual interest pertinent to protection of systems that process sensitive or other unclassified information."[12] The technical working group would review:

> prior to public disclosure all matters regarding technical systems security techniques to be developed for use in protecting sensitive information in federal computer systems to ensure they are consistent with the national security of the United States. If NIST and NSA are unable to resolve such an issue within 60 days, either agency may elect to raise the issue to the Secretary of Defense and the Secretary of Commerce. It is recognized that such an issue may be referred to the President through the NSC for resolution.[13]

The MOU also stated NIST would:

> Request the NSA's assistance on all matters related to cryptographic algorithms and cryptographic techniques including but not limited to research, development evaluation, or endorsement.[14]

The Computer Professionals for Social Responsibility (CPSR)'s Washington office director, Marc Rotenberg, testified to Congress arguing the MOU, "undermines the [Computer Security] Act, transferring the authority that Congress intended to remain at the Commerce Department [NIST's parent agency] to Fort Meade [NSA]."[15] Another testimony from Milton J. Scolar, Special Assistant to the Comptroller General within the General Accounting Office, was supportive of Rotenberg's assessment:

---

8 Ibid, Appendix II:2.1.5.
9 Ibid, Appendix II:2.1.6.
10 United States General Accounting Office, 1987, 7; United States Congress, 1987.
11 National Institute of Standards and Technology and National Security Agency, 1989.

12 Ibid.
13 Ibid.
14 Ibid.
15 Rotenburg, 1993, 7.

The document as a whole...allows such prerogatives to NSA as it seems to me go a long way towards nullifying any initiative that NIST might undertake to which NSA would at the same time object...The memo to me does not project the full sense that it is NSA that will be responsible to NIST. Rather, it suggests that where there is any disagreement between NIST and NSA, that it will be NSA that keeps its hands on the levers of control.[16]

NIST met with the NSA to discuss the public key initiative in 1989, stating they "would prefer having one public key (asymmetric) cryptographic algorithm that does both digital signature and key distribution."[17] NIST argued it would be "difficult to support two different algorithm standards where one could suffice," and also, "it would be difficult to support standards contrary to wider user acceptance"—the subtext being the public would expect RSA to be the standard given its industry dominance and the rigorous cryptanalytic testing to which it had been subjected.[18] NIST favored RSA. Senior NIST scientist Dr. Roy Saltman described RSA as a "most versatile public-key system," and acknowledged the algorithm as the *de facto* international standard.[19] NIST requested NSA assistance in evaluating a series of their candidate algorithms, including RSA. NIST's criteria included: the algorithm must be public, implementable in both software and hardware, and the algorithm should be capable of both authentication (digital signatures) and confidentiality (key exchange).[20] The NSA were also asked by NIST to provide "new algorithms when existing algorithms do not meet NIST requirements."[21] NSA acknowledged the challenge of launching any algorithm they should produce; "any public key solution provided by NSA must be capable of withstanding close public scrutiny and discussion," they told the first meeting of the joint NSA-NIST Technical Working Group in May 1989.[22]

Despite frequent NSA-NIST meetings to discuss potential public key encryption standards, it was seven months after NIST's first assistance request they were informed NSA had excluded RSA as a candidate.[23] NSA informed NIST they were developing their own digital signature algorithm, but it would not meet NIST's criteria of being capable of key exchange.[24] The author, and later patent holder, of Fort Meade's algorithm was NSA employee David W. Kravitz, who had written the algorithm whilst on sabbatical at the Center for Communications Research within Princeton's Institute for Defense Analyses.[25] To achieve a digital signature, a hashing algorithm is executed against the file for which a user is seeking to create a signature, resulting in a string of characters called a hash.[26] The hashing algorithm to be used was the government's Secure Hashing Algorithm (SHA-1), which would become a

---

[16] Scolar, 1989, 37–38.
[17] National Institute of Standards and Technology, 1989, 472.
[18] McNulty, 1997, 479.
[19] Schneier and Banisar, 1997, 304.
[20] National Institute of Standards and Technology, 1989, 472–473.
[21] Ibid, 472.
[22] McNulty, 1997, 475.
[23] United States General Accounting Office, 1993, Appendix II:2.1.7.
[24] Ibid.
[25] National Institute of Standards and Technology, 1991.
[26] Also sometimes known as a message digest.

standard in 1993.[27] The hash is then encrypted using the author's private key, which results in a digital signature. A recipient of the file then uses the author's public key to decrypt the digital signature thus revealing the file hash. The recipient then uses the hashing algorithm to generate their own hash of the file—if the hashes match, the file is authenticated as belonging to the author (assuming the correct ownership of the keys). The NSA position paper justifying why RSA was eliminated in favor of Kravitz's algorithm (albeit based on the public El Gamal algorithm) was classified top secret codeword, and was only available to view at NSA's headquarters by "properly cleared senior NIST officials."[28]

Through 1989 and 1990 NIST and NSA met weekly with little progress on the original goal of agreeing on an algorithm capable of both authenticity and confidentiality, Lynn McNulty would later reflect:

> We went to a lot of meetings with our NSA counterparts, and we were allowed to write a lot of memos, but we on the technical side of NIST felt we were being slow rolled…in retrospect it is clear that the real game plan that NSA had drawn up was…key escrow.[29]

Key escrow is a system where encryption keys are stored by the government so they can access communications when they possess a warrant. The government's key escrow would be announced in 1993, and became known as the Clipper chip.

A NIST report of January 1990 noted, "It's increasingly evident that it is difficult, if not impossible, to reconcile the concerns and requirements of NSA, NIST, and the general public through using this approach."[30] The FBI were also concerned about public key encryption and its impact on their interception activities. FBI Director William Sessions wrote to the directors of the CIA and NSA, the Attorney General, and the Defense and Commerce Secretaries, requesting a meeting to agree a public key policy for "eventual submission to the National Security Council"; the FBI soon joined the working group developing the DSS.[31] NIST's control over the project was ebbing. Expressing their frustration, a NIST memo noted patent issues with the DSS would need to be addressed, "if we ever get our NSA problem settled."[32]

To surmount NIST's recalcitrance to progress a standard incapable of both signatures and key exchange, an internal NSA note of October 19, 1990 detailed a scheduled meeting with NIST's Ray Kammer to present their "entire package (hashing function, digital signature key exchange and data confidentiality standard proposals)."[33] The memo noted, "if Kammer does not accept our proposal we will have to consider escalating the problem."[34] The escalation path is unclear; nevertheless, it

---

[27] SHA-1 was found to have a "minor flaw" that was discovered by NSA after it had been launched as a standard, making it "less secure that original thought," though NSA noted it was "still extremely reliable" (National Institute of Standards and Technology, 1994b). An update was swiftly deployed, the incident was another indicator to industry that the NSA were in fact continually evaluating the algorithms they created as national standards, it was also an indicator that NSA's coding prowess was fallible.

[28] Sobel, 1993.
[29] Diffie and Landau, 1999, Chapter 3.
[30] Sobel, 1993.
[31] Schneier and Banisar, 1997, 305.
[32] Sobel, 1993.
[33] Unknown NSA Author, 1990, 481.
[34] Ibid.

would likely be to the President, via the Defense Secretary. NSA Director William Studeman wrote to NIST director John Lyons in February 1991 to apply further pressure:

> We are aiming to publish detailed descriptions of the algorithms we have selected for hashing and digital signatures. We anticipate no problem with the hashing algorithm, but our digital signature proposal is likely to arouse some controversy...With your support we hope to be able to cut short debate and get on with the things that need to be done to provide the necessary protection.[35]

Kammer agreed to the NSA proposal in April 1991, shortly thereafter the DSS was publicly announced.[36] The public were informed the DSS would provide authentication that a certain individual/organization (key holder) authored a file, but would not provide for key exchange. As well as replacing handwritten signatures, NIST advised digital signatures could "serve as a useful tool in protecting Government and commercial software against hackers and viruses."[37] NIST declared their intention to make the DSS available worldwide on a royalty-free basis—NIST believed their algorithm was patentable, and no other patents applied to their algorithm.[38]

In September 1991, Jim Bidzos, President of RSA Data Security Incorporated (RSADSI), was enraged at news that a rival was being introduced to his companies, and the industries established public key product: RSA.[39] Bidzos wrote to Democratic Representative Tim Valentine from North Carolina, Chair of the Technology and Competitiveness subcommittee, demanding a Congressional inquiry into the DSS' origins.[40] Bidzos argued, "NIST's approach gives the appearance of trying to reverse a major worldwide trend in industry and standards making."[41] Bidzos wrote that rather than "going the extra mile" to work with industry in developing a public key cryptography standard, "NIST shuns industry cooperation and offers flawed proposals developed secretly with NSA."[42] Ron Rivest, another of those set to financially suffer should RSA not be selected as the algorithm of choice, wrote:

> It is past the time for national cryptographic standards to be designed in secret backroom negotiations according to hidden agendas. NIST should assume leadership role by abandoning its current proposal and starting fresh.[43]

Should the government revert and elect to use the RSA algorithm, the government would have free usage, as the academics involved all received federal funding for the associated research, commercial entities, however, would have to pay RSA a license fee. Bidzos argued industry had already indicated its willingness to purchase RSA encryption technologies: "a well-studied and well-respected public-key system is worth paying a reasonable price for."[44] Bidzos argued in not adopting the *de facto*

---

[35] Schneier and Banisar, 1997, 307.
[36] Ibid, 306.
[37] National Institute of Standards and Technology, 1989, 472.
[38] National Institute of Standards and Technology, 1991.
[39] Bidzos, 1991.
[40] Ibid.
[41] Ibid.
[42] Ibid.
[43] Rivest et al., 1992, 47.
[44] Bidzos, 1991.

RSA businesses that had already deployed RSA rather than waiting for the decade late DSS would be "punished," having the "undesirable effect of discouraging the adoption of innovative technologies."[45] Whilst Bidzos' comment on the usurping of RSA as the principal public key algorithm were highly biased, they were not necessarily unrepresentative of the cryptologic community. The maximum DSS key size at 512 bits was considered too weak; Bidzos commented, "Any proposal, such as NIST's, that contains unnecessary restrictions on allowable key sizes…contains the cause of its own eventual demise."[46] Bidzos wrote he was "deeply concerned that it is likely NIST and NSA intend to restrict use of DSS to specific conditions facilitating their own ability to 'break the system.'"[47] Bidzos argued:

> a "breakable" system is effected by forcing the use of a single number or small group of numbers that the government can "break," but they believe no one else can. A number of the size proposed by NIST seems just about right for this scenario.[48]

Such a capability, Bidzos argued would give the "government unwarranted, unnecessary, and undesirable powers to violate personal privacy."[49] Bidzos argued there was also a risk of a "digital Pearl Harbor," whereby a foreign government also broke the digital signature standard bringing about "a devastating loss of the security of the entire national financial and business transaction systems."[50] Rivest questioned the rationale for having a fixed key-size:

> A national standard based on a fixed 512-bit key size would serve our country very poorly—such a proposal unnecessarily risks catastrophic failure of the integrity of our financial, industrial, and governmental information processing systems.[51]

Martin Hellman argued whilst a minimum key-size should be enforced to ensure an adequate level of security, there was no rationale for an upper limit—if one were imposed, Hellman advised it be increased to 1024-bit.[52] NIST responded to the criticism by increasing the key length to Hellman's recommended 1024 bits.[53] In the decades to come, the invocation of national crises as the result of not following their preferred path would be consistently conjured by digital rights activists, and later also by government officers in pursuit of funding.

Rivest also saw malevolent intent in NIST's patent application for DSS, a move he believed NIST's only motivation was to "force users, via licensing requirements, to use key sizes shorter than they might naturally wish to use."[54] Rivest labeled the DSA's selection process as "flawed…the DSS algorithm was created by the NSA, and adopted by NIST as its proposal, without any input from U.S. industry."[55] Rivest wrote, "the closed-door approach toward the development of DSS…created a

---

[45] Ibid.
[46] Ibid.
[47] Ibid.
[48] Ibid.
[49] Ibid.
[50] Ibid.

[51] Rivest et al., 1992, 43.
[52] Ibid, 47.
[53] Ibid, 54.
[54] Ibid, 41.
[55] Ibid, 45.

confrontational, rather than cooperative, situation between NIST and the U.S. industry."[56] Rivest added that, despite the comments period increasing from three to six months after industry criticism, such a period remained insufficient to "perform the mathematical study required to validate a new proposal."[57] To further compound this challenge, design criteria for the DSS was not released—a freedom of information act request by CPSR to liberate the design criteria was denied.[58] Rivest believed a weak DSS was the first step in a larger plan to "install weak cryptography as a national standard, and that NIST is doing so in order to please the NSA and federal law enforcement agencies"; he continued:

> While the DSS is nominally a proposal for only a signature standard, there are several public key encryption algorithms known that could make use of distributed DSS public keys. A strong signature algorithm invites extension to a strong public key encryption algorithm; concern about this possibility is probably the major reason NIST selected a scheme based on "weak cryptography" as its proposal. Should DSS be extended later to a public key encryption standard, weak cryptography will then be built into the national encryption standard, as well as the national signature standard.[59]

Bruce Schneier had similar concerns:

> There should be a NIST standard for public-key encryption. NIST is committing a grave injustice to the American people by not implementing a public-key encryption standard. It is suspicious that NIST proposed a digital signature standard that cannot be used for encryption.[60]

Martin Hellman drew attention to the vulnerability of using DSS as a common modulus system, and the absence of sufficient warnings about its use. Hellman reflected that whilst common modulus systems have the advantage of speed of key generation, they also have a negative trait:

> using a common modulus is analogous to having all personnel within an organization use combination locks with 10-digit combinations, but with the first nine digits being common to all users. This simplifies setting the combination...but allows an opponent to amortize the cost of an attack on one lock over the large number of locks that are then easily picked...clear warnings are needed about reduced security.[61]

However, there were alternate modes of use other than common modulus for DSS.

Bidzos, Rivest, and Hellman all had conflicts of interest with regard to the DSS algorithm. Bruce Schneier reflected on the "maelstrom of criticisms and accusations":

> it was more political than academic...they [RSADSI] wanted RSA, not another algorithm, used as the standard...RSADSI makes a lot of money licensing the RSA

---

[56] Ibid.
[57] Ibid.
[58] Ibid, 46.

[59] Ibid.
[60] Schneier, 1993, 306.
[61] Rivest et al., 1992, 48.

algorithm, and a royalty-free digital signature standard would directly affect the bottom line.[62]

NIST responded to criticisms by arguing the DSS was developed in accordance with established processes, adhering to CSA, and by drawing on NSA expertise:

> In the normal standards development process, NIST identifies the need for a standard, produces technical specifications of a standard using inputs from different sources, and then solicits government and public comment on the proposal. After the comment period, the comments are analyzed, appropriate changes are made and a standard is issued…This public process is being followed.[63]

NSA responded to the criticisms, quite curiously, through an interview with *Houston Chronicle* journalist Joe Abernathy:

> We state categorically that the chances of anyone—including NSA—forging a signature with the DSS when it is properly used and implemented is infinitesimally small.[64]

Further, the NSA stated they reviewed the "arguments purporting insecurities with the DSS, and we remain unconvinced of their validity."[65] NSA commented the "DSS had been subjected to intense evaluation," which led to its endorsement for use in "signing unclassified data processing in certain intelligence systems and even for signing classified data in selected systems."[66] The NSA stated that the DSS was even being used "in a pilot project for the Defense Message System to assure the authenticity of electronic messages of vital command and control information."[67] NSA articulated their role during the DSS selection:

> NIST requested that NSA evaluate candidate algorithms proposed by NIST for a digital signature standard and that NSA provide new algorithms when existing algorithms did not meet U.S. government requirements. In the two-year process of developing a digital signature for U.S. government use, NIST and NSA examined various publicly-known algorithms and their variants, including RSA.[68]

The NSA further stated they had "no role in limiting the power of cryptographic schemes used by the public within the U.S." and with regards to exports of cryptography NSA:

> analysis indicates that the U.S. leads the world in the manufacture and export of information security technologies. Of those cryptologic products referred to NSA by the Department of State for export licenses, we consistently approve over 90%.[69]

---

[62] Schneier, 1993, 305.
[63] Rivest et al., 1992, 53.
[64] National Security Agency, 1992.
[65] Ibid.
[66] Ibid.
[67] Ibid.
[68] Ibid.
[69] Ibid.

The CPSR's freedom of information request for DSS development documents was finally granted in 1993. The cache revealed the extent of the NSA's involvement. CPSR's lawyer David Sobel commented, "the super-secret NSA dominates the process of establishing security standards for civilian computer systems in contravention of the intent of legislation Congress enacted in 1987 [the CSA]."[70] Sobel added:

> DSS was the first test of the CSA's division of labor between NIST and NSA…The newly released documents suggest that NSA continues to dominate the government's work on computer security and to cloak the process in secrecy, contrary to the clear intent of Congress.[71]

Brook's General Accounting Office report also found discrepancies between the respective legal remits and the reality on the ground during development of the DSS assessing, "Although the CSA of 1987 reaffirmed NIST's responsibility for developing federal information-processing standards for the security of sensitive, unclassified information, NIST follows NSA's lead in developing certain cryptographic standards."[72]

The Computer System Security and Privacy Advisory Board (CSSPAB) wrote to NIST to express their "grave concerns" with the draft DSS proposal.[73] The 13-strong industry-government CSSPAB was established as part of the CSA in order to "identify emerging managerial, technical, administrative, and physical safeguard issues relative to computer systems and privacy."[74] The CSSPAB comprised one chair, four government seats, four vendor seats, and four non-government/vendor seats. Willis Ware of the RAND corporation, a non-profit think tank, was Chair in March 1992; government seats were occupied by representatives from NASA, NSA, and the Departments of Treasury and Transport.[75] Given their observance of the "mostly negative" public comments, the CSSPAB sent Ware to express their concerns to NIST's chairman, John Lyons.[76] Lyons told Ware the public would have to clearly explain the DSS' negative impacts should a change be desired.[77] With NIST unsympathetic to CSSPAB's concerns, it was decided in March 1992, CSSPABs should call for a national public review of cryptology policy, as "the factors which led to the selection of this [digital signature] algorithm are indicative of larger issues, compounding the need for a national review."[78] The CSSPAB issued a series of resolutions stating they would not endorse the DSS until this review was completed, and neither should the Commerce Director.[79] Support for such a review was given by most branches of government; however, NSA Director Vice Admiral John M. McConnell expressed his agencies' "serious reservations about a public debate on cryptography."[80] McConnell wrote:

---

[70] Sobel, 1993.
[71] Ibid.
[72] United States General Accounting Office, 1993, 3.
[73] Computer System Security and Privacy Advisory Board, 1992a, 5.
[74] Ibid, 1.
[75] Ibid, 2

[76] Ibid, 8.
[77] Ibid.
[78] Ware, 1992, 2; Computer System Security and Privacy Advisory Board, 1993a, 7.
[79] Computer System Security and Privacy Advisory Board, 1992b and 1992c.
[80] McConnell, 1992.

We do, however, support the need to ensure that government decision makers are made aware of the oft-conflicting interests of the various stakeholders who seek to influence cryptographic policy. To the extent that we can be assured that national security interests will not be jeopardized in a public debate, we are willing to pursue with NIST actions that address the concerns raised by the board.[81]

The CSSPAB also wrote to the outgoing Bush administration, and the incoming Clinton administration advising them of national cryptology's importance, and urging their support for the review.[82] The additional key escrow controversy in early 1993 contributed to President Clinton instructing his administration to conduct the desired national encryption policy review in May 1993—the National Security Council would chair the review.[83]

DSS also faced significant patent problems. Public Key Partners (PKP), who held the Diffie-Hellman and RSA patents, claimed the DSS violated their intellectual property. In an attempt to remove the patent obstacles, NIST announced its intent to grant an exclusive worldwide license to PKP in June 1993.[84] PKP's Robert Fougner stated, "only those parties who enjoy commercial benefit from making or selling products, or certifying digital signatures, will be required to pay royalties to practice the DSA," therefore the DSS would be royalty-free for personal, noncommercial, and government use.[85] The CSSPAB advised NIST their PKP plan, "may have latent consequences that would be negative for the country and general public"; the CSSPAB passed a resolution stating, "the original goal that the Digital Signature Standard would be available to the public on a royalty free basis has been lost," and the "economic consequences for the country have not been addressed in arriving at…the exclusive licensing arrangement with Public Key Partners."[86] The news was met with hostility by industry, causing a position reversal in April 1994, when the White House declared, "the Administration has determined that such technology should not be subject to private royalty payments, and it will be taking steps to ensure that royalties are not required for use of a digital signature."[87]

NIST announced the DSS' approval on May 13, 1994, stating it had resolved the concerns raised by 109 individuals and organizations, and had "addressed the possible patent infringement claims, and has concluded that there are no valid claims."[88] The news was not warmly received, even the Department of Treasury and Inland Revenue Services threatened to adopt RSA over the DSS.[89] An even more damming verdict came in June 1995, when many major technology players including Apple, Microsoft, and Netscape collaborated with RSA Data Security to form Verisign, which would become one of the world's most important digital-signature certification

---

[81] Ibid.
[82] Computer System Security and Privacy Advisory Board, 1993a, 7–8.
[83] Computer System Security and Privacy Advisory Board, 1994a, 1, 7.
[84] National Institute of Standards and Technology, 1993.
[85] Ibid.
[86] Ware, 1993, and Computer System Security and Privacy Advisory Board, 1993b.
[87] The White House, 1994a.
[88] National Institute of Standards and Technology, 1994a.
[89] Schneier and Banisar, 1997, 306.

authorities using RSA algorithms in competition to NIST's DSS.[90] By 1997, the DSS was making little progress; Bruce Schneier and David Banisar reflected, "To date, implementations of the DSS has been minimal."[91]

The government's handling of DSS had demonstrated itself to be inept and unattuned to public sentiment, yet the Clinton administration had opened another front in the crypto wars which in many ways would define the conflict: key escrow.

6.2   KEY ESCROW: CLIPPER CHIP GENESIS

To deliver key exchange and confidentiality, the NSA were quietly working to complete the Clipper chip in the early 1990s, a project initiated at the behest of the Justice Department, but also with roots in NIST's 1989 request.[92]

Key escrow is a form of regulation which tries to resolve the technical problem at the heart of the crypto wars: the provision of strong encryption defending citizens against digital threats, whilst allowing the government an "exceptional access" (back door) mechanism. There are two main theoretical issues with key escrow. Firstly, cryptologists have repeatedly derided the practicality of exceptional access methods within encryption algorithms.[93] Any form of access method, or encryption weakness, is also a vulnerability non-government actors can theoretically exploit. Secondly, key escrow relies on trusting the government not to abuse the accesses with which it is trusted—something very hard in the US with the then-recent history of Watergate and other incidents which damaged government trustworthiness. In the twenty-first century, the Trump administration has also demonstrated why governments should not be trusted absent verification mechanisms. Therefore, a transparent and robust system of checks and balances would be required for escrow to have any chance of gaining citizenry acceptance, and openness and security/intelligence operations are often in direct conflict. When considering key escrow, or any security control or regulation, implementation should depend on a risk calculation. Is the risk greater in leaving the technology unregulated, or in regulating, but accepting any associated risks with such regulation—the principal risk of key escrow is governmental abuse of power, an abuse that could contribute to an erosion of democracy. Ron Rivest made just this point when writing to Senators in 1997. Rivest argued technology should only be regulated when it was possible to do so, and when the benefits of regulations outweighed the costs.[94] Rivest argued cryptography didn't meet either of these conditions, as regulating encryption was like "trying to command the sea to retreat."[95] Rivest commented key escrow was like "soaking your flame-retardant materials in gasoline," risking a "catastrophic failure of the exact sort you were trying to prevent."[96] Rivest argued that should organized crime corrupt "just a few officials or judges…the security of our national information infrastructure [could end up] disappearing in the flames of keys 'recovered' by organized crime."[97]

---

[90] Reference for Business, 2002.
[91] Schneier and Banisar, 1997, 307.
[92] Sessions, 1993.
[93] Abelson et al., 2015.

[94] Rivest, 1997.
[95] Ibid.
[96] Ibid.
[97] Ibid.

Clipper was not the first time the NSA attempted to insert their algorithms into commercial products. The Commercial COMSEC Endorsement Program (CCEP) was a project in the mid-1980s to allow select industry partners to include classified US algorithms within their products, which would subsequently be NSA-certified.[98] Jim Bidzos reflects the CCEP was "Clipper in a black box"; the algorithm would not be able to be inspected to validate the absence of a covert NSA access mechanism.[99] The project was ultimately unsuccessful as industry had invested heavily in DES equipment, and a solution based on secret US technology could not serve the international market.[100] Further research is needed on this initiative.

More recently, in 1992, the FBI's Advanced Telephony Unit had written a paper entitled *Impact of Emerging Telecommunications Technology on Law Enforcement*, to reinforce their arguments, likely in preparation for any challenges to the Clipper policy the incoming Clinton administration may have presented. The secret document laid out the challenge facing law enforcement: "technology advances in the telecommunications industry will facilitate the development and production of affordable...cryptographically excellent encryption devices for voice, data and image transmissions."[101] The report explained telecommunications encryption products preventing government access were already being deployed.[102] The FBI predicted in the worst-case scenario that by 1994 only 40% of intercepted product would be unencrypted, with no useable product remaining by 1995.[103] Highlighting the value of intercept, the FBI stated between 1985 and 1991, wiretaps delivered seven thousand convictions, resulting in $295 million of fines, $756 million of recoveries, restitutions, and forfeitures, and $1.8 billion of prevented economic loss.[104] The FBI advocated a national cryptography strategy that "affords legitimate users of cryptography protection which their adversaries cannot defeat," whilst ensuring "cryptographic devices and systems are capable of real-time decryption by law enforcement"; most controversially, the FBI argued policy should "prohibit cryptography that cannot meet the standard enumerated."[105] The FBI believed "to permit unregulated use of excellent cryptography would establish an electronic sanctuary for conducting criminal activities, unfettered by legal process."[106]

Launching the controversial key escrow scheme amidst the political turbulence of an election year, in 1992 would be unwise. The ideal scenario was to launch Clipper near the start of a new presidential term allowing two years for any public disquiet to subside before mid-terms. The FBI and NSA also recognized the "pitfalls" of advancing Clipper with the current Bush administration, the most serious being if news of the "exploitable" chip emerged before the incoming Clinton administration approved the solution. FBI Director William Sessions was advised:

---

[98] United States House of Representatives, 1985, 101.

[99] Bidzos, 1994a.

[100] Diffie and Landau, 1999, 73.

[101] Advanced Telephony Unit, Federal Bureau of Investigation, 1992, 20.

[102] Ibid, 1.

[103] Ibid, 21.

[104] Ibid, 8.

[105] Ibid, 22.

[106] Ibid, 24.

If that happened, it might result in their being pushed toward disavowing the prior Bush administration approach in order to avoid the controversy, rather than the Clinton administration moving forward with us in a consolidated effort to convince Congress and the public of the merits of our position.[107]

However, there was a problem. In late 1992, AT&T were preparing to launch a line of secure telephones superior to anything on the market. It was the first attempt to sell a secure phone to the mass market, and 10,000 units would likely be produced by April 1993.[108] The AT&T Telephone Security Device (TSD) 3600 model used DES, it was portable, and could be connected to any hardwire telephone.[109] An FBI briefing memo described the 3600 technology as "superior to and more user friendly than similar telephone encryption devices," and at $1000 it was also half the price of similar devices.[110] The device was the size of a small book, and didn't weigh much more; it was connected between the phone and the handset with only two buttons and an LCD, the user simply clicked the "go secure" button to encrypt causing the 3600 to digitize the audio and encrypt the bitstream.[111]

Such a capability acceleration was directly opposed to the desires of the NSA and FBI. Intervention was needed before Clinton's inauguration. The Attorney General delegated the AT&T problem to FBI Director Sessions.[112] The Clipper chip's development was accelerated.[113] The government would need to request AT&T use the Clipper chip instead of DES to ensure market forces did not make their key escrow plans irrelevant. Sessions called AT&T's director, if they agreed to use Clipper in the 3600 the government would buy nine thousand units at a cost of $9 million.[114] The inducement worked, and for now at least, the market was kept in check.

FBI Director Sessions wrote to George Tenet, Special Advisor to the newly sworn-in President Clinton, and Senior Director for Intelligence Programs at the National Security Council on behalf of a working group comprising FBI, NSA, and the Department of Justice on February 19, 1993.[115] The top-secret letter informed Tenet:

Recent advances in communications technology, particularly telecommunications technology, and the increased availability and use of encryption threaten to significantly curtail, and in many instances preclude, effective law enforcement.[116]

Technical solutions would be needed to counteract this threat, "which need to be incorporated into all encryption products. To ensure this occurs, legislation mandating the use of Government-approved encryption products or adherence to Government encryption criteria is required."[117]

---

[107] Davis, 1992.
[108] Diffie and Landau, 1999, 233; Sessions, 1993.
[109] Crypto Museum, 2018.
[110] Sessions, 1993; Crypto Museum, 2018.
[111] Crypto Museum, 2018; Diffie and Landau, 1999, 233.
[112] Sessions, 1993.
[113] Baker, 1994.
[114] Davis, 1992; Levy, 2001, Chapter 8, The Clipper Chip; Sessions, 1993.
[115] Session, 1993.
[116] Ibid.
[117] Ibid.

The Clipper chip was authorized by President Clinton in a confidential directive of April 15, 1993, in which he stated, "the fact of law enforcement access to the escrowed keys will not be concealed from the American public."[118] Clinton wrote, "I do not intend to prevent the private sector from developing, or the government from approving, other microcircuits or algorithms that are equally effective in assuring both privacy and a secure key-escrow system."[119] Clipper was to deliver real-time voice, fax, and data encryption, and intercept capability.[120] Concurrently, Clinton issued a Presidential Review Directive instructing an interagency review on a number of cryptography topics, to include the impact of key escrow and whether it could be implemented in software.[121] Ten months later, the review assessed prevailing export controls were "in the best interest of the nation and must be maintained."[122] The White House publicly announced Clipper a day later.[123] Clipper was presented as a "voluntary program to improve the security and privacy of telephone communications while meeting the legitimate needs of law enforcement."[124] The voluntary nature suggests the Clinton administration believed a mandatory scheme would be unpalatable to the public, or not proportionate to the threat. Alternatively, it could be that a plan was developed to first establish Clipper and then to make key escrow mandatory. The announcement argued:

> We need the "Clipper Chip" and other approaches that can both provide law-abiding citizens with access to the encryption they need and prevent criminals from using it to hide their illegal activities.[125]

The White House felt a balance was struck between competing interests:

> The Administration is not saying, "since encryption threatens the public safety and effective law enforcement we will prohibit it outright"…nor is the U.S. saying that "every American, as a matter of right, is entitled to an unbreakable commercial encryption product." There is a false "tension" created in the assessment that this issue is an "either-or" proposition. Rather, both concerns can be, and in fact are, harmoniously balanced through a reasoned, balanced approach such as is proposed with the "Clipper Chip."[126]

The release explained the "state-of-the-art microcircuit" was developed by "government engineers," and:

> Each device containing the chip will have two unique "keys," numbers that will be needed by authorized government agencies to decode messages encoded by the device. When the device is manufactured, the two keys will be deposited separately in two "key-escrow" databases that will be established by the Attorney General. Access to

---

[118] The White House, 1993b.
[119] Ibid.
[120] The White House, 1994b.
[121] Ibid.
[122] Baker, 1994.

[123] The White House, 1993a.
[124] Ibid.
[125] Ibid.
[126] May, 1993a.

these keys will be limited to government officials with legal authorization to conduct a wiretap.[127]

The announcement argued Clipper "provides law enforcement with no new authorities to access the content of the private conversations of Americans."[128] It was subsequently announced escrowed keys would be stored with NIST, and the Automated Systems Division of the Treasury Department, who were chosen "because of their abilities to safeguard sensitive information, while at the same time being able to respond in a timely fashion when wiretaps encounter encrypted communications."[129] The release stated the Attorney General would procure several thousand AT&T Clipper devices to "demonstrate the effectiveness," and to further instill faith in the technology.[130] "Respected experts" would be given access to the Clipper algorithm to "assess its capabilities and publicly report their findings," though the algorithm would be kept secret from the general public.[131] AT&T's Ed Hickey separately stated Clipper would give their customers "far greater protection in defeating hackers or eavesdroppers attempting to intercept a call."[132] Hickey added Clipper would "support both the government's efforts to protect the public and the public's right to privacy."[133][134]

The announcement made The New York Times' front page, with NSA's involvement reported by John Markoff.[135] Clipper was initially an internal NSA term, rather than an official product name, but the administration had started using the term and it stuck.[136] The name was unfortunate and became the basis of many criticisms, William Safire later wrote in The New York Times the government initiative "clips the wings of individual liberty."[137]

Clipper programming would be executed in a specially created sensitive compartmentalized information facility (SCIF) within California-based Mykotronx.[138] Mykotronx were selected to complete the logic design for the Clipper chip in late 1991.[139] According to the White House, Mykotronx were selected due to their "expertise to quickly design custom design cryptographic chips...secure facilities and [top-secret] cleared personnel."[140] VSLI Technology, also of California, were chosen as the chip foundry "based primarily on its technological capabilities to fabricate microcircuits resistant to reverse engineering."[141]

The two 80-bit "seed" keys would be generated on separate computers at the Mykotronx SCIF, before being transferred to floppy disks which would then be inserted into a single computer to generate a final 80-bit composite programming

---

127 The White House, 1993a.
128 Ibid.
129 United States Department of Justice, 1994.
130 The White House, 1993a.
131 Ibid.
132 Banisar, 1993.
133 Ibid.
134 A later, heavy-weight, key escrow implementation was the Capstone chip, operating at ten megabits per second it incorporated SKIPJACK,

the Digital Signature Standard and the Diffie-Hellman key exchange algorithm.
135 Markoff, 1993a.
136 Levy, 2001, Chapter 8, The Clipper Chip.
137 Safire, 1994.
138 Sessions, 1993.
139 The White House, 1994b.
140 Ibid.
141 Ibid.

key, or unit key, for insertion to the Clipper chip.[142] As well as a unit key, each Clipper chip had a unique serial number. Clipper chips cost $30 when sold in 10,000 batches. Clipper operated at 12 megabits (million bits) per second.[143]

When two Clipper devices need to interact, they first negotiate a session key which is used to encipher 64-bit blocks of data. A Law Enforcement Access Field (LEAF) uses the chip's unit key to encipher the session key, which is joined with the chip's serial number and enciphered with the family key (common to all Clipper chips). To decipher the traffic, a government agent uses the family key to decipher the LEAF and extract the sending chip's serial number. The agent delivers the serial number and a legal warrant to the escrow agencies, who release the two-key parts, allowing the agent to extract the session key and decipher the message.[144]

6.3   KEY ESCROW: PUBLIC RESPONSE

The digital rights community offered an overwhelmingly negative response to the Clipper chip; however, there were those more open to a key escrow system. Jerry Berman, EFF's Executive Director offered a surprisingly positive response:

> the escrow system is an intriguing proposal, but the details of this scheme must be explored publicly before it is adopted. What will give people confidence in the safety of their keys? Does disclosure of keys to a third party waive an individual's Fifth Amendment rights against self-incrimination?[145]

The White House stated the Clipper algorithm, SKIPJACK, must remain classified to prevent non-escrowed, adversarial usage.[146] EFF Chairman Mitch Kapor commented, "A system based on classified, secret technology will not and should not gain the confidence of the American public."[147] Steve Jackson of Steve Jackson Games agreed:

> The manner in which this proposal has been put forward is improper and incomplete. An algorithm intended for private and commercial purposes should not be classified as a "national security matter." And it is wholly improper to ask for meaningful "citizen input" while the algorithm itself is secret.[148]

EFF also highlighted concerns at Clipper's genesis:

> Clipper Chipset was designed and is being produced and a sole-source, secret contract between the National Security Agency and two private firms: VLSI and Mycotronx. NSA work on this plan has been underway for about four years. The manufacturing contract was let 14 months ago.[149]

---

[142] Sessions, 1993.
[143] Denning, 1993, 320.
[144] Ibid, 321.
[145] May, 1993a.

[146] White House, 1994b.
[147] May, 1993a.
[148] Jackson, 1993
[149] May, 1993a.

Whitfield Diffie gave the following analogy when explaining Clipper to Congress:

> The effect is very much like that of the little keyhole in the back of the combination
> locks used on the lockers of school children. The children open the locks with the
> combinations, which is supposed to keep the other children out, but the teachers can
> always look in the lockers by using the key.[150]

Professor George Davida of the University of Wisconsin labeled the Clipper chip as
the "monster twin" of the digital signature standard.[151] Davida pointed out the term
"escrow" was described by Webster's Dictionary as "a deed, a bond, money, or piece
of property held in trust, so Davida commented:

> Privacy held in trust? By Police? By intelligence agents?...holding privacy in escrow
> is like holding someone's wife in escrow for a night. This is no escrow. This is an
> indecent proposal.[152]

Davida argued the US had become a "cryptographic third world" as a result of government market interference, "the effects of government control is taking its toll
on research in cryptography: the number of papers on design of new systems is
minuscule compared to the number of papers that deal with the one or two systems
in place."[153]

The cypherpunks were skeptical of Clipper. Their physical as well as digital footprint was expanding in 1993. Cypherpunk meetings were taking place in London and
Boston, as well as the original Bay Area gatherings, a Southern California chapter
was also planned.[154] Tim May commented on Clipper, "the Clinton and Gore folks
have shown themselves to be enthusiastic supporters of Big Brother," and warned the
cypherpunks to "Be afraid, be very afraid."[155] Derek Zahn urged the cypherpunks to
start "sharpening our rhetorical knives," Eric Hughes promised, "no compromises,"
whilst Detweiler posted, "Someone please wake me from this nightmare...let's man
the battlestations."[156]

The cypherpunks and wider digital rights activists had expected the Clinton
administration to herald a new age of liberalized cryptography controls. John Perry
Barlow comments the administration members he met seemed:

> extremely smart, conscious freedom-lovers...I was sure that after they were fully
> moved in, they"d face down the NSA and the FBI, let Clipper die a natural death, and
> lower the export embargo on reliable encryption products.[157]

However, by the time Clipper was announced, Barlow commented that the transformation of his administration friends made him feel "like I was in another remake

---

[150] Diffie, 1993.
[151] Davida, 1993, 1.
[152] Ibid, 3.
[153] Ibid, 2.

[154] May, 1993b.
[155] May 1994c; May, 1993a.
[156] Zahn, 1993; Hughes, 1993a; Detweiler, 1993.
[157] Barlow, 1994.

of the *Invasion of the Body Snatchers*."[158] Barlow says, "They'd been subsumed by the vast minefield on the other side of the security clearance membrane, where dwell the monstrous bureaucratic organisms that feed on fear. They'd been infected by the institutionally paranoid NSA."[159] Barlow reflects how his friends "used all the tell-tale phrases," Mike Nelson who was leading the National Information Infrastructure program told Barlow, "If only I could tell you what I know, you'd feel the same way I do," to which Barlow replied he was inoculated against that argument during Vietnam.[160] Barlow had good access to the administration, even on occasion hitching a ride aboard Air Force Two with the US Vice President, he reflected, "when I talk to people in the administration their big hobgoblin is the 'nuclear-armed' terrorist."[161] Barlow assessed eliminating the possibility of such an attack, by whatever means necessary was the principal concern of Clinton and Gore, "to which even the future of American liberty and prosperity is secondary."[162] Barlow believed, "They have been convinced that such plots are more likely to ripen to hideous fruition behind a shield of encryption."[163] This world view was likely reinforced by the terrorist bombing of the World Trade Center in February 1993. Whilst the attack only killed six people, it was supposed to be much more potent, with the explosion intended to topple the north tower into the south tower, killing thousands.[164] Barlow comments staffers were immune to the argument "anyone smart enough to steal a nuclear device is probably smart enough to use PGP or some other uncompromised crypto."[165] Barlow's response to the use of nuclear-armed terrorists to justify Clipper reflected that of many cypherpunks:

> I'm willing to take my chances with the few terrorists and drug lords there are out there rather than trusting government with the kind of almost unlimited surveillance power which Clipper...would give them. It's a tough choice. But when you look at the evil perpetrated by government over this century in the name of stopping crime, it far exceeds that done by other organized criminals.[166]

Perry Barlow believed they were engaged in a:

> revolutionary war...Clipper is a last ditch attempt by the United States, the last great power from the old Industrial Era, to establish imperial control over cyberspace. If they win, the most liberating development in the history of humankind could become, instead, the surveillance system which will monitor our grandchildren's morality. We can be better ancestors than that.[167]

David Sobel believed the security establishment had engaged the Clinton administration with:

---

[158] Ibid.
[159] Ibid.
[160] Ibid.
[161] Time Online Odeon, 1994.
[162] Barlow, 1994.
[163] Ibid.
[164] Federal Bureau of Investigation, 2008.
[165] Barlow, 1994.
[166] Time Online Odeon, 1994.
[167] Barlow, 1994.

horror stories about terrorist attacks, more World Trade Center bombings...I think politically, anyone in a decision-making position...is likely to take what they would probably consider to be the cautious approach. And I would assume that's what the administration believes it's doing here.[168]

John "Captain Crunch" Draper also argued criminals would unlikely use the system:

Now, if I were a criminal, do you think I would be dumb enough to "register" my phone with the government. Of course not. I would probably get mine on the black market, or through some other illicit means!![169]

Cypherpunk Sandy Sandfort argued whilst the government was "being coy about it," their intent was to ban non-Clipper encryption.[170] Cypherpunk Phil Karn agreed, writing a voluntary Clipper made "no sense whatsoever...one simply cannot escape the conclusion...[Clipper] is a prelude to a ban on all other encryption schemes, or at least a ban on those the government can't crack."[171] Phil Zimmermann concurred, believing citizens were being treated like an "enemy population," and felt "to make Clipper completely effective, the next logical step would be to outlaw other forms of cryptography."[172] It would be August 1995 before an EPIC FOIA request resulted in disclosure of the FBI Advanced Telephony Unit's 1992 recommendation non-escrowed encryption should be outlawed, David Sobel of EPIC commented that the document:

demonstrates that the architects of the Clipper program—the NSA and the FBI—have always recognized that key-escrow must eventually be mandated. As privacy advocates and industry have always said, Clipper does nothing for law enforcement unless the alternatives are outlawed.[173]

Further FOIA-acquired declassified files affirm legislation against all non-Clipper encryption producers was discussed by the FBI and NSA; however, the latter believed it would be "difficult."[174] Continuing suspicions of encryption's outlawing led NIST to issue a special press release in May 1994, following their testimony to Congress in which Ray Kammer stated, "Let me be clear...this Administration does not seek legislation to prohibit or in any way restrict the domestic use of cryptography."[175] Detweiler wanted to know, "Why is it that this process [Clipper] has been wholly shielded from public view until now?"[176] Cypherpunk Hal Finney disagreed with Sandfort's belief that cryptography would be made illegal, believing, "The plan instead is to make it [key escrow] a *de facto* standard for all encrypted voice communications," and arguing, "the government will initially exert as much influence as it can to prevent any competing standard from getting a toehold."[177] Finney believed

[168] Voice of America, 1994.
[169] Draper, 1993.
[170] May, 1993c.
[171] Karn, 1993.
[172] Bulkeley, 1994; Zimmermann, 1999.
[173] Electronic Privacy Information Center, 1995.

[174] National Security Agency, 1993.
[175] National Institute of Standards and Technology, 1994c.
[176] Detweiler, 1993.
[177] Finney, 1993.

the government had waited until the Clipper Chips were ready in volume, to provide AT&T and key escrow with an advantage in the market:

> It's doubtful that anyone else could even come up with a standard that soon, let alone get it into hardware…If the standard does become established, it could be tough to defeat it. How easy is it going to be to sell a phone which is incompatible with everybody else's for secure communication?[178]

John Perry Barlow agreed:

> The administration is trying to impose Clipper on us by manipulating market forces. By purchasing massive numbers of Clipper devices, they intend to induce an economy of scale which will make them cheap while the export embargo renders all competition either expensive or nonexistent.[179]

Whilst John Perry Barlow was not amongst those who saw imminent government machinations to ban all non-escrowed encryption in the US, he was concerned such plans could "develop in the presence of some pending 'emergency'" such as a terrorist attack or other high-profile threat.[180] Barlow noted the administration's earlier comment that no citizen had a right to "unbreakable commercial encryption products," asking:

> Now why, if it's an ability they have no intention of contesting, do they feel compelled to declare that it's not a right? Could it be that they are preparing us for the laws they'll pass after some bearded fanatic has gotten himself a surplus nuke and used something besides Clipper to conceal his plans for it?

Detweiler felt whilst Clipper was "an illegitimate child…borne of grotesque bedfellows (e.g. Denning, Clinton, and the NSA)," it was "bringing into public view important issues of cryptography."[181] An anonymous cypherpunk warned against an overly emotive narrative being projected to the public:

> An assertion of the power of the ideas expressed on this list will put the Cypherpunks in the discourse of public policy. Obviously, it should be well thought out and expressed in the most positive way. Calm, cool, calculated response will gain the cpunks respect, a knee jerk, emotional response will only get our ideas ignored.[182]

The cypherpunks considered branding Clipper as the "wiretap chip" to color public opinion.[183] May reflected on the fleeting attention of media consumers to whom they must direct their messaging, journalists consistently requested "pithy quotes" and soundbites of him to reach their short attention span audiences causing May to

---

[178] Ibid.
[179] Barlow, 1994.
[180] Ibid.

[181] Detweiler, 1993.
[182] Anonymous Poster, 1993.
[183] May, 1993d.

"shake my head in despair," before trying to fulfill their requests.[184] Eric Hughes had become proficient at providing such pithy quotes to help the cypherpunks' message; he was quoted in *The New York Times*' Clipper coverage arguing, "This plan [Clipper] creates the ears of Big Brother, just as Orwell warned."[185] May considered targeting the broad public as a means to change the Clipper policy imprudent, arguing, "Crypto is too abstract for most people. I doubt anything we say can change this. And 'privacy' is a complicated theme."[186] May believed instead that "the key is to reach the relatively small fraction of policy shapers, both outside government and inside."[187] May believed whilst the "suits" of EFF or CPSR talked with "Congresscritters," there was a "more guerilla-oriented" role for the cypherpunks to play creating a "good cop bad cop" dynamic.[188] May advocated active measures, "More covert efforts to disrupt Clipper-type activities," telling the cypherpunks to "use your own imagination here."[189] One active measure was to use "Big Brother Inside" stickers, emulating the "Intel Inside" stickers; May posted, "While I will not encourage you to surreptitiously place these stickers on boxes containing the products of the aforementioned companies, let your conscience be your guide. Wink."[190] May argued, "Subversive actions that generate media attention, that trigger other people to begin to do things...and that create new communities...are much more effective."[191] Phil Zimmermann would later suggest the cypherpunks start referring to key escrow instead as key forfeiture.[192] Eric Hughes had dinner with John Gilmore and John Perry Barlow in late May after their trip to "DC with the rest of the EFF Board to talk to politicos." Gilmore and Barlow told Hughes, "Clinton has signed onto Clipper full-bore 100%...They're going to deploy Clipper without regard to public sentiment." Hughes said, "This is serious, make no mistake. If...the government does restrict everything to be Clipper, all anonymity and pseudonymity efforts are worthless."[193]

Cypherpunk Matt Blaze pointed out a hardware-only Clipper solution would disadvantage the US in the global market. Blaze wrote to NIST, explaining software encryption can be added to a product at virtually no increase in marginal cost, whereas "hardware-based encryption...can add over a hundred dollars to end price of each unit." This additional cost would either result in US products without encryption, or products with encryption manufactured overseas without key escrow, therefore Blaze wrote, "it is doubtful that the proposed standard will achieve sufficient mass-market penetration to have much impact on the security of our communications networks."[194] Phil Karn agreed, "The Escrowed Encryption Standard is not only fatally flawed on any number of Constitutional considerations, its sole reliance on hardware implementation makes it completely impractical and uneconomical for the mass consumer market." Karn argued in advancing such a scheme, NIST, "far

---

184 Ibid.
185 Markoff, 1993b.
186 May, 1993d.
187 May, 1993g.
188 May, 1994c.
189 Ibid.

190 Ibid.
191 May, 1993g.
192 Zimmermann, 1994.
193 Hughes, 1993b.
194 Blaze, 1993.

from being an independent and impartial agency...has proven itself to be merely a pawn for the National Security Agency, the Federal Bureau of Investigation and other powerful intelligence and law enforcement agencies."[195]

Clipper was not fairing much better in Congress. Senator Patrick Leahy commented, "The Administration is rushing to implement the Clipper chip program without thinking through crucial details."[196] Jack Brooks, addressing the House, argued attempts to "limit encryption is just plain fanciful." Rather than, "promoting scattershot policies, which restrict American industries' ability to design, produce, and market technology," Brooks argued that the government "would be better served by finding real, and targeted ways to deal with international terrorists and criminals."[197] William Safire's "Sink the Clipper Chip" opinion piece in *The New York Times* made a similar argument:

> Billions now spent on passive technical surveillance must be shifted to active means of learning criminal or aggressive plans. Human informers must be recruited or placed, as "sigint" declines and "humint" rises in the new era; psychic as well as monetary rewards for ratting must be raised; governments must collude closely to trace transfers of wealth.[198]

Vice Admiral McConnell did not believe Clipper would harm US exports; "if it has any effect at all, it could increase exports," he commented. McConnell stated it was difficult to predict how the foreign market would react, he acknowledged those foreign companies fearful of US interceptions would likely avoid Clipper. However, McConnell believed the superior strength of SKIPJACK may encourage sales, and some foreign companies wanting to trade with the US government may buy SKIPJACK products. There was the possibility of other foreign governments wishing to procure a version of Clipper, though whilst there had been "preliminary discussions," no further progress had been achieved.[199]

The external panel of cryptologists assembled by the administration to review the SKIPJACK algorithm included Dorothy Denning, who the cypherpunks viewed, in Phil Karn's words, as a "naïve pawn of the government," who "lost whatever credibility she had in the crypto community by her [Clipper] position," and Walter Tuchman, who worked on DES at IBM.[200] The reviewers were briefed by the head of the NSA evaluation team who described their evaluation process and results.[201] They were also given further history of the algorithm, SKIPJACK's "immediate heritage" dated to 1980 and was representative of a family of NSA encryption algorithms known as "type 1," which protect data of all classification levels.[202] SKIPJACK was initially designed for use in government communications systems, and was expected to last "at least" 15 years.[203] SKIPJACK's initial design took place in 1987.[204] The algorithm is described as:

---

[195] Karn, 1993.
[196] Levy, 1994.
[197] Brooks, 1994.
[198] Safire, 1994.
[199] McConnell, 1994.

[200] May, 1994a; Brickell et al., 1993.
[201] Brickell et al., 1993.
[202] Ibid.
[203] The White House, 1994b.
[204] Brickell et al., 1993.

a 64-bit "electronic codebook" algorithm that transforms a 64-bit input block into a 64-bit output block. The transformation is parameterized by an 80-bit key, and involves performing 32 steps or iterations of a complex, nonlinear function.[205]

The head of NSA's evaluation team told the reviewers he believed SKIPJACK could only be broken by "brute force, there is no better way."[206] The White House stated SKIPJACK endured "intense expert scrutiny comparable to that used in the analysis of cryptography intended for classified government systems."[207] SKIPJACK's 80-bit keys offered more than a trillion trillion key possibilities.[208] At 24 bits longer than 56-bit DES, SKIPJACK provided an increased key space by 2^{24}, which according to the NSA made it 16 million times stronger.[209] NSA estimated a "modern super-computer" would take over a billion years to search the key space.[210] NSA stated, "while the government does not issue warranties for algorithms it makes available to the public or indemnify users against the failure or compromise of an algorithm, we are confident of its security."[211] The reviewers estimated using a single processor on an 8-processor Cray Y-MP supercomputer performing 89,000 encryptions per second would result in the key space exhaustion in 400 billion years.[212] Utilization of all eight processors could reduce the time to around a billion years, and looking to the future, a machine capable of 100,000 encryptions per second, which would likely cost $50 million, could reduce the attack time to 4 million years.[213] An "even more speculative attack," on a hypothetical "special purpose $1.2 billion machine" build with "1.2 billion $1 chips with a 1 GHz clock" could exhaust the key space in a year, though such a machine was heavily theoretical.[214] Another comparison drawn was that the cost of breaking SKIPJACK would not be equal to the cost of breaking DES today for another 36 years.[215]

The reasons SKIPJACK was classified as Secret, the reviewers wrote in their report, was as aspects of the algorithm incorporate techniques "representative of algorithms used to protect classified information," and as:

Disclosure of the algorithm would permit the construction of devices that fail to properly implement the LEAF, while still interoperating with legitimate SKIPJACK devices. Such devices would provide high quality cryptographic security without pre-serving the law enforcement access capability that distinguishes this cryptographic initiative.[216]

The reviewers summarized that "SKIPJACK is based on some of NSA's best tech-nology, considerable care went into its design and evaluation in accordance with

205 Ibid.
206 Ibid.
207 The White House, 1994b.
208 Brickell et al., 1993.
209 Ibid.
210 The White House, 1994b.

211 Ibid.
212 Brickell et al., 1993.
213 Ibid.
214 Ibid.
215 Ibid.
216 Ibid.

the care given to algorithms that protect classified data."[217] Their ultimate findings were:

1. "Under an assumption that the cost of processing power is halved every eighteen months, it will be 36 years before the cost of breaking SKIPJACK by exhaustive search will be equal to the cost of breaking DES today. Thus, there is no significant risk that SKIPJACK will be broken by exhaustive search in the next 30–40 years."

2. "There is no significant risk that SKIPJACK can be broken through a shortcut method of attack."

3. "While the internal structure of SKIPJACK must be classified in order to protect law enforcement and national security objectives, the strength of SKIPJACK against a cryptanalytic attack does not depend on the secrecy of the algorithm."[218]

The influential Computer System Security and Privacy Advisory Board held two days of hearings on Clipper before issuing resolutions in June 1993 stating, "serious concerns regarding the key escrow initiative and that more time was needed to achieve a better understanding of the issues."[219] The resolutions further stated:

key escrowing encryption technology not be deployed beyond current implementations planned within the Executive Branch, until the significant public policy and technical issues inherent with this encryption technique are fully understood.[220]

The pressure from the public caused government hesitation. Acting Director of NIST Ray Kammer announced a delay in Clipper's implementation pending a review to complete in the fall.[221]

Democratic Congressman Edward Markey of Massachusetts, chair of the House Subcommittee on Telecommunications and Finance, noted Clipper raised an "arched eyebrow amongst the whole committee"—hearings were swiftly convened.[222] Marc Rotenberg, CPSR's Washington office director, testified on June 9, 1993:

To evaluate the Clipper proposal it is necessary to look at a 1987 law, the Computer Security Act, which made clear that in the area of unclassified computing systems, the National Institute of Standards and Technology (NIST) and not the National Security Agency (NSA), would be responsible for the development of technical standards.[223]

Rotenburg argued Clipper undermined the CSA, declaring that "it reflects the interests of one secret agency with the authority to conduct foreign signal intelligence and another government agency responsible for law enforcement investigations."[224]

---

[217] Ibid.
[218] Ibid.
[219] National Computer System Security and Privacy Advisory Board, 1993a.
[220] Ibid.
[221] Rotenburg, 1989.
[222] Ibid.
[223] Ibid.
[224] Ibid.

NSA's Clinton Brooks would later contest this interpretation of the CSA, stating in Congressional testimony:

> Our function as an advisor in the field of information security became more active with the passage of the Computer Security Act of 1987. The Act authorizes the National Bureau of Standards (now NIST) to draw upon the technical advice and assistance of NSA.[225]

Brooks accentuated the role of NSA as a technical advisor, rather than instigator of strategy, during the Clipper program:

> the FBI and NIST sought our technical advice and expertise in cryptography to develop a means to allow for the proliferation of robust encryption technology without sacrificing law enforcement's cur rent capability to access communications under lawfully authorized conditions.[226]

NSA's Stewart Baker would later also address this issue:

> NSA has more expertise in cryptography than any other entity in the country, public or private...To say that NSA shouldn't be involved in this issue is to say the government should try to solve this difficult technical and social problem with both hands tied behind its back.[227]

NIST's Raymond Kammer later commented of the CSA, "The act says we can draw on N.S.A...They're the pre-eminent scientists in cryptography in the world. We tasked the agency to design a technology to fit the needs of the civilian community."[228]

Diffie's testimony took a more philosophical view of the Clipper chip and the use of technology to restrict privacy, he told the committee:

> No right of private conversation was enumerated in the constitution. I don't suppose it occurred to anyone at the time that it could be prevented. Now, however, we are on the verge of a world in which electronic communication is both so good and so inexpensive that intimate business and personal relationships will flourish between parties who can at most occasionally afford the luxury of traveling to visit each other.
> If we do not accept the right of these people to protect the privacy of their communication, we take a long step in the direction of a world in which privacy will belong only to the rich.[229]

Diffie added:

> Where technology has the capacity to support individual rights, we must enlist that support rather than rejecting it on the grounds that rights can be abused by criminals.

---

[225] Brooks, 1994.
[226] Ibid.
[227] Baker, 1994.

[228] Markoff, 1993b.
[229] Diffie, 1993.

If we put the desires of the police ahead of the rights of the citizens often enough, we will shortly find that we are living in a police state.[230]

Further pressure was added from industry when the Digital Privacy and Security Working Group, an alliance of technology companies and civil rights groups including the ACLU, Apple, EFF, IBM, the Business Software Alliance, and Microsoft, wrote to President Clinton on December 6, 1993, confirming their "tentative acceptance" of Clipper, "but only if it is available as a voluntary alternative to widely available, commercially accepted, encryption programs and products."[231] The implication was industry would treat Clipper as a niche product designed to meet a government-only need.

Cryptologists did not guise their disdain for Clipper in the diplomatic language of the corporate world, nor did they believe even a voluntary Clipper would be able to be ignored as perhaps business leaders did. Three dozen cryptography experts, led by CPSR, wrote to President Clinton in January 1994 asking for Clipper's withdrawal.[232] The experts wrote, "Few in the user community believe that the proposal would be truly voluntary," they cited the government's "enormous influence in the marketplace, and the likelihood that competing standards would survive is small."[233] An electronic version of the letter was put online as a petition—more than fifty thousand people signed.[234] Another benefit of an escrowed standard was it would pressure government departments to buy Clipper equipment; Jim Bidzos stated, "By using the standards making authority of NIST, NSA is attempting to force the entire U.S. government to purchase Clipper equipment since only NIST-standard equipment may be purchased by government agencies."[235]

The Commerce Secretary approved FIPS 185, the Escrowed Encryption Standard (EES) in February 1994.[236] The Federal Register announcement re-emphasized the voluntary nature of the standard. Samuel Kramer, Associate Director of NIST stated the vast majority of the 298 public comments during the standards approval process were negative.[237] NIST estimated establishing the escrow system would cost $14 million, with the annual operating costs being $16 million.[238] Addressing the lack of a software implementation of SKIPJACK, Kramer wrote, "because software is easy to change, secure software implementations of the key escrow technique have been difficult to devise."[239] Kramer stated NIST had asked for the software industries' assistance in solving this challenge in August 1993, and was trying to establish partnerships to develop escrow encryption in software.[240] Many of the comments received sought further assurance Clipper was not the first step in a plan to ban all

---

[230] Ibid.
[231] McCandlish, 1993.
[232] Computer Professionals for Social Responsibility, 1994a.
[233] Ibid.
[234] Computer Professionals for Social Responsibility, 1994b.

[235] Bidzos, 1994a.
[236] National Institute of Standards and Technology, 1994d.
[237] Ibid.
[238] Ibid.
[239] Ibid.
[240] Ibid.

non-escrowed cryptography, so to address this request the White House issued a
release stating:

> Today, any American can purchase and use any type of encryption product. The
> Administration does not intend to change that policy. Nor do we have any intention
> of restricting domestic encryption or mandating the use of a particular technology.[241]

The White House soon realized the perception struggle they were confronting, staffers started referring to Clipper as "our Bay of Pigs," and "the Bosnia of
Telecommunications."[242] NSA engaged with the media to try and convince the public, especially the scientific and technology communities, of Clipper's merit. Stewart
Baker, Chief Counsel for the NSA wrote an article in *Wired* magazine, a literary and
cultural staple of the technology community. Baker wrote, "With all the enthusiasm
of Baptist ministers turning their Sunday pulpits over to the Devil, the editors of
WIRED have offered me the opportunity to respond to some of the [Clipper] urban
folklore."[243] If this article were part of a charm offensive, it was a radical failure ful-
filling many stereotypes of an NSA bereft of emotional intelligence. Addressing the
claim encryption was vital to liberty, Baker wrote:

> This sort of reasoning is the long-delayed revenge of people who couldn't go to
> Woodstock because they had too much trig homework. It reflects a wide—and kind of
> endearing—streak of romantic high-tech anarchism that crops up throughout the com-
> puter world. The problem with all this romanticism is that its most likely beneficiaries
> are predators.[244]

After all but branding digital privacy activists "nerds," and likely further alienating
their counterculture roots, Baker argued:

> We can't afford as a society to protect pedophiles and criminals today just to keep alive
> the far-fetched notion that some future tyrant will be brought down by guerrillas wear-
> ing bandoleers and pocket protectors and sending PGP-encrypted messages to each
> other across cyberspace.[245]

Whilst Baker's characterization of the cypherpunks was an exaggeration, there was
an element of truth in his words. For instance, cypherpunk Nate Sammons posted to
the list in March 1994:

> I cannot help but think that having the gov looking in on us will be good. I know, get
> my head shrunk, but look: It gives us something to fight for. Look at me: Somewhat of a
> slacker who for a long while thought there was nothing worth fighting for...now there's
> the government to fight! What better entity to wage war against? It's the classic "valiant

---

[241] The White House, 1994c.   [244] Ibid.
[242] Barlow, 1994.   [245] Ibid.
[243] Ibid.

fight" the "good guys against the bad guys" fight. It's the kind of fight you may even feel yourself wanting to fight...I can't help thinking what a kick I'll get out of seeing my kids in the future saying, upon them finding my "Cypherpunk Criminal" T-Shirt in the attic, "Gosh! Dad was a Cypherpunk! Wow!"[246]

Baker professed a key escrow world would look, "only a little different from the one we live in now." Baker argued rather than the government changing the surveillance status quo, it was digital privacy activists who:

> want to create a brave new world, one in which all of us—crooks included—have a guarantee that the government can't tap our phones. Yet these proponents have done nothing to show us that the new world they seek will really be a better one.[247]

Baker argued encryption was oversold as a "privacy protector," before commenting, "the biggest threats to our privacy in a digital world come not from what we keep secret but from what we reveal willingly." Given the future of social media, Baker's was a prescient point. Baker stated companies would still be able to develop unescrowed encryption for domestic consumption; however, they would be "hastening a brave new world of criminal immunity," and those companies would not be "able to ride piggyback on federal research efforts," nor could they sell such a product to both private and public sector customers. Baker also contested the virtue of encryption for cyber security, stating it was "at best, a small part of network security."[248]

Tensions reached a zenith when an NSA employee threatened to kill Jim Bidzos in June 1994.[249] Bidzos was a belligerent opponent of the initiative, going as far as to write, "I believe it may even be possible to conclude that Clipper is the visible portion of a large-scale covert operation on U.S. soil by NSA."[250] Bidzos had come to believe:

> The success of this company [RSA] is the worst thing that can happen to them [NSA]. To them, we're the real enemy, we're the real target...If the U.S. adopted RSA as a standard, you would have a truly international, interoperable, unbreakable, easy-to-use encryption technology. And all those things together are so synergistically threatening to the N.S.A.'s interests that it's driving them into a frenzy.[251]

Bidzos reflected, "If we are ever in danger of undermining the NSA, they will either buy us or shoot us."[252] However, as a significant figure in the cryptographic industry, doubtless holding government contracts, Bidzos had continuing contact with the NSA. Whilst meeting with three NSA representatives, two of whom Bidzos says he "respected and trusted," the third representative threatened to run him over in the car park, about which Bidzos commented, "he looked at me and very coldly and said he would do me...he clearly threatened me."[253] Bidzos described the two other officers

---

246 Sammons, 1994.
247 Ibid.
248 Ibid.
249 May, 1994b.

250 Bidzos, 1994a.
251 Levy, 1994.
252 May, 1994b.
253 Bidzos, 1994b; May, 1994b.

as "shocked and literally speechless, staring into their laps."[254] Bidzos offered the representative a chance to withdraw his words and apologize, but he elected not to. "I am certain that he was not speaking for the agency," Bidzos commented, "but when it happened he was quite serious, at least appeared to be. There was a long silence after he made the threat, with a staring contest. He was quite intense."[255] After details of the threat were published in the *San Jose Mercury*, the NSA representative's boss called Bidzos offering an apology, but the incident further reinforced the animosity between the government and private sector.[256] Tim May commented after the incident, "I think things are really heating up...it looks like they're playing hardball."[257]

Assistant US Attorney Walker said, "If you ask the public, 'Is privacy more important than catching criminals?' They'll tell you, 'No.'"[258] However, a *Time/CNN* poll of 1,000 Americans in June 1994, found more than two-thirds believed it more important to protect the privacy of phone calls than to preserve the ability of police to conduct wiretaps.[259] Eighty percent opposed Clipper.[260] EFF's Jerry Berman comments, "The idea that the Government holds the keys to all our locks, before anyone has even been accused of committing a crime, doesn't parse with the public, it's not America."[261] The White House argued key escrow strengthened Fourth Amendment protections, as "law enforcement cannot obtain the contents of communication without first obtaining the key component."[262] Further, the White House briefed, "Systems are being designed to ensure that keys are destroyed when the authority to conduct a particular electronic surveillance has expired."[263] NSA's Clinton Brooks argued Clipper was a privacy-enhancing technology, as it would deliver widespread use of encryption, whereas before its launch virtually nobody used encryption.[264] NSA's Stewart Baker would later say, despite the negative response to Clipper:

> the government went forward with key escrow, not because the key escrow proposal received a universally warm reception, but because none of the proposal's critics was able to suggest a better way to accommodate society's interests in both privacy and law enforcement.[265]

The hostile press coverage continued with a scathing OpEd in *The New York Times* from William Safire, who wrote:

> To the tune of "I Got Algorithm," the Eavesdrop Establishment is singing that it will help us protect our privacy—but not from intrusion by the Feds. In effect, its proposal demands we turn over to Washington a duplicate set of keys to our homes, formerly our castles, where not even the king in olden times could go.[266]

---

254 Bidzos, 1994b.
255 Ibid.
256 Levy, 2001, Slouching Towards Crypto, Chapter 9.
257 May, 1994b.
258 Meeks, 1994.
259 Elmer-Dewitt, 1994.
260 Ibid.
261 Levy, 1994.
262 The White House, 1994b.
263 Ibid.
264 Brooks, 1994.
265 Baker, 1994.
266 Safire, 1994.

Safire continued, "the solution that faceless Clinton officials are putting forward shows outdated law enforcement rooted in abysmal understanding of the information explosion."[267]

To make things worse for the administration, cypherpunk Matt Blaze found a vulnerability in the LEAF in late 1994. Blaze was able to use an exhaustive search to create a LEAF that passed the Clipper's checksum validations, but provided the wrong details to any interceptors thus preventing decryption.[268] Blaze explained:

> With only access to the chip's standard interface, one could easily create a "rogue" device that could happily interoperate with legitimate escrowed peers, enjoy the use of the strong SKIPJACK cipher, but be impervious to the key escrow back door. The only thing stopping you was a 16 bit exhaustive search, a very low barrier.[269]

There was a catch: the attack took around 42 minutes, making it infeasible for real-time communications such as secure telephone conversations, though the attack could be viable for email communications, and with further refinement and additional hardware it was possible that attack time could be reduced.[270]

In Blaze's paper explaining his findings he wrote, "We are particularly grateful for the spirit of openness and collegiality displayed by the members of NSA in reviewing these results."[271] Blaze's engagement with NSA was one of the rare examples of friendly (or at least not openly hostile) collaboration between those on opposite sides of the encryption debate. Blaze was careful in early interactions with the agency to "avoid needlessly inflammatory commentary on the wisdom of key escrow or on whether NSA should be trusted," and as a result the NSA trusted Blaze with prototypes of *Tessera*, a next-gen key escrow device, likely hoping his impartial analysis would adhere to scientific findings rather than political opinions.[272] Blaze also worked for AT&T, so the NSA perhaps assessed they could leverage that relationship to influence Blaze's actions if required.

The discovery reached the front of *The New York Times*. Blaze commented in the article, "Nothing I've found affects the security of the Clipper system...This does quite the opposite. Somebody can use it to circumvent the law-enforcement surveillance mechanism."[273] Martin Hellman reflected, "The Government is fighting an uphill battle...people who want to work around Clipper will be able to do it."[274] The NSA disagreed; Director of Policy Michael A. Smith argued, "Anyone interested in circumventing law-enforcement access would most likely choose simpler alternatives...More difficult and time-consuming efforts, like those discussed in the Blaze paper are very unlikely to be employed."[275] Such a statement that there were easier ways to circumvent Clipper was unlikely reassuring to the public, though NSA did

---

[267] Ibid.
[268] Blaze, 1995.
[269] Blaze, 2011.
[270] Blaze, 1995.
[271] Blaze, 1994.

[272] Blaze, 2011, 2.1.
[273] Markoff, 1994b.
[274] Ibid.
[275] Ibid.

have a point, and the latency issues would certainly have been a strong hindrance to the use of Blaze's attack.[276]

It was also possible adversaries could add a layer of encryption on top of SKIPJACK to circumvent it. For instance, an email client using SKIPJACK could send a PGP, or DES message as the email body, subsequently the SKIPJACK encryption would be applied, and to the government the encrypted traffic would be consistent with SKIPJACK. However, should the government decipher the SKIPJACK cipher text they would find another layer of encrypted text—the NSA conceded this was a vulnerability, though it would require user awareness to achieve.[277] The NSA never came up with a strong argument for why criminals would choose to use an escrowed technology, instead arguing this was not SKIPJACK's primary purpose—in written testimony to Congress Vice Admiral Mike McConnell stated:

> Key escrow encryption is not meant to be a tool to catch criminals. It will make excellent encryption available to legitimate businesses and private citizens without allowing criminals to use the telecommunications system to plan and commit crimes with impunity.[278]

The FBI's lead New York agent Jim Kallstrom was blunter in responding to this issue:

> Thank God most criminals are stupid!…If the smartest segment of the population ever went into crime, we would really have a problem. Will some criminals catch on to the system, and buy their encryption from, let's say, Israel? Yes. Will that be a problem? Yes. But it will be a substantially smaller problem than if we didn't do anything.[279]

Douglas R. Miller of the Software Publishers Association evidenced the availability of foreign encryption, "We…located 340 foreign cryptographic products sold by foreign countries."[280] However, NSA Director McConnell dismissed the ability of companies and adversaries to access these foreign encryption products, framing his narrative to present the only competition to Clipper as home-brewed cryptography: "Serious users of encryption do not entrust their security to software distributed via networks or bulletin boards."[281] McConnell explained:

> There is simply too much risk that viruses, Trojan Horses, programming errors, and other security flaws may exist in such software which could not be detected by the user. Serious users of encryption, those who depend on encryption to protect valuable data

---

[276] Further research into Clipper's technical vulnerabilities, often focusing on the LEAF, occurred within the years after Blaze's findings. Notable within this body of research was Yair Frankel and and Moti Yung's 1995 article *Encryption Escrow Systems Visited: Attacks, Analysis and Designs.* However, no technical issue alone proved sufficient to catalyze Clipper's demise.

[277] McConnell, 1994.
[278] Ibid.
[279] Fallows, 1994.
[280] Levy, 1994.
[281] McConnell, 1994.

and cannot afford to take such chances, instead turn to other sources in which they can have greater confidence. [282]

One promising front for the digital privacy activists during the second crypto war was Democratic Representative Maria Cantwell. Cantwell of Washington State, the home of Microsoft, took aim at the export regulations by adding a pro-cryptography amendment to H.R. 3627, the Export Administration Act's reauthorization bill in 1993.[283] The government needed the export regulations to hold until key escrowed products were accepted as the way forwards and could by exported preventing foreign targets acquiring strong cryptography absent a US access mechanism. Introducing the amendment to the House of Representatives, Cantwell stated, "American software companies, some of America's star economic performers, have estimated they stand to lose between $6 and $9 billion in revenue each year."[284] Cantwell explained American companies "hold a 75 percent worldwide market share and many derive over 50 percent of their revenues from foreign sales…hardware manufacturers earn more than 60 percent of their revenues from exports."[285] Cantwell told the House encryption technologies had been available for over a decade and were readily available worldwide yet, "Incredible as it may seem to most of my colleagues, the Executive Branch has seen fit to regulate exports of American computer software with encryption capabilities," this is "well-intentioned, but completely misguided and inappropriate policy [having] all the practical effect of shutting the barn door after the horses have left."[286] Cantwell declared the "export control system is broken. It was designed as a tool of the cold-war, to help fight against enemies that no longer exist."[287] Cantwell explained her bill:

> would give the Secretary of Commerce exclusive authority over dual use information security programs and products, eliminates the requirement for export licenses for generally available software with encryption capabilities, and requires the Secretary to grant such validated licenses for exports of other software with encryption capabilities to any country to which we already approve exports for foreign financial institutions.[288]

The digital privacy community mobilized; rallied by the EFF they sent Cantwell 5600 messages of support.[289] John Gilmore said the bill was "the dream we've all been working toward."[290] Software companies such as Apple, IBM, Hewlett Packard, Microsoft, and Sun Microsystems also expressed their support in a letter to the President.[291] The White House was not so keen, Vice President Gore called Cantwell to ask her to withdraw the bill—she respectfully declined.[292]

The amendment was referred to the House and Senate Intelligence Committees for review; Gilmore described the committees as "watchdogs for the NSA…[who]

---

[282] Ibid.
[283] United States Congress, 1993.
[284] Godwin, 1994.
[285] Ibid.
[286] Ibid.
[287] Ibid.
[288] Ibid.
[289] McCandlish, 1994.
[290] Ibid.
[291] Ibid.
[292] Levy, 2001, Chapter 8, The Clipper Chip.

tend to follow the agency's wishes when they wave the magic 'national security' wand"; Gilmore believed their intent was to "kill or severely maim" the amendment.[293] The committees did indeed strike Cantwell's amended text, replacing it with a promise to conduct two studies to inform future policy, the first would look at the economic impact of cryptography policy, and the second, on the general availability of cryptography overseas—both were to be completed by 1995.[294]

Writing to Cantwell in July 1994, Gore reiterated that the administration, "disagrees with you on the extent to which existing controls are harming U.S. industry in the short run and the extent to which their immediate relaxation would affect national security."[295] Vice President Gore told Cantwell when the results of the two studies into encryption policy were complete, "we will reassess our existing export controls based on the results of these studies."[296] Gore also urged cooperation for the administration's key escrow policy, stating it could be realized by:

> entering into a new phase of cooperation among government, industry representatives and privacy advocates with a goal of trying to develop a key escrow encryption system that will provide strong encryption, be acceptable to computer users worldwide, and address our national needs as well.[297]

Gore also opened up the possibility of exploring variations of the government's current proposals:

> The Administration understands the concerns that industry has regarding the Clipper Chip. We welcome the opportunity to work with industry to design a more versatile, less expensive system. Such a key escrow system would be implementable in software, firmware, hardware, or any combination thereof, would not rely upon a classified algorithm, would be voluntary, and would be exportable.[298]

Cantwell welcomed the Vice President's willingness to compromise, saying, "I view this as going down a new path, with a new set of criteria."[299] Nathan Myhrvold, senior vice president for advanced technology at Microsoft was also elated, stating, "Maria Cantwell has gone head to head with the powers that be and they blinked. The Clipper chip is dead at least for any kind of data stuff."[300] Myhrvold's assessment of Clipper's death would prove to be greatly exaggerated. When Cantwell received a call from the White House asking whether they could rescind the letter it became evident the Vice President's letter was not the result of a government-wide policy but of a White House maneuver designed to placate Cantwell. Cantwell declined to allow the letter to be withdrawn.[301]

---

[293] McCandlish, 1994.
[294] Office of Technology Assessment, 1996, 63.
[295] Gore, 1994.
[296] Ibid.
[297] Ibid.
[298] Ibid.
[299] Markoff, 1994a.
[300] Ibid.
[301] Levy, 2001, Chapter 8, The Clipper Chip.

6.4   KEY ESCROW: SON OF CLIPPER

Following Gore's letter, NIST announced a "renewed dialogue" and a series of workshops with industry to explore the Vice President's offer.[302] NIST indicated that under a new Clipper policy 64-bit escrowed encryption would be available for expedited export and keys could be managed by foreign countries, "with which the U.S. Government has formal agreements consistent with U.S. law enforcement and national security requirements."[303] The renewed policy became known as the "Son of Clipper," or Clipper II. The workshops were acrimonious; David Sobel wrote of them, "participants expressed widespread dissatisfaction with the direction of government encryption policy"; he added, "The clear message...was that any form of mandatory key-escrow technology would not be acceptable."[304] Sobel declared, "As long as the NIST continues to promote this policy it is acting against the better interests of the American people."[305] Robert Hollyman, President of the Business Software Alliance, stated in the workshops "the Administration's 'new' encryption policy appears to be little more than the old policy in new clothing," adding:

> An even more ominous interpretation of the Administration's recent announcements also suggests itself—the government is pursuing a "Son of Clipper" strategy that could lead to the *mandatory* use of key escrow encryption.
> How so? Clearly the government is trying to force America's software companies to include government sought key escrow features in its software as the "price" for export approval. Because of the companies' strong desire to develop and sell a single version of their programs worldwide, the government thus hopes to be able to have users abroad and in the United States.[306]

Another front opened in June 1995 when Republican Senator Chuck Grassley of Iowa introduced S. 974, the Anti-Electronic Racketeering Act, containing language effectively outlawing the online dissemination of encryption.[307] The legislation read:

> it shall be unlawful to distribute computer software that encodes or encrypts electronic or digital communications to computer networks that the person distributing the software knows or reasonably should know, is accessible to foreign nationals and foreign governments, regardless of whether such software has been designated as nonexportable.[308]

As the Internet is a global network, all resources were available to "foreign nationals"; therefore, the legislation effectively made online dissemination of encryption illegal. However, there was an exception:

---

[302] National Institute of Standards and Technology, 1995.
[303] United States Department of Commerce, 1995.
[304] Sobel, 1995b.
[305] Ibid.
[306] Ibid.
[307] United States Congress, 1995.
[308] Ibid, Section 1030.

It shall be an affirmative defense to prosecution under this section that the software at issue used a universal decoding service or program that was provided to the Department of Justice prior to the distribution.[309]

Essentially, if the encryption algorithm was escrowed, or potentially had another mechanism allowing government access, it could be disseminated online and therefore exported. The bill had no co-sponsors and little support. Phil Dubois, who was facing off with the government as Phil Zimmermann's lawyer, labeled the legislation "an abomination."[310] David Sobel of EPIC believed the bill to be:

> an attempt to mandate the result the Administration sought to achieve with the failed Clipper Chip initiative—ensuring law enforcement access to *all* encrypted communications through government-escrowed keys.[311]

Whilst it is possible this was the case, given the absence of support for the bill in Congress, and the lack of nuance in the legislation's language, it did not bear the hallmarks of a Clinton administration initiative. Cypherpunk Shabbir Safdar commented whilst the bill comprised "all the things that would irk us [it] isn't immediately going anywhere, and there's more dangerous legislation on the floor that is looking a lot like a loaded gun."[312] Safdar advised the cypherpunks to "not go running off every time some DC bozo writes a terrible bill," and they should "not try to divide the forces of the net on bills that aren't yet a serious threat."[313] Robbie Westmorland worried the cypherpunks raising the alarm could amplify the bill which was at the earliest legislative stage.[314] Paul Elliott agreed, hoping "the bill might be quietly forgotten."[315] To the relief of the cypherpunks, the bill passed gently into the night.

6.5 CRYPTOGRAPHY'S ROLE IN SECURING THE INFORMATION SOCIETY (CRISIS)

In November 1993, Congress instructed the National Research Council, a body whose composition included members of the National Academies of Science and Engineering, to establish a committee to study and advise on national cryptographic policy.[316] The committee comprised sixteen members representing a range of interests. Committee members included a former NSA deputy-director, a former attorney general, as well as business and academic representatives such as Martin Hellman.[317] Their research was underwritten by public law 103–160, instructing all federal departments, including the NSA, to "cooperate fully" with the study.[318] Thirteen of the research group received security clearances enabling them to receive classified NSA briefings.[319] The committee stated whilst, "some secrets are still legitimate"

---

[309] Ibid.
[310] Washington Technology, 1995.
[311] Sobel, 1995a.
[312] Safdar, 1995.
[313] Ibid.

[314] Elliott, 1995.
[315] Ibid.
[316] National Research Council, 1996.
[317] Dam, 1997.
[318] National Research Council, 1996, ix.

they wanted to disclose as much information as possible to the public without compromising the NSA's legitimate interests.[320] The committee recognized the NSA's traditional position of "if you knew what we knew, you would agree with us," was not conducive to transparent debate on cryptographic policy, and therefore announced they would attempt to "act as a surrogate for well-intentioned and well-meaning people who fear that the worst is hidden behind the wall of secrecy."[321]

On behalf of the cypherpunks, John Gilmore compiled a list of questions to send the NRC to be used in questioning law enforcement agencies.[322] The questions were reflective of the cypherpunk community, with topics ranging from the relevant and probing, to queries befitting conspiracy theorists.[323] On receiving the cypherpunk question list, NRC representative Herb Lin kindly requested Gilmore reformulate the list into "sensible questions."[324]

After studying the issues, the cleared members of the committee concluded whilst classified material was important to operational matters, "it is neither essential to the big picture of why cryptography policy is the way it is nor required for the general outline of how technology will and policy should evolve in the future," and therefore, "the debate over national cryptography policy can be carried out in a reasonable manner on an unclassified basis."[325] This approach was not intended to diminish the legitimate challenges encryption presented to law enforcement and intelligence agencies; the report drew from a recent government assessment to highlight the threat:

> specialized technical operations (including computer intrusions, telecommunications targeting and intercept, and private-sector encryption weaknesses) account for the largest portion of economic and industrial information lost by U.S. corporations.[326]

The report, *Cryptography's Role in Securing the Information Society*, was issued in 1996. The committee chair, Kenneth W. Dam, wrote, "the committee is not unaware of the acronym for this report—CRISIS—and it believes that the acronym is apt."[327] However, Dam believed the crisis was a *"policy* crisis, rather than a technology crisis, an industry crisis, a law enforcement crisis, or an intelligence-gathering crisis" [original italics][328] The committee assessed, "widespread commercial and private use of cryptography in the United States and abroad is inevitable in the long run and that its advantages, on balance, outweigh its disadvantages."[329] The report concluded, "the overall interests of the government and the nation would best be served by a policy that fosters a judicious transition toward the broad use of cryptography."[330] However, the report advised, "respecting legitimate national needs of law enforcement and intelligence for national security and foreign policy purposes to

[319] Ibid, xiv.
[320] Ibid.
[321] Ibid.
[322] Gilmore, 1995a.
[323] Gilmore, 1995b.
[324] Gilmore, 1995a.

[325] National Research Council, 1996, 4.
[326] National Counterintelligence Center, 1995.
[327] National Research Council, 1996, xv.
[328] Ibid.
[329] Ibid, 13.
[330] Ibid.

the extent consistent with good information protection."[331] The committee assessed, "current national cryptography policy is not adequate to support the information security requirements of an information society."[332] Recommendations included: "No law should bar the manufacture, sale, or use of any form of encryption within the United States," and "National cryptography policy...should be more aligned with market forces."[333] Regarding export policy, the report noted, "Export controls also have had the effect of reducing the domestic availability of products with strong encryption capabilities"; this was because rather than produce two versions of their products, one with stronger cryptography available for domestic use, and one with weaker cryptography for export, vendors would typically only build a single version to minimize production cost. The committee advised, "Export controls on cryptography should be progressively relaxed but not eliminated."[334]

Controversially, the committee recommended a new law criminalizing the use of encryption when used as part of an illegal act, in the same manner as using the mail system to conduct crime resulted in additional penalties being levied upon offenders.[335] The committee recognized the danger of such laws being used to prosecute targets when the underlying crime cannot be proven, or when encryption is on the "periphery" to the actual crime under investigation, they advised that this was not the intent of their recommendation, and that it would be "largely the integrity of the judicial and criminal justice process that will be the ultimate check on preventing its use for such purposes."[336]

The committee urged the government to accelerate their adaption to the new era of encryption: "High priority should be given to research, development, and deployment of additional technical capabilities for law enforcement and national security for use in coping with new technological challenges."[337] The committee advised 56-bit DES should be easily exportable, the currently allowed strength was 40 bits, which research had shown was increasingly vulnerable to brute force attacks.[338] Export would be dependent on manufacturers providing "full technical specifications of their product and reasonable technical assistance upon request in order to assist the U.S. government in understanding the product's internal operations."[339]

Tim May posted on the report, "I'm not as disappointed as I expected to be," saying:

> I think this NRC report comes down strongly enough in favor of cryptography use for business and individuals that it will effectively *derail* and *stall* current Administration proposals...and delay key escrow systems for at least several years. This should be enough to ensure our victory.[340]

---

[331] Ibid, 1.

[332] Ibid, 6.

[333] Ibid, 7.

[334] Ibid, 8.

[335] Ibid, 332.

[336] Ibid.

[337] Ibid, 10.

[338] Wiener, 1994.

[339] United States Department of State, 1996, 9.

[340] May, 1996.

Hal Finney was frustrated with the report, believing it adopted too much "of the point of view of those forces which will oppose the use of cryptography."[341] Finney argued:

> At best it seems to be a recognition that change is inevitable, and that the most that can be hoped for is to ease the transition to a world where people have free access to privacy tools. But in the meantime it appears designed to delay the transition rather than advance it.[342]

Finney recognized the increased recommendation for export from 40 to 56 bits was a step forward, and believed 56 bits likely represented the maximum key length NSA was able to break.[343] Rich Graves posted whilst the underlying technical recommendations, such as the limitation of 56 bits was not entirely congruent with the positive messaging of the report, the general public and politicians would only understand the more positive headline that "NRC Report Backs Crypto Exports and *Real* Security"; he told the cypherpunks to "Work the headline, claim that they agree with you 100% (even though you know that they don't), and continue to say what you believe. It's called politics."[344] The committee suggested a clear strategic direction, but left many of the tactical and technical questions unresolved, in particular how a legal access method could be built. Bidzos commented, "The next battleground is going to be Capitol Hill because the Administration isn't going to give up easily."[345]

6.6   KEY ESCROW: CLIPPER III

The Interagency Working Group on Cryptography Policy published a draft paper entitled *Enabling Privacy, Commerce, Security and Public Safety in the Global Information Infrastructure* on May 20, 1996.[346] It became known as Clipper III. The paper outlined an evolution to the key escrow policy, allowing for "key management infrastructure, voluntary and supported by private sector key management organizations," and would "permit users and manufacturers free choice of encryption algorithm."[347] The working group outlined a number of principals of the new system. As well as voluntary participation, the system would see industry lead development of escrowed products and associated protocols, and export controls on escrowed products would be progressively relaxed.[348] Following on from the report, the White House formally announced the new key escrow policy on July 12, 1996; the administration proposed an escrow framework to be developed by industry and available for domestic and international use.[349] "Trusted private sector parties" would hold the recovery keys, with a mechanism also in place for individuals and corporations to recover their own keys when required.[350] The administration stated the approach was similar to that adopted by other countries, and would "permit nations to establish an

---

[341] Finney, 1996.
[342] Ibid.
[343] Ibid.
[344] Graves, 1996.
[345] Markoff, 1996.

[346] Executive Office of the President, 1996.
[347] Ibid.
[348] Ibid.
[349] The White House, 1996a.
[350] Ibid.

internationally interoperable key management infrastructure with rules for access appropriate to each country's needs and consistent with law enforcement agreements."[351] The government would work with industry to develop appropriate standards for key recovery systems allowing them to gain export permission.[352] Notable in the press release was the favoring of the term "key recovery" rather than "key escrow," the latter having evidently suffered from the debate which had now raged for three years.

Senator Conrad Burns commented, "It's three strikes and you're out...I would say that the third version of the administration's Clipper Chip proposal is a swing and a miss."[353] Twenty-seven members of Congress, including Bob Goodlatte and Zoe Lofgren, urged the President to withdraw his key escrow policy and ease export restrictions in May 1996.[354]

FBI Director Freeh testified before congress calling for "socially-responsible" encryption products in July 1996. Freeh noted a number of examples where cryptography was hindering, or would soon hinder, law enforcement. Examples included a spy, Aldrich Ames, who was advised by his Russian handlers to transmit American secrets using encryption, a child pornography target who used encryption to transmit obscene images, a "major" drug trafficking investigation where a target used telephone encryption, and anti-government militias who were advocating cryptography usage.[355]

Freeh also sought to present international key escrow as an inevitability, declaring:

> There is now an emerging opinion throughout much of the world that there is only one solution to this national and international public safety threat posed by conventional encryption...key escrow encryption.[356]

Attorney General Janet Reno supported this view, stating:

> A consensus is now emerging throughout much of the world that the best way to achieve this balance is by creating a system, otherwise known as Key Escrow, to entrust the encryption keys with a neutral third party.[357]

Freeh argued whilst "some strong encryption products can be found overseas, they are simply not ubiquitous, and, as of yet, they have not become embedded in the basic operating systems and applications found overseas.[358] Freeh stated international partners raised "strong concerns" when the export of stronger US encryption was broached, fearing America would "be flooding the global market with unbreakable cryptography, increasing the likelihood of its use by criminal organizations and terrorists throughout Europe and the world." Freeh reflected, "Ironically, the

---

[351] Ibid.
[352] Ibid.
[353] Office of Senator Conrad Burns, 1996.
[354] Campbell, Goodlatte and Eshaoo, 1996.
[355] Freeh, 1996.
[356] Ibid.
[357] Reno, 1996.
[358] Freeh, 1996.

relaxation of export controls in the U.S. may well lead to the imposition of import controls overseas."[359] Freeh believed:

> If strong, key escrow encryption products proliferates both overseas and domestically which will not interoperate (at least in the long-term) with non-key escrow products, then escrowed encryption products will become the worldwide standard and will be used by almost everyone, including the criminal elements.[360]

Freeh added that key escrow:

> permits law enforcement and national security agencies to protect the American public from the tyranny of crime and terrorism. We believe, as do many others throughout the world, that technology should serve society, not rule it; and that technology should be designed to promote public safety, not defeat it.[361]

On October 1, 1996, Vice President Al Gore offered an incentive to industry to cooperate with key escrow. Gore announced 56-bit encryption, such as DES, would be exportable after a one-time review, and, "contingent upon industry commitments to build and market future products that support key recovery"; the accommodation was to last two years, after which the only unescrowed encryption permitted for export would be 40 bits and below. The export of 56-bit encryption was a significant upgrade from the currently exportable 40-bit cryptography systems. However, export licenses would only be granted for six-month periods—if companies should fail to demonstrate progress towards key escrow, they could lose their licenses.[362]

Eleven companies quickly formed the "key recovery alliance" to "develop an exportable, worldwide approach to strong encryption" in October 1996.[363] The companies included Apple, DEC, HP, IBM, and RSA, some of the largest technology producers in the world—two years of being able to export 56-bit encryption was a substantial prize.[364] Jim Bidzos was among the most boisterous of key escrow opponents, but he was now part of the alliance: "Export controls are a fact of life," he commented, adding:

> The key recovery alliance's approach will allow companies to use cryptography with differing levels of security in an interoperable way…in an imperfect world this technique will at least allow you to take advantage of what governments around the world will allow.[365]

IBM's Irving Wladawsky-Berger stated, "Key recovery will truly open the Internet for serious business, once businesses are confident that their electronic transactions are safe and they control the recovery of keys, a flood of new market opportunities will open."[366] The alliance quickly grew to more than fifty companies.[367] Heidi

---

[359] Ibid.
[360] Ibid.
[361] Ibid.
[362] The White House, 1996b.
[363] Apple et al., 1996.
[364] Ibid.
[365] Ibid.
[366] Ibid.
[367] United States House of Representatives, 1997, 41.

Kukis from Vice President Gore's office commented, "I think we have a critical mass of companies willing to work with us."[368] David Sobel of EPIC commented:

> While some companies might choose to cast their lot with the government's key-escrow policy, the marketplace is likely to reject the approved products...users want strong security, not guaranteed government access to their communications.[369]

Despite their words and actions, it is unknown whether the commercial organizations truly intended to support key escrow.

In an internal government memo, William Reinsch conceded in November 1996, that escrowed products were "more costly and less efficient than non-escrowed products."[370] Reinsch also acknowledged the "real risk that multinational corporations will move production of these non-key recovery products offshore to avoid new U.S. restrictions."[371] The foreign community was divided over key escrow. In the OECD France and the UK sided with America's key recovery proposals, Australia, Canada, Denmark, and Finland all opposed on the grounds of civil liberties in March 1997.[372] The Europe Commission also rejected US proposals for key recovery in October 1997, their report feared the proposal could undermine digital commerce and Internet adoption "If citizens and companies have to fear that their communication and transactions are monitored with the help of key access or similar schemes, they may prefer remaining in the anonymous off-line world."[373] William Reinsch commented:

> I am a little surprised...My question to the European Commission is, where do they think the market is going? Our sense is that corporations engaged in electronic commerce want key recovery in some form, because they want to recover their own records and to monitor their own employees.[374]

FBI Director Freeh, speaking to a Senate subcommittee for the first time publicly acknowledged the FBI's desire for domestic cryptography controls in September 1997:

> What we would recommend from a law enforcement point of view is that the legislation contain a provision that would require the manufacturers of encryption products and services, those which will be used in the United States or imported into the United States for use, include a feature which would allow for the immediate, lawful decryption of the communications or the electronic information.[375]

The comment was part of a response to questions rather than part of a pre-prepared statement—it quickly became evident his message did not have the administration's approval. Reinsch stated, "The administration has been very clear to the director that he has an obligation to tell Congress what's in the interests of law enforcement, and

---

368 Lash, 1996.
369 Ibid.
370 Reinsch, 1996.
371 Ibid.

372 Ackerman, 1998.
373 Andrews, 1997.
374 Ibid.
375 United States Senate, 1997.

he did that. That doesn't mean he was speaking for everybody."[376] Reinsch added, "What he [Freeh] proposed was not the administration's policy."[377] Becca Gould of the Business Software Alliance called the plan awful, commenting, "It's basically saying the government should have a back-door key to all private citizens' records."[378]

Representatives David Weldon and Ronald Dellums added an amendment to the SAFE bill, one of many encryption-related bills transiting through Congress, the amendment would make it illegal to sell non-escrowed encryption in the US:

> As of January 1, 1999, it shall be unlawful for any person to manufacture for sale or distribution within the U.S., distribute within the U.S., sell within the U.S., or import into the U.S. any product that can be used to encrypt communications or electronic information, unless that product includes features, such as key recovery, trusted third party compatibility or other means, that permit immediate decryption upon receipt of decryption information by an authorized party without the knowledge or cooperation of the person using such encryption product.[379]

A few days later, an even more aggressive amendment was added by Congressmen Oxley and Manton—their text would ban all encryption technologies unless it permits "immediate access to the plaintext."[380] Immediate access would be infeasible with the key escrow access methods previously outlined; therefore, the processes would need to be reworked, potentially devaluing some of the in-built protections against abuse. Oxley commented, "Law abiding citizens have no reason to fear this [amendment]."[381] The Oxley-Manton amendment was virulently opposed by a broad spectrum of groups. Business leaders wrote to Congress, as did privacy lobbyists.[382] Jerry Berman of the Center for Democracy and Technology commented, "This is not the first step toward the surveillance society—it is the surveillance society."[383] Cypherpunk Anthony Garcia wrote to former FBI officer Congressman Oxley giving his name and address, declaring, "I fully intend to willfully break your stupid law exactly one minute after the moment it goes into effect," Garcia told Oxley, "So, get ready to arrest me, Big Mike. Get out your old FBI shield and shine it up, because I AM GOING TO BREAK YOUR LAW. GOT IT?"[384] A collection of eminent law professors wrote a letter to Congress to protest the "unprecedented proposal that has been advanced to impose criminal penalties on the manufacturing or distribution of domestic encryption products that do not contain a government-mandated backdoor."[385] The professors argued the legislation would cause the US to "no longer be a leader protecting individual rights internationally; we would instead become the architect of the most comprehensive surveillance plan the world has seen since the

[376] Pressman, 1997.
[377] Ibid.
[378] Chandrasekaran, 1997.
[379] United States Congress, 1997a.
[380] United States Congress, 1997b.
[381] Clausing, 1997.
[382] Markoff, 1997b.
[383] Markoff, 1997a.
[384] Garcia, 1997.
[385] Aoki et al., 1997.

end of the Cold War." The Professors argued the plan was as "unconstitutional as it is unwise." The Professors wrote:

> Congress faces a historic choice about the shape of free speech and privacy in the next century. In making this choice, there will no doubt be many questions of profound importance to our constitutional values. But there is little doubt that the Intelligence Committee substitute and the Oxley-Manton amendment would inspire the creation of an unprecedented system of global surveillance, expanding law enforcement authority and circumventing the protections of the First and Fourth amendments. It is too radical a change to make with so little thought. We urge you to resist it.[386]

"That would move us into an entirely new world of surveillance, a very intrusive surveillance, where every communication by every individual can be accessed by the FBI." "Where is probable cause?" Senator Lott asked, "Why has the FBI assumed that all Americans are going to be involved in criminal activities? Where is the Constitution?" Lott argued, "the FBI proposal would: Invade our privacy; be of minimal use to the FBI; would require nonexistent technology; would create new administrative burdens; and would seriously damage our foreign markets." Lott added, "I have learned that even the administration does not support this new FBI proposal. So why does the FBI believe it must now subject all Americans to more and more surveillance?" Lott concluded, "Americans should not be forced to only communicate in ways that simply make it more convenient for law enforcement officials. This is not our national tradition. It is not consistent with our heritage."[387]

After four hours of debate, the Oxley-Manton amendment was defeated in the House Commerce Committee by 35–16 in September 1997.[388] With Oxley-Manton's demise, a slow recognition perhaps started to fall upon the security and intelligence agencies—commerce and privacy would be prioritized over security by Congress and the American people—that state would not change until September 11, 2001.

Clipper was fading from existence by 1998. Key escrow/recovery was never officially withdrawn, but with multiple failed attempts, a Congress increasingly hostile to encryption controls, courts affirming that constitutional protections applied to cyberspace, and a burgeoning technology industry the government quietly allowed Clipper to sail into oblivion. Very few of the AT&T 3600s were ever built, apart from those procured by the Department of Justice in an attempt to seed the market.[389] NSA declassified SKIPJACK in July 1998.[390] Though it is unclear what struck the killing blow, and no funeral was ever held, key escrow was dead. The other major fight of the second crypto war, the challenging of the export regulations, was still unfolding; to tell that story we have to go back to 1991.

---

[386] Ibid.
[387] Lott, 1997.
[388] Clausing, 1997.

[389] Diffie and Landau, 1999, xv.
[390] Schneier, 1998.

REFERENCES

ARTICLES

Abelson, H., Anderson, R., Bellovin, S. M., Benaloh, J., Blaze, M., Diffie, W., Gilmore, J., Green, M., Landau, S., Neumann, P. G., Rivest, R. L., Schiller, J. I., Schneier, B., Specter, M. A., and Weitzner, D. J. (2015). Keys under Doormats: Mandating Insecurity by Requiring Government Access to All Data and Communications. *Journal of Cybersecurity* **1**(1), 69–79.

Ackerman, W. M. (1998). Encryption: A 21st Century National Security Dilemma. *International Review of Law, Computers & Technology* **12**(2), 371–394.

Denning, D. (1993). The Science of Computing: The Clipper Encryption System. *American Scientist* **81**(4), 319–323.

Garfinkel, S. (1995). *PGP: Pretty Good Privacy* (New York: O'Reilly Media Inc).

Rivest, R. L., M. E. Hellman, and J. C. Anderson (1992). Responses to NIST's Proposal. *Communications of the ACM* **35**(7). 41–52.

BOOKS

Diffie, W. and Landau, S. (1999). *Privacy on the Line: The Politics of Wiretapping and Encryption* (Massachusetts: MIT Press).

Levy, S. (2001). *Crypto: Secrecy and Privacy in the New Cold War* (New York: Viking Penguin).

National Counterintelligence Center. (1995). *Annual Report to Congress on Foreign Economic Collection and Industrial Espionage* (United States Government).

National Research Council. (1996). *Cryptography's Role in Securing the Information Society* (Washington, DC: The National Academies Press).

Schneier, B. (1993). *Applied Cryptography Protocols, Algorithms, and Source Code in C.* (New York: John Wiley & Sons).

Schneier, B. and Banisar, D. (1997). *The Electronic Privacy Papers: Documents on the Battle for Privacy in the Age of Surveillance.* (New York: John Wiley & Sons Inc.).

CHAPTERS IN BOOKS

McNulty, L. (1997). Letter from Lynn McNulty, NIST, to James Hearn, NSA, and Raymond Kammer, 19 May 1989. In *The Electronic Privacy Papers: Documents on the Battle for Privacy in the Age of Surveillance.* Edited by Bruce Schneier and David Banisar (New York: John Wiley & Sons Inc.), 479–480.

Unknown NSA Author. (1990). Technical Support to NIST, 19 October 1990. In *The Electronic Privacy Papers: Documents on the Battle for Privacy in the Age of Surveillance.* Edited by Bruce Schneier and David Banisar (New York: John Wiley & Sons Inc.), 481.

Zimmermann, P. (1994a). Pretty Good Privacy: Public Key Encryption for the Masses. In *Building in Big Brother: The Cryptographic Policy Debate.* Edited by Hoffman, L. (New York: Springer-Verlag), 93–109.

CYPHERPUNK MAILING LIST ARCHIVES 1992–1998

Anonymous Poster. (1993). "No Subject." MessageID: "9304170312.AA19797@pmantis.be rkeley.edu." April 16, 2019.

Bidzos, J. (1994a). "NSA Agents Threaten to Kill Bidzos of RSA?" MessageID: "9406290514. AA02321@RSA.COM." June 28, 1994.

Blaze, M. (1995). "My life as an international arms courier." MessageID: "9501062154.AA0 4543@merckx.info.att.com." January 6, 1995.

Detweiler, L. (1993). "BIGBROTHER: a public attack plan in 14 points." MessageID: "9304 180255.AA22660@longs.lance.colostate.edu." April 17, 1993.

Draper, J. (1993). "My comments on the Clipper or Tapper chip." MessageID: "9304190711. AA12484@netcom4.netcom.com." April 19, 1993.

Elliott, P. (1995). "Re: Why no action alert, coalition opposing S. 974?" MessageID: "3012 a599.flight@flight.hrnowl.lonestar.org." July 23, 1995.

Finney, H. (1993). "IMPORTANT!" MessageID: "9304181952.AA16918@alumni.cco.calt ech.edu." April 18, 1993.

Finney, H. (1996). "Re: NRC Cryptography Report: The Text of the Recommendations." MessageID: "199605302304.QAA14424@jobe.shell.portal.com." May 31, 1996.

Garcia, A. (1997). "FWD: Dear Representative Oxley." MessageID: "199709242252.R AA14004@Starbase.NeoSoft.COM." September 25, 1997.

Gilmore, J. (1995a). "Re: NRC panel wants questions for Law Enforcement on crypto policy." MessageID: "9507261951.AA23210@toad.com." July 26, 1995.

Gilmore, J. (1995b). "NRC Panel, Law Enforcement questions." MessageID: "9508020134. AA07797@toad.com." August 1, 1995.

Godwin, M. (1994). "Text of info file on Cantwell bill." MessageID: "199402081756. MAA21918@eff.org." February 8, 1994.

Graves, R. (1996). "Re: Optimism re NRC Cryptography Report." MessageID: "pine.GUL. 3.93.960531155935.11396G-100000@Networking.Stanford.EDU." June 1, 1996.

Hughes, E. (1993a). "a cypherpunk's clipper reaction." MessageID: "9304170302.AA10041@ soda.berkeley.edu." April 16, 1993.

Hughes, E. (1993b). "Clipperpunks Write Code?" MessageID: "9306011656.AA17722@soda. berkeley.edu." June 1 1993.

May, T. C. (1993a). "White House announcement on encryption—FORWARDED." MessageID: "9304161638.AA19495@netcom3.netcom.com." April 16, 1993.

May, T. C. (1993b). "Key Registration and Big Brother—Time to Fight!" MessageID: "9304162117.AA29302@netcom.netcom.com." April 16, 1993.

May, T. C. (1993c). "IMPORTANT—WE WON......NOT!" MessageID: "9304170419. AA26923@netcom.netcom.com." April 16, 1993.

May, T. C. (1993d). "Fighting the Wiretap Chip Plan." MessageID: "9304181911.AA04196@ netcom.netcom.com." April 18, 1993.

May, T. C. (1994a). "Demonizing Denning." MessageID: "199410060803.BAA06601@ne tcom6.netcom.com." October 6, 1994.

May, T. C. (1994b). "NSA Agents Threaten to Kill Bidzos of RSA?" MessageID: "199406272 302.QAA09581@netcom4.netcom.com." June 27, 1994.

May, T. C. (1994c). "The Coming Police State." MessageID: "199403100158.RAA27863@ mail.netcom.com." March 9, 1994.

May, T. C. (1996). "Optimism re NRC Cryptography Report." MessageID: "add44f85020210 04f975@[205.199.118.202]." June 1, 1996.

McCandlish, S. (1993). "ANNOUNCEMENT: DPSWG Crypto-Policy Statement to White House." MessageID: "199312072217.RAA07526@eff.org." December 7, 1993.

McCandlish, S. (1994). "EFFector Online 07.10—Action needed *immediately* for crypto bill!" MessageID: "199406150214.WAA06044@eff.org." June 14, 1994.

Sammons, N. (1994). "RE: The Coming Police State." MessageID: "199403110544.VAA113 84@netcom10.netcom.com." March 10, 1994.

Safdar, S. (1995). "Re: Why no action alert, coalition opposing S. 974?" MessageID: "1995 07192226.SAA10293@panix4.panix.com." July 19, 1995.

Zahn, D. (1993). "circling the wagons." MessageID: "9304162000.AA29054@lynx.cs.wisc. edu". April 16, 1993.

Zimmermann, P. (1994). "Key Forfeiture, not Key Escrow." MessageID: "m0qspDz-0002wCC@maalox.ppgs.com." October 6, 1994.

MISCELLANEOUS

Scolar, M. J. (1989). Military and Civilian Control of Civilian Computer Security Issues: Hearing before the Subcommittee on Legislation and National Security of the House Committee on Government Operations, 101st Cong. quoted in Banisar, D.

NEWSPAPER ARTICLES

Bulkeley, W. M. (1994). Cipher Probe: Popularity Overseas of Encryption Code Has the U.S. Worried, *The Wall Street Journal*, April 28, p.1.

WEBSITES

Advanced Telephony Unit, Federal Bureau of Investigation. (1992). *Impact of Emerging Telecommunications Technology on Law Enforcement.* Available: https://www.cs. columbia.edu/~smb/Telecommunications_Overview:1992.pdf [Accessed February 18, 2019].

Andrews, E. L. (1997). *Europeans Reject U.S. Plan On Electronic Cryptography.* Available: https://www.nytimes.com/1997/10/09/business/international-business-europeans-rej ect-us-plan-on-electronic-cryptography.html [Accessed January 6, 2020].

Aoki, K. et al. (1997). *Law Professors' Letter Opposing Mandatory Key Escrow.* Available: http://groups.csail.mit.edu/mac/classes/6.805/articles/crypto/short-pieces-1997/law-p rof-crypto-letter.html [Accessed January 6, 2020].

Apple et al. (1996). *Joint Press Announcement: High-Tech Leaders Join Forces to Enable International Strong Encryption.* Available: https://www.epic.org/crypto/key_escrow/j oint_announce_10_2_96.html [Accessed December 18, 2019].

Baker, S. (1994). *Don't Worry Be Happy.* Available: https://www.wired.com/1994/06/nsa-c lipper/ [Accessed December 7, 2019].

Barlow, J. P. (1994). *Jackboots on the Infobahn.* Available: https://www.wired.com/1994/04/ privacy-barlow/ [Accessed December 11, 2019].

Bidzos, J. (1991). *Letter from Jim Bidzos to Tim Valentine, Chairman, Subcommittee on Technology and Competitiveness, House Committee on Space, Science and Technology, September 20, 1991.* Available: http://www.mekabay.com/overviews/risks/risks12_199 1-07-01_1991-12-24.pdf [Accessed August 25, 2019].

Bidzos, J. (1994b). *Some Thoughts on Clipper, NSA, and One Key Escrow Alternative.* Available: https://web.archive.org/web/19970320185713/http://www.eff.org/pub/Priv acy/Clipper/bidzos_clipper.article [Accessed December 11, 2019].

Blaze, M. (1993). *Comments to National Institute for Standards and Technology (NIST) on Clipper.* Available: https://web.archive.org/web/20010510211939/http://www.cpsr. org/cpsr/privacy/crypto/clipper/clipper_nist_escrow:comments/blaze_comments.txt [Accessed December 5, 2019].

Blaze, M. (1994). *Protocol Failure in the Escrowed Encryption Standard*. Available: https://www.mattblaze.org/papers/eesproto.pdf [Accessed December 11, 2019].

Blaze, M. (2011). *Key Escrow from a Safe Distance*. Available: https://www.mattblaze.org/escrow-acsac11.pdf [Accessed December 11, 2019].

Brickell, E. F., Denning, D., Kent, S.T., Maher, D. P, and Tuchman, W. (1993) *SKIPJACK Review: Interim Report—The SKIPJACK Algorithm, 28 July 1993*. Available: https://www.epic.org/crypto/clipper/skipjack_interim_review.html [Accessed December 5, 2019].

Brooks, C. (1994). *Dr. Clinton C. Brooks, National Security Agency Testimony before the House Science, Space and Technology Committee's Technology, Environment, and Aviation Subcommittee, May 3 1994*. Available: https://web.archive.org/web/19970320185726/http://www.eff.org/pub/Privacy/Clipper/brooks_nsa_clip-dt.testimony [Accessed December 11, 2019].

Brooks, J. (1994). *Floor Statement of Congressman Jack Brooks, U.S. House of Representatives, 15 June 1994*. Available: https://web.archive.org/web/19970320185720/http://www.eff.org/pub/Privacy/Clipper/brooks_crypto_061594.statement [Accessed December 13, 2019].

Campbell, T., Goodlatte, B., Eshaoo, A. et al. (1996). *Letter to President Bill Clinton From Numerous Congress Members, 15 May 1996*. Available: https://www.epic.org/crypto/key_escrow/house_letter_5_15_96.html [Accessed December 31, 2019].

Chandrasekaran, R. (1997). *Freeh Seeks Encryption Decoding Key*. Available: https://www.washingtonpost.com/wp-srv/politics/special/encryption/stories/cr090497.htm [Accessed December 18, 2019].

Clausing, J. (1997). *House Panel Rejects FBI Plan on Encryption*. Available: https://archive.nytimes.com/www.nytimes.com/library/cyber/week/092597encrypt.html [Accessed January 7, 2020].

Computer Professionals for Social Responsibility, et al. (1994a). *Letter to the President Regarding Clipper Chip*. Available: https://www.epic.org/crypto/clipper/crypto_experts_letter_1_94.html [Accessed December 13, 2019].

Computer Professionals for Social Responsibility. (1994b). *The Clipper Chip*. Available: https://www.epic.org/crypto/clipper/ [Accessed December 15, 2019].

Computer System Security and Privacy Advisory Board. (1992a). *1991 Annual Report of the Computer System Security and Privacy Advisory Board*. Available: https://csrc.nist.rip/groups/SMA/ispab/documents/annual-reports/1991_annual-report_natl-computer-system.pdf [Accessed October 5, 2019].

Computer System Security and Privacy Advisory Board. (1992b). *Computer System Security and Privacy Advisory Board Resolution #2, March 18, 1992*. Available: https://csrc.nist.rip/groups/SMA/ispab/documents/annual-reports/1992_annual-report_natl-computer-system.pdf [Accessed October 5, 2019].

Computer System Security and Privacy Advisory Board. (1992c). *Computer System Security and Privacy Advisory Board Resolution #3, March 18, 1992*. Available: https://csrc.nist.rip/groups/SMA/ispab/documents/annual-reports/1992_annual-report_natl-computer-system.pdf [Accessed October 5, 2019].

Computer System Security and Privacy Advisory Board. (1993a). *1992 Annual Report of the Computer System Security and Privacy Advisory Board*. Available: https://csrc.nist.rip/groups/SMA/ispab/documents/annual-reports/1992_annual-report_natl-computer-system.pdf [Accessed October 5, 2019].

Computer System Security and Privacy Advisory Board. (1993b). *Computer System Security and Privacy Advisory Board Resolution #s93–4, July 30, 1993*. Available: https://csrc.nist.gov/CSRC/media/Projects/ISPAB/documents/annual-reports/1993_annual-report_natl-computer-system.pdf [Accessed October 5, 2019].

Computer System Security and Privacy Advisory Board. (1994). *1993 Annual Report of the Computer System Security and Privacy Advisory Board*. Available: https://csrc.nist.go v/CSRC/media/Projects/ISPAB/documents/annual-reports/1993_annual-report_nat l-computer-system.pdf [Accessed October 5, 2019].

Crypto Museum. (2018). *AT&T TSD-3600-E*. Available: https://www.cryptomuseum.com/c rypto/att/tsd3600/ [Accessed December 9, 2019].

Cypherpunks. (1992–1998). *Cypherpunks Mail List Archive 1992–1998*. Available: https:// lists.cpunks.org/pipermail/cypherpunks/2013-September/000741.html [Accessed July 10, 2015].

Dam, K. W. (1997). *Letter from Kenneth W. Dam to the Senate Judiciary Committee, 9 July 1997*. Available: http://groups.csail.mit.edu/mac/classes/6.805/articles/crypto/short-pi eces-1997/dam-july-9.txt [Accessed January 6, 2020].

Davida, G. (1993). *Letter to National Institute and Standards and Technology on Clipper, September 24 1993*. Available: https://web.archive.org/web/20011116063928/http://cp sr.org/cpsr/privacy/crypto/clipper/clipper_nist_escrow:comments/davida_comments. ps [Accessed December 5, 2019].

Davis, J. R. (1992). *Letter from J. R. Davis to FBI Director William Sessions, 23 December 1992*. Available: https://www.epic.org/crypto/clipper/foia/att3600_12_23_92.html [Accessed December 9, 2019].

Diffie, W. (1993). *The Impact of a Secret Cryptographic Standard on Encryption, Privacy, Law Enforcement and Technology: Testimony to House Science Subcommittee, 11 May 1993*. Available: https://www.epic.org/crypto/clipper/diffie_testimony.html [Accessed December 7, 2019].

Electronic Frontier Foundation. (1996c). *Court Declares Crypto Restrictions Unconstitutional*. Available: https://www.eff.org/press/archives/2008/04/21-37 [Accessed June 6, 2020].

Electronic Privacy Information Center. (1995). *EPIC Press Release*. Available: https://we b.archive.org/web/19970323035553/http://www.eff.org/pub/Privacy/Clipper/Clipper_ FOIA/epic_clipper_secrets.announce [Accessed December 17, 2019].

Elmer-Dewitt, P. (1994). *Who Should Keep the Keys?* Available: http://content.time.com/t ime/magazine/article/0,9171,980329,00.html [Accessed December 15, 2019].

Executive Office of the President. (1996). *Draft paper, "Enabling Privacy, Commerce, Security and Public Safety in the Global Information Infrastructure."* Available: https ://www.epic.org/crypto/key_escrow/white_paper.html [Accessed December 1, 2019].

Fallows, J. (1994). *Open Secrets*. Available: https://www.theatlantic.com/magazine/archive/ 1994/06/open-secrets/376359/ [Accessed December 11, 2019].

Federal Bureau of Investigation. (2008). *First Strike: Global Terror in America*. Available: https://archives.fbi.gov/archives/news/stories/2008/february/tradebom_022608 [Accessed January 8, 2020].

Freeh, L. (1996). *Statement of Louis J. Freeh Director Federal Bureau of Investigation on July 25, 1996 before the Committee on Commerce, Science, and Transportation United States Senate Regarding Impact of Encryption on Law Enforcement and Public Safety*. Available: https://web.archive.org/web/19971010093406/http://www.crypto.com/ events/072596/freeh.html [Accessed December 31, 2019].

Gore, A. (1994). *Correspondence from Al Gore, Vice President of the United States, to Representative Maria Cantwell, 20 July 1994*. Available: https://en.wikipedia.org/ wiki/Maria_Cantwell [Accessed November 25, 2019].

Jackson, K. (1993). *Letter to National Institute of Standards and Technology Regarding Clipper, 26 September 1993*. Available: https://web.archive.org/web/20011116061211/ http://cpsr.org/cpsr/privacy/crypto/clipper/clipper_nist_escrow:comments/steve_jacks on_comments.txt [Accessed December 5, 2019].

Karn, P. (1993). *Letter to National Institute of Standards and Technology Regarding Clipper, 27 September 1993*. Available: https://web.archive.org/web/20010510212312/ http://www.cpsr.org/cpsr/privacy/crypto/clipper/clipper_nist_escrow:comments/karn_ comments.txt199 [Accessed December 5, 2019].

Lash, A. (1996). *Computer Alliance Supports Encryption Policy*. Available: https://web.arc hive.org/web/19970605171214/http://www.news.com/News/Item/0,4,4063,00.html [Accessed December 18, 2019].

Levy, S. (1994). *Battle of the Clipper Chip*. Available: http://www.nytimes.com/1994/06/12/m agazine/battle-of-the-clipper-chip.html?src=pm&pagewanted=1 [Accessed December 11, 2019].

Lott, T. (1997). *October 21 [1997], U.S. Senate Majority Leader Trent Lott, Statement before the Senate on the encryption debate*. Available: http://groups.csail.mit.edu/mac/classes/ 6.805/articles/crypto/short-pieces-1997/lott-oct-21.html [Accessed January 6, 2020].

Markoff, J. (1993a). *Electronics Plan Aims to Balance Government Access with Privacy*. Available: https://www.nytimes.com/1993/04/16/us/electronics-plan-aims-to-balance -government-access-with-privacy.html [Accessed December 7, 2019].

Markoff, J. (1993b). *Big Brother and the Computer Age*. Available: https://www.nyt imes.com/1993/05/06/business/big-brother-and-the-computer-age.html [Accessed December 7, 2019].

Markoff, J. (1994a). *Gore Shifts Stance on Chip Code*. Available: https://www.nytimes.com/1 994/07/21/business/gore-shifts-stance-on-chip-code.html [Accessed November 26, 2019].

Markoff, J. (1994b). *Flaw Discovered in Federal Plan for Wiretapping*. Available: https://ww w.nytimes.com/1994/06/02/us/flaw-discovered-in-federal-plan-for-wiretapping.html [Accessed December 11, 2019].

Markoff, J. (1996). *White House Challenged on Data Security*. Available: https://ww w.nytimes.com/1996/05/31/business/white-house-challenged-on-data-security.html [Accessed May 5, 2019].

Markoff, J. (1997a). *Law Proposed to Regulate Encoding Devices*. Available: http://gro ups.csail.mit.edu/mac/classes/6.805/articles/crypto/short-pieces-1997/nyt-sep-6.txt [Accessed January 4, 2020].

Markoff, J. (1997b). *Scientists Campaign for Computer-Data Security*. Available: https://ar chive.nytimes.com/www.nytimes.com/library/cyber/week/092497encrypt-side.html [Accessed June 7, 2020].

McConnell, J. M. (1992). *Correspondence to William H. Ware, Chair, Computer Security and Privacy Advisory Board, 23 July 1992*. Available: https://csrc.nist.rip/groups/S MA/ispab/documents/annual-reports/1992_annual-report_natl-computer-system.pdf [Accessed October 5, 2019].

McConnell, J. M. (1994). *Senate Subcommittee on Technology and the Law Hearing on the Administration's Key Escrow Encryption Standard: Written Questions for VADM McConnell*. Available: https://epic.org/crypto/clipper/nsa_responses.html [Accessed December 11, 2019].

Meeks, B. (1994). *Electrosphere: The End of Privacy*. Available: http://groups.csail.mit.edu/ mac/classes/6.805/articles/clipper/privacy.meeks.html [Accessed December 13, 2019].

National Computer System Security and Privacy Advisory Board. (1993). *1993 Annual Report of the National Computer System Security and Privacy Advisory Board*. Available: https://csrc.nist.rip/csspab/reports/93-rpt.txt [Accessed December 4, 2019].

National Institute of Standards and Technology and National Security Agency. (1989). *Memorandum of Understanding between NIST and NSA*. Available: https://web.arc hive.org/web/20010617230041/https://www.epic.org/crypto/csa/nist_nsa_mou.html [Accessed August 12, 2020].

National Institute of Standards and Technology. (1991). *A Proposed Federal Information Processing Standard for Digital Signature Standard (DSS)*. Available: https://www.epic.org/crypto/dss/dss_fr_notice_1991.html [Accessed August 25, 2019].

National Institute of Standards and Technology. (1993). *Notice of Proposal for Grant of Exclusive Patent License*. Available: http://catless.ncl.ac.uk/Risks/14.74.html [Accessed October 5, 2019].

National Institute of Standards and Technology. (1994a). *Approval of Federal Information Processing Standards Publication 186, Digital Signature Standard (DSS)*. Available: https://www.govinfo.gov/content/pkg/FR-1994-05 [Accessed October 5, 2019].

National Institute of Standards and Technology. (1994b). *NIST Announces Technical Correction to Secure Hash Standard*. Available: https://www.nist.gov/news-events/news/1994/04/nist-announces-technical-correction-secure-hash-standard [Accessed October 25, 2019].

National Institute of Standards and Technology. (1994c). *Voluntary Nature of Telecommunications Security Initiative Stressed by NIST Official in Testimony*. Available: https://web.archive.org/web/19970323035534/http://www.eff.org/pub/Privacy/Clipper/Clipper_FOIA/clipper_nist.defense [Accessed December 13, 2019].

National Institute of Standards and Technology. (1994d). *Federal Register Volume 59, Number 27 (Wednesday, February 9, 1994)*. Available: https://www.govinfo.gov/content/pkg/FR-1994-02-09/html/94-2919.htm [Accessed December 15, 2019].

National Institute of Standards and Technology. (1995). *Commerce's NIST Announces Process for Dialogue on Key Escrow Issues*. Available: https://www.epic.org/crypto/key_escrow/NIST_escrow:release.html [Accessed December 18, 2019].

National Security Agency. (1992). *Correspondence to Joe Abernathy*, Houston Chronicle, *10 June 1992*. Available: https://epic.org/crypto/dss/nsa_abernathy_letter.html [Accessed September 29, 2019].

National Security Agency. (1993). *Options to Address Encryption Effects on Law Enforcement*. Available: https://www.epic.org/crypto/ban/options1.gif [Accessed December 9, 2019].

Office of Senator Conrad Burns. (1996). *Burns: Clipper III Strikes Out: New Clinton Computer "Wiretap" Plan Circulates With Few Changes, 20 May 1996*. Available: https://www.epic.org/crypto/key_escrow/burns_on_white_paper.html [Accessed December 31, 2019].

Office of Technology Assessment. (1996). *Information Security and Privacy in Network Environments*. Available: https://books.google.co.uk/books?id=Rk6q8K9hPs4C&pg=PA63&lpg=PA63#v=onepage&q&f=false [Accessed November 26, 2019].

Pressman, A. (1997). *Clinton Administration Backs Away From FBI on Encryption*. Available: http://groups.csail.mit.edu/mac/classes/6.805/articles/crypto/short-pieces-1997/reuter-sep-4.txt [Accessed December 18, 2019].

Reference for Business. (2002). *VeriSign, Inc.—Company Profile, Information, Business Description, History, Background Information on VeriSign, Inc.* Available: https://www.referenceforbusiness.com/history2/29/VeriSign-Inc.html [Accessed October 24, 2019].

Reinsch, W. A. (1996). *Memorandum for Deputies Subgroup on Cryptography, 25 November, 1996*. Available: https://www.epic.org/crypto/key_escrow/reinsch_memo.html [Accessed January 1, 2020].

Reno, J. (1996). *Law Enforcement in Cyberspace Address by the Honorable Janet Reno United States Attorney General Presented to the Commonwealth Club of California, June 14 1996*. Available: https://web.archive.org/web/19970514094425/http://www.epic.org/privacy/wiretap/reno_speech.html [Accessed December 31, 2019].

Rivest, R. (1997). *Letters to Senators of the Senate Judiciary Committee, 10 June 1997*. Available: http://groups.csail.mit.edu/mac/classes/6.805/articles/crypto/short-pieces-1997/rivest-june-10.txtAssociate [Accessed January 5, 2020].

Rotenburg, M. (1989). *Testimony of Marc Rotenburg, Director of Computer Professionals for Social Responsibility's Washington D.C. Office, to The Subcommittee on Legislation and National Security, Committee on Government Operations, US House of Representatives, 4 May 1989*. Available: https://www.epic.org/crypto/csa/Rotenber g-Testimony-CSA-1989.pdf [Accessed August 13, 2020].

Rotenburg, M. (1993). *Testimony of Marc Rotenburg, Director of Computer Professionals for Social Responsibility's Washington D.C. Office, to The Subcommittee on Telecommunications and Finance. Committee on Energy and Commerce, 9 June 1993*. Available: https://www.epic.org/crypto/clipper/cpsr_markey_testimony_6_9.htm l [Accessed December 7, 2019].

Safire, W. (1994). *Opinion: Sink the Clipper Chip*. Available: https://www.nytimes.com/1994/02/14/opinion/essay-sink-the-clipper-chip.html [Accessed December 11, 2019].

Schifreen, R. (1992). *Data Protection and Security for Personal Computers: Manager's Guide to Improving the Confidentiality, Availability and Integrity of Data on Personal Computers and Local Area Networks*. Available: https://books.google.co.uk/books?id =jpODDwAAQBAJ&printsec=frontcover&source=gbs_ge_summary_r&cad=0#v =onepage&q&f=false [Accessed February 25, 2020].

Schneier, B. (1998). *Crypto-Gram, 15 July 1998*. Available: https://www.schneier.com/crypt o-gram/archives/1998/0715.html [Accessed January 5, 2020].

Sessions, W. S. (1993). *Letter to George J. Tenet, Special Assistant to the President and Senior Director for Intelligence Programs, National Security Council, February 9 1993*. Available: https://www.epic.org/crypto/clipper/foia/crypto_threat_2_19_93.html [Accessed December 5, 2019].

Sobel, D. L. (n.d.). *Governmental Restrictions on the Development and Dissemination of Cryptographic Technologies: The Controversy over the Digital Signature Standard*. Available: https://www.epic.org/crypto/dss/sobel_dss_paper.html [Accessed September 23, 2019].

Sobel, D. L. (1993). *New NIST/NSA Revelations*. Available: https://www.epic.org/crypto/dss/new:nist_nsa_revelations.html [Accessed October 24, 2019].

Sobel, D. L. (1995a). *New Bill Would Outlaw Non-Escrowed Encryption*. Available: https://www.epic.org/crypto/ban/epic.html [Accessed December 16, 2019].

Sobel, D. L. (1995b). *Comments on Draft Export Criteria for Key Escrow Encryption*. Available: https://www.epic.org/crypto/key_escrow/sobel_criteria.html [Accessed December 18, 2019].

The White House. (1993a). *Statement of the White House Press Secretary, 16 April 1993*. Available: https://web.archive.org/web/20000118230308/http://www.pub.whitehouse. gov/uri-res/I2R?urn:pdi://oma.eop.gov.us/1993/4/19/6.text.1 [Accessed December 1, 2019].

The White House. (1993b). *Presidential Directive Authorizing the Clipper Initiative, 15 April 1993*. Available: http://groups.csail.mit.edu/mac/classes/6.805/articles/crypto/clipper-directive.html [Accessed December 7, 2019].

The White House. (1994a). *Statement of the White House Press Secretary*. Available: https://www.eff.org/effector/7/3 [Accessed October 6, 2019].

The White House. (1994b). *White House Responses to Questions Submitted by the Digital Privacy and Security Working Group, 29 July 1994*. Available: https://web.archive.org/web/19970320191301/http://www.eff.org/pub/Privacy/Clipper/wh_clipper.answers [Accessed December 12, 2019].

The White House. (1994c). *Statement of the Press Secretary, 4 February 1994*. Available: https://www.epic.org/crypto/clipper/white_house_statement_2_94.html [Accessed December 15, 2019].

The White House. (1996a). *Administration Statement on Commercial Encryption Policy, 12 July 1996.* Available: https://www.epic.org/crypto/key_escrow/wh_cke_796.html [Accessed December 31, 2019].

The White House. (1996b). *Vice President On Clipper 4, Electronic Privacy and Information Center (1 October 1996).* Available:https://www.epic.org/crypto/key_escrow/clipper4_statement.html [Accessed June 12, 2020].

Time Online Odeon. (1994). *Online Debate Between John Perry Barlow of the Electronic Frontier Foundation, and Dr. Dorothy Denning, over the Clipper Chip Scheme, from the Time Online Forum of America On Line.* Available: https://web.archive.org/web/19 970320185649/http://www.eff.org/pub/Privacy/Clipper/barlow:v_denning.transcript [Accessed December 11, 2019].

United States Census Bureau. (2010). *Computer and Internet Use in the United States: 1984 to 2009.* Available: https://www2.census.gov/programs-surveys/demo/tables/co mputer-internet/time-series/computer-use-1984-2009/appendix-tablea.xls [Accessed February 17, 2019].

United States Congress. (1987). *Computer Security Act of 1987.* Available: https://csrc.nist.go v/csrc/media/projects/ispab/documents/csa_87.txt [Accessed April 2, 2020].

United States Congress. (1993). *H.R.3627—To Amend the Export Administration Act of 1979 with Respect to the Control of Computers and Related Equipment.* Available: https:// www.congress.gov/bill/103rd-congress/house-bill/3627/text [Accessed May 21, 2019].

United States Congress. (1995). *S.974—Anti-Electronic Racketeering Act of 1995.* Available: https://www.congress.gov/bill/104th-congress/senate-bill/974 [Accessed December 16, 2019].

United States Congress. (1997a). *H.R. 695—Security and Freedom Through Encryption (SAFE) Act, Draft Amendment.* Available: https://web.archive.org/web/199904300610 50/http://www.cdt.org/crypto/fbi_draft_text.html [Accessed January 6, 2020].

United States Congress. (1997b). *H.R. 695—Security and Freedom Through Encryption (SAFE) Act Amendment Offered by Mr Oxley of Ohio and Mr Manton of New York.* Available: https://web.archive.org/web/19980210082328/http://www.cdt.org/crypto/l egis_105/SAFE/Oxley_Manton.html [Accessed January 6, 2020].

United States Department of Commerce. (1995). *Draft Software Key Escrow Encryption Export Criteria.* Available: https://www.epic.org/crypto/key_escrow/criteria.html [Accessed December 18, 2019].

United States Department of Justice. (1994). *Attorney General Makes Key Escrow Encryption Announcements.* Available: https://www.epic.org/crypto/clipper/reno_announcement_feb_94.html [Accessed December 11, 2019]

United States General Accounting Office. (1987). *Statement of Milton J. Socolar, Special Assistant to the Comptroller General Before the Subcommittee on Legislation and National Security Committee on Government Operations.* Available: https://www.gao .gov/assets/110/101795.pdf [Accessed September 22, 2019].

United States General Accounting Office. (1993). *Communications Privacy: Federal Policy and Actions.* Available: https://www.gao.gov/assets/220/218755.pdf [Accessed April 2, 2019].

United States House of Representatives. (1985). *Hearings before the Subcommittee on Transportation, Aviation, and Materials of the Committee on Science and Technology, House of Representatives, Ninety-Ninth Congress, First Session, 27 June 1985.* Available: https://books.google.co.uk/books?id=ST8sAAAAMAAJ [Accessed January 5, 2020].

United States House of Representatives. (1997). *Hearing on H.R. 695 Safety and Freedom Through Encryption (SAFE)—March 20.* Available: http://commdocs.house.gov/comm ittees/judiciary/hju41233.000/hju41233_0f.htm [Accessed May 19, 2019].

United States Senate. (1997). *Senate Judiciary Committee Terrorism, Technology & Government Information Subcommittee, 3 September 1997.* Available: https://cryptome.org/jya/fbi-gak.txt [Accessed December 18, 2019].

Voice of America. (1994). *Communications World, 26 February 1993.* Available: https://www.epic.org/crypto/clipper/voa_clipper.html [Accessed December 13, 2019].

Ware, W. H. (1992). *Correspondence to Barbara Hackman Franklin, Secretary of Commerce, 1 April 1992.* Available: https://csrc.nist.rip/groups/SMA/ispab/documents/annual-reports/1992_annual-report_natl-computer-system.pdf [Accessed October 5, 2019].

Washington Technology. (1995). *Fighting Over Computer Crime Law.* Available: https://washingtontechnology.com/articles/1995/07/27/fighting-over-computer-crime-law.aspx [Accessed December 16, 2019].

Wiener, M. J. (1994). *Efficient DES Key Search.* Available: http://citeseerx.ist.psu.edu/viewdoc/download;jsessionid=86D868AE29E7F26B3384949B0D5BE4CA?doi=10.1.1.130.7347&rep=rep1&type=pdf [Accessed October 13, 2019].

Zimmermann, P. (1999). *Why I Wrote PGP.* Available: https://www.philzimmermann.com/EN/essays/WhyIWrotePGP.html [Accessed December 5, 2019].

7 Crypto War II (1991–2002)
Export Battles

It seems to me that the combination of...digital technology and

robust encryption has brought informatized society to a

very sharp balance point between

two lousy choices.

On one side lies a technological foundation upon which the most

massive totalitarianism could be built.

On the other is a jungle in which any number of

anarchic guerrillas might hide,

upon whom little order could ever be imposed.

John Perry Barlow, 1995

7.1 OUTLAWING CRYPTOGRAPHY: 1991 COMPREHENSIVE COUNTER-TERRORISM ACT

Whilst the Digital Signature Standard and Clipper chip were quietly being developed behind the scenes, it was the Senate's proposed *Comprehensive Counter-Terrorism Act of 1991* (S.266) which ignited the second crypto war. Introducing the bill, Democratic Senator Joe Biden of Delaware stated, "in recent discussions with terrorism experts from the Federal Bureau of Investigation and other law enforcement agencies I've discovered that several gaps exist in our anti-terrorism laws."[1] Digital interception was one of those gaps. The relevant clause within the draft text reads:

[This bill] expresses the sense of the Congress that providers of electronic communications services and manufacturers of electronic communications service equipment should ensure that communications systems permit the Government to obtain the plain text contents of voice, data, and other communications when appropriately authorized by law.[2]

---

[1] C-Span, 1991.   [2] United States Congress, 1991a, Section 2201.

The language indicated companies must either provide a government access method to encrypted communications, commonly known as a "backdoor," or technologies must not use encryption. Either option was anathema to digital privacy activists. Cypherpunk Phil Karn branded the clause an "infamous resolution against cryptography."[3] *The New York Times* reported the data access language was inserted by the Justice Department in response to new encryption systems preventing government wiretaps. A senate aid anonymously told *The New York Times* the language was intended to be a compromise against a more restrictive White House counterterrorism bill, though what such a bill would have looked like is unknown.[4] The FBI issued a statement supporting S.266 in April:

> affording a criminal subject the means, through encryption, of securely communicating in furtherance of an illicit activity is tantamount to providing a sanctuary immune from judicially authorized collection of evidence.[5]

Cypherpunk Perry Metzger contacted John Bentivoglio, a Biden aid who claimed authorship of the text.[6] Bentivoglio stated the language was "intended more to get communications providers to help with the tapping of things like cellular phones," and this was not the "proverbial crack in the dike [...] the Senator has no intention of following through with additional legislation to enforce a ban on secure cryptosystems."[7] Writing in the Electronic Frontier Foundation's (EFF's) online magazine, *EFFector*, Metzger urged others to contact the Senators on the reviewing Judiciary Committee to protest the clause. Metzger asked they "be nice; these men are the ones who we have to count on to rescue us."[8]

More and more, the technology industry required influence in Washington DC. The lucrative computing market enabled technology business leaders to embark upon political lobbying in the early 1990s. These leaders often presented the issues for which they advocated as morally virtuous, though these causes were also typically crucial to their global business operations. This is not to say the technological vanguard did not hold also genuine affinity to issues such as digital privacy—many were steeped in the counter-culture and liberal politics. The digital rights groups emerging in the 1980s/90s proved a significant obstacle, in the courts and press, to government cryptology policies. Most prominent amongst these groups was the EFF, co-founded by cypherpunk John Gilmore, John Perry Barlow, and Mitch Kapor in 1990.[9] Jeff Moss, founder of the preeminent hacker conference DefCon comments, "the EFF is the closest thing hackers have to a religion."[10]

The EFF formed following a Secret Service operation against Steve Jackson Games (SJG) in 1990. SJG were accused of possessing an architectural document of the emergency services (911) telephony infrastructure illegally copied from BellSouth Labs.[11] The Secret Service feared that with knowledge of the mechanics

---

[3] Karn, 1993.
[4] Markoff, 1991.
[5] United States General Accounting Office, 1993, 31.
[6] Electronic Frontier Foundation, 1991a.
[7] Ibid.
[8] Ibid.
[9] Electronic Frontier Foundation, no date.
[10] Moss, 2019.

of the 911 system hackers could overwhelm it, resulting in genuine calls not reaching the emergency services.[12] A search and seizure warrant was executed against SJG—all electronic equipment was seized.[13] This resulted in SJG being unable to deliver their latest game, consequently, half of their staff were made redundant.[14] When the Secret Service returned the computers, all the emails stored on them were erased.[15] Steve Jackson searched for a civil liberties organization to defend his company against what he believed to be free speech and privacy violations, but no existing groups understood technology well enough to offer support.[16] During discussions of SJG on the Whole Earth 'Lectronic Link (WELL) electronic bulletin board a small group of those with the financial resources to address such problems united.[17] Cypherpunk John Gilmore, former Lotus Development Corporation President Mitch Kapor, and John Perry Barlow founded the EFF, which would lobby for privacy rights, and the preservation of the constitution in the digital era.[18] Another notable group emerging in the early 1990s was the Computer Professionals for Social Responsibility (CPSR.)[19]

A delegation from the CPSR, EFF, and RSA Data Security Inc. (RSADSI) visited Washington to argue for the Comprehensive Counter-Terrorism Act data access clause's removal in early June 1991—within a week the offending language was discarded.[20,21] But the bill had stoked fear in the digital privacy community that similar legislation may soon be passed. Further, Senator Leahy's sub-committee agreed to continue the dialogue with the digital privacy activists, and to study encryption policy issues.[22] To help inform Leahy's encryption policy formulation CPSR, RSADSI, and EFF quickly convened a workshop on privacy and encryption in Washington D.C.[23]

The workshop was held in July 1991. The resultant press statement highlighted the concerns of the digital privacy activists who accused the government of failing to "take advantage of opportunities to promote communications privacy."[24] The statement made a number of recommendations. Firstly, it advocated for encryption policy to be removed from the national security and intelligence communities. Secondly, it advised any government encryption policy recommendations be "critically reviewed." Thirdly, it indicated government departments should work free of the NSA's influence to promote the general availability of cryptography. Finally, it advised that export controls for cryptography be relaxed, stating "the cost of export control restrictions are enormous," and that "foreign companies are often able to

[11] Electronic Frontier Foundation, no date.
[12] Ibid.
[13] Ibid.
[14] Ibid.
[15] Ibid.
[16] Ibid.
[17] Ibid.
[18] Ibid.
[19] Computer Professionals for Social Responsibility, 2008.

[20] The same language was also included in S.618 section 545 the House of Representatives proposed Violent Crime Bill Act of 1991, this also failed to pass.
[21] United States General Accounting Office, 1993, 31; Garfinkel. 1995, 98; Electronic Frontier Foundation, 1991b.
[22] Electronic Frontier Foundation, 1991b.
[23] Ibid.
[24] Computer Professionals for Social Responsibility, 1991.

obtain these products from other sources." The statement also highlighted the changing geopolitical climate. The Berlin Wall fell in 1989, and the Soviet Union was disintegrating. In May 1991, the leaders of the Committee for Multilateral Export Controls (COCOM), an organization designed to prevent strategic Western technologies reaching the Soviet Union, met in Europe to debate revisions to existing controls.[25,26] Cryptography was discussed. The CPSR concluded, "At the urging of the National Security Agency, our [America's] delegates blocked efforts to relax restrictions on cryptography."[27] The actions of the digital privacy community were not limited to political lobbying. In particular, S.266 caused one cryptologist, a cryptologist who at the time knew little about the Internet and could barely use email, to accelerate an encryption project that would bring him into direct conflict with the US government and endanger his liberty.[28] That cryptologist was Philip R. Zimmermann.

7.2 ENCRYPTION FOR THE MASSES: PHIL ZIMMERMANN

Zimmermann first read about S.266 on a Usenet board; the text was accompanied by an anonymous comment, "I suggest you begin to stock up on Crypto gear while you can still get it."[29] The "sense of congress" language was not binding, but in keeping with the cryptologist communities' distrust of government, Zimmermann believed such devices were often used to "deploy the political groundwork to make it possible later to make it into hard law."[30]

Zimmermann grew up in Miami. He read his first book on encryption, Herbert S. Zim's *Codes and Secret Writing*, at the age of ten, in 1964.[31] From Zim's book, Zimmermann learned Morse code and Braille, as well as how to make invisible ink from lemon juice—his passion for cryptology was kindled.[32]

Zimmermann graduated from Florida Atlantic University in 1978, his first major had been physics, but he found it too hard, "the calculus got me," he comments.[33] Zimmermann proved a quicker study in his subsequent major: computer science.[34] Fellow student Steve Welch met Zimmermann late one night in the computer lab during the earliest days after his transfer. Welch notes Zimmermann knew "nothing about computers, [but] within one week, he was a better programmer than I was."[35] Whilst studying, Zimmermann read Martin Gardner's "Mathematical Games" article detailing the discovery and refinement of public key encryption—Zimmermann wrote to Rivest asking for a copy of the paper further describing their work.[36] It was

---

25 COCOM disbanded in 1994 and was replaced in 1996 by the Wassenaar Arrangement on Export Controls for Conventional Arms and Dual-Use Goods and Technologies (Wassenaar Arrangement, 2018).

26 Greenhouse, 1991, 1.

27 Computer Professionals for Social Responsibility, 1991.

28 Harrington, 1996, Empire Section.

29 Greenberg, 2012, Chapter 2.

30 Lebkowsky, 1993.

31 Zimmermann, 1994a.

32 Garfinkel, 1995, 89.

33 Zimmermann, no date-a; Harrington, 1996.

34 Ibid.

35 Ibid.

36 Schwartz, 1995; Garfinkel, 1995, 89.

this article that eight years later catalyzed Zimmermann's project to bring public key cryptography to the masses, and to make encryption "a force for social change."[37]

Zimmermann became an activist after graduating. The Watergate scandal initially drew Zimmermann to politics; he commented, "I began to question a lot of things that government does during that time."[38] Zimmermann spent a year working on a rape crisis center helpline, during which time he says, "I became more of a humanist."[39] As part of his political research, Zimmermann became acutely aware of the threat to his family from nuclear warfare, "We'd had our first child," Zimmermann recalls, "I began to think about the future and the threats to that future."[40] Zimmermann recalls in the 1980s "[it] looked like things were going to go badly. There was talk of the evil empire. Reagan was going berserk with the military budget. Things looked pretty hopeless."[41] Zimmermann feared the US would initiate a nuclear war, "Our side was building weapons that were designed to launch a first strike."[42] The Zimmermann family decided New Zealand, a nuclear-free territory, was the best chance for their safety—they successfully applied for visas and work permits in early 1982.[43] It was during this time Zimmerman and his wife attended a nuclear freeze conference in Denver. Daniel Ellsberg, famed for leaking a highly critical top-secret government study of US policy in Vietnam (known as the Pentagon Papers) spoke at the event, Zimmermann found the experience, "sobering but empowering."[44] The Zimmermanns were inspired. Ellsberg's actions had resulted in an informed public, helped buttress press freedoms, and shaped public opinion driving pressure for policy change. The Zimmermanns felt they should equally try to effect change, speaking of the Campaign for Nuclear Weapons Freeze, Zimmermann says, "It seemed plausible that this was a political movement that had some chance of success…we decided to stay and fight."[45]

Zimmermann was a dedicated student. He read widely on military strategy and became part of the nuclear freeze community in Boulder. Fellow campaigner Chet Tchozewski comments, "Phil was invaluable to us, not only as a speaker… but because of his technical knowledge and his remarkable intellectual capacities."[46] Tchozewski also reflected on Zimmermann's philosophy, "he's thought deeply about civil disobedience and is influenced by Gandhi and Thoreau, as well as by science."[47] Zimmermann would be arrested twice at anti-nuclear demonstrations, both times Ellsberg was also arrested.[48]

Whilst working with the nuclear freeze community, Zimmermann started thinking about how to protect their communications and digital records:

> Mostly they were taking floppy disks with membership information. It didn't take much to know we needed to keep our communications secret. So I began to read the scholarly papers on the subject…I began to work on the problems.[49]

[37] Schwartz, 1995.
[38] Harrington, 1996.
[39] Ibid.
[40] Ibid.
[41] Dexheimer, 1993.
[42] Garfinkel, 1995, 86.
[43] Harrington, 1996.
[44] Garfinkel, 1995, 87.
[45] Ibid.
[46] Harrington, 1996.
[47] Ibid.
[48] Dexheimer, 1993.
[49] Harrington, 1996.

Zimmermann began seriously studying cryptology in 1984, two years later his first paper on the topic was published.[50,51] Rivest became a contact of Zimmermann's during this period, with the former critiquing Zimmermann's paper during its peer review.[52] Despite his publishing success, Zimmermann recognized from consuming the cryptology literature that he was not as talented as he once believed, "I thought I was a smart guy...until I read enough in the field to see how bad I really was...I'm not the best cryptographer in the world. I figured that out pretty quickly."[53] To protect the nuclear activists' data, Zimmermann contacted Charlie Merritt for assistance. Merritt had been active in cryptography since 1977, when a friend sent him a copy of the Gardner article asking whether such an encryption system could be implemented on a microcomputer—Merritt believed it could.[54] Merritt started a company to create an encryption system for Z80-based computers running the Control Program/ Monitor (CP/M) operating system in 1980, he soon had workable code.[55] Merritt commented, "we thought it would take a week or two to generate a 'pretty big' key. Encryption of a file might take 20 minutes," but they achieved much better results with 256-bit keys generated in ten minutes and small files encrypted in thirty seconds.[56] Merritt and the two colleagues with whom he formed the company called the encryption system DEDICATE/32 (32 bytes/256 bit keys).[57] By 1983, Merritt was receiving regular visits from NSA employees who informed him the RSA algorithm was classed as a munition, and could not be exported to countries except Canada without government permission. Merritt believes the NSA effectively "shut us down. Pretty near ruined us."[58] As a result of being confined to the domestic and Canadian markets, Merritt purchased some computer magazines and started calling companies that may need DEDICATE/32.[59] Before long Merritt reached Metamorphic Systems, Zimmermann's startup attempting to make the faster Intel 8088 chips work with the relatively slow Apple II computers, which many considered a superior operating system.[60] Merritt and Zimmermann shared an anti-government philosophy. Merritt once also protested against the Vietnam war—he and Zimmermann began exchanging cryptology knowledge; "I'd been holding a grudge for years [against NSA], when Zimmermann called me. I was happy to help."[61] Merritt describes Zimmermann as one of the "most gee-whiz-whoopie enthusiastic characters" he had ever met.[62] Zimmermann wanted to know everything about how Merritt made RSA work on microcomputers, something he had thought computationally infeasible.[63] For the next few years, Zimmermann called Merritt once a week to discuss how

[50] Zimmermann, P. (1986). A Proposed Standard Format for RSA Cryptosystems. *Computer* 19(9), 21–34.
[51] Hoffman, 1996.
[52] Zimmermann, 1986, 34.
[53] Harrington, 1996.
[54] Garfinkel, 1995, 88.
[55] Ibid.
[56] Ibid.
[57] Ibid.
[58] Ibid, 89.
[59] Ibid.
[60] Ibid, 88.
[61] Harrington, 1996, and Ibid, 89–91.
[62] Garfinkel, 1995, 89.
[63] Ibid.

cryptography could be made viable for the Apple II.[64] Merritt was demotivated after years of battling the NSA and operating in a restricted market, but Zimmermann, "had a vision I had given up," Merritt reflects, "He had drive, I felt beat."[65] During summer 1986, Merritt traveled to Boulder to spend a week teaching Zimmermann how to perform multi-precision arithmetic operations, a vital pre-requisite for RSA key generation.[66]

During his time in Boulder, Merritt also met RSADSI CEO Jim Bidzos, for whom Merritt was contracting the previous year. Bidzos recommended they meet at a steak house; Merritt recalls the plan was to "eat thick slabs of dead cow, drink, and smoke some fine cigars," as a way to get to know one another in the flesh. Zimmermann was also invited. The dinner did not go well. The political philosophies of Zimmermann and Bidzos starkly contrasted—highlighted by Bidzos having volunteered for the US Marines, despite not being an American citizen. During the dinner, Bidzos gave Zimmermann and Merritt a copy of RSADSI's new product: MailSafe. MailSafe was an email encryption program written by Rivest and Adleman, similar to that which Zimmermann was coding. Zimmermann claims during the meal Bidzos promised him another gift, a free license for the RSA algorithm, something Bidzos denies. At the end of Merritt's visit to Boulder, he estimated Zimmermann possessed 95% of his knowledge. Merritt says Zimmermann "was now a 'real danger' to the national security machine."[67]

In the Comprehensive Counter-Terrorism Act data access clause, Zimmermann identified his opportunity to challenge the national security machine; he believed the backdoor provision, "foretold the shape of things to come."[68] Zimmermann recognized the US was "moving toward a future when the nation will be crisscrossed with high capacity fiber optic data networks linking together all our increasingly ubiquitous personal computers," and that "e-mail will be the norm for everyone, not the novelty it is today."[69] Zimmermann also understood the removal of the surveillance labor constraint occurring as citizens transitioned from letters to email:

> If the government wants to violate the privacy of ordinary citizens, it has to expend a certain amount of expense and labor to intercept and steam open and read paper mail, and listen to, and possibly transcribe spoken telephone conversation. This kind of labor-intensive monitoring is not practical on a large scale. This is only done in important cases when it seems worthwhile. More and more of our private communications are going to be routed through electronic channels…E-mail messages are just too easy to intercept and scan for interesting keywords. This can be done easily, routinely, automatically, and undetectably on a grand scale.[70]

As well as recognizing the unique threat facing citizens, Zimmermann understood science was on the verge of providing citizens new capabilities to protect themselves, "There's never been a time in our history where it's been possible to place

---

[64] Ibid.
[65] Ibid., 90.
[66] Ibid.
[67] Ibid, 90–92.

[68] Zimmermann, 1997.
[69] Zimmermann, 1991.
[70] Ibid.

information beyond the reach of the collective efforts of society, but with modern cryptography you can."[71]

Zimmermann wanted to ensure cryptography was delivered to citizens before the Comprehensive Counter-Terrorism Act, or other similar legislation, outlawed encryption.[72] Zimmermann believed even those acting outside the law deserved privacy protection: "You may be doing something that you feel shouldn't be illegal, but is...There's nothing wrong with asserting your privacy. Privacy is as apple-pie as the Constitution."[73] Addressing the argument that if one has nothing to hide, one does not require encryption; Zimmermann wrote:

> If you really are a law-abiding citizen with nothing to hide, then why don't you always send your paper mail on postcards? Why not submit to drug testing on demand? Why require a warrant for police searches of your house? Are you trying to hide something? You must be a subversive or a drug dealer if you hide your mail inside envelopes. Or maybe a paranoid nut.[74]

Zimmermann started work on his encryption software, later christened *Pretty Good Privacy* (PGP), in 1986.[75] Zimmermann's intent was not only to protect American citizens, but human rights groups worldwide though due to export laws he could not publicly voice that objective during the 1990s.[76]

With S.266's announcement, Zimmermann accelerated PGP's development. Zimmermann's estimations of how long it would take to complete PGP were "pathologically optimistic"—it took him a further six months to finish the program—prioritizing PGP's development over his day job resulted in Zimmermann missing five mortgage payments and coming dangerously close to losing his home.[77] Launching PGP as a commercial product would be difficult. The main hurdle was the Diffie-Hellman and RSA patent licenses held by Public Key Partners (PKP), which Bidzos controlled—Zimmermann would be unable to sell the product without licensing from PKP. Zimmermann claims he never intended to profit from PGP, but planned to give it "away for free so that it would achieve wide dispersal, to inoculate the body politic."[78]

Zimmermann finished his program in June 1991, and named it in tribute to "Ralph's Pretty Good Grocery," a sponsor of Prairie Home Companion radio show.[79] With S.266 in progress, Zimmermann had rushed out the software, he confessed the code was "hastily written, and it shows."[80] On June 5, 1991, Zimmermann started to distribute PGP version 1.0 for Microsoft DOS. The first recipient was Allan Hoeltje who posted PGP to Peacenet, a service provider Zimmermann says "specialized in grassroots political organizations, mainly in the peace movement. Peacenet was accessible to political activists all over the world."[81] The next recipient was Kelly

---

[71] Arachelian, 1994.
[72] Ibid.
[73] Zimmermann, 1991.
[74] Ibid.
[75] Lebkowsky, 1993.
[76] Zimmermann, 2012.

[77] Harrington, 1996, Empire Section.
[78] Zimmermann, 1991, 1996.
[79] Bulkeley, 1994.
[80] Garfinkel, 1995, 99.
[81] Zimmermann, 2001a.

Goen.[82] Jim Warren, a journalist, recalls Goen calling him over the first weekend of June to update him with tales of his progress in spreading PGP:

> He [Goen] was driving around the Bay Area with a laptop, acoustic coupler, and cellular phone. He would stop at a pay phone, upload a number of copies for a few minutes, then disconnect and rush off to another phone miles away. He said he wanted to get as many copies scattered as widely as possible around the nation before the government could get an injunction and stop him.[83]

Zimmermann instructed PGP users to upload the code to any electronic bulletin boards they had access to: "please disseminate the complete PGP release package as widely as possible. Give it to all your friends."[84] Attempting to cover himself from a legal perspective, Zimmerman wrote in PGP's documentation:

> The Government has made it illegal in many cases to export good cryptographic technology, and that may include PGP. This is determined by volatile State Department policies, not fixed laws…I will not export this software in cases when it is illegal to do so…I assume no responsibility for other people exporting it.[85]

In 1991, Zimmermann claims to have known little of how Usenet newsgroups worked, or in fact even what they were. Zimmermann asked Goen to tag the PGP Usenet postings as "US only," later he claimed not to have realized Usenet tags were advisory only with no impact on the posts dissemination.[86] There was nothing to stop PGP going global, but then in the digital age what could have stopped the code spreading when so many people had copies? Zimmermann reflects:

> It's hard to see how something like that could be published, and thousands of people could have it, and it could not leak overseas. It's like saying that *The New York Times* shouldn't be exported, how can you prevent that when a million people have a copy? It's blowing in the wind, you can't embargo the wind.[87]

Zimmermann recalls the release set off a "feeding frenzy," commenting that "there was a lot of pent-up demand for a tool like this."[88] Volunteers from around the globe contacted Zimmermann wanting to contribute to PGP's development, to help port the software to other platforms, and to support promotion of PGP.[89]

Only a week after PGP launched, the data access language in S.266 was removed as a result of political lobbying. Zimmermann reflects that after all his efforts, "PGP didn't have any impact, it turned out, at all."[90] This would prove very much an understatement. Despite not impacting the S.266 debate, Zimmermann released the first computationally viable and free implementation of public key cryptography for

---

[82] Ibid.
[83] Levy, 2001, Crypto Anarchy.
[84] Zimmermann, 1991.
[85] Zimmermann, 1991.
[86] Zimmermann, 2001a.

[87] Lebkowsky, 1993.
[88] Zimmermann, 2001a.
[89] Ibid.
[90] Lebkowsky, 1993.

microcomputers; as Zimmermann explains, "PGP is RSA public key cryptography for the masses."[91] PGP's differentiator, Zimmermann comments that it "performs the RSA function faster than most other software implementations."[92] PGP combines the RSA algorithm for key exchange (512, 1024, or 1280 bit) with traditional single-key symmetric algorithms for data exchange, ensuring the secure exchange of keys with the rapid exchange of data.[93] Zimmermann called the symmetric encryption algorithm he wrote for PGP, *Bass-O-Matic*. PGP creates a temporary session key to encrypt the data, then encrypts that session key using the recipient's public key—the recipient then uses their private key to decipher the symmetric key and subsequently decipher the message.[94] Public keys are kept in "key certificates" which include the key owner's user ID (their name), a timestamp of when the key pair was generated, and the key material itself.[95] Private keys are stored in their own certificates, and are password protected. PGP can also be used to sign a document, the private key is used to sign, the public key can then be used to validate the signature was applied by the genuine owner of the paired key (presuming neither key is compromised). PGP used the LZHUF compression algorithm, written in Japan by Haruyasu Yoshizaki.[96]

7.3   PGP: V2.0 AND CYPHERPUNKS' LAUNCH

Zimmerman acknowledged the dangers of "home-cooking" encryption algorithms. In an early experience at college, Zimmermann had created an algorithm he thought sound to only later discover it was trivial to break, he retained a degree of healthy skepticism married to cautious optimism:

> I'm not as cock-sure about the security of PGP as I once was about my brilliant encryp-
> tion software from college. If I were, that would be a bad sign…source code is avail-
> able, so other cryptographers are welcome to review its design. It's reasonably well
> researched. It's based on the work of a number of reputable cryptographers. [97]

Zimmermann had christened his home-baked symmetric encryption algorithm Bass-O-Matic, after a blender that liquifies fish, in the same way PGP "liquified" data.[98] Baked into the heart of PGP, Bass-O-Matic was a largely untested algorithm—a fact Zimmermann needed to remedy if PGP were to provide protection to the masses.

Every year since 1981, cryptologists gathered during late summer at the Santa Barbara campus of the University of California for the annual crypto conference. In 1991, Zimmermann attended with the intent of having world-class cryptographers analyze Bass-O-Matic.[99] Zimmermann approached Adi Shamir, who offered to review the code if Zimmermann sent it to Israel—though to do so would violate export laws.[100] Eli Biham, of Israel's Weizmann Institute of Science, was more helpful. Over lunch with Zimmermann, Biham leafed through several pages of printed

---

91 Zimmermann, 1991.   96 Ibid.
92 Ibid.   97 Ibid.
93 Schneier, 1995, 436.   98 Levy, 1993.
94 Zimmermann, 1991.   99 Garfinkel, 1995, 100.
95 Ibid.   100 Ibid, 102.

out code and found a plethora of errors. After ten minutes, it was clear Bass-O-Matic was vulnerable to attacks such as differential cryptanalysis—PGP version 2 would need a replacement algorithm.[101]

As PGP 2.0 was being developed, Zimmermann transitioned from programmer to project manager and design authority, most of the coding was now taking place outside the US and beyond reach of its legal system.[102] It also meant importing the finished PGP product to the US would avoid the issue of exporting domestically produced code. Cypherpunk Hal Finney comments Zimmermann's greatest skill was personal relations, he was able to "shepherd a network of easily distracted programmers" to complete complex tasks.[103] Zimmermann determined the International Data Encryption Algorithm (IDEA) would be the replacement for the flawed Bass-O-Matic. IDEA was developed as a potential replacement for DES by Xuejia Lai and James L. Massey at the Swiss Federal Institute of Technology.[104] Zimmermann recognized both Lai and Massey had earned "distinguished reputation[s] in the cryptologic community," and in combination with the rigorous testing endured by IDEA, the algorithm could be considered trustworthy.[105] In creating his own algorithm, Zimmermann violated a core tenet of cryptography, and launched Bass-O-Matic without the validation of a sustained attack by world-class cryptanalysts. Zimmermann was likely aware of the error, his calculation was probably based on it being better to have an imperfect product launched before S.266 became law, rather than a perfect product that could not be distributed after the legislation passed. Perhaps referencing his earlier error, Zimmermann commented in the documentation for PGP version 2 that the new algorithm was not a "home-grown algorithm."[106] IDEA was released in 1990 and had withstood sustained cryptanalytic attack. Zimmermann believed IDEA may also be more capable of preventing Biham and Shamir's differential cryptanalysis techniques than was DES.[107] Zimmermann suspected IDEA was better than DES, likely due to IDEA's 128-bit key against DES' 56 bits, and the fact it ran faster in software.[108] Ascom Tech AG granted Zimmermann a license to use IDEA, including for commercial purposes, so there would be no patent-related challenges.[109] However, the RSA algorithm patent challenge remained.

The first physical meeting of the cypherpunks took place in September 1992, only days after PGP 2.0's release. Cypherpunk Arthur Abraham distributed diskettes of PGP 2.0 to the attendees.[110]

Tim May posted after the meeting to the cypherpunks' mailing list his belief they were entering the "long awaited 'Crypto Singularity,'" a point at which the advances of cryptography would become irreversible. May believed factors including PGP, fully encrypted remailers, which allowed the anonymous sending of emails, and journalist interest in cryptography all contributed to the imminent singularity. May wrote to the cypherpunks, "Things may get very interesting and very sticky in the

---

[101] Ibid.
[102] Lebkowsky, 1993.
[103] Finney, 1994.
[104] Lai and Massey, 1990.
[105] Zimmermann, 1992.
[106] Ibid.
[107] Ibid.
[108] Ibid.
[109] Ibid.
[110] May, 1994, 7.5.1.

next several months," commenting such a time frame for cryptography's disruption of society was, "quite a bit faster than I'd expected." May speculated the government may try to make a "high-publicity case involving drugs or child molesters...as a pretext to crack down on cryptographic technologies."[111]

Zimmermann did not consider himself a cypherpunk, he once quipped, "I'm not a Cypherpunk—I wear a suit when I visit clients,' but he did share their digital privacy and free-speech ideals.[112] Zimmermann joined the cypherpunk mailing list, but departed after only a few days as the volume of messages proved a distraction from his work—he intermittently returned but with minimal engagement.[113] Zimmermann held mixed feelings towards the cypherpunks. The ideological gap with the cypherpunks was often quite pronounced; May once commented Zimmermann's 'achievement with PGP was considerable, but I know from first-hand experience that his political views are very non-libertarian and are, in fact, counter to liberty.'[114] Others agreed, explicitly stating Zimmermann was not a cypherpunk.[115] Nevertheless, the cypherpunks held a variety of political views, and May represented the most extreme faction. Despite May's condemnations, Zimmermann's actions were often consistent with liberal cypherpunks. Indeed, many cypherpunks supported him and contributed to the further development of PGP. For instance, cypherpunk Derek Atkins, an MIT computer science student, became a PGP programmer, bug-tracker, and even project lead for later versions of PGP.[116]

Shortly after version 2.0 launched, Zimmermann received a call that led to him becoming a figurehead for the entire cryptography movement whilst also facing jail.

7.4   PGP: INVESTIGATION OF PHIL ZIMMERMANN

In 1993, Zimmermann received a call from US Customs Special Agent Robin Sterzer. Sterzer wanted to ask him some questions about PGP.[117] She informed Zimmermann he was not obliged to answer the questions.[118] At first, Zimmermann thought Sterzer was calling to ask for advice on how to break some PGP-encrypted files, so he tried to explain how PGP worked before Sterzer told Zimmermann she intended to travel from her office in San Jose, California, to meet him face-to-face in Boulder, Colorado, to discuss the software and its export.[119] The announcement of travel caused Zimmermann to realize Sterzer "wasn't just looking for a tutorial on PGP"—he called criminal defense lawyer Phil Dubois.[120] On their meeting in Dubois' office, Zimmermann was "freaked out" when he saw files related to the defense of a murderer, "I thought oh my god, this guy defends criminals—what am I doing here?"[121] But Zimmerman knew he needed a criminal lawyer with "street smarts," he wanted someone experienced with drug cases, of dealing with the

---

111 May, 1992.
112 Bulkeley, 1994.
113 Lebkowsky, 1993.
114 May, 1994.
115 Frissell, 1996.
116 Atkins, no date.

117 Zimmermann, 2003a, 20:25.
118 White, 1993.
119 Zimmermann, 2003a, 21:00.
120 Ibid, 21:20.
121 Ibid, 21:50.

federal authorities, and who had served in the public defender's office so could operate with minimal resources—Dubois met these criteria.[122] However, there was one
challenge: Dubois was still discovering the Internet, having only gone online during fall 1993—to defend Zimmermann he would need to endure a steep and rapid
learning curve.[123] Dubois being able to work with limited resources was particularly important—Zimmermann almost bankrupted himself completing PGP, should
charges be filed he would need someone who could operate with little funding. To try
and increase his war chest, Zimmermann even asked the cypherpunks' mailing list
if they knew of anyone in need of his data security consulting skills.[124] To help out,
Dubois agreed not to bill for all of his time working on the case.[125]

The investigators arrived in February 1993. Previously they had met with Jim
Bidzos. Zimmermann states Bidzos left the investigators with the impression that:

> PGP was stolen property. That it was owned by PKP. And indeed, there was some sig-
> nificance to the fact that PGP and PKP had some similarities to their names, differing
> only by the middle letter.[126]

The meeting focused on the patent issues as much as the potential export violation; "in fact, they spent slightly more time talking about the former than the latter," Zimmerman recalls.[127] Zimmermann told the agents that patent conflicts "are
supposed to be resolved by civil action between the patent holder and the alleged
infringer, not between customs and me." The agents informed Zimmermann he was
not, nor was there any, target of the current investigation, "They just said that they
wanted to hear about PGP and collect information." Their investigation was soon
formalized, with Zimmermann facing export-related charges that could result in his
incarceration for a maximum of five years, and a fine of up to a million dollars.[128]

In September 1993, the EFF announced it would provide the Zimmermann case
financial aid as it:

> may involve fundamental issues in the application of the U.S. Constitution to digital
> media. At stake is the right of privacy, public access to secure cryptography, the right
> to publish digital writings, and the right of equal protection under the law.[129]

As well as supporting Zimmermann with financial and legal aid, the EFF declared
it would support similar cases where the government sought to prevent the spread
of cryptography, and it would initiate a campaign to "promote the Constitutionally
guaranteed rights to develop, discuss, and use cryptographic technology."[130]

Despite the potential legal challenges Zimmermann faced, in August 1993, he
announced an agreement with ViaCrypt (part of Lemcom Systems) to sell a commercial version of PGP.[131] Given the potential patent infringements businesses had

---

[122] Ibid, 22:25.
[123] Zimmermann, 1993c.
[124] Zimmermann, 1993b.
[125] Dubois, 1996a.
[126] Garfinkel, 1995, 112.

[127] Ibid.
[128] Markoff, 1996.
[129] Electronic Frontier Foundation, 1993.
[130] Ibid.
[131] Zimmermann, 1993d.

been unwilling to use PGP, but as ViaCrypt was already licensed for the RSA patents, the new agreement resolved any commercial patent ambiguity.[132] Zimmermann announced ViaCrypt PGP would be available for $100 per user.[133]

As the investigation progressed, a cypherpunk member using the alias "Prince Niccolo di Bernardo Machiavelli" posted to the mail list imploring the cypherpunks to do more to aid Zimmermann, who he considered "one of our own."[134] Machiavelli added:

> Phil and the PGP development team have laid the basis for a lot of the Cypherpunk tools we take for granted...I think Phil deserves better than the silence his plight has received as of late. I know if we put our collective heads together, we can come up with many ways to help him out. Organized fund raisers might be a good way to start, or perhaps a fax campaign to make the media and legislators aware of his situation...If we don't take care of our own, who will?[135]

Zimmermann asked the cypherpunks remain muted on his case, fearing their actions could put Assistant US attorney William P. Keane, who was leading the investigation, into an "irretrievably adversarial position."[136] Zimmermann recognized, "the issues involved in this investigation are of the greatest importance and transcend my personal interests."[137] However, Zimmermann cautioned the cypherpunks against taking actions that would graduate the "investigation into a full-scale federal prosecution."[138] Zimmermann's lawyer Phil Dubois urged the cypherpunks not to enact their planned protest at the upcoming meeting with Keane, "What Phil needs [...] is a quiet environment in which serious legal issues can be discussed candidly in an effort to avoid the necessity for any trial."[139] In late 1993 Zimmermann learned the investigation had progressed to a grand jury.[140]

7.5 PGP: PUBLICITY AND ENCRYPTION'S GREATER GOOD ARGUMENT

Coverage of the Zimmermann investigation appeared in mainstream publications including *Scientific American*, *Time*, *The New York Times*, *The Wall Street Journal*, and *Wired*.

By 1993, examples of criminal use of PGP were emerging. Police in Sacramento, California, stated they were unable to read the computer diary of a convicted pedophile because of PGP, which potentially prevented them from finding additional leads against his suspected child-pornography ring.[141] In a *Denver Westword* article, lead detective Brian Kennedy called Zimmermann a "dirtbag," commenting, "he's an irresponsible person who takes credit for his invention without taking responsibility

---

132 Ibid.
133 Ibid.
134 Machiavelli [alias], 1994.
135 Ibid.
136 Zimmermann, 1993c.
137 Ibid.
138 Ibid.
139 Zimmermann, 2003b, 21:20; Zimmermann, 1994d.
140 Braddock, 1995.
141 Dexheimer, 1993.

for its effect. He's protected people who are preying on children. I hope that someday he'll get what he deserves."[142] Zimmermann commented, "The thought of a child molester out there using PGP does keep me up at nights," but he felt the societal benefit outweighed the costs.[143] In encryption's defense, Zimmermann poses the question of whether automobiles should be banned as "a pedophile can drive up the street and pull little girls into his car."[144] The duality in PGP was perhaps best expressed by the very same Sacramento Police force. Federal funding allowed local computer expert William Sternow to train around 500 officers who now used PGP to protect their official communications, possibly including those concerning investigation into the pedophile ring Kennedy was referencing.[145]

In a *New York Times* article, Nicholas Wade argued technology such as PGP was enabling a greater threat from terrorists:

> Not so long ago, high technology was seen as the likely handmaiden of totalitarian government…by a strange turn of events, what is now in progress is the very opposite of that nightmare. So many powerful technologies are streaming into private hands that Government is struggling to protect even the bare minimum of its legitimate domains.[146]

Wade asked whether the "humiliation of Big Brother isn't being taken beyond reasonable limits," arguing some government monopolies, such as the use of force, are "not so bad." Wade wrote, "If you believe the F.B.I. is bugging your conversations, you'll want to see Zimmermann in the inventors' hall of fame; if terrorism and organized crime seem the more immediate threats, the universal right to absolute privacy looks less compelling." Wade was concerned technologies such as secure phones were being used by terrorists who could "bring down not just a few buildings but large sections of a modern economy." Wade concluded, "Big Brother is dead. The only serious likelihood of his resurrection lies in reaction to the chaos and disintegration that an era of Little Brothers might bring."[147]

Zimmermann was cognizant of the threats that privacy technologies enabled, such as those articulated by Wade; he commented:

> I am worried about what happen if unlimited security communications come about, but I also think there are tremendous benefits. Some bad things would happen, but the trade-off would be worth it. You have to look at the big picture.[148]

Zimmerman argued governments "have more ways to investigate than just tapping. Criminals leave their footprints in the real world."[149] In 1994, FBI Director Louis J. Freeh spoke at the American Law Institute to make the case for the Digital Telephony legislation intended to make telecommunications providers and

---

[142] IbidIbid.I.
[143] Ibid.
[144] Ibid.
[145] Ibid.

[146] Wade, 1994.
[147] Ibid.
[148] Levy, 1994a, 283.
[149] Harrington, 1996.

manufacturers facilitate government access on their digital services and equipment.[150] Freeh declared interception capabilities as "the number one law enforcement, public safety, and national security issue facing us today."[151] Freeh's speech was emotive, the cypherpunks would likely even have said emotionally manipulative. Freeh told the assembled lawyers, "If you think crime is bad now, just wait and see what happens if the FBI one day soon is no longer able to conduct court-approved electronic surveillance."[152] Freeh warned of "disastrous consequences without legislation…Federal Law Enforcement will be crippled…National Security Endangered. Lives will be lost."[153] Freeh continued:

> Without an ability to wiretap, the country will be unable to protect itself against foreign threats, terrorism, espionage, violent crime, drug trafficking, kidnapping, and other crimes. Indeed, we may be unable to intercept a terrorist before he sets off a devastating bomb. Unable to thwart a foreign spy before he can steal secrets that endanger the entire country. Unable to arrest traffickers smuggling in huge amounts of drugs that will cause widespread violent crime and death. Unable to rescue abducted children before they are murdered by their kidnappers.[154]

Freeh added:

> I never want to be in the position of telling a Father or Mother of a kidnapped child that the FBI doesn't have a capability…to [access] criminal communications…and you, likewise, never want to be that parent or grandparent who gets such a call from the FBI when it's your child or grandchild who is at risk.[155]

The use of wiretaps was common in the US, though perhaps less common than many would imagine. In 1993, 976 State and Federal wiretaps were executed, representing a six percent increase on 1992.[156] The majority (73%) of those wiretaps were in New York, New Jersey, and Pennsylvania.[157] Between 1983 and 1993, the use of wiretaps increased by around 30%, only eleven interception applications to judges were refused during this period.[158] Narcotics accounted for 70% of wiretaps in 1993.[159] The average 1993 wiretap cost $57,256—a 23% increase over the previous year.[160] 2,428 people were arrested as a result of electronic surveillance in 1993, 413 were convicted.[161] Whilst these numbers are relatively small in a population of over three hundred million, wiretaps were likely deployed against the most dangerous of criminals, those against whom other investigatory methods had failed.

Zimmermann believed parts of the government were creating a cryptographic Manichean narrative accompanying the demonization of hackers. To counter this positioning, he needed clear examples of PGP being used in a "positive upbeat application that normal people can relate to."[162] Zimmermann asked the cypherpunks

---

150 Freeh, 1994.
151 Freeh, 1994, 134.
152 Ibid, 125.
153 Freeh, 127.
154 Freeh.
155 Freeh, 134.
156 United States Department of Justice, 1994, 12.
157 Ibid.
158 Ibid, 12, 18.
159 Ibid, 14.
160 Ibid.
161 Justice, 17–18.
162 Zimmermann, 1994e.

for such examples which should be more than "disaffected paranoid libertarians embracing it for the theoretical benefits for a free society. We need to be able to cite examples of real people using PGP for good ends."[163]

Zimmermann already had some examples of democracy activists using PGP. For instance, in Burma (Myanmar), Zimmermann highlighted opposition groups and freedom fighters using PGP, "They're being trained to use PGP in Burma in jungle training camps on portable computers. They take this knowledge to other jungle training camps and teach them too."[164] Zimmermann explains, "it's raised morale quite a bit because before PGP came along captured documents would lead directly to the arrest and torture and execution of entire families."[165]

There was more positive coverage in the press for Zimmermann, who was becoming a minor celebrity within the technology world. In August 1995, Zimmermann was announced as one of six recipients for the *Chrysler Award for Innovation in Design* for PGP, which was cited as enabling emails to be "sent securely all over the world without risk of interception by any third party."[166] Chrysler purchased a full-page spread in the *New York Times* to publicize the winners.[167] Cypherpunk Sandy Sandfort commented:

> Phil has gotten an amazing amount of positive press. In the scheme of things, this may prove to be more beneficial for the Cypherpunkish agendas than even his creation of PGP. Phil's image—cryptographer as puppy-dog—will help us a lot more than the "evil kiddieporn/terrorist/hacker" image the FBI…would prefer the public to see.[168]

Despite the growing profile of the encryption issue, the government did little to address the expanding gap between cryptography reality and policy. In June 1993, attempting to demonstrate the anachronism of government policies, the Software Publishers Association (SPA), representing more than a thousand companies, published research arguing export controls had caused the US to lose its global dominance of the encryption market.[169] The SPA found, contrary to government claims strong encryption was not available outside of the US, 143 foreign encryption products, compared to 133 US products on the market. The SPA study identified at least 48 of those using DES, 15 were described as "mass market encryption software programs."[170] The report noted PGP and DES were widely available on the Internet. Ilene Rosenthal, SPA's general counsel argued:

> Unilateral US export controls do not make any sense given the widespread legal availability of foreign encryption programs…foreign companies will buy foreign encryption products if they cannot buy from American companies…as a result, the U.S. Government will only succeed in crippling an American industry's exporting ability.[171]

---

[163] Ibid.
[164] Arachelian, 1994.
[165] Ibid.
[166] Chrysler, 1994.
[167] Ibid.

[168] Sandfort, 1995.
[169] Software Publishers Association, 1993.
[170] Ibid.
[171] Ibid.

The government's response was muted. In 1994 the State Department announced a number of small reforms to encryption export policy. These reforms included manufacturers being able to ship their encryption products directly to customers within approved regions absent individual licenses for each end-user.[172] Export licenses would also be expedited, with an objective of response within two working days.[173] The reforms included a personal use exemption for those temporarily traveling overseas.[174] The sum effect of these reforms was minimal.

7.6 PGP: RESOLVING THE PATENT ISSUE AND MIT PROTECTION

One of the biggest challenges to PGP's non-commercial growth remained the patent violation. May highlighted this to the cypherpunks, commenting whilst PGP moved encryption forward:

> bootleg crypto…is *not* going to spread the way we want strong crypto to…it's not legal…[users] are exposing themselves to serious liabilities if they use it. This alone will begin to strangle PGP in its crib, so to speak.[175]

Ever since PGP's release, Bidzos had claimed it infringed on PKP patents. On first learning of PGP Bidzos went apoplectic, labeling Zimmermann, "gutless and a liar."[176] Bidzos accused Zimmermann of violating both patent law, in using the RSA algorithm, and export law—he further criticized Zimmermann for hiding behind his associates who disseminated PGP.[177] Bidzos wrote to those hosting PGP on their servers to demand removal of the software due to the patent violation—allowing such a precedent to rest unchallenged would have threatened PKP and RSADSI's most valuable assets, their Diffie-Hellman and RSA patents.[178] Bidzos approached Zimmermann several months after PGP's release when it became evident his efforts to have the code removed from the Internet were failing, "We told him that if he stopped distributing PGP, we wouldn't sue, and he signed an agreement."[179] Zimmermann signed the agreement, but Bidzos commented, "he's been violating the agreement ever since."[180] Zimmermann says he respects copyright laws, "But what we're talking about is a patent on a math formula. It's like Isaac Newton patenting Force = Mass × Acceleration. You'd have to pay royalty every time you threw a baseball."[181]

In 1993, Jeffrey Schiller, network manager for MIT, and MIT Professor James Bruce started working with Bidzos to find a resolution to the alleged PGP patent infringement.[182] Bruce states MIT had a "strong belief that heavy-duty cryptography…needed to be in the hands of the general public."[183] Their first meeting in January 1994 included Ron Rivest, and John Preston of MIT's Technology Licensing

---

172 United States Department of State, 1994b.
173 Ibid.
174 Ibid.
175 May, 1993b.
176 Garfinkel, 1995, 101.
177 Ibid.

178 Ibid, 100.
179 Dexheimer, 1993.
180 Ibid.
181 Ibid.
182 Levy, 1994b.
183 Ibid.

office, but there was no immediate breakthrough. Bidzos was adamant Zimmermann would not receive a "free" license.[184]

The eventual solution came not as a result of a concession from Bidzos, but from a stroke of luck. RSADSI had published a cryptography library, RSAREF, with free noncommercial licenses.[185] RSAREF used RSA to help users implement Privacy Enhanced Mail (PEM), an email encryption program. RSAREF failed to gain market share as users had to pay for public key certification before use.[186] In March 1994, RSAREF 2.0 was released. On examination, Zimmermann realized the new code could act as a base for PGP's use of RSA, which in turn would inherit the RSAREF licenses built into the software.[187] Zimmermann inserted the RSAREF code into PGP and removed the patent-violating code—PGP 2.5 was born.[188] In May 1994, MIT announced it would place its institutional strength behind Zimmermann by becoming the hub for PGP 2.5 dissemination.[189] Schiller commented PGP 2.5, "strictly conforms to the conditions of the RSAREF 2.0 license."[190] Zimmermann reflected:

> It took a lot of manuevering [sic] by me and my lawyers and by my friends at MIT and MIT's lawyers to pull this off…This is a major advance in our efforts to chip away at the formidable legal and political obstacles placed in front of PGP.[191]

MIT's sponsorship was important—it was an American intellectual icon with vast resources at its disposal should the US government seek to challenge it in the courts. The MIT FTP server did not, theoretically, allow export overseas. The server provided a questionnaire to the PGP requestor asking them to affirm they were an American citizen, and requesting they declare they would not export the code.[192] Zimmermann stated these precautions were the same as those used by other websites in order to comply with export controls, but they were trivial to circumvent.[193] After posting PGP to their server, MIT received no government complaints. Zimmermann hoped MIT's "moral authority" would continue to shield PGP into the future.[194] In a 1995 conference, MIT's Jeffrey Schiller shared a stage with NSA lawyer Ronald Lee and attempted to get clarification MIT's export protections were sufficient; Lee refused to provide a straight answer, or provide further guidelines as to what actions would be classed as a violation of the export laws.[195] Even with export precautions, such as they were, placed on the MIT server, the new version of PGP was in Europe a day after its launch.[196] Zimmermann reflected, "Information wants to be free. Apparently, that applies to free software more than anything else."[197]

---

[184] Ibid.
[185] Zimmermann, 1994c.
[186] Garfinkel, 1995, 104.
[187] Zimmermann, 1994c.
[188] Levy, 1994b.
[189] Schiller, 1994.
[190] Ibid.
[191] Zimmermann, 1994g.
[192] Arachelian, 1994.
[193] Zimmermann, 1994c.
[194] Arachelian, 1994; Zimmermann, 1994f.
[195] Levy, 2001. Slouching toward Crypto.
[196] Arachelian, 1994.
[197] Ibid.

7.7   PGP: CIRCUMVENTING EXPORT CONTROLS

Challenging the export laws in the digital realm was not enough for MIT and Zimmermann, together they decided to see whether the same PGP code not eligible for digital export, could be exported in print. The freedom to publish printed content, in contrast to digital content, was a well-established and constitutionally protected right. Should the government attempt to prevent printed content being published or exported, the civil liberties, academic, and journalist communities would likely make common cause with, and rally behind, MIT and Zimmermann. It was also impractical to control printed items such as books; Zimmermann commented, "it would be politically difficult for the Government to prohibit the export of a book that anyone may find in a public library or a bookstore."[198] Zimmermann first met Robert V. Prior, editor in the Computer Science department at MIT Press, in mid-1994, shortly after they planned to publish a book on PGP.[199] Prior commented:

> MIT Press and MIT were fully aware of the controversy surrounding PGP…and made the decision to publish…for both sound business reasons…and in a desire to see non-classified and pedagogically important information be made widely available.[200]

The six-hundred-page book included the full C code for PGP printed in characters suitable for optical character recognition. This meant the book could be scanned into a computer and converted back to software once it was overseas, thereby circumventing export laws. MIT wrote to the Office of Defense Trade Controls at the State Department on January 24, 1995, informing them of MIT's intent to publish. MIT conveyed their assessment the PGP book was not covered by the ITAR, and gave the State Department the opportunity to express any export objections.[201] Prior confirmed copies of the book were dispatched to the Defense and Commerce Departments on February 25, with their expectation the review would take 20–30 days.[202] When that period elapsed, Prior again wrote the State Department on April 26 asking for "expedited handling" for MIT's CJ request as the publishing date was in May.[203] MIT received no response. They decided to publish, including in foreign countries, on June 6, four months after sending the initial request to the government.[204] On the same day, Prior received a call from his State Department contact, Sam Capino, who told him Commerce agreed the PGP book was not ITAR-controlled.[205] Prior claims Capino informally told him the NSA recommended the PGP book be ITAR-controlled, though Capino refused to provide this information in written form.[206] Prior stated:

> The tale basically ends here. We never received any response to our letter, either to confirm that our interpretation of the ITAR was correct or to inform us that it was not

---

[198] Zimmermann, 1995a.
[199] Prior, 1996.
[200] Ibid.
[201] Ibid.
[202] Ibid.

[203] Ibid.
[204] Ibid.
[205] Ibid.
[206] Ibid.

correct. We decided to publish the book in spite of the fact that we had not received a response from the Government and despite the fact that we had been told informally that NSA recommended that the book be controlled under the ITAR.[207]

Zimmermann recognized that the book:

comprised entirely of thousands of lines of source code looks pretty dull. But then so does a nondescript fragment of concrete—unless it happens to be a piece of the Berlin Wall, which many people display on their mantels as a symbol of freedom opening up for millions of people...Perhaps in the long run, this book will help open up the US borders to the free flow of information.[208]

EFF co-founder John Perry Barlow wrote the forward to MIT's Official PGP User Guide. Barlow's forward captured the sentiments of the cypherpunks as well as perhaps any words committed to paper, they bear examining in detail:

I love irony, and there lies in this book an irony as striking as any I know...[PGP] written by an apparently unformidable gnome on a tight budget, now terrifies a security monolith which required half a century, uncounted billions of dollars, and the collective IQs of a few thousand geniuses to develop...

[PGP] could very well be the root tendril which will grow into the National Security State and shatter it. If that is true, it's probably only a little hyperbolic to claim that you are holding a work as liberating as Common Sense, or, viewed through another set of bunker slits, as socially disruptive as *Mein Kampf*.[209]

Barlow articulated the combination of the digital age and encryption technologies was resulting in society coming to:

[a] very sharp balance point between two lousy choices. On one side lies a technological foundation upon which the most massive totalitarianism could be built. On the other is a jungle in which any number of anarchic guerrillas might hide, upon whom little order could ever be imposed.[210]

Barlow continued:

Any government that can automatically generate an intimate profile of every one of its citizens is a government endowed with a potential for absolute power that will eventually, to use Lord Acton's phrase, corrupt absolutely. Few civil liberties are likely to survive such capacities in the hands of increasingly panicky authoritarians who run the embattled old bureaucracies of the Meat World.[211]

But PGP, Barlow explained, was one of a number of tools as "unbalancingly powerful in their power to conceal as are the other side's in the service of revelation." Barlow added that these tools allow users to:

---

[207] Ibid.
[208] Zimmermann, 1995a.
[209] Barlow, 1995.
[210] Ibid.
[211] Ibid.

simply vanish from the governmental radar. They are at greater liberty than ever before to conduct any endeavor...In many ways, they can effectively resign from the community of the governed and enter a condition in which their actions are ordered by conscience and culture alone.[212]

Barlow added culture is a strong governance force, as is the case in his home town Wyoming, where "something like the Code of the West is still more important than the law of its instruments."[213] Barlow did acknowledge the possibility of returning to such models, and whether diverse societies such as America can be governed by norms culture alone, was a valid question.

Barlow argued the Bill of Rights "continues to apply only when the government feels no pain from its application."[214] Barlow stated he did not trust the government to regulate information, nor to judge what communications were appropriate to surveil, which he viewed as, "rather like having a peeping tom install one's window blinds."[215] Barlow recognized the potential impact of giving privacy tools such as PGP to citizens:

> I would even rather extend to people the general condition of anonymity, hoping they will not use it much, knowing that without identity, there is little impetus for responsibility, and that without responsibility, the Social Contract is abrogated.[216]

Barlow encouraged readers to be "circumspect" about using privacy tools such as PGP, given their power as the "ultimate defensive weapon, the ability to disappear, countervail against the all-seeing electronic eye." However, he believed citizens should be "armed" with digital protection as he predicted that "any government which can see everything we do all the time will sooner or later feel compelled to add omnipotence to omniscience, which are, in the Virtual Age, much the same thing anyway." Barlow recognized that should privacy tools be used by the citizenry there could be "anarchy, maybe even chaos," but in such a scenario it was possible "human beings will turn out to be better, less paranoid, less worthy of inspiring paranoia, than many of us think."[217]

In September, Michael Hortmann of Germany's Bremen University informed the cypherpunks his students had scanned the PGP source code from the MIT book and were uploading the files to Bremen's FTP server making them available for all—the circumvention of US export laws was complete.[218] MIT printed 1500 copies of their PGP book, in February 1996 they sold out.[219] As the export-circumvention methodology had been demonstrated, and the government had taken no action, a reprint was unnecessary.[220]

However, several months later, a potential US response to MIT's PGP book did come to light. Hal Abelson, Professor of Computer Science and Engineering

---

[212] Ibid.
[213] Ibid.
[214] Ibid.
[215] Ibid.

[216] Ibid.
[217] Ibid.
[218] Hortmann, 1995.
[219] Gilmore, 1996a.

at MIT, and a long-standing PGP developer, reported to the cypherpunks that Sandia National Laboratories, a government body funding MIT and other academic research, attempted to insert contractual language giving Sandia the right to prior review of any resulting MIT research to identify potential export control violations. When MIT queried this a Sandia lawyer, Bruce Winchell, informed MIT the State Department had "made it clear" to Sandia they were very concerned MIT did not have procedures in place to monitor the dissemination of material subject to export controls. Winchell also said the PGP source code book came very close to violating the export laws. Abelson expressed his frustration that after the State Department's failure to engage with MIT regarding the PGP book, for MIT to now learn of a "back channel communication from State to DOE [Department of Energy] to Sandia," prompting the latter, "to act as a policeman for MIT *vis-à-vis* export controls," was very concerning. Abelson wrote, "This is troubling for what it says about how the State Department is dealing with export issues surrounding information about cryptography, and about the extent to which policies are being administered in a clear and aboveboard manner."[221]

7.8 PGP: CONCLUSION OF THE ZIMMERMANN INVESTIGATION

In February 1995, Zimmermann's defense team traveled to California to meet with the assistant US attorney to attempt to persuade him not to indict. Dubois reported to the cypherpunks the meeting was "cordial," and the assistant US attorney, "listened carefully and agreed to consider our arguments." Dubois told the cypherpunks he was providing this information with the "hope of avoiding speculation and misinformation"—this statement suggests Dubois was accustomed to the cypherpunks' mercurial nature. The cypherpunks provided Zimmermann and Dubois with a "warm reception" during their visit to California.[222]

With the investigation progressing, it became clear Zimmermann needed additional financial assistance to face any charges—Dubois established a defense fund. Hugh Miller, Assistant Professor of Philosophy at Loyola University Chicago, and Zimmermann's friend, introduced the defense fund to the cypherpunks. Miller told the cypherpunks they stood upon the precipice of an important battle following the revolution "unleashed" by Diffie and Hellman in 1976.[223] Fourteen months after being told he was the subject of a grand jury investigation, Zimmermann was to meet with Keane in two weeks' time, on January 12, 1995.[224] Miller wrote, "An indictment, if one is pursued by the government after this meeting, could be handed down very shortly thereafter."[225] Zimmermann would need money—lots of money. He was thousands of dollars in debt on legal fees; Dubois estimated Zimmermann's legal fees could be as high as $300,000.[226] Miller told the cypherpunks Zimmermann's case presented "significant issues and will establish legal

---

[220] Ibid.
[221] Abelson, 1996.
[222] Dubois, 1995.
[223] Braddock, 1995.

[224] Ibid.
[225] Ibid.
[226] Ibid.

precedent" on digital privacy.[227] Miller believed the government "hopes to establish the proposition that posting a "munition" on a BBS [Bulletin Board System] or on the Internet is exportation," he believed this would "resurrect Checkpoint Charlie—on the Information Superhighway."[228] Miller recognized Zimmermann's contribution to the cypherpunks:

> Phil has assumed the burden and risk of being the first to develop truly effective tools with which we all might secure our communications against prying eyes, in a political environment increasingly hostile to such an idea...Now is the time for us all to step forward and help shoulder that burden with him.[229]

People from all over the world answered Miller's call, giving from $1 up to an anonymous $10,000 donation, the fund eventually reached a mid-five-figure sum.[230] Other contributions were made to Zimmermann's cause, such as frequent flyer miles allowing Zimmermann's defense team to travel as required for the case.[231] Eventually Zimmermann commanded an array of allies to help him fight the investigation, this included lawyers Ken Bass, Curt Karnow, Eben Moglen, and Bob Corn-Revere, who donated hundreds of hours of their time, and members of the Electronic Privacy Information Center (EPIC), the EFF, CPSR, and the American Civil Liberties Union (ACLU) who in Dubois' words provided, "financial, legal, and moral support, and kept the public informed."[232]

Michael J. Yamaguchi, the US Attorney for the North District of California, announced there would be no prosecutions relating to the Usenet posting of PGP, on January 10, 1996; the investigation was closed.[233] The announcement was delivered to Dubois by fax—perhaps an unintended representation of the attorney offices' technological state.[234] Zimmermann, evidently overwhelmed, thanked the cypherpunks, writing, "The medium of email cannot express how I feel about this turn of events."[235] No reason for dropping the case was given. Some on the cypherpunks' mailing list speculated the investigation may have ended as "NSA finally managed to crack PGP."[236] Though Zimmermann doubted such an event would have a direct bearing on his case as the NSA would keep such a capability "under tight wraps, and would certainly not tell a federal prosecutor about it. The NSA would never trust the cops with a secret of that magnitude."[237] Zimmermann added, "If the NSA could break it, it would make more sense for them to just sit back and allow a prosecution to proceed, which would make PGP even more popular, and thus give the NSA even more opportunities to exploit their secret capability."[238] Other cypherpunks such as Attila (alias), even suspected Zimmermann may finally have caved to pressure to add a PGP NSA backdoor.[239] Mark Bainter posted he was informed by a "newly made"

---

[227] Ibid.
[228] Ibid.
[229] Ibid.
[230] Dubois, 1996b; Harrington, 1996.
[231] Dubois, 1995.
[232] Dubois, 1996b.
[233] United States Attorney, 1996.

[234] Dubois, 1996b.
[235] Zimmermann, 1996b.
[236] Duvos, 1996.
[237] Zimmermann, no date-b.
[238] Ibid.
[239] Attila, 1996.

acquaintance that Zimmermann had told this acquaintance at DefCon that he co-operated with the government providing them a way to crack PGP keys since version 2.3.[240] It seems most likely this was a deceitful individual trying to impress a new contact, rather than a government conspiracy to discredit PGP, but the latter was possible. It is equally possible Bainter was lying of his own recognizance. Zimmermann states, "I didn't cut any deals, and would not have done so even if it was the only way to stay out of prison." Zimmermann even offered up an alternate conspiracy theory: "The government actually started these nasty rumors of backdoors in PGP, because in fact they don't know how to break it. What better way to scare people away from using it?"; however, Zimmermann confessed he did not truly believe this as "I'm not a conspiracy nut."[241]

There was always a degree of paranoia regarding PGP's security. Some tried to discredit PGP publicly from behind their own shield of anonymity. For instance, in 1993 on the mailing list an individual calling himself "Raymond Paquin," who claimed to be a university professor of mathematics who could not reveal his identity as he claimed to conduct classified work, argued PGP was fatally flawed.[242] However, Paquin did not offer evidence to support his claim. Whether Paquin was authentic, a government agent, or a non-government individual making trouble (as seems most likely), is unknown.

Others thought the investigation was closed as the statute of limitations was either shortly due to expire, or had already expired, dependent on for which specific act prosecution was being contemplated.[243] Bill Frantz hypothesized the prosecution, "could not build a trail of evidence between Zimmermann and the export."[244] Curtis Karnow, an intellectual-property lawyer on Zimmermann's legal team wondered whether the prosecutor may have been "affected by Phil Zimmermann's folk-hero status," arguing, "Thousands of people see Phil as a voice of conscience and someone who has dedicated his life to protecting people's rights."[245] Dubois offered the cypherpunks another theory: lack of prosecution could be because the ITAR was unconstitutional. Dubois offered further analysis:

> it might be that the government did not want to risk a judicial finding that posting it cryptographic software on a site in the U.S., even if it's an Internet site, is not an "export."
>
> There was also the risk that the export-control law would be declared unconstitutional. Perhaps the government did not want to get into a public argument about some important policy issues: should it be illegal to export cryptographic software? Should U.S. citizens have access to technology that permits private communication? And ultimately, do U.S. citizens have the right to communicate in absolute privacy?[246]

There was also a question of whether non-prosecution established a future precedent for export violations. Dubois advised the cypherpunks, "Nobody should conclude

---

[240] Bainter, 1996.
[241] Zimmermann, no date-b.
[242] Anonymous Poster, 1993.
[243] Hallam-Baker, 1996.

[244] Frantz, 1996.
[245] Bulkeley, 1996.
[246] Dubois, 1996b.

that it is now legal to export cryptographic software."[247] Speaking to *The New York Times*, one of many national papers covering the case, Zimmermann said, "In the long run, the export controls are going to have to fall. The opposition is so strong in the computer industry that the Government cannot ignore the changes in the world. This technology is not just for spies any more."[248] Marc Rotenberg, director of EPIC said, "We hope this signals a change on the part of the Federal Government, we hope that it reflects a recognition that encryption developers should be encouraged and not indicted."[249] EFF staff attorney Shari Steele commented, "We are so excited that the Justice Department has finally realized they don't have any facts to pursue this witch hunt."[250] Mark Rasch, a former Justice Department lawyer who worked on export and computer cases reflected the government, "had recognized that criminal prosecution is a terrible tool with which to make national policy."[251]

Amongst the cypherpunks, feelings were mixed about the result. Sameer Parekh argued, "We've made no progress. Phil has lost lots of time and gained lots of gray hairs, and everyone who donated to his defense fund lost money. The US can still harass people if they want, and make their life hell."[252] Tim May agreed, believing the government would look for a more "winnable" case: "In many ways, what Phil and/or some of his friends may or may not have done was too "stale." None of the Four Horsemen were involved directly, and Phil's case generated publicity that tended to make him a hero, not an Enemy of the People."[253] Alex Strasheim agreed, posting, "It's great that Phil's off the hook, but there's nothing to stop them from doing the same thing to someone else tomorrow. What's more, everyone here knows that, and so the government gets what it really wants: a chilling effect on crypto development."[254] Bill Stewart commented the government, "demonstrated that you can tie up a person for years, and cause him to spend huge legal expenses, without being stopped by the Constitutional right to a speedy trial, and by not prosecuting they're preserving the powers of Fear, Uncertainty, and Doubt."[255] Stewart wrote that the government could:

And they can always argue that "Well, the case against Phil didn't have quite enough direct evidence to prosecute, but we caught SAMEER and three of his customers Red-handed, and plan to prosecute those crypto-narco-anarco-porno-terrorist Commie-sympathizing Nazi-protecting Foreign-looking money-laundering EEEVIL conspirators from BERKELEY to the fullest extent of the law!*" and spend a couple of years harassing them, and then find another victim after that.[256]

Alex Strasheim agreed the government's actions were designed to chill cryptographic development, "our position is similar to that of a little kid in grade school who's getting beat up by a bully every day. We need to make friends with a big guy

247 Ibid.
248 Markoff, 1996.
249 Ibid.
250 Bulkeley, 1996.
251 Markoff, 1996.

252 Parekh, 1996.
253 May, 1996a.
254 Strasheim, 1996a.
255 Stewart, 1996.
256 Ibid.

who can keep the bully off our back."[257] The "big guys" were partners like MIT, who the government could not so easily "push around."[258] If such partners hosted a more ambitious cryptography repository Strasheim believed the chilling effect could be offset.[259] Though some cypherpunks were more positive, Ed Carp wrote, "by abandoning their case…they have seriously weakened their case against anyone else that they feel has violated the ITAR in a similar manner—it's called 'selective enforcement' and courts have been taking a dim view of that sort of thing."[260] Marc Rotenberg of EPIC, who was also a lawyer, saw more nuance in the situation, "The decision [to discontinue the investigation] doesn't [establish a judicial precedent]… but it may mean the government will be more careful in considering future prosecutions."[261] Cypherpunk Jim Bell believed the government's ability to "harass" cryptographers had been "severely limited by their failure to indict Zimmermann."[262] Cypherpunk Vladimir Nuri wondered whether the ITAR had "teeth" at all, as Goen had not been prosecuted:

> the "Feds" are AWARE that KELLY GOEN was the one who distributed it [PGP]. did they prosecute him either? NO!!! did they have evidence that Goen was the one that knowingly "exported" the code? PROBABLY!!! WHAT DOES THIS TELL YOU?!?!?![263]

Assistant US attorney William P. Keane acknowledged the technical and political "cutting-edge issues" Zimmermann's case represented.[264] Of the decision to drop the investigation, Keane said, "sometimes the right thing is to do nothing."[265] That explanation fell short of sating the cypherpunks' appetite for answers; Patrick Finerty posted, "I would hope that after persecuting this man [Zimmermann] for years they would offer some reasonable explanations about their (real) motivations and why they decided to drop the case."[266] With regards to the implications, Keane said, "If there is any policy decision, it's certainly not going to come from the prosecutor in Silicon Valley."[267] Cypherpunk Hal Finney worried the end of the investigation could damage their efforts to change policy:

> unfair and unjustified as the pending charges against Phil were, they did at least raise people's consciousness about the problems in current policies. Phil did an excellent job of keeping these issues in front of people.[268]

To celebrate his freedom, Zimmermann's wife held a "Phil got off the hook" party, attended by his family, friends, lawyers, and colleagues from his nuclear protest days.[269] A post from cypherpunk Alex Strasheim summed up the cypherpunks' admiration of Zimmermann:

---

[257] Strasheim, 1996b.

[258] Ibid.

[259] Ibid.

[260] Carp, 1996.

[261] Harrington, 1996.

[262] Bell, 1996a.

[263] Nuri, 1996.

[264] Markoff, 1996.

[265] Ibid.

[266] Finerty, 1996.

[267] Markoff, 1996.

[268] Finney, 1996.

[269] Harrington, 1996.

Phil changed the world. Maybe not as much as people like Roosevelt or Reagan, but a lot more than most people do...He used technology to effect positive political changes around the world...And he stood up under a personal attack from the government. They came at him, but he took it and won.[270]

7.9 CODE AS CONSTITUTIONALLY PROTECTED SPEECH I: DANIEL BERNSTEIN

Daniel Bernstein was born in 1971.[271] Bernstein excelled at High School in New York. Already in his final year by the age of 15, he commented, "I can't remember a time when I wasn't interested in math."[272] That school year, Bernstein became one of the youngest ever winners when he was awarded fifth place in the prestigious Westinghouse Science Talent Search, which President George W. Bush once referred to as the "Super Bowl of Science," for his research on new algorithms to calculate infinite numbers such as pi.[273] The young Bernstein already had an activist streak with his hobbies including lobbying for environmental causes.[274]

In the late 1980s, whilst reading for a degree in mathematics at New York University, the computer account of one of Bernstein's computer accounts was hacked; Bernstein recalled, "How disgusted I was at finding out that he [the hacker] had been rifling through my files."[275] Bernstein spent hours trying to understand whether the intruder had destroyed, or simply copied files—the breach triggered an interest in computer security.[276] Some years later, Bernstein helped design a system to monitor the activities of an intruder into the University's computer network.[277] Whilst monitoring the intruder, Bernstein realized cryptography could have helped prevent the attack.[278]

Bernstein started his PhD in Mathematics at Berkeley, University of California, in 1991.[279] During his studies, Bernstein was exposed to the government's encryption export regulations. Bernstein recalls, "I heard that the government controlled encryption exports, but that it permitted exports of encryption technology in the form of specialized 'one-way hash functions.' This struck me as silly."[280]

Hash functions are mathematical algorithms allowing a unique fixed string (a hash) to be generated from a file. Should one digital bit of the file be changed, a completely different hash should be generated. This trait is very useful for file integrity checks. For instance, a file could be "hashed" before being transmitted over email, the accompanying hash would be sent with the message (or ideally, placed in a separate location accessible to the user to reduce the chance of person-in-the-middle attacks), allowing the recipient to generate a new hash of the file they have received

---

[270] Strasheim, 1996c.
[271] Bernstein, 2008.
[272] Verhovek, 1987.
[273] Ibid and Huler, 1991.
[274] Verhovek, 1987.
[275] Cassidy, 1996.

[276] Bernstein, 1996a.
[277] Ibid.
[278] Ibid.
[279] Bernstein, 2008.
[280] Bernstein, 1996a.

in order to confirm it matches the sent hash. This allows the recipient to confirm the file had not been damaged (or manipulated) in transit. Mathematical algorithms used for hashes are often based on the same idea as Diffie and Hellman's public key cryptography—they are easy to compute in one direction (hash generation), but near impossible, to reverse engineer (recreating a file from a hash).

Bernstein developed a simple algorithm capable of converting legally exportable one-way hash functions into encryption systems. Bernstein called his algorithm Snuffle.[281]

Snuffle itself was not an encryption system. Instead, Snuffle converted a one-way hash function, such as Xerox's widely available freeware Snerfru 2.0, into a private-key encryption system with minimal effort. Bernstein explains, "The portions of snuffle.c [enabling encryption] and unsnuffle.c [enabling decryption] which actually perform encryption and decryption contain just 15 lines each of C code with no cryptographic technology *per se*."[282] All cryptographic code resided within the hash function; Bernstein commented, "If the hash function is strong, the system encrypts strongly. If the hash function is weak, the system encrypts weakly."[283] Bernstein was exploiting a regulatory loophole—as hash functions were not controlled by ITAR they could be exported and Bernstein's code enabled foreigners to easily transform the hashes into encryption systems.[284] Bernstein explains, "A program like Pretty Good Privacy is all set to go; my program is a machine that gives you a method of encrypting data, but you have to do a lot more work to make it usable."[285]

In June 1992, Bernstein wrote to the State Department to initiate a Commodity Jurisdiction Request (CJR), a government process determining whether a crypto-logic artifact intended for export required a license, for which the author would subsequently apply.[286] Bernstein wanted to publish Snuffle5.0 and the accompanying documentation to the popular online newsgroup "Science of Cryptography," known to the digital community as sci.crypt, this would constitute export under the law.[287] Bernstein told the State Department Snuffle could "convert any one-way hash function into a zero-delay private-key encryption system."[288] Zero-Delay meant Snuffle was ideal for encrypted online chats, the notion of further digital anonymity would surely have disturbed law enforcement at a time when they were already concerned with losing access to targets. In the early 1990s, criminals were migrating online to enable their illicit activities. In a highly publicized PR campaign two years earlier, the US Secret Service had announced Operation SUNDEVIL, part of a "hacker crackdown," the purpose of which, Assistant Director Gary M. Jenkins explained, was to send, "a clear message to those computer hackers who have decided to violate the laws of this nation."[289] Adding Bernstein's encryption to the equation was anathema to law enforcement, especially as crime was increasingly transnational.

---

[281] Ibid.
[282] Bernstein, 1992.
[283] Bernstein, 1996a.
[284] Ibid.
[285] Cassidy, 1996.

[286] Bernstein, 1992.
[287] Ibid.
[288] Ibid.
[289] Bromberg, 1991.

Bernstein hoped whilst Snuffle enabled cryptographic functionality once combined with Snerfru or other hashes, the technicality that it did not itself contain cryptographic technology would enable exportation. In a severe understatement of the implications of his code, Bernstein closed his letter with, "In effect what I want to export is a description of a way to use existing technology in a more effective manner."[290] Two months later, William B. Robinson, Director of the Office of Defense Trade Controls (ODTC) at the State Department which administered the ITAR regulations, wrote to Bernstein informing him Snuffle was a defense article requiring an export license.[291] The NSA inputted to, and potentially drove, the State Department decision, with Mark Koro and Greg Stark of NSA's Encryption Export Control Branch judging Snuffle to fall within the ITAR restrictions.[292] Bernstein was "shocked," commenting, "I had thought that I would be free to publish my ideas."[293]

Bernstein challenged the ruling in March 1993.[294] In July, Bernstein spoke with Charles Ray, special assistant to Robinson at the ODTC to discuss the situation.[295] Bernstein tried to ascertain from Ray whether if he exploited what he believed to be an ITAR loophole, the public exemption rule, the State Department would consider the act illegal, despite his holding to the letter of the law. Bernstein recounted to Ray that the ITAR specified if content were published and available in libraries to the public, it was considered public domain information, and was therefore exempt from export controls.[296] Bernstein wanted to know if someone placed an item in a library would this act not trigger the public exemption rule.[297] Ray acknowledged the loophole Bernstein was referring to:

I know it says that, but I think you have to use a little common sense there. I think if someone created something that they knew was [on the] [ITAR] Munitions List and wanted to get around the law and took it to a library, I think the motivation has to be considered.[298]

Ray believed such an act "could be considered a violation of the Arms Export Control Act [ITAR]."[299] Bernstein argued the First Amendment protected his right to publish. Ray disagreed, "I don't think that's quite what the freedom of the press statutes were meant to protect."[300] Ray argued the freedom of the press "carries with it a responsibility to comply with the existing legislation and regulations."[301] The message was clear: should Bernstein attempt to circumvent ITAR via the public exemption rule (even though he may not have broken a literal interpretation of the law), the government would still prosecute him for violating the State Department's interpretation of the "spirit" of the law.

In April, Bernstein requested written answers to fourteen questions, focusing on the same public exemption clause, from Robinson himself, presumably knowing to

---

290 Bernstein, 1992.
291 United States Department of State, 1992.
292 Giles, 1995.
293 Bernstein, 1996a.
294 Bernstein, 1993a.
295 Bernstein and Ray, 1993.

296 Ibid.
297 Ibid.
298 Ibid.
299 Ibid.
300 Ibid.
301 Ibid.

initiate judicial proceedings against the State Department would require such documentation.[302] After almost two months with no reply from the State Department, Bernstein wrote to Californian Democratic Congressman Ronald Dellums for assistance.[303] Bernstein explained he was dealing with Clyde Bryant, the Chief of Compliance and Enforcement Branch, ODTC, who had been a "consistently uncooperative government employee."[304] Bernstein called the delay in response to his questions "outrageous," adding, "I'm not sure Mr. Bryant *ever* plans to respond to my letters" [original italics].[305] Bernstein requested Dellums intervene to accelerate the State Department's response—he did so on 24 May.[306] On 27 May, Bryant wrote to Bernstein informing him the State Department, "are unable to advise you as to whether what you hypothetically referred to is licensable"; Bryant advised Bernstein to provide specific technical data and a detailed explanation of its use for a CJR review.[307]

Bernstein wrote to Robinson on June 30 informing him, "I intend to perform certain actions which might violate the regulations administered by your office."[308] Clearly infuriated, Bernstein told Robinson, "You have achieved your apparent goal of censorship by leaving me in fear that I _might_ be committing a crime. Such behavior is unacceptable in a free society."[309] Bernstein declared to Robinson:

I will not register with [O]DTC. I will publish Snuffle 5.0 without any license from [O] DTC. I will never again ask [O]DTC whether any particular item is a defense article, and I will not apply for any license from [O]DTC.[310]

Bernstein added:

I have published many thousands of pages of information and I will publish many more. I see no reason to waste the time to determine whether I am publishing defense articles. Nor do I see any reason to submit any of my information to [O]DTC censorship. Unfortunately your office appears to have the policy that ITAR does require prior review and licensing for some publications.[311]

Bernstein again requested an answer to his fourteen questions on the ITAR regulations, and reiterated that he created Snuffle as a hobby, and the ITAR provisioned an exemption for "scientific purposes, including research and development," (ITAR 122.1(b)(4)) which he believed his work fell within and demanded a "good-faith attempt to answer my questions in a timely and informative manner."[312]

After two weeks, Robinson had not responded.[313] Bernstein wrote to Congressman Dellums informing him the State Department was "engaging in unconstitutional censorship."[314] Bernstein believed the State Department had not responded to his

[302] Bernstein, 1993b.
[303] Bernstein, 1993c.
[304] Ibid.
[305] Ibid.
[306] Ibid. and Bernstein, 1993e.
[307] United States Department of State, 1993a.
[308] Bernstein, 1993d.
[309] Ibid.
[310] Ibid.
[311] Ibid.
[312] Ibid.
[313] Bernstein, 1993e.
[314] Ibid.

questions as they knew they were "acting in violation of the Bill of Rights."[315] Bernstein added, "Both Mr. Bryant and Mr. Robinson failed to answer this question: Does ITAR exert prior restraint on otherwise lawful publication?"[316] Bernstein was also able to speak with some NSA representatives who told him Snuffle was considered "strategic," the meaning of which Bernstein inferred meant it would not be easy to break cryptography systems built upon Snuffle.[317] Bernstein comments, "They offered to help me rewrite it to make it not strategic"—he declined.[318]

Switching to another tactic, on July 15, Bernstein divided his original CJR into five separate components and resubmitted them to the Department of State for approval—with the intent of identifying which component of Snuffle were subject to export controls.[319] The five separate requests were:

1. Snuffle encryption system paper
2. Snuffle encryption software
3. Snuffle decryption software
4. Description of how to use Snuffle
5. Instruction for programming a computer to use Snuffle

Bernstein posted to sci.crypt to brief his fellow cryptologists on his experience in late July:

> My battle with the State Department has entered its second year and continues to thicken. For many months I did not tell the story of this battle, for I thought that the censors were reasonable men, and that quiet negotiation would succeed while confrontation would surely fail. I now know that I was wrong.[320]

Bernstein released documentation of his exchanges with the State Department to "show you a bit of how the censors work."[321]

Robinson wrote Bernstein on September 7 in reply to his defiant June 30 letter. Robinson informed Bernstein, "The fact that you created Snuffle 5.0 as a hobby does not in itself exempt you being a manufacturer of defense articles as defined in the ITAR." Robinson stated Snuffle was not in the public domain as defined by ITAR, and it would be unlawful to export Snuffle without a license.[322] Bernstein enclosed the forms for Bernstein to register as an arms manufacturer, a requirement for all exporters of items on the ITAR list which were considered to be dual-use, and closed the letter with, "I trust that this letter and its enclosures provide the information that you have requested and need to take proper action regarding your stated intentions."[323]

---

315 Ibid.
316 Ibid.
317 Levy, 2001, Slouching towards Crypto.
318 Ibid.
319 Bernstein, 1993f.

320 Bernstein, 1993g.
321 Ibid.
322 Ibid.
323 United States Department of State, 1993b.

Writing back to Robinson on September 20, Bernstein asked all future correspondence be copied to Shari Steele, EFF's director of legal services, suggesting he was planning to take his case to the judicial system.[324] Bernstein was clearly enraged, writing:

I am disgusted that you refer to me as an "arms manufacturer" simply because I have thought up and written down certain information. What happened to freedom of thought and freedom of expression in this country? Don't you have anything more useful to do than harass working mathematicians?[325]

Bernstein asked Robinson to explain the discrepancy between the scientific research and development ITAR clause and the State Department's refusal to clarify Snuffle as academic research.[326]

In a subsequent letter to Robinson, Bernstein also argued the infeasibility of providing an export license application to include "all end-users, grouped by country, and must include a signed statement from each end-user" when posting information online.[327] Bernstein commented, "it appears that ITAR bars publication, via the sheer impracticality of applying for a publication license."[328] Likely recognizing Robinson's unwavering position, Bernstein appealed the Snuffle CJR classification to Ambassador Michael Newlin, the State Department's Acting Director for the Center for Defense Trade on September 22.[329] Just over a week later, Bernstein's five CJ requests were denied. They were treated as a single request, meaning the State Department had not enabled Bernstein to identify which aspects of Snuffle were falling foul of ITAR.[330]

The EFF announced it was sponsoring Bernstein's federal lawsuit against the State Department in February 1995.[331] The EFF's John Gilmore stated, "This suit is one front in the crypto-wars. Nobody really knows how these wars will end up or which front will be the one that finally collapses."[332] The EFF's press release stated the government opposed encryption, "fearing that its citizens will be private and secure from the government as well as from other vandals."[333] The EFF declared the export-control system an "impermissible prior restraint on speech, in violation of the First Amendment." The EFF stated software was published rather than manufactured and are, "constitutionally protected works of human-to-human communication." The EFF argued restrictions on publishing, "unconstitutionally abridge the right to speak, to publish, to associate with others, and to engage in academic inquiry and study." Further, the EFF contended ITAR restricted citizen's ability to protect their privacy—another Constitutionally protected right. Specifically, the EFF argued ITAR:

---

[324] Bernstein, 1993h.
[325] Ibid.
[326] Ibid.
[327] Bernstein, 1993i.
[328] Ibid.
[329] Bernstein, 1993j.
[330] United States Department of State, 1993c; Lowell, 1995, para 14.
[331] Electronic Frontier Foundation, 1995.
[332] Cassidy, 1996.
[333] Electronic Frontier Foundation, 1995.

- Allowed the government to restrict publication without judicial review[334]
- Provided "too few procedural safeguards for First Amendment rights"
- Created a "licensed press" by requiring cryptography authors to register with the government
- Forbade general publication by requiring recipients of cryptography to be individually identified
- Created ambiguity of what acts were considered illegal
- Was overly broad as it prohibited protected activities (such as speaking with foreigners in the US) and prohibited software being exported on the basis cryptography may be subsequently added[335]

The EFF expected it would take years to win the case, and, "the government will use every trick and every procedural delaying tactic available to avoid having a court look at the real issues."[336] The EFF were confident a court would validate their argument that ITAR violated the constitution, and government "attempts to restrict both freedom of speech and privacy will be shown to have no place in an open society."[337] Cindy Cohn, of McGlashan and Sarrail in California agreed to be the lead attorney on a pro bono basis, with EFF providing additional support and paying any expenses.[338] Cohn would later argue:

> From a legal standpoint, the Bernstein case is not complex, nor does it break any dramatic new ground. It simply asks the courts to recognize that the First Amendment extends to science on the Internet, just as it does to science on paper and in the classroom. For it is this scientific freedom which has allowed us to even have an Internet, as well as the many other technologies which we enjoy today.[339]

In his legal complaint Bernstein claimed "irreparable injury" to his reputation and livelihood was being caused by the export controls.[340] Cohn argued, "there is no 'sliding scale' of First Amendment protection under which the degree of scrutiny fluctuates in accordance with the degree to which the regulation touches on foreign affairs."[341] Cohn asked the courts to provide an injunction allowing Bernstein to publish his works without fear of prosecution, and ultimately for ITAR to be declared unconstitutional.[342]

Prior restraint on freedom of speech was a particularly contentious issue, the principal legal question was whether computer code was sufficiently "expressive" to trigger First Amendment protection. Cohn highlighted Freeman v. Maryland, in which the Supreme Court held that if the government should wish to implement a prepublication licensing scheme it must contain a mechanism to make a prompt

---

[334] In 1989, the Arms Control Export Act was amended to preclude judicial reviews of items the government designated to fall within the ITAR regulations (United States Congress, 1989, Section 6).
[335] Ibid.
[336] Ibid.

[337] Ibid.
[338] Ibid.
[339] Cohn, 1998a.
[340] Cohn, 1995a, para 88.
[341] Cohn, 1995b, Conclusion.
[342] Cohn, 1995a, para 197.2.

decision (no more than two weeks), the courts must make the decision to prevent publication (the government could only bring forth the case), and the government must bear the burden of proof that the publication will cause the relevant damage as to outweigh the constraint on the freedom of speech.[343] Cohn explains:

> Even a claim of national security or public safety must be carefully weighed against our fundamental rights, and must be supported with hard evidence of direct, immediate and irreparable harm, not just conjecture and a few frightening scenarios.[344]

Cohn argues the Founding Fathers themselves intended cryptography to be available to the public: "In sharp contrast to the Administration's arguments today, they viewed cryptography as an essential instrument for protecting information, both political and personal."[345] Cohn highlighted:

> Even the Constitution and the Bill of Rights themselves were often encoded, as Thomas Jefferson and James Madison exchanged drafts of those seminal documents Cryptography was used by a virtual Who's Who of the American Founding Fathers— not only Jefferson and Madison but Benjamin Franklin, Alexander Hamilton, John and Abigail, Adams, Aaron Burr, and many others.[346]

The government argued the courts lacked authority to intervene in this matter, and the "speech" in question was functional rather than expressive, meaning it did not attain First Amendment protection.[347] Cohn recalls:

> The key legal question raised by Appellants…is whether publication and communication of encryption source code in electronic form is sufficiently "expressive" to fall under the well-established prior restraint doctrine…
> More than 20 years ago, the Justice Department's Office of Legal Counsel found that the "requirement of a license as a prerequisite to 'exports' of cryptographic information clearly raises First Amendment questions of prior restraint."[348]

Cohn highlights, "the agencies have known for 20 years that this scheme is unconstitutional. Their own lawyers told them so."[349]

The case was assigned to Marilyn Hall Patel, a Federal Judge since 1980.[350] For several months throughout 1995 both parties submitted initial written arguments to Judge Patel, with the government again arguing the courts lacked jurisdiction over the case.[351] Then there was a sudden change in position from the State Department. On June 29, 1995, almost two years after telling Bernstein his Snuffle academic paper and other accompanying textual advice required a CJR, the State Department reversed their decision, though the license requirement on the code itself remained.[352]

---

[343] Cohn, 1998a.
[344] Ibid.
[345] Ibid.
[346] Ibid.
[347] Coppolino, 1995.
[348] Cohn, 1998a.
[349] Ibid.
[350] Federal Judicial Center, no date.
[351] Coppolino, 1995.
[352] United States District Court for the Northern District of California, 1996d.

Whilst it is unclear what catalyzed this position reversal, it is likely government law-yers reviewed the department's decision and became aware that attempting to restrict dissemination of an academic paper was potentially a violation of free speech under the First Amendment.

The first scheduled oral arguments were to be held in San Francisco on October 10, 1995, to determine if the case should progress to a full hearing.[353] By this point, Bernstein had completed his PhD which likely conveyed him more credibility as a scientist whose works were being restricted.[354] The press asked Gilmore whether the cypherpunks would hold a demonstration, to which he commented, "what we will demonstrate is how the legal system can turn against the bureaucrats and authoritar-ians who currently hold crypto hostage."[355] The EFF wanted to fill the courtroom with as many supporters as possible.[356] Gilmore told the cypherpunks that, like the ongoing Phil Karn case,[357] "this lawsuit really has the potential to outlaw the whole NSA crypto export scam," he proclaimed a "Cypherpunks' dress-up day" to sup-port Bernstein, joking, "Hey, I've seen Tim May in a suit once, why not again?"[358] Gilmore told the cypherpunks to make a positive impression on the judge, advising them, "Banners and inflammatory t-shirts are probably not a good idea...we'll have to be quiet and orderly while we're in the courthouse."[359] For a collective including anarchists who wished to see the government abolished, it was a serious challenge for Gilmore to prevent any of their actions disadvantaging the case. Cypherpunk Attila (alias) agreed they should not intimate the judge "with a crowd of anti-social rowdies," he urged the cypherpunks to "show respect for the judge [as] the demeanor of both the protagonists and the 'court' influences the judge."[360] Gilmore told the cypherpunks the proceedings would "teach most observers something about how the courts work, and how the NSA and State Dept. use bureaucratic tricks to avoid facing the real issues."[361] Gilmore jokingly told the cypherpunks they would have the opportunity to "shake hands with an NSA lawyer flown in for the occasion"—the lawyer in question was Susan Arnold, accompanied by Anthony J. Coppolino of the Justice Department.[362]

The debate in the courtroom was energetic. Judge Patel asked insightful ques-tions in her attempt to understand whether First Amendment rights were being cur-tailed.[363] Patel did not adhere to the narrowest interpretation of the case before her, that of whether Snuffle should be on the ITAR munition's list. Instead, Patel sought to understand the broader issue of software as speech, to which Coppolino replied, "that's not the case before you."[364] The government did not want to engage in the wider issue of whether as a general rule source code was classified as speech, which would trigger much stronger Constitutional protections and set a higher threshold

---

[353] Gilmore, 1995a.
[354] Bernstein, 2008.
[355] Gilmore, 1995b.
[356] Gilmore, 1995a.
[357] See Section 7.10.
[358] Gilmore, 1995a.
[359] Ibid.

[360] Attila, 1995.
[361] Gilmore, 1995a.
[362] Ibid; United States District Court for the Northern District of California, 1995.
[363] Ibid.
[364] Ibid.

for overruling those protections in the name of national security.[365] Patel wanted to know how source code in some contexts could be considered speech, such as when it was used to drive word processor technologies, but in other cases it would not be; "if it's speech in one context, why isn't it speech in this context?" she asked Coppolino.[366] Coppolino explained that ultimately the issue was a technical evaluation of whether Snuffle was an encryption technology, and that it was at the government's discretion to make that decision, to which Patel replied, "it's not up to the government to determine what is speech."[367]

It was six months before Judge Patel gave her initial opinion in April 1996, but for the cypherpunks the wait was worthwhile. Patel attacked the government's arguments, and affirmed source code as free speech:

> This court can find no meaningful difference between computer language, particularly high-level languages as defined above, and German or French…like music and mathematical equations, computer language is just that, language, and it communicates information either to a computer or to those who can read it…thus, even if Snuffle source code…is essentially functional, that does not remove it from the realm of speech…for the purposes of First Amendment analysis, this court finds that source code is speech.[368]

Patel addressed the government's argument that Snuffle was functional rather than expressive,

> Defendants argue in their reply that a description of software in English informs the intellect but source code actually allows someone to encrypt data. Defendants appear to insist that the higher the utility value of speech the less like speech it is. An extension of that argument assumes that once language allows one to actually do something, like play music or make lasagne, the language is no longer speech. The logic of this proposition is dubious at best. Its support in First Amendment law is nonexistent.[369]

Responding to the government's argument that the court lacked jurisdiction in this case, Patel stated, "with respect to constitutional questions, the judicial branch not only possesses the requisite expertise to adjudicate these issues, it is also the best and final interpreter of them"; she added, "federal courts have consistently addressed constitutional issues in the context of national security concerns." Commenting on the government's position reversal on the Snuffle academic paper, Patel wrote, "It is disquieting than an item defendants now contend could not be subject to regulation was apparently categorized as a defense article and subject to licensing for nearly two years, and was only reclassified after plaintiff initiated this action." Patel added the academic paper on the scientific underpinnings of Snuffle was "speech of the

---

[365] Ibid.
[366] Ibid.
[367] Ibid.

[368] United States District Court for the Northern District of California, 1996a.
[369] Ibid.

most protected kind." Patel denied the government's request to dismiss the case and ordered progression to a full hearing.[370]

The EFF wrote, "The decision holds importance to the future of secure electronic commerce and lays the groundwork needed to expand First Amendment protection to electronic communication."[371] John Young joked to the cypherpunks that the result, "Shows what a scary cpunk-packed courtroom can do to tip the scales of blind justice."[372] To celebrate Cohn organized a volleyball victory party at the Grey Whale Cove beach, which she playfully described as a "clothing-optional beach," Gilmore forwarded the invite to the cypherpunks, adding, "remember how much fun it was to get all dressed up in banker's clothes to go to the Bernstein court hearing and show the judge that we cared? Well, now it's time to get UNdressed and come to the beach to celebrate the results!" Cohn joked, "the first person to spot a naked NSA guy wins a prize!"[373]

Cohn asked for the courts to either find in Bernstein's favor or allow the case to trial, arguing, "the undisputed facts demonstrate that the ITAR Scheme is a Kafkaesque procedural labyrinth pervaded by unfettered discretion and delay."[374]

By September 1996, the government again asked for the case against them to be dismissed, contesting ITAR did not constitute prior restraint on scientific publication.[375] Cohn argued in seeking to dismiss the case, "Defendants again unabashedly seek to rewrite history, ignore facts, and unilaterally eliminate issues in this case," Cohn concluded her letter to the Judge by boldly asking she invalidate the ITAR.[376] Judge Patel scheduled a hearing on September 20 to hear arguments.[377]

As the second court date approached, Gilmore declared another "Cypherpunks' dress-up day":

Watch the noose tighten around the scrawny neck of the vile crypto export controls! Be part of reclaiming your freedom to teach cryptography and to share your crypto expressions worldwide! Garb yourself in a ritual costume used by powerful and famous people![378]

At court, quite contrary to the stereotype, the singular government lawyer Anthony Coppolino faced four lawyers representing Bernstein.[379] Judge Patel asked Coppolino, "Are you all by yourself?...I thought the government had batteries of lawyers," to which he replied, "No, we staff leanly."[380] One of the key contention points was whether the government censored Bernstein's academic Snuffle paper. The government explained the academic paper was "comingled" with the Bernstein software during the first CJR, and whilst a separate CJR had later been applied for it was equally treated as a bundle along with the Snuffle code; Coppolino stated, "we did

370 Ibid.
371 Electronic Frontier Foundation, 1996a.
372 Young, 1996.
373 Gilmore, 1996b.
374 Cohn, 1996a.
375 United States Department of Justice, 1996.
376 Cohn, 1996b.

377 United States District Court for the Northern District of California, 1996b.
378 Gilmore, 1996c.
379 United States District Court for the Northern District of California, 1996b.
380 Ibid.

not intend to regulate his ideas or his paper."[381] The regulation of academic/scientific ideas, or ideas in general, was clearly in the realms of protected First Amendment rights, and the Judge spent a lot of time exploring this area. Coppolino defended the government's position in clipped speech:

> Don't care about the idea. The ideas are freely published. The algorithms are frequently published for peer review…Algorithms are published. Theories are published. Conferences occur on how these things work. Don't care about that. Care about the actual implementation of the idea on a computer to create a function.[382]

Cohn argued the government was asking the judge to:

> create a new lesser protected category for speech, based upon what they've called functionality. A term that they haven't really defined very well…that that's very dangerous. There's absolutely no support in the case law anywhere for a lesser protected category of speech, based upon functionality. And they've cited none.[383]

After a lengthy exploration of the topic, the debate returned to whether source code was considered speech. Patel likely knew the case was destined for a higher court, stating that more judges with "perhaps even more wisdom" would likely allow the government to protest her previous opinion that code was constitutionally protected speech.[384]

A month later Judge Patel issued her opinion. Patel reiterated source code was speech deserving of First Amendment protection, only to be overridden in times of war in order to prevent "direct, immediate and irreparable damage to our nation," the government's justification for preventing cryptography "speech" did not meet these criteria.[385] Patel ruled the ITAR did not place "even minimal limits on the discretion of the licensor and hence nothing to alleviate the danger of arbitrary or discriminatory licensing decisions."[386] Judge Patel's condemnation was focused on the ITAR Munitions list, which she stated, "is directed very specifically at applied scientific research and speech on the topic of encryption. That it regulates encryption in the interest of national security does not alone justify a prior restraint."[387] Patel also reiterated criticism for the absence of a time limit on ITAR decisions, the lack of a judicial review provision, meaning, "there is no burden on the ODTC to go to court to justify the denial."[388] As a result of these shortcomings, Judge Patel opined the munitions list "acts as an unconstitutional prior restraint in violation of the First Amendment," therefore the munitions list was "unenforceable," and Bernstein was safe from prosecution.[389] The digital privacy community were elated at the ruling. Gilmore commented:

---

[381] Ibid.
[382] Ibid.
[383] Ibid.
[384] Ibid.
[385] United States District Court for the Northern District of California, 1996c.

[386] Ibid.
[387] Ibid.
[388] Ibid.
[389] Ibid.

We're pleased that Judge Patel understands that our national security requires protecting our basic rights of free speech and privacy. There's no sense in "burning the Constitution in order to save it." The secretive bureaucrats who have restricted these rights for decades in the name of national security must come to a larger understanding of how to support and preserve our democracy.[390]

Jim Bidzos said, "This is a positive sign in the crypto wars—the first rational statement concerning crypto policy to come out of any part of the government."[391] Greg Broiles warned the cypherpunks, "while the ruling has considerable historical, cultural, and symbolic significance, it's dangerous to assume that it means that export restrictions on crypto are dead."[392] "The Deviant" (alias) disagreed, seeing the outcome as universally positive, "The fact that one judge says his [her] ruling only applies to one person is irrelevant; his [her] decision can, and probably will, be used as precedent in other cases, which is the good that it really serves in the first place."[393]

A few months after Judge Patel's ruling, President Clinton issued executive order 13026 of November 15, 1996, transferring regulation of non-military encryption to the Commerce Control List, overseen by the Department of Commerce.[394] The Commerce Control List was a tool of the Export Administration Regulations (EAR).[395] Violation of the EAR could result in penalties of up to $250,000 and ten years imprisonment.[396] In a likely response to the Bernstein case, the executive order included the following language:

the export of encryption software, like the export of other encryption products described in this section, must be controlled because of the software's functional capacity, rather than because of any informational value of such software.[397]

President Clinton also instructed should the new provisions prove inadequate, cryptography would again be controlled under ITAR.[398] The new regulations were released on December 30, and were strikingly similar to the provisions Bernstein and others had fought for the past four years.[399] John Gilmore labeled the transference of powers a "pointless shell game...it's his political decision whether to ignore and anger industry leaders, but he can't ignore a federal district court judge."[400] Cohn commented, "The government apparently decided to ignore Judge Patel's findings... instead of...attempting to fix the regulations, they simply issued new ones with the same problems."[401] Cohn commented they would return to Judge Patel "to have the new regulations declared facially unconstitutional...this time we believe that a nationwide injunction against their enforcement is merited."[402]

---

[390] Electronic Frontier Foundation, 1996b.
[391] Ibid.
[392] Broiles, 1996.
[393] The Deviant [alias], 1996.
[394] The White House, 1996a.
[395] Ibid.
[396] United States Department of Commerce, 2001.

[397] The White House, 1996b.
[398] Ibid.
[399] United States Department of Commerce, 1996.
[400] Electronic Frontier Foundation. 1996c.
[401] Ibid.
[402] Ibid.

In her August 1997 opinion following renewed arguments from both parties, Judge Patel stated she did not believe the government's intent was to "avoid the constitutional deficiencies of its regulations by rotating oversight of them from department to department"; however, she was critical of the new regulations.[403] Judge Patel also expressed frustration at both parties:

> this court's rather narrow determination that source code is speech protected by the First Amendment does not serve to remove encryption technology from all government regulation. Both parties exaggerate the debate needlessly. Plaintiff does so by aggrandizing the First Amendment, by assuming that once one is dealing with speech that it is immaterial what the consequences of that speech may be. Defendants do so by minimizing speech, by constantly referring to "mere speech" or "mere ideas" in their briefs and assuming that the functionality of speech can somehow be divorced from the speech itself.[404]

Judge Patel stated the new regulations were "even less friendly to speech than the ITAR," and the, "exception for printed materials...is so irrational and administratively unreliable that it may well serve to only exacerbate the potential for self-censorship," she added the distinction, "makes little or no sense and is untenable." Judge Patel also decried the absence of standards for assessing applications, opining the regulations, "appears to impose no limits on agency discretion." Patel cited a recent Supreme Court case (Reno v. American Civil Liberties Union), in which the Court found speech on the Internet was entitled to First Amendment protection. Applied to encryption, this ruling reiterated the "dramatically different treatment of the same materials depending on the medium by which they are conveyed is not only irrational, it may be impermissible under traditional First Amendment analysis." Judge Patel declared the EAR unconstitutional on the grounds of prior restraint, and gave Bernstein immunity against its enforcement upon him. However, Patel felt whilst she could order a nationwide injunction against the EAR given its failure to adhere to the constitution, given the legal questions at issue are "novel, complex, and of public importance, the injunctive relief should be as narrow as possible pending appeal."[405]

Bernstein stated, "This is wonderful news, I hope I can get some of my ideas published before they change the law again."[406] EFF's Executive Director Lori Fena stated:

> Once again, it took a federal court to sort out technology and the Constitution [...] let this decision signal the other two branches of government that when making laws pertaining to the Internet, they must honor their oaths to uphold the Constitution.[407]

John Gilmore wrote:

> Our right to create, use, and deploy encryption come from our basic civil rights of free speech, freedom of the press, freedom from arbitrary search, due process of law, and

---

[403] United States District Court for the Northern District of California, 1997.
[404] Ibid.
[405] Ibid.
[406] Electronic Frontier Foundation, 1997b.
[407] Ibid.

privacy. Judge Patel has affirmed those roots in the First Amendment. Our Founding Fathers used encryption—and even invented some—and did not intend any "crypto exceptions" to the Bill of Rights.[408]

On the cypherpunk mailing list, Vladimir Z. Nuri was elated at Patel's ruling against regulations, "erected by a government way out of control and subject to covert machinations by a massively funded/favored constituency known as the SPOOKS, under the patriotic guise of NATIONAL SECURITY," he added, "I sincerely hope that this is the first straw that breaks that fraudulent camel's back [...] let the whole corrupt structure fall like the rotten house of cards that it is."[409]

The Justice Department requested, and was granted, a stay of Bernstein's injunction citing his actions posed "immediate and irreparable harm on the government's interests."[410]

In the summer of 1999, a ninth-circuit three-judge panel comprising Judges Myron H. Bright, Betty B. Fletcher, and Thomas G. Nelson heard the case.[411] Fletcher and Bright agreed with Judge Patel's original opinion, whilst Nelson dissented—giving Bernstein a 2–1 victory.[412] The assenting opinion read:

> the EAR regulations (1) operate as a prepublication licensing scheme that burdens scientific expression, (2) vest boundless discretion in government officials, and (3) lack adequate procedural safeguards. Consequently, we hold that the challenged regulations constitute a prior restraint on speech that offends the First Amendment.[413]

Fletcher stated, "Bernstein's right to speak, not the rights of foreign listeners to hear," was the concern of the court.[414] Fletcher judged the broad definition of export, including the use of Internet fora and domestic communications with foreign nationals, meant, "we think it plain that the regulations potentially limit Bernstein's freedom of speech in a variety of both domestic and foreign contexts."[415] Fletcher reasserted the judgment that "source code is merely text, albeit text that conforms to stringent formatting and punctuation requirements."[416] Fletcher wrote:

> While the articulation of such a system in layman's English or in general mathematical terms may be useful, the devil is, at least for cryptographers, often in the algorithmic details. By utilizing source code, a cryptographer can express algorithmic ideas with precision and methodological rigor that is otherwise difficult to achieve.[417]

---

[408] Ibid.
[409] Nuri [alias], 1997.
[410] United States Department of Justice, 1997; United States Court of Appeals for the Ninth Circuit, 1997.
[411] United States Court of Appeals for the Ninth Circuit, 1999a.
[412] Ibid.
[413] Ibid.
[414] Ibid.
[415] Ibid.
[416] Ibid.
[417] Ibid.

Accordingly, Fletcher judged:

> encryption software, in its source code form and as employed by those in the field of
> cryptography, must be viewed as expressive for First Amendment purposes, and thus
> is entitled to the protections of the prior restraint doctrine.[418]

Fletcher attacked the government's argument, about which he wrote:

> distilled to its essence, suggests that even one drop of "direct functionality" over-
> whelms any constitutional protections that expression might otherwise enjoy [...] we
> reject the notion that the admixture of functionality necessarily puts expression beyond
> the protections of the Constitution.[419]

In her summary, Judge Fletcher took a more philosophical view:

> Whether we are surveilled by our government, by criminals, or by our neighbors, it is
> fair to say that never has our ability to shield our affairs from prying eyes been at such a
>   low ebb. The availability and use of secure encryption may offer an opportunity
> to reclaim some portion of the privacy we have lost. Government efforts to control
> encryption thus may well implicate not only the First Amendment rights of cryptog-
> raphers intent on pushing the boundaries of their science, but also the constitutional
> rights of each of us as potential recipients of encryption's bounty.
>   Viewed from this perspective, the government's efforts to retard progress in cryp-
> tography may implicate the Fourth Amendment.[420]

Judge Fletcher closed:

> Because the prepublication licensing regime challenged by Bernstein applies directly
> to scientific expression, vests boundless discretion in government officials, and lacks
> adequate procedural safeguards, we hold that it constitutes an impermissible prior
> restraint on speech.[421]

The dissent opinion of Judge Nelson argued the primary purpose of encryption
source code was to encrypt, and whilst it may "occasionally be used in an expressive
manner, it is inherently a functional device." Nelson also argued, "in the overwhelming majority of circumstances, encryption source code is exported to transfer functions, not to communicate ideas...only a few people can actually understand what a
line of source code would direct a computer to do."[422]

The government swiftly appealed, requesting the case be reheard *en banc*, in
front of an eleven judge panel given the cases' importance.[423] The government
argued previous hearings were erroneous, and the judicial majority's "extraordinary

---

[418] Ibid.
[419] Ibid.
[420] Ibid.

[421] Ibid.
[422] Ibid.
[423] United States Department of Justice, 1999.

conclusion" opened the "door to the unrestricted export of encryption products."[424] Cohn was unsurprised by the government appeal, commenting it was the "intention of the Government to delay justice for Professor Bernstein and the millions of others who are restricted by the encryption regulations for as long as possible."[425] The ninth circuit voted to rehear the case—the previous three-judge ruling was withdrawn.[426]

In October 1999, before the hearing could take place the White House announced a series of modifications to the export rules—the case was to be suspended until March 2000 to allow analysis of how the changes may impact the Bernstein case.[427] The export modifications were part of a wider "new approach" to governing cryptography catalyzed by the pressure in Congress bought about by several pro-cryptography bills. Deputy Assistant for National Security Affairs James Steinberg stated, "we are presenting today…a more balanced approach to the issue than the proposals that are now before Congress."[428] The new rules announced were that any commodity encryption (e.g., mass-produced) utilizing any key length, was exportable without a license (under a license "exception") to individuals, businesses, and non-government end-users in any country except the seven designated state supporters of terrorism (Cuba, Iran, Iraq, Libya, North Korea, Sudan, and Syria).[429] Retail encryption products with key lengths over 64 bits could be exported to all end users, including governments with the exception of the state supporters of terrorism.[430] Three principles underwrote the new export system. Firstly, there would be a one-time technical review of encryption products in advance of sales.[431] Secondly, a post-export reporting system for sales of encryption using keys over 64 bits would be implemented.[432] Thirdly, there would be a mechanism to allow the government to review sales of encryption to foreign governments, military organizations, and "nations of concern."[433] With regard to the technical review, Under-Secretary of State William Reinsch described the main focus as classifying a product as retail or custom.[434] One can hypothesize it was economically efficient for the government to set task forces to work on finding vulnerabilities they could exploit within a finite number of encryption algorithms used globally, but should a plethora of customized algorithms flood the market it would become less economically feasible. Therefore, the government would likely set additional checks before allowing encryption algorithms or highly customized implementations for a singular client or small group of clients, to gain market access. Secretary of Commerce William Daley stated, "These regulatory changes basically open the entire commercial sector as a market for strong U.S. encryption products."[435]

When asked at the White House Press Conference whether the government believed it could break encryption stronger than 64-bit Attorney General Janet Reno

[424] Ibid.
[425] Electronic Frontier Foundation, 1999.
[426] United States Court of Appeals for the Ninth Circuit, 1999b.
[427] Ibid; The White House, 1999.
[428] The White House, 1999b.
[429] The White House, 1999.
[430] Ibid.
[431] Ibid.
[432] The White House, 1999b.
[433] The White House, 1999.
[434] The White House, 1999b.
[435] Ibid.

replied, probably to the distress of the NSA, "we have looked carefully at this, and think that it is going to be possible."[436] Bruce Schneier commented the change in policy "represent[s] a reversal of their long-standing hostility towards strong encryption."[437] The government refuted this was a "relaxation" of the export rules, but rather, as Deputy Secretary of Defense John Hamre stated, "a very different approach with very, very simple rules that everyone can understand," as opposed to the complex array of guidelines previously surrounding export laws—but there could be no mistaking, this was a significant relaxation and reversal of position.[438]

The changes announced to the encryption regulations were published on January 14, 2000.[439] They included specific updates to address open source software:

> unrestricted encryption source code not subject to an express agreement for the payment of a licensing fee or royalty for commercial production or sale of any product developed using the source code can, without review, be...exported and reexported under License Exception.[440]

The exporter would be required to notify the Commerce Department via email when they exported, or posted online, content falling under this exception.[441] Uploading data to the Internet, even when it was known terrorist countries could download the content, or were active subscribers to a wider newsgroup like sci.crypt, would not be treated as "knowledge" as EAR termed it, or a prohibited export.[442] Providing "technical assistance" to foreigners working on such source code would also fall under the exception.[443] Sales of encryption to governments and Internet and telecommunications providers would continue to be strictly controlled.[444] Supplicants could export thirty days after making a classification request unless otherwise notified by the government, though if the "review is not proceeding in an appropriate fashion" the government could "suspend eligibility" for the license exemption.[445] Symmetric encryption of 64 bits was also to be treated as mass-market software/retail software, meaning it could be exported after a classification review.[446]

The ACLU, EFF, and EPIC released a joint statement in response to the new encryption export regulations on January 12, 2000.[447] The parties judged the regulations as progress, but believed, "fundamental constitutional defects [...] have not been remedied."[448] The flaws identified by the parties included the government still having to be notified of electronic "export" of publicly available source code, despite such code being freely exportable when on paper.[449] The parties argued the regulations

---

[436] Ibid.
[437] Schneier, 1999.
[438] The White House, 1999b.
[439] United States Department of Commerce, 2000.
[440] Ibid.
[441] Ibid.
[442] Ibid.
[443] Ibid.

[444] United States Department of Commerce, 1999
[445] United States Department of Commerce, 2000.
[446] Ibid.
[447] American Civil Liberties Union, Electronic Frontier Foundation, and Electronic Privacy Information Center, 2000.
[448] Ibid.
[449] Ibid.

remained a "completely discretionary licensing scheme," and the First Amendment was still violated by preventing transmission of source code not publicly available.[450] The regulations also retained prohibition of "technical assistance" to foreign nationals.[451] Whitfield Diffie and Susan Landau were more positive about the changes:

> The new rules…are a clever compromise between the needs of business and the needs of the intelligence community. Products employed by individual users, small groups or small companies are fairly freely exportable. Products intended for protecting large communications infrastructures—and it is national communication systems that are the primary target of American communications intelligence—are explicitly exempted from retail status.[452]

EFF attorney Shari Steele commented, "The government has made some concessions, but they are not enough to make the regulations constitutional."[453] Barry Steinhardt, Associated director of the ACLU conceded the new regulations were a "step forwards," but argued that as the administration had "tacitly admitted that it can't and shouldn't control the use of encryption, it should have announced a simple deregulation, rather than regulatory maze."[454] Dean Morehous, Chairman of technology and intellectual property at law firm Thelen Reid also acknowledged the improvement, but nonetheless was critical of the new regulations:

> Still, the new rules evince a continuing "encryption non-proliferation" attitude by the Government, even when dealing with technology that is already widely available both domestically or abroad. The intimidating complexity of the new rules and the ever-present threat of significant sanctions serve this policy approach well.[455]

Two days after their release, Cohn wrote to James Lewis, Director of Strategic Trade and Foreign Policy Controls at Commerce on behalf of Bernstein seeking clarity on the new regulations, which she termed "complex and ambiguous."[456] Of particular contention to Cohn was the continuing difference of rules for printed and digital code, and whether machine/object code derived directly from source code that was publicly available (e.g., was sold rather than released) would fall under a different set of guidelines.[457] Cohn also highlighted licenses were still required for "protected speech" (source code) that was not publicly available, and there was a continued lack of judicial oversight of government restraints.[458]

Lewis promptly replied that Bernstein's "concerns are unfounded…the new regulations do not interfere with his [Bernstein's] planned activities as you have described them."[459] Lewis confirmed machine code was exportable under the new regulations.[460] This statement was viewed by Bernstein and his legal team as being

---

450 Ibid.
451 Ibid.
452 Diffie and Landau, 2005, 15–16.
453 American Civil Liberties Union, Electronic Frontier Foundation, and Electronic Privacy Information Center, 2000.
454 Ibid.
455 Morehous, 2008.
456 Cohn, 2000.
457 Ibid.
458 Ibid.
459 Lewis, 2000.
460 Ibid.

in contradiction to the regulations.[461] Lewis closed by writing, "Viewed in its full perspective, the new regulation simply requires that concurrent notice is provided to the government of an export of encryption source code in electronic form and that such software no knowingly and directly be exported to a proscribed destination."[462] Despite this statement, later in the year Commerce made several changes to the EAR to align it to the guidance returned to Bernstein.[463] Bernstein continued negotiating with the Commerce Department to gain further concessions to regulatory language he believed prevented him from conducting academic work, however, by September 2001, engagement with Commerce deteriorated and no further regulatory changes were made.[464]

Bernstein's case had been one of the most consequential in history—it had forced a judicial reckoning of the constitutionality of the export regulations which had resulted in the recognition of encryption as an expression of free speech and forced severe concessions in the regulations. But his case was only one of three making its way through the courts and delivering this overall effect, the second case was that of Bruce Schneier and Phil Karn.

7.10 CODE AS CONSTITUTIONALLY PROTECTED SPEECH III: APPLIED CRYPTOGRAPHY

Bruce Schneier's, *Applied Cryptography: Protocols, Algorithms, and Source Code in C* was published in November 1993.[465] Schneier informed readers, "There are two kinds of cryptography in this world: cryptography that will stop your kid sister from reading your files, and cryptography that will stop major governments from reading your files. This book is about the latter."[466] Costing $44.95, Schneier described the 600-page book as a "lively introduction to the field of cryptography and a comprehensive reference work."[467] Schneier offered readers the option of purchasing an accompanying disk for thirty dollars that contained "probably the largest collection of cryptographic source code outside a military institution."[468] Schneier initially convinced his publisher, John Wiley & Sons, to distribute the source code disk with the book, as was common practice with many software books, but after learning about the ITAR restrictions, the publishers decided against such an act.[469] Instead, Schneier would physically mail the disk to US and Canadian addresses when purchased separately.[470] Source code for the following algorithms were included within the book: Vigenere; Enigma; DES; Lucifer; Feal-8; NewDES; IDEA (Used in PGP); MD5; and the Secure Hash Algorithm.[471] Schneier asked Daniel Bernstein if he could include the source code for Snuffle 5.0, written to covert hash functions, something

[461] Cohn and Tien, 2002, 22.

[462] Lewis, 2000.

[463] Cohn and Tien, 2002, 23.

[464] Ibid, 24–25.

[465] Schneier, 1993.

[466] Ibid, XV.

[467] Ibid.

[468] Ibid.

[469] Schneier, 1996.

[470] Ibid.

[471] Schneier, 1993, X.

not covered by the ITAR, into cryptographic capabilities.[472] As Snuffle itself did not include any cryptographic code (the requisite code was contained in whichever hash function was used with Snuffle), it was theoretically exportable.[473] However, the State Department had informed Bernstein he would still need an export license, something Bernstein was in the process of contesting. Fearful of the legal implications of including Snuffle in Schneier's cryptographic compendium before that contestation was concluded, Bernstein turned down Schneier's offer.[474]

Schneier hoped *Applied Cryptography* would do "more to further the spread of cryptography around the globe than any single (encryption) product could."[475]

Schneier wrote his book was being published at a "tumultuous time" given government efforts to control cryptology, observing, "Some dangerously Orwellian assumptions are at work here: that the government has right to listen to private communications, and that there is something wrong with a private citizen trying to keep a secret from the government."[476] Referencing the Clipper Chip, Schneier wrote that whilst governments had always been able to conduct surveillance, this was the first time in history people were "forced to take active measures to make themselves available for surveillance."[477] Schneier continued, "These initiatives are not simply government proposals in some obscure area; they are preemptive and unilateral attempts to usurp powers that previously belonged to the people."[478] Schneier retained a distrust of governments common to cryptographers:

> the same law enforcement authorities who illegally tapped Martin Luther King Jr.'s phones can easily tap a phone protected with Clipper. In the recent past, local police authorities have either been charged criminally or sued civilly in numerous jurisdictions—Maryland, Connecticut, Vermont, Georgia, Missouri, and Nevada—for conducting illegal wiretaps. It's a poor idea to deploy a technology that could some day facilitate a police state.[479]

Schneier advised:

> The lesson here is that it is insufficient to protect ourselves with laws; we need to protect ourselves with mathematics. Encryption is too important to be left solely to governments. This book gives you the tools you need to protect your own privacy; cryptography products may be declared illegal, but the information will never be.[480]

Schneier thanked an array of cryptographers who contributed to his book including Whitfield Diffie, Eli Biham, Matt Blaze, and Phil Zimmermann: it was truly a community effort. The second edition was published in 1995, a major update at twice the length of the original, it included a specific note of thanks to the cypherpunks for their inputs.[481]

---

[472] Bernstein, 1996a.
[473] Ibid.
[474] Ibid.
[475] Steinert-Threlkeld, 1994.
[476] Schneier, 1993, XVI.

[477] Ibid.
[478] Ibid.
[479] Ibid.
[480] Ibid.
[481] Schneier, 1995.

Al Stevens wrote in his review for the popular *Dr Dobb's Journal* that *Applied Cryptography* was "the definitive work on cryptography for computer program- mers."[482] Stevens described the text as containing a "monumental body of knowl- edge," he continued to write, "I do not know of another work that encapsulates as much information about cryptography and then supplies the computer code to imple- ment the algorithms that it describes."[483] Within six months, fifteen-thousand copies were sold, with between fifteen-hundred and two-thousand of those selling over- seas.[484] Christian D. Odhner reflected to the cypherpunks, "Applied Cryptography could easily be renamed 'The Cypherpunk's Bible.'"[485] Years later, in a rare moment of levity between a cypherpunk and the government, Schneier would give a copy of Applied Cryptography to CIA director John Deutch, who in return presented Schneier a CIA medallion, known as a challenge coin, Schneier comments:

> I looked at it, held it up in front of me, and asked: "Will this help me if I'm ever stuck in a foreign country and need to get out?" Without missing a beat, he [Deutch] replied: "Just speak into it."[486]

It was cypherpunk Phil Karn, acting independently of Schneier, who wrote to the State Department's ODTC and the NSA to request a 14-day expedited CJR for *Applied Cryptography* in February 1994.[487] Karn argued as the book was read- ily available, it qualified as "mass market software."[488] William Robinson of the ODTC wrote back informing Karn *Applied Cryptography* was not subject to the State Department's licensing jurisdiction as it was already in the public domain; the source code disks, however, were not covered by this ruling.[489]

Karn's next step was to see if the same code included in the *Applied Cryptography* book which the State Department confirmed was not subject to export controls would be approved for a CJR in digital form, as a disk. Karn wrote the State Department to request another 14-day expedited CJR explaining, "Character by character, the information is exactly the same. The only difference is the medium: magnetic impulses on mylar rather than inked characters on paper," in March 1994.[490] Five weeks later, Karn was still awaiting a reply; "They either ignore my calls or put me off with 'it's coming soon,'" he commented.[491] Karn wrote to the State Department asking why he had not received a ruling, given the difference between the previous CJR and this was only the media upon which the data was presented; Karn argued a second CJR should not be required, "after all, typing skills are hardly unique to Americans."[492] Three weeks later, State informed Karn that after consultation with the NSA, the *Applied Cryptography* diskette had been designated a defense article as per the ITAR munitions list.[493] State argued the diskette was not an exact copy of the contents found in the book as "Each source code listing has been partitioned

482 Stevens, 1994.
483 Ibid.
484 Steinert-Threlkeld, 1994.
485 Snyder, 1994.
486 Schneier, 2020.
487 Schneier, 2020; Karn, 1994a.

488 Karn, 1994a.
489 United States Department of State, 1994a.
490 Karn, 1994b.
491 Karn, 1994f.
492 Karn, 1994c.
493 United States Department of State, 1994c.

into its own file and has the capability of being easily compiled into an executable subroutine...this is certainly an added value to any end-user that wishes to incorporate encryption into a product.'[494] The State Department commented several of the algorithms would not be exportable if they were incorporated into products, and therefore were not exportable on disk.[495] Karn wrote William Bulkeley at the Wall Street Journal stating he believed "not even the government" was so "stupid" as to believe refusing the disk export permission would slow cryptography's spread, rather he assessed they were "using fear and intimidation in a desperate attempt to delay the inevitable, no matter what the consequences."[496]

Karn appealed, declaring State's judgment "arbitrary, capricious and wholly indefensible."[497] Karn countered State's "added value" position by arguing it was trivial to translate the *Applied Cryptography* text to code using optical character recognition.[498] Karn also argued the judgment violated the constitutionally protected rights of freedom of speech and freedom of the press. Karn cited cases supporting his claims constitutional rights were not lessened when directed abroad (Bullfrog Films, Inc v. Wick [1988]) and referenced any system of prior restraint would face courts with a "heavy presumption" against its constitutional validity and demanding a "heavy burden of showing justification for the imposition" (New York Times Co v. US [1970]).[499] Karn stated he was prepared to "seek judicial relief," should the appeal not be successful.[500] The appeal took four months before Dr. Martha C. Harris, State's Deputy Assistant Secretary reaffirmed the view that the *Applied Cryptography* diskette would need an export license.[501] Harris argued the diskette's cryptographic content was at such a "strategic level as to warrant continued State Department licensing."[502] Harris also stated their ruling was consistent with First Amendment protections.[503]

Karn enlisted the services of lawyers Kenneth C. Bass and Thomas J. Cooper to further appeal his case via the judicial system. Both Bass and Cooper had worked as executive branch attorneys, such knowledge positioned them well to challenge the system.[504] Before Bass and Cooper could progress to the judicial case they needed to make one final appeal to Harris' boss, Assistant Secretary of State Thomas McNamara, to evidence exhaustion of all options of redress via the State Department—Bass and Cooper were pessimistic about their chances of success.[505] Bass and Cooper reiterated Karn's arguments, adding further legal precedents, and wrote:

> this case illustrates a fundamental inability of our government to deal with computerized information in a rational manner...it is particularly ironic that representatives of

[494] Ibid.
[495] Ibid.
[496] Karn, 1994e.
[497] Karn, 1994d.
[498] Ibid.
[499] Ibid.

[500] Ibid.
[501] United States Department of State, 1994d.
[502] Ibid.
[503] Ibid.
[504] Bass and Cooper, 1994.
[505] Ibid.

an Administration, which is publicly so supportive of the coming Information Super Highway, could take a policy position that is so at odds with its implementation and reality.[506]

Bass and Cooper argued the decision was "based on an irrational distinction [between print and digital], constitutionally flawed interpretations of the law, and an erroneous view of the facts."[507] The lawyers highlighted the ITAR's public domain exemption did not discriminate by the dissemination form, supporting their claim the distinction between book and diskette was unjustified.[508] Bass and Cooper argued State's dismissal of their First Amendment claims was "untenable," writing, "To brush this issue aside with a conclusory statement totally lacking in legal analysis reflects a surprising insensitivity to the importance of the Constitutional rights that are involved in this case."[509] Bass and Cooper also referred to the 1978 memo written by the Justice Department Office of Legal Counsel's (OLC) Assistant Attorney General John Harmon to Dr. Frank Press, science advisor to the President, in which Harmon indicated, "existing provisions of the ITAR are unconstitutional insofar as they establish a prior restraint on disclosure of cryptographic ideas and information developed by scientists and mathematicians."[510] Bass and Cooper stated the OLC view was reaffirmed in 1981 and 1984, and, "To the best of our knowledge, those OLC opinions remain the latest and most authoritative legal opinions within the Executive Branch on the applicability of the First Amendment to the dissemination of cryptologic information."[511] In February 1995, Bass and Cooper met with the Justice Department and the NSA to further explain their arguments, yet by May no progress had been made.[512] The lawyers wrote to McNamara stating, "the licensing delays...fit a pattern of procrastination by federal agencies which appears to be based on the publicly stated policy of the National Security Agency to attempt to deter the further spread of strong cryptography as much as they can."[513] Bass and Cooper concluded, "The continued delay in rendering a decision in this matter is inexplicable except on the assumption that the Executive Branch intends, by its inaction, to chill the activities of Mr. Karn and others."[514] Bass and Cooper informed McNamara that Karn had instructed them to initiate a judicial review by June 15, regardless of whether State responded.[515] McNamara shortly after reaffirmed State's ruling.[516] McNamara highlighted the ITAR procedure may be used when there is doubt if an article is covered by the US Munitions List.[517] McNamara argued the technical exemption within ITAR was referring to "know-how" information, rather than "functional" information, "Rather than merely containing information that, for example, explains the theory of how cryptographic software works, the disk contains actual cryptographic software that may be utilized to encrypt information."[518]

---

[506] Ibid.
[507] Ibid.
[508] Ibid.
[509] Ibid.
[510] Ibid.; Harmon, 1978.
[511] Bass and Cooper, 1994.
[512] Bass and Cooper, 1995a.

[513] Ibid.
[514] Ibid.
[515] Ibid.
[516] United States Department of State, 1995.
[517] Ibid.
[518] Ibid.

McNamara assessed their ruling "does not implicate the First Amendment since such software is subject to licensing not because it might contain 'information,' but because it can function to encrypt communications."[519] McNamara also told Karn's legal team the ruling was not subject to judicial review.[520] Bass and Cooper replied, arguing McNamara had not addressed the "fundamental inconsistency" between the State's ruling on the book regarding the diskette.[521] Bass and Cooper assessed further engagement "futile," and believed they had demonstrated exhaustion of administrative redress.[522] The lawyers initiated judicial proceedings, requesting State's ruling be overturned as it violated Karn's First Amendment right to free speech.[523] A number of testimonies were provided by the defense, including from Deputy Director of the NSA, William P. Cromwell.[524] Cromwell's argument expanded upon previous arguments about the difference between the book, which provided "know-how," and the diskette which acted as an "engine" for a cryptographic device.[525] Cromwell argued Optical Character Recognition technology converting text into code, "may not produce error-free reproductions of the scanned material," and turning the text into executable code requires someone with knowledge of the source code language and cryptography fundamentals.[526] In contrast, Cromwell argued, the diskette's code was error-free. Cromwell evidenced this by referencing an error in the book within the FEAL-8 source code that was corrected on the diskette.[527] The government re-stated this case was not within the judicial system's remit, that designation of defense articles subject to export licenses was an executive branch discretion.[528] The government argued this was a national security, rather than a constitutional, issue.[529] Turning to the issue of free speech, the government cited a number of judicial precedents to challenge the extent of what can be labeled as "speech."[530] The government argued the restriction was not upon the discussion of scientific ideas, but materials enabling their implementation—Americans were still free to discuss and publish articles on cryptology.[531] With regard to the public availability exemption, the government argued, "the public availability of a functioning defense article does not alter the fact that wider, uncontrolled, dissemination of a greater number of those articles in foreign lands may increase the harm to the government's interests."[532] In a retort to Karn's accusation, the government was acting in an "irrational" manner; the government testified, "In the face of the important governmental interests at stake, the idea that government cannot have any say in where, to whom, and for what purpose, powerful encryption technology is being exported is the 'irrational' position."[533] The government asked the case be dismissed.[534] Karn later testified to

---

[519] Ibid.
[520] Ibid.
[521] Bass and Cooper, 1995b.
[522] Ibid.
[523] Bass and Cooper, 1995c.
[524] Cromwell, 1995.
[525] Ibid.
[526] Ibid.
[527] Ibid.

[528] United States Department of Justice, 1995.
[529] Ibid.
[530] Ibid.
[531] Ibid.
[532] Ibid.
[533] Ibid.
[534] Ibid.

Congress that the government believes, "no-one—not the Courts, not Congress, and least of all a private citizen like myself—has the wisdom to question their policies."[535]

Karn's lawyers argued the diskettes' only function was source code storage, in the same way as the book stored text—to turn it into workable code required more than an hour's work by a skilled programmer, therefore it could not be considered functional encryption code.[536] Bass and Cooper requested a trial to explore the contested facts.[537] Phil Zimmermann also testified in Karn's support. Zimmermann stated he was "informally advised" by undisclosed sources the CJR request for his PGP book, which resulted in the NSA recommending it be export-controlled under ITAR, whilst Commerce disagreed.[538] For Commerce to oppose the powerful NSA on this issue demonstrated the value cryptographic exports represented to the US economy. The government again asked the judge to dismiss the case in December.[539]

District Judge Charles Richey dismissed the case in March 1996.[540] Richey was no stranger to surveillance cases. Two years earlier Richey judged in favor of the Electronic Privacy Information Center (EPIC), ordering the FBI to release information pertinent to their alleged inability to conduct intercepts due to modern technology.[541] Karn was not so fortunate. Richey found in the defendant's favor on all points, and painted a dim picture of Karn:

> The plaintiff, in an effort to export a computer diskette for profit, raises administrative law and meritless constitutional claims because he and others have not been able to persuade the Congress and the Executive Branch that the technology at issue does not endanger the national security.[542]

Richey judged the diskette's export a "political question."[543] The judge erroneously stated Karn was seeking profit, though this was not the case as the diskette belonged to Schneier.[544] Karn advanced to the Court of Appeals.[545] Bass and Cooper continued their established position arguing the different treatment of book and diskette was "equivalent to an assertion that it was permissible for The Washington Post to publish the Pentagon Papers as a series of newspaper installments, but impermissible to disseminate the identical information by putting it on the Post's Internet website"; they argued, "had such a ludicrous assertion been advanced, we are confident that it would have been seen for what it was and soundly rejected."[546] Bass and Cooper highlighted a recent separate case, Bernstein v. Department of State, where Judge Patel ruled source code constituted speech, which was indirectly in opposition to the arguments made by the government and accepted by Judge Richey in Karn's case.[547] This was important, as in Karn's case the defense team used the O'Brien

---

[535] Karn, 1997.
[536] Bass and Cooper, 1995d.
[537] Ibid.
[538] Zimmermann, 1995b.
[539] United States Department of Justice, 1995b, and Bass and Cooper, 1995e.
[540] Richey, 1996.
[541] United States District Court for the District of Columbia, 1994b.
[542] Richey, 1996.
[543] Ibid.
[544] Ibid.
[545] Bass and Cooper, 1996a.
[546] Bass and Cooper, 1996b.

test to assess whether the diskette's restriction would violate constitutional rights. However, the O'Brien test was designed for cases where conduct and speech take place together (for instance the burning of a flag whilst delivering hate speech). If Judge Patel's ruling that source code is "pure speech" was held as precedent, the O'Brien test was not the correct instrument with which to assess whether export of the diskette could be restricted.[548] Instead the government would need to satisfy the "clear and present danger" standard consistently applied to prior restraints on speech.[549] Bass and Cooper argued for a trial to establish whether the government's position met the "clear and present danger" threshold.[550]

The difference of judgments in disparate parts of the country highlighted the growing divisions in cryptography policy. Phil Karn's case was thrown out of court in Washington in the most unequivocal manner, whilst the government received a similar treatment in California. Perhaps the disjoint was influenced by the geographies; Californian Judge Patel sat at the heart of the technology industry, whilst Judge Richey presided over a court in Washington D.C., the hub of the federal security and intelligence apparatus. Karn's lawyer Ken Bass commented, "The two opinions reflect two totally different philosophies on how the First Amendment applies to cryptography."[551] Lee Tien, a lawyer supporting Cindy Cohn commented of Karn's case, "They had a very compelling piece of Alice and Wonderland stupidity that had its advantages. It is simple, concrete, and there is doctrine that applies," Bernstein approached the court differently, saying, "our complaint was like a kitchen sink. We laid out every conceivable constitutional infirmity."[552] Such contrasts in judicial findings added to the likelihood a ruling by the Supreme Court would be required to resolve the constitutional questions.

Just before the first court of appeals session was to take place, the President transferred export controls for civilian encryption from the ITAR, administered by the State Department, to the Export Administration Regulations (EAR), administered by the Bureau of Export Administration at the Department of Commerce.[553]

The court session went ahead. Gilmore urged the cypherpunks to attend as it was the "first time [a] crypto export case has hit a Court of Appeals, and your rights are very much at stake here."[554] Gilmore wrote in the Electronic Frontier Foundation's online newsletter, the *EFFector*:

> Phil Karn's case illustrates both the irrationality of the encryption rules and the depths of the bureaucratic mazes which protect them. The idea that the First Amendment protects the author of a book, but not the author of an identical floppy disk, is ridiculous.
>
> All books, magazines, and newspapers are written on computers today before print publication, and many are also published online. Yet here we have Government lawyers not only defending their right to regulate machine-readable publication, but also arguing that the courts are not permitted to re-examine the issue.

---

[547] Ibid.
[548] Ibid.
[549] Ibid.
[550] Ibid.

[551] Voorhees, 1996.
[552] Ibid.
[553] The White House, 1996a.
[554] Gilmore, 1997.

Their argument amounts to "Trust us with your fundamental liberties." Unfortunately, a decade of NSA actions have amply demonstrated that they are happy to sacrifice fundamental liberties when it gives them an edge in some classified spy program.

Unless there's a clear and present danger to our nation's physical security (which we have seen no evidence of), our citizens' right to speak and publish freely is much more important to American national security than any top-secret program.[555]

By mutual consent, the parties agreed in court that a new request would be made of the new executive department responsible for whether the diskette would require an export license.[556] A new export request for the diskette was made to the Commerce Department given the transfer of powers.[557] In November 1997 Commerce informed Karn the diskette would not be approved for export as it was "contrary to the national security interests of the United States."[558] Commerce offered to reconsider should Karn identify specific end-users and end-uses, but such a requirement was incompatible with Karn's free speech argument.[559] Karn's lawyers promptly took their complaint back to the judicial system, the government requested dismissal, but this time the Judge, in February 1999 granted an evidentiary hearing.[560] However, the case would never reach court.

In April 1997 the Commerce Department had announced the formation of the President's Export Council Subcommittee on Encryption (PECSENC).[561] PECSENC would comprise around twenty-five members who would "assure a balanced representation among the exporting community and those Government agencies with a mandate to implement policy regarding encryption."[562] PECSENC's 1998 report into the US export controls found commercial impact "palpable. For many software applications, business customers simply demand security and encryption; it is a checklist item, and its absence is a deal breaker."[563] The authors noted many US software companies were embarking upon "cooperative arrangements" with foreign encryption suppliers able to "provide complete security solutions by encouraging their foreign partners to marry foreign-made crypto with U.S. commercial applications."[564] The authors noted whilst this practice was not "unlawful *per se*," it was "highly risky under US law…given the stakes, many companies have been prepared to take risks…and it is expected that more will do the same."[565] The author's assessed US export policy had "fostered the development of cryptographic software and hardware skills outside the United States. German, Swiss, Canadian, Russian, and Israeli cryptography companies have all benefited from this unintended consequence of

[555] Electronic Frontier Foundation, 1997.
[556] Kenneth Bass, Frank W. Hunger, et al., 1997.
[557] Bass, Hunger, et al., 1997.
[558] United States Department of Commerce, 1997.
[559] Ibid.
[560] Bass and Cooper, 1998a and 1998b; United States Department of Justice, 1998; Oberdorfer, 1999.

[561] Department of Commerce, 1997b.
[562] Ibid.
[563] President's Export Council Subcommittee on Encryption, 1998, 122.
[564] Ibid.
[565] Ibid.

U.S. encryption policy."[566] On September 16, 1999, before the Karn case reached court, the government announced changes to the export regulations.[567]

The new encryption regulations became operational on January 14, 2000.[568] Significant changes liberalized controls even further than drafts suggested. In particular, provision was added for unrestricted export of open-source source code without any form of review from the government, although notification was still required.[569] The Applied Cryptography diskette was now exportable. Karn allowed his case to be dismissed as moot; he commented, "While this was admittedly not as satisfying as actually winning in court, for all practical purposes I got everything I wanted."[570] Karn reflected, "I think things are in much better shape than they were when I started my quest six and a half years ago."[571]

The third legal case challenging the cryptography regulations in the judicial system belonged to Professor Peter Junger.

7.11 CODE AS CONSTITUTIONALLY PROTECTED SPEECH III: PETER JUNGER

Peter Junger had been a Professor of law at Ohio's Case Western Reserve University since the early 1970s.[572] Born in 1933, Junger grew up in Wyoming, and graduated from Harvard Law School in 1958.[573] After graduation, Junger worked in real estate law in New York until 1970 before he started teaching.[574] Fellow law professor Wilbur Leatherberry comments Junger was "a voracious…and an eclectic reader," and he could "consume all of your time. Still, it was difficult to resist when he came into your office, because he always had something interesting to say."[575] His output includes writings on topics from human rights to Buddhism, and he would eventually become President of the Cleveland Buddhist Temples.[576]

Junger first taught a course entitled "Computers and the Law" in 1986. The syllabus covered software and algorithms, patents, copyright laws, and government cryptology regulations.[577] Junger's course did not just consider cryptography from a legal perspective, but as a tool for the use of his students, as Junger believed:

> lawyers have a legal and ethical duty to protect the confidences of their clients, I am convinced that lawyers who use electronic mail or other computer technologies to communicate with their clients, or to store information supplied by their clients, are in some circumstances ethically, and perhaps even legally, required to use cryptography to maintain the confidentiality of that information.[578]

---

[566] Ibid.
[567] See Section 7.9 for details of regulatory changes.
[568] United States Department of Commerce, 2000.
[569] Ibid.
[570] Karn, 2010.
[571] Ibid.
[572] Vasvari, Scarselli, and O'Neill, 1996b.
[573] Suchetka, 2006.
[574] Ibid.
[575] Ibid.
[576] Junger, 2002.
[577] Junger, 1996.
[578] Vasvari and Scarselli, 1996c.

In 1993, Junger even wrote his own "simple" encryption program in 8086 assembly language to demonstrate to his students how cryptography worked, and to demonstrate the "nature of an algorithm."[579] Junger realized teaching or publishing his encryption program may be subject to ITAR restrictions, as foreign students were often in his classes.

Junger contacted the Commerce Department's Bureau of Export Administration and spoke to Dale Jensen on May 7, 1993.[580] Jensen informed Junger he needed to apply to the State Department to determine whether Commerce or State had jurisdiction over the "exportability" of his algorithm, such a determination would likely take two months.[581] Regarding the eight-week decision period, Jensen informed Junger, "you are now in the world of bureaucracy, not of common sense."[582] Junger called the State Department's ODTC, reaching Major Gary Oncale.[583] Junger recalls Oncale, "could not—or would not," reveal the criteria used to determine jurisdiction for Junger's request.[584] Oncale told Junger there was "no established criteria for determining whether a license would be required, since each determination is made on a 'case by case' basis."[585] Oncale gave Junger an NSA phone number he could call to attempt to understand whether his program would need a license, but Oncale could not reveal the name of the person who would answer the phone.[586] The unidentified NSA woman told Junger she did not believe discussing the program in class would be an issue, but posting the program on the Internet was a "gray area" that could present problems.[587] Junger pressed the anonymous woman for more specific information, but told him, "she could not answer hypothetical questions," and gave Junger a general information telephone number he could call for further information.[588] In 1995, Junger again attempted to discover more information about the criteria used to determine whether his encryption program would be subject to export controls if he taught it in his August 1996 class. Previously Junger had been forced to exclude non-American/Canadian students from his lecture hall.[589] Junger also wanted to teach information about DES, Triple-DES, RSA, and PGP.[590] Junger reached Karen Hopkinson, an NSA employee seconded to the ODTC, but she would not provide further information on whether the program would be exempt from ITAR.[591] Shortly after, a federal budget crisis shut ODTC down.[592] Junger's course was starting imminently, and he wanted to issue a book that would accompany the course, publish relevant software online for his students, and of course teach the encryption content itself to domestic and foreign students.[593] It was time for another approach.

Junger hired three lawyers, Raymond Vasvari, Kevin Francis O'Neill, and Gino Scarselli in August 1996, and took his case to court, seeking an injunction against

---

[579] Junger, 1996.
[580] Junger, 1996.
[581] Ibid.
[582] Ibid.
[583] Ibid.
[584] Ibid.
[585] Ibid.
[586] Ibid.

[587] Ibid.
[588] Ibid.
[589] Ibid.; Vasvari, Scarselli, and O'Neill, 1996a.
[590] Vasvari, Scarselli, and O'Neill, 1996a.
[591] Junger, 1996.
[592] Ibid.
[593] Ibid.

the government allowing him to "teach, publish and otherwise disclose unclassified cryptographic information to foreign students and other foreign persons without first obtaining a license or approval from the government."[594] In their press release announcing the action, Scarselli argued that "The material at issue in this case can be found in any university library, but the regulations make no exceptions for even the most basic software," adding, "It's not as though we are talking about classified information."[595] Vasvari commented, "These regulations allow the government to dictate what a Professor may and may not teach, even though the material involved poses no threat to national security."[596] Junger's lawyers argued:

> The challenged regulations are unconstitutional because they constitute a blatant system of overbroad and vague prior restraints that violate rights of academic freedom, political speech and freedom of association. Moreover, there is no evidence whatsoever that Congress authorized a licensing scheme on the free, nonmilitary disclosure of unclassified technical and scientific information within the United States or on the internet.[597]

EFF's John Gilmore offered his assistance as a technical advisor to Junger's legal team.[598] An anonymous donation of $5000 helped to fund the case, to which Junger and other donors added, increasing the war chest to around $7000.[599] Junger's case was the third to launch against the export regulations, following Phil Karn and Daniel Bernstein's suits. Scarselli states the lawyers of Karn and Bernstein provided "a great deal of help and support."[600] A common feature of the Bernstein and Junger cases was the opposition provided by Tony Coppolino, who Scarselli describes as "one of the Justice Department's best trial attorneys."[601]

Junger's complaint argued no provisions for judicial review of ODTC decisions constituted a "prepublication registration and licensing scheme, and thus a prior restraint on free expression, in violation of the First Amendment."[602] Junger's lawyers argued:

> The First Amendment allows Prof. Junger to decide what he wants to teach, how it should be taught and to whom he can teach…The First Amendment also protects the rights of professors and students to receive and exchange information…Thus, the First Amendment protects Prof. Junger's rights to publish and exchange cryptographic information with foreign professors, researchers and students without having to obtain a license.[603]

Junger's lawyers argued the ITAR was overly broad and vague as it was "written and as interpreted by the defendants, have been drafted and applied in such a confusing

---

594 Vasvari, Scarselli, and O'Neill, 1996a; Vasvari and Scarselli, 1996c.
595 Vasvari and Scarselli, 1996.
596 Ibid.
597 Vasvari., Scarselli, and O'Neill, 1996b.
598 Vasvari and Scarselli, 1996a.
599 Vasvari and Scarselli, 1996c.
600 Scarselli, 2007, 328.
601 Ibid, 328.
602 Vasvari, Scarselli, and O'Neill, 1996a.
603 Ibid.

way that the plaintiff cannot be sure what cryptographic information is exempt," and there were:

> no published criteria or standards available to him or the public on which the defendants base their decisions to grant or deny licenses for the export of cryptographic information other than guidelines for the export of mass market encryption software.[604]

A third argument was the ITAR placed restrictions on Junger's academic freedom and political speech.[605] Junger's team asked the Judge to declare ITAR unconstitutional in violation of the First and Fifth Amendments (separation of powers), they also requested a preliminary and permanent injunction to prevent ITAR's enforcement against Junger.[606] Furthermore, Junger's lawyers raised the 1978 memo written by the OLC's John Harmon in which he stated, "further Congressional authorization would obviously be necessary in order to extend governmental controls to domestic as well as foreign disclosures of public cryptographic information."[607] Junger's lawyers also highlighted the advice issued by the OLC in 1981 and 1984, which concluded the ITAR could be unconstitutionally broad in some applications, such as when applied to lecturers discussing theoretical ideas with foreigners visiting the United States.[608]

Shortly after the complaint's submission, Junger's case was strengthened by California's Judge Patel who ruled in the Daniel Bernstein case that source code constituted speech protected by the First Amendment.[609] Junger's lawyers amended their complaint requesting a permanent injunction to remove the need for anyone to "obtain a license or approval from the government before disclosing to any other person or persons by speech, publication or any other means or by any medium, any unclassified information about cryptography."[610]

In the press release, Junger drew on another recent digital case to argue in favor of cryptography:

> Computer programs are written and published by human beings just as, for example, pornography is. The Supreme Court recently held in Reno v. ACLU that the full protection of the First Amendment extends to pornography in cyberspace. I find it hard to believe that programmers are not entitled to at least as much constitutional protection as pornographers.[611]

Shortly after, Junger stated:

> It is quite clear to me, that the…government are attempting to restrain the communication of information about cryptographic software not only abroad, but also within the

---

[604] Ibid.
[605] Ibid.
[606] Ibid.
[607] Vasvari, Scarselli, and O'Neill, 1996b; Harmon, 1978.
[608] Vasvari, Scarselli, and O'Neill, 1996b; Olson, 1981; Simms, 1984.

[609] United States District Court for the Northern District of California, 1996a.
[610] Vasvari, Scarselli, and O'Neill, 1996b.
[611] Vasvari and Scarselli, 1996b.

United States, because they do not want us actually to be able to use cryptography to preserve the privacy of our thoughts and our communications.

It is as if the government required one to get a license before explaining how to make or use an envelope, even though it did not forbid the use of envelopes themselves. After all, all that cryptographic software is, is a way of making electronic envelopes.[612]

Judge Donald Nugent issued a preliminary injunction on behalf of Junger and his students in late 1996, stating, "There is little, if any, likelihood that disclosures of cryptographic information by Prof. Junger or his students would compromise the national security of the United States."[613] Nugent ruled the ITAR cryptographic export regulations, "constitute a prepublication registration and licensing scheme that does not provide for judicial review and thus constitute an unconstitutional prior restraint in violation of the First Amendment."[614] Judge Nugent added the regulations were "overbroad and vague...and as applied to the plaintiff's conduct, in violation of the First and Fifth Amendments to the United States Constitution."[615] Nugent added the rights of foreign students and professors within the US were also having their First Amendment right to receive information breached.[616] Nugent concluded freedom of association under the First Amendment was also violated by ITAR.[617]

Judge Nugent added, "the government does not have a compelling interest to regulate all cryptographic information, including privately developed, unclassified information."[618] Nugent took aim directly at the AECA, stating that it:

does not authorize the registration or licensing of disclosures of unclassified cryptographic information within the United States, including disclosures of unclassified cryptographic information on the internet.[619]

Nugent added:

By requiring registration and a license prior to the disclosure of cryptographic software and/or cryptographic technical data within the United States, the defendants are engaged in controlling the exchange of cryptographic information between persons within the United States and restricting the dissemination of cryptographic information on the internet. The defendants have therefore adopted a *de facto* policy of restricting the domestic dissemination of unclassified cryptographic information without Congressional authorization in violation of the constitutional doctrine of separation of powers.[620]

---

[612] Vasvari and Scarselli, 1996c.
[613] United States District Court Northern District of Ohio Eastern Division, 1996.
[614] Ibid.
[615] Ibid.
[616] Ibid.
[617] Ibid.
[618] Ibid.
[619] Ibid.
[620] Ibid.

Judge Nugent also found:

> AECA unconstitutionally deprives the Judiciary of its responsibility to review poten-
> tial restrictions on information and expression in violation of the constitutional doc-
> trine of separation of powers.[621]

On November 15, 1996, Clinton issued executive order 13026 transferring the regulation of non-military encryption from ITAR to the Commerce Department's EAR.[622]

On June 12, 1997, Scarselli submitted three applications to the Commerce
Department requesting commodity classifications for a total of 13 cryptography programs and other items on behalf of Junger.[623]

In the first application Scarselli requested classifications for PGP, a Perl implementation of RSA, a C implementation of RC4, and two algorithms Junger had written: Fiddle in C, and Twiddle in 8086 Assembly.[624] The Commerce Department
determined all except Twiddle required export licenses.[625] In the second application, Scarselli requested classification of chapter one of Junger's *Computers and the
Law* book (in electronic form), including instructions for creating an executable version of Twiddle (Junger's OTP program) and Paul Leyland's encryption program in
ANSI C.[626] The Commerce Department responded the "non-software" elements of
the chapter were not EAR classified, Twiddle was also export permitted.[627] However,
the software components, such as the RSA Perl code, were export-controlled, so that
chapter segment could not be published.[628]

Scarselli also sought clarification as to whether posting links to encryption software overseas was considered an export, the Commerce Department confirmed such
an act would not violate the EAR.[629] In the third application, Scarselli submitted
three classification requests to the Department of Commerce to ascertain whether
five encryption programs (XOR [single byte key], XOR [one-time pad], ROT13,
RC2, and RC4) were exportable.[630] James Lewis, Director of the Office of Strategic
Trade and Foreign Policy Controls, replied on July 4, that the Commerce Department
was unable to classify algorithms, only specific software implementations.[631]

Junger and Scarselli issued a press release, in October 1997, in which Scarselli
wrote, "the fact that it is only [encryption software] publication on the Internet and
in other electronic form that is restricted does not help the government, because the
Supreme Court held this year that the Internet is entitled to the full protection of the
First Amendment."[632] Scarselli added:

> This is not a complicated case involving complex issues of computer science...Once
> you recognize that computer programs are written and published just like any other

---

[621] Ibid.
[622] The White House, 1996a.
[623] Scarselli, 1997.
[624] Lewis, 1997.
[625] Ibid.
[626] Ibid.

[627] Ibid.
[628] Scarselli, 1997.
[629] Lewis, 1997b.
[630] Scarselli, 1997b.
[631] Lewis, 1997.
[632] Junger and Scarselli, 1997.

text—like mathematical proofs and musical scores, for example—it becomes clear that the regulatory scheme, which requires a would-be publisher to apply for and obtain a license before he can publish, is a classic example of a prior restraint and it's unconstitutional.[633]

Junger drew attention to the wider implications of his suit:

> If the government's functionality argument were to be upheld, it would mean that the government could suppress the writing and publication of any software which might be used in ways the government does not like. And not just software. Any writing that delights or instructs or persuades has functionality. The government's functionality argument could justify requiring you to get a license before you publish a legal form book or a political pamphlet or a book of sermons. And it is exactly that type of censorship that led the adoption of the First Amendment.[634]

Junger's complaint requested the judiciary declare EAR unconstitutional, and issue a permanent injunction preventing government prosecutions of those exporting encryption.[635]

Hunger and Coppolino reflected on the scope creep of Junger's complaint.[636] Initially, Junger was just trying to teach his class, now he was mounting a full challenge against the export regulations by seeking to export additional algorithms.[637] The government argued the focus should be on Junger and his activities, rather than the EAR's constitutionality:

> In the final analysis, this is a simple case, greatly complicated by plaintiff's presentation of the facts and law.
>
> Courts have consistently deferred to the President's judgment as to which commodities should be controlled for export to protect the nation's national security and foreign policy interests. Though in the guise of a "free speech" claim, this case presents no different issue.
>
> Powerful encryption products, including software, can unquestionably harm the government's interests abroad, and efforts to limit this harm through export licensing requirements do not run afoul of the First Amendment.[638]

Hunger and Coppolino reiterated:

> The EAR is not a complete prohibition on the exportation of encryption products, including software, but, rather, establishes a licensing process so that the government can determine where the product is going, for what purpose, and whether the particular export poses a national security or foreign policy concern.[639]

---

[633] Ibid.
[634] Ibid.
[635] Scarselli, 1997.
[636] Hunger and Coppolino, 1997.
[637] Ibid.
[638] Junger and Scarselli, 1997.
[639] Ibid.

The government argued the regulations served a "permissible purpose to protect the government's interests abroad and do not otherwise impinge on the broad discourse that occurs daily in the field of cryptography."[640] The government maintained cryptography was more functional than expressive:

> Encryption source code is not merely technical information or "know-how" that "relates to" a technical function, or explains a cryptographic theory, or "describes" how the software functions. It is itself the item essential to encrypting data on a computer. Without the underlying source code software, a computer cannot encrypt...For encryption software, whatever informative value it has for some, it is not merely informative, but directly functional as well.[641]

Hunger and Coppolino argued against Junger's use of the term "publish":

> the notion that the Internet is merely a means of "publication" of ideas is quite misleading when it comes to posting a software program. Plaintiff consistently uses the term "publish" or "publication" when, in fact, an "export" is at issue.
> There is no restriction on plaintiff's right to "publish" software in the United States. Similarly, there is no restriction on his right to use the Internet to publish articles or course materials, or communicate with students or colleagues for academic reasons... Rather, the narrow issue here concerns the global dissemination of actual encryption software. Plaintiff must concede that the Internet is an international telecommunications medium, through which items posted are available all over the globe...The posting of software to the Internet does not merely allow it to be "read" by someone for informative reasons. Indeed, that is perhaps the least common reason software is posted online.[642]

With increasingly belligerent language, Scarselli wrote in Junger's response, "The defendants have it completely backwards. The enjoyment of First Amendment liberties is the right of Americans, not a benefit that the government bestows at its discretion."[643]

Judge James Gwin issued his opinion and dismissed the case on July 2, 1998. Gwin opined:

> The Court finds that the Export Regulations are constitutional because encryption source code is inherently functional, because the Export Regulations are not directed at source code's expressive elements, and because the Export Regulations do not reach academic discussions of software, or software in print form.[644]

The court accepted the government's argument it was seeking to restrict the distribution of encryption software, rather than ideas on encryption.[645] Gwin noted two

---

[640] Ibid.
[641] Ibid.
[642] Ibid.
[643] Scarselli and O'Neill, 1998.

[644] United States District Court Northern District of Ohio Eastern Division, 1998.
[645] Ibid.

other major encryption export cases (Bernstein and Karn) resulted in contradictory judgments.[646] Gwin argued Judge Patel's ruling in the Bernstein case that anything written in a language necessarily is protected speech was "unsound":

> "Speech" is not protected simply because we write it in a language. Instead, what determines whether the First Amendment protects something is whether it expresses ideas.[647]

Judge Gwin argued:

> the court in Bernstein I misunderstood the significance of source code's functionality. Source code is "purely functional"...in a way that the Bernstein Court's examples of instructions, manuals, and recipes are not. Unlike instructions, a manual, or a recipe, source code actually performs the function it describes. While a recipe provides instructions to a cook, source code is a device, like embedded circuitry in a telephone, that actually does the function of encryption.[648]

Judge Gwin stated whilst source code is "conduct that can occasionally have communicative elements," that "does not necessarily extend First Amendment protection to it." Judge Gwin added, "source code is by design functional: it is created and, if allowed, exported to do a specified task, not to communicate ideas." Judge Gwin also dismissed the vagueness challenge stating the regulations are "quite detailed."[649]

It was a major setback for the digital rights activists following their successes with Judge Patel in the Bernstein case. EFF's Shari Steele commented, "The Ohio [Gwin] court clearly doesn't understand the communicative nature of software."[650] Cindy Cohn, Bernstein's lawyer, responded with a scathing post attacking Judge Gwin's ruling, "where is the evidence to support his conclusions? The government submitted no empirical studies of source code 'exports' from which one could conclude how often source code is 'expressive.'"[651] Cohn challenged, "I know of no authority which holds that the number of people who communicate in a given language is the basis on which we decide whether that communication is speech."[652] Cohn wrote:

> Software on paper isn't any less "functional" than software in electronic form. It simply requires one more, simple, step to make it functional. In the case of the single page of source code which is Snuffle, in the Bernstein case, the difference cannot be more than ten minutes worth of typing or a few minutes to scan and correct errors prior to compiling. *This* is the difference our national security rests upon?[653]

Cohn also drew on the wider implications of Judge Gwin's ruling:

> Judge Gwin decided, despite the evidence, that source code isn't often read by anyone and so shouldn't really deserve First Amendment protection...The result is that we

---

646 Ibid.
647 Ibid.
648 Ibid.
649 Ibid.

650 Reuters, 1998.
651 Cohn, 1998b.
652 Ibid.
653 Ibid.

have a new category of lesser protected expression, speech which is also "functional," without any clear or understandable definition of the term "functional." And all those computer scientists and their settled methods of communicating with each other apparently don't count when it comes to the First Amendment.

The larger ramifications of this holding, if it becomes law for the rest of us, are frightening. Taken to its extreme, this holding could be the exception that swallows the rule of Reno v. ACLU [that Constitutional protections apply to the Internet].

If the fact that something can "function" means it is not speech, every web page written in HTML could be held not protected, since at some level each page is a "functioning" computer program. Certainly, any web page or other electronic publication which contains a Java applet is a "functioning" program.[654]

EFF President Barry Steinhardt concurred with Cohn's analysis, "If the [Gwin ruling] would become the law of the land, we'd have no First Amendment protection for a wide range of expression in the digital age."[655] Professor Junger responded that despite their lack of funding the case was "so important that we will have to scrape up the resources somehow to bring an appeal."[656] However, former NSA attorney Stewart Baker assessed the higher courts would unlikely overturn Gwin's ruling, "This is a conservative court. They're inclined to defer to the government on national security issues."[657] Baker added, "The court is reluctant to speak broadly in an area that would be cutting back the government's authority. It requires more enthusiasm for second-guessing the government than I think most judges have."[658] On the cypherpunk mailing list Ernest Hua wrote:

Why doesn't Gwin understand that the moment one successfully claims that a specific class of source code is not speech by the virtue of the fact that a compiler can transform it automatically into executable code which performs a function, then ANY speech of ANY sort is fundamentally vulnerable to being classified as functional as soon as a compiler can transform it into real machine code.[659]

Hua added:

Gwin said that encryption is a special class of software which is MORE functional. This is definitely a misunderstanding, to say the least. I don't see how any particular class of software is necessarily more or less functional than other classes of software. In the functional sense, all software, when compiled and executed is functional, period (whether it performs according to its original design is irrelevant.)[660]

However, there was some agreement with Judge Gwin's opinion, Ed Gerck wrote:

Your 4-instruction source code above is not a device today—it cannot perform any function. It has only syntatics [sic], not the "how to." But, if there were a machine that

[654] Ibid.
[655] CNET, 1998.
[656] Junger and Vasvari, 1998.
[657] CNET, 1998.
[658] Ibid.
[659] Hua, 1998a.
[660] Hua, 1998b.

could supply the proper semantics (i.e., actually perform the functions 1–4) then your source code above would be a device...

In that, Gwin is correct. Can the source code actually perform a function? Then, it is a device. Irrespective of the needed platform, in the same way that an electric shaver is a device irrespective of the local availablity [sic] of an appropriate power outlet.[661]

Despite the ongoing conflicts in the judicial system, the government did make an export concession to the global financial sector in 1998. Commerce Secretary William M. Daley announced encryption products of any bit length would be exportable to eligible financial institutions in 45 countries without a license, after a one-time review.[662] Daley stated, "These new guidelines will affect encryption exports for almost 70 percent of the world's financial institutions, including all of the 100 largest banks."[663] The financial sector welcomed the removal of restrictions, as Kawika Daguio, an American Bankers Association lobbyist, commented, "What we've heard sounds great. We've been arguing [for several years] that the regulatory structure we have guarantees we're good citizens."[664] It is unsurprising the financial sector was the first to receive a removal of export restrictions, the sector was the highest risk, underpinned American's global commercial supremacy, possessed powerful and well-established lobbyists, and, as Daguio highlighted, was highly regulated. Though the wider community did not share the banking sector's enthusiasm, Ed Gillespie, executive director of lobbying group Americans for Computer Privacy stated, "To take a piecemeal approach [to loosening encryption restrictions] is the wrong direction, we need a blanket lifting of restrictions."[665]

Junger's lawyers filed an appeal in August 1998, arguing that the court:

applied a deeply flawed analysis in order to arrive at the conclusion that encryption source code is more functional than expressive, and that this should somehow deprive source code, which the district court nonetheless recognized as a form of expression, of the fullest degree of First Amendment protection.[666]

Oral arguments took place on December 17, 1999 before a three-judge panel of the Sixth Circuit Court of Appeals. Scarselli stated, "at oral argument, it was apparent that the court of appeals was more receptive to our First Amendment argument than the district court," this was despite Chief Judge Boyce F. Martin commenting source code to him was "gobblygook."[667]

The Court of Appeals Sixth Circuit delivered its opinion on April 4, 2000. Chief Judge Martin wrote the unanimous opinion, with concurring Judges being Eric Clay and Herman Weber.[668] Martin invoked a previous Supreme Court ruling, which stated, "all ideas having even the slightest redeeming social importance," including those concerning, "the advancement of truth, science, morality, and arts" have

---

661 Gerck, 1998.
662 Daley, 1998.
663 Ibid.
664 Corcoran, 1998.
665 Ibid.

666 Vasvari, Scarselli, and O'Neill, 1998.
667 Scarselli, 2007, 329.
668 United States Court of Appeals, Sixth Circuit, 2000.

First Amendment protection.[669] Martin wrote this protection "is not reserved for purely expressive communication" citing, "The Supreme Court has recognized First Amendment protection for symbolic conduct, such as draft-card burning, that has both functional and expressive features."[670] Martin wrote:

> Particularly, a musical score cannot be read by the majority of the public but can be used as a means of communication among musicians. Likewise, computer source code, though unintelligible to many, is the preferred method of communication among computer programmers.[671]

Judge Martin ruled as source code is an "expressive means" for the exchange of information and ideas about computer programming it was protected by the First Amendment.[672]

Judge Martin therefore reversed the district court's decision, and, given the recent changes to the EAR, remanded the case for further consideration as to whether a complaint could be launched with the judgment that source code was constitutionally protected speech.[673]

Vasvari commented it was "hard to overstate" the importance of the judgment, writing:

> For the first time, a federal appellate court has decided that computer programming languages are entitled to the protections of the First Amendment. This extends to a new medium of expression the sort of protection which music, poetry, scientific articles, and other forms of technical expression have always enjoyed.[674]

Junger had won—the Judge Cohn's ruling of almost half a decade earlier was substantiated, computer code was protected by the First Amendment.

However, the degree of protection afforded to computer code by the Constitution continues to be a lively debate. Computing technology is advancing, and whilst cryptography was regulated as a munition by the ITAR and EAR, 3D printers now allow code to generate firearms beyond the regulation of the state. As technological capabilities continue to advance, expect further contestation of the degree of Constitutional protection bestowed upon computer code.

7.12   ENCRYPTION AND CONGRESS

Congress had been a crypto wars battlefield for some years by the mid-nineties, historically the security-intelligence establishment was always victorious. The CRISIS report released in 1996, which broadly advocated for stronger encryption and relaxed export rules, marked the start of a gradual shift that would occur over the remainder of the decade. Another important report was issued in close proximity to CRISIS.

---

[669] Ibid.
[670] Ibid.
[671] Ibid.

[672] Ibid.
[673] Ibid.
[674] American Civil Liberties Union, 2000.

The President's National Security Advisor had ordered a report on the impact of encryption export policies on the US software industry in late 1994. The NSA and Commerce Department collaborated on the report to be completed by July 1995, but which was eventually delivered in 1996.[675] The full report was classified SECRET, but a redacted version was publicly released. The authors estimated encryption software only accounted for 1–3% of the software market, but acknowledged significant growth expectations.[676] The report found the "impact of U.S. export controls on the international market shares of general-purpose products is probably negligible," arguing, "customers are often unaware of the encryption features in these products and primarily base purchases on the features implementing the primary function of the product (e.g., word processing or database)."[677] The report added there were few "viable foreign competitors" for general-purpose products with encryption.[678] The report recognized that due to export laws, "Many smaller, security-specific software firms...elected to limit their sales to the domestic market only."[679] However, contrasting the narrative of the digital privacy activists the report argued there was "little evidence that U.S. export controls have had a negative effect on the availability of products in the U.S. marketplace," as a result of vendors only building weaker and export-friendly products.[680] Despite this view from the government report, the mood in Congress was changing.

One important factor for Congress' gradual shift towards liberalization was growth of the technology sector's lobbying power. In the early 1990s, the dominance of a small number of technology companies had generated questions over whether such dominance was anti-competitive, and a foreshadowing of monopolies similar to that of Standard Oil in the early twentieth century. The Standard Oil case led to the company being dismantled into dozens of smaller entities to re-establish a competitive commercial landscape, could such a thing happen to the 1990s technology companies? Microsoft became an anti-trust target when the Federal Trade Commission launched an investigation into potential collusion between Microsoft and IBM, in 1990.[681] The Microsoft case morphed and grew for the remainder of the millennium. The technology sector no doubt realized to manage such threats required a stronger presence in Washington. Politics was an alien culture to many who grew up believing rules should be sacrificed on the altar of technological progress. Geography also worked against the technology executives—the corridors of power were a continent away making it harder to cultivate influential politicians. The growing financial clout, and efforts of technology lobbyists gradually induced Congress members to take an interest in the challenges facing technology companies, one of the most prominent being the encryption issue.

In the early 1990s, Congressional hearings were held on a number of encryption-related topics, such as the Digital Telephony Act. Forays were made to pass

---

[675] Interagency Working Group on Encryption and Telecommunications Policy, 1996, I-1.
[676] Ibid, ES-1.
[677] Ibid, ES-4.
[678] Ibid, ES-2.
[679] Ibid, ES-4.
[680] Ibid.
[681] Wired, 2002.

legislation, such as the insertion of the "sense of congress" language in S.266, which would have given the government warranted access to the plain text of encrypted data, but no such legislation advanced. Notable cryptologists gave testimony to Congress about the strategic socio-political implications of encryption. PGP inventor Phil Zimmermann spoke to the House of Representatives Subcommittee for Economic Policy, Trade, and the Environment in 1993.[682] Zimmermann told Congress computers were initially developed in secret during World War Two to break enemy codes, "Governments formed their attitudes toward cryptographic technology during this period...these attitudes persist today."[683] Zimmerman explained the digital revolution was resulting in "a disturbing erosion of our privacy," before describing the removal of the surveillance labor constraint:

> In the past, if the Government wanted to violate the privacy of ordinary citizens, it had to expend a certain amount of effort to intercept and steam open and read paper mail, and listen to and possibly transcribe spoken telephone conversation. This is analogous to catching fish with a hook and a line, one fish at a time. Fortunately for freedom and democracy, this kind of labor-intensive monitoring is not practical on a large scale.[684]

Zimmermann explained emails are easier to intercept and scan for keywords: "This can be done easily, routinely, automatically, and undetectably on a grand scale. This is analogous to driftnet fishing—making a quantitative and qualitative Orwellian difference to the health of democracy."[685] Zimmerman highlighted the threat to democracy from encryption restrictions, stating:

> some elements of the Government seem intent on deploying and entrenching a communications infrastructure that would deny the citizenry the ability to protect its privacy. This is unsettling because in a democracy, it is possible for bad people to occasionally get elected—sometimes very bad people.
> Normally, a well-functioning democracy has ways to remove these people from power. But the wrong technology infrastructure could allow such a future government to watch every move anyone makes to oppose it. It could very well be the last government we ever elect.[686]

Zimmermann advised when creating policy for new technologies it would be good civic hygiene to ensure technologies that would "best strengthen the hands of a police state" can not be deployed.[687] Speaking three years later to another subcommittee, Zimmermann argued export policies needed to change as encryption is "simple arithmetic" to digital hardware, and the rest of the world was laughing "at the US because we are rallying against nature, trying to stop it...is like trying to legislate the tides and weather."[688] Zimmermann added:

---

[682] Zimmermann, 1993.
[683] Ibid.
[684] Ibid.
[685] Ibid.

[686] Ibid.
[687] Ibid.
[688] Zimmermann, 1996.

Like every new technology, this comes at some cost. Cars pollute the air and cause traffic jams. Cryptography can help criminals hide their activities. People in the law enforcement and intelligence communities are going to look at this only in their own terms. But even with these costs, we still can't stop this from happening in a free market global economy.[689]

Zimmermann added:

At no time in the past century has public distrust of the government been so broadly distributed across the political spectrum, as it is today…Advances in technology will not permit the maintenance of the status quo, as far as privacy is concerned. The status quo is unstable. If we do nothing, new technologies will give the government new automatic surveillance capabilities that Stalin could never have dreamed of.

The only way to hold the line on privacy in the information age is strong cryptography. Cryptography strong enough to keep out major governments.[690]

The two principal legislative vehicles for controlling dangerous or dual-use exports were the State Department's Munitions List (part of the Arms Export Control Act) and the Commerce Department's Commerce Control List (part of the Export Administration Act).[691] The lists' contents gradually began to overlap, and so in November 1990, President Bush had ordered a review of overlapping dual-use items with an intent to remove them from the Munitions List unless they posed a significant National Security risk.[692]

The Department of State led the inter-agency review to identify items to move to the Commerce Control List.[693] Mass-market software with cryptographic capabilities was one of the items reviewed.[694] Initially, in April 1991, the Departments of State and Defense agreed to keep software with cryptographic capabilities on the Munitions List to enable the NSA to review all such products.[695] However, by January 1992, the State Department reversed its position, believing Commerce could manage mass-market software.[696] The Defense Department objected, believing Commerce lacked the control system to manage encryption.[697] The NSA appealed to the Under Secretary of State for International Security Affairs and the President's Assistant for National Security Affairs to maintain the controls with the State Department.[698] The administration agreed.

In an effort to ease export regulations, Democratic Representative Meldon Levine of California had added an amendment to the 1991 reauthorization of the Export Administration Act to transfer mass-market software to the Department of Commerce, rather than State's jurisdiction when the encryption "contain certain

---

[689] Ibid.
[690] Ibid.
[691] United States General Accounting Office, 1993, 24.
[692] Ibid.
[693] Ibid.
[694] Ibid.
[695] Ibid.
[696] Ibid.
[697] Ibid.
[698] Ibid.

specified technical characteristics."[699] Levine was encouraged by the Software Publishers Association (SPA), a body representing US software providers.[700] According to *The Washington Post*, in what they called a "wrongheaded and unrealistic" move, the Bush administration threatened to veto the bill should the amendment not be removed.[701] Whilst the amendment was withdrawn from the legislation, Levine's actions further pressured the National Security Council and NSA to compromise rather than outright block SPA, who were specifically looking for the ability to export DES.[702] Public opinion was slowly starting to shift in favor of those against the administration. For instance, a June 1992 *Washington Post* article stated the government was "clinging to the futile hope that it can stem the tide of technology," and had failed to acknowledge the technological "sea change."[703] The article argued the Department of Defense "won't yield to common sense [policy] unless compelled to do so."[704]

Agreement between the SPA and the Bush administration was reached in July 1992.[705] The agreement allowed Ron Rivest's 40-bit Ciphers 2 and 4 (RC2 and RC4) to be exported. SPA General Counsel Ilene Rosenthal commented:

> Although this was an important first step toward the much-needed decontrol of exports of mass market software with encryption capability, the National Security Agency and the National Security Council must continue the process of decontrol.[706]

The National Security Council also agreed to meet twice yearly with software industry representatives to consider further export liberalization.[707] 40-bit RC-4 was soon incorporated into export products, including in the market-dominant Netscape Navigator browser.

However, 40-bit RC4 (around a million million keys) proved increasingly fragile. A 40-bit RC4 message was broken in France by Damien Doligez in 1995.[708] Doligez executed an exhaustive attack with around 120 workstations; the key was found in eight days after searching just over half the key space.[709] In January 1996, an MIT undergraduate student, Andrew Twyman, used an $83,000 graphics computer to achieve the same task in an equal eight days—with a search rate of 830,000 keys per second, he could have searched the entire keyspace in fifteen days.[710] NSA would have many times this computing power available, so one can reasonably hypothesize they could break RC4 when it was approved for export. Cryptography Professor Keith Martin comments, "It is safe to assume that [in the early 1990s] the NSA deemed an exhaustive search for a 40-bit key feasible."[711]

---

[699] United States Congress, 1991b; United States National Archives and Records Administration, 1992, 32148.

[700] United States General Accounting Office, 1993, 26.

[701] Hirschhorn and Peyton, 1992.

[702] United States General Accounting Office, 1993, 26.

[703] Hirschhorn and Peyton, 1992.

[704] Ibid.

[705] Rosenthal, 1993.

[706] Ibid.

[707] United States General Accounting Office, 1993, 26.

[708] National Research Council, 1996, 124.

[709] Ibid.

[710] Ibid.

[711] Martin, 2020, 211.

With the crypto war becoming more polarized and publicized as the 1990s progressed, a series of bills were introduced in Congress, often in a strike-counter-strike pattern. In March 1996, Democratic Senator Patrick Leahy of Vermont introduced Senate Bill S. 1587, the Encrypted Communications Privacy Act (ECPA), with a companion bill introduced in the House. Leahy stated the bill allowed Americans to "use any encryption, regardless of encryption algorithm selected, key length chosen, or implementation technique, or medium used." The bill would also grant the Commerce Secretary control of cryptographic export policy, allow license-free export without key escrow where comparable capabilities were available overseas, and criminalize the use of encryption in furtherance of a crime. The bill provided a legal framework for key escrow, though its use was optional.[712]

The ECPA received a mixed reception by the digital privacy community. Todd Lappin commented in *Wired*:

> Surprise, surprise. Several members of Congress have finally heard the cry for strong encryption to protect privacy and commerce on the Internet. At long last, they've waded into the battle by introducing legislation that aims a silver bullet straight at the heart of the Clinton administration's botched...proposals.[713]

The Association for Computing Machinery, the Institute of Electronical and Electronics Engineers, and the Voters Telecommunications Watch all expressed support.[714] The Center for Democracy and Technology stated the bill, "represent[s] a major step towards breaking the stranglehold on encryption technologies," and it "represents a rejection of the Clinton Administration's invasive and unworkable...policies."[715] Cypherpunk Jim Gillogly wrote the bill was "good news for a change"; Matt Blaze added, "I think the bill is a huge step forward and deserves support," he also corresponded with Leahy, thanking him for his "continued leadership in this area."[716] Others offered more limited support. Simon Garfinkel, a leading PGP proponent, wrote in *The New York Times*, "although the new bill would still prohibit American companies from exporting innovative programs, it would at least allow them to compete with foreign companies on an equal footing."[717] Whilst expressing some reservations, Peter Junger said Senator Leahy and other sponsors of the bill "should be congratulated."[718] John Gilmore stated, "The bill is a good start, and with healthy debate and modification, it could become acceptable legislation."[719] An EFF statement warned of pending anti-cryptography counter-bill being prepared by the Clinton administration:

> at the behest of the FBI and NSA. It is unknown at present what such a bill would look like in detail, but it is unlikely to be favorable to Internet users' privacy rights, digital commerce, system security, or freedom of expression. The current bills give those of

---

[712] United States Congress, 1996.
[713] Lappin, 1996.
[714] Banisar, 1996 and Voters Telecommunications Watch, 1996.
[715] Palacios, 1996.

[716] Gillogly, 1996; Blaze, 1996.
[717] Garfinkel, 1996.
[718] Junger, 1996b.
[719] Electronic Frontier Foundation, 1996d.

us concerned about these issues a head start in educating legislators, the media, and the public before the storm hits.[720]

However, as the digital rights community conducted further detailed analysis of the bill, a number of language ambiguities were identified raising concerns of how the text may be interpreted by law enforcement—many turned away from the legislation. Cypherpunk Jim Bell commented, "We raked that bill over the coals, found it seriously flawed, and generally pro-encryption people don't seem to be defending it at all. It contained many aspects which have the prospect of future danger to the use of encryption."[721] Many also felt the legislation too broad; the ACM and IEEE argued:

> the inclusion of issues that are tangential to export, such as key escrow and encryption in domestic criminal activities, is not necessary. The relaxation of export controls is of great economic importance to industry and users, and should not become entangled in more controversial matters.[722]

Denning argued the bill was not in the national interest. Writing to Leahy, Denning wrote that the bill "is not in balance with society's needs," and that it would "erode the ability of our law enforcement and intelligence agencies to carry out their missions."[723] To some within the digital rights movements, Denning's antagonism to the bill was itself an endorsement of its virtue, whilst having reservations about the bill, Declan McCullagh commented, "Any legislation that Dorothy Denning attacks so virulently must be worth passing."[724] The media were increasingly following the moves and counter-moves in Congress, with *The New York Times* trying to highlight the importance of the issue at a time when indecent images were the public's internet policy focus, "The key issue for the Net is not smut, it is the use of encryption."[725]

On May 2, 1996, Senator Patrick Leahy announced he was "proud" to become the first member of Congress to post a message to the Internet both signed and encrypted with PGP.[726] His posting was to support another pro-encryption bill, released two months after ECPA, Leahy wrote:

> Today, a bipartisan group of Senators has joined me in supporting legislation to encourage the development and use of strong, privacy-enhancing technologies for the Internet by rolling back the out-dated restrictions on the export of strong cryptography.[727]

Leahy wrote he had long been concerned about online privacy issues; as a result, he and a number of other Senators introduced a new bill in the Senate, the "Promotion of Commerce On-Line in the Digital Era (PRO-CODE) Act of 1996" to remove the export restraints on "generally available or mass market encryption products." Leahy added, "It is clear that the current policy towards encryption exports is hopelessly

---

[720] Ibid
[721] Bell, 1996d.
[722] Banisar, 1996.
[723] Bell, 1996c.

[724] Ibid.
[725] Caruso, 1996.
[726] Leahy, 1996.
[727] Ibid.

outdated, and fails to account for the real needs of individuals and businesses in the global marketplace."[728]

The privacy argument was increasingly being augmented with the security argument for, rather than against, encryption. Leahy told the senate:

> Strong encryption has an important use as a crime prevention shield, to stop hackers, industrial spies and thieves from snooping into private computer files and stealing valuable proprietary information. We should be encouraging the use of strong encryption to prevent certain types of computer and online crime.[729]

Leahy concluded, "The time is right for Congress to take steps to put our national encryption policy on the right course."[730] John Gilmore recounts the impact of having Leahy in the cypherpunks' corner, "It meant that there was one person in Washington who had a clue about [encryption], which previously it looked like there were zero people."[731] But it was not just one person, Senator Conrad Burns was one of a number of the bill's co-sponsors; in a letter to the Internet community Burns wrote, "Until we get the federal government out of the way and encourage the development of strong cryptography for the global market, electronic commerce and the potential of the Internet will not be realized."[732] Burns added:

> The last thing the Net needs are repressive and outdated regulations prohibiting the exports of strong privacy and security tools and making sure that the government has copies of the keys to our private communications. Yet this is exactly the situation we have today.[733]

The framing of the bill as enabling economic growth, rather than privacy, was sure to have wider appeal to Congress. Senator Burns told Congress:

> A study by the Computer Systems Policy Project found that within just the next four years, American companies could lose $60 billion in revenues and American workers could lose 216,000 high-tech jobs. Our bill is a jobs bill that I'm sure the administration can agree with.[734]

The language of the bill reinforced this message:

> The full potential of the Internet for the conduct of business cannot be realized as long as it is an insecure medium in which confidential business information and sensitive personal information remain at risk of unauthorized viewing, alteration, and use.[735]

[728] Ibid.
[729] Leahy, 1996b.
[730] Ibid.
[731] Franceschi-Bicchierai, 2016.
[732] Burns, 1996b.
[733] Ibid.
[734] Burns, 1996a.
[735] United States Congress, 1996b, 2.a.5.

The bill firmly placed blame for stifling the encryption market's growth:

> Businesses have been discouraged from further developing and marketing products with encryption capabilities because of regulatory efforts by the Secretary of Commerce, acting through the National Institute of Standards and Technology.[736]

The bill highlighted the government's key escrow policies as hindering commercial progress, arguing the government, "has ignored the fact that there is no demonstrated commercial demand for features which give government easy access to information."[737] Further, the bill's authors highlighted numerous non-key escrow alternatives available from foreign suppliers, as well as free of charge via the Internet.[738] The bill's authors also attacked government attempts to manipulate the market with their buying power:

> The Secretary of Commerce, acting through the National Institute of Standards and Technology, has attempted to leverage the desire of United States businesses to sell commercial products to the United States Government, and sell a single product worldwide, to force the businesses to include features in products sold by the businesses in the United States and in foreign countries that will allow the Federal Government easy access to the plain text of all electronic information and communications.[739]

The bill's authors argued:

> United States businesses should be encouraged to develop and market products and programs offering encryption capabilities; and the Federal Government should be prohibited from promulgating regulations and adopting policies that discourage the use and sale of encryption.[740]

The bill banned key escrow, and allowed export of any encryption generally available to the public (including online).[741] Essentially, short of exporting encryption developed specifically for military applications, or the sending of encryption to terrorism-supporting countries, export of mass-market encryption would be legal.[742] Senator Burns asked Congress members:

> How many of you would feel secure sending your credit card number over the Internet especially when you learn that reported invasions by computer hackers increased ninefold between 1990 and 1994? Or when Internet World magazine estimates that the actual number of unwanted computer penetrations in 1992 alone was 1.2 million?[743]

Burns promised to hold two online town halls with Internet users to solicit their feedback.[744] The cryptology community responded positively. Phil Zimmermann argued:

---

[736] Ibid, 2.a.10.
[737] Ibid, 2.a.12 and 2.a.15.
[738] Ibid, 2.a.15.
[739] Ibid, 2.a.12.
[740] Ibid, 2.a.16.

[741] Ibid, 5.b.
[742] Ibid, 5.b.
[743] Burns, 1996a.
[744] Ibid.

[PRO-CODE] is our best chance for giving Americans access to this essential tool of liberty [cryptography]. Let us bequeath to our children a society that lets them whisper in someone's ear, even if the ear is a thousand miles away.[745]

However, by July 1996, Zimmermann's optimism was fading:

Unfortunately, no matter how wonderful the ProCODE bill may be (and it is), it isn't going anywhere this year. There's no time left. And in the Senate, national security interests have strong allies who would move to block the bill if it suddenly slithered out of committee.[746]

However, Zimmermann saw a silver lining believing they had been able to, "educate Congress, and the debate is shifting in our favor." Citing a recent Congressional hearing, Zimmermann noted the growing fears of "a cyber equivalent of Pearl Harbor," as articulated by Deputy Attorney General Jamie Gorelick, which could work in their favor.[747]

As Congress returned for its 1997–1998 session, Senator Burns re-introduced PRO-CODE with additional language to create an Information Security Board (ISB).[748] The ISB would meet quarterly and was intended to "provide a forum to foster communication and coordination between industry and the federal government," aiming to share knowledge of "general, nonproprietary, and nonconfidential developments in important information security technologies, including encryption."[749] The ISB would be attended by policy-makers, and would report:

general, nonproprietary, and nonconfidential information to appropriate Federal agencies to keep law enforcement and national security agencies abreast of emerging technologies so they are able effectively to execute their responsibilities.[750]

This inclusion was likely made in an attempt to assure law enforcement and intelligence agencies they would be provided with timely information to aid in their management of relaxed export rules. The cypherpunks were concerned about the ISB's intent: Greg Broiles worried the ISB would be able to compel testimony, Alan Olsen worried, "It sounds like a nice little rubber hose committee," joking the ISB could be called, "The House Committee on Unamerican Encryption."[751] Rubber hose cryptanalysis is a euphemism for the extraction of cryptographic secrets via coercion (such as the beating of suspects with a rubber hose).

As the earlier cryptography bills failed to gain enough momentum to proceed through Congress, H.R. 695, a bipartisan bill with over 60 cosponsors entitled the Safety and Freedom Through Encryption (SAFE) Act, was introduced by Republican

---

745 Ibid.
746 Ibid.
747 Ibid.
748 United States Congress, 1997b.

749 Ibid, 6.b.
750 Ibid, 6.c.
751 Broiles, 1997; Toto, 1997.

Representative Robert Goodlatte of Virginia in February 1997.[752] Included in the bill was "sense of congress" language arguing export control imposition without an agreed international approach to prevent other countries exporting strong encryption, an approach the President had failed to deliver, was "detrimental to the competitiveness" of the US.[753] The SAFE bill allowed US citizens, either at home or abroad, to use any encryption, "regardless of the algorithm selection, encryption key length chose, or implementation or medium used."[754] SAFE proposed removing encryption export restrictions providing, "a product offering comparable security is commercially available outside the United States from a foreign supplier," with exceptions for foreign militaries and terrorists.[755] The bill made the use of encryption to facilitate a crime punishable with up to five years in jail.[756] Representative John Conyers stated foreign competitors' marketing campaigns were highlighting they could offer encryption far stronger than the "trivially-cracked" U.S. products.[757] Democratic Representative Zoe Lofgren of California argued, "due to a myopic Federal government policy regulating this technology, our country risks losing its advantage in this vital industry; many within the industry believe that we are already some length down that path."[758] Lofgren added:

> Rather than continuing to pursue this flawed and unworkable policy, I would urge the national security and law enforcement community to assume a cooperative posture with our domestic technology industry, and utilize the minds of the foremost scientists in the world.[759]

William Reinsch argued on behalf of the government that SAFE would "not be helpful…it proposes export liberalization far beyond what the administration can entertain." Deputy Attorney General Robert Litt highlighted a number of cases where encryption had prevented their investigations. Litt recounted how Aldrich Ames, a CIA agent recruited as a KGB spy, was directed by his handlers to encrypt files containing secrets before transmission to Moscow. Another example given was of Ramzi Yousef, recently convicted of conspiring to blow up ten US-owned airliners, and an alleged "mastermind" of the 1993 World Trade Center bombing, who, along with his co-conspirators, "apparently stored information about their terrorist plot in an encrypted computer file." Other cases cited included those involving child pornography, drug trafficking, and criminal hacking.[760] Litt also addressed the fourth amendment's provision for privacy:

> our Founding Fathers recognized that an absolute right to privacy was incompatible with an ordered society, and so our Nation has never recognized such an absolute right. Rather, the fourth amendment strikes a careful balance between an individual's right to privacy and society's need, on appropriate occasions and when authorized by a court

---

752 United States Congress, 1997.
753 Ibid, Sec. 4.A.1.
754 Ibid, Sec. 2802.
755 Ibid, Sec. 3.
756 Ibid, Sec. 2805.

757 United States House of Representatives, 1997.
758 Ibid.
759 Ibid.
760 Ibid.

order, to intrude into that privacy. Our encryption policy should try to preserve that time-tested balance.[761]

Litt argued:

> Unbreakable encryption would upset this delicate constitutional balance, which is one of the bedrock principles of our legal system, by effectively nullifying a court's issuance of a search warrant or wiretap order. The notion that advances in technology should dictate public policy is backwards.[762]

Litt stated the government disagreed the cryptography "genie is out of the bottle." He believed whilst strong encryption could be found overseas, the products were not ubiquitous due to US export controls. Litt argued the "quality of encryption products abroad varies greatly, with some encryption products not providing the level of protection advertised." Litt stated most "legitimate businesses and individuals" who wanted strong encryption would not rely on software downloaded from the Internet from "untested sources," preferring instead to deal with known and reliable suppliers. Litt argued, "Our allies agree with us that unrestricted export of encryption would severely hamper law enforcement objectives." Litt advised it would be "profoundly unwise" to remove export controls, arguing that should the US do so, other countries would respond by "imposing their own import controls or restricting the use of strong encryption by their citizens."[763] Tim May commented in May 1997:

> I've been watching these so-called "crypto liberation" bills, Pro-CODE and SAFE, wend their ways through the legislative process. Both are severely flawed. Both should be rejected. Passing laws with flaws is worse than doing nothing, than just relying on the good old Constitution for our rights.[764]

A few weeks later, a counter-bill was introduced, the Secure Public Networks Act (SPNA).[765] The SPNA stated domestic cryptography would be unregulated and key escrow explicitly forbidden. The bill also criminalized the use of encryption when it was "knowingly" used in "furtherance of the commission of a criminal offense."[766] Penalties for such a crime were up to five years in jail for a first offense, and up to ten years in jail for a second offense.[767] The bill made the breaking of encryption for the purpose of violating privacy or property rights a crime.[768] The bill stated any encryption system purchased by the government, or with government funds, would be required to have a key escrow system.[769] The Commerce Department would control encryption policy.[770] The bill made 56-bit DES, or equivalent strength encryption exportable after a one-time review.[771] All encryption strengths would be allowed if the system were key escrowed.[772] Decisions on prohibited exports would not be

---

761 Ibid.
762 Ibid.
763 Ibid.
764 May, 1997.
765 Congress, 1997c, 101–102.
766 Ibid, 105.
767 Ibid, 105.
768 Ibid
769 Ibid, 202–205.
770 Ibid, 301.
771 Ibid, 302.
772 Ibid, 304.

subject to judicial review.[773] If key escrow were not built into the encryption system, and the key size was greater than 56 bits, the export decision would be based on whether the end-user had access to similar strength encryption.[774] Government would only need a subpoena, rather than a judicial warrant, to access escrowed keys.[775] The legislation also indicated certificate authorities would need to escrow their public keys:

> The Secretary or a Certificate Authority for Public Keys registered under this Act may issue to a person a public key certificate that certifies a public key that can be used for encryption only if the person…stores with a Key Recovery Agent registered under this Act sufficient information, as specified by the Secretary in regulations, to allow timely lawful recovery of the plaintext of that person's encrypted data and communications.[776]

Whilst the act had earlier claimed encryption would not be regulated within the US, this was a significant restriction; the EFF commented:

> While its sponsors claim that it would not make key recovery mandatory, SPN would require the use of key recovery systems in order to obtain the "public key certificates" needed to participate in electronic commerce and would require key recovery for all secure networks built with any federal funds.[777]

The bill would also create a public-private information security board to make policy recommendations to Congress and the President.[778]

Introducing the bill, Senator Bob Kerrey stated, "our ability to be able to communicate, for national security reasons, and our ability to be able to communicate for law enforcement reasons and know those communications are secure is the first order of business of the Secure Public Networks Act." Kerrey argued the "alternative to the rule of law in this dynamic area is chaos and anarchy."[779]Kerrey stated it was "simply not true," that the legislation was "an attempt by Government to gain access over the privacy of individuals…there is protection after protection after protection in this legislation guarding against that." Kerrey argued the act "protects and strengthens the privacy rights of the individual without damaging the interest of public safety."[780] Kerrey argued it was not the government, but hackers who posed the greatest privacy threat:

> These hackers and crackers are skilled way beyond my capacity to understand what they are doing, except to know that they have the ability to come in and steal information that has great value, to manipulate that data and do not just a little bit of mischief but put our commercial and our national security interests at risk.[781]

---

[773] Ibid, 306.
[774] Ibid, 307.
[775] Ibid, 106.
[776] Ibid, 405.
[777] Electronic Frontier Foundation, 1997e.

[778] Congress, 1997c, 801.
[779] Ibid.
[780] Kerrey, 1997.
[781] Ibid.

Kerrey also acknowledged, "Our Nation's policy on encryption is only a single piece of the puzzle," a global solution would be needed if key escrow were to be viable in a heavily networked world. Kerrey informed the Senate the legislation, "calls on the President to continue consultations and negotiations with foreign countries to ensure secure public networks are built on a global scale," by which he presumably meant key escrow, rather than general information security practices. Kerrey informed the Senate that "as the largest purchaser of computer software and hardware, the Federal Government can create important incentives to help the market fulfill this need." In closing, Kerrey argued his bill would "provide the security needed for us to be able to move Government operations into the new paradigm of network activity."[782]

The legislation was met with dismay by the digital privacy rights community, who found the new paradigm an acute divergence from their desired future. CPSR's Andy Oram labeled the legislation a "brute force attack on encryption."[783] Oram commented the authors, "have read everything that civil libertarians and encryption experts had to say about computer encryption—and put everything they hated into one bill."[784] Oram argued whilst the key escrow system may not be universally mandatory, "the law requires its use under a variety of circumstances...intended to bring it into universal use."[785] Oram wrote the potential for abuse of the system was "clear to anyone who has read about the FBI COINTELPRO campaign of the 1960s and 1970s."[786] Oram argued whilst McCain and Kerrey introduced the bill, it had the "imprint of the Clinton Administration all over it."[787] Oram believed the legislation was "part of a campaign by the NSA, the FBI, and the Clinton Administration to impose a new surveillance capability on the U.S. public—and indirectly, the rest of the world"; Oram further contended the bill was part of a "damage-control operation to stop two bills that could open the way to strong encryption on the Internet [PRO-CODE and SAFE]."[788] The cypherpunks felt the same—Greg Broiles labeled the legislation "evil."[789] Kenneth Dam, chair of the National Research Council (NRC) study on cryptographic policy stated the legislation was "inconsistent with the general thrust of the NRC CRISIS report. The SPNA is a highly aggressive promotion of key recovery for the private sector, establishing that technology as a pillar of national cryptography policy."[790] Dam further added, "the bill attempts to use something that all parties agree is needed for electronic commerce, namely a public key infrastructure (PKI), as leverage for obtaining approval for something fundamentally unrelated, namely key recovery for domestic use."[791]

The SPNA made it out of the Commerce committee in June 1997, but failed to progress further in the Senate.[792] Cypherpunk Michael Pierson summed up how many must have felt given the volume of maneuvering around cryptographic political activity:

---

[782] Ibid.
[783] Oram, 1997.
[784] Ibid.
[785] Ibid.
[786] Ibid.
[787] Ibid.
[788] Ibid.
[789] Broiles, 1997b.
[790] Dam, 1997.
[791] Ibid.
[792] Oram, 1997.

Watching the rapid-fire succession of Administration rulings and gambits, and the developments of various contending legislative proposals and industry initiatives, along with all the debate over the differing implications and portents of this distracting plethora of moves and countermoves, has made for quite an intriguing spectacle.[793]

The next cryptography bill to emerge was S. 2067, the Encryption Protects the Rights of Individuals from Violation and Abuse in Cyberspace (E-PRIVACY) Act in June 1998. Introducing the bill, Republican Senator John Ashcroft of Missouri wrote in three years of working on encryption policy, "I have not seen any real attempt by the White House to resolve this problem. In fact, over the course of that time the Administration has moved further from negotiation by taking increasingly extreme positions on this critical national issue."[794] Ashcroft argued Clinton administration policies could cost the country 200,000 jobs and $60 billion by the year 2000.[795] There was an increasingly urgent need to pass legislation—a sunset clause from a 1996 Clinton decision allowing export of 56-bit DES encryption would come into effect in December 1998, after which only 40-bit encryption would be exportable.[796]
Leahy further critiqued the administration:

In the Senate we have a name for debate that delays action on legislative matters. We call it a filibuster. On encryption policy, the Administration has been willing to talk, but not to forge a real solution. That amounts to a filibuster. The longer we go without a sensible policy, the more jobs will be lost, the more we risk eroding our privacy rights on the Internet, and the more we leave our critical infrastructures vulnerable.[797]

Senator Conrad Burns told Congress, "If anyone was looking for the compromise to resolve this difficult but important issue, this [E-PRIVACY bill] is it."[798] Ashcroft said, "We are offering this as what we think is an appropriate solution…We're also saying to them [the Clinton administration], 'Let's look at where the world is.'"[799] Senator Patty Murray agreed, "It is time for the United States to acknowledge that we no longer exclusively control the pace of technology."[800] For example, a Dutch subsidiary of Network Associates, a US software producer, started selling PGP in March 1998.[801] Leahy stated, "I hope this bill will break the logjam [and the practice of] people talking past each other."[802] Senator Larry Craig addressed key recovery:

Addressing this from an economic perspective, customers—especially foreign customers—are unwilling to purchase American encryption products with backdoors and third-party access. This is particularly true since they can buy stronger encryption overseas from either foreign-owned companies or American-owned companies on foreign soil without these invasive features.[803]

---

[793] Pierson, 1997.
[794] United States Congress, 1998.
[795] Branson, 1998.
[796] United States Congress, 1998.
[797] Ibid.
[798] Tech Law Journal, 1998.
[799] Branson, 1998.
[800] United States Congress, 1998.
[801] Branson, 1998.
[802] Ibid.
[803] United States Congress, 1998.

The bill:

> Prohibits…requiring, compelling, setting standards for, or conditioning any approval
> or the receipt of any benefit on, a requirement that a decryption key, access to a decryp-
> tion key, key recovery information, or other plaintext access capability.[804]

Furthermore, the proposed legislation:

> Prohibits and sets penalties for knowingly and willfully, during the commission of a
> Federal felony, encrypting any incriminating communication or information relating
> to that felony with intent to conceal it to avoid detection by a law enforcement agency
> or prosecutor.[805]

The bill requires entities in possession of encrypted data to provide the government,
when in possession of a warrant, with "necessary decryption assistance," though
such assistance should be the minimum required to meet the warrant's requirements.
The Commerce Secretary would control exports. Encryption algorithms/strengths
available abroad would be exportable after a newly formed public-private Encryption
Export Advisory Board confirmed the foreign product's availability, or its arrival
within eighteen months, and a one-time 15-day product review. The bill also established the National Electronic Technologies (NET) Center, within the Department
of Justice. The NET Center would "serve as a center for Federal, State, and local
law enforcement authorities for information and assistance regarding decryption,"
and "for industry and government entities to exchange information and methodology
regarding information security." The NET Center would also "examine encryption
techniques and methods to facilitate the ability of law enforcement to gain efficient
access to plaintext of communications and electronic communications," and "conduct research to develop efficient methods, and improve the efficiency of existing
methods, of accessing plaintext of communications and electronic information." The
NET Center would be able to draw on assistance from other federal agencies, such as
the NSA, and would be able to request the secondment of staff from those agencies
to the NET Center.[806]

As with other bills, a mixed reception was afforded the proposed legislation.
Whilst the Business Software Alliance and Americans for Computer Privacy, a
recently formed advocacy group, announced their support, the Clinton administration did not.[807] EPIC had two concerns with the bill. Firstly, they believed criminalizing encryption would have negative implications, drawing on a historic precedent
EPIC's statement read:

> a typewritten ransom note poses a more difficult challenge for forensic investiga-
> tors than a handwritten note. But it would be a mistake to criminalize the use of a

---

[804] United States Senate, 1998.   [806] Ibid.
[805] Ibid.   [807] McKay, 1998, and Tech Law Journal, 1998.

typewriter simply because it could make it more difficult to investigate crime in some circumstances.[808]

EPIC also felt criminalization would send "mixed message to users and businesses—that we want people to be free to use encryption but will be suspicious when it is used."[809] Furthermore, EPIC worried about criminalization's law enforcement implications:

> a provision which criminalizes the use of encryption, even in furtherance of a crime, would give prosecutors wide latitude to investigate activity where the only indicia of criminal conduct may be the mere presence of encrypted data. In the digital age, where techniques to protect privacy and security will be widely deployed, we cannot afford to view encryption as the potential instrumentality of a crime, just as we would not today view the use of a typewriter with suspicion.[810]

EPIC's second concern was the provision allowing other federal agencies to provide the NET Center "assistance," including the secondment of staff:

> existing federal expertise in the areas of electronic surveillance and decryption resides at the National Security Agency (NSA), the bill in effect authorizes unprecedented NSA involvement in domestic law enforcement activities. Such a result would be contrary to a half-century-old consensus that intelligence agencies must be strictly constrained from engaging in domestic "police functions."[811]

EPIC's David Sobel commented, "While we support the goal of lifting [export restrictions on encryption] it should not be done at the cost of creating new domestic problems."[812] E-PRIVACY's fate was to join its comrades in the cryptography legislation graveyard, Congress was simply too polarized to act on the issue.

7.13   SUBVERTING FOREIGN GOVERNMENTS' CRYPTO

"It was the intelligence coup of the century," the CIA wrote, "Foreign governments were paying good money to the U.S. and West Germany for the privilege of having their most secret communications read."[813] Whilst this book focuses on how cryptology mediates the power relationship between citizen and state, rather than between states, one example of the latter is worthy of inclusion as it demonstrates the art of the possible with regarding the subversion of secure communications: that is the story of Crypto AG.

The Washington Post and ZDF obtained documents including a CIA history, and BND account, of the Crypto AG operation in 2020—the authenticity of these documents was not disputed by their governments. Their reporting showed a systemic

---

[808] Electronic Privacy Information Center, 1998.   [811] Ibid.
[809] Ibid.   [812] Branson, 1998.
[810] Ibid.   [813] Miller and Mueller, 2020.

global undermining of foreign nations' cryptography equipment by the American and German intelligence agencies for most of the latter part of the twentieth century.[814]

Perhaps ironically, the story starts with Russian-born Boris Hagelin, who fled to the US as the Nazis marched on Europe. Hagelin designed a cryptography machine, the M-209; the US army purchased 140,000 M-209s during the war, making Hagelin a millionaire. After the War, Hagelin developed a new device, the CX-52, American codebreakers could not break it and worried about its proliferation to foreign governments. William Friedman, who led the US Army Signals Intelligence Service, had struck up a friendship with Hagelin, and over dinner in 1951 asked Hagelin, whose company was now Switzerland-based, to restrict sales of Crypto AG's most sophisticated devices to a US list of approved countries. Other countries would receive older, less secure, Crypto AG equipment. Hagelin would be paid as much as $700,000 in compensation for lost sales. By 1960, despite internal conflict between the NSA and the CIA as to the wisdom of the scheme, a licensing agreement was in place with Hagelin which paid him $855,000 to renew the initial agreement, $70,000 a year as a retainer, and $10,000 infusions for "marketing" expenses to ensure Crypto AG— rather than its rivals—won key contracts in foreign nations. Friedman had blocked suggestions of asking Hagelin to allow NSA design input or authority into Crypto AG machines as he felt Hagelin would deem such an advance a step too far, but as mechanical encryption machines were supplanted by electronic machines this state of affairs changed.[815]

In 1967, Crypto AG marketed a new electronic encryption device, the H-460, with inner workings designed by the NSA. Rather than inserting a backdoor, or having the device leak encryption keys, the NSA architected the H-460s to be weak enough to allow their supercomputers and cryptanalysts to break the code—but they still needed to intercept the communications. Two versions of Crypto AG devices were manufactured, one secure version for US allies, the other insecure version for all others. By 1970, the CIA and the BND agreed to jointly purchase Crypto AG, a Liechtenstein law firm helped them obscure the origins of the $5.75m payment to Hagelin.[816]

By 1975, Crypto AG's revenues grew to $19 million, with 250 employees generating sales globally. In the 1980s, the initial code name of "Thesaurus" was changed to "Rubicon," (it would later change again to "Minerva") as the customer list grew to include Saudi Arabia, Iran, Italy, Indonesia, Iraq, Libya, Jordan, and South Korea. There were disagreements between the BND and the CIA; the former were often accused of focusing too much on financial profit, whilst the latter catalyzed tension as they increasingly wanted to sell Crypto AG technology to NATO allies, to which the Germans disagreed. The CIA and BND protected Crypto AG's market position by smearing rivals and bribing clients; on one occasion Saudi customers were hosted in Switzerland where their "favorite pastime was to visit the brothels, which

---

[814] Ibid.   [816] Ibid.
[815] Ibid.

the company [Crypto AG] also financed." Crypto AG's employees were well paid, but some started to develop suspicions—on one occasion an employee was fired for modifying a Syrian deployment of Crypto AG, which caused the traffic to become unreadable to NSA.[817]

Few employees knew of the true ownership and objectives of Crypto AG, and with increasing questions from the engineering department, it became necessary in 1979 to position a CIA/BND technical asset at the top of Crypto AG to tame the restive engineering team. Swedish mathematics professor Kjell-Ove Widman, a military reservist and well-known cryptologist, was installed as scientific advisor reporting directly to the CEO—his "technical prominence" could not be challenged which helped deflect questions of staff and clients alike. Widman developed a set of principles with the BND and the CIA for manipulating cryptographic algorithms; they would in the future have to be "undetectable by usual statistical tests," and when discovered, "easily masked as implementation or human errors." Widman is branded the "irreplaceable man...[the] most important recruitment in the history of the Minerva program," in the CIA history of the operation.[818]

The most severe issue in the operation's history came when Crypto AG sales-man Hans Buehler was arrested by one of their largest customers, Iran. Iran had suspicions regarding Crypto AG for several years, yet Buehler was not cognizant of the CIA-BND's relationship to the firm. Buehler commented, "I was questioned for five hours a day for nine months...I was never beaten, but I was strapped to wooden benches and told I would be beaten. I was told Crypto [AG] was a spy cen-ter."[819] It was nine months later before the BND paid a $1 million ransom to recover Buehler—the CIA refused to contribute due to their policy of not paying ransoms.[820]

In 1993, the German government's support of the operation ended—the Cold War was over and without an existential threat, a unified German government elected to have the CIA buy them out of the Crypto AG partnership for $17m. By the mid-1990s, Crypto AG was no longer profitable, software encryption was supplanting encryption machines—CIA cash infusions kept operations running.[821]

The Baltimore Sun reported on the program in 1995; whilst light on details, the report caused a series of countries including Argentina, Italy, Saudi Arabia, Egypt, and Indonesia to abandon the firm—employees also started to turn away from the company.[822]

The CIA history concludes in 2004, though the report notes, "at the turn of the cen-tury MINERVA was still alive and well." Crypto AG Swiss headquarters was sold in 2017, the next year the company's assets were divided and sold for an estimated $50–70m. The intelligence gain over almost half a century was likely significant. Some examples given by the history include the US passing intelligence to the UK during the Falkland War, 80–90% of Iran's communications being readable during its war with Iraq, and confirmation of Libya's responsibility for the 1986 bombing of a West

---

817 Ibid.
818 Ibid.
819 Shane and Bowmanthe, 1995.

820 Miller and Mueller, 2020.
821 Ibid.
822 Ibid.

German club which US soldiers frequented (two of whom were killed). During the response to the latter, Reagan's presentation of the evidence against Libya revealed the US had seen communications from Libya's Embassy in East Berlin implicating the Crypto AG machines as one source of the compromise—though his statements do not seem to have caused clients to desert the cryptography company. During the 1980s, 40% of the NSA's machine decryptions, and 90% of the BND's diplomatic reports were sourced from MINERVA. Despite many operational problems over the decades, Crypto AG "yielded a bonanza," according to the CIA history.[823]

7.14 THE TOWERS FALL

Almost everyone in the West recalls where they were on September 11, 2001, when, as Barack Obama later elegantly recalled:

> a bright September day was darkened by the worst attack on the American people in our history. The images of 9/11 are seared into our national memory—hijacked planes cutting through a cloudless September sky; the Twin Towers collapsing to the ground; black smoke billowing up from the Pentagon.[824]

Thousands died. America became bereft of a sense of security forged in the generations since it was last attacked at Pearl Harbor. The devastating assault was amplified by twenty-four-hour news outlets beaming the spectacular footage easily mistakable for a Hollywood blockbuster. It was a concomitant strike at the heart of American capitalism, culture, and military. As the toxic clouds nestling between Manhattan skyscrapers dissipated, a feeling of anxiety solidified. Americans demanded an explanation for why their extortionately expensive intelligence apparatus failed to uncover the deadly attack. The public's next question was how such cataclysmic terror could be prevented from revisiting America?

Fear and dismay were soon married with anger. Society searched for scapegoats. The wrath of some Americans fell upon cryptologists, the midwives to digital encryption technologies, the use of which was one possible explanation for the failure of intelligence agencies to intercept the hijackers' communications. PGP creator Phil Zimmermann came under scrutiny for his role in delivering cryptography to the world and consequently those who would do America harm. No evidence existed of PGP, or encryption, being used by terrorists. Zimmermann received hate mail, one anonymous author wrote, "Phil—I hope you can sleep at night with the blood of 5,000 people on your hands."[825] The author argued PGP was a "weapon of war" leveling the battlefield between "zealots" and the US.[826] Zimmermann had wept over the terrorist attacks before assessing whether he still felt comfortable advocating for cryptography, he comments:

---

[823] Ibid.
[824] Obama, 2011.
[825] Zimmermann, 2001b.
[826] Ibid.

the outcome…was the same as it was during the years of public debate, that strong cryptography does more good for a democratic society than harm, even if it can be used by terrorists…I have no regrets about developing PGP.[827]

Zimmermann added:

in these emotional times, we in the crypto community find ourselves having to defend our technology from well-intentioned but misguided efforts by politicians to impose new regulations on the use of strong cryptography.[828]

Zimmermann cautioned:

Under the present emotional pressure, if we make a rash decision to reverse such a careful decision, it will only lead to terrible mistakes that will not only hurt our democracy, but will also increase the vulnerability of our national information infrastructure.[829]

President George W. Bush declared a State of National Emergency three days after the attacks.[830] Bush's father, former President George H. Bush advised victory would require "we…free up the intelligence system from some of its constraints."[831] Cryptography soon became a constraint under scrutiny. Americans were fearful. A 2002 survey of 2519 Americans found pre-9/11 39% strongly agreed they felt safe, post-9/11 only 17% strongly agreed they felt safe.[832] 78% were willing to give up certain freedoms to gain security, and 30% favored making it easier for the government to access private communications.[833] A Princeton Survey Research Associates poll found 54% of Americans favored "reducing encryption of communications to make it easier for the FBI and CIA to monitor the activities of suspected terrorists," even if that "infringe[s] on people's privacy and affect[s] business practices."[834]

Addressing the Senate a week after the attacks, Republican Senator Judd Gregg of New Hampshire commented, "in the electronics area it is very obvious that our intelligence-gathering communities…have severe problems because of the limitations of law…placed on them."[835] Gregg argued companies using encryption should cooperate to address the access issue as, "There is no excuse for anybody to be underwriting that type of activity in our country."[836] Gregg proposed using America's economic clout to influence the encryption market:

The people making these products want to sell their products in the United States…I believe we should use the leverage of the American market as a way to say, if you are going to sell this type of equipment anywhere in the world, and you want to sell something in the United States also, you have an obligation to comply with our needs for our national security under a strict legal judicial structure.[837]

---

[827] Ibid.
[828] Ibid.
[829] Ibid.
[830] Bush, G. W., 2001a
[831] Bush, G. H., 2001b.
[832] Gallup, 2002.

[833] Ibid.
[834] Witt, 2001.
[835] United States Senate, 2001
[836] Ibid.
[837] Ibid.

Less than a month later, Gregg declared he would not seek encryption legislation, despite having initially said the opposite, but the incident was a firm post-9/11 indicator some in Congress were leaning towards legislation.[838]

Six months after 9/11, the ACLU voiced concern at the "ongoing pattern of erosion" of American civil liberties.[839] ACLU's Anthony D. Romero commented the most "disturbing change" post-9/11 was "the government's apparent dismissal of the idea that our society can and must be both safe and free."[840] ACLU were particularly concerned with new security measures which "erode and evade judicial review"; Romero commented, "Checks and balances are the cornerstone of our democracy... The Founders put the judiciary in place to protect our rights, a role they can't play if Congress explicitly forbids them from even reviewing law enforcement actions."[841] But despite the climate, encryption policy remained intact. The immediate security legislation passed post-9/11, the Uniting and Strengthening America by Providing Appropriate Tools Required to Intercept and Obstruct Terrorism (PATRIOT) Act did not address encryption, despite Congress' earlier posturing. John Gilmore comments, "The panicky public reaction to the attack of 9/11 was unable to upset the balance of relatively sane encryption policy that it had taken decades to set right."[842]

However, the criminalization of encryption was considered in the PATRIOT Act's successor, the Domestic Security Enhancement Act of 2003, which derisively became known by its opponents as PATRIOT II. A draft version of the Department of Justice-authored document, marked "confidential—not for distribution" was published online by The Center for Public Integrity in February 2003.[843] The Act stated:

Any person who, during the commission of a felony under Federal law, knowingly and willfully encrypts any incriminating communication or information relating to that felony—

1) in the case of a first offense under this section, shall be imprisoned not more than 5 years, fined under this title, or both and

2) in the case of a second or subsequent offense under this section, shall be imprisoned not more than 10 years, fined under this title, or both[844]

The encryption text was located in section 404 of the bill. 404 is a Web (HTTP) response code, or error message, meaning page/resource not found. Whether the placing of the encryption text in section 404 was a coincidence or an insider joke by the authors suggesting it was an "error" to use encryption for criminal purposes is unknown. The language is also ambiguous in that penalties apply to criminals who "knowingly or willfully" use encryption—this does not address the scenario of the user being unaware they were using encryption. The inclusion was not well received by the technology industry; the Electronic Frontier Foundation commented:

---

838 McCullagh, 2001.   842 Curtin, 2005, Forward.
839 ACLU, 2002.   843 United States Department of Justice, 2003.
840 Ibid.   844 Ibid, 58.
841 Ibid.

Just as the government encourages Americans to lock their doors and take other personal precautions against crime and terrorism, it should encourage Americans to use encryption. USAPA II steps in exactly the opposite direction...This provision creates a disincentive for Americans to protect their data and information from identity thieves, stalkers and other criminals.[845]

The legislation did not advance, though it was another indicator the government's encryption concerns persisted.

7.15 THE SECOND CRYPTO WAR: SUMMARY

The Internet does not exist in a vacuum—this is perhaps the greatest lesson of the second crypto war. Whilst John Perry Barlow declared the Internet's independence in 1996, the "old world" consistently mediated the "new world." The extent to which individuals could evade online accountability was curtailed by the lack of robust anonymity tools. Then again, most activists did not covet anonymity. The cypherpunks were among the digital world's intellectual elite—few of their order maneuvered from the shadows—in fact, in partnership with the digital rights groups, they embraced one instrument of the old world in particular: the judiciary. The administration vehemently argued their position, yet, overall the courts favored digital privacy activists. The adjudication of old laws was not supplemented by the ascent of new legislation. Congress failed: lots of debate was coupled with little action. The efficacy of existing security laws was decreasing, the digital risks to their citizens were increasing, and Congress failed to provide decisive instruction or new authorities as to how these changes should be managed by the government apparatus.

At the RSA conference in 2000, Jim Bidzos popped open a bottle of champagne on a stage he shared with NSA and Justice Department representatives—he believed the digital privacy activists were victorious in the crypto wars.[846] Bidzos' assessment was myopic and braggadocio. The reality was infinitely more complex. Aristotle once stated, "it is not enough to win a war; it is more important to organize the peace"; by this measure, all parties were in dereliction of duty. The government was unreconciled to the new normal—the uneasy peace could not endure. The primary failing of the digital privacy activists was their belief technology alone could regulate the Internet. Bruce Schneier reflected on his Applied Cryptography book of 1993:

I described a mathematical utopia: algorithms that would keep your deepest secrets safe for millennia...In my vision cryptography was the great technological equalizer; anyone...could have the same security as the largest government...two years later, I went so far as to write: "It is insufficient to protect ourselves with laws; we need to protect ourselves with mathematics."

It's just not true. Cryptography can't do any of that...

Cryptography is a branch of mathematics...it involves numbers, equations, and logic.

---

[845] Electronic Frontier Foundation, 2003.   [846] Levy, 2001.

Security...involves people...Digital security involves...complex, unstable, buggy computers.

Mathematics is perfect; reality is subjective. Mathematics is defined; computers are ornery. Mathematics is logical; people are erratic, capricious, and barely comprehensible...

I didn't talk at all about the context...I was pretty naïve.[847]

Schneier concludes, "If you think technology can solve your security problems, then you don't understand the problems and you don't understand the technology."[848]

As the twenty-first century crested, the first digital natives were born, those citizens knowing nothing other than an Internet-infused world, an environment where distinction between the "real" and "digital" worlds was anachronistic: Humanity was increasingly being shaped by technology, and the governance of technology remained a societal ineptitude.

REFERENCES

ARTICLES

Huler, S. (1991). Nurturing Science's Young Elite: Westinghouse Talent Search. *The Scientist* **5**(8), 20.

Lai X. and Massey, J. L. (1990). A Proposal for a New Block Encryption Standard. *Lecture Notes in Computer Science*, **473**. 389–404.

Scarselli, G. J. (2007). Tribute to Professor Peter Junger. *Case Western Reserve Law Review*, **58**(2), 325–331.

Zimmermann, P. (1986). A Proposed Standard Format for RSA Cryptosystems. *Computer* **19**(9), 21–34.

BOOKS

Greenberg, A. (2012). *This Machine Kills Secrets: How Wikileakers, Cypherpunks, and Hacktivists Aim to Free the World's Information* (New York: Random House).

Levy, S. (2001). *Crypto: Secrecy and Privacy in the New Cold War* (New York: Viking Penguin).

Martin, K. (2020). *Cryptography: The Key to Digital Security, How It Works, and Why It Matters.* (New York: W.W. Norton).

National Research Council. (1996). *Cryptography's Role in Securing the Information Society* (Washington, DC: The National Academies Press).

Schneier, B. (1993). *Applied Cryptography Protocols, Algorithms, and Source Code in C.* (New York: John Wiley & Sons).

Schneier, B. (1995). *Applied Cryptography Protocols, Algorithms, and Source Code in C. 2nd Edition.* (New York: John Wiley & Sons).

---

[847] Schneier, 2000.   [848] Ibid.

CHAPTERS IN BOOKS

Freeh, L. J. (1994). Speech of Louis J. Freeh, Director Federal Bureau of Investigations at the American Law Institute, May 19 1994. In *The Electronic Privacy Papers: Documents on the Battle for Privacy in the Age of Surveillance*. Edited by Schneier, B. and Banisar, D. (New York: John Wiley & Sons Inc.), 124–134.

Levy, S. (1994a). The Cypherpunks vs. Uncle Sam. In *Building in Big Brother: The Cryptographic Policy Debate*. Edited by Hoffman, L. J. (New York: Springer-Verlag), 262–283.

United States Department of Justice. (1994). Report on Applications for Orders Authorizing or Approving the Interception of Wire, Oral, or Electronic Communications. In *The Electronic Privacy Papers: Documents on the Battle for Privacy in the Age of Surveillance*. Edited by Schneier, B. and Banisar, D. (New York: John Wiley & Sons Inc.), 10–25.

CYPHERPUNKS' ARCHIVE AND ARCHIVAL POSTS

Abelson, H. (1996). "m0udsPo-000G1BC@htp.ai.mit.edu." MessageID: "MIT harassed over publication of PGP book." July 10, 1996.

Anonymous Poster. (1993). "Further PGP Security Doubts." Message ID: "199308261827. AA25477@xtropia." April 26, 2019.

Arachelian, A. R. (1994). "Censorship in Cyberspace 5/6." MessageID: "9411302012. AA01012@photon.poly.edu." November 30, 1994.

Attila (alias). (1995). "Re: REMINDER: SF Federal Building, Oct 20, 1015AM: Bernstein case." MessageID: "Pine.BSD.3.91.951019133453.8166A-100000@usr2.primenet. com." October 19, 1995.

Attila (alias). (1996). "Selling your sole to DOJ ...err, devil Zimmermann?" MessageID: "199608300621.AAA29460@InfoWest.COM." August 30, 1996.

Bainter, M. (1996). "PGP backdoor? (No, I'm not paranoid.)." MessageID: "3134C779.7C84@ adspp.com." February 29, 1996.

Banisar, D. (1996). "ACM/IEEE Letter on Crypto." MessageID: "n1383746530.3760@epic. org." April 2, 1996.

Bell, J. (1996a). "Re: Can the inevitability of Software privacy be used to defeat the ITAR?" MessageID: "199607112332.QAA09668@mail.pacifier.com." July 12, 1996.

Bell, J. (1996c). "Re: Dorothy Denning attacks Leahy's crypto bill." MessageID: "m0tzIxu-0008yqC@pacifier.com." March 20, 1996.

Bell, J. (1996d). "Re: CDT Policy Post 2.19—27 Reps Urge President to Abandon Key-Escrow Encryption Policy." MessageID: "199605181744.KAA10141@newmail.paci fier.com." May 19, 1996.

Blaze, M. (1996). "My letter to Leahy supporting the crypto bill." MessageID: "199603051509. KAA27596@crypto.com." March 5, 1996.

Braddock, C. A. (1995). "(fwd) Re: Phil Zimmermann." MessageID: "53ae08506afed0671ca 88cb1b531a06e@NO-ID-FOUND.mhonarc.org." January 7, 1995.

Broiles, G. (1996). "Reflections on the Bernstein ruling." MessageID: "3.0.32.199612202345 18.006a1ef4@law.uoregon.edu." December 20, 1996.

Broiles, G. (1997). "Re: The Pro-CODE Bill could make things worse!." MessageID: "3.0. 32.19970306211056.006e7930@mail.io.com." March 6, 1997.

Broiles, G. (1997b). "Kerrey bill introduced in Senate." MessageID: "3.0.2.32.1997061714 4146.009656c0@mail.io.com." June 18, 1997.

Carp, E. (1996). "Re: Zimmermann case is dropped." MessageID: "199601120100.TAA023 04@dal1820.computek.ne." January 12, 1996.

Deviant, the [alias]. (1996). "Re: Bernstein (export laws unconstitutional) decision update."
MessageID: "Pine.LNX.3.95.961221074912.234A-100000@batcave.intrex.net."
December 20, 1996.

Dubois, P. (1995). "Zimmermann." MessageID: "199502072300.AA20868@teal.csn.org."
February 7, 1995.

Dubois, P. (1996a). "Zimmermann Legal Defense Fraud." MessageID: "199602070236.
TAA13753@teal.csn.net." February 7, 1996.

Dubois, P. (1996b). "News Release." MessageID: "199601130542.WAA06898@teal.csn.net."
January 13, 1996.

Duvos, M. (1996). "Re: Zimmermann case is dropped." MessageID: "199601112225.OAA173
91@netcom23.netcom.com." January 12, 1996.

Finerty, P. (1996). "Re: BIG NEWS: PRZ investigation dropped!" MessageID: "pine.LNX.
3.91.960111133332.1141I-100000@zifi.genetics.utah.edu." January 11, 1996.

Finney, H. (1994). "Re: Programming languages debate." MessageID: "199404260345.U
AA04412@jobe.shell.portal.com." April 25, 1994.

Finney, H. (1996). "Re: Disclosure of Public Knowledge to Foreigners." MessageID: "1996
04031545.HAA12637@jobe.shell.portal.com." April 4, 1996.

Frantz, B. (1996). "Re: more RANTING about NSA-friendly cpunks." Message ID: "1996
01282130.NAA29294@netcom6.netcom.com." January 29, 1996.

Frissell, D. (1996). "Re: SS Obergruppenfuhrer Zimmermann (NOT!)" MessageID: "2.2.
32.19960124014532.0095ac74@panix.com." January 24, 1996.

Gerck, E. (1998). "RE: Junger et al." MessageID: "pine.LNX.3.95.980707003846.742Q-10
0000@laser.cps.softex.br." July 6, 1998.

Gillogly, J. (1996). "Encrypted Communications Privacy Act." MessageID: "199602270007.
QAA08147@mycroft.rand.org." February 27, 1996.

Gilmore, J. (1995a). "Oct 20th SF C'punks meeting: at the ITAR Constitutional trial court."
MessageID: "9510032330.AA11251@toad.com." October 3, 1995.

Gilmore, J. (1995b). "REMINDER: SF Federal Building, 20 October 1995, 1015AM:
Bernstein case." MessageID: "9510190245.AA20897@toad.com." October 18, 1995.

Gilmore, J. (1996a). "PGP source code book sold out!" MessageID: "9602272119.AA08088@
toad.com." February 28, 1996.

Gilmore, J. (1996b). "SF area: Bernstein victory beach volleyball party, this Sunday."
MessageID: "199604302019.NAA11079@toad.com." May 1, 1996.

Gilmore, J. (1996c). "Bernstein hearing, Nov 8, 10:30AM: injunction against export controls."
MessageID: "199611020127.RAA01285@toad.com." November 1, 1996.

Gilmore, J. (1997). "URGENT: Fri 10 Jan 9:30AM Wash, DC: Karn appeals, come to the
hearing!" MessageID: "199701082255.OAA20606@toad.com." January 8, 1997.

Hallam-Baker, P. (1996). "Re: Zimmermann case is dropped." MessageID: "9601112236.
AA04283@zorch.w3.org." January 12, 1996.

Hortmann, M. (1995). "new source of PGP sourcecode." MessageID: "199509221554.R
AA22108@bettina.informatik.uni-Bremen.de." September 22, 1995.

Hua, E. (1998a). "RE: Junger et al." MessageID: "413AC08141DBD011A58000A0C924A
6D52C359A@mvs2.teralogic-inc.com." July 6, 1998.

Hua, E. (1998b). "RE: Junger et al." MessageID: "413AC08141DBD011A58000A0C924A
6D52C359C@mvs2.teralogic-inc.com." July 6, 1998.

Junger, P. D. (1996a). "Executive order on crypto." MessageID: "199611160154.UAA23706@
pdj2-ra.F-REMOTE.CWRU.Edu." November 15, 1995.

Junger, P. D. (1996b). "A lengthy preliminary analysis of the Leahy bill." MessageID: "m0tw
BMF-0004L1C@pdj2-ra.F-REMOTE.CWRU.Edu." March 12, 1996.

Karn, P. (1993). "Re: purloined letter." MessageID: "9301051802.AA17738@servo." January
5, 1993.

Karn, P. (1994e). "WSJ editorial email or fax?" MessageID: "199404290519.WAA13283@se rvo.qualcomm.com." April 28, 1994.

Karn, P. (1994f). "Re: Schneier's source code." MessageID: "199404271805.LAA07284@se rvo.qualcomm.com." April 29, 1994.

Machiavelli, N. (Prince) [alias]. (1994). "Phil's Plight." MessageID: "199412280403. UAA22893@infinity.c2.org." December 27, 1994.

May, T. C. (1992). "The Crypto Singularity." MessageID: "9211130018.AA11046@netcom. netcom.com." November 12, 1992.

May, T. C. (1993b). "Re: No Compromise in Defense of Our Privacy Rights. PGP FIRST!" MessageID: "9304300247.AA09058@netcom.netcom.com." April 29, 1993.

May, T. C. (1996a). "Re: Zimmermann case is dropped." MessageID: "ad1aff2216021004007 f@[205.199.118.202]." January 12, 1996.

May, T. C. (1997). "SAFE Bill is a Disaster—'Use a cipher, go to prison.'" MessageID: "199705010008.RAA29286@you.got.net." May 1, 1997.

Nuri, V. (1996). "Re: more RANTING about NSA-friendly cpunks." MessageID: "199601290 535.VAA08104@netcom8.netcom.com." January 30, 1996.

Nuri, V. (1997). "Re: Stewart Baker on Bernstein encryption decision (fwd)." MessageID: "199708261910.MAA04330@netcom3.netcom.com." August 27, 1997.

Palacios, B. (1996). "No Subject." MessageID: "v02130505ad622688ad73@[204.157.127.16]. " March 6, 1996.

Parekh, S. (1996). "Re: Zimmermann case is dropped." MessageID: "199601112329. PAA15617@infinity.c2.org." January 12, 1996.

Pierson, M. (1997). "Maneuvering [sic] the Instruments of Control Through Deception." MessageID: "199706051125.GAA07090@vcspucci.iquest.com." June 5, 1997.

Sandfort, S. (1995). "Re: Modern Journalism (was: All about Bernstein)." MessageID: "pine .SUN.3.91.950826151407.6069A-100000@crl7.crl.com." August 26, 1995.

Snyder, B. (1994). "Re: Applied Cryptography." MessageID: "199404302219.SAA01323@du nx1.ocs.drexel.edu." April 30, 1994.

Software Publishers Association (Press Release 4 June 1993), Posted by Mulivor, P. (1993). "SPA Press Release." MessageID: "9306061624.AA09694@relay2.UU.NET." June 4, 1993.

Stewart, B. (1996). "Re: Zimmermann case is dropped." MessageID: "199601120811.A AA25133@ix11.ix.netcom.com." January 13, 1996.

Strasheim, A. (1996). "Re: Zimmermann case is dropped." MessageID: "199601120205. UAA02271@proust.suba.com." January 11, 1996.

Strasheim, A. (1996b). "Re: Zimmermann case is dropped." MessageID: "199601121722. LAA04179@proust.suba.com." January 11, 1996.

Strasheim, A. (1996c). "Re: SS Obergruppenfuhrer Zimmermann (NOT!)." MessageID: "199601240015.SAA03590@proust.suba.com." January 24, 1996.

Toto [alias]. (1997). "Re: Pro-CODE Crypto Bill." MessageID: "331A4CB4.6206@ sk.sympatico.ca." March 2, 1997.

Voters Telecommunications Watch. (1996). "(INFO) Leahy/Goodlatte introduce crypto bill." MessageID: "199603051717.MAA13628@panix3.panix.com." March 6, 1996.

Young, J. (1996). "Re: Bernstein case decisision (fwd)." MessageID: "199604171634.M AA26903@pipe3.nyc.pipeline.com." April 18, 1996.

Zimmermann, P. (1993b) "Need Consulting Work." MessageID: "9306170107.AA05669@ columbine.cgd.ucar.EDU." June 16, 1993.

Zimmermann, P. (1993c). "Statement from Zimmermann on PGP investigation." MessageID: "9309191832.AA24906@columbine.cgd.ucar.EDU." September 19, 1993.

Zimmermann, P. (1993d). "Coming Soon: Commercial version of PGP!" MessageID: "9308 250853.AA06179@columbine.cgd.ucar.EDU." August 25, 1993.

Zimmermann, P. (1994a). "Herbert S. Zim dies." MessageID: "m0rHJIa-0002MZC@maalox.ppgs.com." December 12, 1994.

Zimmermann, P. (1994c). "Zimmermann Statement on PGP 2.6." MessageID: "9405290539.AA24788@columbine.cgd.ucar.EDU." May 28, 1994.

Zimmermann, P. (1994d). "January meeting with Zimmermann's prosecutor." MessageID: "m0rNcLy-0002IJC@maalox.ppgs.com." December 30, 1994.

Zimmermann, P. (1994e). "Positive uses for PGP." MessageID: "9404030811.AA03068@columbine.cgd.ucar.EDU." April 3, 1994.

Zimmermann, P. (1994f). "RE: PGP 1.5." MessageID: "9405130620.AA09814@columbine.cgd.ucar.EDU." May 12, 1994.

Zimmermann, P. (1994g). "Zimmermann on PGP 2.6 myths." MessageID: "9408180644.AA16037@columbine.cgd.ucar.EDU." August 27, 1994.

Zimmermann, P. (1996b). "Zimmermann case is dropped." MessageID: "199601081035.KAA02532@maalox." January 12, 1996.

United States Attorney, Posted by McCullagh, D. (1996). "US DoK Zimmermann Press Release." January 12, 1996.

White, G. (1993). "PGP Customs investigation." MessageID: "9302132122.AA13118@nexsys.nexsys.net." February 13, 1993.

INTERVIEWS AND CORRESPONDENCE BY AUTHOR

Schneier, B. (2020). Correspondence with Author, June 8, 2020.

MISCELLANEOUS

Moss, J. (2019). *Blackhat Security Conference Opening Remarks, 7 August 2019.* Author in attendance.

NEWSPAPER ARTICLES

Bulkeley, W. M. (1996). Cryptographer Zimmermann Is Told By U.S. That Investigation Is Over, *The Wall Street Journal*, January 15, p. 5.

Chrysler. (1994). 1995 Chrysler Awards, *The New York Times*, p. A9.

Dexheimer, E. (1993). Secrets Agent, *Denver Westword*, September 29, p. 12.

Greenhouse, S. (1991). U.S. and Allies Move to Ease Cold War Limits on Exports, *New York Times*, May 25, p. 1. Available: https://www.nytimes.com/1991/05/25/business/us-and-allies-move-to-ease-cold-war-limits-on-exports.html [Accessed March 14, 2019].

Harrington, M. (1996). Cyber Rebel, *Denver Post Sunday*, March 3, Empire Section.

Schneier, B. (1999). *New U.S. Export Rules and Anti-Privacy Encryption Legislation.* 15 October 1999. Available: https://www.schneier.com/crypto-gram/archives/1999/1015.html#NewUSExportRulesandAnti-PrivacyEncryptionLegislation [Accessed May 27, 2019].

Schwartz, J. (1995). Privacy Program: An On-Line Weapon?, *Washington Post*, April 3, p. A01. Available: https://www.washingtonpost.com/archive/politics/1995/04/03/privacy-program-an-on-line-weapon/3d61a997-0b28-49e8-9ac3-47b541ef16b6/[Accessed April 10, 2019].

Shane, S. and Bowman, T. (1995). No Such Agency Part Four: Rigging the Game. *The Baltimore Sun*, December 4, pp. 9–11.

Steinert-Threlkeld, T. (1994). Cryptography Tests Rights of Electronic Word. *Dallas Morning News*, July 23, p. 5F.

Wade, N. (1994). Method and Madness, *New York Times*, September 4, p. 23.

WEBSITES

ACLU. (2002). *On Eve of Sixth-Month Anniversary of September 11th, ACLU Says Terrorist Attacks Have Changed American Law, Society.* Available: https://web.archive.org/web/20020613030841/https://www.aclu.org/news/2002/n030802c.html [Accessed January 16, 2020].

American Civil Liberties Union, Electronic Frontier Foundation, and Electronic Privacy Information Center. (2000). *Civil Liberties Groups Say New Encryption Export Regulations Still Have Serious Constitutional Deficiencies.* Available: https://www.acl u.org/press-releases/civil-liberties-groups-say-new-encryption-export-regulations-sti ll-have-serious?redirect=news/civil-liberties-groups-say-new-encryption-export-regul ations-still-have-serious-constitutional [Accessed July 9, 2019].

American Civil Liberties Union. (2000). *In Legal First, Federal Appeals Court is Unanimous: First Amendment Applied to Programming Code.* Available: https://www.aclu.org/press-releases/legal-first-federal-appeals-court-unanimous-first-amendment-applies-p rogramming-code [Accessed August 2, 2019].

Atkins, D. (n.d.). *Resume.* Available: http://www.mit.edu/people/warlord/resume.pdf [Accessed April 21, 2020].

Barlow, J. P. (1995). *Foreword: A Pretty Bad Problem.* Available: https://philzimmermann.co m/EN/essays/index.html [Accessed June 25, 2020].

Bass, K., Hunger, F. W, Holder, E. H., Coppolino, A. J., and Garvey, V. M. (1997). *Stipulation and Proposed Scheduling Order.* Available: https://web.archive.org/web/199901281720 06/http://people.qualcomm.com/karn/export/stip.html [Accessed May 26, 2019].

Bass, K. and Cooper, T. J. (1994). *Letter from Kenneth C. Bass and Thomas J. Cooper to Thomas E. McNamara of 5 December 1994.* Available: https://web.archive.org/w eb/19981202214652/http://people.qualcomm.com/karn/export/mcnamara-appeal.html [Accessed May 24, 2019].

Bass, K. and Cooper, T. J. (1995a). *Letter from Kenneth C. Bass and Thomas J. Cooper to Thomas E. McNamara of 28 April.* Available: https://web.archive.org/web/1998120 3000445/http://people.qualcomm.com/karn/export/mcnamara-letter.html [Accessed May 24, 2019].

Bass, K. and Cooper, T. J. (1995b). *Letter from Kenneth C. Bass and Thomas J. Cooper to Thomas E. McNamara of 19 July.* Available: https://web.archive.org/web/19990127211839/http://pe ople.qualcomm.com/karn/export/mcnamara-letter2.html [Accessed May 24, 2019].

Bass, K. and Cooper, T. J. (1995c). *United States District Court for the District of Colombia: Philip R. Karn Jr. Complaint.* Available: https://web.archive.org/web/199902221543 31/http://people.qualcomm.com/karn/export/complaint.html [Accessed May 25, 2019].

Bass, K. and Cooper, T. J. (1995d). *Plaintiff's Opposition to Defendants' Motion to Dismiss or, in the Alternative, for Summary Judgment.* Available: https://web.archive.org/web/20000817000056/http://people.qualcomm.com/karn/export/karnresp.html [Accessed May 25, 2019].

Bass, K. and Cooper, T. J. (1995e) *Plaintiff's Supplemental Memorandum in Opposition to Defendants Motion to Dismiss or, in the Alternative, for Summary Judgment.* Available: https://web.archive.org/web/19990128113934/http://people.qualcomm.com/ karn/export/response.html [Accessed May 26, 2019].

Bass, K. and Cooper, T. J. (1996a). *Notice of Appeal.* Available: https://web.archive.org/w eb/19990221152741/http://people.qualcomm.com/karn/export/appeal_notice.html [Accessed May 26, 2019].

Bass, K. and Cooper, T. J. (1996b). *Brief of the Appellant Phillip R. Karn JR.* Available: https ://web.archive.org/web/20000817000207/http://people.qualcomm.com/karn/export/ karnbrf.html [Accessed May 26, 2019].

Bass, K. and Cooper, T. J. (1998). *Amended Complaint*. Available: https://web.archive.org/w eb/19990221131311/http://people.qualcomm.com/karn/export/amended_complaint.ht ml [Accessed May 27, 2019].

Bass, K. and Cooper, T. J. (1998b). *Plaintiff's Memorandum in Opposition to Defendants' Motion to Dismiss or for Summary Judgment and in Support of Plaintiff's Cross-Motion for Partial Summary Judgment*. Available: https://web.archive.org/web/20 001202140400/http://people.qualcomm.com/karn/export/oppos.html [Accessed May 26, 2019].

Bernstein, D. (1992). *Letter from Daniel Bernstein to the Department of State, 30 June 1992*. Available: https://cr.yp.to/export/1992/0630-bernstein.txt [Accessed June 2, 2019].

Bernstein, D. (1993a). *Letter from Daniel Bernstein to William B. Robinson, Department of State, 19 March 1993*. Available: https://cr.yp.to/export/1993/0319-bernstein.txt [Accessed June 2, 2019].

Bernstein, D. (1993b). *Letter from Daniel Bernstein to William B. Robinson, Department of State, 2 April 1993*. Available: https://cr.yp.to/export/1993/0402-bernstein.txt [Accessed June 4, 2019].

Bernstein, D. (1993c). *Letter from Daniel Bernstein to Andrew Henderson, 20 May 1993*. Available: https://cr.yp.to/export/1993/0520-bernstein.txt [Accessed June 3, 2019].

Bernstein, D. (1993d). *Letter from Daniel Bernstein to William B. Robinson, Director, Office of Defence Trade Controls, Bureau of Politico-Military Affairs, 30 June 1993*. Available: https://cr.yp.to/export/1993/0630-bernstein.txt [Accessed June 2, 2019].

Bernstein, D. (1993e). *Letter from Daniel Bernstein to Andrew Henderson, 14 July 1993*. Available: https://cr.yp.to/export/1993/0714-bernstein.txt [Accessed June 2, 2019].

Bernstein, D. (1993f). *Letter from Daniel Bernstein to Office of Defence Trade Controls, U.S. Department of State, 15 July 1993*. Available: https://cr.yp.to/export/1993/0715-bernst ein.txt [Accessed June 4, 2019].

Bernstein, D. (1993g). *Post to Sci.Crypt Newsgroup, 30 July 1993*. Available: https://cr.yp.to/ export/1993/0730-bernstein.txt [Accessed June 2, 2019].

Bernstein, D. (1993h). *Letter from Daniel Bernstein to William B. Robinson, Director, Office of Defence Trade Controls, Bureau of Politico-Military Affairs, 20 September 1993*. Available: https://cr.yp.to/export/1993/0920-bernstein.txt [Accessed June 2, 2019].

Bernstein, D. (1993i). *Letter from Daniel Bernstein to William B. Robinson, Director, Office of Defence Trade Controls, Bureau of Politico-Military Affairs, 21 September 1993*. Available: https://cr.yp.to/export/1993/0921-bernstein.txt [Accessed June 2, 2019].

Bernstein, D. (1993j). *Letter from Daniel Bernstein to Ambassador Michael Newlin, Acting Director Center for Defense Trade, Department of State*, 22 September 1993. Available: https://cr.yp.to/export/1993/0922-bernstein.txt [Accessed June 2, 2019].

Bernstein, D. (1996). *Declaration of Daniel J. Bernstein: Daniel J. Bernstein v. United States Department of State et al*. Available: https://cr.yp.to/export/1996/0726-bernstein.txt [Accessed June 9, 2019].

Bernstein, D. (1996b). *Declaration of Daniel J. Bernstein in Support of Plaintiff's Motion for Preliminary Injunction: Daniel J. Bernstein v. United States Department of State*. Available: https://cr.yp.to/export/1996/1004-bernstein.txt [Accessed June 9, 2019].

Bernstein, D. and Ray, C. (1993). *Excerpts from Conversation between Daniel Bernstein and Charles Ray, State Department*. Available: https://cr.yp.to/export/1993/0326-transcript.txt [Accessed June 2, 2019].

Bernstein, D. (2008). *Curriculum Vitae*. Available: https://cr.yp.to/cv/cv-20080915.pdf [Accessed July 12, 2019].

Branson, A. (1998). *Senators Float New Encryption Bill*. Available: https://www.washingt onpost.com/wp-srv/politics/special/encryption/stories/ls051298.htm   [Accessed November 29, 2019].

Bromberg, C. (1991). *In Defense of Hackers.* Available: https://www.nytimes.com/1991/0 4/21/magazine/in-defense-of-hackers.html [Accessed July 14, 2019].

Bulkeley, W. M. (1994). *Cipher Probe: Popularity Overseas of Encryption Code Has the U.S. Worried.* Available: https://www.burmalibrary.org/reg.burma/archives/199405/msg00 012.html [Accessed May 29, 2020].

Burns, C. (1996a). *Floor Statement by Senator Conrad Burns Introduction of "Pro-CODE" bill May 2, 1996.* Available: https://www.epic.org/crypto/legislation/burns_floor.html [Accessed May 22, 2019].

Burns, C. (1996b). *Open Letter to the Internet Community.* Available: https://www.epic.org/ crypto/legislation/burns_letter.html [Accessed May 22, 2019].

Bush, G. H. (2001a). *Text: Former President George Bush.* Available: https://www.washingtonpos t.com/wp-srv/nation/transcripts/bushsrtext_091301.html [Accessed January 25, 2020].

Bush, G. W. (2001b). *Declaration of National Emergency by Reason of Certain Terrorist Attacks.* Available: https://georgewbush-whitehouse.archives.gov/news/releases/20 01/09/20010914-4.html [Accessed January 25, 2020].

Caruso, D. (1996). *The Key Issue for the Net Is Not the Smut, It Is the Use of Encryption.* Available: https://www.nytimes.com/1996/03/25/business/technology-digital-commerc e-key-issue-for-net-not-smut-it-use-encryption.html [Accessed November 27, 2019].

Cassidy, P. (1996). *Reluctant Hero.* Available: https://www.wired.com/1996/06/esbernstein/ [Accessed July 15, 2019].

C-Span. (1991). *Senate Session.* Available: https://www.c-span.org/video/?15912-1/senate-session&start=16444 [Accessed February 17, 2019].

CNET. (1998). *Professor Loses Crypto Case.* Available: https://www.cnet.com/news/prof essor-loses-crypto-case/ [Accessed August 3, 2019].

Cohn, C. A. (1995a). *Daniel J. Bernstein v. United States Department of State et al.* Available: https://cr.yp.to/export/1995/0221-cohn.txt [Accessed June 6, 2019].

Cohn, C. A. (1995b). *Plaintiff's Opposition to Motion to Dismiss: Daniel J. Bernstein v. United States Department of State et al.* Available: https://cr.yp.to/export/1995/0922-c ohn-1.txt [Accessed June 6, 2019].

Cohn, C. A. (1996a). *Plaintiff's Memorandum of Points and Authorities in Support of Motion for Partial Summary Judgment and/or Summary Adjudication of Issues: Daniel J. Bernstein v. United States Department of State et al.* Available: https://cr.yp.to/export/1 996/0726-cohn-2.txt [Accessed June 9, 2019].

Cohn, C. A. (1996b). *Plaintiff's Opposition to Defendant's Motion for Summary Judgment: Daniel J. Bernstein v. United States Department of State et al.* Available: https://cr.yp.t o/export/1996/0830-cohn.txt [Accessed June 9, 2019].

Cohn, C. A. (1996c). *Motion for Preliminary Injunction: Daniel J. Bernstein v. United States Department of State et al.* Available: https://cr.yp.to/export/1996/1004-cohn-1.txt [Accessed June 12, 2019].

Cohn, C. A. (1996d). *Plaintiff's Memorandum of Points and Authorities in Support of Motion for Preliminary Injunction: Daniel J. Bernstein v. United States Department of State.* Available: https://cr.yp.to/export/docs.html [Accessed June 9, 2019].

Cohn, C. A. (1998a). *Testimony of Cindy A Cohn. before the Senate Judiciary Committee's Subcommittee on Constitution, Federalism and Property Rights on Tuesday, 17 March 1998.* Available: https://cr.yp.to/export/1998/0317-cohn.txt [Accessed July 14, 2019].

Cohn, C. A. (1998b). *Correspondence to bernstein-announce@toad.com from Cindy Cohn, 14 July 1998.* Available: https://cryptome.org/jya/pdj13.htm [Accessed August 3, 2019].

Cohn, C. A. (2000a). *Correspondence to James Lewis, Office of Strategic Trade and Foreign Policy Controls, Bureau of Export Administration, Department of Commerce, 16 January 2000.* Available: https://cr.yp.to/export/2000/0116-cohn.html [Accessed July 10, 2019].

Cohn, C. A. (2000b). *Correspondence to Ms. Cathy Catterson, Clerk, United States Court of Appeals for the Ninth Circuit, 3 March 2000.* Available: https://cr.yp.to/export/2000/0 303-cohn.html [Accessed July 10, 2019].

Cohn, C. A. and Tien, L. (2002). *Daniel J. Bernstein v. United States Department of Commerce: Plaintiff's Second Supplemental Complaint.* Available: https://cr.yp.to/exp ort/2002/0107-winter.html [Accessed July 11, 2019].

Computer Professionals For Social Responsibility. (1991). *Winter_Spring1991.txt.* Available: http://cpsr.org/prevsite/publications/newsletters/old/1990s/Winter_Spring1991.txt/ [Accessed February 23, 2019].

Computer Professionals for Social Responsibility. (2008). *About CPSR.* Available: http://cpsr. org/about/ [Accessed April 4, 2019].

Coppolino, A. J. (1995). *Bernstein v. United States Department of State et al.* Available: https ://cr.yp.to/export/1995/0504-coppolino.txt [Accessed June 6, 2019].

Corcoran, E. (1998). *U.S. to Ease Limits on Export of Data-Scrambling Technology.* Available: http://www.washingtonpost.com/wp-srv/WPlate/1998-07/07/0641-07079 8-idx.html [Accessed August 3, 2019].

Cromwell, W. P. (1995). *Declaration of William P. Cromwell.* Available: https://web.arc hive.org/web/19990222173228/http://people.qualcomm.com/karn/export/crowell.html [Accessed May 25, 2019].

Curtin, M. (2005). *Brute Force: Cracking the Data Encryption Standard.* (New York: Copernicus Books).

Cypherpunks. (1992–1998). *Cypherpunks Mail List Archive 1992–1998.* Available: https:// lists.cpunks.org/pipermail/cypherpunks/2013-September/000741.html [Accessed July 10, 2015].

Daley, W. M. (1998). *Remarks to the Bureau of Export Administration's 1998 Update Conference, 7 July 1998.* Available: https://cryptome.org/jya/daley-expo.htm [Accessed August 3, 2019].

Dam, K. (1997). *Kenneth Dam (Chair of the NRC Study), Letter to the Senate Judiciary Committee.* Available: http://groups.csail.mit.edu/mac/classes/6.805/articles/crypto/ short-pieces-1997/dam-july-9.txt [Accessed June 7, 2020].

Diffie, W., and Landau, S. (2005). *The Export of Cryptography in the 20th Century and the 21st.* Available: https://privacyink.org/pdf/export_control.pdf [Accessed July 17, 2019].

Electronic Frontier Foundation. (n.d.). *A History of Protecting Freedom Where Law and Technology Collide.* Available: https://www.eff.org/about/history [Accessed April 4, 2019].

Electronic Frontier Foundation. (1991a). *Effector Online Volume 1 Issue 6.* Available: https:// www.eff.org/effector/1/6 [Accessed February 19, 2019].

Electronic Frontier Foundation. (1991b). *Effector Online Volume 1 Issue 7.* Available: https:// www.eff.org/effector/1/7 [Accessed February 19, 2019].

Electronic Frontier Foundation. (1993). *Effector Online Volume 6 Issue 2.* Available: https:// www.eff.org/effector/6/2 [Accessed April 28, 2019].

Electronic Frontier Foundation. (1994). *Effector Online Volume 7 Issue 5.* Available: https:// www.eff.org/effector/7/5 [Accessed November 2, 2019].

Electronic Frontier Foundation. (1995). *EFF Sues to Overturn Cryptography Restrictions.* Available: https://www.eff.org/press/archives/2008/04/21-42 [Accessed June 5, 2019].

Electronic Frontier Foundation. (1996a). *Federal Court Denies Government's Motion to Dismiss Bernstein Case, Acknowledges Source Code as Speech.* Available: https://ww w.eff.org/press/archives/2008/04/21-40 [Accessed June 7, 2019].

Electronic Frontier Foundation. (1996b). *Court Declares Crypto Restrictions Unconstitutional.* Available: https://www.eff.org/press/archives/2008/04/21-37 [Accessed June 9, 2019].

Electronic Frontier Foundation. (1996c). *Professor Asks for Constitutional Review of New Encryption Regulations.* Available: https://www.eff.org/press/archives/2008/04/21-36 [Accessed June 16, 2019].

Electronic Frontier Foundation. (1996d). *Effector Online Volume 9 Issue 3.* Available: https://www.eff.org/effector/9/3 [Accessed November 27, 2019].

Electronic Frontier Foundation. (1997a). *Effector Online Volume 10 Issue 1.* Available: https://www.eff.org/effector/10/1 [Accessed May 26, 2019].

Electronic Frontier Foundation. (1997b). *Crypto Export Restrictions are Unconstitutional.* Available: https://cr.yp.to/export/1997/0826-eff.txt [Accessed June 30, 2019].

Electronic Frontier Foundation. (1997c). *Court Allows Unlicensed Crypto Export.* Available: https://cr.yp.to/export/1997/0829-eff.txt [Accessed July 1, 2019].

Electronic Frontier Foundation. (1997d). *US Export Control Laws on Encryption Ruled Unconstitutional.* Available: https://cr.yp.to/export/1999/0507-eff.txt [Accessed July 5, 2019].

Electronic Frontier Foundation. (1997e). *Effector Online Volume 10 Issue 10.* Available: https://www.eff.org/effector/10/10 [Accessed November 26, 2019].

Electronic Frontier Foundation. (1999). *DOJ Seeks Rehearing of Landmark Ruling in Bernstein Encryption Case.* Available: https://www.eff.org/press/archives/2008/04/21 -27 [Accessed July 9, 2019].

Electronic Frontier Foundation. (2002). *Professor Pushes for Revised Encryption Regulations.* Available: https://www.eff.org/press/archives/2008/04/21-24 [Accessed July 10, 2019].

Electronic Frontier Foundation. (2003). *EFF Analysis of "Patriot II," Provisions of the Domestic Security Enhancement Act of 2003 that Impact the Internet and Surveillance.* Available: https://web.archive.org/web/20080116033319/http://w2.eff.org/Censorship/ Terrorism_militias/patriot-act-II-analysis.php [Accessed February 1, 2020].

Electronic Privacy Information Center. (1998). *EPIC Preliminary Analysis of E-PRIVACY Encryption Bill.* Available: https://epic.org/crypto/legislation/epriv_analysis.html [Accessed November 29, 2019].

Federal Judicial Center. (n.d.). *Patel, Marilyn Hall* Available: https://www.fjc.gov/history/ju dges/patel-marilyn-hall [Accessed July 13, 2019].

Franceschi-Bicchierai, L. (2016). *20 Years Ago, A Senator Became the First US Lawmaker to Use Encryption.* Available: https://motherboard.vice.com/en_us/article/ezppgz/senat or-patrick-leahy-pgp-encryption-letter-20-years [Accessed May 2, 2019].

Gallup. (2002). *Which Freedoms Will Americans Trade for Security?* Available: https://ne ws.gallup.com/poll/6196/which-freedoms-will-americans-trade-%20security.aspx [Accessed January 20, 2020].

Garfinkel, S. L. (1995). *The Continuing Investigation of Phil Zimmermann*—Wired. Available: https://www.wired.com/1995/03/the-continuing-investigation-of-phil-zim mermann/ [Accessed April 28, 2019].

Garfinkel, S. L. (1996). *Peeking at Your P.C.* Available: https://www.nytimes.com/1996/0 4/06/opinion/peeking-at-your-pc.html [Accessed November 28, 2019].

Giles, L. F. (1995). *Declaration of Louis F. Giles, National Security Agency in Daniel J. Bernstein v. United States Department of State et al.* Available: https://cr.yp.to/export/1 995/08.15-giles.html [Accessed June 6, 2019].

Giles, L. F. (2002). *Declaration of Louis F. Giles, National Security Agency in Daniel J. Bernstein v. United Department of State et al.* Available: https://cr.yp.to/export/2002/0 4.29-giles.html [Accessed July 11, 2019].

Harmon, J. (1978). *Constitutionality Under the First Amendment of ITAR Restrictions on Public Cryptography—Memorandum from Assistant Attorney General John Harmon, Office of Legal Counsel, Department of Justice to Dr Frank Press, Science Advisor to the President (11 May 1978).* Available: https://www.justice.gov/olc/page/file/936106/ download [Accessed April 16, 2019.

Hirschhorn, E. and Peyton, D. (1992). *Uncle Sam's Secret Decoder Ring.* Available: https ://www.washingtonpost.com/archive/opinions/1992/06/25/uncle-sams-secret-decoder-ring/3eafe084-bb60-4eac-9e7f-3e566a52c513/ [Accessed November 23, 2019].

Hoffman, R. D. (1996). *Interview with Author of PGP (Pretty Good Privacy), February 2 1996.* Available: https://www.animatedsoftware.com/hightech/philspgp.htm [Accessed April 10, 2019].

Hunger, F. W. and Coppolino, A. J. (1997). *Defendants' Second Cross-Motion for Summary Judgement.* Available: https://web.archive.org/web/20060912162502/http://samsara .cwru.edu/comp_law/jvd/pdj5.html [Accessed August 4, 2019].

Interagency Working Group on Encryption and Telecommunications Policy. (1996). *A Study of the International Market for Computer Software and Encryption.* Available: https ://www.bis.doc.gov/index.php/documents/technology-evaluation/24-a-study-of-the-i nternational-market-for-computer-software-with-encryption-nsa-1995/file [Accessed May 22, 2019].

Junger, P. (1996). *Declaration of Peter Junger.* Available: https://web.archive.org/web/19 970318220518/http://www.eff.org/pub/Privacy/ITAR_export/Junger_v_DoS/junger .declaration [Accessed July 20, 2019].

Junger, P. (2002). *Peter D. Junger.* Available: https://web.archive.org/web/20060129193852/ http://samsara.law.cwru.edu/cv.html [Accessed August 3, 2019].

Junger, P. and Scarselli, G. (1997). *Press Release: Summary Judgment Motion Filed in Suit Attacking Restrictions on the "Export" of Software Brief Claims Publication of Computer Software Is Protected by First Amendment Export Regulations Restrict Only Publication of Encryption Software, Not Its Use.* Available: https://web.archive.org/ web/20060912162651/http://samsara.cwru.edu/comp_law/jvd/pr_brief.txt [Accessed August 4, 2019].

Junger, P. and Vasvari, R. (1998). *Federal District Court Holds That Software Publishers Are Not Protected by the First Amendment Government Wins Summary Judgment in Junger v. Daley.* Available: https://web.archive.org/web/20060912162408/http://samsa ra.cwru.edu/comp_law/jvd/pressrel-070798.txt [Accessed July 20, 2019].

Karn, P. (1994a). *Mass Market Software with Encryption −15 Day Expedited Review Requested.* Available: https://web.archive.org/web/20000816235747/http://people. qualcomm.com/karn/export/book-cjr.html [Accessed May 23, 2019].

Karn, P. (1994b). *Commodity Jurisdiction Request for "APPLIED CRYPTOGRAPHY SOURCE CODE DISK."* Available: https://web.archive.org/web/199902241217 32/http://people.qualcomm.com/karn/export/floppy-cjr.html [Accessed May 23, 2019].

Karn, P. (1994c). *CJ Case 0081-94, "Applied Cryptography Source Code Disk."* Available: https://web.archive.org/web/19990128104904/http://people.qualcomm.com/karn/ex port/request1.html [Accessed May 23, 2019].

Karn, P. (1994b). *Appeal in CJ Case 081–94, "Applied Cryptography Source Code Disk."* Available: https://web.archive.org/web/19990224164735/http://people.qualcomm.com/ karn/export/harris-appeal.html [Accessed May 23, 2019].

Karn, P. (1997). *Statement of Philip R. Karn, Jr. Before the House Judiciary Committee Subcommittee on Courts and Intellectual Property, March 20, 1997.* Available: https ://web.archive.org/web/19990224233458/http://people.qualcomm.com:80/karn/export/ houseoral.html [Accessed May 26, 2019].

Karn, P. (2010). *The Applied Cryptography Case: Only Americans Can Type!* Available: http://www.ka9q.net/export/ [Accessed May 26, 2019].

Kerrey, B. (1997). *Senator Kerrey's Floor Statement Introducing the Secure Public Networks Act of 1997.* Available: https://cryptome.org/jya/s909.htm#Read2 [Accessed November 24, 2019].

Lappin, T. (1996). *Cyber Rights Now.* Available: https://www.wired.com/1996/06/cyber-righ ts-15/ [Accessed November 27, 2019].

Leahy, P. (1996a). *Letter from Senator Patrick Leahy (D-VT) on Encryption to EFF Action Mailing List.* MessageID: "9604028310.AA831063527@smtpgwys.senate.gov." 2 May 1996. Available: https://web.archive.org/web/20081103050340/https://w2.eff.or g/Privacy/Crypto_export/Crypto_bills_1996/leahy_pgp_960502_net.letter [Accessed November 22, 2019].

Leahy, P. (1996b). *Statement of Senator Patrick Leahy on Introduction of "Promotion Of Commerce On-Line In The Digital Era" (PRO-CODE), Thursday May 2, 1996.* Available: https://web.archive.org/web/19970215020102/http://www.cdt.org/crypto/9 60502_Leahy_stmnt.html [Accessed November 22, 2019].

Lebkowsky, J. (1993). *THE INTERNET CODE RING! An Interview with Phil Zimmerman, creator of PGP.* Available: https://tucops.info/tucops3/etc/crypto/live/aoh_pgpup.htm [Accessed April 4, 2019].

Levy, S. (1993). *Crypto Rebels.* Available: https://www.wired.com/1993/02/crypto-rebels/ [Accessed June 7, 2020].

Levy, S. (1994b). *Cypher Wars: Pretty Good Privacy Gets Pretty Legal.* Available: https://ww w.wired.com/1994/11/cypher-wars/ [Accessed April 30, 2019].

Lewis, J. (1997a). *Correspondence from James Lewis, Office of Strategic Trade and Foreign Policy Controls, Bureau of Export Administration, Department of Commerce, to Gino J. Scarselli, Lawyer for Peter D. Junger, 3 July 1997.* Available: https://web.archive. org/web/20060912162741/http://samsara.cwru.edu/comp_law/jvd/pdj-bxa-gjs070397 .html [Accessed August 4, 2019].

Lewis, J. (1997b). *Correspondence from James Lewis, Office of Strategic Trade and Foreign Policy Controls, Bureau of Export Administration, Department of Commerce, to Gino J. Scarselli, Lawyer for Peter D. Junger, 7 August 1997.* Available: https://web.archive. org/web/20060912162558/http://samsara.cwru.edu/comp_law/jvd/pdj-bxa-gjs080797 .html [Accessed August 4, 2019].

Lewis, J. (2000). *Correspondence from James Lewis, Office of Strategic Trade and Foreign Policy Controls, Bureau of Export Administration, Department of Commerce, to Cindy Cohn, Lawyer for Daniel Bernstein, 17 February, 2000.* Available: https://cr.yp.to/exp ort/2000/0218-doc.html Accessed [July 10, 2019].

Lowell, W. J. (1995). *Declaration of William J. Lowell: Daniel J. Bernstein v. United States Department of State et al.* Available: https://cr.yp.to/export/1995/08.15-lowell.html [Accessed June 6, 2019].

Markoff, J. (1990). *Drive to Counter Computer Crime Aims at Invaders.* Available: http:// www.nytimes.com/1990/06/03/us/drive-to-counter-computer-crime-aims-at-invaders .html?pagewanted=all [Accessed July 14, 2019].

Markoff, J. (1991). *Move on Unscrambling Of Messages Is Assailed.* Available: https://ww w.nytimes.com/1991/04/17/business/move-on-unscrambling-of-messages-is-assailed.h tml [Accessed February 10, 2019].

Markoff, J. (1996). *Data-Secrecy Export Case Dropped by I.S.* Available: https://ww w.nytimes.com/1996/01/12/business/data-secrecy-export-case-dropped-by-us.html [Accessed April 20, 2019].

May, T. C. (1994). *Cyphernomicon V0.666.* Available: https://www.cypherpunks.to/faq/cyph ernomicron/cyphernomicon.txt [Accessed August 20, 2017].

McCullagh, D. (2001). *Senator Backs off Backdoors.* Available: https://www.wired.com/200 1/10/senator-backs-off-backdoors/ [Accessed January 25, 2020].

McKay, N. (1998). *Privacy Campaign Plods Ahead.* Available: https://web.archive.org/ web/19991220010934/http://www.wired.com/news/news/politics/story/15467.html [Accessed November 29, 2019].

Miller, G. and Mueller, P. F. (2020). *The CIA Secretly Bought a Company that Sold Encryption Devices Across the World. Then its Spies Sat Back and Listened.* [Online]. Available: https://www.washingtonpost.com/graphics/2020/world/national-security/cia-crypto-encryption-machines-espionage/ [Accessed June 26, 2020].

Morehous, D. (2008). *Problems Remain with New Rules Liberalizing Export of Software Products Incorporating Encryption Functionality.* Available: https://corporate.findlaw.com/business-operations/problems-remain-with-new-rules-liberalizing-export-of-software.html [Accessed July 17, 2019].

Obama, B. (2011). *Osama Bin Laden Dead.* Available: https://obamawhitehouse.archives.gov/blog/2011/05/02/osama-bin-laden-dead [Accessed January 15, 2020].

Oberdorfer, L. F. (1999). *Order.* Available: https://web.archive.org/web/19991128031159/http://people.qualcomm.com/karn/export/lbo_ruling.html [Accessed May 26, 2019].

Olson, T. B. (1981). *Constitutionality of Proposed Revisions of the Export Administration Regulation.* Available: https://www.justice.gov/file/22716/download [Accessed August 5, 2019].

Oram, A. (1997). *The McCain-Kerrey "Secure Public Networks Act": Brute Force Attack on Encryption.* Available: http://cpsr.org/prevsite/cpsr/nii/cyber-rights/web/mccain-kerrey.html/ [Accessed November 24, 2019].

President's Export Council Subcommittee on Encryption [PECSENC]. (1998). *Findings of the President's Export Council Subcommittee on Encryption (September 18, 1998).* Available: https://www.govinfo.gov/content/pkg/CHRG-106shrg69984/pdf/CHRG-106shrg69984.pdfp (page 121 onwards) [Accessed May 30, 2019].

Prior, R. V. (1996). *Declaration of Robert V. Prior: Daniel J. Bernstein v. United States Department of State.* Available: https://cr.yp.to/export/1996/1004-prior.txt [Accessed June 9, 2019].

Reuters. (1998). *Encryption Challenge Fails.* Available: https://www.wired.com/1998/07/encryption-challenge-fails/ [Accessed August 2, 2019].

Richey, C. R. (1996). *Memorandum Opinion of Charles R. Richey, United States District Court Judge.* Available: https://web.archive.org/web/20000817000154/http://people.qualcomm.com/karn/export/richey_decision.html [Accessed May 26, 2019].

Rosenthal, I. (1993). *CFP'93—Export Controls on Mass Market Software with Encryption Capabilities.* Available: http://cpsr.org/prevsite/conferences/cfp93/rosenthal.html/ [Accessed November 23, 2019].

Scarselli, G. (1997a). *Junger v. Daley: Supplemental and Amended Complaint.* Available: https://web.archive.org/web/20060912162639/http://samsara.cwru.edu/comp_law/jvd/compl.html [Accessed July 20, 2019].

Scarselli, G. (1997b). *Correspondence to the Department of Commerce, June 12, 1997.* Available: https://web.archive.org/web/20060912162558/http://samsara.cwru.edu/comp_law/jvd/pdj-bxa-gjs080797.html [Accessed August 1, 2019].

Scarselli, G. J. and O'Neill, K. F. (1998). *Plaintiff's Reply Brief in Support of his Motion for Summary Judgment and in Opposition to the Defendants' Motion for Summary Judgement.* Available: https://web.archive.org/web/20060912162733/http://samsara.cwru.edu/comp_law/jvd/pdj7.html [Accessed August 4, 2019].

Schiller, J. (1994). *MIT PGP Announcement.* Available: https://town.hall.org/cyber94/pgp.html [Accessed May 11, 2019].

Schneier, B. (1996). *Declaration of Bruce Schneier: Daniel J. Bernstein v. United States Department of State et al.* Available: https://cr.yp.to/export/1996/0726-schneier.txt [Accessed June 9, 2019].

Schneier, B. (1996). *Declaration of Bruce Schneier: Daniel J. Bernstein v. United States Department of State et al.* [Online]. Available: https://cr.yp.to/export/1996/0726-schneier.txt [Accessed June 9, 2019].

Schneier, B. (2000). *Preface*. Available: https://www.schneier.com/books/secrets_and_lies/pref.html [Accessed March 30, 2020].

Shane, S. and Bowmanthe, T. (1995). *Rigging The Game: Spy Sting*. Available: https://web.archive.org/web/20190106104412/https://www.baltimoresun.com/news/bs-xpm-1995-12-10-1995344001-story.html [Accessed February 13, 2020].

Simms, L. D. (1984). *Memorandum for Davis R. Robinson Legal Adviser Department of State —Re: Revised Proposed International Traffic in Arms Regulation*. Available: https://www.justice.gov/olc/page/file/936161/download [Accessed August 5, 2019].

Stevens, A. (1994). *Programmer's Bookshelf: Applying Cryptanalysis*. Available: https://web.archive.org/web/20140811000926/https://collaboration.cmc.ec.gc.ca/science/rpn/biblio/ddj/Website/articles/DDJ/1994/9405/9405n/9405n.htm [Accessed May 15, 2019].

Sterling, B. (2002). *The Hacker's Crackdown*. Available: http://www.mit.edu/hacker/hacker.html [Accessed July 14, 2019].

Suchetka, D. (2006). *Peter Junger, led Buddhist Temple, studied and taught computer law*. Available: https://web.archive.org/web/20070520081321/https://www.cleveland.com/news/plaindealer/index.ssf?/base/news/1164360994108030.xml&coll=2 [Accessed July 20, 2019].

Tech Law Journal. (1998). *New Encryption Bill Introduced in Senate*. Available: http://www.techlawjournal.com/encrypt/80514.htm [Accessed November 29, 2019].

The White House. (1996a). *Executive Order 13026 of November 15, 1996: Administration of Export Controls on Encryption Products*. Available: https://www.govinfo.gov/content/pkg/FR-1996-11-19/pdf/96-29692.pdf [Accessed May 7, 2019].

The White House. (1996b). *Memorandum for the Vice President et al on Encryption Export Policy, November 15, 1996*. Available: https://cr.yp.to/export/1997/04.25-coppolino.html [Accessed June 21, 2019].

The White House. (1999a). *Statement by the Press Secretary: Administration Announces New Approach to Encryption*. Available: https://www.epic.org/crypto/legislation/cesa/WH_release_9_16.html [Accessed May 27, 2019].

The White House. (1999b). *Special White House Briefing: Encryption Technology*. Available: https://cryptome.org/jya/crypto-us-up.htm [Accessed May 27, 2019].

United States Congress (1989). *H.R.91—Anti-Terrorism and Arms Export Amendments Act of 1989*. Available: https://www.congress.gov/bill/101st-congress/house-bill/91/text [Accessed August 3, 2020].

United States Congress. (1991a). *S.266—Comprehensive Counter-Terrorism Act of 1991*. Available: https://www.congress.gov/bill/102nd-congress/senate-bill/266 [Accessed February 10, 2019].

United States Congress. (1991b). H.R.3489—Omnibus Export Amendments Act of 1991. Available: https://congress.gov/bill/102nd-congress/house-bill/3489/text?q=%7B%22search%22%3A%5B%22johnson%22%5D%7D [Accessed November 23, 2019].

United States Congress. (1996a). *S.1587—Encrypted Communications Privacy Act of 1996*. Available: https://www.congress.gov/bill/104th-congress/senate-bill/1587 [Accessed November 27, 2019].

United States Congress. (1996b). *S.1726—Promotion of Commerce On-Line in the Digital Era (Pro-CODE) Act of 1996*. Available: https://www.congress.gov/bill/104th-congress/senate-bill/1726/text [Accessed May 22, 2019].

United States Congress. (1997a). *H.R. 695—Security and Freedom Through Encryption (SAFE) Act*. Available: https://www.congress.gov/bill/105th-congress/house-bill/695/text [Accessed May 19, 2019].

United States Congress. (1997b). *S.377—Promotion of Commerce On-Line in the Digital Era (Pro-CODE) Act of 1997*. Available: https://www.congress.gov/bill/105th-congress/senate-bill/377/text [Accessed November 23, 2019].

United States Congress. (1997c). *S.909—Secure Public Networks Act*. Available: https://ww w.congress.gov/bill/105th-congress/senate-bill/00909 [Accessed November 24, 2019].

United States Congress. (1997d). *H.R. 695—Security and Freedom Through Encryption (SAFE) Act, Draft Amendment*. Available: https://web.archive.org/web/199904300610 50/http://www.cdt.org/crypto/fbi_draft_text.html [Accessed January 6, 2020].

United States Congress. (1997e). *H.R. 695—Security and Freedom Through Encryption (SAFE) Act Amendment Offered by Mr Oxley of Ohio and Mr Manton of New York*. Available: https://web.archive.org/web/19980210082328/http://www.cdt.org/crypto/l egis_105/SAFE/Oxley_Manton.html [Accessed January 6, 2020].

United States Congress. (1998). *Introduction of Encryption Protects the Rights of Individuals from Violation and Abuse in Cyberspace (E-PRIVACY) Act, S. 2067*. Available: https ://cyber.harvard.edu/eon/ei/elabs/security/crime1.htm [Accessed November 29, 2019].

United States Court of Appeals, Sixth Circuit. (2000). *Opinion: Boyce F. Martin Jr*. Available: https://casetext.com/case/junger-v-daley. [Accessed July 20, 2019].

United States Court of Appeals for the Ninth Circuit. (1997). *Order: Daniel J. Bernstein v. United Department of State et al*. Available: https://cr.yp.to/export/1997/0922-order.txt [Accessed July 15, 2019].

United States Court of Appeals for the Ninth Circuit. (1999a). *Daniel J. Bernstein v. United Department of State et al: Opinion*. Available: https://cr.yp.to/export/1999/0506-order. html [Accessed July 1, 2019].

United States Court of Appeals for the Ninth Circuit. (1999b). *Daniel J. Bernstein v. United Department of State et al: Order*. Available: https://casetext.com/case/bernstein-v-us -department-of-justice [Accessed July 1, 2019].

United States Court of Appeals for the Ninth Circuit. (1999c). *Daniel J. Bernstein v. United Department of State et al: Order*. Available: https://cr.yp.to/export/1999/1028-order. html [Accessed July 1, 2019].

United States Department of Commerce. (1996). *Department of Commerce Regulations on Export of Encryption Products*. Available: https://www.govinfo.gov/content/pkg/FR-1 996-12-30/html/96-33030.htm [Accessed June 30, 2019].

United States Department of Commerce. (1997a). *Letter from Patricia Sefcik, Director of Encryption Policy Controls Division US Department of Commerce to Philip Karn, 20 November*. Available: https://web.archive.org/web/19990222025524/http://pe ople.qualcomm.com/karn/export/bxa_license_denial.html [Accessed May 26, 2019].

United States Department of Commerce. (1997b). *President's Export Council Subcommittee on Encryption; Notice of Establishment*. Available: https://www.govinfo.gov/content/ pkg/FR-1997-04-24/html/97-10664.htm [Accessed May 30, 2019].

United States Department of Commerce. (1999). *Daniel J. Bernstein v. United States Department of State et al: Appellant's Motion to Reschedule Oral Argument*. Available: https://cr.yp.to/export/docs.html [Accessed July 9, 2019].

United States Department of Commerce. (2000). *Revisions to Encryption Items*. Available: https://www.govinfo.gov/content/pkg/FR-2000-01-14/html/00-983.htm [Accessed May 28, 2019].

United States Department of Commerce. (2001). *EAR: Enforcement and Protective Measures*. Available: https://cr.yp.to/export/ear2001/764.pdf [Accessed July 14, 2019].

United States Department of Commerce. (2002). *Revisions and Clarifications to Encryption Controls in the Export Administration Regulations-Implementation of Changes in Category 5, Part 2 ("Information Security"), of the Wassenaar Arrangement List of Dual-Use Goods and Other Technologies*. Available: https://www.federalregister.gov/ documents/2002/06/06/02-13990/revisions-and-clarifications-to-encryption-controls-i n-the-export-administration [Accessed July 11, 2019].

United States Department of Justice. (1995a). *Memorandum of Points and Authorities in Support of Defendants' Motion to Dismiss, or in the Alternative, for Summary Judgement.* Available: https://web.archive.org/web/20000817000039/http://people.qualcomm.com/karn/export/memorandum.html [Accessed May 25, 2019].

United States Department of Justice. (1995b). *Reply Memorandum in Further Support of Defendant's Motion to Dismiss, or in the Alternative, for Summary Judgement.* Available: https://web.archive.org/web/19990128085747/http://people.qualcomm.com/karn/export/repmem.html [Accessed May 26, 2019].

United States Department of Justice. (1996). *Daniel J. Bernstein v. United Department of State et al.: Defendant's motion for summary judgment.* Available: https://cr.yp.to/export/1996/07.26-coppolino-motion.html [Accessed June 9, 2019].

United States Department of Justice. (1997). *Daniel J. Bernstein v. United Department of State et al.: Defendant's Notice of Motion and Motion for a Stay Pending Appeal and to Shorten Time Ex Parte Motion.* Available: https://cr.yp.to/export/1997/0827-coppolino.txt [Accessed June 30, 2019].

United States Department of Justice. (1998). *Defendant's Second Motion to Dismiss, or, in the Alternative, for Summary Judgment (Re: Commerce Department Regulations).* Available: https://web.archive.org/web/19990223225005/http://people.qualcomm.com/karn/export/dismiss_motion2.html [Accessed May 26, 2019].

United States Department of Justice. (1999). *Daniel J. Bernstein v. United Department of State et al.: Petition for Panel Hearing & Rehearing En Banc.* Available: https://cr.yp.to/export/1999/0621-mcintosh.html [Accessed July 9, 2019].

United States Department of Justice. (2000). *Letter from Scott R. McIntosh to Ms. Catterson, Clerk, United States Court of Appeals for the Ninth Circuit, 3 March 2000.* Available: https://cr.yp.to/export/2000/03.03-mcintosh.html [Accessed July 10, 2019].

United States Department of Justice. (2003). *Domestic Security Enhancement Act of 2003, 9 January 2003.* Available: http://www-tc.pbs.org/now/politics/patriot2-hi.pdf [Accessed February 1, 2020].

United States Department of State. (1992). *Letter from William B. Robinson, Director, Office of Defence Trade Controls, Bureau of Politico-Military Affairs to Daniel Bernstein, 20 August 1992.* Available: https://cr.yp.to/export/1992/0820-robinson.txt [Accessed June 2, 2019].

United States Department of State. (1993a). *Letter from Clyde G. Bryant, Jr., Chief of Compliance and Enforcement Branch, Office of Defence Trade Controls, Bureau of Politico-Military Affairs to Daniel Bernstein, 27 May 1993.* Available: https://cr.yp.to/export/1993/0527-bryant.txt [Accessed June 2, 2019].

United States Department of State. (1993b). *Letter from William B. Robinson, Director, Office of Defence Trade Controls, Bureau of Politico-Military Affairs to Daniel Bernstein, 7 Sep 1993.* Available: https://cr.yp.to/export/1993/0709-robinson.txt [Accessed June 2, 2019].

United States Department of State. (1993c). *Letter from William B. Robinson, Director, Office of Defence Trade Controls, Bureau of Politico-Military Affairs to Daniel Bernstein, 5 October 1993.* Available: https://cr.yp.to/export/1993/1005-robinson-1.txt [Accessed June 2, 2019].

United States Department of State. (1994a). *REQUEST FOR COMMODITY JURISDICTION DETERMINATION FOR: "Applied Cryptography" Cryptographic Book by Bruce Schneier.* Available: https://web.archive.org/web/19990221204918/http://people.qualcomm.com/karn/export/book-response.html [Accessed May 23, 2019].

United States Department of State. (1994b). *Statement of State Department's New Export Regulations.* Available: http://cpsr.org/prevsite/program/clipper/state-dept-new-export-regs.html/ [Accessed May 6, 2019].

United States Department of State. (1994c). *REQUEST FOR COMMODITY JURISDICTION DETERMINATION FOR: "Applied Cryptography Source Code Disk."* Available: https ://web.archive.org/web/19990224102110/http://people.qualcomm.com/karn/export/ floppy-cjr-response.html [Accessed May 23, 2019].

United States Department of State. (1994d). *Martha C. Harris response to Phil Karn's appeal for export exemption of Applied Cryptography Diskette.* Available: https://web.archive. org/web/19990224205347/http://people.qualcomm.com/karn/export/harris-ruling.h tml [Accessed May 24, 2019].

United States Department of State. (1995). *Thomas E. McNamara letter to Phil Karn's appeal for export exemption of Applied Cryptography Diskette.* Available: https://we b.archive.org/web/19990127224140/http://people.qualcomm.com/karn/export/mcnam ara-response.html [Accessed May 24, 2019].

United States Department of State. (1997) *Defendant's Notice of Motion for a Stay Pending Appeal and to Shorten Time: Daniel J. Bernstein v. United States Department of State.* Available: http://cr.yp.to/export/1997/0827-coppolino.txt [Accessed July 15, 2019].

United States District Court for the District of Columbia. (1992b). *Electronic Privacy Information Center V. Federal Bureau of Investigation: Judgement* [Online]. Available: https://web.archive.org/web/19970707090155/http://www.epic.org/open_gov/foia/fbi _survey_95/FBI_Survey_opinion.html [Accessed November 9, 2019].

United States District Court for the Northern District of California. (1995). *Transcript: Daniel J. Bernstein v. United States Department of State.* Available: https://cr.yp.to/exp ort/1995/1020-transcript.txt [Accessed June 7, 2019].

United States District Court for the Northern District of California. (1996a). *Opinion: Daniel J. Bernstein v. United States Department of State.* Available: https://cr.yp.to/export/1 996/0415-order.txt [Accessed June 7, 2019].

United States District Court for the Northern District of California. (1996b). *Transcript: Daniel J. Bernstein v. United States Department of State.* Available: https://cr.yp.to/exp ort/1996/0920-transcript.txt [Accessed June 9, 2019].

United States District Court for the Northern District of California. (1996c). *Proposed Order Granting Preliminary Injunction: Daniel J. Bernstein v. United States Department of State et al.* Available: https://cr.yp.to/export/1996/1004-cohn-2.txt [Accessed June 9, 2019].

United States District Court for the Northern District of California. (1996d). *Opinion: Daniel J. Bernstein v. United States Department of State et al.* Available: https://cr.yp.to/exp ort/1996/1206-order.txt [Accessed July 15, 2019].

United States District Court for the Northern District of California. (1997). *Opinion: Daniel J. Bernstein v. United States Department of State.* Available: https://cr.yp.to/export/1 997/0825-order.html [Accessed June 24, 2019].

United States District Court for the Northern District of California. (2002). *Plaintiff's Notice of Substitution of Counsel.* Available: https://cr.yp.to/export/2002/08.02-bernstein- subst.pdf [Accessed July 11, 2019].

United States District Court for the Northern District of California. (2003). *Opinion: Daniel J. Bernstein v. United States Department of State.* Available: https://casetext.com/case/ bernstein-v-us-department-of-commerce-2 [Accessed July 8, 2019].

United States District Court Northern District of Ohio Eastern Division. (1996). *Preliminary Injunction: Judge Donald C. Nugent.* Available: https://web.archive.org/web/1997031 8220530/http://www.eff.org/pub/Privacy/ITAR_export/Junger_v_DoS/junger_inju nction.draft [Accessed July 20, 2019].

United States District Court Northern District of Ohio Eastern Division. (1998). *Opinion & Order: Judge James S. Gwin.* Available: https://www.courtlistener.com/opinion/25 76599/junger-v-daley/ [Accessed July 20, 2019].

United States General Accounting Office. (1993). *Communications Privacy: Federal Policy and Actions*. Available: https://www.gao.gov/assets/220/218755.pdf [Accessed 2 April 2019].

United States House of Representatives. (1997). *Hearing on H.R. 695 Safety and Freedom Through Encryption (SAFE)—March 20*. Available: http://commdocs.house.gov/comm ittees/judiciary/hju41233.000/hju41233_0f.htm [Accessed May 19, 2019].

United States National Archives and Records Administration. (1992). *Federal Register 57:139, 20 July, 1992*. Available: https://www.govinfo.gov/content/pkg/FR-1992-07-20/pdf/FR-1992-07-20.pdf [Accessed November 23, 2019].

United States Senate. (1998). *S.2067—Encryption Protects the Rights of Individuals from Violation and Abuse in Cyberspace (E-PRIVACY) Act*. Available: https://www.con gress.gov/bill/105th-congress/senate-bill/2067 [Accessed November 29, 2019].

United States Senate. (2001). *Senate Congressional Record, 19 September 2001*. Available: https://cr.yp.to/export/2002/09.03-bernstein-dp-a.pdf & https://cr.yp.to/export/2002/0 9.03-bernstein-dp-b2.pdf [Accessed January 20, 2020].

Vasvari, R., Scarselli, G., and O'Neill, K. F. (1996a). *Brief in Support of Plaintiff's Motion for Preliminary Motion for Preliminary Injunction*. Available: https://web.archive.org/ web/19970318220504/http://www.eff.org/pub/Privacy/ITAR_export/Junger_v_DoS/j unger.brief [Accessed July 20, 2019].

Vasvari, R., Scarselli, G., and O'Neill, K. F. (1996b). *Complaint for Declaratory and Injunctive Relief*. Available: https://web.archive.org/web/20060912162211/http://sa msara.cwru.edu/comp_law/jvc/complaint.html [Accessed July 20, 2019].

Vasvari, R., Scarselli, G., and O'Neill, K. F. (1998). *Proof Brief of Appellant Peter D. Junger*. Available: https://web.archive.org/web/20060912162434/http://samsara.cwru.edu/ comp_law/jvd/pdj-brief.html [Accessed August 3, 2019].

Vasvari, R. and Scarselli, G. (1996a). *Law Professor Sues Federal Government over Computer Privacy Issues*. Available: https://www.eff.org/press/archives/2008/04/21-22 [Accessed July 20, 2019].

Vasvari, R. and Scarselli, G. (1996b). *New Complaint Filed in Suit Challenging Constitutionality of Regulations Forbidding Publication of Software on Internet Suit Seeks to Enjoin Enforcement of Regulations on "Export" of Encryption Software*. Available: https://web.archive.org/web/20060912162348/http://samsara.cwru.edu/ comp_law/jvd/pr.txt [Accessed July 20, 2019].

Vasvari, R. and Scarselli, G. (1996c). *Plaintiff Seeks Summary Judgment in Cleveland Case Challenging Licensing of "Exports" of Cryptographic Information*. Available: https:// web.archive.org/web/20060912162151/http://samsara.cwru.edu/comp_law/jvc/pressre 12.html [Accessed July 20, 2019].

Verhovek, S. H. (1987). Two Girls Win Westinghouse Competition. Available: https://ww w.nytimes.com/1987/03/03/science/two-girls-win-westinghouse-competition.html [Accessed July 13, 2019].

Voorhees, M. (1996). *A Tale of Two Crypto Court Cases: Are Karn & Bernstein Judges on the Same Planet, 5 March 1996*. Available: https://web.archive.org/web/19980708221023/ http://www.infolawalert.com/stories/050396b.html [Accessed July 18, 2019].

Wassenaar Arrangement. (2018). *About Us*. Available: https://www.wassenaar.org/about-us/ [Accessed March 17, 2019].

Wired. (2002). *U.S. V. Microsoft: Timeline*. Available: https://www.wired.com/2002/11/u-s-v -microsoft-timeline/ [Accessed November 14, 2019].

Witt, E. (2001). *Clarification and Exact Wording of Encryption Poll Question*. Available: https://web.archive.org/web/20010924105713/http://www.politechbot.com/p-02530. html [Accessed January 20, 2020].

Zimmermann, P. (n.d.a). *Phil Zimmermann, Background*. Available: https://philzimmerma nn.com/EN/background/index.html [Accessed April 10, 2019].

Zimmermann, P. (n.d.b). *Phil Zimmermann—Frequently Asked Question.* Available: https://
   philzimmermann.com/EN/faq/index.html [Accessed May 12, 2019].
Zimmermann, P. (1991). *PGP Guide.* Available: http://www.erresoft.com/firmadigitale/PG
   P_Guide_vol_1.html [Accessed April 6, 2019].
Zimmermann, P. (1992). *PGP User's Guide Volume II: Special Topics (v2.2).* Available: http:
   //www.mit.edu/afs.new/sipb/project/pgp/doc/pgpdoc2.txt [Accessed May 11, 2019].
Zimmermann, P. (1993). *Testimony of Philip Zimmermann to Subcommittee for Economic
   Policy, Trade, and the Environment US House of Representatives, 12 Oct 1993.*
   Available: https://fas.org/irp/congress/1993_hr/931012_zimmerman.htm [Accessed
   April 20, 2019].
Zimmermann, P. (1995a). *Author's Preface to the Book: "PGP Source Code and Internals."*
   Available: https://philzimmermann.com/EN/essays/index.html [Accessed May 11,
   2019].
Zimmermann, P. (1995b). *Declaration of Philip R. Zimmermann in Support of Plaintiffs'
   Opposition to Defendants' Motion to Dismiss.* Available: https://web.archive.org/w
   eb/19990128224429/http://people.qualcomm.com/karn/export/zimm.html [Accessed
   May 25, 2019].
Zimmermann, P. (1996a). *Testimony of Philip R. Zimmermann to the Subcommittee on
   Science, Technology, and Space of the US Senate Committee on Commerce, Science,
   and Transportation (26 June 1996).* Available: https://philzimmermann.com/EN/testi
   mony/index.html [Accessed April 3, 2019].
Zimmermann, P. (1997). *Author Preface to the Book: "PGP Source Code and Internals."*
   Available: https://philzimmermann.com/EN/essays/BookPreface.html [Accessed May
   20, 2019].
Zimmermann, P. (1999). *Why I Wrote PGP.* Available: https://www.philzimmermann.com/
   EN/essays/WhyIWrotePGP.html [Accessed December 5, 2019].
Zimmermann, P. (2001a). *PGP Marks 10th Anniversary (5 June).* Available: https://philzim
   mermann.com/EN/news/PGP_10thAnniversary.html [Accessed April 15, 2019].
Zimmermann, P. (2001b). *No Regrets About Developing PGP.* Available: https://interviews.
   slashdot.org/story/01/09/24/162236/philip-zimmermann-and-guilt-over-pgp [Accessed
   January 15, 2020].
Zimmermann, P. (2012). *Philip Zimmermann's Internet Hall of Fame 2012 Induction Speech
   (23 April 2012).* Available: http://opentranscripts.org/transcript/philip-zimmermann
   -internet-hall-of-fame-2012-induction-speech/ [Accessed April 4, 2019].
Zimmermann, P. (2003a). *DEF CON 11—Phil Zimmerman—A Conversation with Phil
   Zimmermann (2003).* Available: https://www.youtube.com/watch?v=4ww8AAkW
   FhM [Accessed April 19, 2019].
Zimmermann, P. (2003b). *Philip Zimmermann on PGP (7 October 2003).* Available: https://
   www.youtube.com/watch?v=Ka7BqjmaWJA [Accessed April 5, 2019].

8 Crypto War III (2013–Present)
The Snowden Era

Awesome new technology…creates a serious tension between two values we all treasure: privacy and safety.

That tension should not be resolved by corporations that sell stuff for a living.

It also should not be resolved by the FBI, which investigates for a living.

It should be resolved by the American people deciding how we want to govern ourselves in a world we have never seen before.

We shouldn't drift to a place—or be pushed to a place by the loudest voices—

because finding the right place, the right balance,

will matter to every American for a very long time.

Former FBI Director James Comey, 2016

8.1 SNOWDEN IGNITES CRYPTO WAR III

Civil rights leader or traitor? NSA contractor Edward Snowden divided opinions and captivated the media when stories derived from his theft of classified US intelligence documents were published in 2013. Former NSA and CIA Director General Michael Hayden commented that Snowden's actions represented "the greatest hemorrhaging of legitimate American secrets in…history."[1]

The first story detailed how the Justice Department issued a court order to Verizon, one of the US' largest communication companies, to provide the government with metadata on all customer telephone calls on an "ongoing and daily basis."[2] Metadata comprises information about a communication, rather than the communication's content itself; for a telephone call this includes the call originator, call recipient, and date, time, and duration of call. The court order covered metadata for April to July 2013.[3] The top secret order forbade disclosure of the metadata

---

[1] Pilkington, 2016.
[2] United States Foreign Intelligence Surveillance Court, 2013.
[3] Ibid.

transfer.[4] The order relied on the "business records" provision of the PATRIOT Act, 50 USC section 1861.[5]

A day later the next story broke: PRISM.[6] Journalists Glenn Greenwald and Ewen MacAskill reported how the top secret PRISM program provided, "direct access to the systems of Google, Facebook, Apple, and other US internet giants," allowing data collection including, "email, video and voice chat, videos, photos, voice-over-IP chats (e.g., Skype), file transfers, social networking details, and more."[7] The authors alleged the complicity of the technology companies, but Google and Apple denied involvement.[8] NSA documents showed the PRISM program originated in 2007 when Microsoft was added to the program, followed by Yahoo in 2008; Google, Facebook, and PalTalk in 2009; YouTube in 2010; Skype and AOL in 2011; and Apple in 2012.[9] A "senior administration" figure commented the collection was authorized under Section 702 of the Foreign Intelligence Surveillance Act (FISA), and did not permit targeting of US citizens or those located in the US.[10] A leaked document lauded PRISM as "one of the most valuable, unique and productive accesses for NSA," resulting in more than 77,000 intelligence reports.[11]

ACLU's James Jaffer stated, "This is [an] unprecedented militarisation of domestic communications infrastructure."[12] Jesselyn Radack of the Government Accountability Project commented:

> Instead of focusing on Snowden and shooting the messenger, we should really focus on the crimes of the NSA. Because whatever laws Snowden may or may not have broken, they are infinitesimally small compared to the two major surveillance laws and the Fourth Amendment of the Constitution that the NSA's violated.[13]

UN Secretary-General Ban-Ki Moon was more favorable to the US government, commenting that the Snowden disclosures created problems outweighing the benefits of public disclosure.[14]

Speaking just weeks before the first Snowden story broke, President Obama acknowledged post 9/11 security measures, like expanded surveillance, "raised difficult questions about the balance that we strike between our interests in security and our values of privacy."[15] However, Obama noted countering terrorist plots presented particular challenges "in an age when ideas and images can travel the globe in an instant," and when "a person can consume hateful propaganda, commit themselves to a violent agenda, and learn how to kill without leaving their home."[16] Obama said the government has to "strike the appropriate balance between our need for security and preserving those freedoms that make us who we are."[17] The President continued:

---

4   Ibid.
5   Greenwald, 2013a.
6   Greenwald and MacAskill, 2013.
7   Ibid.
8   Ibid.
9   Ibid.
10 Ibid.

11 Greenwald and MacAskill, 2013.
12 Ibid.
13 Foreign Policy, 2013
14 Pilkington, 2013.
15 Obama, 2013a.
16 Ibid.
17 Ibid.

Now, all these issues remind us that the choices we make about war can impact—in sometimes unintended ways—the openness and freedom on which our way of life depends. And that is why I intend to engage Congress…to determine how we can continue to fight terrorism without keeping America on a perpetual wartime footing.[18]

Obama stated law enforcement powers would be reviewed to understand how "we can intercept new types of communication, but also build in privacy protections to prevent abuse."[19] Commenting as the Snowden stories started to break, Obama explained:

what you've got is two programs that were originally authorized by Congress… bipartisan majorities have approved…them, Congress is continually briefed on how these are conducted. There are a whole range of safeguards involved, and federal judges are overseeing the entire program.[20]

Obama declared, "nobody is listening to your telephone calls," adding:

That's not what this program is about. As was indicated, what the intelligence community is doing is looking at phone numbers and durations of calls. They are not looking at people's names, and they're not looking at content. But by sifting through this so-called metadata, they may identify potential leads with respect to folks who might engage in terrorism…if the intelligence community then actually wants to listen to a phone call, they've got to go back to a federal judge [to get a warrant].[21]

Obama argued:

you can't have 100 percent security and also then have 100 percent privacy…We're going to have to make some choices as a society. And what I can say is that…these programs…make a difference in our capacity to anticipate and prevent possible terrorist activity.[22]

Obama concluded:

in the abstract, you can complain about Big Brother and how this is a potential program run amuck, but when you actually look at the details, then I think we've struck the right balance.[23]

President Obama's policy response came six months later, when he announced Presidential Policy Directive 28 (PPD28) on Signals Intelligence in January 2014.[24] Introducing PPD28, Obama reflected, "[As a] Senator, I was critical of several practices, such as warrantless wiretaps," and recounted his "healthy skepticism toward our surveillance programs after I became President."[25] After reviewing intelligence

---

[18] Ibid.
[19] Ibid.
[20] Obama, 2013b.
[21] Ibid.

[22] Ibid.
[23] Ibid.
[24] Obama, 2014.
[25] Ibid.

programs, he ordered changes including an increase in oversight, auditing, and compliance.[26] However, Obama explained he did not halt the programs:

> not only because I felt that they made us more secure, but also because nothing in that initial review, and nothing that I have learned since, indicated that our intelligence community has sought to violate the law or is cavalier about the civil liberties of their fellow citizens...The NSA, consistently follow protocols designed to protect the privacy of ordinary people. They're not abusing authorities in order to listen to your private phone calls or read your emails.[27]

Obama reflected he would not be President but for the "courage of dissidents like Dr. King, who were spied upon by their own government," and it was not enough for governments to say:

> Trust us, we won't abuse the data we collect. For history has too many examples when that trust has been breached. Our system of government is built on the premise that our liberty cannot depend on the good intentions of those in power; it depends on the law to constrain those in power.[28]

Obama declared, "the standards for government surveillance must be higher."[29] Whilst not mentioning him by name, Obama stated the "sensational way" in which the Snowden disclosures occurred, "often shed more heat than light," and revealed, "methods to our adversaries that could impact our operations...for years to come."[30] In a digital world, Obama argued, "We cannot prevent terrorist attacks or cyber threats without some capability to penetrate digital communications."[31] Obama stated:

> As the nation that developed the Internet, the world expects us to ensure that the digital revolution works as a tool for individual empowerment, not government control. Having faced down the dangers of totalitarianism and fascism and communism, the world expects us to stand up for the principle that every person has the right to think and write and form relationships freely—because individual freedom is the wellspring of human progress.[32]

Obama explained the new directive would strengthen executive oversight, increase transparency, and implement an independent privacy panel to testify before the FISA court on important cases.[33] The use of national security letters, orders which compel companies to provide details to the government but prevent the disclosure such an order was issued, would be revised. Obama stated the government should be "more transparent" in the use of these letters, and their "secrecy will not be indefinite,

---

26 Ibid.
27 Ibid.
28 Ibid.
29 Ibid.
30 Ibid.
31 Ibid.
32 Ibid.
33 Ibid.

unless the government demonstrates a real need for further secrecy." Obama added communications providers would be able to "make public more information than ever before about the orders that they have received to provide data to the government." Addressing the bulk collection of Americans' metadata, Obama stated telephone numbers were only queried where there was a "reasonable suspicion that a particular number is linked to a terrorist organization," he added:

> Why is this necessary? The program grew out of a desire to address a gap identified after 9/11. One of the 9/11 hijackers…made a phone call from San Diego to a known al-Qaeda safe house in Yemen. NSA saw that call, but it could not see that the call was coming from…the United States.[34]

Obama went on to explain:

> the program…consolidates these records into a database that the government can query if it has a specific lead—a consolidation of phone records that the companies already retained for business purposes. The review group turned up no indication that this database has been intentionally abused…I believe it is important that the capability…is preserved.[35]

Obama conceded whilst bulk metadata collection was authorized by Congress and FISA courts, it had "never been subject to vigorous public debate." Obama announced the bulk metadata program would continue but without government holding the metadata, though he acknowledged there was no plan of how to achieve such an objective. Obama also said the database would only be queried after a "judicial finding or in the case of a true emergency," and phone numbers could only be investigated when they were two steps removed from a terrorist organization, rather than the current three.[36] Obama also outlined the acceptable uses of signals intelligence under PPD28:

> the United States does not collect intelligence to suppress criticism or dissent, nor do we collect intelligence to disadvantage people on the basis of their ethnicity, or race, or gender, or sexual orientation, or religious beliefs…[or] competitive advantage to U.S. companies.[37]

For weeks to follow, Snowden's disclosures continued to be published. Particularly controversial projects included GCHQ's TEMPORA, which was described as the "ability to tap into and store huge volumes of data drawn from fiber-optic cables for up to 30 days so that it can be sifted and analyzed."[38] Another story detailed Microsoft's cooperation with the NSA, enabling government access to Hotmail and Outlook.com accounts.[39] But perhaps the most damaging story was Operation BULLRUN.

---

[34] Ibid.
[35] Ibid.
[36] Ibid.

[37] Ibid.
[38] MacAskill et al., 2013.
[39] Greenwald et al., 2013.

8.2   NSA ENCRYPTION ACCESS PROGRAM: OPERATION BULLRUN

NSA encryption access operations were detailed in *The Guardian*, *ProPublica*, and *The New York Times* in September 2013.[40] Operation BULLRUN was named after an American Civil War battle; its GCHQ counterpart was branded Operation EDGEHILL, after an English Civil War battle.[41] The article in *The Guardian* claimed, "US and British intelligence agencies have successfully cracked much of the online encryption relied upon by hundreds of millions of people to protect the privacy of their personal data, online transactions, and emails."[42] The methods used to achieve access to encryption included:

> covert measures to ensure NSA control over setting of international encryption standards, the use of supercomputers to break encryption with "brute force," and—the most closely guarded secret of all—collaboration with technology companies and internet service providers themselves.[43]

BULLRUN's initiation date is unknown; however, a 2010 GCHQ document stated, "For the past decade, NSA has lead [sic] an aggressive, multi-pronged effort to break widely used internet encryption technologies," placing its origins at the second crypto war's close.[44] It is possible the NSA realized they had lost the public battle for access to encrypted data and consequently increased investment in covert access. It is also possible BULLRUN was a successor to another classified program. BULLRUN investment for 2013 was $254.9m—more than twelve times the $20m PRISM investment.[45] The NSA described "strong decryption programs as the "price of admission" for the US to maintain unrestricted access to and use of cyberspace."[46] Further technical details of BULLRUN capabilities were unknown.

One of the primary BULLRUN activities was to "actively engage US and foreign IT industries to covertly influence and/or overtly leverage their commercial products' designs," and to "insert vulnerabilities into commercial encryption systems." The objective was to "make the systems in question exploitable through SIGINT collection…with foreknowledge of the modification. To the consumer and other adversaries, however, the systems' security remains intact." This description is reminiscent of the Clipper chip's goals. The Snowden archive did not identify companies working with the government, though some targeting information is provided. GCHQ were targeting the "big four": Google, Facebook, Yahoo, and Hotmail. GCHQ also established a HumInt (human intelligence) Operations Team (HOT), described as being "responsible for identifying, recruiting, and running covert agents in the global telecommunications industry."[47] The article also detailed the NSA's Commercial Solutions Center, established to allow industry security products to be

40 Ball, Borger, and Greenwald, 2013.   44 Ibid.
41 Ibid.   45 Ibid.
42 Ibid.   46 Ibid.
43 Ibid.   47 Ibid.

assessed by, and pitched to, government clients, and which had a secondary role to "to leverage sensitive, co-operative relationships with specific industry partners," and to, in the reporters' words, "insert vulnerabilities into security products." As a result of BULLRUN, the NSA expected to gain access to "data flowing through a hub for a major communications provider," and to a "major internet peer-to-peer voice and text communications system," in 2013. GCHQ's 2010 EDGEHILL goals were to gain access to three major (unnamed) Internet companies and 30 types of Virtual Private Networks (VPNs).[48] GCHQ hoped to have access to encryption used by 15 major Internet companies and 300 VPNs by 2013.[49]

The principal concern should BULLRUN capabilities be leaked was "damage to industry relations"; a 2009 GCHQ document revealed, "Loss of confidence in our ability to adhere to confidentiality agreements would lead to loss of access to proprietary information that can save time when developing new capability." A secondary concern, rated a "moderate risk," was the public's reaction which could cause "unwelcome publicity for us and our political masters." These risks had to be weighed against GCHQ's assessment: "SIGINT utility will degrade as information flows changes, new applications are developed (and deployed) at pace and widespread encryption becomes more commonplace."[50]

Bruce Schneier commented, "By deliberately undermining online security in a short-sighted effort to eavesdrop, the NSA is undermining the very fabric of the internet." Snowden himself commented that despite BULLRUN, "Encryption works. Properly implemented strong crypto systems are one of the few things that you can rely on."[51]

However, the Snowden revelations also offered potentially corroborating information to a rumor long in circulation: the NSA's sabotage of a prominent global encryption standard.

In August 2007, Microsoft's Dan Shumow and Niels Ferguson gave a five-minute "turbo talk" entitled, "On the Possibility of a Back Door in the NIST SP800–90 Dual EC PRNG" at the annual Santa Barbara crypto conference.[52] NIST SP800–90 was a recently released standard for pseudo-random number generation (PRNG)— its international companion was ISO 18031. The informal presentation contained only nine slides, but its contents, given the political context, were more deserving of the keynote address than a five-minute turbo talk. The authors had discovered a flaw in an SP800–90 PRNG algorithm called Dual_EC_DRBG, with DRBG standing for deterministic random bit generator.[53] PRNGs are at the heart of cryptography, being used to generate the prime numbers vital to public key encryption, initialization vectors, random authentication challenges, and having a host of other applications. Generating random numbers is one of cryptography's hardest problems, a problem

[48] Ibid.
[49] Ibid.
[50] Ibid.

[51] Ibid.
[52] Shumow and Ferguson, 2007.
[53] Ibid, 6.

that has resulted in numerous PRNG algorithms being found to contain flaws.[54] Schneier sums up their importance, "Break the random-number generator, and most of the time you break the entire security system."[55] SP800–90 contained four approved PRNGs: a block cipher; a hash function; a hash-based message authentication code (HMAC); and an elliptic curve (Dual_EC_DRBG). Schneier describes the latter as "three orders of magnitude slower than its peers," Schneier believed it was only in the standard because "it's been championed by the NSA."[56] Within the standard there are a series of fixed numbers (constants) used to determine the elliptic curve which is responsible for the randomness of the algorithm. Shumow and Ferguson found the constants had a mathematical relationship to a second unknown set of numbers—these numbers, Schneier commented in 2007:

> act as a kind of skeleton key. If you know the secret numbers, you can predict the output of the random-number generator after collecting just 32 bytes of its output…you only need to monitor one TLS internet encryption connection in order to crack the security of that protocol. If you know the secret numbers, you can completely break any instantiation of Dual_EC_DRBG.[57]

Shumow and Ferguson explicitly stated, "we are not saying…NIST intentionally put a backdoor in this PRNG."[58] However, they added, "The prediction resistance of this PRNG…is dependent on solving one instance of the elliptic curve discrete log problem. (And we do not know if the algorithm designer knew this beforehand)."[59] At the conference the reaction to the presentation was surprisingly muted, a Microsoft manager in attendance commented, "I think folks thought, 'Well that's interesting,' and 'Wow, it looks like maybe there was a flaw in the design,' but there wasn't a huge reaction."[60] Schneier's subsequent commentary was more alarmed:

> we have no way of knowing whether the NSA knows the secret numbers…We have no way of knowing whether an NSA employee working on his own…has the secret numbers. We don't know if someone from NIST…has them. Maybe nobody does. We don't know where the constants came from…We only know that whoever came up with them could have the key to this backdoor. And we know there's no way for NIST—or anyone else—to prove otherwise. This is scary stuff.[61]

Schneier concluded:

> If this story leaves you confused, join the club. I don't understand why the NSA was so insistent about including Dual_EC_DRBG in the standard. It makes no sense as a trap door: it's public, and rather obvious. It makes no sense from an engineering perspective: it's too slow for anyone to willingly use it.[62]

---

[54] Schneier, 2007.
[55] Ibid.
[56] Ibid.
[57] Ibid.
[58] Shumow and Ferguson, 2007, 8.
[59] Ibid.
[60] Zetter, 2013.
[61] Schneier, 2007.
[62] Ibid.

Schneier stated the irregularity "can only be described as a backdoor...both NIST and the NSA have some explaining to do."[63]

The US government leveraged their purchasing power to have vendors implement the suspect algorithm under the FIPS certification requirement.[64] Dual_EC_DRBG was implemented as an optional PRNG in a number of products including Microsoft's SChannel (used in Internet Explorer and in web server Internet Information Services [IIS]) and OpenSSL's FIPS module; RSA's BSAFE crypto libraries used Dual_EC_DRBG as a default PRNG—although there is little evidence of how widely it was employed in practice.[65] A primary use case for these libraries was generating random numbers for establishing SSL/TLS connections, which are used for everything from secure web browsing to Virtual Private Networks (VPNs).[66] A Reuters report of December 2013 details how two sources "familiar with the contract" informed them the NSA had paid RSA $10 million to include Dual_EC_DRBG as the default PRNG in its BSAFE library.[67] RSA was reported to have adopted the algorithm before NIST approved it.[68] RSA responded stating, "we have never entered into any contract or engaged in any project with the intention of weakening RSA's products, or introducing potential 'backdoors.'"[69] NIST responded to calls to abandon the algorithm:

> We have no evidence that anyone has, or will ever have, the "secret numbers" for the backdoor that were hypothesized...that would provide advance information on the random numbers generated by the algorithm. For this reason, we are not withdrawing the algorithm at this time.

NIST added the standard endured a "rigorous" review process, including a public comment period, before publication—the algorithm also included a "method for randomly generating points [constants] if there is a concern about a backdoor."[70] Whilst a method for generating new constants was available, NIST never explained in the standard why a user may choose to do so.[71] The NIST standard itself also did not include the alternative constant generation algorithm, instead users needed to purchase an American National Standards Institute (ANSI) standard to access the algorithm.[72] Matthew Green comments this was akin to "putting the details in the bottom of a locked filing cabinet stuck in a disused lavatory with a sign on the door saying 'Beware of the Leopard.'"[73] Green commented, "To the best of our knowledge, nobody has ever used ANSI's alternative generation procedure in a single one of the *many* implementations of Dual EC DRBG in commercial software."[74]

The story remained in abeyance until in September 2013; *The New York Times* claimed it found correlating data in the Snowden archives confirming NSA's role in manipulating the Dual_EC_DRBG algorithm. The raw Snowden / NSA files themselves were not released, therefore the public were forced to rely on *The New York Times'* assessment of the data. The newspaper detailed how:

---

63 Ibid.
64 Zetter, 2013.
65 Checkoway, Fredrikson et al., no date.
66 Ibid.
67 Menn, 2013.
68 Ibid.

69 https://web.archive.org/web/20201108141548if_/
https://community.rsa.com/thread/189597
70 Kelsey, 2014, 32.
71 Ibid.
72 Green, 2015.
73 Ibid.
74 Ibid.

Classified N.S.A. memos appear to confirm that the fatal weakness, discovered...in 2007, was engineered by the agency. The N.S.A. wrote the standard and aggressively pushed it on the international group.[75]

A subsequent article added:

Internal N.S.A. memos describe how the agency subsequently worked behind the scenes to push the same standard on the International Organization for Standardization [ISO]. "The road to developing this standard was smooth once the journey began," one memo noted. "However, beginning the journey was a challenge in finesse."[76]

At the time, Canada's Communications Security Establishment ran the standards process for the international organization, but classified documents describe how ultimately the N.S.A. seized control. "After some behind-the-scenes finessing with the head of the Canadian national delegation and with C.S.E., the stage was set for N.S.A. to submit a rewrite of the draft," the memo notes. "Eventually, N.S.A. became the sole editor."[77]

The ISO is a group of 164 countries that negotiate standards across a range of fields enabling international interoperability.[78] Once a standard is accepted its contents, such as the Dual_EC_DRBG algorithm, rapidly spread around the world. A later editorial by *The New York Times* was more explicit in its assessment:

the National Security Agency, secretly inserted a "backdoor" into the system that allowed federal spies to crack open any data that was encoded using its technology... documents leaked by Edward Snowden, the former N.S.A. contractor, make clear that the agency has never met an encryption system that it has not tried to penetrate.[79]

Whether the author(s) of this statement was(were) involved in the original assessment of the Snowden files, or had found additional data to support their assessment solidifying attribution and intent is unknown; however, no supplemental evidence was presented. This is not to say the author(s) may or may not have been correct, but the caution of the earlier assessments was abandoned without explanation.

NIST were caught between the NSA and the technology community. Matthew Green commented, "I know from firsthand communications that a number of people at NIST feel betrayed by their colleagues at the NSA."[80] NIST re-opened the standard for public comment, stating they wanted to assure the cryptographic community the "transparent, public process used to rigorously vet our standards is still in place."[81] NIST added they "would not deliberately weaken a cryptographic standard," and, "If vulnerabilities are found...[they would] address them as quickly as possible."[82] However, there was a less conciliatory tone within NIST's statement on the issue:

[75] Perlroth, Larson, and Shane, 2013.
[76] Perlroth, 2013.
[77] Ibid.
[78] International Organization for Standardization, 2020.
[79] New York Times Editorial Board, 2013.
[80] Perlroth, 2013.
[81] National Institute for Standards and Technology, 2013a.
[82] Ibid.

There has been some confusion about the standards development process...NIST's mandate is to develop standards and guidelines to protect federal information and information systems. Because of the high degree of confidence in NIST standards, many private industry groups also voluntarily adopt these standards.[83]

This text could be interpreted as, "NIST standards are not produced for the public, but for the government—if you use them you are responsible for any consequences." NIST also addressed their collaboration with NSA:

The NSA participates in the NIST cryptography development process because of its recognized expertise. NIST is also required by statute to consult with the NSA.[84]

In a separate advisory, NIST recommended Dual_EC_DRBG no longer be used until the security concerns were resolved.[85] However, there remained some skepticism as to whether Dual_EC_DRBG contained a backdoor. Journalist Kim Zetter wrote:

The Times...hasn't released the memos that purport to prove the existence of a backdoor, and the paper's direct quotes from the classified documents don't mention any backdoor in the algorithm or efforts by the NSA to weaken it or the standard. They only discuss efforts to push the standard through committees for approval.[86]

Jon Callas, Chief Technology Officer of Silent Circle, which produces encrypted phones, saw the Shumow and Ferguson presentation in 2007 and was not alarmed.[87] After reading the 2013 *New York Times* articles Callas commented:

If [NSA] spent $250 million weakening the standard and this is the best that they could do, then we have nothing to fear from them...this was really ham-fisted. When you put on your conspiratorial hat about what the NSA would be doing, you would expect something more devious, Machiavellian...and this thing is just laughably bad. This is Boris and Natasha sort of stuff.[88]

Paul Kocher, Chief Scientist at Cryptography Research discounted the "bad cryptography" explanation, "Bad cryptography happens through laziness and ignorance... but in this case, a great deal of effort went into creating this and choosing a structure that happens to be amenable to attack," Kocher added:

What's mathematically creative [with the algorithm] is that when you look at it, you can't even prove whether there is a backdoor or not, which is very bizarre in cryptography...usually the presence of a backdoor is something you can prove is there, because you can see it and exploit it...I've never seen a vulnerability like this.[89]

---

[83] Ibid.
[84] Ibid.
[85] National Institute for Standards and Technology, 2013b.

[86] Zetter, 2013.
[87] Ibid.
[88] Ibid.
[89] Ibid.

Bruce Schneier agreed:

> If we were living in a kinder world, that [bad coding] would be a plausible expla-
> nation…but we're living in a very malicious world…NSA…have so undermined the
> fundamental trust in the internet, that we don't know what to trust. We have to suspect
> everything. We're never sure. That's the greatest damage.[90]

Recognizing Dual_EC_DRBG would never be trusted again, NIST withdrew it from
SP800–90A in 2014.[91]

In late 2013, NIST announced a review of their standard development procedures
in an effort to re-establish public trust.[92] The review of NIST was conducted by a
group branded the Visiting Committee on Advanced Technology (VCAT), an external panel including Ron Rivest of RSA fame, Edward Felten of Princeton University,
and Google's Vint Cerf.[93]

The VCAT delivered its report in 2014. NIST told the VCAT they spent "a lot
of time trying to figure out what happened [with Dual_EC_DRBG]," but evidence
dispersed over a decade, and the fact that it was poorly documented made their task
arduous.[94] NIST conceded there were "many reasons, we should have rejected or
modified Dual_EC_DRBG," which they acknowledged was provided by the NSA.[95]
As well as the constants issue which NIST wrote, "may have been generated to allow
NSA to know a backdoor," there was also a "slight statistical bias," which meant the
level of randomness was not as high as it should have been.[96] Fixing the bias would
have made exploiting the alleged backdoor much harder.[97] NIST identified both of
these issues during development.[98] NIST's John Kelsey asked Don Johnson, who
worked for Cygnacom, a commercial encryption company supporting development
of PRNG standards, where the constants came from during development, to which
Johnson replied, they were the "(in essence) the public key for some random private
key"; Johnson added that the NSA would not allow him to discuss the constants
publicly.[99] NIST had asked the NSA directly where and how the constants originated
as early as 2004, and Niels Ferguson highlighted the issue to NIST in 2005.[100] NSA
responded the constants were generated in a secure and classified manner, originally
for the national security community.[101] The NSA told NIST they wished to keep the
algorithm and its constants in its current form to preserve the NSA's "existing investment" and allow their clients to get FIPS validated—but it would be "reasonable to
allow other users to generate their own [constants]."[102] NIST told the VCAT they did
not believe there was a backdoor in the algorithm, stating it was, "extremely slow,

---

90 Ibid.
91 National   Institute   for   Standards   and
    Technology, 2014a.
92 National   Institute   for   Standards   and
    Technology, 2016.
93 National   Institute   for   Standards   and
    Technology, 2014b, 1.
94 Kelsey, 2014, 22.

95 Ibid, 3.
96 Ibid, 10.
97 Kelsey, 2014, 36.
98 Ibid, 21.
99 Green, 2015.
100 Kelsey, 2014, 23–24.
101 Ibid, 24.
102 Ibid, 24.

and seemed unlikely to see much use…putting a trapdoor in seemed kind of point-less."[103] NIST also expected as it was so slow it was only NSA's existing national security customers who would use Dual_EC_DRBG.[104] However, NIST recognized they framed the backdoor question incorrectly, rather than asking "Do we think there is a trapdoor in Dual_EC_DRBG?" they told VCAT they should instead have asked themselves, "should we include an algorithm in our standards that **could** have a trapdoor?" [original bold].[105] The VCAT were briefed how after the 2007 presen-tation NIST cryptographer John Kelsey wrote to the SP800-90A standards editing committee apologizing, "for not realizing before how big an issue this [the NSA constants] would be."[106] At their next editing committee meeting it was debated whether the algorithm should be withdrawn. However, as they believed the issue had previously been addressed with the option for users to generate their own constants, NIST took no action.[107] Regarding the issue of statistical bias, NIST deferred to NSA any comments. With hindsight, NIST recognized they should have remedied the bias issue by elongating the truncation of the Dual EC DRBG.[108] The VCAT were told over 50 cryptographic modules NIST validated implemented the algorithm, but NIST explained that does not necessarily mean the algorithm was widely used.[109]

The VCAT panel offered individual findings; Vint Cerf assessed:

> In my opinion, NIST representatives were particularly and probably overly hard on themselves in analyzing the Dual_EC_DRBG matter, but the retrospective analysis reinforces my view that NIST must achieve sufficient depth of cryptographic and math-ematical knowledge to render itself fully capable of evaluating strength and weakness of proposed algorithms without dependence on NSA.[110]

Felten assessed it was highly likely the NSA inserted a trapdoor, though "the evi-dence I have seen indicates that NIST believed at the time, in good faith, that there was not a trapdoor. However… NIST failed to exercise independent judgment but instead deferred extensively to NSA with regard to DUAL_EC."[111] Felten stated the bias could have been fixed, but, "NSA asserted that the fix was not needed, and NIST accepted this assertion."[112] Felten added:

> It was discovered later that had NIST addressed the bias problem by changing the standard to discard some of the biased bits, this would have had the side effect of elimi-nating the potential trapdoor in DUAL_EC. This might be a reason why NSA argued against addressing the bias problem.[113]

---

[103] Ibid, 26.
[104] Ibid, 26.
[105] Ibid, 27.
[106] Ibid, 30.
[107] Ibid, 34.
[108] Ibid, 37.
[109] Ibid, 18.
[110] National Institute for Standards and Technology, 2014b, 23.
[111] Ibid, 32.
[112] Ibid.
[113] Ibid, 33.

Felten found NIST did not have an elliptic curves expert on staff causing them to defer to NSA.[114] Another VCAT member, Microsoft's Steven Lipner, was less explicit in his assessment of there being an NSA backdoor:

> While there were no clear signs of a deliberate attempt by NIST—or NSA—to undermine the security of the algorithm, NIST's discussion revealed and acknowledged numerous process shortcomings that allowed a potentially weak algorithm to be standardized.[115]

Ron Rivest's view differed:

> Recent revelations and technical review support the hypothesis that, nonetheless, the NSA has been caught with "its hands in the cookie jar" with respect to the development of the Dual-EC-DRBG standard. It seems highly likely that this standard was designed by the NSA to explicitly leak users' key information to the NSA (and to no one else).[116]

Rivest continued:

> The Dual_EC_DRBG standard apparently (and I would suggest, almost certainly) contains a "backdoor" enabling the NSA to have surreptitious access. The backdoor is somewhat clever in that the standard is not designed to be "weak" (enabling other foreign adversaries to perhaps exploit the weakness as well) but "custom" (only the creator (NSA)…will have such access). Of course, the ability to restrict access to NSA only supposes that NSA can keep secret its knowledge of the…[constants]…and that no adversary can compute the [constants].[117]

Rivest wondered whether this could have been a comprise solution by NSA—an access method they believed only their agency could exploit.[118] Rivest commented:

> Politics requires, however, that such an approach not be achieved by stealth, but rather by explicit approval through a democratic political process, backed by widespread popular approval. In fact, such popular approval does not now (and probably will never) exist, and there is really no chance that explicitly giving the NSA (or more broadly, the government) unfettered access to encrypted data through a back-doored standard would meet with democratic political approval.[119]

Rivest asked which other standards may be "tainted" by NSA's involvement, "should others be withdrawn?"[120] Rivest agreed NIST must strengthen its own cryptographic capacity as "NIST can no longer rely so naively on guidance from the NSA."[121] Rivest also advised the relationship between NIST and the NSA should be restructured, and

---

114 Ibid, 34.
115 Ibid, 43.
116 Ibid, 81.
117 Ibid.
118 Ibid.
119 Ibid.
120 Ibid.
121 Ibid, 84.

all standards-related communications between the parties should be on the public record.[122]

Civil rights groups added their calls to that of the VCAT for the memorandum of understanding between the NSA and NIST, first published in 1989, but updated in 2010, to be refined.[123] In a letter to NIST and the White House, the civil rights groups argued for NIST to "publicly explain the extent and nature of the NSA's consultation on future standards and any modifications thereto made at NSA's request," and to "under no circumstances, consider the signals intelligence needs of the NSA or any other intelligence or law enforcement need of any agency."[124]

NSA's response to the Dual_EC_DRBG accusations came through several comments by its leadership over the subsequent years. Speaking at the Infiltrate security conference in 2014, Richard "Dickie" George, NSA technical director between 2003 and 2011, offered background context on the inclusion of the Dual_EC_DRBG variables in the standard. George stated the genesis of the Dual_EC_DRBG variables was a challenge the NSA confronted in developing classified phones, such as the Secure Telephone Unit 3 (STU-III), in the 1980s which were used by customers including the President. Whilst the NSA had jurisdiction of the technology and standards in use for classified communications equipment, NIST had jurisdiction for the unclassified equivalents. In order for the STU-III to be accredited for both classified and unclassified communications, both NIST and NSA standards had to be satisfied. George explains for the STU-III, "the problem was it wasn't approved for unclassified communications and so the guys [users] had to have two phones on their desk [one for classified, one for unclassified]."[125] George explains the STU could not be approved by NSA for unclassified communications as:

> our algorithms…are classified [and] weren't in the NIST standards. So, I had to go down to my friends at NIST, and I know them well…I said can you waive this [requirement] so that the people in the government can use one phone not two phones….eventually—they were not happy about it—but they did waive it. They said please don't put us in this position again…because we don't want to start granting waivers on these standards, we want people to use the standards.[126]

George explained to prevent a recurrence of the problem, NSA developed the Suite-B set of algorithms for which they used NIST algorithms, but:

> we [NSA] like to use our randomizers, and we were gonna use the Dual Elliptic Curve randomizer. And I said, if you can put this in your standard, nobody else is gonna use it, because it looks ugly, it's really slow. It makes no sense for anybody to go there. But I'll be able to use it. And so they stuck it in, and I said by the way, you know these parameters that we have here, as long as they're in there so we can use them, you can let anybody else put any parameters in that they want.[127]

---

[122] Ibid.
[123] Access Advocacy for Principled Action in Government, et al., 2014.
[124] Ibid, 3.

[125] George, 2014, 31:46.
[126] Ibid, 31:59.
[127] Ibid, 32:47.

NSA Director of Research Michael Wertheimer reflected in 2015:

> With hindsight, NSA should have ceased supporting the Dual_EC_DRBG algorithm immediately after security researchers discovered the potential for a trapdoor. In truth, I can think of no better way to describe our failure to drop support for the Dual_ EC_DRBG algorithm as anything other than regrettable. The costs to the Defense Department to deploy a new algorithm were not an adequate reason to sustain our support for a questionable algorithm.
>
> Indeed, we support NIST's April 2014 decision to remove the algorithm. Furthermore, we realize that our advocacy for the DUAL_EC_DRBG casts suspicion on the broader body of work NSA has done to promote secure standards. Indeed, some colleagues have extrapolated this single action to allege that NSA has a broader agenda to "undermine Internet encryption." A fair reading of our track record speaks otherwise. Nevertheless, we understand that NSA must be much more transparent in its standards work and act according to that transparency.[128]

The cryptologist community did not respond positively to Wertheimer's comments, Matthew Green commented:

> on closer examination, the letter doesn't express regret for the inclusion of Dual EC DRBG in national standards. The transgression Dr. Wertheimer identifies is merely that NSA *continued* to support the algorithm after major questions were raised.[129]

One further twist in the story was an extension to Dual_EC_DRBG which makes it vastly easier to exploit. The "Extended Random" (ER) extension was requested by the US Defense Department which argued the algorithm's nonces "should be at least twice as long as the security level."[130] ER was proposed by Eric Rescorla of RTFM, a cyber security company, and the NSA's Margaret Salter in an Internet draft in March 2008.[131] ER's funding was acknowledged as being provided by the US Department of Defense.[132] ER reduces the Dual_EC_DRBG attack cost from 231 to 215 as the attacker no longer needs to guess the extra sixteen missing bits, this makes the attack up to 65,000 faster.[133] Matthew Green commented, "If using Dual Elliptic Curve is like playing with matches, then adding Extended Random is like dousing yourself with gasoline."[134] Researchers confirmed one use of ER implemented in BSAFE-Java code exposed, "sufficient quantity of contiguous output bytes to enable quick recovery of the session keys."[135] Researchers experimenting with other implementations found "otherwise innocuous implementation decisions greatly affect exploitability."[136] Researchers discovered RSA's B-Safe-C was the easiest to exploit, whilst Open-SSL was more challenging.[137] RSA's Chief Technologist Sam Curry reflected,

---

128 Wertheimer, 2015, 166.
129 Green, 2015.
130 Rescorla and Salter, 2009.
131 Ibid.
132 Ibid, Section 6.
133 Bernstein, Lange and Niederhagen, 2015, 19; Checkoway, Fredrikson et al., no date.
134 Menn, 2014.
135 Checkoway, Fredrikson et al., 2014, 326.
136 Ibid, 334.
137 Ibid.

"We could have been more skeptical of NSA's intentions. We trusted them because they are charged with security for the U.S. government and U.S. critical infrastructure."[138] Curry declined to say whether the NSA paid RSA to include ER in the BSafe security suite.[139] The researchers surveyed the Internet in 2014 and found very few servers using ER (386 of 8 million scanned).[140]

The final Snowden NSA encryption documents showed the agency held a database of encryption keys for specific commercial products called a "key provisioning service"; if the required key was not available, the request was sent to a "key recovery service," in an attempt to acquire it.[141] Further technical details were unavailable.

8.3   SNOWDEN'S IMPACT

The Snowden disclosures focused public attention on digital privacy like never before. The story was made for Hollywood, and a documentary capturing Snowden's ascent from obscurity to infamy helped enthrall the public. The mystique was enriched by its prolonged and uncertain conclusion with Snowden trapped in a Russian airport. Or was he? Rumors circulated Snowden was an agent of the powerful Russian FSB, one of the KGB's successor agencies, though Snowden claims he was not.[142] Snowden proclaimed himself a loyal servant of the American people, and said he would face trial in the US if he were able to mount a public interest defense, where the jury would consider whether his actions were justified, rather than ruling simply on whether he made an unauthorized disclosure of classified files, for which he would surely be found guilty.[143] A few years later, the exile received the full silver screen treatment with Oliver Stone making a Snowden biographical movie starring Joseph Gordon-Levitt.

However, despite the increased public attention, there was mixed evidence as to whether security and privacy opinions had changed. A Pew Research survey of 1004 Americans found 54% believed NSA tracking of telephone records was an acceptable way to investigate terrorism; 41% believed it unacceptable.[144] 62% believed it more important to investigate terrorism even at the expense of citizens' privacy, 34% believed privacy should be pre-eminent—even at the expense of investigations.[145] These figures were largely unchanged from a similar 2006 poll, suggesting Snowden's disclosures whilst bringing surveillance to the fore, did not change mainstream attitudes, though one should be hesitant to place too much faith in a survey with such a small sample set.[146]

Many in the technology community felt betrayed at the revelations. Jeff Moss, a figurehead for the hacker community, asked the government to stay away from the annual DefCon security gathering in Las Vegas.[147] DefCon is the spiritual home of

---

[138]   Menn, 2014.
[139]   Ibid.
[140]   Checkoway, Fredrikson et al., 2014, 325.
[141]   Perlroth, Larson, and Shane, 2013.
[142]   Davies, 2019.

[143]   Ibid.
[144]   Pew Research Center, 2013.
[145]   Ibid.
[146]   Ibid.
[147]   Moss, 2013.

the hacker movement, attracting more than ten thousand hackers every year. When Moss formed DefCon two decades earlier he'd fostered a community where spies, law enforcement officers, and hackers could all come together to learn from one another, and inevitably it proved a fertile recruitment ground for the government.[148] Whilst the hacker community was instinctively suspicious of government agents, there was also a begrudging respect for their technical mastery and mission, the latter of which became more pronounced post-9/11. Before the Snowden revelations broke, a state of peaceful co-existence existed between the parties, to the point where the previous year NSA Chief Keith Alexander keynoted the conference. In asking the government to stay away from DefCon, Moss commented:

> Recent revelations have made many in the [hacker] community uncomfortable about this relationship [with the government]…it would be best for everyone involved if the feds call a "time-out" and not attend DEF CON this year. This will give everybody time to think about how we got here, and what comes next.[149]

The US government was in particular need of the hacking community during the early 2010s. The government was increasingly aware of the risk to national strength posed by a lack of, or the undermining of, cyber security capabilities such as encryption. In 2010, Under Secretary of Defense William J. Lynn had revealed a 2008 breach of classified networks, the most significant breach of US military computers ever.[150] In 2012, NSA Director General Keith Alexander stated intellectual property theft represented the "greatest transfer of wealth in history," commenting it cost US companies around $250 billion per year, with a further $114 billion lost to cybercrime; Alexander added, "that's our future disappearing in front of us."[151] Lynn observed, "Although the threat to intellectual property is less dramatic than the threat to critical national infrastructure, it may be the most significant cyberthreat that the United States will face over the long term."[152] Whilst encryption was a problem, it was also part of a solution to intellectual property theft and critical national infrastructure security. Much of the critical infrastructure requiring protection was located in the private sector, which was predominantly protected by those who attended DefCon and similar conferences—damaging relations with the hacker community endangered not only recruitment of their number to direct government work, but also the working level relationships required to defend the country.

The most significant impact of the Snowden disclosures was a renewed effort by industry to deploy ubiquitous cryptography. Companies aspired to encrypt all web traffic, to offer end-to-end (E2E) encryption for sensitive exchanges such as instant messages (e.g., WhatsApp), and to provide full-disk encryption (FDE) for devices themselves.

---

[148] Finkle, 2013.
[149] Moss, 2013.
[150] Lynn, 2010.

[151] Rogin, 2012.
[152] Lynn, 2010.

Let's Encrypt, which planned to make it easier to encrypt web traffic, was one of the most impactful post-Snowden projects. Let's Encrypt's Josh Aas commented in 2014:

> It's clear at this point that encrypting is something all of us should be doing. Then why don't we use TLS [HTTPS] everywhere? Every browser in every device supports it. Every server in every data center supports it. Why don't we just flip the switch? The challenge is server certificates.[153]

Aas' colleague Alex Halderman offers historical context:

> Traditionally, implementing HTTPS has required website operators to choose a certificate authority, prove their identity to them, pay as much as a few hundred dollars for a certificate, wait for it to arrive, then follow a complicated series of steps to install it. You have to repeat the process every year or two, and if you don't do it on time, your website might go down. So a lot of websites, particularly smaller ones, just left their sites unencrypted.[154]

On average a single-domain certificate cost $178 per year.[155] Halderman explains that in the 1990s, encryption was just used for digital financial transactions; however, "since then, the internet has become a much more dangerous place…Snowden showed us that governments were surveilling traffic on a global scale," and thus ubiquitous encryption was now needed to protect citizens from the State.[156] However, Let's Encrypt has pre-Snowden origins, with two separate projects attempting to solve the Certificate Authority (CA) problem.[157] The first project was led by Halderman at Michigan University and EFF's Peter Eckersley who started developing a protocol for automatically issuing and renewing certificates in 2012.[158] Concurrently, a team led by Josh Aas and Eric Rescorla at Mozilla were trying to build a free and automated CA. The groups merged forming the Internet Security Research Group (ISRG) in 2013.[159] Donations from EFF, Mozilla, Cisco, and Akamai helped sustain the ISRG.[160]

To solve the certificate issue, Let's Encrypt designed a "fully robotic" certificate issuing process to allow for scalability and ease of use—with this model they could offer free certificates.[161] The next challenge was having browsers trust an unknown CA; the easiest way to do this was to partner with an established CA and have Let's Encrypt's certificates cross-signed by the established CA, this way they would inherit their partner's trusted status.[162] Let's Encrypt partnered with IdenTrust, a root authority trusted by Apple, Microsoft, and Mozilla.[163]

---

[153] Aas, 2014.
[154] Moore, 2019.
[155] Aas, Barnes, Case et al., 2019, 2.
[156] Moore, 2019.
[157] Aas, Barnes, Case et al., 2019, 3.
[158] Ibid.

[159] Ibid.
[160] Ibid, 4.
[161] Ibid, 1.
[162] Ibid, 4.
[163] Ibid.

Let's Encrypt issued their first certificate in July 2015, triggering a rapid advance of web encryption.[164] Between 2016 and 2019 global encryption rose an average 10% per year, rising from 40% to 80%, according to Firefox statistics.[165] By January 2019, Let's Encrypt had issued over 538 million certificates for 223 million domain names allowing it to claim to be the world's largest "HTTPS CA, accounting for more currently valid certificates than all other browser-trusted CAs combined."[166] Reflecting on their success Let's Encrypt wrote:

> We hope that in the near future, clients will start using HTTPS as the default Web transport. Eventually, we may marvel that there was ever a time when Web traffic traveled over the Internet as plaintext.[167]

Apple were also at the heart of the encryption movement—as a global business, any perception the US government could readily access its data or devices was anathema to maintaining foreign market share. Apple also had a decades' long history of marketing the privacy and anti-establishment nature of its products. For instance, in 1984 Apple produced a Super Bowl advert in which the protagonist ran from riot police before destroying a cinema screen broadcasting propaganda to a captive audience before displaying the caption, "1984 won't be like 1984." Since that point, a degree of independence from the US government, and even antagonism towards it, had become crucial to preserving credibility in foreign markets—especially those markets of the US' political adversaries. Many other technology companies were in a similar position. A significant danger of the Snowden disclosures was that the global market would turn away from American products, believing them all to be readily accessible by the US government, and develop indigenous alternative products, thus accelerating the Internet's balkanization.

In September 2014, Apple deployed default FDE, with decryption keys tied to the user's password which were stored exclusively on the device.[168] Apple CEO Tim Cook announced, "Apple cannot bypass your passcode and therefore cannot access this data. So it's not technically feasible for us to respond to government warrants for the extraction of this data from devices in their possession running iOS 8."[169] The value of E2E encryption, and most forms of FDE encryption, is the practice of holding keys exclusively on the end-user device (e.g., iPhone). Consequently, service providers are unable to read their client's data. Therefore, if the government serves a warrant upon a company for user data, the company cannot comply, they simply don't have the access, or at best can provide an encrypted blob. This does not come without cost to the user—should they forget their password, or lock themselves out of their account, there is no way to recover the data (unless a compensating mechanism is employed). ACLU Technologist Christopher Soghoian commented, "Apple's old policy for extracting user data from iPhones for law enforcement: Come back with a

---

[164] Aas, 2015.
[165] Let's Encrypt, 2020.
[166] Aas, Barnes, Case et al., 2019.
[167] Ibid, 13.
[168] Farivar, 2014.
[169] Ibid.

warrant. Their new policy: Get lost."[170] Chicago's former Chief of Police Detectives John Escalante predicted, "Apple will become the phone of choice for the pedophile."[171] Google's Android 5.0 (Lollipop) enabled default FDE in November 2014 as they gradually moved all Google traffic to be encrypted. Google figures show a steady rise from 50% of their traffic encrypted in 2014, to 94% by the close of 2019.[172] WhatsApp also enabled default E2E in November 2014.[173] Before moving to the US, WhatsApp's founder Jan Koum grew up in the Soviet Union, where he says, "everything you did was eavesdropped on, recorded, snitched on."[174] Koum was unwilling to aid the US government, stating:

> Nobody should have the right to eavesdrop, or you become a totalitarian state—the kind of state I escaped as a kid to come to this country where you have democracy and freedom of speech. Our goal is to protect it. We have encryption between our client and our server. We don't save any messages on our servers, we don't store your chat history. They're all on your phone.[175]

Over the coming months and years, almost all major services enacted similar default encryption, and vocally projected their privacy credentials to a global public apprehensive of US surveillance.

An indicator of the effectiveness of default encryption was presented by Manhattan's District Attorney Cyrus Vance when he stated 111 investigations were hindered due to fully encrypted mobile phones between September 2014 and October 2015.[176] Vance reported the cases related to "homicide, attempted murder, sexual abuse of a child, sex trafficking, assault, and robbery."[177] Vance commented, "it is reasonable to believe that in many of these cases the data that is out of the reach of law enforcement would have been relevant to the case and to the investigation of additional crimes or perpetrators."[178] Vance also included a comment by a prison inmate who, speaking to a friend, said:

> The DA Cyrus Vance who's prosecuting me is beefing with Apple because they put these phones that can't be [un]encrypted. If our phones is running on the iO8 software, they can't open my phone. That might be another gift from God.[179]

The geopolitical reaction to Snowden was significant with the international community expressing its dismay at US surveillance practices. In a United Nations December 2013 resolution entitled "the right to privacy in the digital age," the UN stated they were:

> Deeply concerned at the negative impact that surveillance and/or interception of communications, including extraterritorial surveillance and/or interception of

---

[170] Ibid.
[171] Timberg and Miller, 2014.
[172] Greenberg, 2014; Google, 2019.
[173] Donohue, 2014.
[174] Rowan, 2014.

[175] Ibid.
[176] Manhattan District Attorney's Office, 2015, 9.
[177] Ibid.
[178] Ibid.
[179] Ibid, 12.

communications, as well as the collection of personal data, in particular when carried out on a mass scale, may have on the exercise and enjoyment of human rights.[180]

President Obama had earlier accused those who criticized the program of hypocrisy:

> Some of the folks who have been most greatly offended publicly we know privately engage in the same activities directed at us, or use information that we've obtained to protect their people. And we recognize that.[181]

Tim Berners-Lee, inventor of the World Wide Web, called for a global digital bill of rights, a digital "Magna Carta."[182] Berners-Lee stated the issues of government surveillance, "crept up on us...our rights are being infringed more and more on every side, and the danger is that we get used to it."[183] Berners-Lee added:

> Unless we have an open, neutral internet we can rely on without worrying about what's happening at the backdoor, we can't have open government, good democracy, good healthcare, connected communities and diversity of culture. It's not naïve to think we can have that, but it is naïve to think we can just sit back and get it.[184]

Former NSA and CIA director Michael V. Hayden warned the debate should "proceed carefully."[185] Hayden lamented, "Sweeping charges, bumper stick explanations, score settling, demagoguery, and outright ignorance have characterized this discussion so far."[186] Hayden admitted, "a balanced discussion is going to be hard and extraordinary effort will be required if metadata collection and programs...revealed by Snowden are to be judged on their merits and not merely swept away by the broader politics of the day."[187] For a fact-based discussion to take place, Hayden explained the "the administration and intelligence community are going to have to be *very* forthcoming with facts" [author italics].[188]

In Congress, Republican Representative Thomas Massie of Kentucky and Democratic Representative Zoe Lofgren of California attempted to prevent the NSA and CIA from negatively modifying encryption standards in 2014 by offering an amendment to the 2015 National Defense Appropriations Act. The Massie-Lofgren amendment reads:

> None of the funds made available by this Act may be used by the National Institute of Standards and Technology to consult with the National Security Agency or the Central Intelligence Agency to alter cryptographic computer standards, except to improve information security.[189]

---

[180] United Nations, 2014.
[181] Obama, 2013c.
[182] Kiss, 2014.
[183] Ibid.
[184] Ibid.
[185] Hayden, 2014, 15.
[186] Ibid.
[187] Ibid, 16.
[188] Ibid.
[189] Massie, 2014a.

Massie commented if standards were manipulated, "everyone that uses that standard is at risk of having their financial and medical records stolen, and being subject to hackers. Hackers will find these backdoors if they exist."[190] The amendment passed the House of Representatives 291–123 in June.[191] However, in December 2014, negotiations between the House and Senate to pass the Appropriations Act the amendment was stripped out. Massie commented, "A veto-proof majority of Republicans and Democrats voted for my NSA reform amendment this summer. If this amendment is killed in a back room is that the will of the people?"[192] The same day it became evident the Massie-Lofgren amendment had died, Democratic Senator Ron Wyden introduced the Secure Data Act, and Representative Lofgren introduced the same legislation in the House.[193] The short bill stipulated:

> no agency may mandate that a manufacturer, developer, or seller of covered products design or alter the security functions in its product or service to allow the surveillance of any user of such product or service, or to allow the physical search of such product, by any agency.[194]

The bill exempted equipment falling under the CALEA legislation.[195] Wyden stated encryption "is the best way to protect our constitutional rights at a time when a person's whole life can often be found on his or her smartphone."[196] Wyden added:

> strong computer security can rebuild consumer trust that has been shaken by years of misstatements by intelligence agencies about mass surveillance of Americans. This bill sends a message to leaders of those agencies to stop recklessly pushing for new ways to vacuum up Americans' private information, and instead put that effort into rebuilding public trust.[197]

The Secure Data Act failed to get out of the Commerce, and Intelligence and Judiciary Committees. However, Wyden saw positives in the failure, believing as a result of their attempt, "there is growing interest both in the Senate and House for legislation to protect Americans' security and liberty by outlawing government mandates for backdoors and other cybersecurity weaknesses."[198]

8.4   FBI TARGETS ENCRYPTION KEYS OF SNOWDEN'S EMAIL PROVIDER, LAVABIT

Two FBI agents knocked on the front door of Ladar Levison's Texas home in June 2013. The agents were seeking access to an email account Edward Snowden used to call a press conference in Moscow's Sheremetyevo Airport, where he was stranded.[199] The email account was run by Levison's company, Lavabit. Levison grew up in San

[190] Whittaker, 2015.
[191] Reitman, 2014.
[192] Massie, 2014b.
[193] United States Congress, 2014.
[194] Ibid.
[195] Ibid.
[196] Wyden, 2014.
[197] Ibid.
[198] Geller, 2016.
[199] Levison, 2014a; Lokshina, 2013.

Francisco. He built his first computer at the age of ten and ran a bulletin board whilst still at school. At fourteen, Levison slipped away from home without saying a word, in order to make a pilgrimage to DefCon.[200] Lavabit offered secure email services designed to frustrate US interception and access tools—encryption protected the data in transit and at rest, Lavabit themselves could not read the email content, therefore they could not turn it over to the government, even if served with a warrant. Lavabit had 410,000 clients worldwide.[201] Lavabit's website states:

> Lavabit believes that a civil society depends on the open, free and private flow of ideas. The type of monitoring promoted by the PATRIOT Act restricts that flow of ideas because it intimidates those afraid of retaliation. To counteract this chilling effect, Lavabit developed its secure e-mail platform. We feel e-mail has evolved into a critical channel for the communication of ideas in a healthy democracy. It's precisely because of e-mail's importance that we strive so hard to protect private e-mails from eavesdropping.[202]

Despite this, Levison was not completely anti-establishment. Fully encrypted services were only offered to paying users of Lavabit services; the website notes, "with paying customers, there is a money trail. If the account is used for illegal purposes that money trail can be used to track down the account owner."[203] However, financial footprints can be obscured—a fact Levison would have known. Levison claims to have cooperated with "upwards of a dozen court orders" for specific users.[204]

The FBI agents presented Levison with a court order instructing him to facilitate the FBI placing interception technologies on Lavabit's network to enable metadata from Snowden's account to be intercepted.[205] The Judge ordered the interception order be kept secret, as its disclosure risked alerting Snowden to the government investigation and causing him to abandon Lavabit's services.[206] When court documents were eventually released, the investigation's target was redacted and the secrecy order prevented Levison from conveying this information; it was 2016 before a government redaction error confirmed public suspicions Snowden was the target.[207]

The court order was later enhanced to include an interception requirement for all Snowden-related content.[208] The court order stated, "Lavabit shall furnish agents from the Federal Bureau of Investigation, forthwith, all information, facilities, and technical assistance necessary to accomplish the installation and use of the pen/trap device."[209] The inclusion of the term "use of" was argued by the Department of Justice to include providing decryption keys to enable "use of" the intercepted product—Levison disputed this interpretation. The DOJ recounts Levison indicated he had the technical ability to decrypt the traffic but did not want to "defeat [Lavabit's]

---

[200] Rogers, 2013.
[201] Lavabit, 2012; Levison, 2014a.
[202] Lavabit, 2012.
[203] Ibid.
[204] NBC News, 2013.
[205] Levison, 2014a.

[206] United States District Court Eastern District of Virginia, 2013, 2–3.
[207] Zetter, 2016.
[208] United States District Court Eastern District of Virginia, 2013, 36.
[209] Ibid, 8.

own system."[210] Levison did not comply with the court order, telling the FBI agents he wanted to consult a lawyer as to his options.[211] Levison's objection was that if he surrendered Lavabit's encryption keys, there would be no technical barriers to prevent the FBI from intercepting the traffic of all of the company's 410,000 clients. Levison claims the agents "said they needed…customer passwords—which were sent securely—so that they could access the plain-text versions of messages from customers using my company's encrypted storage feature."[212] Levison was advised the FBI would only store data associated with the account for which they had legal authorization: Edward Snowden's. This did not satisfactory Levison.[213]

Judge Theresa Buchanan ordered Levison to comply with the intercept requirement warning Levison he would be subject to "any penalty within the power of the court"; in barely legible handwriting the typed sentence was appended with "including the possibility of criminal contempt of court," on June 28.[214] The FBI claimed they made "numerous attempts" to meet with Levison in the subsequent days and weeks without success, though Levison claims he was speaking with the FBI regularly.[215] Levison was summoned to a Virginia court on July 16 to "show cause why Lavabit…failed to comply with the orders," and was instructed to bring to the hearing "the public and private encryption keys used by lavabit.com in any SSL or TLS sessions."[216]

It was far from the first time the FBI attempted to acquire encryption keys. The earliest evidence of FBI operations to acquire their target's encryption keys came in 2001 when, during prosecution of suspected loan shark Nicodemo Scarfo, the Bureau was forced by Judge Nicholas Politan to disclose how the accused's PGP encrypted communications were accessed.[217] The FBI explained how, with relevant court authorizations, they covertly entered Scarfo's office to install key-stealing malware on his computer.[218] The FBI Laboratory configured the malware—known as a key logger system (KLS)—which was based on "previously developed techniques."[219] The deployment of the FBI code to the suspect's machine was executed in May 1999, suggesting the FBI's forays into computer exploitation began before that date.[220] Retrieval of the data required physical access to the machine, therefore FBI agents covertly re-entered Scarfo's office several times to retrieve their digital haul, which included the PGP passphrase and other "key-related information."[221]

In 2001 it was also reported the FBI was developing a capability codenamed MAGIC LANTERN, malware designed to harvest user encryption keys and associated keying data remotely.[222] The FBI's Paul Bresson confirmed MAGIC

---

[210] Ibid, 12.
[211] Ibid.
[212] Levison, 2014a.
[213] United States District Court Eastern District of Virginia, 2013, 45.
[214] Ibid, 16.
[215] Ibid, 20.
[216] Ibid, 31; Levison 2014.

[217] United States District Court Eastern District of New Jersey, 2001b, 3.
[218] United States District Court Eastern District of New Jersey, 2001a, 2–4.
[219] Ibid.
[220] Ibid.
[221] Ibid, 10.
[222] Sullivan, 2001.

LANTERN's existence, but stated, "It is a workbench project...we can't discuss it because it's under development."[223] In 2007 court documents revealed FBI capabilities had evolved to remote operations—the Bureau were no longer reliant on breaking and entering techniques making their use of the technique scalable and responsive.[224] The court documents revealed a case in which the perpetrator sent bomb threats to a Washington high school via email and taunted FBI investigators they lacked the digital skills to trace him.[225] The FBI gained a warrant and deployed a tool called a Computer and Internet Protocol Address Verifier (CIPAV) to identify the suspect.[226] The CIPAV would be delivered via an "electronic messaging program controlled by the FBI" and would be able to send information on the target device back to the FBI, including: true IP address, MAC address, list of running programs, operating system, Internet browser, registered computer name, current logged-in user, last URL visited.[227] The operation was successful and the perpetrator was identified as a student of the school.[228]

In Levison's case, MAGIC LANTERN or similar capabilities were not an option—as well as Levison likely having more advanced technical defenses than typical investigatory targets, he was not the subject of the investigation, but a third party. Therefore, the FBI needed Levison to hand over the keys. In trying to deliver the subpoena for his court appearance, FBI agents stated they knocked at Levison's door only to witness, "Levison leave the rear of his apartment, get in his car, and drive away."[229] Before the hearing, Levison offered to conduct the interception himself and provide the FBI with the data, he demanded a fee of $4000 to compensate him for writing the necessary code and offered to deliver the intercept product at the end of the court-ordered 60 days, with the option to provide intercept more frequently for an additional $1500 compensation.[230] Levison also requested $2000 for the re-issuing of SSL certificates to his clients, though it was not clear to the FBI whether this was included within the $4000 quoted.[231] The FBI argued this demand did not fall under the definition of "reasonable expenses" as allowed for by the pen register legislation.[232] The FBI further stated Levison could comply with the pen register order by "simply allowing the FBI to install the pen register device and providing the FBI with the encryption keys."[233] The DOJ requested the judge fine Levison $1000 per day after the scheduled hearing if he failed to yield to the court order.[234] The morning of the hearing, the DOJ secured a search warrant specifically for Lavabit's encryption keys to resolve any ambiguity in the initial pen register request.[235] Levison asked Judge Hilton to unseal the case to allow public debate—Hilton refused, citing the risk to the investigation.[236] Levison attempted to have the

223 Reuters, 2001.
224 United States District Court Western District of Washington, 2007.
225 Ibid.
226 United States District Court Western District of Washington, 2007, 2–3.
227 Ibid, 5 and 13.
228 Poulsen, 2007.
229 United States of America, 2013, 14.
230 United States District Court Eastern District of Virginia, 2013, 46.
231 Ibid.
232 Ibid.
233 Ibid, 47.
234 Ibid.
235 Ibid, 51.
236 Ibid, 54.

search warrant for his encryption keys revoked, arguing, "Lavabit will pay the ultimate price—the loss of its customers' trust and business—should the Court require
that the Master Key be turned over."[237] Levison also argued that as the encryption
keys would allow all Lavabit users to be monitored, the search warrant was overbroad
and thus violated the Fourth Amendment.[238] Levison's lawyer asked Judge Claude
Hilton for a mechanism to ensure the government would not go outside the scope of
the warrant, with Levison's offer of he himself conducting the intercept proffered as
a solution.[239] Judge Hilton replied, "You want to do it in a way that the government
has to trust you…to come up with the right data…and you won't trust the government. So why would the government trust you?"[240] The FBI assured the judge their
software would sift the data and only extract Snowden's communications.[241] The
court dismissed Levison's request and ordered the encryption keys be delivered to
the FBI.[242] Levison complied—in a manner—on August 2 he provided the encryption keys…on eleven pages in an illegible 4-point font.[243] The government wrote to
the judge asking that from August 5, a $5000 fine be levied against Levison for each
day of non-compliance—Judge Hilton granted the request.[244] Levison handed in an
electronic copy of the encryption keys to the FBI's Dallas office on August 7—the
same day he closed Lavabit.[245] With the company deceased, the encryption keys
were of no use to the FBI. Levison posted on Lavabit's website he had been forced to
"make a difficult decision: to become complicit in crimes against the American people or walk away from nearly ten years of hard work by shutting down Lavabit."[246]
Levison explained legalities prevented him from communicating the events leading
him to this decision.[247] Levinson closed his message warning, "without congressional action or a strong judicial precedent, I would strongly recommend against anyone
trusting their private data to a company with physical ties to the United States."[248]
Levison later explained:

> if the feds had known I was planning to shutdown they would have gotten a court order
> requiring me to continue operating the service. If I had shutdown the service after
> receiving such an order I would have almost certainly been charged with obstruction
> of justice. I've been told that other service providers have threatened a shutdown and
> received such orders.[249]

Who the other companies were is unknown. Maryland-based Silent Circle, which
offered a similar secure mail service, announced they would also close on August
9, telling their customers, "We see the writing [on] the wall, and we have decided
that it is best for us to shut down Silent Mail now. We have not received subpoenas,
warrants, security letters, or anything else by any government, and this is why we

---

237 Ibid, 74.
238 Ibid, 70–73.
239 Ibid, 127–128.
240 Ibid, 128.
241 Ibid, 132.
242 Ibid, 133.
243 Ibid, 140–141.

244 Ibid, 142 and 153–154.
245 United States of America, 2013, 20.
246 Levison, 2013a.
247 Ibid.
248 Ibid.
249 Levison, 2013b.

are acting now."[250] In October the Lavabit records were unsealed, allowing the public to understand events leading to the closure of Lavabit. EFF's Jennifer Lynch commented, "Obtaining a warrant for a service's private key is no different than obtaining a warrant to search all the houses in a city to find the papers of one suspect."[251] Snowden was "inspired" by Lavabit's actions, commenting, "employees and leaders at Google, Facebook, Microsoft, Yahoo, Apple, and the rest of our internet titans must ask themselves why they aren't fighting for our interests the same way small businesses are."[252] The government made no comment.

Levison appealed his contempt of court sanctions, his defense fundraised over $100,000 of the total $150,000 it would eventually require.[253] The DOJ's brief to the court argued:

> Just as a business cannot prevent the execution of a search warrant by locking its front gate, an electronic communications service provider cannot thwart court-ordered electronic surveillance by refusing to provide necessary information about its systems.[254]

As data belonging to other users of Lavabit was not to be reviewed by the FBI, the government reiterated their argument that "other information not subject to the warrant was encrypted using the same set of keys is irrelevant...all other data would be filtered electronically, without reaching any human eye[s]."[255] In what could potentially be considered a message to other companies contemplating dissent, the DOJ wrote, "Marketing a business as 'secure' does not give one license to ignore a District Court of the United States."[256] Levison's appeal was rejected.[257] Levison commented of the experience:

> courts must not be allowed to consider matters of great importance under the shroud of secrecy, lest we find ourselves summarily deprived of meaningful due process. If we allow our government to continue operating in secret, it is only a matter of time before you or a loved one find yourself in a position like I did—standing in a secret courtroom, alone, and without any of the meaningful protections that were always supposed to be the people's defense against an abuse of the state's power.[258]

Levison also reflected on protecting Edward Snowden:

> I'm glad it was him and not a degenerate or a scoundrel that I was left defending...My fear was that I would be forced to defend a terrorist or a child pornography ring or organized crime or something of that nature. Instead, the person they went after that led to the eventual shutdown was a whistleblower exposing government abuse. That's at the very heart of why I think privacy is so important.[259]

---

[250] Callas, 2013.
[251] Electronic Frontier Foundation, 2013.
[252] Greenwald, 2013b.
[253] Levison, 2014b.
[254] United States of America, 2013.
[255] Ibid.
[256] Ibid.
[257] United States Court of Appeals for the Levison Circuit, 2014.
[258] Levison, 2014a.
[259] Conger, 2016.

Lavabit's experience was a foreshadowing of the Apple San Bernardino case about to erupt in California—the difference was Apple retained an army of lawyers, and argued their case in full view of the world, rather than in sealed courtrooms.

8.5 GOING DARK: FBI ENCRYPTION FEARS

In October 2014, the Washington Post issued an editorial stating, "smartphone users must accept that they cannot be above the law if there is a valid search warrant." The editorial asked, "with all their wizardry, perhaps Apple and Google could invent a kind of secure golden key they would retain and use only when a court has approved a search warrant."[260] The conflation of secure devices and a user being above the law was a common refrain. As attorney Marc Zwillinger pointed out:

> The fact that the Constitution offers a process for obtaining a search warrant where there is probable cause is not support for the notion that it should be illegal to make an unbreakable lock. These are two distinct concepts.[261]

The public response was predictable. Vice's Sarah Jeong commented, "The specter of future warrants should not shape the internet exactly how law enforcement would like it to be shaped, particularly when it put[s] ordinary people at risk of harm."[262] Techdirt's Mike Masnick asked:

> I'm not sure which members of the Washington Post editorial board is engaged in mythical "golden key" cryptography studies, but to most folks who have even the slightest understanding of technology, they ought to have recognized that what they basically said is: "a back door is a bad idea, so how about creating a magic back door?"[263]

Whilst the comments of the Washington Post were not substantive policy suggestions, the language of "golden keys" would endure as a short-hand for a back door into encrypted systems. Just over a week later, on October 16, 2014, FBI Director James Comey, who had then spent a year at the FBI's helm, made his "Going Dark" speech.[264] The FBI's Going Dark program had been active since at least 2006, with its scope comprising:

> efforts to utilize innovative technology; foster cooperation with industry; and assist... law enforcement partners in a collaborative effort to close the growing gap between lawful interception requirements and our capabilities.[265]

The going dark narrative was previously employed in 2010 by then FBI General Counsel Valerie Caproni when she commented, "They [technology companies] can

---

[260] Washington Post Editorial Board, 2014.
[261] Zwillinger, 2014.
[262] Jeong, 2015.
[263] Masnick, 2014.
[264] Comey, 2014.
[265] Lynch, 2011.

promise strong encryption. They just need to figure out how they can provide us plain text."[266] Comey explained:

> technology has become the tool of choice for some very dangerous people…sophisticated criminals will come to count on these means [encryption] of evading detection. It's the equivalent of a closet that can't be opened. A safe that can't be cracked.[267]

Comey argued the post-Snowden perception the government was "sweeping up all of our communications," was erroneous:

> Some believe that the FBI has these phenomenal capabilities to access any information at any time—that we can get what we want, when we want it, by flipping some sort of switch. It may be true in the movies or on TV. It is simply not the case in real life.[268]

Comey worried the combination of E2E and FDE encryption would enable targets to "Go Dark," preventing agents from accessing crucial evidence. Comey believed the law had not kept pace with encryption technology arguing, "encryption threatens to lead all of us to a very dark place," and soon, "an order from a judge to monitor a suspect's communication may amount to nothing more than a piece of paper." Comey invoked a phrase popular amongst the youth, "Fear of Missing Out," or FOMO, which he said the FBI was experiencing:

> With Going Dark, those of us in law enforcement and public safety have a major fear of missing out—missing out on predators who exploit the most vulnerable among us… missing out on violent criminals who target our communities…missing out on a terrorist cell using social media to recruit, plan, and execute an attack.[269]

Comey commented Apple and Google's FDE would cause problems, "Both companies are run by good people, responding to what they perceive is a market demand. But the place they are leading us is one we shouldn't go to without careful thought and debate as a country." Comey stated whilst data backed up to the cloud for Apple and Google was available, this data was not everything on the device, and savvy criminals stored their data exclusively on devices protected by FDE. Comey also argued any available unencrypted metadata was "incomplete information" as it does not provide content.[270] Comey noted brute force attacks against encryption were not feasible:

> Even a supercomputer would have difficulty with today's high-level encryption, and some devices have a setting whereby the encryption key is erased if someone makes too many attempts to break the password, meaning no one can access that data.[271]

---

266 Caproni, 2011; Savage, 2010.
267 Comey, 2014.
268 Ibid.
269 Ibid.
270 Ibid.
271 Ibid.

Further, Comey stated compelling criminals to provide access was not an option due to legalities, and criminals would not willingly unlock data due to what it could reveal:

> if we had a child predator in custody, and he could choose to sit quietly through a 30-day contempt sentence for refusing to comply with a court order to produce his password, or he could risk a 30-year sentence for production and distribution of child pornography, which do you think he would choose?[272]

Comey requested technology companies, "take a step back, to pause, and to consider changing course…there should be no law-free zone in this country." Comey called for "open and honest debates about liberty and security," positing there was no conflict between the two as "we in law enforcement, national security, and public safety are looking for security that enhances liberty." Comey stated, "Perhaps it's time to suggest that the post-Snowden pendulum has swung too far in one direction—in a direction of fear and mistrust"; Comey said whilst skepticism of government power was healthy, he asked:

> Are we no longer a country governed by the rule of law, where no one is above or beyond that law? Are we so mistrustful of government—and of law enforcement— that we are willing to let bad guys walk away…willing to leave victims in search of justice?[273]

Comey declared, "We aren't seeking a back-door approach. We want to use the front door, with clarity and transparency, and with clear guidance provided by law." Specifically, Comey noted the provisions of the Communications Assistance for Law Enforcement Act (CALEA), passed almost two decades ago, compelling communications and broadband suppliers to build interception capabilities into their infrastructure, did not apply to the thousands of Internet companies now providing some form of communications services to clients (e.g., Facebook). Comey wanted those companies not subject to CALEA to provide intercept capabilities, voluntarily, and then as a result of legislation. Comey stated, "We aren't seeking to expand our authority to intercept communications. We are struggling to keep up with changing technology and to maintain our ability to actually collect the communications we are authorized to intercept." Comey finished with a call for a "reasoned and practical approach," but confessed he lacked the "perfect solution," but felt it was "important to start the discussion."[274]

But it was far from the start of discussion. Whilst Comey was coming to the crypto wars for the first time, the discussion had been ongoing for a generation, as was pointed out by EFF's Cindy Cohn, a crypto wars veteran, who noted Comey's "twenty-year old talking points."[275] Cohn stated:

---

[272] Ibid.
[273] Ibid.

[274] Ibid.
[275] Cohn, 2014.

Now just as then, the FBI is trying to convince the world that some fantasy version of security is possible—where "good guys" can have a backdoor or extra key to your home but bad guys could never use it. Anyone with even a rudimentary understanding of security can tell you that's just not true.[276]

Cohn argued, "The FBI should not be in the business of trying to convince companies to offer less security to their customers."[277] Cohn wrote:

if the FBI…convinces Congress to change the law, or even if it convinces companies like Apple that make our tools and hold our data to weaken the security they offer to us, we'll all end up less secure and enjoying less privacy. Or as the Fourth Amendment puts it: we'll be less "secure in our papers and effects."[278]

ACLU Washington office Director Laura Murphy stated, "Comey is wrong in asserting that law enforcement cannot do its job while respecting Americans' privacy rights." Murphy continued, "Whether the FBI calls it a front door or a backdoor, any effort by the FBI to weaken encryption leaves our highly personal information and our business information vulnerable to hacking by foreign governments and criminals." ACLU praised Apple and Google who were "unwilling to weaken security for everyone to allow the government yet another tool in its already vast surveillance arsenal."[279]

In March 2015, NSA Director Admiral Michael Rogers, speaking at Princeton University, continued Comey's narrative, commenting, "I don't want a back door, I want a front door, and I want the front door to have multiple locks, big locks…so that no single entity can get in."[280] Rogers' suggestion for some form of split-key cryptography was identical in concept to that of the failed 1990s Clipper chip. Rogers countered concerns that a split-key approach would introduce a new vulnerability by arguing:

this is like when you get a safe deposit box in your bank and you tell yourself, "well I'm the only one with a key, this is safe"…I'm thinking, you're not the only one with a key…I'm a little uncomfortable with the idea "you're just creating vulnerability."[281]

However, Rogers did stress this topic was a national conversation and the country would have to decide how it wanted to manage the exceptional access challenge.

Digital privacy activists responded with dismay at the suggestion. The Center for Democracy and Technology's Joseph Hall commented, "split-key encryption is not a serious proposal…Rogers should come back with a proposal the technical community hasn't already identified as irresponsible, costly, and impractical." Hall further added, "It's time to stake that trial balloon to the ground of technical reality."[282] It

---

276 Ibid.
277 Ibid.
278 Ibid
279 ACLU, 2014.

280 Rogers, 2015, 39:20.
281 Rogers, 2015, 40:01.
282 Hall, 2015.

seemed clear that if the US government again attempted such an escrow initiative, it would confront the same public opposition as it had during the 1990s.

In early 2016, academics at Harvard University released a paper contesting the "going dark" argument, the authors included Bruce Schneier and colleagues from a range of backgrounds including technical, government, and legal.[283] The authors questioned whether the "going dark" metaphor was appropriate, "Are we really headed to a future in which our ability to effectively surveil criminals and bad actors is impossible? We think not." The authors agreed some forms of communications would become harder to intercept, however, they argued:

> Short of a form of government intervention in technology that appears contemplated by no one outside of the most despotic regimes, communication channels resistant to surveillance will always exist...We argue that communications in the future will neither be eclipsed into darkness nor illuminated without shadow.[284]

The authors argued some data would remain unencrypted as digital companies relied on being able to see user activity for monetization purposes (e.g., targeted advertisements) and metadata would likely remain unencrypted by necessity. The authors also argued growth of the Internet of Things would open up new surveillance opportunities (e.g., being able to gain warrants to have Smart TVs activate their cameras to monitor targets).[285]

8.6   APPLE DEFIES THE COURTS: SAN BERNARDINO AND EXCEPTIONAL ACCESS

Syed Rizwan Farook left his office at San Bernardino's Health Department before returning with his wife, Tashfeen Malik, on December 2, 2015.[286] Farook and Malik then fired more than a hundred bullets at Farook's colleagues before fleeing.[287] Shortly afterward, the assailants were killed in a police shootout.[288] Fourteen people died and 21 were injured in what was the worst domestic terrorist attack since 9/11.[289] FBI Director James Comey stated there were "indications of radicalization by the killers and of the potential inspiration by foreign terrorist organizations."[290] However, Comey added there was "no indication that these killers are part of an organized larger group."[291] Comey stated hundreds of FBI agents were "trying to understand the motives of these killers and trying to understand every detail of their lives."[292] It soon emerged Malik had pledged allegiance to Islamic State via Facebook.[293] Before they were killed in a shootout with the police, the terrorists attempted to conceal and destroy electronic evidence—it was this electronic evidence, in particular an iPhone

---

[283] Olson, Schneier, and Zittrain, 2016.
[284] Ibid.
[285] Ibid.
[286] Berman, 2016.
[287] Ibid.
[288] Ibid

[289] Federal Bureau of Investigation, 2015.
[290] Ibid.
[291] Ibid.
[292] Ibid.
[293] Schmidt and Pérez-Peña, 2015.

5C running iOS9—that became the nexus of a legal and media battle between the FBI and Apple. The FBI asked Apple to unlock the device; they refused.

Whilst the investigation was progressing, in January 2016 technology executives and government security leaders gathered in San Jose, California, for a summit to discuss a broad range of topics including encryption and Islamic State propaganda. During the meeting Tim Cook, who State Department's Richard Stengel believed was talking for the assembled industry leaders, told the government representatives, including the FBI's James Comey, White House Chief of Staff Denis McDonough, and NSA Director Michael Rogers, that "the horse has left the barn on encryption. It's not going away and will only get more powerful."[294] Cook argued the government needed to recognize this reality and consequently ask, "How do you optimize your ability to find a terrorist in a world where there is encryption, that is the question?"[295] On the prospect of a back door, Cook commented, "If I felt that this was the thing that would protect us all, I'd be for it."[296] The meeting then progressed to other topics, perhaps the government executives feeling that further pressing the encryption issue would sour their wider agenda with the technology leaders.

On February 16, 2016, the FBI asked Apple to unlock the iPhone again, this time with an All Writs Act court order.[297] The order instructed Apple to provide "reasonable technical assistance to achieve three important functions:

(1) bypass or disable the auto-erase function whether or not it has been enabled
(2) enable the FBI to submit passcodes to the SUBJECT DEVICE for testing electronically via the physical device port, Bluetooth, Wi-Fi or other protocol available
(3) ensure that when the FBI submits passcodes to the SUBJECT DEVICE, software running on the device will not purposefully introduce any additional delay between passcode attempts"

To achieve this the order instructed Apple to provide a "signed iPhone Software file, recovery bundle, or other Software Image File that can be loaded onto the subject device."[298] The update would allow a passcode to be input electronically, rather than manually, making it easier to unlock iPhones by an exhaustion, or brute force, attack.[299]

Apple CEO Tim Cook responded to what he labeled the FBI's "unprecedented" request stating:

While we believe the FBI's intentions are good, it would be wrong for the government to force us to build a backdoor into our products. And ultimately, we fear that this demand would undermine the very freedoms and liberty our government is meant to protect.[300]

---

294   Stengel, 2019, 207.
295   Ibid, 206.
296   Ibid, 207.
297   United States Department of Justice, 2016.
298   Ibid.
299   Cook, 2016.
300   Ibid.

Cook wrote he had "no sympathy for terrorists," and wished to see justice done—Apple had provided the FBI with all the data in their possession, and even made engineers available to advise their agents. However, with FDE Apple placed some user data beyond their organization, trusting encryption at the end-point to protect the user, as, "we [Apple] believe the contents of your iPhone are none of our business." Cook explained:

> we have done everything...within our power and within the law to help them. But now the U.S. government has asked us for something we simply do not have, and something we consider too dangerous to create. They have asked us to build a backdoor to the iPhone.[301]

Cook commented, "In the wrong hands, this software...would have the potential to unlock any iPhone in someone's physical possession." Cook argued:

> The FBI may use different words to describe this tool, but make no mistake: Building a version of iOS that bypasses security in this way would undeniably create a backdoor. And while the government may argue that its use would be limited to this case, there is no way to guarantee such control.[302]

Cook argued despite the government suggesting the tool would be used on only one occasion:

> Once created, the technique could be used over and over again, on any number of devices. In the physical world, it would be the equivalent of a master key, capable of opening hundreds of millions of locks—from restaurants and banks to stores and homes. No reasonable person would find that acceptable.[303]

Cook stated Apple could identify "no precedent for an American company being forced to expose its customers to a greater risk of attack," or for such a use of the 1789 All Writs Act upon which the FBI's request relied.[304] The All Writs Act allows courts to "issue all writs necessary or appropriate in aid of their respective jurisdictions and agreeable to the usages and principles of law."[305] The question was whether the issuance of such an order in this case was a circumvention of Congressional responsibility to pass laws, and could serve to undermine the public's confidence in the oversight of the national security apparatus. Cook labeled the FBI's demands "chilling," and its interpretation of the All Writs Act would allow it to:

> demand that Apple build surveillance software to intercept your messages, access your health records or financial data, track your location, or even access your phone's microphone or camera without your knowledge.[306]

---

[301] Ibid.
[302] Ibid.
[303] Ibid.

[304] Ibid.
[305] Legal Information Institute, no date.
[306] Cook, 2016.

Cook stated Apple were challenging FBI demands with the "deepest respect for American democracy and a love of our country," but felt they must, "speak up in the face of what we see as an overreach by the U.S. government."[307]

Apple's legal petition to have the FBI's court order overturned raised further arguments, such as once the access method was created, "it is only a matter of time before foreign governments demand the same tool."[308] The government's argument that the access tool would be only used against the iPhone in question was also refuted:

> The government says: "Just this once" and "Just this phone." But the government knows those statements are not true; indeed, the government has filed multiple other applications for similar orders, some of which are pending in other courts. And as news of this Court's order broke last week, state and local officials publicly declared their intent to use the proposed operating system to open hundreds of other seized devices—in cases having nothing to do with terrorism.[309]

Apple's lawyers accused the FBI of augmenting democratically granted investigatory powers by, "seeking through the courts a dangerous power that Congress and the American people have withheld."[310] Apple closed by arguing society was willing to make security sacrifices for privacy preservation:

> examples abound of society opting not to pay the price for increased and more efficient enforcement of criminal laws. For example, society does not tolerate violations of the Fifth Amendment privilege against self-incrimination, even though more criminals would be convicted if the government could compel their confessions. Nor does society tolerate violations of the Fourth Amendment, even though the government could more easily obtain critical evidence if given free rein to conduct warrantless searches and seizures.
>
> At every level of our legal system…society has acted to preserve certain rights at the expense of burdening law enforcement's interest in investigating crimes and bringing criminals to justice. Society is still debating the important privacy and security issues posed by this case. The government's desire to leave no stone unturned, however well intentioned, does not authorize it to cut off debate and impose its views on society.[311]

The technology industry, cryptologists, and civil liberties groups rallied around Apple, providing supporting testimonies for its court case.[312] Google CEO Sundar Pichai commented that assisting law enforcement with data readily available was "wholly different than requiring companies to enable hacking of customer devices and data," which could be a "troubling precedent."[313] WhatsApp CEO Jan Koum posted, "We must not allow this dangerous precedent to be set. Today our freedom and our liberty is at stake."[314] Snowden commented it was, "the most important tech

---

[307] Ibid.
[308] United States District Court for the Central District of California Eastern Division, 2016.
[309] Ibid.
[310] Ibid.
[311] Ibid.
[312] Apple, 2016.
[313] Pichai, 2016.
[314] Koum, 2016.

case in a decade," and that "the FBI is creating a world where citizens rely on Apple to defend their rights, rather than the other way around."[315] In many ways the case caught public attention in a way the Snowden disclosures had not, one commentator summed up the lure of the case:

> Apple is almost a religion, and not just in America, but all over the world, from Japan to Romania. It has millions of fans who follow it with cult-like dedication. So when Apple is attacked, people listen and are interested in all the technical details of encryption; nobody even thinks to say "I've got nothing to hide."[316]

Comey replied to Apple's narrative, arguing the case:

> isn't about trying to set a precedent or send any kind of message. It is about the victims and justice…we simply want the chance, with a search warrant, to try to guess the terrorist's passcode without the phone essentially self-destructing and without it taking a decade to guess correctly. That's it.[317]

Comey added, "We don't want to break anyone's encryption or set a master key loose on the land."[318] Comey acknowledged the FBI did not know what was on the phone, "Maybe the phone holds the clue to finding more terrorists. Maybe it doesn't. But we can't look the survivors in the eye, or ourselves in the mirror, if we don't follow this lead."[319] Comey hoped, "folks will take a deep breath and stop saying the world is ending," but he did acknowledge the strategic tension between "privacy and safety," commenting:

> That tension should not be resolved by corporations that sell stuff for a living. It also should not be resolved by the FBI, which investigates for a living. It should be resolved by the American people deciding how we want to govern ourselves in a world we have never seen before. We shouldn't drift to a place—or be pushed to a place by the loudest voices—because finding the right place, the right balance, will matter to every American for a very long time.[320]

Future President Donald Trump called for a boycott of Apple products, asking a political rally, "who do they think they [Apple] are?"[321]

The court case never had the opportunity to unfold—on March 20 the FBI found an unnamed third party to provide them access to Farook's iPhone.[322] The third party was reportedly the Israeli firm Cellebrite, though the technical vulnerability they exploited is unknown.[323] Comey reflected the court case "stimulated a bit of a marketplace around the world which didn't exist before then for people to try

---

[315] Snowden, 2016a and 2016b.
[316] Ciobotea, 2016.
[317] Comey, 2016a.
[318] Ibid.
[319] Ibid.

[320] Ibid.
[321] Brandom, 2016.
[322] United States District Court for the Central District of California, 2016, 3.
[323] Cohen, 2016.

and figure out could they break into an Apple 5C running iOS 9."[324] Whilst the exact price for the access is unknown, Comey stated it was more than $1.2m, and the investment was "worth it" (this figure may have been for repeated use of the exploit.)[325] Comey was also happy the litigation was no longer needed as, "litigation is not a great place to resolve hard values questions that implicate all kinds of things that all of us care about."[326]

It was likely the FBI were not keen to have a court trial—perhaps the public sentiment from the case was not as favorable as expected. The story had been keenly reported by the media, leading the 24-hour news cycle and even being discussed on political chat shows such as the *Stephen Colbert Late Show* where Colbert grilled the Attorney General on the case.[327] FBI Counsel Jim Baker later reflected on the legal failure of the case: "I thought that the San Bernardino case provided Congress with ample basis to change the law to help resolve the larger problem because of the number of victims and the direct connection to terrorism. Obviously, I was wrong."[328]

The FBI's withdrawal of the case was likely also influenced by a recent, though less publicized, legal ruling in New York. Following the arrest of Jun Feng, an alleged methamphetamine dealer, the FBI petitioned the courts using the 1789 All Writs Act, the same legislation used in the San Bernardino case, to compel Apple to unlock the seized iPhone 5s (running iOS7) in October 2015.[329] Being an older version of the iPhone, in this case Apple had the ability to unlock the device. Judge Orenstein ruled application of the All Writs Act must be "agreeable to the usages and principles of the law," as per the legislation's text, in his opinion of February 29, 2016.[330] On at least 70 previous occasions, the government invoked the All Writs Act to compel Apple to unlock suspects' devices.[331] The crux of the legal issue was whether the government was using the All Writs Act to employ powers Congress had considered and determined not to provide to the government.[332] The 1995 CALEA legislation passed to allow interception of digital telephony explicitly forbade its application to entities providing "information services," a definition Apple stated it fell within.[333] Apple argued the omission of information services from the CALEA legislation evidenced that Congress considered whether information services should be subjected to the legislation, and decided they should not.[334] Orenstein found in favor of Apple, stating, "what the government seeks here is to have the court give it authority that Congress chose not to confer," adding, "the government's argument here is manifestly irreconcilable with the statute."[335] Further, Orenstein added the government's reading of the law:

> which allows a court to confer on the executive branch any investigative authority
> Congress has decided to withhold, so long as it has not affirmatively outlawed it, would

---

[324] The Aspen Institute, 2016, 5.
[325] Ibid, 6.
[326] Ibid, 5.
[327] Garofalo, 2016.
[328] Baker, 2019.
[329] Orenstein, 2016.

[330] Ibid, 1.
[331] Ibid, 28.
[332] Ibid, 26.
[333] Ibid, 19.
[334] Ibid, 15.
[335] Ibid, 30.

transform the All Writs Act from a limited gap-filing statute that ensures the smooth functioning of the judiciary itself into a mechanism for upending the separation of powers by delegating to the judiciary a legislative power bounded only by Congress's superior ability to prohibit or preempt. I conclude that the constitutionality of such an interpretation is so doubtful as to render it impermissible.[336]

Orenstein stated it was clear "the government is relying on the All Writs Act as a source of authority that is legislative in every meaningful way," and the government's position would, "produce impermissibly absurd results."[337] Orenstein stated the government:

has made the considered decision that it is better off securing such crypto-legislative authority from the courts...rather than taking the chance that open legislative debate might produce a result less to its liking.[338]

Orenstein concluded:

How best to balance those interests [security vs. privacy] is a matter of critical importance to our society, and the need for an answer becomes more pressing daily, as the tide of technological advance flows ever farther past the boundaries of what seemed possible even a few decades ago. But that debate must happen today, and it must take place among legislators who are equipped to consider the technological and cultural realities of a world their predecessors could not begin to conceive. It would betray our constitutional heritage and our people's claim to democratic governance for a judge to pretend that our Founders already had that debate, and ended it, in 1789.[339]

Speaking in Congress the next day, Director Comey expressed his confusion, "I don't fully get it, honestly, because CALEA is about data in motion, and this is about data at rest."[340] Comey sought to minimize the decision:

this is the kind of thing judges do. They take acts of Congress and try to understand, so what does it mean, especially given changing circumstances. So I expect it'll be bumpy, there will be lots of lawyers paid for lots of hours of work, but we will get to a place where we have the courts with an understanding of its reach.[341]

However, Comey reiterated his view that balancing conflicting equities was not a job for the FBI:

It is not our job to tell the American people how to resolve that problem. The FBI is not some alien force imposed upon America from Mars. We are owned by the American people, we only use the tools that are given to us under the law. And so our job is simply to tell people there is a problem. Everybody should care about it, everybody should want to understand if there are warrant-proof spaces in American life...

---

[336] Ibid, 27.
[337] Ibid, 28.
[338] Ibid, 29.
[339] Ibid, 49.

[340] United States House of Representatives, 2016, 14.
[341] Ibid.

I don't know what the answer is. It may be the American people, through Congress and the courts, decide it's too hard to solve, or law enforcement can do its job well enough with strong encryption covering our communications and our papers and effects, or that it's something that we have to find a way to fix to achieve a better balance.[342]

The FBI appealed the decision. However, the case was quietly withdrawn in April 2016 when the DOJ gained access to the phone through other means.[343] It was the end of the FBI's legal offensive.

A 2018 investigation into the FBI's conduct during the San Bernardino incident by the DOJ's Inspector General found irregularities in the Bureau's behavior. The report found conflicting testimony as to whether all available measures to unlock the iPhone were employed before initiating legal action against Apple.[344] The report stated a senior FBI officer "became concerned" a subordinate "did not seem to want to find a technical solution, and that perhaps he knew of a solution but remained silent in order to pursue his own agenda of obtaining a favorable court ruling against Apple."[345] The officer believed the Farook case was the "poster child" case for the going dark challenge.[346] Senator Wyden commented, "It's clear now that the FBI was far more interested in using this horrific terrorist attack to establish a powerful legal precedent than they were in promptly gaining access to the terrorist's phone."[347] The Center for Democracy and Technology's Greg Nojeim commented, "The inspector general is clearly concerned that the whole of the FBI is not committed to finding technical solutions that do not involve the weakening of encryption."[348] Susan Landau stated the finding "raises the question of how seriously the FBI has really been thwarted when devices are locked—and how much of the going dark debate is the FBI simply seeking easier ways to do investigations."[349]

When the FBI accessed the Farook phone, it was of limited value. Law enforcement sources told CNN that whilst new data was recovered from the device, it showed no contact with ISIS or other targets, though that in itself could be considered valuable as it was a data point that supported the theory the terrorists operated in isolation as "lone wolves"—it is also possible the suspects had other, undiscovered devices.[350] It seems likely if the data recovered proved useful, the FBI would have been very vocal in declaring the intelligence haul to support their arguments for an Apple access method.[351] However, the other possibility is a highly-sensitive lead was developed and the FBI did not want to tip the target(s) to their investigation—though it seems by this point in 2020 the public would have been told of any value which resulted from such a scenario.

---

[342] Ibid, 7.
[343] United States District Court Eastern District of New York, 2016.
[344] United States Department of Justice, 2018.
[345] Ibid.
[346] Ibid.
[347] Geller, 2018.
[348] Ibid.
[349] Ibid.
[350] Perez, Brown, and Prokupecz, 2016.
[351] Ibid.

Director Comey maintained his commentary on the going dark challenge throughout 2015, stating Islamic State in Syria were "recruiting and tasking dozens of troubled Americans to kill people, a process that increasingly takes part through mobile messaging apps that are end-to-end encrypted."[352] Comey warned, "There is simply no doubt that bad people can communicate with impunity in a world of universal strong encryption."[353] Comey referenced another case where two terrorists attempted an attack in Garland, Texas. Comey stated:

> Before they left to try to commit mass murder, one of them exchanged 109 messages with somebody we know is a terrorist outside the United States. I have no idea what they said. I still can't tell you what they said. Because they communicated with... [a] messaging app that is end-to-end encrypted...It was important. It was important enough to exchange 109 messages across an ocean to talk about what was about to happen that day but I can't tell you what it was. That's a problem. That's a problem with democracy.[354]

As of mid-2019, the FBI had not accessed the messages.[355] Comey's narrative was slowly becoming more aggressive, arguing encryption was a problem with democracy itself, rather than his earlier narrative calling for a balanced debate and a choice by society.

Policy solutions to address the going dark challenge were not appealing. Obama's encryption working group reported on options for exceptional access.[356] The internal document noted there was "no one-size-fits-all" technical approach, and that each "type of encryption will require unique technical solutions."[357] The authors assessed for some of the technical challenges there was no clear solution, and recognized, "inaccessible encryption will always be available to malicious actors."[358] The authors also noted an additional challenge being many services and encryption products use open source software, for which there is no central authority for government to partner with in developing access solutions.[359] None of the options were progressed, the authors noted:

> some technologists, civil society, and companies may perceive any government access as an attempt to obtain widespread, non-targeted access for bulk collection purposes. Accordingly, those communities almost certainly will be unlikely to trust limitations enforced through policy or law, and will be more likely to be satisfied by those enforced through technology.[360]

Collaboration with industry was declared the best option; however, the authors recommended not suggesting technical solutions as:

---

352 Comey, 2015a.
353 Ibid.
354 Comey, 2015b.
355 Barr, 2019.
356 Encryption Working Group, 2015, 1.

357 Ibid.
358 Ibid, 2.
359 Ibid, 3.
360 Ibid, 2.

given industry and civil society's combative reaction to government statements to date, any proposed solution almost certainly would quickly become a focal point for attacks and the basis of further entrenchment by opposed parties. Rather than sparking more discussion, government proposed technical approaches would almost certainly be perceived as proposals to introduce "backdoors" or vulnerabilities…and increase tensions rather than build cooperation.[361]

The working group suggested offering a series of principles, rather than solutions, was a potential way forwards to "focus public or private conversation on practicalities and policy trade-offs rather than whether the government is seeking to weaken encryption or introduce vulnerabilities into technology products and services."[362] The suggested principles included a focus on targeted rather than bulk access, no unilateral government access (no "golden keys"), technologically enforced limits, minimizing negative impacts on innovation, international adoption, and avoiding the undermining of trust in security.[363] The authors did briefly explore four access ideas. The first was to modify hardware for physical devices to include an "independent, physical encryption port," to which the provider would maintain a set of keys to enable decryption on receipt of a warrant.[364] The authors noted this approach would be expensive for providers, but could limit the potential for abuse by governments and malicious actors.[365] A second option was having a provider-enabled remote access using update procedures to upload government software, which could offer "far reaching access" to the device.[366] However, the authors recognized this could "call into question the trustworthiness of established software update channels," which could cause users to "turn off software updates, rendering their devices significantly less secure."[367] A third option was remote access with multiple participants holding the key, similar to the Clipper chip—the authors stated this would be "complex to implement and maintain."[368] A final option was to use remote access to force an unencrypted backup which could be provided to the government.[369] When the working group's document found its way online, National Security spokesman Mark Stroh confirmed the proposals were not being pursued.[370]

It is worth briefly examining the pre-eminent example cited by lawful intercept opponents to understand its significance to the argument interception capabilities decrease security. This is the case of Athens-based Vodafone-Panafon.[371] During winter 2004/2005, attackers activated the legal intercept provisions of Vodafone-Panafon's Ericsson telephony network equipment to monitor the calls of over a hundred targets.[372] Victims included the Greek Prime Minister and his wife, the Ministers of National Defense, Foreign Affairs and Justice, and the Mayor of Athens.[373] The compromise method is unclear.[374] However, we know four Ericsson

---

361 Ibid, 3.
362 Ibid, 4.
363 Ibid.
364 Ibid, 5.
365 Ibid.
366 Ibid.
367 Ibid.
368 Ibid, 6.
369 Ibid.
370 Peterson and Nakashima, 2015.
371 Prevelakis and Spinellis, 2007.
372 Ibid.
373 Ibid.
374 Ibid.

switches were breached allowing the attackers to utilize the legitimate interception software, intended for government use, to create duplicate streams of the targets' phone calls and forward them to a third attacker-owned phone.[375] The calls were encrypted between the phones and their nearest base stations, but on the internal component of Vodafone's network there was no encryption.[376] Investigators stated the switches were "reprogrammed with a finesse and sophistication rarely seen before."[377] The breach was detected when the attackers updated their software, causing network errors which resulted in legitimate text messages being undelivered.[378] Whilst the attacker was never identified, historian James Bamford argued there were signs the CIA and NSA were responsible.[379] Whilst this case is a good illustration of how interception capabilities can increase the vulnerability of a system, there were numerous indicators best practices were not followed by the Greeks. In comparison, the proposed Clipper chip would have possessed much greater safeguards, both procedural and technical. Could such an attack have succeeded against a mature interception capability? Certainly not with the same ease, although given the potential intelligence bounty, a determined and well-resourced actor would have the motivation to dedicate much blood and treasure to the achievement of such a goal. Few systems, if any, could sustain such an assault—this is why the most sensitive networks are air-gapped (isolated) from other networks (e.g., the Internet).

8.7 BURR-FEINSTEIN EXCEPTIONAL ACCESS LAW

In April 2016 Republican Senator Richard Burr of North Carolina and Democratic Senator Dianne Feinstein of California released draft legislation entitled the *Compliance with Court Orders Act of 2016*, which stated:

> all providers of communications services and products (including software) should protect the privacy of United States persons through implementation of appropriate data security and still respect the rule of law and comply with all legal requirements and court orders.[380]

The bill instructed, "all persons receiving an authorized judicial order for information or data must provide, in a timely manner, responsive, intelligible information or data, or appropriate technical assistance to obtain such information or data."[381] Burr and Feinstein held influential positions on the Senate's Select Committee on Intelligence as Chairman and Vice-Chairman respectively. Introducing the draft, Burr stated:

> I have long believed that data is too insecure, and feel strongly that consumers have a right to seek solutions that protect their information—which involves strong

---

[375] Ibid.
[376] Ibid.
[377] Ibid
[378] Ibid.

[379] Bamford, 2015.
[380] United States Senate, 2016, 2.
[381] Ibid.

encryption. I do not believe, however, that those solutions should be above the law. I am hopeful that this draft will start a meaningful and inclusive debate on the role of encryption and its place within the rule of law.[382]

Feinstein added:

No entity or individual is above the law. The bill we have drafted would simply provide that, if a court of law issues an order to render technical assistance or provide decrypted data, the company or individual would be required to do so. Today, terrorists and criminals are increasingly using encryption to foil law enforcement efforts, even in the face of a court order. We need strong encryption to protect personal data, but we also need to know when terrorists are plotting to kill Americans.[383]

The response from industry groups and civil liberties organizations was predictably negative. The Internet Association, a broad assembly of large technology organizations stated, "Mandating the weakening of encryption will put the United States' national security and global competitiveness at risk without corresponding benefits."[384] The EFF's Nate Cardozo declared should the legislation pass the EFF would "lead the effort" to tie the bill up in court for years.[385] Joseph Lorenzo Hall, chief technologist at the Center for Democracy and Technology commented, "This basically outlaws end-to-end encryption…it's effectively the most anti-crypto bill of all anti-crypto bills."[386] Senator Ron Wyden stated:

I will do everything in my power to block [the] Burr-Feinstein anti-encryption bill. It makes Americans less safe…Americans who value their security and liberty must join together to oppose this dangerous proposal. I intend to oppose this bill in committee and if it reaches the Senate floor, I will filibuster it.[387]

The White House was rumored to have offered input to the Burr-Feinstein bill, but declined to offer public support, according to Reuters.[388]

As the San Bernardino attacks lapsed from the forefront of people's memories, so did any support the bill had in Congress—it died in committee in late May 2016.[389]

The attempt to advance federal legislation on encryption occurred just as Californian State legislation on encryption was also failing. In January 2016, California Assembly member Jim Cooper, a former Sheriff Deputy, had introduced legislation that would result in technology companies being fined $2500 for each smartphone they sold unable to be decrypted or unlocked.[390] The bill was later amended to introduce the fine when companies were unable to decrypt the data, rather than at the point of sale.[391] The bill was vociferously opposed and it died

---

382 Burr, 2016.
383 Ibid.
384 Internet Association, 2016.
385 O'Neill, 2016.
386 Greenberg, 2016.

387 Wyden, 2016.
388 Hosenball and Volz, 2016.
389 Volz, 2016.
390 Cooper, no date; California Legislative, 2016.
391 California Legislative, 2016.

in committee in April 2016.[392] Similar bills in Louisiana and New York also were proposed and perished around this period; all stipulated a fine of £2500 per device, suggesting either imitation or collaboration.[393] It is likely those who proposed the bills knew they would be unsuccessful, but the simultaneous attempts of officials in three powerful states to pass such legislation would surely have conveyed the message to technology leaders and Washington politicians that the status quo was under siege. Several Congress members heard this message and sought to counter the State's activities by introducing the Ensuring National Constitutional Rights for Your Private Telecommunications (ENCRYPT) Act in the house in February 2016.[394] The ENCRYPT Act proclaimed no government entity may:

> mandate or request that a manufacturer, developer, seller, or provider of covered products or services design [or] alter the security functions…to allow…surveillance…or to allow the physical search of such product…or have the ability to decrypt or otherwise render intelligible information that is encrypted or otherwise rendered unintelligible using its product or service.[395]

Nor could a product be excluded from the market due to its use of encryption.[396] The ENCRYPT Act repeatedly failed to progress beyond committee, despite being reintroduced in 2018 and late in 2019, the latter an attempt to pass the legislation which was announced at DefCon.[397]

Obama addressed the encryption issue again in March 2016. The President cautioned against taking an "absolutist view" on the issue, arguing strong encryption without constraints would "not strike the kind of balance that we have lived with for 200, 300 years…it's fetishizing our phones above every other value. And that can't be the right answer."[398] Obama stated:

> I suspect that the answer is going to come down to how do we create a system where the encryption is as strong as possible, the key is as secure as possible, it is accessible by the smallest number of people possible for a subset of issues that we agree are important.[399]

However, Obama recognized he lacked the expertise to design such a system. Digital privacy activists generally agree if an exceptional access method could be developed without introducing a systemic weakness in the digital ecosystem (something currently believed to be technically impossible) it could be acceptable if accompanied by robust oversight provisions; the problem Obama did not address was the one which had perplexed policy-makers for a generation—how such a capability could be developed. Obama added, "But…I am way on the civil liberties side of this

---

[392] Electronic Frontier Foundation, 2016; Reitman, 2016.

[393] James, 2016; WAFB, 2016; The New York State Senate, 2016.

[394] United States Congress, 2016.

[395] Ibid.

[396] Ibid.

[397] Lieu, 2019.

[398] The White House, 2016.

[399] Ibid.

thing…I am not interested in overthrowing the values that have made us an exceptional and great nation simply for expediency. But the dangers are real." Obama
explained, "we make compromises all the time…and this notion that somehow our
data is different and can be walled off from those other tradeoffs we make I believe
is incorrect." Obama also cautioned against inaction:

> Because what will happen is if everybody goes to their respective corners and the tech
> community says, you know what, either we have strong, perfect encryption, or else it's
> Big Brother and an Orwellian world—what you'll find is that after something really
> bad happens, the politics of this will swing and it will become sloppy and rushed, and
> it will go through Congress in ways that have not been thought through. And then you
> really will have dangers to our civil liberties.[400]

Obama added his concern that "the people who understand this best and who care
most about privacy and civil liberties have sort of disengaged or taken a position that
is not sustainable for the general public as a whole over time."[401]

Policy options remained poor. The National Academies of Science, Engineering,
and Medicine offered a framework for policy-makers in the form of a set of questions designed to "maximize its [encryption policy] effectiveness while minimizing
harmful side effects," in February 2018.[402] The framework recommended asked the
following questions of any proposed solution:

1. To what extent will the proposed approach be effective in permitting law
   enforcement and/or the intelligence community to access plaintext at or
   near the scale, timeliness, and reliability that proponents seek?
2. To what extent will the proposed approach affect the security of the type of
   data or device to which access would be required, as well as cybersecurity
   more broadly?
3. To what extent will the proposed approach affect the privacy, civil liberties,
   and human rights of targeted individuals and others?
4. To what extent will the proposed approach affect commerce, economic
   competitiveness, and innovation?
5. To what extent will financial costs be imposed by the proposed approach,
   and who will bear them?
6. To what extent is the proposed approach consistent with existing law and
   other government priorities?
7. To what extent will the international context affect the proposed approach,
   and what will be the impact of the proposed approach internationally?
8. To what extent will the proposed approach be subject to effective ongoing
   evaluation and oversight?

---

[400] Ibid.
[401] Ibid.

[402] National Academies of Sciences, Engineering,
and Medicine, 2018, Summary.

Whilst the framework can be considered useful, it did, as the EFF pointed out, "collapse the question of *whether* the government should mandate 'exceptional access' to the contents of encrypted communications with *how* the government could accomplish this mandate."[403]

By late 2016 efforts for a new legislative exceptional access solution were ruled out. FBI Director Comey commented:

> the administration has decided not to seek a legislative remedy at this time, we will continue the conversations we are having with private industry, state, local, and tribal law enforcement, our foreign partners, and the American people.[404]

Comey had recently stated conversations with industry were improving, though he recognized there was no "simple answer."[405] Comey stated engagement was now:

> healthier, because people have stripped out a lot of the venom. Folks are not questioning as much as they used to each other's motives because we are in a place where we recognize we care about the same stuff.[406]

8.8   GHOST USERS: CRYPTO WARS IN THE UK

In the UK, Prime Minister David Cameron entered the encryption debate in response to the January 2015 Paris terrorist attacks. Cameron stated:

> *In extremis*, it has been possible to read someone's letter, to listen to someone's call, to mobile communications…The question remains: are we going to allow a means of communications where it simply is not possible to do that? My answer to that question is: no, we must not. The first duty of any government is to keep our country and our people safe.[407]

A few months earlier, new GCHQ Director Robert Hannigan wrote an open letter to technology companies asking for their assistance with gaining access to encrypted data.[408] Hannigan branded the problem facing governments as "huge," and could "only be met with greater co-operation from technology companies."[409] Hannigan also spoke of the changing use of the Internet by terrorists:

> Where al-Qaeda and its affiliates saw the internet as a place to disseminate material anonymously or meet in "dark spaces," ISIS has embraced the web as a noisy channel in which to promote itself, intimidate people, and radicalize new recruits.[410]

[403] Electronic Frontier Foundation, 2018.
[404] Comey, 2016b.
[405] United States Senate, 2015.
[406] Ibid.
[407] Emm, 2015.
[408] Hannigan, 2014.
[409] Ibid.
[410] Ibid.

Hannigan explained ISIS had refined their use of the Internet:

> The grotesque videos of beheadings were remarkable not just for their merciless brutality, which we have seen before from al-Qaeda in Iraq, but for what ISIS has learnt from that experience. This time the "production values" were high and the videos stopped short of showing the actual beheading. They have realized that too much graphic violence can be counter-productive in their target audience and that by self-censoring they can stay just the right side of the rules of social media sites, capitalizing on western freedom of expression.[411]

Hannigan stated:

> techniques for encrypting messages or making them anonymous which were once the preserve of the most sophisticated criminals or nation states now come as standard. These are supplemented by freely available programs and apps adding extra layers of security, many of them proudly advertising that they are "Snowden approved." There is no doubt that young foreign fighters have learnt and benefited from the leaks of the past two years.[412]

Hannigan argued that British intelligence agencies:

> cannot tackle these challenges at scale without greater support from the private sector, including the largest US technology companies which dominate the web. I understand why they have an uneasy relationship with governments. They aspire to be neutral conduits of data and to sit outside or above politics. But increasingly their services not only host the material of violent extremism or child exploitation, but are the routes for the facilitation of crime and terrorism. However much they may dislike it, they have become the command-and-control networks of choice for terrorists and criminals, who find their services as transformational as the rest of us.[413]

Hannigan stated GCHQ were "happy to be part of a mature debate on privacy in the digital age," but warned that "privacy has never been an absolute right and the debate about this should not become a reason for postponing urgent and difficult decisions." Hannigan called for a "new deal between democratic governments and the technology companies in the area of protecting our citizens," which should be "rooted in the democratic values we share," but warned that would mean "addressing some uncomfortable truths." Hannigan concluded the article with a warning similar to that from US leaders: "Better to do it now than in the aftermath of greater violence."[414]

It was not long before a major change in UK legislation offered the possibility of disrupting the status quo. The Investigatory Powers Act of 2016 granted the UK government the ability to issue Technical Capability Notices (TCNs), which includes the requirement for subjects to remove "electronic protection applied by or on behalf

---

411 Ibid.   413 Ibid.
412 Ibid.   414 Ibid.

of that operator to any communications or data."[415] There is some ambiguity over to whom this applies, with subjects identified as "telecommunications operator[s]," which is described as a telecommunication service:

in which a service is to be taken to consist in the provision of access to, and of facilities for making use of, a telecommunication system include any case where a service consists in or includes facilitating the creation, management or storage of communications transmitted, or that may be transmitted, by means of such a system.[416]

A telecommunications operator[s] is described as a telecommunications system which:

means a system (including the apparatus comprised in it) that exists (whether wholly or partly in the United Kingdom or elsewhere) for the purpose of facilitating the transmission of communications by any means involving the use of electrical or electromagnetic energy.[417]

These definitions suggest software, websites, and devices (e.g., iPhones) are in scope of the legislation. The Secretary of State would be required to consult with a technical advisory board, and the subjects of any TCN before its issuing.[418] TCN could also be issued to "persons outside the United Kingdom."[419] Non-disclosure rules would prevent recipients from revealing they received TCNs.[420] Whilst it is known that TCNs have been used, the extent and success of their applications are unknown.[421]

Apple responded to the legislation by writing to the UK parliament arguing, "A key left under the doormat would not just be there for the good guys. The bad guys would find it too."[422] Apple argued, "The best minds in the world cannot rewrite the laws of mathematics…any process that weakens the mathematical models that protect user data will by extension weaken the protection."[423]

However, within Britain political parties have very different outlooks on the security services and exceptional access. These divisions were highlighted when a British terrorist killed four people outside of parliament in March 2017. Investigations found the terrorist sent messages using WhatsApp minutes before launching the attack. Home Secretary Amber Rudd stated it was "completely unacceptable" messages with end-to-end encryption could not be accessed by authorities.[424] Rudd added, "We need to make sure that organizations like WhatsApp, and there are plenty of others like that, don't provide a secret place for terrorists to communicate with each other."[425] Rudd concluded, "These people have families, have children as well, they

---

[415] United Kingdom Government, 2016a, 2 and 5c.
[416] United Kingdom Government, 2016b.
[417] Ibid.
[418] United Kingdom Government, 2016a, 7.
[419] Ibid, 8.
[420] United Kingdom Government, 2016c.

[421] Investigatory Powers Comissioner's Office, 2018, 2.14.
[422] Geller, 2015.
[423] Ibid.
[424] Sparrow, 2017.
[425] Ibid.

should be on our side, and I'm going to try to win that argument."[426] However, this
was far from a universal view; the Liberal Democrats home affairs spokesman Brian
Paddick said giving the security services access to encrypted messages would be
"neither a proportionate nor an effective response" to the Westminster attack.[427]
Paddick added, "These terrorists want to destroy our freedoms and undermine our
democratic society. By implementing draconian laws that limit our civil liberties, we
would be playing into their hands."[428] Labour Party leader Jeremy Corbyn argued the
government already had "huge, huge powers of investigation," and questioned the
need for additional capabilities.[429]

The debate continued in November 2018 when Ian Levy, Technical Director
of the National Cyber Security Centre, GCHQ's outward-facing arm, and Crispin
Robinson, the agency's Technical Director for Cryptanalysis, wrote an article proposing a series of principles for exceptional access.[430] Levy and Robinson together
represented the technical leadership of the dual missions of GCHQ: communications security and communications exploitation. The authors argued the exceptional
access debate was lacking details, and consequently was being, "debated as a purely
academic abstraction concerning security, liberty, and the role of government."[431]
The authors proposed, "If we can get all parties to look at some actual detail, some
practices and proposals—without asking anyone to compromise on things they fundamentally believe in—we might get somewhere."[432] Rather than branding the challenge "going dark," Levy and Robinson used the term "going spotty," which reflected
the latest thinking and the arguments postulated by researchers from Harvard
University.[433] The authors offered a series of principles the UK used to govern their
access to "mass-scale, commodity, end-to-end encrypted services."[434] Among the
principles was the acknowledgment that, "Even when we have a legitimate need, we
can't expect 100 percent access 100 percent of the time," the authors believed the
public narrative considered security as binary, they argued, "This isn't true—every
real system is a set of design trade-offs."[435] Another principle offered was:

> Targeted exceptional access capabilities should not give governments unfettered access
> to user data…we definitely *don't* want governments to have access to a global key that
> can unlock any user's data. Government controlled global key escrow systems would
> be a catastrophically dumb solution in these cases.[436] [Original italics]

To rule out such technical solutions was a sensible move given how unpalatable
they were to the technology community as the Clipper chip proved in the 1990s.
The authors went further, stating, "solutions should be designed so the service

---

[426] Ibid.
[427] Ibid.
[428] Ibid.
[429] Ibid.
[430] Levy and Robinson, 2018.
[431] Ibid.

[432] Ibid.
[433] Ibid; Olson, Schneier, and Zittrain, 2016.
[434] Levy and Robinson, 2018.
[435] Ibid.
[436] Ibid.

provider—in the form of a real human—is involved in enacting every authorized request, limiting the scale of use." This was a direct counterbalance to concerns of mass surveillance; however, it should be noted Levy and Robinson had implied a separate set of principles govern acquisition of such data. The authors acknowledged exceptional access systems "could have defects and some of this could be security vulnerabilities," but "The public has been convinced that a solution in this case is impossible, so we need to explain why we're not proposing magic." Levy and Robinson proposed any solution be "subject to some form of peer review and incremental implementation," as well as a "form of public audit," though such an audit must protect investigations. The authors believed "with a bit of work, technology solutions can assure the public of the scale of use of an exceptional access solution, without damaging intelligence and law enforcement outcomes."[437] Levy and Robinson also addressed the argument "lawful hacking" was a solution to the access challenge by pointing to a big hole in the technology communities argument:

> Lawful hacking of target devices initially sounds attractive as the panacea to governments' lawful access requirements—just hack the target's device and get what you want. But that requires governments to have vulnerabilities on the shelf to use to hack those devices, which is completely at odds with the demands for governments to disclose all vulnerabilities they find to protect the population. That seems daft.[438]

The authors further argued:

> vulnerabilities can be found and exploited by anyone—not just governments—and so this will very likely engender a shady marketplace of vulnerabilities and exploit chains that would be available to anyone with the cash. There are other problems with this approach, but asking governments to rely exclusively on lawful hacking of target devices is likely to have some nasty second order effects.[439]

Levy and Robinson offered one access solution, drawing from a century-old voice intercept device: crocodile clips. The authors argued as physical crocodile clips became virtual clips, many digital exchanges used conference calling functionality to enact lawful interception.[440] The authors stated:

> It's relatively easy for a service provider to silently add a law enforcement participant to a group chat or call. The service provider usually controls the identity system and so really decides who's who and which devices are involved—they're usually involved in introducing the parties to a chat or call. You end up with everything still being end-to-end encrypted, but there's an extra "end" on this particular communication.[441]

The additional user would become known as a "ghost" user. The authors believed ghost users were no more intrusive than traditional voice intercept solutions and

---

[437] Ibid.   [440] Ibid.
[438] Ibid.   [441] Ibid.
[439] Ibid.

"certainly doesn't give any government power they shouldn't have."[442] Levy and Robinson added:

> We're **not** talking about weakening encryption or defeating the end-to-end nature of the service. In a solution like this, we're normally talking about suppressing a notification on a target's device, and **only** on the device of the target and possibly those they communicate with. That's a very different proposition to discuss and you don't even have to touch the encryption.[443] [original bold]

The authors commented, "The problem of gaining access to a seized encrypted device is very different and may well end up being harder to do in a proportionate way—there's not enough research to be sure either way." This suggests access to iPhones and Android devices may not be pursued, but instead the focus may be on services such as WhatsApp and Facebook—the authors added unencrypted cloud backups could also be a viable access method. Levy and Robinson argued caution should be taken to solution proposals which claim "the problem is either totally solved or totally insoluble. That's just bad science and solutions are going to be more complex than that." The authors stated more detailed work would be needed with experts critiquing one another, and that should "happen without people being vilified for having a point of view or daring to work on this as a problem." As was a pattern with such government communications, their article was signed off with a warning that the alternative to not collaborating to solve the problem "will almost certainly be bad for everyone."[444]

Industry and civil rights groups responded to the proposal with an open letter to GCHQ.[445] The signatories included Apple, Google, Microsoft, WhatsApp, and a host of other technology companies, civil rights organizations, and technologists. The authors warned ghost users would "pose serious threats to cybersecurity and thereby also threaten fundamental human rights, including privacy and free expression."[446] To instigate a ghost user, the cryptography protocols would have to be modified to manipulate the safety number/security code (a number derived from the keys in the conversation that changes when a change to those in the chat change), and suppress any notifications of users being added.[447] The authors commented that if such changes were made, users would no longer be able to "trust that their communications are secure, as users would no longer be able to trust that they know who is on the other end of their communications, thereby posing threats to fundamental human rights, including privacy and free expression."[448] The authors also argued:

> In order for providers to be able to suppress notifications when a ghost user is added, messaging applications would need to rewrite the software that every user relies on.

---

442 Ibid.
443 Ibid.
444 Ibid.
445 Access Now, Big Brother Watch et al., 2019.
446 Ibid, 1.
447 Ibid, 2.
448 Ibid, 3.

This means that any mistake made in the development of this new function could create an unintentional vulnerability that affects every single user of that application.[449]

The authors also worried about the "cloak of secrecy" which would accompany the UK implementing the ghost users:

the Investigatory Powers Act grants U.K. officials the power to impose broad non-disclosure agreements that would prevent service providers from even acknowledging they had received a demand to change their systems, let alone the extent to which they complied.[450]

As far as the public is aware, the ghost user proposal was not advanced.

8.9   THE TRUMP YEARS

In a show of unity, the governments of the "five-eyes" nations, i.e., Australia, Canada, Great Britain, New Zealand, and the United States, released a joint encryption statement in September 2018.[451] The authors stated, "privacy is not absolute," arguing:

The increasing gap between the ability of law enforcement to lawfully access data and their ability to acquire and use the content of that data is a pressing international concern that requires urgent, sustained attention, and informed discussion on the complexity of the issues and interests at stake. Otherwise, court decisions about legitimate access to data are increasingly rendered meaningless, threatening to undermine the systems of justice established in our democratic nations.[452]

The authors wrote, "Governments should recognize that the nature of encryption is such that there will be situations where access to information is not possible, although such situations should be rare," and "lawful access should always be subject to oversight by independent authorities and/or subject to judicial review."[453] The tone then became more aggressive, with the authors reiterating technology companies were subject to the law, which includes assisting authorities to access communications data.[454] The authors recommended the technology companies "voluntarily establish lawful access solutions," with "customized solutions, tailored to their individual system architectures."[455] However, if voluntary cooperation could not be attained the authors warned, "we may pursue technological, enforcement, legislative, or other measures to achieve lawful access solutions."[456] It was in Australia that new encryption legislation would become a prominent issue in the coming months.

The Australian Federal Police reported over 90% of their interceptions were now encrypted.[457] To remedy this, the Telecommunications and Other Legislation

---

[449] Ibid, 4.
[450] Ibid, 7.
[451] Five Country Ministerial, 2018, 2.
[452] Ibid.
[453] Ibid, 3.
[454] Ibid.
[455] Ibid.
[456] Ibid.
[457] Australian Parliament, 2018a, 2.

Amendment (TOLA) (Access and Assistance) Bill was passed by the government as a vehicle to "enhance cooperation by introducing a new framework for industry assistance, including new powers to secure assistance from key companies in the communications supply chain both within and outside Australia."[458]

The legislation provided three levels of "graduated approach to industry assistance," the Australian government would serve one of the following upon technology companies: technical assistance requests; technical assistance notices; technical capability notices.[459] The technical assistance request is a voluntary request for aid, whilst the technical assistance notice is a mandatory notice for the company to provide assistance as "reasonable, proportionate, practicable, and technically feasible"—both of these powers are within established international norms.[460] However, the technical capability notice was similar to the UK's Investigatory Powers Act; the recipient would be required to "do acts or things to ensure the provider is capable of giving help to…interception agencies where…it is reasonable, proportionate, practicable and technically feasible."[461] The "acts or things" recipients would be tasked to do would principally be removing encryption. When the draft bill was circulated numerous entities, most notably Apple warned the bill was "dangerously ambiguous with respect to encryption and security," and it could "require the development of a tool that can unlock a particular user's device regardless of whether such a tool could be used to unlock every other user's device as well."[462] To address the concern a technical capability notice request could create systemic weaknesses the legislation's accompanying commentary refuted that actions taken under the bill would create such weaknesses by providing an example of its use:

> if…a provider was capable of removing encryption from the device of a terrorism suspect without weakening other devices in the market then the provider could be compelled…to provide help…by removing the electronic protection. The mere fact that a capability to selectively assist agencies with access to a target device exists will not necessarily mean that a systemic weakness has been built. The nature and scope of any weakness and vulnerability will turn on the circumstances in question and the degree to which malicious actors are able to exploit the changes required.[463]

The legislation explicitly addressed the systemic weakness concern, stating actions compelled under the bill:

> must not have the effect of requesting or requiring a designated communications provider to implement or build a systemic weakness, or a systemic vulnerability, into a form of electronic protection; preventing a designated communications provider from rectifying a systemic weakness, or a systemic vulnerability, in a form of electronic protection.[464]

---

458 Ibid.
459 Australian Parliament, 2018a, 3.
460 Ibid.
461 Ibid.

462 Apple, 2018.
463 Australian Parliament, 2018a, 98.
464 Australian Parliament, 2018b, 84.

The bill included provisions to maintain the secrecy of the orders, with penalties of five-year imprisonment for violation.[465]

Despite assurances that systemic weaknesses would not be introduced, industry was concerned. Apple's Erik Neuenschwander commented, "My overall fear would be that if some of the capabilities of that legislation were imposed on any provider, that provider would have to weaken encryption, just by the nature of the technology, for all users."[466] The Australian Human Rights Commission commented the legislation would "authorize intrusive and covert powers that could significantly limit an individual's human rights to privacy and freedom of expression, among other rights."[467]

Speaking in August 2020, ASIO Director-General Mike Burgess confirmed that ASIO had "used the industry assistance powers [TOLA] fewer than 20 times…and the internet has not broken as a result."[468] Burgess indicated the voluntary requests (TARs), rather than the mandatory TAN and TCNs, had been used. Burgess added, "ASIO's preference to use voluntary processes first does not mean the compulsory powers are not needed. There have been points in time when ASIO has come close to issuing a compulsory notice."[469] Given the nature of intelligence operations, Burgess did not elaborate on the data they had been able to access using the TOLA legislation, but as past court cases have demonstrated, perhaps the core exceptional access requirement for law enforcement is access to locked cell phones, it is possible some TARs were used in support of this need.

The "five-eyes" community again came together in July 2019 to declare lawful access, "a shared challenge that requires urgent action by Governments, industry and civil society, focused on reasonable proposals, respecting different perspectives and based on core values."[470] The authors concluded, "we call for detailed engagement between governments, tech companies, and other stakeholders to examine how proposals of this type can be implemented without negatively impacting user safety, while protecting cyber security and user privacy."[471]

The "five-eyes" gathering took place shortly after Mark Zuckerberg announced Facebook would transition to being a more privacy-oriented platform in March 2019.[472] Facebook's reputation had been severely damaged the previous year when it emerged the profiles of tens of millions of users were revealed to political consultancy firm Cambridge Analytica, allowing them to target users based on private information and possibly influence the US election. Facebook's stock price dropped by a quarter, over $100 billion was wiped from their valuation.[473] Zuckerberg was subject to Congressional inquiries, his representatives were summoned to answer for Facebook's actions the world over, and public faith in the social media firm plummeted—Zuckerberg was also vilified by many in part for his wooden performance in

---

465 Ibid, 73–76.
466 Ng, 2019.
467 Australian Human Rights Commission, 2018, 4.
468 Parliamentary Joint Committee on Intelligence and Security, 2020.

469 Ibid.
470 Five Country Ministerial, 2019.
471 Ibid.
472 Zuckerberg, 2019.
473 Lambert and Dave, 2018.

Congress.[474] The Congressional hearings highlighted the generational gaps in understanding of technology between Congress members when Republican Senator Orrin Hatch of Utah struggled to grasp Facebook's business model and asked Zuckerberg how his business was able to make money without charging users for services, to which a nonplussed Zuckerberg replied, "Senator, we run ads," a fact every child with an Internet connection world likely understands.[475] In 2018, the average age of House members was 57.8 years, Senators were an average 61.8 years, making it one of the oldest Congresses in history.[476] This disparity makes it even harder to have debates on digital topics. Zuckerberg explained rather than connecting in the "town square," users now want to "connect privately in the digital equivalent of the living room."[477] Zuckerberg commented, "As I think about the future of the internet, I believe a privacy-focused communications platform will become even more important than today's open platforms."[478]Zuckerberg noted private aspects of their services, such as messaging and ephemeral stories were the fastest growing business areas; he commented, "Many people prefer the intimacy of communicating one-on-one or with just a few friends. People are more cautious of having a permanent record of what they've shared." Zuckerberg believed, "the future of communication will increasingly shift to private, encrypted services where people can be confident what they say to each other stays secure and their messages and content won't stick around forever." On encryption, Zuckerberg stated, "People expect their private communications to be secure and to only be seen by the people they've sent them to—not hackers, criminals, over-reaching governments, or even the people operating the services they're using." Zuckerberg added that Facebook Messenger would soon join WhatsApp in deploying end-to-end encryption.[479] Zuckerberg turned to managing government partners:

> Governments often make unlawful demands for data, and while we push back and fight these requests in court, there's always a risk we'll lose a case—and if the information isn't encrypted we'd either have to turn over the data or risk our employees being arrested if we failed to comply. This may seem extreme, but we've had a case where one of our employees was actually jailed for not providing access to someone's private information even though we couldn't access it since it was encrypted.[480]

Zuckerberg noted there were "real safety concerns" to address before end-to-end encryption could be deployed, commenting:

> Encryption is a powerful tool for privacy, but that includes the privacy of people doing bad things. When billions of people use a service to connect, some of them are going to misuse it for truly terrible things like child exploitation, terrorism, and extortion. We have a responsibility to work with law enforcement and to help prevent these wherever

---

474 Weisbaum, 2018.
475 NBC News, 2018, 0:34.
476 Manning, 2018.
477 Zuckerberg, 2019.

478 Ibid.
479 Ibid.
480 Ibid.

we can. We are working to improve our ability to identify and stop bad actors across our apps by detecting patterns of activity or through other means, even when we can't see the content of the messages, and we will continue to invest in this work. But we face an inherent tradeoff because we will never find all of the potential harm we do today when our security systems can see the messages themselves.[481]

Zuckerberg stated Facebook would consult with safety experts, law enforcement, and governments on the best way to implement safety measures within their new architecture, and they would also engage other platforms to develop a common approach where possible.[482] Zuckerberg reflected there were "tradeoffs to work through," but stated:

> On balance, I believe working towards implementing end-to-end encryption for all private communications is the right thing to do. Messages and calls are some of the most sensitive private conversations people have, and in a world of increasing cyber security threats and heavy-handed government intervention in many countries, people want us to take the extra step to secure their most private data. That seems right to me, as long as we take the time to build the appropriate safety systems that stop bad actors as much as we possibly can within the limits of an encrypted service.[483]

US Attorney General William Barr, Homeland Security Secretary Kevin McAleenan, Australian Home Affairs Minister Peter Dutton, and British Home Secretary Priti Patel wrote to Mark Zuckerberg to protest Facebook's plans to deploy E2E encryption in October 2019.[484] The letter implored Zuckerberg not to proceed "without ensuring that there is no reduction to user safety and without including a means for lawful access to the content of communications to protect our citizens." The authors built their argument on the most black-and-white crime available: child exploitation. The authors stated risks resulting from E2E encryption were "exacerbated in the context of a single platform that would combine inaccessible messaging services with open profiles, providing unique routes for prospective offenders to identify and groom our children."[485] The authors argued, "Security enhancements to the virtual world should not make us more vulnerable in the physical world."[486] To articulate the potential risk, the authors highlighted Facebook's contribution to combating threats on its network:

> In 2018, Facebook made 16.8 million reports to the US National Center for Missing & Exploited Children (NCMEC)—more than 90% of the...total reports that year. As well as child abuse imagery...more than 8,000 reports related to attempts by offenders to meet children online and groom or entice them into sharing indecent imagery or meeting in real life.

---

481 Ibid.
482 Ibid.
483 Ibid.

484 Patel, Barr et al., 2019.
485 Ibid, 2.
486 Ibid, 1.

The UK National Crime Agency (NCA) estimates that, last year, NCMEC reporting from Facebook will have resulted in more than 2,500 arrests by UK law enforcement and almost 3,000 children safeguarded in the UK.

Your transparency reports show that Facebook also acted against 26 million pieces of terrorist content between October 2017 and March 2019. More than 99% of the content Facebook takes action against—both for child sexual exploitation and terrorism—is identified by your safety systems, rather than by reports from users.[487]

The authors commented, "While these statistics are remarkable, mere numbers cannot capture the significance of the harm to children," offering a detailed case study of how Facebook data helped prevent harm to children:

Facebook…identified a child who had sent self-produced child sexual abuse material to an adult male. Facebook located multiple chats between the two that indicated… ongoing sexual abuse. When investigators were able to locate and interview the child, she reported that the adult had sexually abused her hundreds of times over the course of four years, starting when she was 11…The offender…was sentenced to 18 years in prison. Without the information from Facebook, abuse of this girl might be continuing to this day.[488]

The level of detail provided was richer than in previous crypto wars, and few readers could fail to recognize the work Facebook conducted to stop such harm. The authors believed 70% of Facebook's global reporting, 12 million reports globally, would be lost if Facebook enacted their privacy plans.[489]

Facebook's response to the minister's letter came from the heads of WhatsApp and Messenger, Will Cathcart and Stan Chudnovsky.[490] The authors argued their 2.7 billion users have a "right to expect" end-to-end encryption.[491] Cathcart and Chudnovsky turned around the minister's argument regarding the digital-physical relationship of security, arguing:

The "backdoor" access you are demanding for law enforcement would be a gift to criminals, hackers, and repressive regimes, creating a way for them to enter our systems and leaving every person on our platforms more vulnerable to real-life harm. It is simply impossible to create such a backdoor for one purpose and not expect others to try and open it…That is not something we are prepared to do.[492]

The authors invoked Bruce Schneier who earlier in the year stated, "You have to make a choice. Either everyone gets to spy, or no one gets to spy. You can't have 'We get to spy, you don't.' That's not the way the tech works."[493] Nevertheless, the authors declared they were very willing to continue helping law enforcement, "as long as it is consistent with the law and does not undermine the safety of our users."[494] The

487 Ibid, 2.

488 Ibid.

489 Ibid.

490 Cathcart and Chudnovsky, 2019.

491 Ibid, 1.

492 Ibid.

493 Ibid, 2.

authors highlighted a number of ways, outside of the methods which would become infeasible once E2E encryption was deployed, in which they helped law enforcement with the 35,000 staff they had working on "safety and security," a number which doubled in the previous year:

> Artificial Intelligence now enables us to proactively detect many types of bad content on Facebook and Instagram before anyone even reports it, and often before anyone even sees it. WhatsApp detects and bans 2 million accounts every month based on abuse patterns and scans unencrypted information, such as profile and group information for abusive content, like child exploitative imagery.
>
> Our teams are constantly developing new ways to try to detect patterns of activity, by finding bad activity upstream, and by reviewing what we know across the accounts we provide. So, if we know someone is doing something bad on Facebook or Instagram we can often take action on their account on Messenger and WhatsApp, and vice versa.[495]

The authors stated as Facebook enters its "privacy-focused chapter" it would continue to consult with partners, and would, "put our minds and everything we've learned over these years—all the teams, the people and the resources—towards the goal of building the safest private spaces."[496] The messaging was clear: Zuckerberg had steered the ship towards privacy, and Facebook would not be blown off course.

A collection of civil rights groups, technology firms, and technologists also wrote an open letter in response to the Minister's letter to Facebook.[497] The authors expressed their "significant concerns," that the "security and privacy of billions of internet users" would be endangered.[498] The authors argued the technology did not exist to solve the exceptional access problem, and despite encryption, "crime-fighting capacity remains robust given that we are in an age where technology generates so much digital information about individuals and their activities."[499] The authors challenged the Minister's notion that separate solutions could be found for corporate and personal use, arguing, "Critical infrastructure runs on consumer products and services, and is protected by the same encryption," an example of this may be engineers working on critical infrastructures such as energy plants, who may use applications on their personal iPhones or iPads to conduct remote maintenance [whilst this is not best practice it is common].[500] The authors also challenge the veracity of the FBI's quantification of the problem, stating:

> in 2017, the FBI tried to illustrate the impact of encryption on law enforcement when it told Congress that it had seized 7,800 phones that were inaccessible due to encryption. In 2018, this figure was contradicted when an internal FBI estimate of 1,200 phones became public. The FBI committed to providing a revised number, but has not yet done so.[501]

---

494 Ibid.
495 Ibid.
496 Ibid.
497 Access Now and ACLU et al., 2019.

498 Ibid, 1.
499 Ibid.
500 Ibid, 2.
501 Ibid, 6.

The authors were vindicated in their challenge when it emerged in May 2020 the 7,800 number was erroneous—an initial FBI assessment to which *The Washington Post* gained access stated, "programming errors resulted in significant over-counting of [locked] mobile devices reported"—the closer number according to one FBI source was estimated to be 1000–2000.[502] The lack of clarity or exaggeration of the size of the encryption problem, either purposefully or accidentally, has consistently sown distrust throughout the crypto wars.

Barr further pushed his points in a speech on encryption policy in July 2019.[503] Much of the narrative was predictable:

> While we should not hesitate to deploy encryption to protect ourselves from cyber-criminals, this should not be done in a way that eviscerates society's ability to defend itself against other types of criminal threats. In other words, making our virtual world more secure should not come at the expense of making us more vulnerable in the real world. But, unfortunately, this is what we are seeing today.[504]

The simple notion that virtual and "real" world are two separate, nearly demarcated entities represented anachronistic thinking. Barr went on to argue:

> The net effect [of encryption] is to reduce the overall security of society. I am here today to tell you that, as we use encryption to improve cybersecurity, we must ensure that we retain society's ability to gain lawful access to data and communications when needed to respond to criminal activity.[505]

Barr argued encryption created a "law-free zone," which enables "dangerous criminals to cloak their communications and activities behind an essentially impenetrable digital shield, the deployment of warrant-proof encryption is already imposing huge costs on society."[506] Barr added:

> giving criminals the means to operate free of lawful scrutiny, will inevitably propel an expansion of criminal activity. If you remove any possibility that the cops are going to be watching a neighborhood, the criminals already in the neighborhood will commit a lot more crimes.[507]

Barr stated, "Law enforcement has generally not wanted to get too specific about these cases because details can help sophisticated criminals and terrorists evade detection"; however, he offered one of "countless examples" of encryption hindering law enforcement. Barr stated that a Mexican drugs cartel, which smuggled drugs into America and used WhatsApp as their primary communications method, murdered hundreds of Mexican police officers—Barr claimed a decryption capability could have saved these lives.[508] Barr declared, "We are confident that there are technical

---

502 Barrett, 2020.
503 Barr, 2019.
504 Ibid.
505 Ibid.

506 Ibid.
507 Ibid.
508 Ibid.

solutions that will allow lawful access to encrypted data...without materially weakening the security provided by encryption."[509] Barr labeled the technologists' position that encryption access methods could not be developed as "indefensible," stating, "there have been enough dogmatic pronouncements that lawful access simply cannot be done. It can be, and it must be."[510] Barr then offered an analysis of risk that perhaps for the first time acknowledged on behalf of the government that it was not possible to introduce an access method without decreasing the security offered by encryption.[511] Previously the government's position was industry technologists should "nerd-harder," as technologists jokingly labeled their attitude, to find a solution to enable law enforcement access without undermining the integrity of encryption algorithms.[512] Barr stated cybersecurity did not "deal in absolute guarantees, but in relative risks," adding:

> All systems fall short of optimality and have some residual risk of vulnerability—a point which the tech community acknowledges when they propose that law enforcement can satisfy its requirements by exploiting vulnerabilities in their products. The real question is whether the residual risk of vulnerability resulting from incorporating a lawful access mechanism is materially greater than those already in the unmodified product. The Department does not believe this can be demonstrated.[513]

This statement was insightful, and laid a challenge for digital rights activists to quantify the additional risk a lawful access method introduced.[514] Barr then attempted to divide the issue of corporate encryption (e.g., protecting American companies) vs. citizen security:

> Moreover, even if there was, in theory, a slight risk differential, its significance should not be judged solely by the fact it falls short of theoretical optimality. Particularly with respect to encryption marketed to consumers, the significance of the risk should be assessed based on its practical effect on consumer cybersecurity, as well as its relation to the net risks that offering the product poses for society. After all, we are not talking about protecting the Nation's nuclear launch codes. Nor are we necessarily talking about the customized encryption used by large business enterprises to protect their operations. We are talking about consumer products and services such as messaging, smart phones, e-mail, and voice and data applications.

Barr offered an illustration of the trade-off between risk offered by the lack of exceptional access and its presence:

> If one already has an effective level of security—say, by way of illustration, one that protects against 99 percent of foreseeable threats—is it reasonable to incur massive further costs to move slightly closer to optimality and attain a 99.5 percent level of

---

[509] Ibid.
[510] Ibid.
[511] Ibid.

[512] Doctorow, 2018.
[513] Barr, 2019.
[514] Ibid.

protection even where the risk addressed is extremely remote? A company would not make that expenditure; nor should society.

Some argue that, to achieve at best a slight incremental improvement in security, it is worth imposing a massive cost on society in the form of degraded public safety. This is untenable, again using a crude illustration, if the choice is between a world where we can achieve a 99 percent assurance against cyber threats to consumers, while still providing law enforcement 80 percent of the access it might seek; or a world, where we have boosted our cybersecurity to 99.5 percent but at a cost reducing law enforcements access to zero percent—the choice for society is clear.[515]

The language represented a clear move towards a risk-oriented, rather than a binary, approach. Barr conceded his numbers were crude, and it did not represent a break with government policy, as Barr believed society should accept the additional risk in cyberspace for the diminished risk exceptional access could provide. Bruce Schneier commented after Barr's speech it was now possible to "finally have a sensible policy conversation…This is exactly the policy debate we should be having…we can finally move on from the fake security vs. privacy debate, and to the real security vs. security debate."[516]

Barr closed his speech saying whilst collaboration with the private sector to solve the encryption challenge was desirable, "the time to achieve that may be limited."[517]

I think it is prudent to anticipate that a major incident may well occur at any time that will galvanize public opinion on these issues. Whether we end up with legislation or not, the best course for everyone involved is to work soberly and in good faith together to craft appropriate solutions, rather than have outcomes dictated during a crisis…

The status quo is exceptionally dangerous, unacceptable, and only getting worse… It is time for the United States to stop debating *whether* to address it, and start talking about *how* to address it.[518]

Jim Baker, General Counsel of the FBI between 2014 and 2017, commented Barr was wrong to brand cyberspace a "law-free zone," arguing, "It's just that the law that applies in this area is not what Barr or the Justice Department want the law to be."[519] Barr added, "under current law, the most the government can do with respect to encrypted systems where the manufacturer or service provider does not hold the encryption keys is to demand that companies provide it with an encrypted blob for which they have no mechanism to decrypt." In office, Baker had argued robustly for an exceptional access method underpinned by new legislation, but since leaving the FBI he changed his position; Baker comments he now accepts that "Congress is unlikely to act," and his "assessment that the relevant cybersecurity risks to society have grown disproportionately over the years when compared with other risks." Baker felt Barr was "miscalculating the relative costs and benefits and potentially putting the country at greater risk as a result."[520] Baker also highlighted that:

---

515 Ibid.
516 Schneier, 2019.
517 Barr, 2019.

518 Ibid.
519 Baker, 2019.
520 Ibid.

many people on all sides of the debate will admit in private is that the United States has not experienced a terrorist or other attack of sufficient magnitude where encryption clearly played a key role in preventing law enforcement from thwarting it so as to change the contours of the public debate and motivate Congress to act.[521]

Baker commented he was unaware of a technical solution to the problem, but government should not undermine the broader security eco-system to achieve their goals; he stated governments should not, for example:

> use the means through which companies update software as a way to install surveillance software (something the attorney general seems to suggest…).
>
> Updating software promptly is an important way to enhance cybersecurity, and people might not do it if they thought that the government was using that mechanism as a way to install surveillance software.[522]

Baker believed governments should collect communications likely to remain unencrypted, such as metadata, and should "focus on collecting the right data and developing or buying top-notch analytical tools," though he acknowledged, "It is hard to use metadata, for example, to prove criminal intent or to understand exactly what a spy or a terrorist is plotting."[523] Baker ultimately argued:

> In light of the serious nature of this profound and overarching threat, and in order to execute fully their responsibility to protect the nation from catastrophic attack and ensure the continuing operation of basic societal institutions, *public safety officials should embrace encryption*. They should embrace it because it is one very important and effective way—although certainly not the only way and definitely not a complete way—to enhance society's ability to protect its most valuable digital assets in a highly degraded cybersecurity environment.[524]

Baker acknowledged embracing encryption, "will be a bitter pill for some in law enforcement and other public safety fields to swallow, and many people will reject it outright," though argued, "we all need to deal with reality."[525] He added:

> How else do you stop the bad guys *but* by living in reality and aggressively taking the fight to them based on an accurate assessment of the facts? I am most certainly not advocating surrender, but public safety officials need to take a different approach to encryption as a way to more effectively thwart our adversaries, protect the American people and uphold the Constitution in light of the existential cybersecurity threat that society faces.[526]

Baker closed with a stinging statement, "If law enforcement doesn't want to embrace encryption as I have suggested here, then it needs to find other ways to protect the

---

521 Ibid.   524 Ibid.
522 Ibid.   525 Ibid.
523 Ibid.   526 Ibid.

nation from existing cyber threats because, so far, it has failed to do so effectively."[527] Baker's comments are particularly important, as having advocated the government position whilst at the FBI, and during the San Bernardino case, his reversal, even with his "if you knew what I knew" access, undermines that argument. Baker was not in the employ of a technology organization, and therefore seemed to be making the statement without bias to any current employers (though of course it cannot be ruled out he was not considering future employment opportunities.)

At the end of December 2019, another case highlighted how encryption could be a hindrance to law enforcement investigations of terrorism. A Saudi Air Force Officer, Lieutenant Mohammed Saeed Alshamrani, training at a Pensacola, Florida military base launched a terrorist attack murdering three US sailors before himself being killed.[528] Alshamrani possessed two iPhones (an iPhone 5 and an iPhone 7) during the attack, one of which he shot in an attempt to destroy it during the firefight with first responders, the other phone was also damaged.[529] Alshamrani posted online on the previous September 11 anniversary, "the countdown has begun," and two hours before the attack, Alshamrani posted anti-American Jihadi messages.[530] The FBI were able to repair the phones, but AG William Barr commented, "both phones are engineered to make it virtually impossible to unlock them without the password"; he argued, "it is very important to know with whom and about what the shooter was communicating before he died."[531] The FBI asked for Apple's help in unlocking the phones, but Barr stated they did not receive "any substantive assistance."[532] Barr reflected, "This situation perfectly illustrates why it is critical that investigators be able to get access to digital evidence once they have obtained a court order based on probable cause."[533] Barr called for "Apple and other technology companies to help us find a solution so that we can better protect the lives of Americans and prevent future attacks."[534] On January 14, 2020, Trump tweeted:

> We are helping Apple all of the time on TRADE and so many other issues, and yet they refuse to unlock phones used by killers, drug dealers and other violent criminal elements. They will have to step up to the plate and help our great Country, NOW! MAKE AMERICA GREAT AGAIN.[535]

In May, Barr revealed the FBI had successfully broken into the phone, which "definitively establishes Alshamrani's significant ties to Al Qaeda in the Arabian Peninsula (AQAP)," and provided, "a clearer understanding of Alshamrani's associations and activities in the years, months, and days leading up to the attack."[536] Barr stated it was not only the FBI's "ingenuity," but "luck" which enabled them to access the phones, such an approach he argued was not scaleable or necessarily repeatable—he again advocated for a legislative solution.[537] Barr also attacked the technology

---

[527] Ibid.
[528] Barr, 2020a.
[529] Ibid.
[530] Ibid.
[531] Ibid.
[532] Ibid.

[533] Ibid.
[534] Ibid.
[535] Trump, 2020.
[536] Barr, 2020b.
[537] Ibid.

companies for supposedly cooperating with autocratic nations in order to advance their business interests but not the democratic U.S. with its civil liberties, privacy rights, and judicial safeguards, commenting:

> it has been widely reported that Apple has worked with both the Communist Party of China and the Russian regime to relocate data centers to enable bulk surveillance by those governments. Apple also has reportedly disabled features and applications on iPhones used by pro-democracy advocates, thereby facilitating censorship and oppression.[538]

Barr continued with another plea for access:

> Right now, across the nation, there are many phones, both at the federal and state level, that law enforcement still cannot unlock despite having court authorization. As commercial encryption becomes even more sophisticated, our odds of success diminish with each passing year. We cannot do our jobs when companies put the ability to defeat court-authorized searches in the hands of terrorists and criminals. For the safety and security of our citizens, we cannot afford to wait any longer.[539]

ACLU's Brett Max commented on Barr's statement, "Every time there's a traumatic event requiring investigation into digital devices, the Justice Department loudly claims that it needs backdoors to encryption, and then quietly announces it actually found a way to access information without threatening the security and privacy of the entire world"[540] The ACLU added, "The boy who cried wolf has nothing on the agency that cried encryption."[541]

Apple "rejected the characterization" they had not provided the FBI with, "substantiative assistance," stating, "Our responses to their many requests…have been timely, thorough, and are ongoing."[542] Apple added, "We responded to each request promptly, often within hours…the queries resulted in many gigabytes of information that we turned over to investigators…we responded with all of the information that we had."[543]

The case becomes more curious when Andy Garrett, CEO at digital forensics firm Garrett Discovery stated, "We've got the tools to extract data from an iPhone 5 and 7 now…everybody does."[544] Digital forensics instructor Sarah Edwards commented, "It's a cat-and-mouse game. Apple locks things, but if someone wants to find a way to get into these devices, they will find a way."[545]

In the aftermath of the Florida attacks, a bipartisan warning was issued to technology companies in a Senate Judiciary Committee in early December 2019.[546] Speaking before the committee, Manhattan District Attorney Cyrus Vance Jr. stated

---

[538] Ibid.
[539] Barr, 2020b
[540] Allam, 2020.
[541] ACLU, 2020.
[542] Lynn, 2010.

[543] Ibid.
[544] McMillian, 2020.
[545] Edwards. 2014.
[546] Ng, 2019.

whilst his team employed "lawful hacking methods," it costs hundreds of thousands of dollars, and was only successful half the time.[547] Vance told the senators, "There are many serious cases where we can't access the device in the time period where it is most important for us to access it."[548] Vance argued, "Without moving toward legislation, we're not going to solve this problem."[549] Republican Senator Lindsey Graham of South Carolina told Apple and Facebook representatives, "My advice to you is to get on with it. This time next year, if you haven't found a way that you can live with it, we will impose our will on you."[550] Republican Senator Marsha Blackburn of Tennessee added, "You all have got to get your act together, or we will gladly get your act together for you, This is not going to continue."[551] Republican Senator Richard Blumenthal of Connecticut stated, "the American people are losing patience, I hope you take that message back [to Apple and Facebook]."[552] Republican Senator Joni Ernst of Iowa added, "I think you'd rather find the solution than have Congress do it for you."[553]

Cloud backups have repeatedly been cited as a way for law enforcement to manage threats even though devices themselves are encrypted—however, users can choose to host data exclusively on their devices. Reuters reported sources informed them Apple dropped plans for encrypting backups as a result of FBI pressure in January 2020.[554] The article reported at a date potentially earlier than 2018 Apple informed the FBI of its plans to offer end-to-end encryption for using backing up their iPhones to the iCloud.[555] The plan however was dropped—a former Apple employee told Reuters, "Legal killed it, for reasons you can imagine…They decided they weren't going to poke the bear anymore."[556] The former employee said Apple did not want to risk being publicly attacked for protecting criminals, sued for placing data outside the government's reach, or give law enforcement an excuse for pursuing new anti-encryption legislation.[557] Another former Apple employee theorized the abandonment of the plan may have instead been due to fears the cost to users would be too high when the lost or had their devices stolen, or forgot their passcodes.[558] A former FBI officer commented that he believed "Apple was convinced," by the FBI's arguments of the damage it would cause to law enforcement operations, adding, "Outside of that public spat over San Bernardino, Apple gets along with the federal government."[559]

A consequence of companies like Apple and Facebook deploying end-to-end encryption is reduced detection of child abuse content. Technology firms recognize the Internet is a boon to child abusers, and consequently take steps to minimize their digital gains. Photograph scanning is one of the strongest child abuse detection methods. Scanning compares pictures on a technology platform with databases of

---

[547] Ibid.
[548] Ibid.
[549] Ibid.
[550] Ibid.
[551] Ibid.
[552] Ibid.
[553] Ibid.

[554] Menn, 2020.
[555] Ibid.
[556] Ibid.
[557] Ibid.
[558] Ibid.
[559] Ibid.

known abuse photographs, typically via a hash comparison, but increasingly leveraging artificial intelligence techniques.[560] However, increasing user security by deploying end-to-end encryption makes scanning technologies ineffective. In 2019, the Senate Judiciary Committee, led by Republican Senator Lindsey Graham of South Carolina, held an inquiry entitled "Protecting Innocence in a Digital World," and on March 5 2020 Graham introduced the Eliminating Abusive and Rampant Neglect of Interactive Technologies Act (EARN IT Act).[561] Cosponsors included Republican Senator Josh Hawley of Missouri, and Democratic Senators Richard Blumenthal of Connecticut and Dianne Feinstein of California.[562] The EARN IT bill establishes a National Commission on Online Child Sexual Exploitation Prevention that will develop best practices to "prevent, reduce, and respond to the online sexual exploitation of children."[563] The commission would comprise 19 members including the Attorney General (who would chair), the Secretary of Homeland Security, and the Chairman of the Federal Trade Commission. Congress would fill the remainder of the positions with those likely to support any regulations guised as a defense against child abuse—for instance, investigators, prosecutors, and child abuse survivors.[564] Two members of the commission would be computer scientists, four members would work for technology companies on the child abuse problem, and only a maximum of two members would have "current experience in matters related to constitutional law, consumer protection or privacy."[565] Given the phrasing of the latter, it would be possible for none to hold privacy expertise. The Commission would have 18 months to make best practice recommendations—highly likely to include encryption "best practices." To submit recommendations, 14 members of the Commission must be in agreement—the Attorney General, Homeland Secretary, and Federal Trade Commission Chair would all hold vetoes. This would mean even should the maximum number of 5 privacy advocates and technologists who understood the problem be appointed to create the appearance of a balanced Commission, the Attorney General could override them. If the recommendations submitted to the Attorney General are not to their liking, the recommendations can be returned for revision. The returning of the recommendations was a concession, in a leaked earlier draft of the bill the Attorney General could simply replace the commission's recommendations with their own if they disapproved.[566] Once best practices were authorized they would need to be debated by Congress, the process for doing so is minimized in the EARN IT bill to limit opportunity for scrutiny.

The best practice non-compliance penalty would be removal of the liability protection technology platforms hold under section 230 of the Communications Decency Act. This immunity has been critical to the evolution of the Internet—making sure users, rather than platforms, are accountable for published content. Section 230 underwrites digital free speech. Had companies such as Facebook and

---

[560] Todorovic and Chaudhuri, 2018.
[561] United States Congress, 2020.
[562] Ibid.
[563] Ibid.

[564] Ibid.
[565] Ibid.
[566] United States Congress, 2020b.

WhatsApp been legally accountable for content published on their platforms by third parties, the liability would have made their business infeasible given compliance costs and potential penalties—not to mention foreign firms without such constraints would have dominated the market. This protection, however, did not shield technology companies from violations of federal criminal law, such as the harboring of child abuse content—in fact, any companies identifying such content must report it to the National Center for Missing and Exploited Children and subsequently cooperate with law enforcement investigations.[567] Even more Machiavellian was a small clause buried deep within the bill—if best practices were not agreed and approved by the Congress within a four year period, technology companies' liability protections would cease nonetheless, heralding devastation upon the US technology sector. The EFF's Elliot Harmon comments the "Attorney General…would have Internet platforms right where he wants them, ready to compromise their users' security and privacy in order to avoid serious repercussions, including both civil and criminal liability."[568] Introducing the bill Senator Graham explained:

> For the first time, you will have to earn blanket liability protection when it comes to protecting minors. Our goal is to do this in a balanced way that doesn't overly inhibit innovation, but forcibly deals with child exploitation.[569]

Senator Hawley commented:

> Tech companies have an extraordinary special safeguard against legal liability, but that unique protection comes with a responsibility. Companies that fail to comport with basic standards that protect children from exploitation have betrayed the public trust granted them by this special exemption. Online platforms' near complete immunity from legal responsibility is a privilege—they have to earn it.[570]

Hawley added:

> The internet is infested with stomach-churning images of children who have been brutally assaulted and exploited, and who are forced to endure a lifetime of pain after these photographs and videos are circulated online…tech companies need to do better…It's time to stop putting the financial interests of Big Tech above protecting kids from predators.[571]

The bill was widely opposed. Senator Ron Wyden labeled the bill "deeply flawed and counterproductive," commenting:

> This terrible legislation is a Trojan horse to give Attorney General Barr and Donald Trump the power to control online speech and require government access to every

---

567 Harmon, 2020.
568 Ibid.
569 United States Committee of the Judiciary, 2020.
570 Ibid.
571 Ibid.

aspect of Americans' lives…This bill is a transparent and deeply cynical effort by…the Trump administration to use child sexual abuse to their political advantage, the impact to free speech and the security and privacy of every single American be damned.[572]

In a letter to Congress, the EFF's Sophia Cope and Aaron Mackey agreed that EARN IT "impermissibly regulates online speech. The Act forces online service providers to make an impossible choice: cave to government pressure regarding their editorial decisions or face significant new criminal and civil liability."[573] Cope and Mackey argued, "the bill does not just directly target unlawful content, such as child pornography or child sex trafficking ads. Rather, the bill regulates *how* online service providers must operate their platforms and manage the speech they host."[574] Separately Harmon wrote, "the bill's authors have shrewdly used defending children as the pretense for an attack on our free speech and security online…Make no mistake: the EARN IT Act is a vehicle to undermine end-to-end encryption."[575] Matthew Green was even more critical, commenting:

> this bill is a backdoor way to allow the government to ban encryption on commercial services. And even more beautifully: it doesn't come out and actually ban the use of encryption, it just makes encryption commercially infeasible for major providers to deploy, ensuring that they'll go bankrupt if they try to disobey this committee's recommendations. It's the kind of bill you'd come up with if you knew the thing you wanted to do was unconstitutional and highly unpopular, and you basically didn't care.[576]

The bill was announced at a particularly bad time. America was locked down, sheltering from Covid-19; the theater of Washington's inept response, included President Trump's suggestion citizens inject themselves with disinfectant to kill the virus, was ensuring the electorate's focus on little else. The opportunity for a bad bill to be passed with the support of well-meaning but ill-informed members of congress judging technology security only in the context of child abuse was acute. The introduction of EARN IT, and the bill's attempt to undermine democratic and considered debate regarding encryption and exceptional access, if that is what was intended, would represent an egregious violation of public trust, and highlights just how dangerous it is to leave such an issue without resolution.

Shortly following EARN-IT, Senator Graham introduced another bill, along with Republican Senators Tom Cotton of Arkansas and Marsha Blackburn of Tennessee: the Lawful Access to Encrypted Data Act (LAEDA).[577] Whilst bereft of the typically forced acronyms of past legislation proposals, LAEDA was more direct in its intent—technology manufacturers and services should proactively design their offerings to provide the government with decrypted data when required, for both data at rest and data in motion. The only way for technology firms to not comply

---

[572] Wyden, 2020.
[573] Cope and Mackey, 2020.
[574] Ibid.

[575] Harmon, 2020.
[576] Green, 2020.
[577] United States Senate, 2020.

would be to "demonstrate…that it is technically impossible…to make any change to the way the hardware, software, or other property of the person behaves."[578] LAEDA also allowed for the government to provide secret evidence to the courts of why they would need such capabilities from companies where "disclosure of the information would harm…national security…or harm the enforcement of criminal law."[579] AG William Barr supported the bill, commenting:

> end-to-end encryption technology is being abused by child predators, terrorists, drug traffickers, and even hackers to perpetrate their crimes and avoid detection. Warrant-proof encryption allows these criminals to operate with impunity. This is dangerous and unacceptable.[580]

Barr added:

> the danger is particularly great for children who are targeted online for sexual exploitation, especially during this time of coronavirus lockdowns…We cannot allow these [technology] companies to elevate their profits and the privacy rights of these abusers over the safety and security of children.[581]

Again, the digital rights community protested at the latest anti-encryption bill. The EFF's Andrew Crocker commented that the bill "ignores expert consensus and public opinion, which is unfortunately par for the course. But the bill is actually even more out of touch with reality than many other recent anti-encryption bills."[582] Riana Pfefferkorn of Stanford University's Center for Internet and Society commented the bill was a "full-frontal nuclear assault on encryption in the United States," she added:

> This bill is the encryption backdoor mandate we've been dreading was coming, but that nobody, during the past six years of the renewed crypto wars, had previously dared to introduce. Well, these three senators finally went there.[583]

As this book went to print, both bills were still making their way through Congress.

8.10   BIDEN VICTORY

In November 2020, Joe Biden was proclaimed the forty-sixth US President. Biden's victory came despite efforts by the Oval Office incumbent to sabotage the election, a feat he had oft accused his opponent of plotting. President Trump's brazenly false claims of victory, his baseless accusations of Democratic Party corruption, and his blatantly illegal demands for a cessation of ballot counting represented an egregious domestic threat to US democracy. Three decades earlier, at the Cold War's end and with communism perceived to be in ruins, Francis Fukuyama had optimistically proclaimed the "end of history" and declared liberal democracy as the "final form of

---

578 Ibid, 16.   581 Ibid.
579 Ibid.   582 Crocker, 2020.
580 Barr, 2020c.   583 Pfefferkorn, 2020.

human government." Yet, the twenty-first century has thus far witnessed the ascent of illiberal democracies and autocratic rule, with President Trump proudly marching at the vanguard. The world's political decay was in part a result of unprecedented technological advances accelerating a globalization which whilst empowering the highly-educated, too frequently eroded the prospects of those without degrees. Trump exploited these emerging societal fissures, accentuated by media polarization, to win the presidency in 2016. Whilst occupying the White House, President Trump subverted many of the institutions, such as the FBI, charged with providing checks on the power of his office. When the judiciary offered resistance by prosecuting the President's associates, President Trump bestowed pardons on the convicted, essentially placing his acolytes above the law, divorcing action from consequence and thus emboldening future illegality. For many digital privacy activists, President Trump's conduct will have reinforced their conviction that systems of power, such as the US surveillance apparatus, must be architected to resist would-be autocrats who would act in violation of democratic principles. Such systems must possess sufficient safeguards so as to withstand their commandeering for the purpose of democratic subversion until the electorate can eject the transgressor from office.

For many around the world, Biden's victory was a sign of hope portending the re-emergence of a more conciliatory form of politics. However, with regards to cryptologic and technological regulations, that hope must be tempered. Biden's digital policy record is far from reflective of many of his other centrist positions. As well as introducing the 1991 Comprehensive Counter-Terrorism Act, which implied encryption should contain government back doors, Biden has repeatedly adopted positions favorable to big business, law enforcement, and national security. There is also a concern that, given Biden's advanced age, he may not be conversant in the technologies within his power to regulate; Biden was almost of pensionable age when the first iPhone was released. An additional factor is the anti-tech sentiment growing within both parties in Congress; the antitrust investigations that continue could yet be expanded to include other issues such as the encryption policies of the technology behemoths. Much will depend on those who surround Biden and offer a counterweight to law enforcement and national security positions—should Biden be overly deferential to such positions, we may yet see encryption regulations that do not reflect the will of the people (a will which remains ambiguous), and are ineffective in achieving their professed goals. However, there is cause for some hope: the new President has repeatedly demonstrated his ability to reassess his positions, and it is highly likely that Biden administration policies will be more thoughtfully conceived, debated, and executed than those of his predecessor.

8.11 THE THIRD CRYPTO WAR: SUMMARY

The third crypto war is yet to conclude—or if it has—our proximity is such we cannot yet place the bookend. Snowden's actions birthed a new generation of digital rights activists to augment the cypherpunks of the 1990s, many of whom were still active, and helped instill a sense of urgency in business leaders to deliver ubiquitous encryption to protect their clients and foreign market viability. The post-Snowden years also saw the barbarous so-called Islamic State (IS) promote its dystopian medieval vision of society via the Internet. There is little doubt digital technologies contributed to the rise of IS. States had to manage home-grown IS terrorists, who, with a little knowledge and the Internet, could cause outsized destruction. Simply put, the danger a lone hostile actor could inflict upon their victims increased exponentially due to digital technologies.

The FBI became the government vanguard as the White House likely recognized the post-Snowden toxicity of the NSA brand and its mass-surveillance associations. In contrast, the FBI were arguing for exceptional access against individual devices when they possessed reasonable cause and a judicial warrant—a scenario much more familiar and acceptable to the citizenry. In the early 2010s, governments were likely able to mostly access the required data to manage the complex threats they faced. However, the post-Snowden security acceleration likely eroded government capabilities, or presaged an erosion, making the FBI desperate enough to risk confronting in court one of the world's most powerful and consumer-fetishized technology companies: Apple. The government lost the encounter. Perhaps the FBI expected public sentiment to favor their arguments presented in the context of a high-profile terrorism investigation. However, the reality was in stark contrast.

The government's mission of safeguarding its citizens from the twenty-first-century risk landscape became infinitely more complex when Snowden highlighted to citizens the civil rights risks which must be managed alongside terrorism, criminal, and nation-state risks. The rise of the erratic Donald Trump, likely also further concentrated citizens' minds on the need for protection against governments, especially as he strove to undermine the democratic process of the 2020 election. The state is today placed in a conundrum where victory seems elusive: citizens are demanding privacy and security without always appreciating the complex relationship between the two.

When we consider the encryption question, it is worth noting the opinions of those government leaders who were at the forefront of the third crypto war. The narrative of many leaders often dramatically changes when they leave office. Former NSA and CIA director, Michael Hayden states, "the downsides of a front or backdoor outweigh the very real public safety concerns."[584] Former Defense Secretary Ashton Carter cautions, "I'm not a believer in backdoors or a single technical approach to what is a complex and complicated problem."[585] Vice-Chairman of the Joint Chiefs of Staff Admiral James A. Winnefeld remarks, "I think I would rather live on the side of secure networks and a harder problem for…the intelligence side."[586] Robert Hannigan, former GCHQ Director comments, "Encryption is an overwhelmingly good thing…Building in backdoors is a threat to everybody and it's not a good idea to weaken security for everybody to tackle a minority."[587]

Edward Snowden states, "We have the technology to end mass surveillance without any legislative action…[encryption] can end mass surveillance…around the world."[588] His belief is saturated with a cypherpunk's technological utopianism

---

[584] Shachtman, 2014.
[585] Kleiner Perkins, 2016.
[586] Winnefeld, 2015.
[587] McMullan, 2017.
[588] Bamford, 2014.

which, whilst laudable and romantic, is flawed. Technology never operates in a vacuum. The third crypto war demonstrates technological constraints upon government must be married with legislative constraints—and such constraints should reflect the desires of the citizenry, a fact receiving scant attention throughout the crypto wars.

REFERENCES

ARTICLES

Foreign Policy. (2013). The Surveillance States and its Discontents. *Foreign Policy*, **203**, 64–67, 74.
Hayden, M. V. (2014). Beyond Snowden: A NSA Reality Check. *World Affairs*, **176**(5), 13–23.

BOOKS

Stengel, R. (2019). *Information Wars: How We Lost the Global Battle against Disinformation and What We Can Do about It.* (United Kingdom: Grove Press).

WEBSITES

Aas, J. (2014). *Let's Encrypt: Delivering SSL/TLS Everywhere.* Available: https://letsencrypt.org/2014/11/18/announcing-lets-encrypt.html [Accessed January 14, 2020].
Aas, J. (2015). *Let's Encrypt Launch Schedule.* Available: https://letsencrypt.org/2015/06/16/lets-encrypt-launch-schedule.html [Accessed January 14, 2020].
Aas, J., et al. (2019). *Let's Encrypt: An Automated Certificate Authority to Encrypt the Entire Web.* Available: https://zakird.com/papers/lets-encrypt.pdf [Accessed January 14, 2020].
Access Advocacy for Principled Action in Government, et al. (2014). *Correspondence to NIST and White House, 20 November 2014.* Available: https://www.ccianet.org/wp-content/uploads/2014/11/Coalition-NIST-Nov2014.pdf [Accessed February 5, 2020].
Access Now, ACLU et al. (2019). *Letter to Priti Patel, William P. Barr, Chad F. Wolf, and Peter Dutton from Civil Society, Technology, Technology Companies and Trade Associations, and Security and Policy Experts, 10 December 2019.* Available: https://newamericadotorg.s3.amazonaws.com/documents/Coalition_Response_Letter_-_Encryption_DOJ_event_and_letter_to_Facebook.pdf [Accessed January 30, 2020].
Access Now, Big Brother Watch et al. (2019). *Open Letter to GCHQ from Civil Society, Technology, Technology Companies and Trade Associations, and Security and Policy Experts, 22 May 2019.* Available: https://newamericadotorg.s3.amazonaws.com/documents/Coalition_Letter_to_GCHQ_on_Ghost_Proposal_-_May_22_2019.pdf [Accessed January 30, 2020].
ACLU. (2014). *ACLU Comment on FBI Director Comey's Encryption Speech.* Available: https://www.aclu.org/press-releases/aclu-comment-fbi-director-comeys-encryption-speech?redirect=technology-and-liberty/aclu-comment-fbi-director-comeys-encryption-speech [Accessed January 9, 2020].
ACLU. (2020). *Tweet 18 May 2020.* Available: https://twitter.com/ACLU/status/1262504664039403526 [Accessed June 7, 2020].

Allam, H. (2020). *FBI: New iPhone Evidence Shows Pensacola Shooter Had Ties To Al-Qaida.* Available: https://www.npr.org/2020/05/18/857932909/fbi-new-iphone-evidence-shows-pensacola-shooter-had-ties-to-al-qaida?t=1591552738516 [Accessed June 7, 2020].

Apple. (2016). *Amicus Briefs in Support of Apple.* Available: https://www.apple.com/newsroom/2016/03/03Amicus-Briefs-in-Support-of-Apple/ [Accessed January 13, 2020].

Apple. (2018). *Submission to the Parliamentary Joint Committee on Intelligence and Security (PJCIS) on the Telecommunications and Other Legislation Amendment (Assistance and Access) Bill 2018.* Available: https://assets.documentcloud.org/documents/5001477/Apple-comments-to-Australian-parliament.pdf [Accessed February 19, 2020].

Australian Human Rights Commission. (2018). *Telecommunications and Other Legislation Amendment (Assistance and Access) Bill 2018.* Available: https://www.humanrights.gov.au/sites/default/files/Australian%20Human%20Rights%20Commission%20submission%20Access%20and%20Assistance%20Bill%20%5Bfinal%5D%2012%20Oct%202018.pdf [Accessed February 19, 2020].

Australian Parliament. (2018a). *Revised Explanatory Memorandum: Telecommunications and Other Legislation Amendment (Assistance and Access) Bill 2018.* Available: https://parlinfo.aph.gov.au/parlInfo/download/legislation/ems/r6195_ems_504ca495-f6b2-46bb-a4a2-9ce169ba2616/upload_pdf/692183_Revised%20Explanatory%20Memorandum.pdf;fileType=application%2Fpdf [Accessed January 22, 2020].

Australian Parliament. (2018b). *Telecommunications and Other Legislation Amendment (Assistance and Access) Bill 2018.* Available: https://parlinfo.aph.gov.au/parlInfo/download/legislation/bills/r6195_aspassed/toc_pdf/18204b01.pdf;fileType=application%2Fpdf [Accessed January 22, 2020].

Baker, J. (2019). *Rethinking Encryption.* Available: https://www.lawfareblog.com/rethinking-encryption [Accessed January 25, 2020].

Ball, J., Borger, J., and Greenwald, G. (2013). *Revealed: How US and UK Spy Agencies Defeat Internet Privacy and Security.* Available: https://www.theguardian.com/world/2013/sep/05/nsa-gchq-encryption-codes-security [Accessed January 12, 2020].

Bamford, J. (2014). *Edward Snowden: The Most Wanted Man in the World.* Available: https://www.youtube.com/watch?v=Nbmr_eM2DnQ [Accessed April 22, 2020].

Bamford, J. (2015). *A Death in Athens.* Available: https://theintercept.com/2015/09/28/death-athens-rogue-nsa-operation/ [Accessed January 27, 2020].

Barr, W. (2019). *Attorney General William P. Barr Delivers Keynote Address at the International Conference on Cyber Security.* Available: https://www.justice.gov/opa/speech/attorney-general-william-p-barr-delivers-keynote-address-international-conference-cyber [Accessed January 26, 2020].

Barr, W. (2020a). *Attorney General William P. Barr Announces the Findings of the Criminal Investigation into the December 2019 Shooting at Pensacola Naval Air Station.* Available: https://www.justice.gov/opa/speech/attorney-general-william-p-barr-announces-findings-criminal-investigation-december-2019 [Accessed January 21, 2020].

Barr, W. (2020b). *Attorney General William P. Barr Announces Updates to the Findings of the Investigation into the December 2019 Shooting at Pensacola Naval Air Station.* Available: https://www.justice.gov/opa/speech/attorney-general-william-p-barr-announces-updates-findings-investigation-december-2019 [Accessed May 24, 2020].

Barr, W. (2020c). *Statement from Attorney General William P. Barr on Introduction of Lawful Access Bill in Senate.* Available: https://www.justice.gov/opa/pr/statement-attorney-general-william-p-barr-introduction-lawful-access-bill-senate [Accessed June 27, 2020].

Barrett, D. (2020). *FBI Repeatedly Overstated Encryption Threat Figures to Congress, Public.* Available: https://www.washingtonpost.com/world/national-security/fbi-repeat edly-overstated-encryption-threat-figures-to-congress-public/2018/05/22/5b68ae90 -5dce-11e8-a4a4-c070ef53f315_story.html [Accessed May 24, 2020].

Berman, M. (2016). *One Year after the San Bernardino Attack, Police Offer a Possible Motive as Questions Still Linger.* Available: https://www.washingtonpost.com/news/ post-nation/wp/2016/12/02/one-year-after-san-bernardino-police-offer-a-possible-moti ve-as-questions-still-linger/ [Accessed January 12, 2020].

Bernstein, D., Lange, T., Niederhagen, R. (2015). *Dual EC: A Standardized Back Door.* Available: https://projectbullrun.org/dual-ec/documents/dual-ec-20150731.pdf [Accessed February 7, 2020].

Brandom, R. (2016). *Donald Trump Calls for a Boycott of Apple Products.* Available: https ://www.theverge.com/2016/2/19/11071684/donald-trump-apple-boycott-encryption-iph one [Accessed January 13, 2020].

Burr, R. (2016). *Intelligence Committee Leaders Release Discussion Draft of Encryption Legislation.* Available: https://www.burr.senate.gov/press/releases/intelligence-committee -leaders-release-discussion-draft-of-encryption-legislation- [Accessed January 24, 2020].

California Legislative. (2016). *AB-1681 Smartphones (2015–2016).* Available: https://leginfo .legislature.ca.gov/faces/billVersionsCompareClient.xhtml?bill_id=201520160AB168 1&cversion=20150AB168199INT [Accessed January 24, 2020].

Callas, J. (2013). *To Our Customers.* Available: https://silentcircle.wordpress.com/2013/08/09 /to-our-customers/ [Accessed February 18, 2020].

Caproni, V. (2011). *Valerie Caproni, General Counsel, FBI, Statement Before the House Judiciary Committee, Subcommittee on Crime, Terrorism, and Homeland Security, Washington, D.C., February 17, 2011.* Available: https://archives.fbi.gov/archives/n ews/testimony/going-dark-lawful-electronic-surveillance-in-the-face-of-new-techn ologies [Accessed January 20, 2020].

Cathcart, W. and Chudnovsky, S. (2019). *Facebook's Public Response to Open Letter on Private Messaging.* Available: https://cdn.vox-cdn.com/uploads/chorus_asset/file/19446144/Facebo ok_Response_to_Barr_Patel_Dutton_Wolf___1_.pdf [Accessed January 22, 2020].

Checkoway, S., et al. (2014). *On The Practical Exploitability of Dual EC in TLS Implementation.* Available: https://www.usenix.org/system/files/conference/usenixse curity14/sec14-paper-checkoway.pdf [Accessed February 7, 2020].

Checkoway, S., et al. (n.d.). *On the Practical Exploitability of Dual EC in TLS Implementations: Summary.* Available: http://dualec.org/ [Accessed February 8, 2020].

Ciobotea, O. (2016). *Why the Apple-FBI Battle Made People Realize the Importance of Privacy Faster than Snowden.* Available: https://venturebeat.com/2016/04/29/why-t he-apple-fbi-battle-made-people-realize-the-importance-of-privacy-faster-than-sn owden/ [Accessed January 13, 2020].

Cohen, T. (2016). *Israeli Firm Helping FBI to Open Encrypted iPhone: Report.* Available: https://www.reuters.com/article/us-apple-encryption-cellebrite/israeli-firm-helping-f bi-to-open-encrypted-iphone-report-idUSKCN0WP17J [Accessed January 13, 2020].

Cooper, J. (n.d.). *Jim Cooper Biography.* Available: https://a09.asmdc.org/article/biography [Accessed January 24, 2020].

Cope, S. and Mackey, A. (2020). *Letter to Senate Judiciary Committee, Re: EARN IT Act (S. 3398) Violates the First Amendment, 9 March 2020.* Available: https://www.eff .org/files/2020/03/10/2020-3-9_eff_earn_it_act_first_amd_letter_final.pdf [Accessed April 26, 2020].

Cohn, C. (2014). *EFF Response to FBI Director Comey's Speech on Encryption.* Available: https://www.eff.org/deeplinks/2014/10/eff-response-fbi-director-comeys-speech-en cryption [Accessed January 9, 2020].

Comey, J. (2014). *Going Dark: Are Technology, Privacy, and Public Safety on a Collision Course? 16 October 2014.* Available: https://www.fbi.gov/news/speeches/going-dark-are-technology-privacy-and-public-safety-on-a-collision-course [Accessed January 9, 2020].

Comey, J. (2015a). *Encryption, Public Safety, and "Going Dark."* Available: https://www.lawfareblog.com/encryption-public-safety-and-going-dark [Accessed January 20, 2020].

Comey, J. (2015b). *Standing Together Against Terrorism and Fear: Tossed by the Waves but Never Sunk.* Available: https://www.fbi.gov/news/speeches/standing-together-against-terrorism-and-fear-tossed-by-the-waves-but-never-sunk [Accessed January 20, 2020].

Comey, J. (2016a). *FBI Director Comments on San Bernardino Matter.* Available: https://www.fbi.gov/news/pressrel/press-releases/fbi-director-comments-on-san-bernardino-matter [Accessed January 13, 2020].

Comey, J. (2016b). *Oversight of the Federal Bureau of Investigation.* Available: https://www.fbi.gov/news/testimony/oversight-of-the-federal-bureau-of-investigation [Accessed January 20, 2020].

Conger, K. (2016). *Ladar Levison Finally Confirms Snowden was Target of Lavabit Investigation.* Available: https://techcrunch.com/2016/06/24/ladar-levison-finally-confirms-snowden-was-target-of-lavabit-investigation/ [Accessed February 18, 2020].

Cook, T. (2016). *A Message to Our Customers.* Available: https://www.apple.com/customer-letter/ [Accessed January 12, 2020].

Crocker, A. (2020). *The Senate's New Anti-Encryption Bill Is Even Worse Than EARN IT, and That's Saying Something.* Available: https://www.eff.org/deeplinks/2020/06/senates-new-anti-encryption-bill-even-worse-earn-it-and-thats-saying-something [Accessed June 27, 2020].

Davies, D. (2019). *Edward Snowden Speaks Out: "I Haven't and I Won't" Cooperate with Russia.* Available: https://www.npr.org/2019/09/19/761918152/exiled-nsa-contractor-edward-snowden-i-haven-t-and-i-won-t-cooperate-with-russia [Accessed February 6, 2020].

Doctorow, C. (2018). *NERD HARDER! FBI Director Reiterates Faith-Based Belief in Working Crypto That He Can Break.* Available: https://boingboing.net/2018/01/12/imaginary-numbers.html [Accessed January 26, 2020].

Donohue, B. (2014). *Android 5.0 Data Better Protected with New Crypto System.* Available: https://www.kaspersky.com/blog/full-disk-encryption-android-5/6423/ [Accessed January 15, 2020].

Edwards, J. (2014). *U.S. Attorney General Criticizes Apple, Google Data Encryption.* Available: https://www.reuters.com/article/us-usa-smartphones-holder/u-s-attorney-general-criticizes-apple-google-data-encryption-idUSKCN0HP22P20140930 [Accessed January 20, 2020].

Electronic Frontier Foundation. (2013). *EFF Has Lavabit's Back in Contempt of Court Appeal.* Available: https://www.eff.org/press/releases/eff-has-lavabits-back-contempt-court-appeal [Accessed February 17, 2020].

Electronic Frontier Foundation. (2016). *Coalition Letter Opposing CA AB 1681.* Available: https://www.eff.org/document/coalition-letter-opposing-ca-ab-1681 [Accessed January 24, 2020].

Electronic Frontier Foundation. (2018). *New National Academy of Sciences Report on Encryption Asks the Wrong Questions.* Available: https://www.eff.org/deeplinks/2018/02/new-national-academy-sciences-report-encryption-asks-wrong-questions [Accessed February 21, 2020].

Emm, D. (2015). *David Cameron, Encryption and National Security.* Available: https://www.huffingtonpost.co.uk/david-emm/david-cameron-encryption_b_6631398.html [Accessed January 28, 2020].

Encryption Working Group. (2015). *Obama Administration's Encryption Working Group Summary of Encryption Policy Options.* Available: https://assets.documentcloud.org/documents/2430092/read-the-obama-administrations-draft-paper-on.pdf   [Accessed January 31, 2020].

Farivar, C. (2014). *Apple Expands Data Encryption Under iOS 8, Making Handover to Cops Moot.* Available: https://arstechnica.com/gadgets/2014/09/apple-expands-data-encryption-under-ios-8-making-handover-to-cops-moot/ [Accessed January 15, 2020].

Federal Bureau of Investigation. (2015). *FBI Will Investigate San Bernardino Shootings as Terrorist Act.* Available: https://www.fbi.gov/news/stories/fbi-will-investigate-san-bernardino-shootings-as-terrorist-act [Accessed January 12, 2020].

Finkle, J. (2013). *Hackers Convention Ask Government to Stay Away Over Snowden.* Available: https://web.archive.org/web/20130722035410/http://www.reuters.com/article/2013/07/11/us-hackers-feds-idUSBRE96A08120130711 [Accessed February 26, 2020].

Five Country Ministerial. (2018). *Statement of Principles on Access to Evidence and Encryption.* Available: https://www.ag.gov.au/About/CommitteesandCouncils/Documents/joint-statement-principles-access-evidence.pdf [Accessed January 21, 2020].

Five Country Ministerial. (2019). *Joint Meeting of Five Country Ministerial and Quintet of Attorneys-General: Communiqué, London* 2019. Available: https://www.gov.uk/government/publications/five-country-ministerial-communique/joint-meeting-of-five-country-ministerial-and-quintet-of-attorneys-general-communique-london-2019 [Accessed January 21, 2020].

Garofalo A. (2016). *Loretta Lynch Defends FBI in Apple Encryption Case to Stephen Colbert.* Available: https://www.ibtimes.com/loretta-lynch-defends-fbi-apple-encryption-case-stephen-colbert-video-2334739 [Accessed January 25, 2020].

Geller, E. (2015). *Apple Warns U.K. Surveillance Law Would Ruin Encryption For All Users.* Available: https://www.dailydot.com/layer8/apple-uk-encryption-law-criticism-letter/ [Accessed February 1, 2020].

Geller, E. (2016). *The Pro-Encryption Bill that Congress is Ignoring.* Available: https://www.dailydot.com/layer8/secure-data-act-encryption-backdoors-stuck-congress-committees/ [Accessed January 25, 2020].

Geller, E. (2018). *MC Exclusive: Manhattan DA Takes Encryption-Breaking Plea to Congress.* Available: https://www.politico.com/newsletters/morning-cybersecurity/2018/03/28/mc-exclusive-manhattan-da-takes-encryption-breaking-plea-to-congress-152422 [Accessed January 25, 2020].

George, R. (2014). *Richard "Dickie" George—Keynote—Life at Both Ends of the Barrel: An NSA Targeting Retrospective.* Available: https://vimeo.com/97891042 [Accessed February 7, 2020].

Google. (2019). *Transparency Report: HTTPS Encryption on the Web.* Available: https://transparencyreport.google.com/https/overview?hl=en_GB [Accessed January 15, 2020].

Green, M. (2015). *A Few Thoughts on Cryptographic Engineering: Hopefully the Last Post I'll Ever Write on Dual EC DRBG.* Available: https://blog.cryptographyengineering.com/2015/01/14/hopefully-last-post-ill-ever-write-on/ [Accessed February 8, 2020].

Green, M. (2020). *EARN IT is a Direct Attack on End-to-End Encryption.* Available: https://blog.cryptographyengineering.com/2020/03/06/earn-it-is-an-attack-on-encryption/ [Accessed April 26, 2020].

Greenberg, A. (2014). *WhatsApp Just Switched on End-to-End Encryption for Hundreds of Millions of Users.* Available: https://www.wired.com/2014/11/whatsapp-encrypted-messaging/ [Accessed January 20, 2020].

Greenberg, A. (2016). *The Senate's Draft Encryption Bill Is "Ludicrous, Dangerous, Technically Illiterate."* Available: https://www.wired.com/2016/04/senates-draft-encryption-bill-privacy-nightmare/ [Accessed January 22, 2020].

Greenwald, G. (2013a). *NSA Collecting Phone Records of Millions of Verizon Customers Daily.* Available: https://www.theguardian.com/world/2013/jun/06/nsa-phone-reco rds-verizon-court-order [Accessed January 10, 2020].

Greenwald, G. (2013b). *Email Service Used by Snowden Shuts Itself Down, Warns against Using US-Based Companies.* Available: https://www.theguardian.com/commentisfre e/2013/aug/09/lavabit-shutdown-snowden-silicon-valley [Accessed February 18, 2020].

Greenwald, G. and MacAskill, E. (2013). *NSA Prism Program Taps in to User Data of Apple, Google and Others.* Available: https://www.theguardian.com/world/2013/jun/06/us-t ech-giants-nsa-data [Accessed January 10, 2020].

Greenwald, G., MacAskill, E., Poitras, L., Ackerman, S., and Rushe, D. (2013). *Microsoft Handed the NSA Access to Encrypted Messages.* Available: https://www.theguardian.com/world/2 013/jul/11/microsoft-nsa-collaboration-user-data [Accessed January 12, 2020].

Hall, J. L. (2015). *The NSA's Split-Key Encryption Proposal is Not Serious—Center for Democracy and Technology.* Available: https://cdt.org/insights/the-nsas-split-key-e ncryption-proposal-is-not-serious/ [Accessed July 3, 2020].

Hannigan, R. (2014). *The Web is a Terrorist's Command-and-Control Network of Choice.* Available: https://www.ft.com/content/c89b6c58-6342-11e4-8a63-00144feabdc0#a xzz3I5Wn36Fv [Accessed January 29, 2020].

Harmon, E. (2020). *The Graham-Blumenthal Bill Is an Attack on Online Speech and Security.* Available: https://www.eff.org/deeplinks/2020/03/graham-blumenthal-bill -attack-online-speech-and-security [Accessed April 26, 2020].

Hosenball, M. and Volz, D. (2016). *Exclusive: White House Declines to Support Encryption Legislation—Sources.* Available: https://www.reuters.com/article/us-apple-encryptio n-legislation-idUSKCN0X32M4 [Accessed January 23, 2020].

Internet Association. (2016). *Statement on the Compliance with Court Orders Act of 2016.* Available: https://internetassociation.org/041116encryption/ [Accessed 24 January 2020].

International Organization for Standardization. (2020). *About Us.* Available: https://www.iso. org/about-us.html [Accessed February 3, 2020].

Investigatory Powers Commissioner's Office (2018). Annual Report of the Investigatory Powers Commissioner. Available: https://ipco.org.uk/docs/IPCO%20Annual%20Repo rt%202018%20final.pdf [Accessed August 31, 2020].

James, E. T. (2016). *House Bill No. 1040.* Available: http://www.legis.la.gov/legis/ViewD ocument.aspx?d=991170 [Accessed January 24, 2020].

Jeong, S. (2015). *A "Golden Key" for Encryption Is Mythical Nonsense.* Available: https ://www.vice.com/en_us/article/3dk9v8/a-golden-key-for-encryption-is-mythical-non sense [Accessed July 4, 2020].

Kelsey, J. (2014). *Dual EC in X9.82 and SP 800–90.* Available: https://csrc.nist.gov/csrc/ media/projects/crypto-standards-development-process/documents/dualec_in_x982_a nd_sp800-90.pdf [Accessed February 4, 2020].

Kiss, J. (2014). *An Online Magna Carta: Berners-Lee Calls for Bill of Rights for Web.* Available: https://www.theguardian.com/technology/2014/mar/12/online-magna-c arta-berners-lee-web [Accessed January 18, 2020].

Kleiner Perkins. (2016). *An Interview with Defense Secretary Ash Carter.* Available: https ://www.kleinerperkins.com/perspectives/interview-with-dod-secretary-ash-carter/ [Accessed April 22, 2020].

Koum, J. (2016). *Facebook Post 17 January 2016.* Available: https://www.facebook.com/jan. koum/posts/10153907267490011 [Accessed January 13, 2020].

Lambert, L. and Dave, P. (2018). *Facebook Shares Drop as Data Privacy Fallout Spreads.* Available: https://uk.reuters.com/article/us-facebook-data-cambridge-analytica/fa cebook-shares-drop-as-data-privacy-fallout-spreads-idUKKBN1OI241 [Accessed January 22, 2020].

Lavabit. (2012). *Security Through Asymmetric Encryption.* Available: http://web.archive.o
rg/web/20120502035558/http://lavabit.com/secure.html [Accessed February 18, 2020].

Legal Information Institute. (no date). *28 U.S. Code § 1651 Writs.* Available: https://www.law
.cornell.edu/uscode/text/28/1651 [Accessed January 20, 2020].

Let's Encrypt. (2020). *Let's Encrypt Stats.* Available: https://letsencrypt.org/stats/ [Accessed
January 14, 2020].

Levison, L. (2013a). *Lavabit Closing Letter.* Available: https://web.archive.org/web/2013110
5161450/https://lavabit.com/ [Accessed February 15, 2020].

Levison, L. (2013b). *I Am Ladar Levison, Owner and Operator of Lavabit, Ask Me Almost
Anything.* Available: https://www.reddit.com/r/IAmA/comments/1qetvk/i_am_lada
r_levison_owner_and_operator_of_lavabit/cdc3zit/ [Accessed February 18, 2020].

Levison, L. (2014a). *Secrets, Lies and Snowden's Email: Why I Was Forced to Shut Down
Lavabit.* Available: https://www.theguardian.com/commentisfree/2014/may/20/why-di
d-lavabit-shut-down-snowden-email [Accessed February 15, 2020].

Levison, L. (2014b). *The Story Continues.* Available: https://rally.org/lavabit [Accessed
February 18, 2020].

Levy, I. and Robinson, C. (2018). *Principles for a More Informed Exceptional Access Debate.*
Available: https://www.lawfareblog.com/principles-more-informed-exceptional-acces
s-debate [Accessed January 30, 2020].

Lieu, T. (2019). *Rep Lieu Announces Encrypt Act Reintroduction at DefCon.* Available: https
://lieu.house.gov/media-center/press-releases/rep-lieu-announces-encrypt-act-reintrod
uction-defcon [Accessed January 25, 2020].

Lokshina, T. (2013). *Facebook Post 00:25, 12 July 2013.* Available: https://www.facebook
.com/tanya.lokshina/posts/515881045133478%20 [Accessed February 17, 2020].

Lynch, J. (2011). *Newly Released Documents Detail FBI's Plan to Expand Federal
Surveillance Laws.* Available: https://www.eff.org/deeplinks/2011/02/newly-releas
ed-documents-detail-fbi-s-plan-expand [Accessed February 2, 2020].

Lynn, W. J. (2010). *Defending a New Domain: The Pentagon's Cyberstrategy.* Available:
https://archive.defense.gov/home/features/2010/0410_cybersec/lynn-article1.aspx
[Accessed January 18, 2020].

MacAskill, E., Borger, J., Hopkins, N., Davies, N., and Ball, J. (2013). *GCHQ Taps Fibre-
Optic Cables for Secret Access to World's Communications.* Available: https://ww
w.theguardian.com/uk/2013/jun/21/gchq-cables-secret-world-communications-nsa
[Accessed January 12, 2020].

Manhattan District Attorney's Office. (2015). *Report of the Manhattan District Attorney's
Office on Smartphone Encryption and Public Safety.* Available: https://web.archive.
org/web/20151123001557/https://www.manhattanda.org/sites/default/files/11.18.15%2
0Report%20on%20Smartphone%20Encryption%20and%20Public%20Safety.pdf
[Accessed January 17, 2020].

Manning, J. E. (2018). *Membership of the 115th Congress: A Profile.* Available: https://
www.senate.gov/CRSpubs/b8f6293e-c235-40fd-b895-6474d0f8e809.pdf   [Accessed
February 22, 2020].

Masnick, M. (2014). *Washington Post's Clueless Editorial On Phone Encryption: No
Backdoors, But How About A Magical "Golden Key"?* Available: https://www.tec
hdirt.com/articles/20141006/01082128740/washington-posts-braindead-editorial-pho
ne-encryption-no-backdoors-how-about-magical-golden-key.shtml [Accessed July 4,
2020].

Massie, T. (2014a). *Amendment to H.R. 2578, As Reported Offered By Mr. Massie of
Kentucky.* Available: https://repcloakroom.house.gov/uploadedfiles/cjs16massie4.pdf
[AccessedFebruary 24, 2020].

Massie, T. (2014b). *Facebook Post 0721 4 December 2014*. Available: facebook.com/Re
pThomasMassie/posts/word-is-spreading-that-the-massielofgrensensenbrennerholt-ns
a-amendment-to-stop-/910370438987121/ [Accessed February 23, 2020].

McMillian, R. (2020). *As Justice Department Pressures Apple, Investigators Say iPhone
Easier to Crack: Security Experts Question Necessity of Latest Battle Over Encryption
as New Tools Emerge*. Available: https://www.wsj.com/articles/as-justice-department
-pressures-apple-investigators-say-iphone-easier-to-crack-11579010143   [Accessed
January 21, 2020].

McMullan, T. (2017). *Former GCHQ Chief: End-to-end Encryption is an "Overwhelmingly
Good Thing."* Available: https://www.alphr.com/politics/1006273/former-gchq-chie
f-end-to-end-encryption-is-an-overwhelmingly-good-thing [Accessed April 22, 2020].

Menn, J. (2013). *Exclusive: Secret Contract Tied NSA and Security Industry Pioneer*.
Available: https://www.reuters.com/article/us-usa-security-rsa/exclusive-secret-c
ontract-tied-nsa-and-security-industry-pioneer-idUSBRE9BJ1C220131220   [Accessed
February 6, 2020].

Menn, J. (2014). *Exclusive: NSA Infiltrated RSA Security More Deeply Than Thought—
Study*.   Available: https://www.reuters.com/article/us-usa-security-nsa-rsa/exclusive
-nsa-infiltrated-rsa-security-more-deeply-than-thought-study-idUSBREA2U0TY2
0140331 [Accessed February 7, 2020].

Menn, J. (2020). *Exclusive: Apple Dropped Plan for Encrypting Backups After FBI
Complained—Sources*. Available: https://www.reuters.com/article/us-apple-fbi-iclou
d-exclusive/exclusive-apple-dropped-plan-for-encrypting-backups-after-fbi-compla
ined-sources-idUSKBN1ZK1CT [Accessed January 31, 2020].

Moore, N. (2019). *How Let's Encrypt Doubled the Internet's Percentage of Secure Websites
in Four Years*. Available: https://www.eurekalert.org/pub_releases/2019-11/uom-hle
111319.php [Accessed January 14, 2020].

Moss, J. (2013). *Feds, We Need Some Time Apart*. Available: https://web.archive.org/web/20
130722211016/http://defcon.org/ [Accessed February 26, 2020].

The New York State Senate. (2016). *Assembly Bill A8093A*. Available: https://www.nysenate
.gov/legislation/bills/2015/a8093 [Accessed January 24, 2020].

National Academies of Sciences, Engineering, and Medicine. (2018). *Decrypting the
Encryption Debate: A Framework for Decision Makers*. Available: https://www.nap.
edu/read/25010/chapter/1 [Accessed January 28, 2020].

National Institute for Standards and Technology. (2013a). *Cryptographic Standards
Statement*. Available: https://www.nist.gov/news-events/news/2013/09/cryptographic-
standards-statement [Accessed February 3, 2020].

National Institute for Standards and Technology. (2013b). *Supplemental ITL Bulletin for
September 2013*. Available: https://csrc.nist.gov/csrc/media/publications/shared/do
cuments/itl-bulletin/itlbul2013-09-supplemental.pdf [Accessed February 4, 2020].

National Institute for Standards and Technology. (2014a). *NIST Removes Cryptography
Algorithm from Random Number Generator Recommendations*. Available: https://ww
w.nist.gov/news-events/news/2014/04/nist-removes-cryptography-algorithm-random-n
umber-generator-recommendations [Accessed February 4, 2020].

National Institute for Standards and Technology. (2014b). *NIST Cryptographic Standards
and Guidelines Development Process*. Available: https://www.nist.gov/system/files/d
ocuments/2017/05/09/VCAT-Report-on-NIST-Cryptographic-Standards-and-Guideli
nes-Process.pdf [Accessed February 4, 2020].

National Institute for Standards and Technology. (2016). *Cryptographic Standards and
Guidelines Development Process*. Available: https://csrc.nist.gov/projects/crypto-st
andards-development-process [Accessed February 4, 2020].

NBC News. (2013). *Lavabit.com Owner: "I Could be Arrested" for Resisting Surveillance Order.* Available: http://investigations.nbcnews.com/_news/2013/08/13/20008036-lavabitcom-owner-i-could-be-arrested-for-resisting-surveillance-order?lite [Accessed February 18, 2020]

New York Times Editorial Board. (2013). *Opinion | Close the N.S.A.'s Back Doors.* Available: https://www.nytimes.com/2013/09/22/opinion/sunday/close-the-nsas-back-doors.html ?_r=0 [Accessed February 4, 2020].

Ng, A. (2019). *Congress Warns Tech Companies: Take Action on Encryption, or We Will.* Available: https://www.cnet.com/news/congress-warns-tech-companies-take-action-on-encryption-or-we-will/ [Accessed January 22, 2020].

Obama, B. (2013a). *Remarks by the President at the National Defense University.* Available: https://obamawhitehouse.archives.gov/the-press-office/2013/05/23/remarks-president-national-defense-university [Accessed January 10, 2020].

Obama, B. (2013b). *Statement by the President.* Available: https://obamawhitehouse.archives.gov/the-press-office/2013/06/07/statement-president [Accessed January 11, 2020].

Obama, B. (2013c). *Remarks by President Obama and Prime Minister Reinfeldt of Sweden in Joint Press Conference.* Available: https://obamawhitehouse.archives.gov/the-press-office/2013/09/04/remarks-president-obama-and-prime-minister-reinfeldt-sweden-joint-press- [Accessed January 18, 2020].

Obama, B. (2014). *Remarks by the President on Review of Signals Intelligence.* Available: https://obamawhitehouse.archives.gov/the-press-office/2014/01/17/remarks-president-review-signals-intelligence [Accessed January 10, 2020].

Olson, M., Schneier, B., and Zittrain, J. (2016). *Don't Panic. Making Progress on the "Going Dark" debate.* Available: https://cyber.harvard.edu/pubrelease/dont-panic/Dont_Panic_Making_Progress_on_Going_Dark_Debate.pdf [Accessed January 16, 2020].

O'Neill, P. H. (2016). *EFF Vows to Tie Up Encryption "Backdoor" Legislation in Court "For Years."* Available: https://www.dailydot.com/layer8/burr-encryption-bill-eff/ [Accessed January 24, 2020].

Orenstein, J. (2016). *Memorandum and Order.* Available: https://cdn1.vox-cdn.com/uploads/chorus_asset/file/6124209/Orenstein-Order-Apple-iPhone-02292016.0.pdf [Accessed January 28, 2020].

Parliamentary Joint Committee on Intelligence and Security (2020). *Parliamentary Joint Committee on Intelligence and Security 07/08/2020 Telecommunications and Other Legislation Amendment (Assistance and Access) Act 2018.* Available: https://parlinfo.aph.gov.au/parlInfo/search/display/display.w3p;query=Id%3A%22committees%2Fcommjnt%2F30904d8b-7cfb-4ef0-99fb-fba2299b57bf%2F0003%22 [Accessed August 22, 2020].

Patel, P., Barr, W. P., McAleenan, K. K., and Dutton, P. (2019). *Open Letter: Facebook's "Privacy First" Proposals.* Available: https://assets.publishing.service.gov.uk/government/uploads/system/uploads/attachment_data/file/836569/Open_letter_from_the_Home_Secretary_-_alongside_US_Attorney_General_Barr__Secretary_of_Homeland_Security__Acting__McAleenan__and_Australian_Minister_for_Home_Affairs_Dutton_-_to_Mark_Zuckerberg.pdf [Accessed January 21, 2020].

Perez, E., Brown, P., and Prokupecz, S. (2016). *Sources: Data from San Bernardino Phone has Helped in Probe.* Available: https://edition.cnn.com/2016/04/19/politics/san-bernadino-iphone-data/index.html [Accessed January 18, 2020].

Perlroth, N. (2013). *Government Announces Steps to Restore Confidence on Encryption Standards.* Available: https://bits.blogs.nytimes.com/2013/09/10/government-announces-steps-to-restore-confidence-on-encryption-standards/?src=twrhp&_r=0 [Accessed February 3, 2020].

Perlroth, N., Larson, J., and Shane, S. (2013). *N.S.A. Able to Foil Basic Safeguards of Privacy on Web*. Available: https://www.nytimes.com/2013/09/06/us/nsa-foils-much-interne t-encryption.html?pagewanted=all [Accessed February 3, 2020].

Peterson, A. and Nakashima, E. (2015). *Obama Administration Explored Ways to Bypass Smartphone Encryption*. Available: https://www.washingtonpost.com/world/national -security/obama-administration-ponders-how-to-seek-access-to-encrypted-data/2015 /09/23/107a811c-5b22-11e5-b38e-06883aacba64_story.html [Accessed January 31, 2020].

Pew Research Center (2013). *Majority Views NSA Phone Tracking as Acceptable Anti-terror Tactic*. Available: https://www.people-press.org/2013/06/10/majority-views-nsa-phone-tracking-as-acceptable-anti-terror-tactic/ [Accessed February 2, 2020].

Pfefferkorn, R. (2020). *There's Now an Even Worse Anti-Encryption Bill Than EARN-IT. That Doesn't Make the EARN-IT Bill OK*. Available: https://cyberlaw.stanford.edu/ blog/2020/06/there%E2%80%99s-now-even-worse-anti-encryption-bill-earn-it-do esn%E2%80%99t-make-earn-it-bill-ok [Accessed June 27, 2020].

Pichai, S. (2016). *Tweet 1547, 17 February 2016*. Available: https://twitter.com/sundarpichai/ status/700104433183502336?lang=en-gb [Accessed January 13, 2020].

Pilkington, E. (2013). *Edward Snowden's Digital "Misuse" Has Created Problems, Says Ban Ki-Moon*. Available: https://www.theguardian.com/world/2013/jul/03/edward-sn owden-digital-misuse-ban-ki-moon [Accessed January 12, 2020].

Pilkington, E. (2016). *Edward Snowden Did This Country a Great Service. Let Him Come Home*. Available: https://www.theguardian.com/us-news/2016/sep/14/edward-snowd en-pardon-bernie-sanders-daniel-ellsberg?page=with%3Aimg-2 [Accessed May 22, 2020].

Poulsen, K. (2007). *FBI's Secret Spyware Tracks Down Teen Who Made Bomb Threats*. Available: https://web.archive.org/web/20161226042048/https://www.wired.com/ 2007/07/fbi-spyware/?currentPage=all2007:FBI's [Accessed February 15, 2020].

Prevelakis, V. and Spinellis, D. (2007). *The Athens Affair: How Some Extremely Smart Hackers Pulled off the Most Audacious Cell-Network Break-In Ever*. Available: https ://web.archive.org/web/20071009120318/http://www.spectrum.ieee.org/jul07/5280 [Accessed January 25, 2020].

Reitman, R. (2014). *EFF Statement on Passage of Massie-Lofgren Amendment Regarding NSA Backdoors*. Available: https://www.eff.org/deeplinks/2014/06/eff-statement-mas sie-lofgren-amendment-passing-house [Accessed February 23, 2020].

Reitman, R. (2016). *Victory: California Smartphone Anti-Encryption Bill Dies in Committee*. Available: https://www.eff.org/deeplinks/2016/04/victory-california-smartphone-an ti-encryption-bill-dies-committee [Accessed January 24, 2020].

Rescorla, E. and Salter, M. (2009). *Internet Draft: Extended Random Values for TLS*. Available: https://tools.ietf.org/html/draft-rescorla-tls-extended-random-02#section-6 [Accessed February 7, 2020].

Reuters. (2001). *FBI 'Fesses Up to Net Spy App*. Available: https://www.wired.com/2001/12/ fbi-fesses-up-to-net-spy-app/ [Accessed February 15, 2020].

Rogers, T. (2013). *The Real Story of Lavabit's Founder*. Available: https://www.dmagazin e.com/publications/d-magazine/2013/november/real-story-of-lavabit-founder-ladar-levison/ [Accessed February 18, 2020].

Rogers, M. (2015). *Challenges and Opportunities in an Interconnected World*. Available: https://gilbertlectures.princeton.edu/news/admiral-michael-rogers-usn [Accssed July 3, 2020].

Rogin, J. (2012). *NSA Chief: Cybercrime Constitutes the "Greatest Transfer of Wealth in History."* Available: https://foreignpolicy.com/2012/07/09/nsa-chief-cybercrime-co nstitutes-the-greatest-transfer-of-wealth-in-history/ [Accessed January 18, 2020].

Rowan, D. (2014). *WhatsApp: The Inside Story.* Available: https://www.wired.co.uk/article/whatsapp-exclusive [Accessed January 20, 2020].

Savage, C. (2010). *U.S. Tries to Make It Easier to Wiretap the Internet.* Available: https://www.nytimes.com/2010/09/27/us/27wiretap.html?pagewanted=2&_r=1 [Accessed February 2, 2020].

Schmidt, M. S. and Pérez-Peña, R. (2015). *F.B.I. Treating San Bernardino Attack as Terrorism Case.* Available: https://www.nytimes.com/2015/12/05/us/tashfeen-malik-islamic-state.html [Accessed January 12, 2020].

Schneier, B. (2007). *The Strange Story of Dual_EC_DRBG.* Available: https://www.schneier.com/blog/archives/2007/11/the_strange_sto.html [Accessed February 3, 2020].

Schneier, B. (2019). *Attorney General William Barr on Encryption Policy.* Available: https://www.lawfareblog.com/attorney-general-william-barr-encryption-policy [Accessed January 26, 2020].

Shachtman, N. (2014). *Even the Former Director of the NSA Hates the FBI's New Surveillance Push.* Available: https://www.thedailybeast.com/even-the-former-director-of-the-nsa-hates-the-fbis-new-surveillance-push [Accessed April 22, 2020].

Shumow, D. and Ferguson, N. (2007). *On the Possibility of a Back Door in the NIST SP800-90 Dual Ec Prng.* Available: http://rump2007.cr.yp.to/15-shumow.pdf [Accessed February 2, 2020].

Snowden, E. (2016a). *Tweet, 0843 17 February 2016.* Available: https://twitter.com/snowden/status/699997565987745792?lang=en [Accessed January 13, 2020].

Snowden, E. (2016b). *Tweet, 0750 17 February 2016.* Available: https://twitter.com/snowden/status/699984388067557376?lang=en [Accessed January 13, 2020].

Sparrow, A. (2017). *WhatsApp Must Be Accessible to Authorities, Says Amber Rudd.* Available: https://www.theguardian.com/technology/2017/mar/26/intelligence-services-access-whatsapp-amber-rudd-westminster-attack-encrypted-messaging [Accessed January 29, 2020].

Sullivan, B. (2001). *FBI Software Cracks Encryption Wall.* Available: http://www.nbcnews.com/id/3341694 [Accessed February 15, 2020].

Timberg, C. and Miller, G. (2014). *FBI Blasts Apple, Google for Locking Police Out of Phones.* Available: https://www.washingtonpost.com/business/technology/2014/09/25/68c4e08e-4344-11e4-9a15-137aa0153527_story.html [Accessed January 19, 2020].

The Aspen Institute. (2016). *The Complexities of Today's Security Challenges.* Available: https://aspensecurityforum.org/wp-content/uploads/2014/07/The-Complexities-of-Todays-Security-Challenges.pdf [Accessed January 13, 2020].

The White House. (2016). *Remarks by the President at South By Southwest Interactive, 11 March 2016.* Available: https://obamawhitehouse.archives.gov/the-press-office/2016/03/14/remarks-president-south-southwest-interactive [Accessed: January 23, 2020].

Todorovic, N. and Chaudhuri, A. (2018). *Using AI to Help Organizations Detect and Report Child Sexual Abuse Material Online.* Available: https://www.blog.google/around-the-globe/google-europe/using-ai-help-organizations-detect-and-report-child-sexual-abuse-material-online/ [Accessed April 26, 2020].

Trump, D. (2020). *Tweet 1536, 14 January 2020.* Available: https://twitter.com/realDonaldTrump/status/1217228960964038658 [Accessed January 20, 2020].

United Kingdom Government. (2016a). *Investigatory Powers Act 2016 Section 253.* Available: http://www.legislation.gov.uk/ukpga/2016/25/section/253/enacted [Accessed January 29, 2020].

United Kingdom Government. (2016b). *Investigatory Powers Act 2016 Section 261.* Available: http://www.legislation.gov.uk/ukpga/2016/25/section/261/enacted [Accessed January 29, 2020].

United Kingdom Government. (2016c). *Investigatory Powers Act 2016*. Available: http://www
.legislation.gov.uk/ukpga/2016/25/part/2/chapter/3/crossheading/restrictions-on-use-o
r-disclosure-of-material-obtained-under-warrants-etc/enacted [Accessed February 22,
2020].
United Nations. (2014). *68/167. The Right to Privacy in the Digital Age*. Available: https://
undocs.org/A/RES/68/167 [Accessed January 16, 2020].
United States Committee of the Judiciary. (2020). *Graham, Blumenthal, Hawley, Feinstein
Introduce EARN IT Act to Encourage Tech Industry to Take Online Child Sexual
Exploitation Seriously*. Available: https://www.judiciary.senate.gov/press/rep/release
s/graham-blumenthal-hawley-feinstein-introduce-earn-it-act-to-encourage-tech-ind
ustry-to-take-online-child-sexual-exploitation-seriously [Accessed April 26, 2020].
United States Congress. (2014). *H.R.5800—Secure Data Act of 2014*. Available: https://ww
w.congress.gov/bill/113th-congress/house-bill/5800/text [Accessed January 25, 2020].
United States Congress. (2016). *H.R.4528—ENCRYPT Act of 2016*. Available: https://ww
w.congress.gov/bill/114th-congress/house-bill/4528/text [Accessed January 25, 2020].
United States Congress. (2020). *S.3398—EARN IT Act of 2020*. Available: https://www.con
gress.gov/bill/116th-congress/senate-bill/3398/text [Accessed April 26, 2020].
United States Congress. (2020b). *Draft Discussion Text 3398—EARN IT Act of 2020*.
Available: https://assets.documentcloud.org/documents/6746282/Earn-It.pdf [Accessed
April 29, 2020].
United States Department of Justice. (2016). *All Writs Act Order*. Available: https://www.jus
tice.gov/usao-cdca/apple-litigation [Accessed February 23, 2020].
United States Department of Justice. (2018). *A Special Inquiry Regarding the Accuracy of
FBI Statements Concerning Its Capabilities to Exploit an iPhone Seized During the
San Bernardino Terror Attack Investigation*. Available: https://oig.justice.gov/report
s/2018/o1803.pdf [Accessed January 18, 2020].
United States District Court for the Central District of California. (2016). *Government's Ex
Parte Application for a Continuance*. Available: https://epic.org/amicus/crypto/appl
e/191-FBI-Motion-to-Vacate-Hearing.pdf [Accessed January 13, 2020].
United States District Court Eastern District of New Jersey. (2001a). *United States of America
V. Nicodemo S. Scarfo and Frank Paolercio: Affidavit of Randall S. Murch*. Available:
https://www.epic.org/crypto/scarfo/murch_aff.pdf [Accessed February 15, 2020].
United States District Court Eastern District of New Jersey. (2001b). *Re—United States of
America V. Nicodemo S. Scarfo et al. Criminal Action No. 00–404 (NHP)*. Available:
https://web.archive.org/web/20010926211132/https://www2.epic.org/crypto/scarfo/o
rder_8_7_01.pdf [Accessed February 15, 2020].
United States District Court Eastern District of New York. (2016). *The Government's
Memorandum of Law in Support of Its Application for an Order Compelling Apple Inc.
to Assist Law Enforcement Agents in the Execution of a Search Warrant*. Available:
https://regmedia.co.uk/2016/03/08/apple_fbi_appeal.pdf [Accessed January 28, 2020].
United States District Court Eastern District of Virginia. (2013). *Court Documents*. Available:
https://www.documentcloud.org/documents/801182-redacted-pleadings-exhibits-1-23.
html [Accessed February 16, 2020].
United States District Court Western District of Washington. (2007). *Application and
Affidavit for Search Warrant*. Available: https://web.archive.org/web/201701040725
09/https://www.wired.com/images_blogs/threatlevel/files/timberline_affidavit.pdf
[Accessed February 15, 2020].
United States House of Representatives. (2016). *The Encryption Tightrope: Balancing
Americans' Security and Privacy*. Available: https://docs.house.gov/meetings/JU/
JU00/20160301/104573/HHRG-114-JU00-Transcript-20160301.pdf [Accessed January
28, 2020].

United States of America. (2013). *Brief of the United States*. Available: https://www.eff.org/document/government-lavabit-brief [Accessed February 17, 2020].

United States Senate. (2015). *Threats to the Homeland: Hearing before the Committee on Homeland Security and Governmental Affairs United States Senate, 8 October 2015*. Available: https://www.govinfo.gov/content/pkg/CHRG-114shrg22380/pdf/CHRG-114shrg22380.pdf [Accessed January 20, 2020].

United States Senate. (2016). *Compliance with Court Orders Act of 2016*. Available: https://www.dailydot.com/layer8/encryption-fbi-harvard-berkman-study/ [Accessed January 16, 2020].

United States Senate. (2020). *The Lawful Access to Encrypted Data Act*. Available:https://www.judiciary.senate.gov/imo/media/doc/S.4051%20Lawful%20Access%20to%20Encrypted%20Data%20Act.pdf [Accessed June 27, 2020]

United States Foreign Intelligence Surveillance Court. (2013). *Application of the Federal Bureau of Investigation for an Order Requiring the Production of Tangible Things from Verizon Business Network Services*. Available: https://assets.documentcloud.org/documents/709012/verizon.pdf [Accessed January 10, 2020].

Volz, D. (2016). *Push for Encryption Law Falters Despite Apple Case Spotlight*. Available: https://www.reuters.com/article/usa-encryption-legislation-idUSL2N18O0BM [Accessed January 24, 2020].

WAFB. (2016). *"Brittney Mills Act" Fails to Pass in La. House Committee*. Available: https://www.wafb.com/story/31866353/brittney-mills-act-fails-to-pass-in-la-house-committee/ [Accessed January 24, 2020].

Washington Post Editorial Board (2014). *Compromise Needed on Smartphone Encryption*. Available: http://www.washingtonpost.com/opinions/compromise-needed-on-smartphone-encryption/2014/10/03/96680bf8-4a77-11e4-891d-713f052086a0_story.html [Accessed July 3, 2020].

Weisbaum, H. (2018). *Trust in Facebook Has Dropped by 66 Percent since the Cambridge Analytica Scandal*. Available: https://www.nbcnews.com/business/consumer/trust-facebook-has-dropped-51-percent-cambridge-analytica-scandal-n867011 [Accessed January 22, 2020].

Wertheimer, M. (2015). *The Mathematics Community and the NSA*. Available: http://www.ams.org//notices/201502/rnoti-p165.pdf [Accessed February 7, 2020].

Whittaker, Z. (2015). *US lawmaker: Next, We Stop the NSA from Weakening Encryption*. Available: https://www.zdnet.com/article/congress-massie-nsa-weakening-encryption-rsa-nist/ [Accessed February 23, 2020].

Winnefeld, J. A. (2015). *Adm. Winnefeld's Remarks at the West Point Cyber Conference*. Available: https://www.jcs.mil/Media/Speeches/Article/589135/adm-winnefelds-remarks-at-the-west-point-cyber-conference/ [Accessed April 22, 2020].

Wyden, R. (2014). *Wyden Introduces Bill to Ban Government-Mandated Backdoors into Americans' Cellphones and Computers*. Available: https://www.wyden.senate.gov/news/press-releases/wyden-introduces-bill-to-ban-government-mandated-backdoors-into-americans-cellphones-and-computers [Accessed January 25, 2020].

Wyden, R. (2016). *Tweet, 2122hrs, 13 April 2016*. Available: https://twitter.com/RonWyden/status/720343774099017728 [Accessed January 24, 2020].

Wyden, R. (2020). *Tweet, 1856hrs, 5 March 2020*. Available: https://twitter.com/RonWyden/status/1235640470015008768/photo/1 [Accessed 26 April 2020].

Zetter, K. (2013). *How a Crypto "Backdoor" Pitted the Tech World against the NSA*. Available: https://www.wired.com/2013/09/nsa-backdoor/ [Accessed February 3, 2020].

Zetter, K. (2016). *A Government Error Just Revealed Snowden Was the Target in the Lavabit Case*. Available: https://www.wired.com/2016/03/government-error-just-revealed-snowden-target-lavabit-case/ [Accessed February 18, 2020].

Zuckerberg, M. (2019). *A Privacy-Focused Vision for Social Networking*. Available: https ://www.facebook.com/notes/mark-zuckerberg/a-privacy-focused-vision-for-social-ne tworking/10156700570096634/ [Accessed January 21, 2020].

Zwillinger, M. (2014). *As Encryption Spreads, U.S. Grapples with Clash between Privacy, Security*. Available: https://www.zwillgen.com/news/as-encryption-spreads-u-s-grap ples-with-clash-between-privacy-security/ [Accessed July 4, 2020].

YOUTUBE VIDEOS

NBC News "Senator Asks How Facebook Remains Free, Mark Zuckerberg Smirks: 'We Run Ads' | NBC News," YouTube video, 1:00, posted by "NBC News," April 10, 2018, Available: https://www.youtube.com/watch?v=n2H8wx1aBiQ [Accessed February 22, 2020].

9 Conclusion

9.1 CONCLUSION: MOVING THE DEBATE FORWARDS

The vitriol permeating the crypto wars often causes us to forget that its belligerents are, for the most part, acting in defense of the citizenry by trying to minimize the risks they judge most prominent. Disagreements as to the most severe risks sustain the conflict. Digital privacy activists are wise to be cautious of digital-era surveillance capabilities aggrandizing state power and resulting in a heightened potential for government abuses which, *in extremis*, could contribute to the fall of democracy. Equally, the prescience of the state, in acting to replicate democratically authorized powers in the digital era and prevent the emergence of ungoverned spaces in which crime, terrorism, and child abuse can flourish, is prudent. However, the government's dogmatic adherence that they are "only" seeking to maintain the status quo existing since telephonies' advent is not credible. The digital exhausts of our devices are much richer than traditional telephony data. Digital telephone services such as Skype are the equivalent of traditional telephones. However, surveillance of the totality of a citizen's digital data, or forensic analysis of their devices, revealing the most intimate details of a citizen's life, is more analogous to having a government informant planted within a citizen's innermost trust circle, with that informant being present at all times. Such capabilities are a significant deviation from the pre-digital status quo, and on the balance of power between citizen and state. Governments must recognize the status quo's disturbance in order to help citizens determine the type of democratic mandate, if any, they wish to grant the state in exercising digital surveillance powers.

This book's aim has been to document the crypto wars to provide a robust foundation for future debates on resolving the exceptional access (EA) dilemma. To fully address EA itself would be the topic of another, much more technical and risk-oriented study. However, having spent half a decade examining the history of this topic, I will offer some thought on EA solutions, which should be received as high-level ideas for further exploration, rather than detailed proposals.

Firstly, rather than state vs. citizen, or security vs. privacy, we must frame this challenge as risk management in the digital age. This is not digital risk management, the world is no longer divorced between physical and digital—it is societal risk management.

For digital privacy activists, the principal risk is an overreaching state—a government that could abuse its power to subvert democracy; President Trump's recent attempts to undermine the election process demonstrate such a scenario is not as outlandish as many would have thought even a few years ago. A related risk is a more general privacy degradation in society. The government assesses the danger of an unregulated space, a space in which threats to the state and citizenry could be incubated and mature, as the most severe risk. The risks from individuals today are more severe than in the pre-digital age. In the twentieth century, for extremists to congregate over distances was challenging, and it was much harder to learn the skills required to carry out mass-murders, such as bomb-making and the forging of biological weapons—in many cases the Internet democratizes such knowledge. The threats from hostile states were also more distant in the pre-digital world. Today, foreign actors can conduct espionage, influence elections, disable critical infrastructure, and perhaps even cause fatalities from within their own borders, whilst leaving little chance for irrefutable attribution. A further risk acknowledged by both parties is an Internet unshielded by encryption, exacerbating all manner of threats including organized crime and child exploitation. Which risk is severest and deserving of the most aggressive treatment, even to the augmentation of other risks, is highly subjective. The FBI, NSA, cypherpunks, and technology executives represent extremes of the argument, and represent a fragment of the population. In a democracy, such a small number of proponents with polarized views and often vested interests should not decide an issue so fundamental to twenty-first-century civil liberties. However, these parties have filed a void vacated by a broadly uninformed, complacent, and disinterested electorate, owing in part to generational divisions. The eldest in our societies often do not understand technology, lacking the ability to comprehend how fundamental digital technologies are to twenty-first-century life and the associated security and privacy threats. The youngest generation, digital natives, know nothing other than a technology-infused world and have no reference as to what "privacy" they may have lost that their parents possessed. It is the generation in between, those who reached adulthood late enough to have experienced the world before society became digitally saturated, yet early enough as to be technologically fluent, who retain the perspective of to differentiate the state of security and privacy during both eras. An additional challenge is that citizens are accustomed to receiving free Internet services—given the absence of a precedent for paying for services, many may place data privacy and security as a subordinate consideration.

9.2   WHERE DO WE GO FROM HERE?

In the twentieth century, civil rights leaped forwards: Emmeline Pankhurst stopped eating, Rosa Parks sat at the front, and Dr. King started dreaming. Under the banner of liberty, legions clamored ashore French beaches to banish an ideology abhorring of civil rights. Whilst many countries lagged behind, global civil rights accelerated perhaps faster than in all previous centuries. War, education, and technology were the great disruptors. Two world wars on a scale hitherto unimaginable drove states to recognize the citizenry, which made the greatest of sacrifices, deserved rewarding with new rights. Whilst the twentieth-century fights for gender equality, race equality, and sexual liberation raged, few recognized the seismic shift occurring in society's infrastructure, and only the most esoteric of futurists predicted the consequences. Today digital technologies mediate almost every aspect of our lives. We earn our wages, connect with friends, and perhaps, if we are lucky, find true love online. Digital technologies are perhaps humanity's most powerful invention, with the closest comparable technological inflection point being the transition from horse to car. Visionaries saw promise and peril. Digital privacy activists foresaw unchecked technology as the midwife to a dystopia surpassing that which even George Orwell could conjure. Such concerns were largely discounted as the ravings of scaremongers, of those who disdained power structures and were possessing of both technological prowess and overactive imaginations. Yet, when we look at the Internet almost three decades after the cypherpunks assembled, many of their fears are manifest. Governments imposed few regulations upon the Internet, hoping to allow it to prosper as a bastion of freedom, yet despite these good intentions, today it fosters villains and heroes in equal measure. Preachers tell us that God shaped humanity in his own image—in the Internet humanity imitated this act. The good and evil we harbor echoes in our creation —sometimes, like a circus mirror, offering distorted reflections. In the pre-digital world, civil rights evolved to protect societies from humankind's darkest impulses. Theoretically, all of these pre-digital rights translate to the digital domain. But sadly, theory is not married with practice. The free market and a regulatory *laissez-faire* approach have resulted in companies turning their clients into the product, sometimes abusing their rights in the process. Digital technology companies have accrued a level of influence over public policy which is not befitting of democratic societies—whilst corporations should be part of the conversation, they should not be the final arbiter of civil liberties issues. That is not to say companies must not challenge legally dubious government actions, such as the FBI's use of the All Writs Act against Apple—indeed, they have an obligation to do so. Governments have at times exploited the lack of avowed digital rights for power aggregation. Such actions were unlikely born of ill-intent. Governments have sought to protect their citizens from an array of new and dangerous threats. Likewise, companies are doing what capitalism has conditioned them to do: creating innovative ways to generate wealth. Accidentally, we have fostered an environment more akin to the Wild West than today's Western world.

Civil rights are not static. The digital revolution and COVID-19 represent severe societal disruptions, the type of disruptions that historically drive re-evaluations of citizens' rights and conversations about the future of such rights—this is needed now more than ever. The Black Lives Matter movement, and the vociferous pleas of the world's younger generation, a generation who will inherit a planet convulsing beneath the stress of humanity, evidence the demand for such a dialogue. The gravest error of governments during the crypto wars has been their failure to acknowledge the need for a new dialogue on civil rights in the digital age. Citizens have not been consulted on how they wish to balance the preservation of their values with the management of digital-era risks: Should privacy be prioritized to the exclusion of government access? Should security concerns be dominant? Is there a preference for a middle ground? All of these questions must be in the context of the complex relationship of security and privacy. It is unsurprising that such a conversation has not occurred. Governments are often under-resourced, with tactical objectives prioritized over attention to wider historic arcs. Additionally, such a rights review would result in political exposure if it ushered in greater citizen privacy provisions subsequently exploited by threat actors. Risking such an undertaking when most citizens are often little aware of this issue would be politically imprudent, if morally virtuous—alas, the latter seldom conveys electoral advantage. It could be argued that as Congress is the will of the people, debates in the Capitol are representative of their desires. After all, this issue is complex and beyond most citizens' comprehension—even those with the pre-requisite knowledge to grasp its nuances unlikely have the time to make a detailed study of the debate and formulate a considered position. This is why we elect politicians: to do the research and make decisions on our behalf. They do it every day. Why should this issue be any different?

The primary argument is that Congress has repeatedly demonstrated its ineptitude regarding civil rights in the digital age. A kinder assessment: there is no congressional consensus on this issue, and tribalism has resulted in the preservation of an unhealthy status quo, rather than policies reflecting considered discourse and refinement. In an age where campaigning policies and debates are often intellectually anemic, and bereft of detailed policy advocation, one also has to question whether a US administration possesses a legitimate mandate to enact any civil liberties policies diverging from the status quo. If politicians cannot reverse the policy stasis, another method will be needed to do so. This is not to say a new rights prioritization, or risk dispersion prioritization, would necessarily differ from the status quo—we simply do not have the data to assess citizens' desires.

The first step in solving this challenge is to conduct an independent study to generate insights into citizen sentiment on digital-era civil liberties and risk dispersion. Offering specifics on how this study should be conducted is beyond the scope of this work of history. However, one model that could be considered is to employ a citizens assembly. Such deliberative democracy vehicles are increasingly in vogue in an age of growing populism. After the widespread, and at times violent, 2019 protests by the French *Gilets Jaunes* (yellow vests), who objected to the government raising fuel taxes to discourage its use in pursuit of achieving climate change objectives, a citizen assembly was convened. The assembly of 150 demographically diverse citizens was to spend days being briefed on the policy options before making recommendations on measures the citizenry would accept to counter climate change. Citizen assemblies have also been successfully used to help unlock other politically gridlocked issues, such as abortion and same-sex marriage in Ireland.[1] The UK is actively sponsoring citizens assemblies, albeit at a local level, under their Innovation in Democracy program.[2] This form of democratic engagement counteracts perceptions that policies that disproportionately hurt the most vulnerable in societies are being taken by an aloof and distant elite. Public participation also acts as a counterweight to political systems which prioritize short-term electoral gains over the long-term needs of current and future generations. Such participation benefits from being removed from party politics and lobbyists, and can offer political cover to elected representatives who support subsequent positions where hard trade-offs are required. The utilization of such a study should expand beyond the EA challenge.

---

[1] Extinction Rebellion, 2019.   [2] UK Government, 2018.

Once we understand how citizens want to disperse their digital-era risk, the next step is to craft technically viable approaches to EA. This will be a matrix of technology-specific solutions. These solutions will need to follow agreed principles. These principles should be decided by another independent study, though many principles already suggested could be considered wise, such as the need to maintain a human-in-the-loop to counter the scalability and potential for abuse. Another principle should be that solutions must have the minimum possible impact on the wider security ecosystem. However, as technical experts have repeatedly emphasized, there is no known EA capability that does not introduce further risks to the digital ecosystem—so societies must decide whether the risk is more severe from the absence of a law enforcement access mechanism, or in a measure of security degradation to aspects of our digital eco-system. We then need to conduct a thorough risk assessment of each EA solution—we will need to develop as objective a framework as possible to quantify the additional vulnerabilities the EA solution introduces. This framework should be built with representation from academia, civil society, and government—bodies such as the National Research Council may be suitable to chair this study.

The next step is to consider risk treatment options. We must assess how risk could be further minimized for each particular EA solution, such as whether safeguards can be implemented to diminish the risk of government abuse or broader unauthorized access. Equally, we must consider how we minimize risks associated with not implementing each EA solution, resulting in consequences such as a lack of access to suspect devices, or inability to scan for child abuse material. The same technological revolution which was midwife to the EA challenge has delivered excellent advances in forensics and other scientific domains, and we will need to explore if other investigatory tools could offset an absence of EA. Again, bodies such as the National Research Council should bring together a wide consortium of stakeholders to make such determinations.

The final step will be to take the information generated and enact decisions aligned to the data on how citizens wish to disperse their digital risk portfolio. This framework and its implementation would need to be enacted by a robust, transparent, and well-resourced oversight mechanism to ensure the government adheres to its mandate.

Of course, there are significant legislative challenges in implementing this solution, not only in the US but beyond. Non-US countries using such a model may struggle to exert influence over technology companies in order to enact EA solutions approved by the citizenry. Foreign technology firms can be influenced to a degree by nations passing laws which exclude violators from their markets, however, such actions may be an act of self-harm when their citizens require access to global platforms to partake in the international economy. Equally, if the US enacts laws dictating EA, which companies honor, this may result in a domino effect around the world as foreign nations, many of whom have governments with different moralities, demand the same security co-operation the US government is afforded. If US technology companies fail to cooperate with foreign governments we may see US products replaced by foreign-government–controlled offerings, further accelerating the Internet's balkanization.

This solution framework is offered solely to catalyze debate as to how we move forwards, and in no way seeks to minimize the complexity of this challenge. This study has been focused on the past rather than the future, and further analysis is required to develop a framework that takes into account citizen sentiment and delivers a democratic mechanism for managing civil liberties in the digital era.

As we build this new framework, we must also guard against the state taking emergency powers as a result of high-profile low-impact threat events such as terrorism attacks. Such powers may have the immediate approval of a fearful citizenry, who could be desperate for reassurance that "something" is being done to reduce their risk exposure; however, these powers may not align to the citizenry's desires absent the distortion of fear. Whilst some security incidents may be "spectacular," such as terrorist attacks, few represent existential threats, and should not justify the curtailment of hard-won civil liberties. In times of crisis, permanent solutions to temporary problems are often deployed, and history demonstrates that the state seldom relinquishes powers once granted. This is not to argue such a provision of emergency powers should not be available to the state, but that if such a provision exists it should operate within a democratically approved framework of checks and balances determined whilst there is not an enemy at the gates. This is particularly important where digital rights are concerned, as the implementation of new security measures can often be rapidly achieved. Where there is an existential threat to the state, there should be a clear mechanism to activate exceptional measures. Such activation criteria should be strictly defined with minimum room for interpretation, to avoid political knee-jerk reactions. The state's most senior judiciary body should concur the required criteria are satisfied. Where emergency powers are granted, sunset clauses should take effect at the earliest opportunity, with clear and strict renewal criteria.

The history explored during this book has demonstrated it is highly unlikely the mathematics of encryption can curtail a state's digital surveillance capabilities. The state has likely, in most historic periods, found ways to access citizens' data despite the actions of the digital privacy activists, though their boisterous opposition and subversive acts likely tempered government actions. Technology does not operate in isolation; absent legal restraints, states will utilize their cunning and brilliance to find ways to access the data they believe is required to protect the citizenry. Whilst technology may at some point reach a stage where this is not possible, it is unlikely such a cyber security capability advance will occur in the imminent future. Therefore, it is up to the citizenry to provide the boundaries for states to operate in, and for governments to facilitate this process if the use of their powers is to be considered legitimate.

The crypto wars have been waged with passionate intensity by its combatants— now is the time to temper such passion with wisdom. Society is starting to recognize that civil rights in the digital age will perhaps be more important to the future of the state–citizen power dynamic than any other issue in the coming generation. It is my hope this history aids in transitioning the half-century war into a sustainable peace—our children deserve to inherit a world in which considered and democratically mandated civil liberty policies serve the aspirations of humanity, rather than inheriting a reality left vulnerable by today's absence of a mechanism to conclude the crypto wars.

REFERENCES

Extinction Rebellion (2019). *The Extinction Rebellion Guide to Citizen's Assemblies.* Available: https://rebellion.earth/wp/wp-content/uploads/2019/06/The-Extinction-Rebellion-Guide-to-Citizens-Assemblies-Version-1.1-25-June-2019.pdf [Accessed June 28, 2020].

UK Government (2018). *Innovation in Democracy Programme: Expression of Interest (EoI).* Available: https://www.gov.uk/government/publications/innovation-in-democracy-programme-expression-of-interest-eoi [Accessed July 26, 2020].

Acknowledgments

It's one a.m. I'm hunched on the top bunk in a cramped cabin on an overnight train between Cairo and Aswan. My roommate is "Coco," a Mexican traveler who on our meeting hours earlier presented me earplugs, saying at once cheerfully and apologetically, "I snorze louds." He was not exaggerating. Such conditions for writing are not unique during the five-year production of a book written upon Vietnamese junk boats, in Spanish cafés, Irish bars, and Las Vegas hotel rooms, on Serbian buses, in the shadows of the Giza Pyramids, and on countless planes, coaches, cars, and in my home city of London, England. I've written most of this book whilst being Chief Technology Officer for Security at DXC Technology, which at the time was the largest provider of cyber security services in the world. I thank Marco Pereira, Chris Moyer, and Dan Hushon for giving me the opportunity to fulfill the challenging CTO role. Marco in particular was a remarkable source of business, strategic, and technological wisdom to me as I negotiated my maiden executive role. At DXC, we confronted many of the major security and privacy issues impacting society; my experiences during those years directly helped me understand the complex topics this history addresses.

I have been inspired by those authors whose works on this topic came before mine, in particular Mr. James Bamford's 1982 *Puzzle Palace* and Mr. Steven Levy's 2001 *Crypto*. I've also been aided by the diligent efforts to unearth and share information by digital civil rights organizations such as the Center for Democracy and Technology, the Electronic Frontier Foundation, the Electronic Privacy Information Center, and Computer Professionals for Social Responsibility. The Web Archive project also deserves credit as a wonderful repository for that which was once online but has since faded into the digital ether.

I would also like to thank my academic mentors, Professor Thomas Rid, Dr. Tim Stevens, Professor Keith Martin, and Dr. Emmett Sullivan, for their patient and insightful guidance.

Further, I would like to thank the wonderful Ms. Gabriella Williams, and the team at Taylor and Francis, for having faith in this book; the production team at Deanta Global; and Michel Velarde, for his brilliant copyediting.

Finally, and most importantly, I thank my family and friends, who endure and support my obsessions with endless patience, encouragement, and understanding.

About the Author

Craig Jarvis is an independent cyber security strategist currently completing a PhD in Cyber Security and History at Royal Holloway, University of London. Craig holds Master's degrees in Cyber Security, International Security, and Classical Music, and studied History at Oxford University. Craig lives in London, UK.

Index

Printed in the United States
by Baker & Taylor Publisher Services

Printed in the United States
by Baker & Taylor Publisher Services